2653

THE MONARCH BOOK

By the same author

Short, Sharp and Off the Point – A Guide to Good (and Bad) Preaching
Marc Europe, 1987, 0-947697-50-0

The Monarch Book of Christian Wisdom

Collected by

ROBERT M E PATERSON

MONARCH
Crowborough

Copyright © Robert M E Paterson 1997
The right of Robert M E Paterson to be identified
as author of this work has been asserted by him in
accordance with the Copyright, Designs
and Patents Act 1988

First Published 1997

All right reserved.
No part of this publication may be reproduced or
transmitted in any form or by any means, electronic
or mechanical, including photocopy, recording or any
information storage and retrieval system, without
permission in writing from the publisher.

Every effort has been made to indicate the copyright
holder where appropriate. Any information received after
publication will be included in the next edition.

Unless otherwise indicated, biblical quotations are from
the Holy Bible, New Revised Standard Version, 1989 and 1995,
Division of Christian Education of the National Council
of the Churches of Christ in the United States of America.

British Library Cataloguing Data
A catalogue record for this book is available
from the British Library.

ISBN 1 85424 360 8

Co-published in South Africa with
SCB Publishers
Cornelis Struik House, 80 McKenzie Street
Cape Town 8001, South Africa.
Reg no 04/02203/06

Designed and produced by Bookprint Creative Services
P.O. Box 827, BN21 3YJ, England for
MONARCH PUBLICATIONS
Broadway House, The Broadway
Crowborough East Sussex, TN6 1HQ.
Printed in Great Britain.

Dedicated
to the memory of my father
David Donaldson Paterson
1899–1969
who tried to teach me
to respect others' wisdom

Born in 1949, Robert Paterson has been Team Rector of Cowbridge in the Church in Wales since 1994. He is known as a teacher of preachers and an occasional broadcaster. Married with three children, he enjoys music and drama, chairs the Welsh Partnership for World Mission, is a member of the Standing Committee of the Governing Body of the Church in Wales and is Secretary of its Liturgical Commission.

FOREWORD

This book is most of a collection begun in the late 1960s with a view to illustrating sermons. Over the years, their scope has grown and, looking at them now, I fear they may also have become a self-portrait in the words of others. I make no apology for there being a number of extended sections: they are, I hope, important concerns of the church today. The book is not intended so much as a source of quotable material but a collection of items which may prompt a thought or a smile.

> Books give not wisdom where none was before,
> But where it is, there reading makes it more.
>
> *Sir John Harington*

I am deeply grateful to Fiona Gardner for the herculean labour of the initial word processing and helping in the correction of the text, and to my family for coping with me. I ask forgiveness and correction for any misplaced words or attributions.

Robert Paterson
Cowbridge
1996

A

ABBA ('Father' in Hebrew) – *see also* PRAYER

This is but a little word, and yet it comprehends everything. The mouth does not speak, but the feelings of the heart are spoken in this way. Even if I am oppressed with anguish and terror on every side and seem to have been forsaken and utterly cast away from your presence, yet I am your child and you are my Father for Christ's sake: I am loved because of the Beloved. Therefore this little word, 'Father', conceived effectively in the heart, passes all the eloquence of Demothenes, Cicero, and of the most eloquent rhetoricians that ever were in the world. For here, the feelings of the heart are expressed with sighs which cannot be expressed by tongue or words of eloquence.

Martin Luther on Galatians 4:6

. . . in no place in this immense literature (the prayer literature of ancient Judaism) is the invocation of God as *abba* to be found . . . *Abba* was an everyday word, a homely, family word. No Jew would have dared to address God in this manner. Jesus did it always, in all His prayers which are handed down to us, with one single exception, the cry from the cross . . .

Joachim Jeremias

You make one leetle prayer. You say: 'Le bon Fadder, oh! I want to come back; I so tire; so hungree; so sorree.'

Ralph Connor: Black Rock, Prayer of a French Canadian

Absent mindedness

When Michael Ramsey (later Archbishop of York and of Canterbury) was on the staff of Boston Parish Church, Lincolnshire, it is said he went out without his key. When he returned, he rang the bell, but his landlady was nervous of strangers and called through the door, 'I'm sorry, Mr. Ramsey is out,' to which Ramsey replied, 'I'll return later.'

From Owen Chadwick: Michael Ramsey, A Life, (Oxford, 1991).

Chadwick says of this story that 'there is excellent evidence of its truth'.

The 14th Earl of Home, Foreign Secretary 1960–63 and later (as Sir Alec Douglas-Home) Prime Minister, used to be reminded by his devoted wife, Elizabeth, where he was. 'Peking, Alec; Peking, Peking,' she would repeat to him as he walked down the steps of the aeroplane – in order to prevent him saying to his hosts, as he stood up before the microphone, 'I'm very happy to be back in Montreal (or Rome or Washington, or Moscow).'

From William Douglas-Home: 'Mr. Home Pronounced Hume', (1979)

Achievement

The world is divided into people who do things – and people who get the credit.

Dwight Morrow

The gospel flattens out notions of deserving.

Bishop Rowan Williams, (1993)

Activism

The many things we have to do, the hundred and one calls on our time and attention, don't get between ourselves and God. On the contrary they are to us in very truth his body and his blood.

Harry A. Williams: 'The Joy of God'

When I was in Oxford, and lived almost like an hermit, I saw not how any busy man could be saved. I scarce thought it possible for a man to retain the Christian spirit amidst the noise and bustle of the world. God taught me better by my own experience. I had ten times more business in America (that is, at intervals) than ever I had in my life. But it was no hindrance to silence of spirit.

John Wesley (1703–1791): from a letter to Miss March, (10 December, 1777)

It was going to be one of Rabbit's busy days. As soon as he woke up he felt important, as if everything depended on him. It was just the day for Organising Something, or for Writing a Notice Signed Rabbit, or for Seeing What Everybody Else Thought About It . . . a . . . sort of day, when everybody said, 'Yes, Rabbit' and 'No, Rabbit,' and waited until he had told them.

A.A. Milne: 'Winnie the Pooh'

Advent

The Advent Ring or Crown is a European and American custom from the Lutheran Church. Four purple candles are set in a circle of evergreen and berried holly leaves and a larger white candle stands in the centre. The circle symbolises the eternal love of God in the same way as the ring of the traditional Celtic cross; the green, the undying faith he inspires in us; the berries remind us of the crown of thorns; the candles, one for each Sunday of Advent, remind us of the true Light who was coming into the world; and the central candle reminds us of the Light who has come into the world.

Traditional

A poor shepherd-boy had no gift for the child Jesus, so he made a tiny crown of leaves from a holly bush. Compared with the expensive presents that others had given, the crown seemed of very little value. So the shepherd-boy began to cry as he presented it. But when the babe touched the crown with his tiny hand, the leaves suddenly gleamed and the teardrops turned to scarlet berries. Thirty-three years later that shepherd saw a man on a cross with a thorny crown on his head. His blood looked like bright berries on his crown. So, through the centuries, the holly crown became a traditional Advent and Christmas decoration, reminding us of the miracle of Christ's birth and his eternal love in dying for us.

Traditional

Advent: From the Latin *Ad Verso* which means 'To crowd out God before Christmas with activities of dubious worth.'

Martin Wroe, Adrian Reith & Simon Parkes: 'The Church English Dictionary', (1991)

Advertising *see also* MEDIA

The codfish lays ten thousand eggs,
The homely hen lays one.
The codfish never cackles
To tell you what she's done.
And so we scorn the codfish,
While the humble hen we prize,
Which only goes to show you
That it pays to advertise.

Anonymous

Advertising may be described as the science of arresting the human intelligence long enough to get money from it.

Stephen Leacock

You can tell the ideals of a nation by its advertisements.

Norman Douglas

Advertisements contain the only truths to be relied on in a newspaper.

Thomas Jefferson (1743–1826): 'Letter to Nathaniel Macon'

Age

The four ages of man are:
Infancy, Childhood, Adolescence and Obsolescence.

Art Linkletter: 'A Child's Garden of Misinformation,' (1965)

In 1987 at King's College Hospital, London, a student nurse saw a frail, elderly woman sitting on the edge of a bed. 'Time for your bath,' said the nurse, only to be told by the lady (who was a little confused) that she had already had one. All went well with the nurse bathing the old lady kindly and firmly. On returning to the ward, the nurse was surprised to see someone else in the old lady's bed. 'That's my sister,' replied the old lady. 'I'd just come to visit her.'

Ed. Stephen Pile: 'The Return of Heroic Failures', (1988)

Derek Osborne (then Vicar of Cromer) to an elderly parishioner in Norfolk:

'Have you lived here all your life?'

'Not yet, Sir!'

'You're a great age: what's your secret?'

'Oh, just keep breathing, Sir.'

I met a lady the other day who said that the years were passing so quickly. She went into the kitchen to make a cup of tea when she was 67, and when she came out she found she was 86.

Matthew Parris: in The Times, (March, 1993)

As a man advances in life he gets what is better than admiration – judgement to estimate things at their own value.

Dr. Samuel Johnson, (1709–1784)

Old lady requires nursing and a little cooking.

Advertisement in The Church Times (c. 1970/71)

Remember your creator in the days of your youth, before the days of trouble come, and the years draw near when you will say, 'I have no pleasure in them;' before the sun and the light and the moon and the stars are darkened and the clouds return with the rain; in the day when the guards of the house tremble, and the strong men are bent, and the women who grind cease working because they are few, and those who look through the windows see dimly; when the doors on the street are shut, and sound of the grinding is low, and one rises up at the sound of a bird, and all the daughters of song are brought low; when one is afraid of heights, and terrors are in the road; the almond tree blossoms, the grasshopper drags itself along and desire fails; because all must go to their eternal home, and the mourners will go about the streets; before the silver cord is snapped, and the golden bowl is broken, and the pitcher is broken at the fountain, and the wheel broken at the cistern, and the dust returns to the earth as it was, and the breath returns to God who gave it.

Ecclesiastes: 12:1–7

Agnosticism

I am not woolly and vague. I have no intellectual certainty, indeed, but I have been given a deep 'inner certitude' of God's unconditional love for me. He accepts me as I am with all my sins and failures and will never let me go. Call it, if you like, the gift of faith; call it, if you like, the seal of the Spirit. I do not care; but that certitude has for me the ring of truth which I cannot escape and from which I do not want to escape. Yes, I am humbly proud to be an agnostic.

Bryan Green in the Church Times, (11 January, 1991), 'The manifesto of a liberated Evangelical'

I took thought and invented what I conceived to be the appropriate title of 'agnostic'. To my great satisfaction, the term took: and when *The Spectator* had stood godfather to it, any suspicion in the minds of respectable people was, of course, completely lulled.

Agnosticism simply means that a man shall not say he knows or believes that for which he has no grounds for professing to believe.

Thomas Henry Huxley (1825–1895): 'Science and Christian Tradition, VII'

I do not see much difference between avowing that there is no God, and implying that nothing definite can for certain be known about him.

John Henry Newman (1801–1890)

The moment a man seriously accepts a deity his interest in 'religion' is at an end. He's got something else to think about. The ease with which we can now get an audience for a discussion of religion does not prove that more people are becoming religious. What it proves is the existence of a large 'floating vote'. Every conversion will reduce this potential audience.

Once the climate of opinion allows such a floating vote to form, I see no reason why it should speedily diminish. Indecision, often very honest, is very natural. It would be foolish, however, not to realise that it is also no hardship. Floating is a very agreeable operation; a decision either way costs something. Real Christianity and consistent Atheism both make demands on a man.

C.S. Lewis: 'Revival or Decay', (1958)

Ambassador

Legatus est vir bonus peregre missus ad mentiendum Republicae causa.
Translated by Sir Henry Wotton (1568 – 1639), its author, as 'An ambassador is an honest man sent to lie abroad for the good of his Country.'

Eight years later, the Latin version – which was not such a good pun as the English – was used in a book by Jasper Scioppus ('a Romanist, a man of restless spirit and a malicious pen') against King James I of England, VI of Scotland. Wotton, then Ambassador to the Court of Venice, was forced to make two public apologies.

Ambition

A churchwarden to a curate:
'If tha wants to git forrards a bit,' he says, it would be fatal to 'speak plaain out' like the 'serious' rector. 'Creep along the hedge-bottoms, an' thou'll be a Bishop yet.'

Alfred Lord Tennyson

Ambition comes when early force is spent
And when we find no longer all things possible.
Ambition comes behind and unobservable.
Sin grows with doing good.

T.S. Eliot: 'Murder in the Cathedral,' Part I, lines 679–682 (Faber and Faber, 1965)

During the reign of the French King Louis XVIII (1814–24, except for a period in 1815), an émigré nobleman who had been a naval cadet in 1789 demanded to be made a Rear Admiral since he considered that he would have achieved that rank had not the Revolution driven him out of France. The authorities admitted the claim but regretted, sorrowfully, that he would have been killed in action at the Battle of Trafalgar in 1805.

Source unknown

Angels

Responsum est, quod Angeli *vocarentur. At ille:* Bene, *inquit; nam et angelicam habent faciem, et tales angelorum in caelis decet esse cohere des.*
(They replied that they were called *Angles.* But he said, *It is good; for they have the countenance of angels, and such should be the co-heirs of the angels in heaven*)

Pope Gregory I (540–604) on seeing two Angle boys in a Rome slave-market, as recounted by Bede: Ecclesiastical History II.i; commonly rendered 'Non Angli sed Angeli', and translated by W.C. Sellar and R.J. Yeatman: 1066 and All That (1930) as 'Not Angels but Anglicans'

For by many stories,
And true, we learn the angels are all Tories.

Lord Byron (1788–1824): 'The Vision of Judgement'

Angels mean 'messengers' and 'ministers'. Their function is to execute the plan of divine providence, even in earthly things.

Thomas Aquinas, (1224–1274)

Even Satan disguises himself as an angel of light.

2 Corinthians: 11:14

When he [the Son] had made purification for sins, he sat down at the right hand of the Majesty on high, having become as much superior to angels as the name he has inherited is more excellent than theirs.
For to which of the angels did God ever say,
'You are my Son;
today I have begotten you?'

The Letter to the Hebrews 1:3b–5a

Then I looked, and I heard the voice of many angels surrounding the throne and the living creatures and the elders; they numbered myriads of myriads and thousands of thousands, singing with full voice,
'Worthy is the Lamb that was slaughtered
to receive power and wealth and wisdom and might
and honour and glory and blessing!'

Revelation: 5:11, 12

War broke out in heaven; Michael and his angels fought against the dragon. The dragon and his angels fought back, but they were defeated, and there was no longer any place for them in heaven. The great dragon was thrown down, that ancient serpent, who is called the Devil and Satan, the deceiver of the whole world – he was thrown down to the earth, and his angels were thrown down with him.

Revelation: 12:7–9 (see also Genesis 3 and Daniel 7 – 12)

Anger

Archbishop McGee, after having soup poured down his collar by a waiter, exclaimed: 'Is there a layman present who will express my feelings?'

So shocked are we at the irreverence and so ashamed of the rational absurdity of letting off our aggressions against God, that we repress them so far as God is concerned and appear to ourselves not to feel them. And then we wonder why, after we have prayed so devoutly, we feel so bloody-minded towards poor inoffensive John Smith or sweet little helpful Mary Jones or, more often, the members of our own family. Your wife, you see, has very often to have thrown at her the rotten eggs you really want to throw at God. And the joke is that God is not in the slightest degree taken in by the pantomime by which you deceive yourself. He knows what we won't admit to ourselves, that the rotten eggs are really meant for him.

Harry A. Williams: 'Tensions'

I am righteously indignant; *you* are annoyed; *he* is making a fuss about nothing.

The New Statesman

Keep your temper. Do not quarrel with an angry person, but give him a soft answer. It is commended by the Holy Spirit and, furthermore, it makes him madder than anything else you could say.

Anonymous (in Reader's Digest, 1949)

I can stand brute force, but brute reason is quite unreasonable. There is something unfair about its use. It is hitting below the intellect.

Oscar Wilde: 'The Picture of Dorian Gray', (1891)

Anglicanism, a collection of parties

That mixture of rivalry, fraternity and confusion we call the Anglican Church.

Robert M.E. Paterson, (1984)

However we interpret it, configure or justify it, Anglicanism is intrinsically pluriform, and to be an intentional Anglican, as opposed to an incidental one, means to affirm the fact of this multiformity. To be an Anglican of any description involves acknowledging that the others are there. Anglicanism can only be at its best if the different species interact and connect with one another.

Human beings seem to find it very difficult to live with complexity and difference. Social as well as intellectual history is bedevilled by the craving for single explanations of complex realities.

Bishop Richard Holloway: in the Church Times, (28 August, 1992), 'Missionary Energy laced with Moralism'

I don't mind being called an Evangelical, but I hate the phrase 'Low Churchman' because I have a very, very high concept of the church. My wing of the church, in which I've been brought up, is the Evangelical wing; but I think I've worked long enough within the Church of England to appreciate that these party labels are meaning less and less.

Archbishop F. Donald Coggan (of York and Canterbury), 5 August, 1974, on television

Low Church: No pictures, no candles, no colour. The same effect can also be achieved by walking around with a large bucket over your head.

Martin Wroe, Adrian Reith & Simon Parkes: 'The Church-English Dictionary', (1991)

Anglicanism, doctrine

To move in one direction then to counterbalance it, to feel enthusiasm then to curb it, is not the same thing as not moving, not feeling. The Thirty-nine Articles is a case in point. The clear-headed Calvinistic zeal with which they were drawn up was sincerely felt; just as sincere, though, is the sheepish disregard the Church of England has had for them ever since.

The combination of the two is quintessentially English.

'The English Spirit, and Anthology of English Spirituality', (D.L.T., 1987), Introduction

[The Anglican Church is] the greatest Bible-reading church in the world. In no other church anywhere is the Bible read in public worship so regularly, with such order, and at such length, as in the Anglican fellowship of churches.

Anglicanism is a form of the Christian faith that demands and expects a great deal from ordinary people.

Bishop Stephen Neill: 'Anglicanism', (1958–1977):

Our worship takes more seriously the ordered reading of the Scriptures than any other church in Christendom.

Canon Alan Dunstan, (1983)

[The Church of England is] a great national society for the promotion of what is commonly called *goodness*.

Matthew Arnold

Mr. Pardoe (M.P.) clearly joined the Liberal Party for the same reasons as he joined the Church of England – he didn't have to believe anything at all!

Michael Foot, M.P., in the House of Commons, (18 March, 1976)

The historic Anglican position is acceptance of the institution of episcopacy and of the two gospel sacraments, but toleration of disagreement on their interpretation; and it needs to be said this toleration is in itself a highly significant ecclesiological matter.

Stephen W. Sykes: 'The Integrity of Anglicanism', (Mowbrays, 1978), Chapter 6

Anglicanism is a very positive form of Christian belief; it affirms that it teaches the whole of Catholic faith, free from the distortions, the exaggerations, the over-definitions both of the Protestant left wing and of the right wing of Tridentine Catholicism. Its challenge can be summed up in the phrases, 'Show us anything clearly set forth in Holy Scripture that we do not teach, and we will teach it; show us anything in our teaching and practice that is plainly contrary to Holy Scripture, and we will abandon it.' It was time (in the late 16th century) that this positive nature of Anglicanism should be made plain to the world.

Bishop Stephen Neill: 'Anglicanism', (1958–1977)

[In the Anglican community] demonstration through debate naturally and necessarily becomes the basic form of discipline in Christian doctrine. The risks of the procedure (unending pluralism, constant muddle, public vacillation and embarrassment) are high; however, its benefits (ripe convictions emerging from a long hard look at alternatives) make the risk worth taking.

J.I. Packer: 'A Kind of Noah's Ark', (Latimer Studies No. 10, 1981)

On the one hand there is a Christian truth, founded upon dogmatic revelation, and delivered forever to a 'people of God' whose existence in the world needs distinct recognition and assured self-identity. On the other hand there is the Church of England – an institution which is quite frankly worldly, in the sense that its leaders define their understanding of Christianity according to an agenda of moral and social concern which appears to differ in no important particulars from the material agenda of the secular intelligentsia.

Edward Norman: in The Times, (1991), 'Siren voices from the pulpit'

Anglicans characteristically are aware of praying in critical continuity with the past . . . Anglicans are characteristically unwilling to seek holiness through amnesia.

Professor William Stafford: in Cathedral Age, (1995), 'Anglican Spirituality'

Anglicanism, prospects

The Church [of England] as it now stands, no human power can save.

Thomas Arnold as Head of Rugby School, (1832)

The Church of England might 'die of its dignity'.

Retort of Bishop A.C. Tait (of London, later Archbishop of Canterbury) on being told that he was not as dignified as his predecessors

The Elizabethan Settlement was as much a political as a theological solution – the sharing of one church by all shades of opinion was a device of government for the peace of the realm, not a profound religious insight. Tolerance of dissent was originally not part of the package, but had to become so once the enforcement of religious uniformity was abandoned as impossible and unjust. It is an attitude manifested not just by doctrinal comprehensiveness but by social 'all-embracingness': the idea, still general in the Church of England, that the Vicar of Bray serves the entire population of Bray, and the population of the parish is the population of the whole neighbourhood which is still notionally deemed to be Anglican. . . . The intellectual content of the Anglican Way is, in its contemporary manifestation, diluted down to a point where its enemies can dismiss it as no more than a half-hearted semi-detachment to Christian faith.

It is not clear to an outsider, any longer, what it is trying to say. And those who are sceptical about doctrines and churches but still have warm feelings towards religion feel less need to belong to anything. For them the Anglican Way has succumbed at last to its own sharpest instrument, Occam's Razor: those ideas which are not necessary should be abandoned. But it deserves a generous obituary when the time comes. It was a most decent and civilised way of faith.

Clifford Longley: in The Times, (19 August, 1989), 'A tolerant church, worthy of a generous obituary'

It has been the tragedy of the Church of England that it has rejected so much that it might well have kept and kept so much that had better been rejected.

Bishop Stephen Neill: 'Anglicanism', (1958–1977)

The Church of England is in a condition not unlike the Soviet Union on the eve of its dissolution. The faith that once animated it has become for too many of its leaders a matter of lip service. Just as the Gorbachev revisionists justified their reforms by constantly invoking the name of Lenin, so in the Church of England traditional language is used to mean something different from what it used to mean. As in Russia, too, loss of belief has been accompanied by impending financial collapse; it is the classical formula for institutional disintegration. There is only one real question left: how long will it take?

William Oddie: in the Sunday Times, (19 December, 1993), 'To hell with the Church of England'

Anglicanism, in the pew

'Alimony Anglicans' pay their dues in order to stay away from Church with a clear conscience.

Anonymous

There's this to be said for the Church [of England], a man can belong to the Church and bide in his cheerful old inn, and never trouble or worry his mind about doctrines at all.

'Coggan' in Thomas Hardy: 'Far from the Madding Crowd', (1874)

An Episcopal (Anglican) Church in the U.S.A. advertised itself thus:
In a church started by a man with six wives, forgiveness goes without saying.

John Arbuthnot, in the John Bull pamphlets (1712):
John had a mother whom he loved and honoured extremely; a discreet, grave, sober, good-conditioned, cleanly old gentlewoman as ever lived; . . . She was neither one of your precise prudes, nor one of your fantastical old belles, that dress themselves like girls of fifteen; . . . She scorned to patch and paint, yet she loved to keep her hands and her face clean. Though she wore no flaunting lace ruffles, she would not keep herself in a constant sweat with greasy flannel; . . . She was no less genteel in her behaviour, well-bred, without affectation, in the due mean between one of your affected courtesying pieces of formality, and your romps that have no regard to the common rules of civility. Though she had a thousand good qualities, she was not without her faults, amongst

which one might perhaps reckon too great lenity to her servants, to whom she always gave good counsel, but often too gentle correction.

Anglicanism, ethos

C. of E. = Comedy of Errors.

Anonymous

While the Anglican church is vindicated by its place in history with a strikingly balanced witness to gospel and church and sound learning, its greater vindication lies in its pointing through its own history to something of which it is a fragment. Its credentials are its incompleteness, with the tension and travail in its soul. It is clumsy and untidy, it baffles neatness and logic. For it is sent not to commend itself as 'the best type of Christianity', but by its very brokenness to point to the universal church wherein all have died.

Michael Ramsey (later Archbishop): 'The Gospel and the Catholic Church', (London, 1936)

[The man who belongs to the Church of England or any Church of the Anglican Communion] . . . belongs to a church which values its cathedrals (and even in this generation builds new ones). He belongs to the church of George Herbert, the pastor, poet and music-maker. He belongs to a church which values music and conducts its worship with colour and dignity. The building he stands in, the robes he wears, the flowers, the organ – all these things belie any attempt to suggest that the quest for beauty and the works of imagination are worthless. Such a man is doomed to disappointment.

John C. King: 'The Gospel Shrinkers', (Hodders, 1970)

A church uniquely designed to frustrate the purposes for which it was created.

Attributed to Bishop Charles Gore

The Church of England is the astonishing survival of centuries of accommodations and compromises: it is perhaps ideally suited to a people who are ideologically inept, and its existence defines a number of negative considerations – it is loved for its very imprecision about formulas of faith which have elsewhere wrought havoc among the compromisers.

Edward Norman: in The Times, (1991), 'Siren voices from the pulpit'

How are we to combine spiritual leadership with our Lord's radical mistrust of power and the example of the Divine Son who did not cling to divinity but emptied himself of it and came among us as a slave? What would a kenotic [self-emptying] episcopate look like? Not, I suspect, like the model on offer in contemporary Anglicanism. Our style is a sort of benign, half-jokey triumphalism. The mitre is both a funny hat and a power statement, and it's not easy to say which we mean by it. Are we trying to make ourselves look ridiculous (a commendable ideal, not difficult to achieve) or more important than everyone else (and then what happens to Philippians 2 and Mark 10?).

Bishop Richard Holloway: in the Church Times, (12 February, 1993)

How many Anglicans does it take to change a light bulb?
Four: one to change it and three to say it didn't need to be changed.

Source unknown

Anglicanism cannot decide whether it is a chaplaincy to Christendom or a voluntary association.

Christopher Cunliffe

The Anglican Church attempts to be a hospital ship and an aircraft carrier at the same time.

Professor Christopher Harries

Anglo-catholicism

The Englishness of Anglo-Catholicism attracts a certain type of customer who loves the poetry of the Roman Catholic faith, but is not at all sure that taking orders from a foreign city is the patriotic thing to do. Being an Anglo-Catholic means you can listen to the Pope, but you can send it all back in 30 days if not absolutely delighted.

Kate Saunders (herself an Anglo-Catholic): in The Sunday Times, (27 May, 1990)

For the Catholic Anglican, in evangelism there is little point to bringing in new Christians if they fail to find Jesus Christ in the lives of those already there.

George Austin, (1991)

This famous comprehensiveness of the Church of England [the underlying principle of the Elizabethan Settlement] was what had given the Anglo-Catholics a claim to a home in the Church of England since the beginning of the Oxford Movement [usually dated from 1833]. Anglo-Catholicism, it can now be seen, is only tenable in the Church of England as long as the majority of non-Anglo-Catholics are prepared to allow it to be. As long as the only price it demands is an attitude of tolerance, they will pay it, But once it demands they should give up something they strongly desire, they will not.

Clifford Longley: in The Times, (11 November, 1989), 'When patience ran out'

High Anglo-Catholics are beneath contempt –
All intellectual and moral wrecks.
They love the frills but hold themselves exempt
From self-denial in the line of sex.

James Fenton and John Fuller: in New Review, (1976), 'Poem against Catholics'

The wing of the church led by slightly bitter, failed actors who still want to appear in a 'show'. Lots of dressing up and props, 'G & Ts' and 'Marvellous performance, darling', plus an adoring if dwindling audience.

Martin Wroe, Adrian Reith and Simon Parkes: 'The Church-English Dictionary', (1991): incorrectly attributed to 'High Church'

He says that if we [members of the Oxford Movement] succeed, we shall be introducing Popery without authority, Protestantism without liberty, Catholicism without universality, and Evangelicalism without spirituality. In the greater part of which censure doubtless you agree.

J.H. Newman: in a letter to the dying R. Hurrell Froude, (Autumn, 1835)

Bishop James Hannington of Eastern Equatorial Africa, martyred in Uganda, and a strong evangelical, was pleased to find Bishop Smythies of the Universities' Mission to Central Africa 'keen on heart conversion, in spite of mitre and cope'.

E.C. Dawson: 'The life of Bishop Hannington', (1877)

Apathy

I have long been convinced that the modern church has been bedevilled not so much by lack of faith as by lack of energy. Inertia is the modern Christian's besetting sin.

George Carey (later Archbishop of Canterbury): 'The Church in the Market Place', (Kingsway, 1984)

Apathy is the Church of England turning over in her sleep.

Anonymous

The only thing necessary for the triumph of evil is for good men to do nothing.

Edmund Burke, (1729–1797)

[Of Pope John Paul II, the 'Polish Pope'] Wojtyla's early life was dominated by the struggle against a godless ideology, but he has come to feel that we now face an even more implacable foe than Communism. The sufferings of the church in Poland and elsewhere ultimately served to strengthen the faith of believers. But what the Communists failed to destroy with force and terror is now in danger of decaying through sheer apathy and neglect.

Michael Dibden: 'Cabal', (Faber & Faber, 1992), the voice in the confessional

Apocrypha

John Bunyan found great comfort in the text: 'Look at the generations of old and see; did ever any trust in the Lord and was confounded? And did any abide in his fear, and were forsaken? Or whom did he ever despise, that called upon him?' He could not find it in the Scriptures, but later he wrote: 'Casting my eye upon the Apocrypha books, I found it in Ecclesiasticus, chapter two, verse ten. This at first did daunt me, because it was not in those texts that we call holy and canonical: yet as this sentence was the sum and substance of many of the promises, it was my duty to take the comfort of it. And I bless God for that word, for it was good to me. That word doth still of times shine before my face.'

Source unknown

I fear not the Apocrypha if the Bible is with it.

Charles Simeon

And the other books (as Hierome saith) the church doth read for example of life and instruction of manners; but yet doth it not apply them to establish any doctrine.

Article VI of the Thirty-nine Articles. [Hierome = Jerome]

The hymn 'Now thank we all our God' by Martin Rinkart (a Lutheran, 1586–1649, who pastored a congregation through the worst days of the Thirty Years' War), is a grace based on verses from the Apocrypha, *Ecclesiasticus 50:22–24 (the blessing of Simon at the re-dedication of the Temple),* with a doxology added.
The English hymn is a translation by Catherine Winkworth. 'Now therefore bless ye the God of all, which only doeth wondrous things every where, which exalteth our days from the womb, and dealeth with us according to his mercy. He grant us joyfulness of heart, and that peace may be in our days in Israel for ever: That he would confirm his mercy with us, and deliver us at his time!'

Traditional

Apologies

A Member of Parliament remarked in the House of Commons: 'The Honourable Member has the manners of a pig.' On being ordered by the Speaker to withdraw that unparliamentary remark, he replied: 'I withdraw my remark. The Honourable Member does not have the manners of a pig.'

Source unknown

The visiting missionary was being entertained for lunch at the Rectory. 'Oh, the apple tart is rather sharp,' said the Rector's wife. 'Would you like some sugar on it?'

'Yes please,' the visitor replied, 'that may improve it.' But he soon realised his mistake and corrected himself. 'I'm sorry, I didn't mean that! What I meant was I would like some sugar but there's nothing that could be done to this tart which would possibly improve it.'

Source unknown

Arts, the

Christianity is almost embarrassed about declaring its central adhesion to dogmatic truths, it is reluctant to admit that it has a mission to people of other faiths, and it is unhappy about insistence on the need for definite subscription to its traditional theology. Its leaders often place moral principle and material needs above revealed spiritual truth and the blunt assertion that people are immersed in sin.

The churches seem unable to quarrel with the widespread belief that religion derives from the emotional sensations of individuals rather than from the objective teaching of the Scripture. So the arts become the accepted repository of truth, and truth is relative to individual sensation.

The churches of the land are now conventional venues of secular concerts and the galleries of secular art. Religion itself is becoming a dimension of the heritage business.

Edward Norman: 'Credo' in The Times, (13 February, 1993)

The artist is a lucky dog . . . In any community of a thousand souls there will be nine hundred doing the work, ninety doing well, nine doing good, and one lucky dog painting or writing about the other nine hundred and ninety-nine.

Tom Stoppard: 'Artist Descending a Staircase', (B.B.C. Radio, 1972)

Ascension

Because He [Christ] is 'in Heaven' He is everywhere on earth; because he is ascended, He is here now. Our devotion is not to hold us by the empty tomb; it must lift up our hearts to heaven so that we too 'in heart and mind thither ascend and with Him continually dwell'*; it must also send us forth into the world to do His will; and these are not two things but one.

Archbishop William Temple: 'Readings in St. John's Gospel' (Collect of Ascension Day)*

The Ascension is not simply a matter of aerodynamics.

Robin E. Nixon, (1969)

He [Jesus] led them [the eleven disciples and their companions] out as far as Bethany, and, lifting up is hands, he blessed them. While he was blessing them, he withdrew from them and was carried up into heaven. And they worshipped him, and returned to Jerusalem with great joy; and they were continually in the temple blessing God.

Luke 24:50–53

. . . as they [the apostles] were watching, he [Jesus] was lifted up, and a cloud took him out of their sight. While he was going and they were gazing up toward heaven, suddenly two men in white robes stood by them. They said, 'Men of Galilee, why do you stand looking up toward heaven? This Jesus, who has been taken up from you into heaven, will come in the same way as you saw him go into heaven.'

Acts 1:9–11

Astronomy

A professor of Astronomy was sitting next to a professor of Theology on a flight. The astronomer teased the theologian: 'Of course, theology is all "Pie in the sky when you die".'

'In the same way that astronomy is all "Twinkle, twinkle little star", I suppose,' replied the theologian.

Source unknown

A cartoon showed an elderly man gazing through his telescope in the attic at the myriad stars of the universe. His wife ushered a friend up the stairs: 'Of course, you know he lives in a little world of his own.'

Source unknown

Atheism

An atheist is a man who has no invisible means of support.

John Buchan: 'Memory Hold the Door', (1940)

It's an interesting view of atheism, as a sort of *crutch* for those who can't stand the reality of God.

Tom Stoppard: 'Jumpers', (1972)

Atheism thrives where religion is most debated.

Welsh saying

Atonement

If the Lord God will judge thee [dying man], say: 'Lord I place the death of our Lord Jesus Christ between me and thy judgement: in no other way do I contend with thee.' If he shall say to thee that thou art a sinner, say: 'Lord, I place the death of our Lord Jesus Christ between thee and my sins.' If he shall say that he is angry with thee say, 'Lord, I place the death of our Lord Jesus Christ between me and thine anger.'

Anselm of Canterbury (1033–1099): 'Admonitis Morienti'

I was moved by the Christmas story but I rejected the atonement on the grounds that I did not need it, or want it, . . . God had sent his only begotten Son into the world to die ***for*** us, but the story did not make it at all clear what ***for*** meant.

A.S. Byatt: 'The God I want'

We are told that Christ was killed for us, that his death has washed out our sins, and that by dying he disabled death itself. Any theories we build up as to how Christ's death did all this are, in my view, quite secondary.

C.S. Lewis: (1898–1963)

Not the labours of my hands
Can fulfil thy law's demands;
Could my zeal no respite know,
Could my tears for ever flow,
All for sin could not atone,
Thou must save, and thou alone.

Augustus Montague Toplady (1740–1778): 'Rock of Ages' (1775)

John [the Baptist] saw Jesus coming toward him and declared, 'Here is the Lamb of God who takes away the sin of the world!'

John 1:29

Every priest stands day after day at his service, offering again and again the same sacrifices that can never take away sins. But when Christ had offered for all time a single sacrifice for sins, 'he sat down at the right hand of God', and since then has been waiting 'until his enemies would be made a footstool for his feet'. For by a single offering he has perfected for all time those who are sanctified.

Hebrews 10:11–14

Authority

Real authority is never taken, it is given.

Bob Mumford

No human order can command a writ of immortality.

Hon. David Bleakley, President of the Church Missionary Society, February 1985

There is only one source of authority which is the freedom and love of the Triune God. In human life, in Scripture, in the creeds, in the decisions of councils, in the liturgical order and canon law, in church leadership, there is only the discovery of authority, not its embodiment.

Stephen W. Sykes: 'The Integrity of Anglicanism', (Mowbrays, 1987), Chapter 7

There is a certain authority that comes from complete spiritual integrity, which is more to do with the way a man looks you in the eye than with his opinions, more to do with the quality of his prayers than the quality of his thoughts ... this ... is a quality valuable in itself, regardless of its impact on society.

Clifford Longley in The Times, (28 July, 1990), 'Carey on the scales'

Christians distinguish between true and false authority, that is, between the tyranny which crushes our humanity and the rational, benevolent authority under which we find our authentic human freedom.

John Stott: 'I Believe in Preaching', (Hodders, 1982)

B

Baptism, general

Writing of indiscriminate baptism, Dom Gregory Dix commented:

The existence of this vast amorphous mass of Pelagian goodwill, at least three or four times as large as the living body of the church which seeks to live by grace, is what muffles the whole impact of the gospel and the whole witness of the Church of England today. Deal with this problem, incorporate these people effectively into the life of the church (or at least prevent their increase), and you may have some prospect of making an impression on the equally large mass of sheer paganism behind.

The 'Theology of Confirmation', (1946)

When a young American Christian was asked whether he believed in baptism, he replied, 'Sure I believe in it, boss! I seen it done.'

Anonymous

Jesus [declares that] preparation by means of water-baptism only is inadequate for the kingdom he preaches; men must be prepared by a radical renewal of themselves, a new birth effected by the Spirit who comes (as it were) as the advance guard of the new age.

C.K. Barrett: Commentary on John 3:5

If we are to leave all questions aside and baptise simply to attest 'the primacy of grace', we shall find that our testimony proclaims what Bonhoeffer called 'cheap grace', and that I think I would call cosmetic grace. If such is the case, we have not only distorted baptism, we have more fundamentally misrepresented God's grace.

Colin Buchanan: 'Policies for Infant Baptism', (Grove Worship No. 98, 1987)

Charles Simeon of Cambridge distinguished between baptism which provides a Christian with a change of *state* and the work of the Spirit which leads to a change of *nature*.

. . .the modern practice of unconditional, indiscriminate baptising is indecent in itself, discreditable to the church, and highly injurious to religion.... Certainly the scandalous laxity which presides over the admission of new members into the Divine Society augurs ill for the future discipline of those members. . . . It is not charity to indulge in the solemn mockery of their use in cases where the assumption of Christianity cannot be reasonably made; it is a grievous and baleful imposture. . . . Is it indeed to Christ that we bring these children, whom we so baptise that they never know they are Christ's? . . . I submit that our present laxity rather hinders than facilitates access to Christ.

Hensley Henson (late Bishop of Hereford then Durham): Oxford University Sermon, 14 June 1896, quoted by C.E. Pocknee: 'Infant Baptism Yesterday and Today', (Mowbrays 1966)

Baptism, infants

Lady Bracknell, on being asked whether Jack Worthing had been baptised:
Every luxury that money could buy, including christening, had been lavished on you by your fond and doting parents.

Oscar Wilde: 'The Importance of Being Earnest', (1895), Act 3

It is sometimes supposed that because Christian initiation was originally received only or mainly by adults, therefore infant baptism, however justifiable, entails a departure from what must be theologically normative. But it is equally possible, and perhaps more reasonable, to regard the New Testament period as in this respect abnormal and exceptional. Not until families and nations were Christian could Christian initiation assume its normal form.

A.R. Vidler: 'The Theology of F.D. Maurice', (London, 1948)

Infant baptism is the sacrament of the empty-handed.

Heiko O. Oberman on Martin Luther's theology

The babe, with a cry brief and dismal,
Fell into the water baptismal;
Ere they'd gathered its plight,
It had sunk out of sight,
For the depth of the font was abysmal.

Edward Gobey: 'The Listening Attic', (1954)

If we want to speak in biblical terms we will say that the church *is* the people of God and that it is called to be the body of Christ. This is why such practices as infant baptism are defensible (though not necessarily contemporary baptismal practice). A child of Christian parents can be treated as capable of becoming a member of the people of God, of making up part of the body of Christ. The calling only becomes effective as understanding develops.

A.T. & R.P.C. Hanson: 'The Identity of the Church', (S.C.M., 1987)

Baptists

There was a very heated church meeting about changing a church's name from 'Baptist Church' to 'Christian Church'. Eventually, one old boy stood up and declared that he'd been a 'Baptist' for over fifty years and no one was ever going to call him a 'Christian'.

Two ministers, a Presbyterian and a Baptist, were discussing baptism. The Presbyterian asked if the Baptist considered that a person was properly baptised if he were immersed in water up to his chin. The answer was, 'Certainly not.'

'And would he be baptised if he were immersed up to his nose?' 'No,' was the reply.

'Well, what if you immersed him up to his eyebrows?' asked the Presbyterian.

'You don't seem to understand,' said the Baptist. He must be totally immersed in water until his head is covered.'

'I see,' said the Presbyterian. 'So it's just a little water on the top of the head that counts!'

Source unknown

When a Roman youth reached manhood, he put on the Toga Virilis, the robe of manhood. The day was accompanied by special ceremonial and was an important day in a young man's life. When Hindu youths of certain castes reach manhood, they put on the Yagnopavitam or sacred cord. The day is also one for special ceremonial and is a great day in the young man's life. Many other religions have similar coming-of-age ceremonies involving special clothing. So a believer at his or her baptism acknowledges that he has 'put on Christ', and is marked as being in a special relationship with the Lord.

Anonymous

Beauty

It is amazing how complete is the delusion that beauty is goodness.

Leo Tolstoy (1828–1910): 'The Kreutzer Sonata'

'Goodness, what beautiful diamonds!'
'Goodness had nothing to do with it, dearie.'

Mae West: 'Night after Night', (1932)

It is said that Bessie Braddock, M.P. once accused Winston Churchill of being drunk, to which he replied: 'Bessie, you're ugly. But tomorrow I shall be sober.'

Apocryphal

If I told you you had a beautiful body, would you hold it against me?

Attributed to Groucho Marx

A face like a hatchet dipped in vinegar.

Anonymous

Youth is happy because it has the ability to see beauty. Anyone who keeps the ability to see beauty never grows old.

Franz Kafka

Beauty without virtue is a flower without perfume.

French saying

Loveliness
Needs not the foreign aid of ornament.
But is, when unadorned, adorned the most.

James Thomson (1700–1748): 'The Seasons, "Autumn"'

If you get simple beauty and nought else,
You get about the best thing God invents.

Robert Browning (1812–1889): 'Fra Lippo Lippi'

One thing I asked of the Lord, that I will seek after:
to live in the house of the LORD all the days of my life,
to behold the beauty of the LORD,
and to inquire in his temple.

Psalm 27:4

Ascribe to the LORD the glory of his name;
worship the LORD in holy splendour.

Psalm 29:2

He [the Servant of the Lord] had no form or majesty that we should look at him,
nothing in his appearance that we should desire him.

Isaiah 53:2

All of us, with unveiled faces, seeing the glory of the Lord as though reflected in a mirror, are being transformed into the same image from one degree of glory to another; for this comes from the Lord, the Spirit.

2 Corinthians 3:18

Changed from glory into glory,
Till in heaven we take our place,
Till we cast our crowns before thee,
Lost in wonder, love and praise.

Charles Wesley (1707–1788) inspired by 2 Corinthians 3:18

Let your adornment be the inner self with the lasting beauty of a gentle and quiet spirit, which is very precious in God's sight.

1 Peter 3:4

Belief

John Stuart Mill suggested that we are usually right in what we affirm and wrong in what we deny.

I am convinced that if a dozen sceptics were to draw up in parallel columns a list of the events narrated in the Gospels which they consider credible and incredible respectively, their lists would be different in several particulars. Belief is literally a matter of taste.

George Bernard Shaw (1856–1950) – revealing a surprising failure to understand the nature of Christian belief

If you believe what you like in the Gospel and reject what you don't like, it is not the Gospel you believe but yourself.

Augustine of Hippo, (354–430)

Men quite happily believe what they want to believe.

Julius Caesar: 'De Bello Gallico, III.xviii'
(This sentiment has been repeated many times in various forms.)

I believe; help my unbelief!

The father of an epileptic boy healed by Jesus: Mark 9:24

Jesus said to them, 'I am the bread of life. Whoever comes to me will never be hungry, and whoever believes in me will never be thirsty. But I said to you that you have seen me and yet do not believe. Everything that the Father gives me will come to me, and anyone who comes to me I will never drive away.'

John 6:35–37

'Do you believe in the Son of Man?' He [the man healed of lifelong blindness] answered, 'And who is he, sir? Tell me, so that I may believe in him.' Jesus said to him, 'You have seen him, and the one speaking with you is he.' He said, 'Lord, I believe.' And he worshipped him. Jesus said, 'I came into this world for judgement so that those who do not see may see, and those who do see may become blind.'

John 9:35–39

This is his commandment, that we should believe in the name of his Son Jesus Christ and love one another, just as he has commanded us. All who obey his commandments abide in him, and he abides in them. And by this we know that he abides in us, by the Spirit that he has given us.

1 John 3:23, 24

Bereavement

Be not hasty to offer advice to those who are bowed down with a weight of trouble. There is a sacredness in grief which demands our reverence; the very habitation of a mourner must be approached with awe.

Charles Simeon: 'Homileticae Horae', Sermon 452

When you know how bitter an experience it is to lose the physical presence of someone you love you know that the comforting of those who mourn isn't saying, 'Well, never mind, it'll be all right.' Sometimes it's just being quiet with somebody, and allowing their grief to penetrate your own soul. You don't have to say anything.

One of the things that comforts me when I'm sad is the knowledge that there are other human beings who know me from all sides. They know the light and the darkness in me, and, because of the closeness of the relationship, they have experienced not only the light but the unpleasantness of the dark as well. But the relationship proves to be totally and absolutely dependable, and I know that I am still loved and valued and respected as a person, almost in spite of myself.

Terry Waite: Meditation on Isaiah 61, in 'Lent for Busy People', (B.R.F.)

The true way to mourn the dead is to take care of the living who belong to them.

Edmund Burke, (1729–1797)

Those who live near the Lord never see one another for the last time.

German saying

Ah, why should we wear black for the guests of God?

John Ruskin, (1819–1900)

. . . the hardness of easy consolation.

George Eliot (Mary Anne Evans)

Martha [sister of Mary and Lazarus] said to Jesus, 'Lord, if you had been here, my brother would not have died. But even now I know that God will give you whatever you ask of him.' Jesus said to her, 'Your brother will rise again.' Martha said to him, 'I know that he will rise again in the resurrection on the last day.' Jesus said to her, 'I am the resurrection and the life. Those who believe in me, even though they die, will live, and everyone who lives and believes in me will never die. Do you believe this?' She said to him, 'Yes, Lord, I believe that you are the Messiah, the Son of God, the one coming into the world.'

John 11:21–27

Do not worry about anything, but in everything by prayer and supplication with thanksgiving let your requests be made known to God. And the peace of God, which surpasses all understanding, will guard your hearts and your minds in Christ Jesus.

Philippians 4:6, 7

Bible, doctrine of – *see also* WORD OF GOD

The Scriptures principally teach what man is to believe concerning

God, and what duty God requires of man.

Shorter Westminster Catechism, (1648)

All the books, and the whole of each book which the church receives as sacred and canonical were written *at the dictation of the Holy Spirit*; and so far is it from being possible that any error can co-exist with Divine inspiration, that not only does the latter in itself exclude any error, but excludes and rejects it with the same necessity as attaches to the impossibility that God himself, who is the supreme Truth, should be the author of any error whatever.

Pope Leo XIII: Encyclical letter 'Providentissimus Deus', (1893). The quotation in italics is from the Council of Trent (1543–1553)

. . . trusting the New Testament is trusting it for a portrait of that person [Jesus]. A portrait, not a photograph. And a portrait not of a dead man, but of one who was for its writers now and for ever the human face of *God*.

Bishop John A.T. Robinson: 'Can we trust the New Testament?', (Mowbrays, 1977)

We present you with this book, the most valuable thing that this world affords. Here is wisdom; this is the royal law; these are the lively oracles of God.

Words at the Presentation of the Bible at a Coronation, spoken by the Moderator of the General Assembly of the Church of Scotland

We need to be conservative in our attitude to Scripture and what Scripture requires, but radical in everything else.

J.R.W. Stott, (E.F.A.C. Bulletin, 1973)

Luther was right when he saw in the Bible the cradle that bore to us the babe of Bethlehem, who is the Christ of Calvary and the eternal Word of God. We do not worship the cradle. We are not bibliolaters. But we thank God for it, Old Testament as well as New, as being that which bears to us him who is the life and light of the world. We can see the variety of workmanship which has gone to the making of it. But we venerate it for the holy burden which it bears and we approach it with the humility it deserves. Through that library of books . . . we hear afresh the voice of the Spirit, saying to the churches and to us as individuals: 'God has spoken. See that you do not refuse to hear the voice that speaks.'

Dr. Donald Coggan, (then Archbishop of York), 16 March 1970 at the Presentation of the New English Bible, Old Testament, Apocrypha and Revised New Testament, at Westminster Abbey

Charles Simeon (1759–1836) on biblical authority: 'No error in doctrine or other important matter is allowed; yet there are inexactnesses in reference to philosophical and scientific matters because of its popular style.'

He distinguished between 'plenary inspiration' [meaning 'those things which man could not know, or which the writer did not know'] and 'supervisory inspiration' [watching over 'the things which the writer did know, to prevent him from going wrong'].

Christian doctrine . . . is the intellectual understanding of the Christian religion and of its interaction with historical events, and the Bible is the check or norm continually to be applied to this understanding to make sure that it is faithful to the original lineaments and significance of the figure of Jesus Christ.

A.T. and R.P.C. Hanson: 'The Identity of the Church', (S.C.M., 1987)

[If a Christian who is part of modern Western culture says, 'I accept Scripture as God's word',] it will be seen as a personal decision, one of a number of possible decisions among which those of the Muslim, the Buddhist, the positivist, and many others must be counted, and one that must be supported by arguments a modern person can accept.

It will not do to say simply, 'The Bible tells me so', if you cannot give reasons for choosing the Bible rather than the Qur'an, the Gita, or *Das Capital*.

Bishop Lesslie Newbigin: 'Foolishness to the Greeks', (S.C.M., 1986)

. . . the resurgence of fundamentalist attitudes in our day, even in educated countries and in charismatic circles that supposedly prize the Spirit above the letter, speaks judgement on the churches for failing to present an intelligent authority of the Bible as a viable alternative to non-biblical spiritualities.

Bishop John A.T. Robinson: 'Can we trust the New Testament?', (Mowbrays, 1977)

Protestants often long for a 'paper pope', to which longing Martin Luther said: 'God and the Scriptures are two different things, as different as Creator and creature.'

Luther's Works

Luther's response, as requested 'without loops and holes' to the charges against him at the Diet of Worms, April 1521: Unless I am convinced by the testimony of the Holy Scriptures or by evident reason – for I can believe neither pope nor councils alone, as it is clear that they have erred repeatedly and contradicted themselves – I consider myself convicted by the testimony of Holy Scripture, which is my basis; my conscience is captive to the word of God. Thus I cannot and will not recant, because acting against one's conscience is neither safe nor sound. God help me. Amen.

(Reichstagsaklen 2.579, 3–5) This was reproduced in the published version of Luther's confession as: 'Here I stand. I cannot do otherwise. God help me. Amen.' (Reichstagsaklen 2.555,37, note 1.)

What pastor has not heard the questions: 'But is God really like that? How do you reconcile such things with the teachings of Jesus?' They are fair questions. And whoever asks them has – whether he is aware of the fact or not – raised the problem of the authority of the Old Testament. He wants to know in what way such narratives can contribute to the Christian's understanding of his God, and how they can furnish guidance for Christian conduct. Nor will it do to turn the question aside with an easy answer, for it is clear that whatever authority such passages possess, they do not provide the Christian with examples which his God wishes him to imitate. Are we, after all, to advocate the death penalty for those who absent themselves from church in order to pick up sticks – well, golf sticks at any rate – on Sunday? Is the Church to deal with its foes by butchering them in the name of Christ? Christ forbids it! Are we, then, to regard such things as but examples of human fanaticism and ignorance or, alternatively, as actions which may have been necessary at the time, but which are in no way to be imitated by us? But, in that event, wherein is their authority?

John Bright: 'The Authority of the Old Testament', (S.C.M., 1967)

Bible, use of

If we made the practice of selecting daily some short portion of Scripture for our meditation throughout the day, the most ignorant among us would soon attain a knowledge which at present appears far beyond his reach.

Charles Simeon (1759–1836)

It is sometimes said that house groups do not succeed in working-class areas. True, some homes are small and noisy, but, remember, we are holding a conversation, not a committee meeting. Conversations take place in small, noisy areas – with constant interruptions, some folk arriving in the middle and others leaving before the end. Nor should we worry too much about sticking to the set topic. As such meetings have no fixed finishing time, but simply run their natural course, we can let the red herrings swim freely!
Here is a not untypical snatch of conversation.
Leader: Why did Zacchaeus climb the tree?
First Member: To see better, I suppose. You've got to be careful, though. Our George climbed a tree in the park, fell out and broke his arm.
Second Member: Poor George, and he's such a nice lad, as well.
The Leader had intended a discussion on how unpopular people long to be accepted, but the resulting discussion centres on the problem of how a loving God can allow unjust suffering!

Never mind, we'll get back to Zacchaeus later, after a cup of tea.

Tony Adamson: 'Inner City Evangelism', (Grove Evangelism No. 22, 1993)

The best home Bible studies are the ones in which the teaching of the Bible is firmly planted in experience: those that try to ape sermons are not only unnecessary but are also doing the wrong job. If you want to kill off a home group from the best of motives, all you have to do is to think of it as a discussion-sermon. In addition to the discussion aspects of home groups, they also provide superb opportunities to convert Bible study into practical and informal prayer.

Robert M.E. Paterson: 'Short, Sharp and Off the Point', (MARC Europe, 1987)

The Grace and Truth catalog offered many items with Scripture emblazoned on them, including birthday cards ('Ye must be born again'), a gospel mail box with handsome nameplate and 'My word shall not pass away. Matthew 24:35' painted on the lid, a telephone-book cover ('Let no corrupt communication pass out of your mouth, but that which is good to the use of edifying. Ephesians 4:29'), a doormat ('Now ye are no more strangers and foreigners, but fellow-citizens with the saints, and of the household of God. Ephesians 2:19'), a wastebasket ('Touch not the unclean thing. 2 Corinthians 6:17'), and even an umbrella ('Giving thanks always for all things. Ephesians 5:20'). There were paper napkins and placemats in the Bible Families, Familiar Parables, Our Lord's Miracles and Bible Prophecies series – once, my friend Lance came to supper and found Armageddon and the Seven-Headed Beast under his plate.

I felt that so much Scripture floating around might tend to harden some hearts, that Scripture should be treated with reverence and not pasted to any flat surface you could find – at least, that was what I said when brethren asked why I didn't carry a 'The Peace of God Passeth All Understanding' bookbag to school. In fact, I was afraid I would be laughed off the face of the earth.

Garrison Keillor: Lake Wobegon Days, (1985), 'Protestant'

In a culture that mounted a frontal assault upon tradition, mediating elites, and institutions [the early U.S. republic], the Bible very easily became . . . 'a book dropped from the skies for all sorts of men to use in their own way.'

Nathan O. Hatch: 'The Democratization of American Society', (Yale, 1989); the quotation is from John W. Nevin.

Definitions have not only devastated God's church but have made heretics and schismatics, and have driven the children of the kingdom to Hell. Let us go back to the old Bible – you will be right there.

Father A.H. Stanton

Some people store their money in a Bible because they know that it's never likely to be opened!

Anonymous

The Bible is like 'a love letter from home' [Augustine of Hippo]. When a person falls in love with Jesus, he falls in love with the word which reveals him. He does not display it but treasures it and can recollect many of its truths. When he is over-critical of it, there would seem to be something wrong with his love for the Author.

Dr. Thomas H.L. Parker (1972)

Sortes Virgilianae – the way not to read the Bible. [Dipping into it to find texts at random.]

. . .when the Scriptures are read in the church, God himself speaks to his people, and it is Christ, present in his word, who proclaims the Gospel. . . . a homily, as a living expression of the work, increases its effectiveness and is an integral part of the service.

The Roman Missal: The General Instruction

There is no 'final' interpretation of holy writ . . . Let us be certain, brethren, that the Lord hath more truth and light yet to break forth out of his holy Word.

John Robinson, pastor of the English Congregation at Leyden, bidding farewell to the Christians on The Speedwell (later called The Mayflower) on 21 July, 1620

Wherever God's Word may be preached, his precepts remain a letter and dead words so long as they are not received by men with a pure heart; only where they pierce to the soul do they become, so to speak, changed into Spirit.

John Calvin

The way to read the Bible is, first and foremost, to read it in big chunks – whole books or even several books. Scripture should not be sipped like wine but drunk freely like beer.

Canon John Fenton: 18 September, 1986

Right from the start, the Church has gone to its task. . . 'with a book in its hand'. That this is so is symbolised by the fact (and it is a fact worth repeating) that the only thing which the Bishop hands to a priest at his ordination – or the Archbishop to the Bishop at his consecration – is a Bible. Here is the one source of his doctrine and the rule of his conduct.

Donald Coggan: 'Convictions', (Hodders 1976)

In interpreting the Bible, we can sometimes be too confident, like the Calvinist who 'looks on statements like that of Paul's possibly becoming a castaway, as a dog looks on a hedgehog: he knows not what to do with it.'

Charles Simeon, (1759–1836)

Experience is necessary for the understanding of the word. It is not merely to be repeated or known, but to be lived and felt.

Martin Luther (1483–1546) quoted from Mackinnon 'Luther', 4:293.

The first necessity . . . for a liturgical movement which will lead to an authentic revival of the church's own piety, is never to try to give back the liturgy to the people without at the same time giving them full and immediate access to the Bible. Only a personal meditation on the word of God in the school of the liturgy itself will enable the Christian people truly to live in that liturgy, *to live that liturgy* again.

Father Louis Bonyer, lectures at Notre Dame in 1954, published in English as 'Life and Liturgy', (1956)

It is funny how modern translations try to take the edge off the Bible and make it slightly more polite. The Bible is full of disturbing and awkward remarks and we always seem to want to tone it down.

Bishop David Jenkins (of Durham): 'God, Jesus and Life in Spirit', (S.C.M., 1988)

The way in which we must read Scripture today is controlled by the fact that we are, from moment to moment in the complex events of our time, dealing with and being dealt with by the same living God who meets us in Scripture, seeking his will, offering our obedience, accepting the share he allots to us of suffering, and looking for the final victory of his cause.

Bishop Lesslie Newbigin: 'Foolishness to the Greeks', (S.C.M., 1986)

There are three cautions about hermeneutical principles [e.g. 'justification by faith', 'the kingdom of God' or 'salvation']. They are never comprehensive enough and leave great tracts of truth that do not fit the framework. So it is important:

i Not to try and make everything fit.
ii To be especially careful in the allegorical use of stories, which can be made to say almost anything.
iii Not to absolutise what was meant to be a help in understanding and explaining truth and turn it into a doctrine by which you start to measure people and practices.

Tom Houston: Prayer and Spiritual Warfare, in 'World Evangelisation', (Number 68, 1994)

Bible, history of

The Bible humanised England; the Bible, nothing else. It is a matter of indifference how attractive we make our services, as long as we keep the open Bible.

Archbishop E.W. Benson (of Canterbury, 1882–1896)

There has never been a significant revival of religion in the history of Christianity which has not been nurtured in a revival of Bible study.

Dr. Ralph Stockman

I have taught you nothing but God's

holy word, and those lessons that I have taken out of God's holy book I have come hither to seal with my blood.

Rowland Taylor, to his parishioners at Hadley (Suffolk) before kissing the stake at which he was to be burned (February, 1555)

The Scripture is alive!

John Rogers, in his trial for heresy during Mary Tudor's reign:

I was taught to hold the Bible in such reverence that when one day, as I was buying a pennyworth of sweets in a little shop in Dublin, the shopkeeper tore a leaf out of a dismembered Bible to wrap them in, I was horrified, and half expected to see him struck by lightning, All the same I took the sweets and ate them; for to my Protestant mind the shopkeeper, as a Roman Catholic, would go to hell as such, Bible or no Bible, and was no gentleman anyhow. Besides, I liked eating sweets.

George Bernard Shaw (1856–1950): from 'The Oxford Book of Literary Anecdotes', Ed. James Sutherland, (1975)

After William Tyndale's first translation of the New Testament into English, Augustine Packington, a London merchant, and Cuthbert Tunstall, Bishop of London, were in Antwerp at the same time. The bishop arranged to buy up the entire stock of unsold copies [almost the entire edition], as a contemporary writer had it: 'The Bishop thinking that he had God by the toe, when indeed (as after he thought) the Devil by the fist'. Packington arranged for Tyndale to supply the books, to be burned at Paul's Cross in London, for two reasons: the new cash would enable Tyndale to correct and re-print many more copies than before 'and the whole world shall cry out upon the burning of God's word'.

Edward Halle: Chronicle

We went to every house in the place, and found each a scene of the greatest ignorance and vice. We saw but one Bible in all the parish, and that was used to prop aflowerpot!

Hannah Moore (1745–1833): letter to William Wilberforce (1759–1833)

. . . one of the earliest acts of the Henrician reform was the placing of an English Bible in churches; and that Cranmer's famous preface to the 1549 Prayer Book was principally concerned with defending the reform of the lectionary and Psalter – the ordered readings of Holy Scripture, rather than the exposition of it, being the centre of Anglican worship. Scripture is independent of, and prior to, the church's exposition of Scripture, and the church relates to it, in the first place, simply by reading it aloud and only secondly by preaching.

Oliver O'Donovan: 'On the Thirty-nine Articles', (Paternoster Press, 1986)

Bible, biblical criticism

Rationalism said the 'facts' of the Gospels (especially miracles, etc.) could be interpreted by nature and reason, without supernature. David Friedrich Strauss rejected even these as historical 'facts': 'The supernatural birth of Christ, his miracles, his resurrection and ascension, remain eternal truths, whatever doubt may be cast on their reality as historical facts.'

D.F. Strauss: 'The Life of Jesus Critically examined', (1835), 36, 38, 40

We are faced with the claim that God is prepared to work knock-down physical miracles in order to let a select number of people into the secret of his incarnation, resurrection and salvation, but he is not prepared to use such methods in order to deliver from Auschwitz, prevent Hiroshima, overcome famine or bring about a bloodless transformation of apartheid . . . Such a God is surely a cultic idol. That is to say, he is a false and misdeveloped picture of the true and gracious God drawn up by would-be worshippers who have gone dangerously and sadly – even if understandably – astray.

Bishop David Jenkins (of Durham): at the Church of England General Synod, (6 July, 1986)

. . . sometimes, released from the straitjacket of literalism (which is almost the antithesis of a 'living', 'active' or 'effective' word), the Bible, which had previously seemed to us to be a static, historical document which we needed to defend and justify, becomes instead a book of blazing originality and profound revelation of truth *here and now*....

It is a positively enriching thing to be released from a narrow literalist view of the Bible to see it as it is, a dynamic word, speaking as eloquently to modern man in his technology as it did to ancient man in his tents.

David Winter: 'But this I CAN believe', (1980)

The difficulties of the 'oral tradition' before the writing down of scriptural texts:

'Is this Wembley?'
'No, it's Thursday.'
'So am I, let's have a drink!'

Traditional

God's thoughts and ways are not like ours and neither is his arithmetic.

Douglas Webster: 'Not Ashamed'

... my certainty of the Christian Faith in its essentials is greater than my certainty of the perfection and infallibility of all the Holy Scriptures; my certainty of that is greater than my certainty of the meaning of many particular texts, and so of the truth of certain books.

Richard Baxter (1615–91): from the 'Reliquiae Baxterianae'

D. L. Moody, the evangelist, on meeting George Adam-Smith, who had just written an excellent commentary on Isaiah, asked him, 'Are you the chap who says there were *two Isaiahs?*' Adam-Smith replied that he was. Moody retorted: 'What on earth did you say that for when most people don't know there's *one* yet?'

The historic event of Christ, as the New Testament records it 'certainly does imply that we are not free to pick and choose, that we cannot treat either the history or the records in a cavalier manner, discarding the inconvenient and the uncomfortable and those events which offend modern taste, or challenge human arrogance.'

Douglas Webster: 'Not Ashamed', (1970)

What triggered off my anger (righteous, I trust) against some of our [theological] 'experts' is this. A clergyman, old, retired, useless if you like, took his own life because his reading of 'new theology' and even some problems on television, finally drove him, in his loneliness and ill-health, to conclude that his own life's work had been founded upon a lie. He felt that these highly-qualified writers and speakers must know so much more than he that they must be right. Jesus Christ did not really rise from the dead, and the New Testament, on which he based his life and ministry, was no more than a bundle of myths.

That made me angry, and I remembered the terrible words of Jesus which, in effect, say that a man would be better off dead than cause one of his little ones to stumble.

I am *not* concerned to distort or dilute the Christian faith so that modern undergraduates, for example, can accept it without a murmur. I am concerned with the truth revealed in and through Jesus Christ. Let the modern world conform to him, and never let us dare to try to make him fit into our clever-clever modern world.

I say quite bluntly that some of the intellectuals (by no means all, thank God), who write so cleverly and devastatingly about the Christian faith, appear to have no personal knowledge of the living God. For they lack awe, they lack humility, and they lack the responsibility which every Christian owes to his weaker brother. They make sure they are never made 'fools for Christ's sake', however many people's faith they may undermine.

I do not care a rap what the *'avant-garde'* scholars say; I do very much care what God says and does.

J.B. Phillips: 'Ring of Truth', (1967), Foreword

. . . the study of the documents requires what Wilhelm Dilthey called 'inner affinity and sympathy.' (Gesammelte Schriften, 5:278) We enter into a conversation with the documents and the authors who stand behind them; we do not simply judge them.

It remains true that the proper place for the Bible is in the church.

The church existed before the creation of scripture; it is the environment of scripture.

Yet unless investigators into the problems of Scripture can remain free; unless they can examine questions of interpretation without being unduly influenced by dogmatic considerations; unless, in short, they are not only church people but also free scholars, how can they hope to understand the Bible and make its insights available for their contemporaries?

R.M. Grant and D. Tracy: 'A Short History of the Interpretation of the Bible', (S.C.M., 1963, 1984)

Bigotry

The anger of men who have no opinion. The people who are most bigoted are the people who have no convictions at all.

G.K. Chesterton (1874–1936)

No doctor can cure those whose minds are blind.

Jewish saying

If we believe absurdities we shall commit atrocities.

François Marie Voltaire (1694–1778)

Birth control

It is now quite lawful for a Catholic woman to avoid pregnancy by a resort to mathematics, though she is still forbidden to resort to physics and chemistry.

H.L. Mencken: 'Minority Report', (1956)

A curate of Clyne Chapel (then a 'proprietary chapel' of a private estate near Swansea) in the 1950s had five children in about as many years. As part of his stipend, the Admiral gave him shooting rights on the estate.

Meeting the curate early one morning, the Admiral asked him, 'Out to bag a couple of rabbits for the family, Mr Evans?' 'No indeed!' came the reply; 'I'm out to shoot that stork.'

Source unknown

The controversy about contraception began with the supposition that God intends sex to be procreative (insofar as nature allows), and that to interfere with that possibility by artificial means is to deny his providence. The contemporary supposition is that sex is primarily a relationship-builder and that responsible parenthood is a Christian duty.

Robert M.E. Paterson, (1995)

Bishops, pastor of the pastors, teacher and missionary

A bishop should be particularly revered when he is silent. The silence of a bishop bears witness to the reality of God, both in the mystery of his divine silence and in the silence of his passion.

Ignatius of Loyola

I come as a learner, with no policy to advocate, no plan already formed to follow. But I come with one burning drive; it is that in all our activities, sacred and secular, ecclesiastical and social, we should help each other to fix our eyes on Jesus . . . Pray for me chiefly that I may never let go of the unseen hand of the Lord Jesus and may live in daily fellowship with him.

Bishop Frederick Temple, at his enthronement at Exeter, 1869, quoted by his son, Bishop William Temple, at his enthronement at Manchester, 1922. (Both men became Archbishop of Canterbury)

. . . it should go without saying that the *first* call on a bishop's time and care should be his clergy, their families and their problems.

Archbishop Donald Coggan: 'Convictions', (Hodders, 1975), 'Spirituality'

An essential qualification for a bishop is that he should be a theologian, that is one who is at least abreast with the main trends of biblical scholarship and theological debate. If he is not, he deprives himself of the right to speak publicly and representatively about doctrinal matters. He is indeed a custodian of the faith. But he is also a watchman. He must recognise the signs of the times. He must continually relate the gospel with which he is entrusted to the intellectual climate and the needs of the age in which he lives. He must not regard himself as simply commissioned to refrain from disturbing the minds of the faithful.

He must also stimulate and educate them.

A.T. & R.P.C. Hanson: 'The Identity of the Church', (S.C.M., 1987)

What I am for you terrifies me: what I am with you consoles me. For you, I am a bishop; with you, I am a Christian. The former is a title of duty; the latter is a title of grace. The former is a danger; the latter is salvation.

Augustine of Hippo, (354–430)

One person is diocese enough for a bishop.

Anonymous, often attributed to Augustine of Hippo

Bishops, prelates

Presbyterianism is no religion for a gentleman.
Episcopacy is no religion for a Christian.

King Charles II

When a Roman Catholic bishop becomes well-respected, the Pope makes him a cardigan.

Child's comment

He [Monseigneur de Giaccone, Archbishop of Lyons] watched her [the Baroness Courtebiche] coming forward through the long, austere apartment, lighted on one side by three high windows; but he did not rise. He himself belonged to the nobility of the long robe. He had the privilege of offering her his ring to kiss, and thus of omitting the courtesies normally shown to a woman. Any excess of politeness that he might have displayed would have involved the whole church, and the church holds herself superior to a baroness.

Gabriel Chevalier: 'Clochemerle', (1936), Chapter 15

It has been said that the only 'oomph' to come from some bishops is the 'oomph' felt by the episcopal cushion.

Anonymous

Merit, indeed! . . . We are come to a pretty pass if they talk of *merit* for a bishopric.

John Fane, Lord Westmorland (1759–1841): 9 December, 1835

Hugh Latimer accused the pre-Reformation English bishops of 'ruffling in their rents, dancing in their dominions . . . munching in their mangers, and moiling in their gay manors and mansions' so that they had no time for preaching.

From J.R.H. Moorman: 'A History of the Church of England', (Black, 1953)

A bishop was coming to stay in the vicarage some time in the early years of the twentieth century. The little eight-year-old son of the vicar was very anxious to see the prelate and pleaded with his father to let him take the bishop his early morning cup of tea. The vicar agreed and told the boy to knock, then say, 'It's the boy, my Lord. It's time to get up.'

The time came and the boy was nervously clutching the tea-cup and rehearsing his lines all the way up the stairs. He knocked on the door and the bishop boomed, 'Who is it?' A little taken aback, the boy announced: 'It's the Lord, my boy. Your time is up!'

Anonymous

Bishops, generally speaking, are generally speaking.

Anonymous

It's no accident that the symbol of a bishop is a crook and the sign of an archbishop is a double-cross.

Dom Gregory Dix

Bishops, archbishops

Robert Runcie, Archbishop of Canterbury during the 1988 Lambeth Conference, in welcoming the bishops on 16 July, meditated on his position.

I asked a friend who is a rabbi what he thought the change had been in the position of the archbishop. He told me this story. There was once a troublesome cat who made a great noise chasing the lady cats of the neighbourhood, disturbing everyone's peace and quiet. Eventually, the owner had it neutered. When friends asked, 'Did it work?' he answered, 'Well, he's still making a lot of noise; but it is now only in an advisory capacity.'

Archbishop: A Christian ecclesiastic of a rank superior to that attained by Christ.

Attributed to H.L. Mencken

The Revd. Michael Ingham, Principal Secretary to the Primate of Canada, Archbishop George Cram, received a request from the Director of the Wisconsin Regional Primate Research Center (John Hearn) for information for the International Director of Primatology. Part of his reply runs as follows:

I think the primates in your study are perhaps of a different species. While it is true that our primate occasionally enjoys bananas, I have never seen him walk with his knuckles on the ground or scratch himself publicly under the armpits. He does have three children, but this is a far cry from 'breeding colonies of primates' as your research project mentions. Like you we do not import our primates from the wild, however. They are elected from among the bishops of our church. This is occasionally a cause of similar, though arcane, comment.

The subject of primate biology might be of great importance in your field but, alas, not so in ours. There are a mere 28 Anglican primates in the whole world. They are all males, of course, but so far we have had no problems of reproduction. They include such distinguished persons as the . . . Archbishop of Canterbury . . . Have you sent letters to them? More importantly, have they responded? They can, I believe, all read and write by themselves so perhaps this might distort your data.

Thank you for writing. I wonder if your extremely efficient database might need just a little refining?
Kindest regards. 11 December, 1991.

Bishops, origins and succession

I must believe in apostolic succession, there being no other way to account for the descent of the Bishop of Exeter from Judas Iscariot.

Sydney Smith

In the government of the church nothing is more absurd than to disregard doctrine and place succession in persons.

John Calvin: 'Institutes of the Christian Religion IV ii, 3', Beveridge translation

The real successor of the apostolate was not the hierarchy but the canon of Scripture, written to prolong their voice, and compiled to replace the vanished witness.

P.T. Forsyth

We may sum up our conclusions in three propositions: Jesus did not institute a ministry for the church; the apostles did not transmit authority to any successors; the ordained ministry in the traditional sense only appears on a local scale at the end of the century. It would not be going too far to claim that the great majority of New Testament scholars of all traditions in the West today would accept the truth of these propositions.

A.T. & R.P.C. Hanson: 'The Identity of the Church', (S.C.M., 1987)

In the early church, bishops were essentially local in their jurisdiction. The decision to found a new church and constitute a bishopric lay with the metropolitan and the other bishops of an ecclesiastical province, at least from the fourth century. But once a bishop was appointed it was clear that he had the sole jurisdiction within what was called his *parochia*. . . .The converse was that he was restricted to his own territory in the exercise of his episcopal function. . . .the clearest statement . . . was that of the Synod of Antioch in 341 (canon 9), which declared that a bishop was independent in the administration of his see and that he could not act outside it without the consent of the metropolitan of the province and the neighbouring bishops.

Since the Reformation the Church of England has followed the patristic pattern very closely. Writers like John Jewell . . . asserted that all intervention had to be provincial in character and by way of metropolitan visitation. This certainly has been Anglican practice.

Dr. Gareth Bennett: in a letter to the Bishop of Birmingham, (1986)

. . . to have a bishop who is historically connected to the bishops of the early church, and is also linked in name and responsibility to every other living bishop in the church is to have a 'symbol of catholicity'.

S.W. Sykes: in a 'Background Paper for the Niagara Report', (ACC/LWF, 1987)

... the episcopate was formed not out of the apostolic order by localisation but out of the presbyteral by elevation: and the title, which originally was common to all [the presbyters], came at length to be appropriate to the chief among them.

Bishop Joseph Barber Lightfoot (of Durham)

Hierome [Jerome] seemeth to match all bishops together, as if they were all equally the Apostles' Successors. And he thinketh not any bishop to be lesse than other, for he that is poorer: or greater than other, for that he is richer. For he maketh the Bishop of Eugubium (a poore towne) equall with the Bishop of Rome. And farther he thinketh that a Bishop is no better than any Priest, saving that the Bishop hath authoritie to order Ministers.

What doethe a bishop, savinge only the Ordering of Ministers, but a prieste may doo the same?

[In every group of priests] one shoulde have a special pre-eminence above the others, and be called *episcopus*, the Bishop.

Bishop John Jewel: extracts from 'Defence', (1567)

Blessing

Anglican doctrine leaves me unclear whether a blessing is an act or a description.

Matthew Paris, in The Times, (1991), ' and moreover'

Prosperity is the blessing of the Old Testament; adversity is the blessing of the New.

Francis Bacon (1561–1626)

Blindness

A man once stood on a soap-box at Hyde Park Corner.

'People tell me that God exists, but I can't see him.

'People tell me that there is life after death, but I can't see it.

'People tell me that there is judgement to come but I can't see it.

'People tell me that there is a heaven and hell, but I can't see them.'

He won cheap applause and climbed down from his pulpit.

Another struggled on to the soap-box.

'People tell me that there is green grass all round, but I can't see it.

'People tell me that there is a blue sky above, but I can't see it.

'People tell me that there are trees nearby: but I can't see them.

'You see, I'm blind.'

David Watson: My God is Real

Horatio, Lord Nelson (1758–1805) at the Battle of Copenhagen:
I have only one eye – I have a right to be blind sometimes. I really do not see the signal.

In the land of the blind, the one-eyed is king.

Apostolius: Paromiae VII. xxiii

This is repeated by Machiavelli in 'La Mandragola' (1524).
Who is blinder than he that will not see?

English saying which appears in a variety of versions, first recorded by Andrew Boorde, (1547)

Boasting

For frantic boast and foolish word –
Thy mercy on thy people, Lord.

Rudyard Kipling (1865–1936): 'Recessional'

The boast of heraldry, the pomp of pow'r,
And all that beauty, all that wealth e'er gave,
Awaits alike th'inevitable hour,
The paths of glory lead but to the grave.

Thomas Gray (1716–1771): 'Elegy Written in a Country Churchyard'

'Let the one who boasts, boast in the Lord.' For it is not those who commend themselves that are approved, but those whom the Lord commends.

2 Corinthians 10:17, 18, quoting Jeremiah 9:24

By grace you have been saved through faith, and this is not your own doing; it is the gift of God – not the result of works, so that no one may boast. For we are what he has made us, created in Christ Jesus for good works, which God prepared beforehand to be our way of life.

Ephesians 2:8–10

Do nothing from selfish ambition or conceit, but in humility regard others as better than yourselves. Let each of you look not to your own interests, but to the interests of others.

Philippians 2:3, 4

Whatever gains I had, these I have come to regard as loss because of Christ. More than that, I regard everything as loss because of the surpassing value of knowing Christ Jesus my Lord. For his sake I have suffered the loss of all things, and I regard them as rubbish, in order that I may gain Christ and be found in him, not having a righteousness of my own that comes from the law, but one that comes through faith in Christ, the righteousness from God based on faith.

Philippians 3:7–9

Books

Reading is sometimes an ingenious device for avoiding thought.

Sir Arthur Helps (1813–1875): 'Friends in Council'

Verily, when the day of judgement comes, we shall not be asked what we have read, but what we have done.

Thomas a Kempis (1380–1471): 'Imitatio Christi'

Some Books are to be Tasted, others to be Swallowed, and some few to be Chewed and Digested; that is, some Books are to be read only in Parts; others to be read but not Curiously; and some few to be read wholly, and with Diligence and Attention.

Sir Frances Bacon (1561–1626)

'Tis the good reader that makes the good book.

Ralph Emerson

Books give not wisdom where was
 none before,
But where some is, there reading
 makes it more.

Sir John Harington

Whenever Benjamin Disraeli, who was a popular writer as well as a parliamentarian, received a book from some up-and-coming writer, he replied immediately: 'I shall waste no time in reading your book.'

At a literary dinner in the middle of the Napoleonic Wars, Thomas Campbell (1777–1844) proposed an outrageous toast to Napoleon Bonaparte! To uproar, he explained that, although the man was a tyrant, still, 'he once shot a bookseller'.

James Sutherland, Ed.: 'The Oxford Book of Literary Anecdotes', (1975)

When Milton wrote *Paradise Lost* he was to receive £5 in advance of publication, a second £5 when the first edition was sold, and an extra £5 for each complete edition sold. Milton lived to receive only £10.

It was said that Dugald Stewart (1753–1828) was bad at returning borrowed books and, by his own admission, also bad at arithmetic. Acquaintances said that he might be bad at arithmetic, but he certainly excelled at book-keeping.

Anonymous

Don't read science fiction books. It'll look bad if you die in bed with one on the nightstand. Always read stuff that will make you look good if you die in the middle of it.

P.J. O'Rourke: in 'National Lampoon', (1979)

Breaking bread *see* EUCHARIST

Britain

Britain lies in a northerly position, but the climate, though very damp, is not nearly so cold as one would expect; if properly drained the country could be made extremely fruitful.

Robert Graves: Claudius in 'Claudius the God'

British Xenophobia takes the form of Insularism, and the Limeys all moved to an island some time ago to 'keep themselves to themselves', which, as far as the rest of the world is concerned, is a good thing.

The 'National Lampoon' Encyclopaedia of Humor, (1973)

C

Care, of others

Caring for the outcasts is labour intensive.

Raymond Fung, (1987)

His room was in a poor, but densely populated part of Liverpool. Children played outside his door. He was found in August. The doctor estimated he had died in mid-February, during the bitterest cold! Nobody had missed him: and he may never have been found, had not some housebreakers tried to rob his gas meter!

In the scullery of her Portsmouth home, the body of a 70-year-old woman was discovered. It was almost decomposed. She had been dead for about four years. For four years, no one could have called on her.

John Dickson Pope

There are ten strong things. Iron is strong but fire melts it. Fire is strong but water quenches it. Water is strong but the clouds evaporate it. Clouds are strong but wind drives them away. Man is strong but fear casts him down. Fear is strong but sleep overcomes it. Sleep is strong but death is stronger. Loving-kindness survives death.

The Talmud

The LORD said to Cain, 'Where is your brother Abel?' He said, 'I do not know; am I my brother's keeper?'

Genesis 4:9

The LORD bless you and keep you;
the LORD make his face to shine upon you, and be gracious to you;
the LORD lift up his countenance upon you, and give you peace.

Numbers 6:24–26 (The Aaronic blessing)

Jesus said to Simon Peter, 'Simon son of John, do you love me more than these?' He said to him, 'Yes, Lord; you know that I love you.' Jesus said to him, 'Feed my lambs.' A second time he said to him, 'Simon son of John, do you love me?' He said to him, 'Yes, Lord; you know that I love you.' Jesus said to him, 'Tend my sheep.' He said to him the third time, 'Simon son of John, do you love me?' Peter felt hurt because he said to him the third time, 'Do you love me?' And he said to him, 'Lord, you know everything; you know that I love you.' Jesus said to him, 'Feed my sheep.'

John 21:15–17

Catechism

The most godly people, therefore, in your congregations will find it worth their labour to learn the very words of a catechism.

Richard Baxter: 'The Reformed Pastor', (1655)

. . . it is the fundamental doctrines of the Catechism which I highest value and daily think of, and find most useful to myself and others. The Creed, the Lord's Prayer and the Ten Commandments do find me now the most acceptable and plentiful matter for all my meditations. They are to me as my daily bread and drink. And as I can speak and write of them over and over again, so I had rather read or hear of them than any of the school niceties which once so much pleased me.

Richard Baxter (1615–91): from the 'Reliquiae Baxterianae'

Catholicity

Scratch an Anglo-Catholic, and you will find an Evangelical. His hymns sometimes strike an evangelical note; he is surprisingly anxious to justify his ministry and doctrine from the Bible. Look carefully into the soul of an Evangelical, and you will find in him a concern for true doctrine which is eminently Catholic, and an allegiance to liturgy which is at least not obviously Protestant.

Bishop Richard Hanson: in The Times, (24 September, 1977)

Ignatius (c. 35–107) describes the local Church in the second century as the gathering of all professing Christians in that geographical place, of whatever social class, meeting with their bishop to celebrate the Lord's Supper. This is what he describes as the 'catholic' Church.

If it [a local church] is to be a 'church' it must also be 'in communion with all other local churches' by means of a world-wide concern, a common basis of the vision and understanding of the gospel and structures to facilitate this communion. Such structures create 'a network of communion of churches, not a new form of church'.

Ian Cundy (later Bishop): 'Historical aspects of the Doctrine of the Church', (1989), quoting John Zizionlas: Being as Communion

The opposite of 'catholic' is not 'protestant' or 'reformed'; it is 'provincial' A healthy catholic emphasis is an essential part of an open-minded biblical faith. The provincial has scarcely considered this; he has decided that something which he vaguely identifies as catholic order is a menace to a proper understanding of a gospel of justification by faith. He has narrowed catholicity down to a point of doctrine when it should be an open attitude of mind.

John C. King: 'The Gospel Shrinkers', (Hodders, 1970)

The designations 'Roman', 'Greek' and 'Protestant' are verbal conventions useful for identifying the differing features of various accounts of the Christian faith, not alternatives to the term 'catholic'.

Stephen W. Sykes: 'The Integrity of Anglicanism', (Mowbrays, 1978), Chapter 4

It [the Church] ought to aim at excluding none whom our Lord Jesus Christ would not exclude. It ought to rule out in principle no type of thought or of temperament, and no forms of devotion, which are in any sense genuinely and defensibly Christian.

A.E.J. Rawlinson: from a sermon in 1925, published in 'Freedom within the Church', (Cambridge, 1928)

. . . by Catholic, I mean going right back to Jesus Christ and the apostles: to their insight into the gospel, their discussion of the meaning of Jesus Christ and what he taught and who he was, their passing on their insights in the gospel through the New Testament writings, and handing them down in the experience of believers during the past 2000 years. This is perhaps better called tradition. That is why I am 'Catholic'. I do not stand alone in my insights into the discovery of God in Christ as Lord and Saviour. This idea of authority has brought great strength to my ministry over many years. It has enabled me to stand up and say not just what I believe to be true but rather what all the Christians down the ages have believed.

Bryan Green: in the Church Times 11 January, 1991: 'The manifesto of a liberated Evangelical'

The present polemics of the self-styled defenders of 'catholicity' in the Church of England, besides being disgracefully ungracious to women, are also deeply ungracious to Christians in other than the Orthodox and Roman Catholic Churches . . . Thus at a time when the central challenge to Christian faith, church and discipline is plainly to do with the credibility of our gospel and our faith in God having any realistic saving relevance to the miseries of our planet, we are expending a great deal of energy and anxiety on eternal quarrels about who should submit to whom. All in the interests of a catholicity which is a fantasy as it is conceived and in danger of being a tyranny as it is practised.

Bishop David Jenkins (of Durham): in The Independent, (26 June, 1993)

The Church is Catholicke, universall, so are all her Actions; All that she does, belongs to all. When she baptises a child, that action concerns mee; for that child is thereby connected to that Head which is my Head too, and engrafted into that body, whereof I am a member.

John Donne, (1623)

Caution

You taught me not to go overboard, lose my head, or make a big deal out of it, but to keep a happy medium, that the truth is in the middle. No extremes. Don't exaggerate. Hold your horses. Keep a lid on it. Save it for later. Be careful. Weigh the alternatives. Wear navy blue. Years later, I am constantly adjusting my feelings downward to achieve that fine balance of caution and melancholy.

Garrison Keillor: 'Lake Wobegon Days', (1985), '95 Theses 95', News

Have more than thou showest,
Speak less than thou knowest,
Lend less than thou owest,
Ride more than thou goest,
Learn more than thou trowest,
Set less than thou throwest.

William Shakespeare: 'King Lear' I.iv

Celtic Christianity

No one knows how the Celtic cross, with its famous wheel behind the cross, came to be; there are many speculative views.
Whatever its origins, there is no doubt that the symbolism of the circle of creation held in tension with the cross of redemption makes a very powerful impression on anyone who today stands in front of one of these crosses.

Esther de Waal: 'A World Made Whole', (Fount, 1991)

One thing we know of Celtic spirituality which cannot seriously be contested is that we know remarkably little for certain about it.

Aled Edwards, (1994)

There is the legend of how St. Patrick on Holy Saturday 433 kindled the Paschal fire on the hill of Slane in defiance of the high king Laeghaire of Tara who sat watching him from the opposite hill of Tara, having decreed that none should light any fire in the land before he did. (Tradition says that, as Patrick fled the king's wrath, he and his followers sang the *Deer's Cry*, St. Patrick's Breastplate, which is, in fact, an eighth century hymn.)

Esther de Waal: 'A World Made Whole', (Fount, 1991)

Celts

His harp was carved and cunning,
His sword prompt and sharp,
And he was gay when he held the sword,
Sad when he held the harp.

For the great Gaels of Ireland
Are the men that God made mad,
For all their wars are merry
And all their songs are sad.

He kept the Roman order,
He made the Christian sign,
But his eyes grew often blind and bright
And the sea that rose in the rocks at night,
Rose to his head like wine.

G. K. Chesterton (a poem about King Alfred), describing a Celtic Chieftain

Censorship

They [*La Prensa*] accused us of suppressing freedom of expression. This was a lie and we could not let them publish it.

Nelba Blandon, Director of Censorship for the Interior Ministry of Nicaragua, quoted in The New York Times, (1984)

Assassination is the extreme form of censorship.

George Bernard Shaw: 'The Rejected Statement'

Chance

Chance is perhaps God's pseudonym when he does not want to sign.

Anatole France (1844–1924): 'Le Jardin d'Epicure'

He that leaveth nothing to chance will do few things ill, but he will do very few things.

Lord Halifax

That power which erring men call chance.

John Milton: 'Comus', (1634)

The laws [of nature] tell you what will happen if nothing interferes. They can't tell you whether something *is* going to interfere.

C.S. Lewis: Religion and Science (1945), in 'God in the Dock', (Collins 1979)

Do not make room for the devil.

Ephesians 4:27

Change

Of the trendiness of clerics:
Anti-clericalism, of a rather mild sort compared with that on the Continent, has always lain just beneath the surface in this country, requiring only a prod or two to bring it to the top. The introduction of the new services has provided such a prod; and the popular Press, in particular the *Daily Telegraph*, has not been slow to cash

in on the resulting upsurge of protest.

In the conversations in which I get embroiled at nearly every social occasion to which I am invited I am constantly hearing the expression, 'these trendy parsons.' It is usually applied to those of the younger clergy who are alleged to take a delight in disturbing elderly members of their congregations by their innovations.

I think that this expression should be used with care. Something very much like it was used two hundred years ago about clergymen who were discarding their wigs and allowing their own hair to be seen. A few years later a vicar who appeared at a vestry meeting in trousers instead of breeches and gaiters was as much disapproved of as would be a clergyman who appeared at a PCC meeting today in jeans.

At Cambridge University, where half the clergy of the established church were educated, there was a rule in at least one college that 'gentlemen must not appear in Hall in trousers.' Only bishops, deans and archdeacons, who tended to be more conservative than the rank-and-file of the clergy, were wearing breeches and gaiters after the turn of the half-century. There was much partisan criticism of clerics who preferred 'the dog-collar' (which is now universally regarded as the clerical badge of office) to the cravat. The dog-collar was regarded, rightly, as Romish.

Until the middle of the nineteenth century the clergy, like all other gentlemen since the end of the seventeenth century, were clean shaven. Inspired by the returning veterans from the Crimean War, whiskers and beards were allowed to grow; and they remained until the end of the century, when clippers were once more employed on the back of the neck and round the ears. The appearance of the hirsute young clergymen of today is very similar to that of their predecessors a hundred years ago.

Anthony Trollope had some very sharp things to say about trendy clergymen. He much preferred conservative characters like Archdeacon Grantly and Mr. Harding.

It was not only in their personal appearance that trendiness was found among the Victorian clergy. In church dreadful things happened. There was an uproar when the clergy discontinued the habit of putting on a preacher's gown before ascending the pulpit. The substitution of open pews in serried ranks for the commodious box pews in which members of the congregation could sleep undetected was deeply resented by those who did not want their slumbers disturbed by enthusiastic sermons. *Hymns Ancient and Modern* were not universally approved, because they let in by the back door numerous heresies. As for the demolition of the minstrels' gallery at the east end of the nave and the introduction of choir stalls in the chancel to accommodate choristers in surplices – this was Popery undisguised!

In fact, nearly everything which the occupant of the pew now regards as the norm in church worship has at one time or another been condemned as trendy or worse.

After I had made a few changes in my own village church a few years ago, an old lady complained that I had altered it from what it had been for hundreds of years. She of all people ought to have known that her own grandfather, the Squire, in connivance with one of my predecessors, had in 1872 transformed the church out of all recognition.

Those who object to the new services today on the grounds that they are trendy should remember that the Holy Communion of the Book of Common Prayer was likened to a Christmas charade by pious Catholics in Cornwall when it first appeared in the parish churches.

Bishop Frank H. West (Suffragan Bishop of Taunton 1962–1977): in the Church Times

God grant us serenity to accept the things we cannot change, courage to change the things we can, and wisdom to know the difference.

Quoted by V. Collancz: 'God of a Hundred Names'

Preservationists seek to put history back, to reproduce the past as though it was now: it is the approach taken by Disney World recreations, an attempt to put the old oak tree back into the acorn. Or else they seek to stop the passage of time, to arrest the clock of history: it is the approach taken by some custodians of ancient monuments, carefully preserved ruins, an attempt to stop the old oak tree decaying or growing.

Conservationists, on the other hand, seek to make the best of the past in the present for the future: it is the approach taken by those who know that time and history are mobile, that the present has to make its contribution to the heritage of the past and must leave room for the contributions of the future. This is an attempt to respect the old oak, to prune it where necessary, to nurture its health, to create good conditions for its future or, perhaps, to let it die.

Robert M.E. Paterson, (1985)

Time does not end. Change does not end. There is no place where I can stand and say, 'This rock is unchanging; this moment is endless.' Nor any place in life where I can stand and say, 'This is what I am, complete and unchanging.' There are forces beyond our willing that beat upon us, and the best we can do is stand against them, firm in our conviction.

Hal Borland: 'This Hill, This Valley'

Maturity is the capacity to endure uncertainty.

Professor John Finley, Harvard University

There are many sights and sounds and ideas and events in the world that disturb us, that offend us, that we would rather not think about. There are many ways to deal with such phenomena; . . . But what, again and again, we do in practice is none of these things; we change the name of what we dislike, and by doing so persuade ourselves that we have changed the thing itself.

Bernard Levin: in The Times, (17 March, 1987)

. . . change is not progress unless the core remains unchanged. A small oak grows into a big oak; if it became a beech, that would not be growth, but mere change.

C.S. Lewis: 'Dogma and the Universe', (1943), in 'God in the Dock', (Collins, 1979)

What might be the Church's seven last words?
'We've never done it that way before.'

Anonymous

The very word *change* causes us discomfiture. The hymn has made us link the word 'change' with 'decay', whereas it can mean new beginning, new growth. Someone remarked that the structures of the church have the engine power of a lawn mower and the brakes of a juggernaut! Such is our instinctive and structural conservatism. But in times of whirlwind developments in communications and yet of galloping disintegration in society, we need to know the difference between the eternally significant in our heritage, and the merely evanescent.

Archbishop Alwyn Rice Jones (of Wales): Board of Mission of Church in Wales, Annual Review, (1994)

Adam to Eve: We live in times of transition, my dear.

Charismatics – *see also* SPIRIT

How many Charismatics does it take to change a light bulb?
Six: one to change it and five to share the experience.

Anonymous

May require an interpreter in conversation. Certainly if conversation is with God. Useful to warm up cold churches. Difficult when it all boils over.

Martin Wroe, Adrian Reith & Simon Parkes: 'The Church-English Dictionary', (1991)

Those who have the gale of the Holy Spirit go forward even in sleep.

Brother Lawrence

A young fellow came to our meeting in Plymouth, as he said, to pick a hole in the preacher's coat; and the Holy Spirit picked a hole in his heart.

George Whitefield, (1714–1770)

Each has a particular gift from God, one having one kind and another a different kind.

1 Corinthians 7:7

Like good stewards of the manifold grace of God, serve one another with whatever gift each of you has received.

1 Peter 4:10

Charity

On 3 February, 1542 Archbishop Thomas Cranmer asked Convocation for a revision of the Great Bible in English. This was carried out, mostly by conservative divines who did not believe in the key Reformation doctrine, justification by faith alone. They, therefore, chose to translate the end of 1 Corinthians 13 as 'faith, hope and charity' following the Latin Vulgate rendering of *caritas*, meaning 'charitable acts of love'. Cranmer, and Bishops Goodrich and Barlow argued, with King Henry VIII's support, that the problem should be sent to the university theologians to decide, because they realised that an accurate rendering of the Greek was 'faith, hope and love'. They won, but 'charity' returned in the 1611 King James Version!

Mrs Thrale reckoned Dr. Samuel Johnson never spent more than £80 a year on himself, nor less than £200 a year on others. He allowed his home to be used as a refuge for the destitute and on his way to and from dinner at some hostelry he would empty his pockets for beggars, or put pennies into the hands of children asleep on doorsteps.

Charm

[Sir Robert] Peel's smile is like the silver plate on a coffin.

J.P. Curran (1750–1817), quoted by Daniel O'Connell in the House of Commons (26 February, 1835)

Children

Dear God,
Last week it rained three days. We thought it would be like Noah's Ark but it wasn't. I'm glad because you could only take two things, remember, and we have three cats. – Donna

Dear Mr. God,
How do you feel about people who don't believe in you? Somebody else wants to know. – A friend, Neil

Dear God,
I know you are supposed to love thy neighbour but if Mark keeps taking my other skate he's going to get it. – Kevin

Dear God,
Are you real? Some people don't believe it. If you are you better do something quick. – Harriet Ann

Insanity is hereditary. You get it from your kids.

Anonymous, (c. 1984)

The quickest way for a parent to get a child's attention is to sit down and look comfortable.

Lane Olinghouse: in the Wall Street Journal

People sometimes ask me, 'Why don't we keep the children in the crèche and Sunday school until they are old enough to understand and believe?' The short answer is, 'Because most of them will have left by then.' On the other hand, anyone who pursues a policy of integrating children into adult worship will never escape criticism. Let me share my convictions:

a. I have learned that 'justification by faith' is not the prerogative of adults.
b. In any church that baptizes babies and children, we have no right to exclude them from our worship.
c. The long-term results of integrating children and adults in worship are noticeable (though it takes at least five years, often ten). There is a lack of teenage culture-shock.
d. There are advantages to adults in worshipping with children.
e. There are advantages to children in worshipping with adults.

So I believe we should be totally committed to a significant proportion of Christian worship being for all ages – and committed in principle as well as in practice. Such worship will be divisive and often quite messy but it is authentically Christian and I know it works.

Robert M.E. Paterson, (1991)

What God had done for his people was to be passed on from generation to generation. The children did not have to have a certain level of understanding in order to take part in the Passover. It was the other way round. They took part in the meal so that they would get that understanding.

David Bell: in 'Together', (magazine of the Church Pastoral Aid Society, 1991)

A parish which gives children their whole and rightful place is a parish which demonstrates an understanding of the nature of the kingdom of God. Jesus himself valued children very highly, and placed them in the midst of his disciples as signs of the kingdom he proclaimed. We too must allow children to be in our midst, where they belong.

Ivor Hughes: in 'Home and Family', (magazine of the Mothers' Union, 1992)

Sunday School:
A small therapy group comprised of victims of parental churchgoing.

Martin Wroe, Adrian Reith and Simon Parkes: 'The Church-English Dictionary', (1991)

How sharper than a serpent's tooth it is to have a thankless child.

William Shakespeare (1564–1616): King Lear

Choice

Between two evils, I always pick the one I never tried before.

Mae West: in 'Klondike Annie', (1936)

You pays your money and you takes your choice.

Anonymous, collected by V.S. Lean

The Christian church today suffers from large numbers who feel that *they* have 'made a decision for Christ', or from those who think that *they* have chosen to join a certain church. Such man-centred notions spell spiritual death, or at least barren sterility. It is only when we begin to see ourselves as chosen, called and commissioned by Christ that we shall have any real sense of our responsibility to present our bodies to him 'as a living sacrifice, holy and acceptable to God'.

David Watson: 'Discipleship', (1981)

Canadian Anglicans [a specific reference but this would apply generally to Christians in the West] certainly did not learn from their church to regard religion as something to be bought and consumed, even less from their Bibles. They learnt it in their high streets and televisions, and took it with them into church . . .

They shopped around, until they found what they wanted in the type and style of services. They went to church when they felt it was what they needed to do. The focus was all the time on the autonomous individual, the choice-making consumer, who selected in the area of religion what he felt would meet his immediate needs or wants, just as he might select a new car, with or without ashtrays and power steering. . .

The implication was that the church had to respond like a good retailer, adapting the products on sale to suit the market. . .

While true enough to modern life, this is a ghastly parody of religion. The danger to the church is that it will fall into the consumerist trap . . . every bishop with his sell-by date, every prayer book with its shelf-life. . .

. . . the warning . . . was that it can go deeper, and that religion itself was beginning to be treated as if it was a piece of personal property or service, chosen according to the same criteria as other things to be bought, with value for money as the only true test. . .

To reduce the obligations of one side of the relationship [between God and his people] to the payment of money, while the other side still delivers the goods, is called prostitution. In religion it is the traffic in sacred things, called simony after Simon the Magician who offered to buy the power of the Holy Spirit. At least the sin of religious consumerism now has a name; and it always helps to name the sin.

Clifford Longley: 'The sin of Simon Magus, first religious consumer', in The Times, (6 January, 1990)

When you have to make a choice and don't make it, that is in itself a choice.

William James

The element of choice available to us today would be unknown to the Christians of the New Testament, in spite of Corinth and the other evidence of division and conflict. Just as Noah did not choose the company with whom he was saved in the ark, so we in one sense cannot choose our company in the church of God.

Ian Cundy (later Bishop of Peterborough): 'Historical aspects of the Doctrine of the Church', (1989)

Christ, the

Arab Christians have for a long time (and still today) referred to Jesus as 'the One who walks by night'.

Kitsch [worthless and pretentious] religious art is the salmonella of the soul. So as long as he [Christ] is such a teddy bear, meek, mild, pastel-coloured, he can keep the children peaceful. But he must not interfere with the pastimes of us grown-ups.

Dewi Morgan: in The Times, (21 December, 1985)

. . . either Jesus was what the Catholic Church said he was, or he did not exist; either he was the Man from heaven, a complete break with the natural order of things, the representative of a transcendental order, supernatural, super-rational, super-everything, or he was nothing.

Bishop Charles Gore of Birmingham, (c. 1909)

When Buddha was dying, his disciples asked how they could best remember him. He told them not to bother. It was his teaching, not his person, that counted. With Jesus it is altogether different.

David Watson: 'Discipleship', (1981)

Polycarp, Bishop of Smyrna, was executed for refusing to offer incense on a pagan altar: The year of his death was between 154 and 177

Eighty-six years I have served him and he has done me no wrong. How can I blaspheme my king who has saved me?

God's only Son doth hug Humanity
Into his very Person.

Edward Taylor, 17th century American poet

Christianity

If we acknowledge the truth of the inroads made by secularism into the 'traditional' Sunday, we have to ask ourselves whether corporate and worshipping Christianity should present itself as one of the following:

(a) a group which says you cannot belong to it if you cannot make its meetings;
(b) a group which is reasonably indifferent as to whether or not you can make its meetings:
(c) a group which is prepared to provide at least some 'main' worship events on other days of the week.

This choice takes us in vastly different directions when each possibility is applied to those seeking baptism for a child or wishing to be converted.

Colin Buchanan: 'The Heart of Sunday Worship', (Grove Worship, 1992)

What the believer possesses as a result of his conversion is not a set of formulae which he can repeat like a parrot, nor a system of doctrines which he accepts as infallibly true, nor a book of oracles out of which he can answer every question: he possesses new eyes.

Alan Richardson

Christianity was born in Palestine. They took it to Greece and they made it a philosophy. They took it to Rome and they made it into an institution. They took it to America and made it into a business enterprise. They took it to England and made it into a tourist attraction.

Tony Campolo: in Tear Times, (Spring 1991)

A local cult called Christianity.

Thomas Hardy (1840 – 1928): 'The Dynasts'

Two things about the Christian religion must surely be clear to anybody with eyes in his head. One is that men cannot do without it; the other, that they cannot do with it as it is.

Matthew Arnold (1822–1888)

It is unnatural for Christianity to be popular.

Billy Graham

The primary declaration of Christianity is not 'This do!' but 'This happened'.

Evelyn Underhill (1875–1941)

. . . foolish preachers, by always telling you how much Christianity will help you and how good it is for society, have actually led you to forget that Christianity is not a patent medicine. Christianity claims to give an account of *facts* – to tell you what the real universe is like.

C.S. Lewis: 'Man or Rabbit?', (1946), in 'God in the Dock' (Collins, 1979)

Christians

I first came across this [indoctrination] at Cambridge where, as an earnest inquirer after truth and being favourably disposed towards Christianity because of my family background, I put myself in the way of Christians in the hope that they might be able to help me in my search. My first discovery was that there were many different breeds of this strange animal and that, instead of regarding me kindly, their immediate concern was to make sure that I hadn't been contaminated by contact with another breed. This done, they proceeded to explain at great length why I should avoid contact with the other breeds, why the other breeds were wrong/immoral/corrupt or just plain stupid, and why their breed was the only one that could help me.

Actually 'help' is the wrong word, because I never at any time felt that anyone was interested in 'helping' me find the truth; they wanted to enrol me in their gang, and were prepared to use almost any means to indoctrinate me. There was the approach of probing one's life like a dentist looking for cavities and then, having found the nerve, pressing on it and saying, 'It hurts, but I can make it better'; there were the aggressive young men who cornered you at parties and demanded, 'Are you saved?' ('For this dance, honey, but I'll keep one for you later'); the élite dinner parties where silver-tongued monsignors from London made you feel how witty, elegant and upper-crust it would be; the parties and meetings where an escape was offered from the pressures of university life – are you lonely? Here we have instant friends; bewildered? Here we have instant answers; confused by this new, strange environment? We can cocoon you.

Richard MacKenna: 'God for Nothing', (Churchman, 1984/85)

Christians cannot be distinguished from the rest of the human race by country or language or customs. They do not . . . use a special form of speech; . . . yet although they . . . follow the customs of the country in clothing and food and other matters of daily living, at the same time they give proof of the remarkable . . . constitution of their commonwealth. They busy themselves on earth, but their citizenship is in heaven . . . to put it simply; what the soul is to the body, the Christians are to the world.

The Letter to Diognetus (late 2nd century)

. . . do not think that Christ is found in ceremonies, in doctrines kept after a fashion, and in constitutions of the church. Who is truly a Christian? Not he who is baptised or anointed or who attends church. It is rather the person who has embraced Christ in the innermost feelings of his heart, and who follows him by his holy deeds. . . . You compel your subjects to know and obey your laws. With far more energy you should exact of yourself knowledge and obedience to the laws of Christ, your king!

Desiderius Erasmus, writing to Charles of Burgundy (later Emperor Charles V): 'The Education of a Christian Prince', (1516)

Christmas – *see also* INCARNATION

Lord Mottistone asked a question in the House of Lords on Wednesday 25 January, 1989:

Couldn't the House of Lords' Christmas card in future have a Christian religious theme? Lord Aberdare, replying, reflected that this had been tried once or twice in the past. He seemed to recall 'An Angel from the Crypt' on one card, and surely there had been another with a picture of 'Seven Bishops being found Not Guilty'? This rather begged the question of which Crypt the Angel was from and what it was the Bishops were not guilty of. But their lordships let that pass. Others rose, mostly to support the idea of putting Christ back into Christmas.

Was there no one to put the opposite view? Yes – you guessed it. The Church of England, in the form of His Grace the Bishop of Truro, rose to the task. The *message*, which issued in the great themes of all men (not just Christians, you see) was really the dignity of human beings. Hope, love, peace, etc. It was the message that counted. And a Happy Ramadan to you, Your Grace.

Matthew Parris: in The Times, 26 January, 1989 , Political sketch

God grant you the light in Christmas,
which is faith;
the warmth of Christmas, which is
love;
the radiance of Christmas, which is
purity;
the righteousness of Christmas,
which is justice;
the belief in Christmas, which is truth;
the *all* of Christmas, which is Christ.

Wilda English

When we say, on Boxing Day, that we're glad Christmas is over for another year, remember, 'To you a Saviour is born . . .'; it's just a beginning.

Eugenia Price

The Word, and unable to speak a word!

Lancelot Andrewes: on John 1:14

You can never truly enjoy Christmas until you can look up into the Father's face and tell him you have received his Christmas gift, Jesus Christ.

John R. Rice

Santa Claus never died for anybody.

Craig Wilson

And is it true? And is it true,
This most tremendous tale of all,
Seen in a stained-glass window's hue,
A Baby in an ox's stall?
The Maker of the stars and sea
Become a Child on earth for me?

No love that in a family dwells,
No carolling in frosty air,
Nor all the steeple-shaking bells
Can with this single Truth compare –
That God was Man in Palestine
And lives to-day in Bread and Wine.

John Betjeman: Christmas, stanzas 6 & 8, (from 'A Few Late Chrysanthemums', 1954 in John Betjemen's Collected Poems, Murray, 1958)

The Christmas story is no pretty seasonal confection: for all its great joy, its implications are in deadly earnest.

Daily Telegraph Leader, (24 December, 1981)

In groves of fir and holly, the country is preparing the sacrificial turkeys in honour of a red-coated figure, apparently invented by an American journalist in the 1820's by combining the legend of St. Nicholas with the practice of Siberian witch doctors, and whose sole purpose seems to be to raise unreasonable desires in children's minds which their parents will be unable to satisfy. Meanwhile, some of us will be celebrating Christmas.

Source unknown

The shops, cafes and travel agencies were all doing a thriving business. Giving and receiving, eating and drinking, skiing and sunning. . . . Any modern Christ who had attempted to intervene would himself have been expelled in short order by the security guards employed to keep this temple of commerce free of beggars, junkies, buskers, religious fanatics and other riff-raff.

Michael Dibden: 'Cabal', (1992), Chapter 7

Sir,
As a Jew, I am distressed and saddened by public treatment of Christmas as a winter jollification rather than a religious celebration. Birmingham Council's designation of civic decorations as 'festive lights' and elimination of religious symbols may have been intended to spare minorities' feelings but I find it patronising and therefore somewhat hurtful.
Yours faithfully,
M.D. Berkson.

Letter to The Times, (13 December, 1993)

Some astronomers believe that the Star of Bethlehem, visible in the Middle East at about the time of

Christ's birth, began to attract attention in late January 6 B.C. as Mars passed near the faint Uranus, a dim yet visible wanderer in those unpolluted skies. From 25 February of the same year, a rare triple conjunction (not repeated for 139 years) would have been visible as Jupiter (father and king of the 'gods' and 'god' of justice) came together with Saturn (ruling planet of Judah and another symbol of justice) while Mars (the 'god' of war), having crossed into the Constellation of Pisces (the fish, representing the Hebrews) from the Constellation of Aries was entering the equinox.

An alternative explanation gives a date of 2 B.C., when the two brightest planets, Venus and Jupiter, moved into line with each other in the Constellation of Leo (the lion), and would have appeared as a dazzling light on 17 June. This, however, does not account for the two sightings (in the east and near Bethlehem) separated by a lengthy journey time.

Matthew's text (Chapter 2) is tantalisingly lacking in detail, and the New Testament points us to Jesus as the true light or star.

Church, doctrine of

The Church is not a bouquet of individuals.

P.T. Forsyth (1848–1921)

The faith-in-Christ people.

James Robertson, (1982)

Even in its invisible essence, it [the Church] is not Christ nor a second Christ nor a kind of extension of the one Christ. Karl Barth makes the point that the presence and activity of Christ in the church has to be made visible by the people of God, that it is the presence of his people (rather than the celebration of the eucharist) which fulfils his promise to be 'there in the midst of them'.

The Reformers highlighted the danger of divinising the Church, what Barth very appropriately calls *sacro egoismo*, for the church is, by nature, a visible community (this side of the grave). What is invisible in the church, he Barth says, is the presence and activity of Jesus Christ, and that is what has to be made outward and visible. The moment the church begins to think that it possesses the fulness of divine grace, it has fallen from that grace.

Digest of parts of Karl Barth: 'Church Dogmatics', IV.3.ii

My reading of the New Testament suggests that the early Christians never went out just telling what Jesus meant to them personally. They would not have separated their faith from that of their fellowship. To say 'Jesus is Lord', which was most probably the earliest Christian confession, joined them to a church where his lordship was acknowledged. To be 'in Christ' and to be 'in the church' is synonymous in the New Testament.

George Carey (later Archbishop): 'The Church in the Market Place', (Kingsway, 1984)

. . . as a people of promise, their very existence in the midst of the nations is a sign of God's wider and final purpose of redemption for humanity and the transformation of the kingdoms of the earth into the kingdom of God.

Chris Wright: 'Ecclesiology – A Biblical Perspective', (1989)

Christianity is a social religion. To turn it into a solitary religion is to destroy it.

John Wesley

. . . many Christians in the Protestant tradition . . . think of the church, if they think of it at all, as a loose federation of saved individuals. Or they attach themselves vaguely to a single charismatic individual who runs his church as rock-stars run their fans, and too often finds the business as lucrative as they. This is a wrong concept of the church, a dangerous distortion of the original idea of the people of God in the Bible and the early church. A low doctrine of the church is not merely feeble and unattractive, it is unorthodox and unscriptural.

A.T. & R.P.C. Hanson: 'The Identity of the Church', (S.C.M., 1987)

It [the Church] embraces all those who in baptism have identified themselves with the justifying grace of the gospel, and inevitably we will not all agree . . . the church described in the New Testament and developed in our theology is a community in which all are accepted because God in Christ has accepted them. Too often in our history, however, we have behaved as if we were a collection, and gathered the like-minded together, whether on social, ethnic or theological grounds.

Ian Cundy (later Bishop of Peterborough): 'Historical aspects of the Doctrine of the Church', (1989)

The phrase 'The Church is the extension of the Incarnation' is non-biblical and open to misunderstanding. But there is enough truth in it to make us take seriously once again what St. Paul meant by the body of Christ, or what St. Luke meant when he spoke of 'all that Jesus began to do and to teach' (Acts 1:1).

Archbishop Donald Coggan (of Canterbury): 'The Ministry of Healing, in Convictions', (Hodders, 1975)

The popular evangelical distinction between the visible and invisible church is unbiblical.

Peter Kuzmic: at the Lausanne II Congress in Manila, (July, 1989)

Those committed to belief in God incarnate, must also be prepared to see the church incarnated in the world.

Bishop Michael Nazir-Ali: 'Evangelisation in Contemporary Cultures', (C.M.S., 1993)

There is no barrier between two
worlds in the church,
The church militant on earth
Is one with the church triumphant in
heaven,
And the saints are in this church
which is two in one.
They come to worship with us, our
small congregation.
The saints our oldest ancestors.

Euros Bowen, (1984)

Church, belonging to

Any local church which seeks not only to handle God's word with integrity but to fashion its life according to God's word ought to be able to hold together in love and trust those who have differing opinions about the work of the Spirit.

David Prior: 'The Suffering and the Glory', (1985)

Perhaps the most lasting pleasure in life is the pleasure of *not* going to church.

Dean William Inge (of St. Paul's, 1911–34)

The church in the last analysis is a community of aliens looking for a home and it is impossible to have Christianity without the church, or to retain the church without concern that it should grow. The church is lightly criticised, but it cannot be lightly dismissed.

Canon Douglas Webster: 'Not Ashamed', (1970)

There is no entering into life unless the church conceives us in her womb, brings us to birth, nourishes us at her bosom and preserves us by her guardianship and discipleship . . . no forgiveness is to be hoped for beyond her embrace, nor any salvation.

John Calvin (1510 – 1564)

Salus extra ecclesiam non est.
(There is no salvation outside the Church.)

Augustine of Hippo (354 – 430)

The Christian church is not a club that we belong to in order that our needs might be met; it is a body, a building, a family, an army – these are some of the pictures used to show that, by accepting the call of Christ, we have responsibilities that we cannot avoid if we are to be his disciples. It is not a matter of our feelings and personal choices; it is a matter of taking with the utmost seriousness the conditions and demands of discipleship that Jesus lays upon us. We are no longer our own. We have been chosen by him, called by him, bought by him; we therefore now belong to him, and by virtue of this fact we also belong to one another, however easy or difficult, joyful or painful, we may find this to be.

David Watson: 'Discipleship', (1981)

. . . that grotesque anomaly, an unchurched Christian.

John R.W. Stott, (1988)

. . . the church shouldn't be an escape or an irrelevance, a place where you put on a false front, but the place where you are given time and space to sense the deepest levels of your existence, the reality underlying all things.

Richard MacKenna: 'God for Nothing', (Churchman, 1984/85)

Any doctrine of the church that includes the assumption that millions of Christians, either now or in the past, must be judged not to be real members of the church at all refutes itself.

A.T. & R.P.C. Hanson: 'The Identity of the Church', (S.C.M., 1987)

The church of the crucified Christ cannot consist of an assembly of like persons who mutually affirm each other, but must be constituted of unlike persons. 'Like seeks after like' as Aristotle says in his discussion of friendship (Ethics Book VIII). But for the crucified Christ, the principle of fellowship is fellowship with those who are different, and solidarity with those who have become alien and have been made different.

Jürgen Moltmann: 'The Crucified God', (S.C.M., 1974)

Church, the institution

It is better that men should be disorderly saved than orderly damned; and that the church be disorderly preserved than orderly destroyed.

Richard Baxter (1615–1691)

The church holds a variety of attitudes on its role:
Is it engaged in maintenance or mission?
Is it a church or a sect?
Is it a club or a movement?
Is it Jesus or institution?

John Poulton (1978)

The church . . . has degenerated either into emotional ritual, or hymn-singing, or secluded and entrenched piety . . . It neither understands the world nor touches it at any point.

Oswin Creighton: in 1917 or 1918

The church should consist of communities of loving defiance. Instead it consists largely of comfortable clubs of conformity.

Ronald J. Sider: 'Rich Christians in an Age of Hunger'

A church of the good and respectable I find mysteriously unappealing.

Bishop Richard Holloway: in Church Times, (28 August, 1992), 'Missionary energy laced with moralism'

I've always figured that if God wanted us to go to church a lot, he'd have given us bigger behinds to sit on and smaller heads to think with.

P.J. O'Rourke: 'Holidays in Hell', (1988)

It would be a good thing if . . . church societies periodically considered the desirability of suicide.

Archbishop William Temple: quoted by Sidney Darke in 'The People's Archbishop', (James Clarke, 1942)

Church, its mission

In spite of what we sometimes hear, the church of Jesus Christ will never die. But the local manifestation of it has no guarantee of success. We depend on the grace and power of God and our faithfulness to his call.

Archbishop George Carey: 'Canterbury Enthronement', (19 April, 1991)

An ecclesiology which wants to maintain a biblical perspective must continue to define the identity of the church primarily in terms of its mission and ethic.

Chris Wright: 'Ecclesiology – A Biblical Perspective', (1989)

The gospel gives birth to the church, and the church is the bearer of the gospel.

Robert M.E. Paterson, (1991)

In our day, everywhere, the church has to learn to exert influence without acquiring political power, to proclaim the Lordship of Christ by being totally available as his servant to all humanity.

Douglas Webster: 'Not Ashamed', (1970)

Unbar the doors! throw open the
  doors!
I will not have the house of prayer,
  the church of Christ,
The sanctuary, turned into a fortress.
The church shall protect her own, in
  her own way, not
As oak and stone; stone and oak
  decay,

Give no stay, but the Church shall endure.
The church shall be open, even to our enemies. Open the door!

T.S. Eliot: 'Murder in the Cathedral', (1935), Part II, lines 316ff (Faber and Faber 1965)

[The church is] the real body of Christ, which continues as he did, powerless and loving. To be confronted by that is to be confronted by the spirit of Jesus...

Richard MacKenna: 'God for Nothing', (Churchman, 1984/85)

Michael Ramsey, Archbishop of Canterbury, was the source of the saying: 'The Church which lives to itself will die by itself.' He indicated that this saying was a digest of the Second Letter to the Corinthians.

Every day people are straying away from the church and going back to God.

Lenny Bruce, (1972)

Evangelization is for no one an individual and isolated act. It is one that is deeply ecclesial. When the most obscure preacher in the most distant land preaches the gospel, gathers his little community together or administers a sacrament, even alone, he is carrying out an ecclesial act, and his action is certainly attached to the evangelizing activity of the whole church.

Pope Paul VI

In some situations... is it [the church] catering for the needs of one segment of the population at the expense of others? Mere presence can be alienating if its visible form is palpably alien to significant sections of the population.

Bishop Michael Nazir-Ali: 'Evangelisation in Contemporary Cultures', (C.M.S., 1993)

Church, scepticism about

The church could be a lot worse. I tell myself that daily. It cheers me up a bit.

Bishop Rowan Williams (of Monmouth, 1993)

The church today is like the Indians in the United States. Their way of life could not be made to fit into modern American Society, and so they have been put into special reservations where 'They cannot do any harm'. So it is with the church. She has become a 'religious reservation' with her own pattern of life.

Robert Adolfs, (c. 1974)

The nearer the church the further from God.

Bishop Lancelot Andrewes (1555–1626)

Look at the life imagined in such a newspaper as *The Nonconformist* – a life of jealousy of the Establishment, disputes, tea meetings, openings of chapels, sermons; and then think of it as an ideal of human life completing itself on all sides, and aspiring with all its organs after sweetness, light and perfection!

Matthew Arnold: 'Culture & Anarchy', (1869)

The churches of the British Isles are old and hard of hearing.

Bishop John Neale: Secretary of the Partnership for World Mission, (1990)

The trouble with the church is that it takes people from where they aren't, to where they don't want to be.

Ernie Southcott

Instead of each of us being called to follow that lonely and desperately hard Calvary road, the church lays a nice bright six-lane highway, and we are all looking for the trappings of success – anything to prove that the absentee landlord still has power, that the organisation is successful. A nice full church, lots of conversions, coming across well on TV or radio, making a good impression as a super going concern full of super people, proving something to ourselves by speaking in 'tongues' – the list is endless.

But does a crucified man have anything to do with success, prestige or popularity? 'The figure of the crucified invalidates all thought which takes success as its standard,' wrote Bonhoeffer; *invalidates* – the whole thing becomes a ghastly sham because the church has become a retreat from reality, dealing with cheap reassurance, rather than the body of Christ which plunges itself into human life, suffering, living, dying for others.

Richard MacKenna: 'God for Nothing', (Churchman, 1984/85)

. . . all too often the church, instead of being the starting-point for the individual's journey, where he is fed, watered and encouraged, is seen as the terminus; a nursery where you are given space to remain childish and unhealed and can avoid all the pain and anxiety of growth.

Richard MacKenna: 'God for Nothing', (Churchman, 1984/85)

If we . . . decreed that all the churches and Christians should vanish overnight, what would happen? I have a secret fear that the only people to notice would be a few local conservation groups.

Richard MacKenna: 'God for Nothing', (Churchman 1984/85)

A church which does not back up its words of faith with acts of personal service is not the church of Jesus Christ.

Archbishop David Penman: at the Lausanne II Congress in Manila, (July, 1989)

Going to church, taking part in church affairs generally, on the whole is not exposure to an exploration into a mysterious and attractive, awe-inspiring and ever deepening reality. On the whole, going to church and being attracted to various church affairs forms a series of operations which protect us from the realities around us. The whole process tends to make people less human and less realistic. I once saw a poster up outside a place I was driving through which said, 'Come to church'. I had a great sense that I ought to get out and put up another poster which said: 'This is the *last* thing you should do.' Which, I still think, is right. People have to know quite a lot about God before they can stand up to going to church.

. . . I would not be a bishop if I were not absolutely clear that even the church cannot keep a good God down.

Bishop David Jenkins (of Durham): 'God, Jesus and Life in the Spirit', (S.C.M., 1988)

Church, the history of

[The twentieth century church] has become more and more focused on things like going to church, where you hear about, talk about and pray to a God who is described in special language which becomes increasingly peculiar to the cultic groups concerned. People have misunderstood the Authorised Version translation of 1 Peter: 'you are a peculiar people.' In a sense, 'by God we are!' And so what they have done has become peculiarer and peculiarer. Therefore it has looked more and more as if people were really concentrating on a rather peculiar and tribalist God.

Bishop David Jenkins (Durham): 'God, Jesus and Life in the Spirit', (S.C.M., 1988)

The Church must be for ever
building, for it is forever
decaying within and attacked from
without.
For this is the law of life; and you
must remember that while there is
time of prosperity
The people will neglect the Temple,
and in time of
adversity they will decry it.

T.S. Eliot Chorus II from The Rock, from Selected Poems, (Faber and Faber, 1954)

We should not fail to note that although the great majority of the world's Christians are white-skinned and live in the West, the main growing-points are among coloured peoples outside the West, and the most serious areas of decay and decadence are among whites and in the West.

Douglas Webster: 'Not Ashamed', (1970)

[It is doubtful whether the majority of Christians were caucasian westerners even in 1970, but the observation remains valid.]

Church, the Scriptures

Now to him who by the power at work within us is able to accomplish abundantly far more than all we can ask or imagine, to him be glory in the church and in Christ Jesus to all generations, for ever and ever. Amen.

Ephesians 3:20, 21

Come to him, a living stone, though rejected by mortals yet chosen and precious in God's sight, and like living stones, let yourselves be built into a spiritual house, to be a holy priesthood, to offer spiritual sacrifices acceptable to God through Jesus Christ. . .

You are a chosen race, a royal priesthood, a holy nation, God's own people, in order that you may proclaim the mighty acts of him who called you out of darkness into his marvellous light.

Once you were not a people, but now you are God's people;
once you had not received mercy, but now you have received mercy.

1 Peter 2:4, 5, 9, 10

Church buildings

Most of the events in the Bible, in both the Old and New Testaments, happen out of doors. The Palm Sunday stories . . . and virtually any other passages at which the Bible might randomly fall open, are descriptions of open-air events.

In striking and disturbing contrast, 'religion' is supposed to 'happen' in contemporary Britain behind closed if not locked doors, usually doors with intersecting parabolic curves at the top. It is presumed to be confined to special and distinct buildings, which is why proposals to tear down or sell such buildings invariably cause such pain in the local community. The actual removal of the place where 'religion happens' is a symbolic removal of religion itself.

Clifford Longley, in The Times, (24 March, 1986)

The longer he [Archbishop J. B. Sumner, 1780–1863, a significant builder of churches] contemplated the difficulties of communicating the Christian faith in a secularising urban culture, the more he became convinced that ecclesiastical buildings were not a suitable or endearing venue for ordinary working people. 'It's too big a jump for such people,' he claimed. 'The only hope is that we carry our message to them.' He went on to recommend the use of cottages and schoolrooms.

Nigel Scotland: 'John Bird Sumner', (Gracewing, 1995)

A Parish Church in the Fifteenth Century:
Not only does everyone go to church on Sundays and in his best clothes: the church is used on weekdays too, for it is impossible to say daily prayers in the little hovels in which most of the villagers live. School is taught in the porch, business is carried out by the cross in the market where the booths are (for there are no shops in the village, only open stalls as in market squares today). In the nave of the church on a weekday there are probably people gossiping in some places, while in others there are people praying. There was no privacy in the Middle Ages, when even princes dined in public and their subjects watched them eat. The nave of the church belonged to the people, and they used it as today we use a village hall or social club. Our new suburban churches, which are used as dance halls during the week with the sanctuary partitioned off until Sunday, have something in common with the mediaeval church. But there is this difference: in the Middle Ages all sport and pleasure, all plays and dancing were 'under God'. God was near, hanging on his Cross above the chancel arch, and mystically present in the sacrament in the pyx hanging over the altar beyond. His crucifixion was carved on the preaching cross in the churchyard.

John Betjeman (1906–84): 'English Parish Churches', Introduction

The church is never a place, but always a people; never a fold, but always a flock; never a sacred building, but always a believing assembly. The church is you who pray, not where you pray. A structure of brick or marble can no more be a church than your clothes of serge or satin can be you. There is in this world nothing sacred but man, no sanctuary of God but the soul.

Source unknown

Every time I see a church,
I always pay a visit,
So when, at last, I'm carried in,
the Lord won't say, 'Who is it?'

Anonymous

Charles Simeon, newly ordained, was given a summer job in charge of St. Edward's Church, Cambridge, while its vicar, Christopher Atkinson, was away. Henry Venn wrote: 'In less than seventeen Sundays he filled it with hearers – a thing unknown there for

Remember that you set apart one day in the week for true festivity, or you will be bored stiff in the technological age you are bringing on yourselves.

Honour your father and your mother but do not seek to prolong their natural term of life so that they are miserable.

You shall not murder future generations by your present greed.

You shall not commit sexual sin by producing more children than is your right.

You shall not steal the inheritance of posterity.

You shall not bear false witness against your overseas neighbours by lying to yourself about the extent of their need.

You shall not covet an ever increasing standard of living.

Bishop Hugh Montefiore (of Kingston, later Birmingham): 'The Commandments', (c 1975)

Thou shalt not spit on holy ground.

Primary School pupil (1981)

Thou shalt not admit adultery.

Confirmation Class member, (1980)

Only 25% of the *Harris* poll survey of religion among Top People (for the *Spectator*) could remember half of the Ten Commandments, with the second and third (blasphemy and the Lord's day) 'so well forgotten that the rest could be renamed the Eight Commandments. This group presumably believes in Sunday Swearing.'

From Clifford Longley: in The Times, (15 December, 1986)

Commitment to Christ

Till you have got a man on his knees to pray, and on his feet to speak for Christ, you have done little or nothing for him spiritually.

Father Peter Green (1871 – 1961)

Commit thy way to Jesus,
Thy burdens and thy cares;
He from them all releases.
He all thy sorrow shares.
He gave the winds their courses,
And bounds the ocean's shore,
He suffers not temptation
To rise beyond thy pow'r.

Lutheran Chorale from St. Matthew Passion, (J.S. Bach, 1729)

. . . it is not enough to get people to church. We need to get them to Christ. I fear there are congregations in which a very large percentage of the regular members have never really faced the question of entire surrender to Christ.

Father Peter Green: 'The Man of God', (1935)

In the third century, Origen, reflecting on Luke's story of the birth of Jesus, wrote:

My brothers, what does it avail you that Christ once took flesh, if he does not come into your soul also? Let us pray that that coming, which was the taking on of flesh, may be daily repeated in our hearts, so that we too can say, 'I live now, not I, but Christ lives in me'.

O Lord God, when thou givest to thy servants to endeavour any great matter, grant us also to know that it is not the beginning but the continuing of the same until it be thoroughly finished which yieldeth the true glory. Through him who for finishing of thy work laid down his life.

Sir Francis Drake (1539–96)

As he [Jesus] went [to Jairus' house], the crowds pressed in on him. Now there was a woman who had been suffering from haemorrhages for twelve years; and though she had spent all she had on physicians, no one could cure her. She came up behind him and touched the fringe of his clothes, and immediately her haemorrhage stopped. Then Jesus asked, 'Who touched me?' When all denied it, Peter said, 'Master, the crowds surround you and press in on you.' But Jesus said, 'Someone touched me; for I noticed that power had gone out from me.' When the woman saw that she could not remain hidden, she came trembling; and, falling down before him, she declared in the presence of all the people why she had touched him, and how she had been immediately healed. He said to her, 'Daughter, your faith has made you well; go in peace.'

Luke 8:42b–48

Jesus said, 'No one who puts a hand to the plough and looks back is fit for the kingdom of God.'

Luke 9:62

Committees

A committee is like a bunch of bananas: it starts off green, turns yellow, and in the end, there's not a straight one left in the bunch.

Anonymous

Psychologists say that committees are best composed of more than five persons and fewer than six.

Anonymous

They take minutes and go on for years.

Cited by Harold Wilson, Labour Prime Minister, (c. 1970)

The most important part of your Parochial Church Council meetings is that unhurried period of quiet thought and prayer which precedes the time you give to consideration of the agenda, when you wait on God to discover His mind and will for the parish.

Archbishop Donald Coggan (of Canterbury): An Institution Sermon on Matthew 13. 43, in 'Convictions', (Hodders, 1975)

God so loved the world that he didn't send a committee.

Anonymous

A group of the unfit appointed by the unwilling to do the unnecessary.

Carl C. Byers

A decision is what a man makes when he can't get anyone to serve on a committee.

Fletcher Knebel

I have never heard about the *Resolutions of the Apostles*, but I have read a good deal about their *Acts*.

Horace Mann, (c. 1974)

Communication

Christianity can be condensed into four words:
Admit, Submit, Commit and Transmit.

Bishop Samuel Wilberforce, 'Soapy Sam', (1805–73)

A wealthy American woman was shopping in London and saw a necklace she rather liked but it was expensive. She called in to the London office of her husband's company and sent a telex: 'Seen a necklace for £5,000. Do you think I should buy it?'

Her husband was not at all in agreement because he knew that his wife had more jewellery than she could ever wear, so he telexed a reply. Unfortunately, the typist slipped up, and instead of receiving the message: 'I do not. Too expensive', the wife read: 'I do. Not too expensive.' – and bought the necklace!

Source unknown

Avoid argument with the verbose: Power of speech is given to all: wisdom to a few.

Cato

Despite good intentions, it is almost always easier to misconstrue the arguments of others if they are not present.

Mark A. Noll: 'The Scandal of the Evangelical Mind', (Eerdmans, 1994)

Communication is more than words, which crack and break down.

Canon Norman Autton, (1980)

I know you believe you understand
what you think I said
but I am not sure you realise
that what you heard
is not what I meant.

Source unknown

Communication is not a one-way process from communicator to audience or readership; it requires mutual trust.

David Runcorn

Communication is either sadism or masochism.

Jean-Paul Sartre

Max Warren, General Secretary of the Church Missionary Society, spoke of the need for 'quadruple-think' by which he meant 'thinking out what I have to say, then thinking out how the other man will understand what I say, and then re-thinking what I have to say, so that, when I say it, he will think what I am thinking! . . . "Quadruple-thinking" involves mental pain and great spiritual sensitivity.'

Max Warren: Crowded Canvas, (Hodders, 1974)

Speech is civilisation itself. The word, even the most contradictory word, preserves contact. It is silence which isolates.

Thomas Mann

A communications expert is an expert in all the ways which have been tried and tested in the past and have failed.

Dafydd Miles Board, (1989)

A misprint of 1 Corinthians 13:1 (AV) read: 'Though I speak with the tongues of men and angels, and have not clarity, I am become as sounding brass or a tinkling cymbal.'

Source unknown

A rich businessman boasted that his new Stradivarius violin was a wonderful instrument. It would pacify all the beasts of the forests and jungles.

He used to play regularly for the wild animals in the jungle until, one day, surrounded by enchanted animals, he was eaten by a strange lion.

'What did you do that for?' exclaimed the other animals!

'I beg your pardon. Could you repeat that, please,' said the Lion.

Which only goes to prove that it's not *what you say*, it's *what they hear* that matters.

Source unknown

A lecture is the process by which information is transferred from the lecturer's notes to the student's notes without passing through the mind of either.

Traditional

Often when he was teaching me to write in Greek the Fox would say, 'Child, to say the very thing you really mean, the whole of it, nothing more or less or other than what you really mean, that's the whole art and joy of words.' A glib saying. When the time comes to you at which you will be forced at last to utter the speech which has lain at the centre of your soul for years, which you have, all that time, idiot-like, been saying over and over, you'll not talk about joy of words. I saw well why the gods do not speak to us openly, nor let us answer. Till that word can be dug out of us, why should they hear the babble that we think we mean? How can they meet us face to face till we have faces?

C.S. Lewis: 'Till We Have Faces', (1956; Collins, 1985), Part Two, Chapter IV

Communism

From each according to his abilities, to each according to his needs.

Karl Marx (1818–83) 'Criticism of the Gothic Programme', (1875)

To grasp the true meaning of socialism, imagine a world where everything is designed by the post office, even the sleaze.

P.J. O'Rourke: 'Holidays in Hell', (1988)

Compassion

Love that feels to the point of pain.

Anonymous

Christianity assumes her true character . . .when she takes under protection those poor degraded beings on whom philosophy looks down with disdain.

William Wilberforce in the House of Commons, (1813)

I would say to that Royal child, worship God by loving peace. It is not *your* humanity to pity a beggar by giving him food or raiment – *I* can do that; that is the charity of the humble and the unknown. Widen you your heart for the more expanded miseries of mankind – pity the mothers of the peasantry who see their sons torn away from their families, pity your poor subjects crowded into hospitals, and calling in their last breath upon their distant country and their young Queen; pity the stupid, frantic folly of human beings who are always ready to tear each other to pieces, and to deluge the earth with each other's blood. This is your extended humanity – and this the great field of your compassion.

Extinguish in your heart the fiendish love of military glory, from which your sex does not necessarily exempt you, and to which the wickedness of flatterers may urge you. Say upon your death-bed, 'I have made few orphans in my reign – I have made few widows – my object has been peace. I have used all the weight of my character, and all the powers of my situation, to check the irascible passions of mankind, and to turn them to the arts of honest industry; this has been the Christianity of my throne, and this the gospel of my sceptre; in this way I

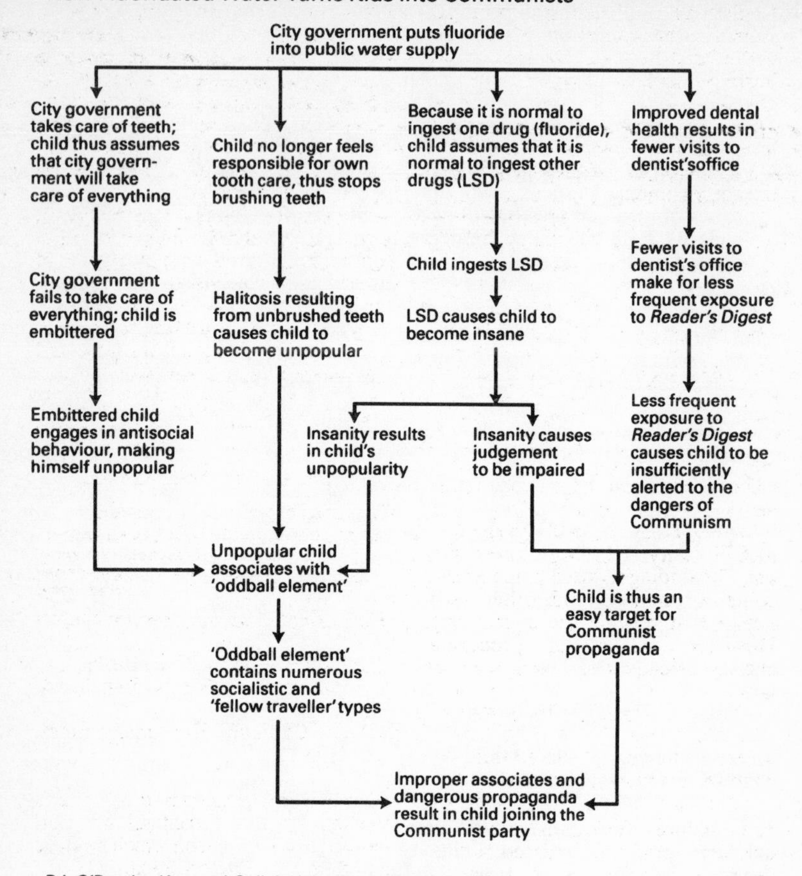

P.J. O'Rourke: 'Age and Guile', (Atlantic and Picador, 1995)

have striven to worship my Redeemer and my Judge.'

Sydney Smith: Sermon on the accession of Queen Victoria, (1837)

A man was attacked and left bleeding in a ditch. Two sociologists passed by and one said to the other, 'We must find the man who did this. He needs help.'

The Good Samaritan for Sociologists: Anonymous

Compromise

A constitution is made for people of fundamentally different views.

Justice Oliver Wendell Holmes

A critic said of Randall Davidson (1848–1930), Archbishop of Canterbury, that he became used to 'sitting on the fence with both ears to the ground.'

Source unknown, though it may have been a Welsh Church leader

. . . there is a trap into which the English in particular are prone to stumble, the confusion of decency with Christianity . . . Decency avoids hurting people's feelings. It looks for compromise and reconciliation. There are times when a religious leader may have to hurt some feelings, when compromise is wrong and reconciliation impossible.

First Leader in the Times, (December, 1987): 'Case Against Dr. Runcie'

Computers

There's a special satisfaction in puzzling out how to work a computer. Once you master it, you can begin to understand the instructions that came with it.

From the Kiplinger Magazine

Scientists discovered a link between silicon and melba toast. After fifteen years exposure to air, silicon turns into melba toast, according to a group of University of California researchers. The findings caused panic among computer makers and other businesses that rely on the silicon chip. However, makers of processed-cheese spreads were elated at the news.

The Off The Wall Street Journal, (1982)

To err is human, but to foul things up completely requires a computer.

Anonymous

Just before Christmas 1994, an unknown prankster created a false dispatch claiming to be from the Associated Press news agency and circulated it on *the Internet*. The story read:

'In a joint press conference at St Peter's Square this morning, Microsoft and the Vatican announced that the software giant will acquire the Roman Catholic Church in return for an unspecified number of shares of Microsoft common stock. If the deal goes through it will be the first time a computer software company has acquired a major world religion.'

Under the terms of the supposed deal, Microsoft would get exclusive electronic rights to the Bible while Pope John Paul II would become the senior vice-president of the combined company's new Religious Software Division.

The fake story also included a promise from Microsoft founder, Bill Gates, that he would 'make the sacraments available online for the first time and revive the popular pre-Counter Reformation practice of selling indulgences'.

Microsoft's long-term strategy, it said, is to develop 'a single core religion to be offered with a choice of interfaces according to the religion desired'.

A statement from Microsoft had to point out: 'The story has no truth and was not generated by the company.'

Matthew May: in The Times, 'Microsoft and the Christmas Papal hoax', (24 December 1994)

Confession – *see also* REPENTANCE

The Lord has put away your sin.
Go in peace and pray for me, a sinner.

Dismissal in the traditional rite of Reconciliation (Confession and Absolution)

The different approaches to confession:
Penitent: 'I've committed murder.'
Protestant: 'Great Scott! How dreadful!'
Roman Catholic: 'How many times, and when?'

Patrick was waiting in the Father's kitchen before confession, and fancied a joint of bacon which he stole and then went into confession.
Pat: I've stolen a joint of bacon!
Priest: You must give it back.
Pat: Will you take it, Father?
Priest: No indeed, I can't take it.
Pat: I've asked the man who owned it and he won't take it back.
Priest: Then you're free to keep it.
Conclusion: Pat saved his bacon and his conscience!

Source unknown

A priest hearing the confessions of children was puzzled to find child after child adding the sin of 'throwing peanuts in the river'. He wondered whether the young consciences were sensitive about wasting food or polluting the river. When the last child came in, he failed to confess to the nuts sin, so the priest pressed the matter. 'Is that all? Isn't there something you have forgotten? What about throwing peanuts in the river?' 'But, Father,' came the bewildered voice, 'I am Peanuts.'

Douglas Woodruff

Confess your sins to one another, and pray for one another, so that you may be healed. The prayer of the righteous is powerful and effective.

James 5:16

If we say that we have no sin, we deceive ourselves, and the truth is not in us. If we confess our sins, he who is faithful and just will forgive us our sins and cleanse us from all unrighteousness.

1 John 1:8, 9

Confirmation

At Philadelphia International Airport it was a busy Friday, with the addition of 5,000 Roman Catholic nuns leaving after a convention at Atlantic City. It was obvious that the flight to Detroit was over-booked, so the ticket agent called out, 'How many of you are confirmed?' He realised his mistake when every nun put her hand up!

Source unknown

Confirmation cannot be called a primary necessity of the Christian's sacramental life . . . it confers nothing in kind or in essential principle from what baptism has already given.

Oliver C. Quick: 'The Christian Sacraments', (1927)

Conscience

Beware lest conscience lose its tenderness.

Richard Baxter: 'The Saints' Everlasting Rest'

Conscience is the inner voice that warns us that someone may be looking.

H.L. Mencken: 'Sententiae', (1920)

Sometimes a clear conscience is the result of a bad memory.

Traditional saying

Little children, let us love, not in word or speech, but in truth and action. And by this we will know that we are from the truth and will reassure our hearts before him whenever our hearts condemn us; for God is greater than our hearts, and he knows everything. Beloved, if our hearts do not condemn us, we have boldness before God.

1 John 3:18–21

Conservatism

A conservative is a person who admires a radical a century after the radical has died.

Anonymous

A conservative is someone who believes in reform. But not now.

Mort Sahl

Contentment

. . . learn to be pleased with everything; with wealth, so far as it makes us beneficial to others; with poverty, for not having too much to care for; and with obscurity, for being unenvied.

Plutarch

When I wish I was rich, then I know I am ill.
Because, to tell the truth, I have enough as I am.
So, when I catch myself thinking: 'Ah, if I was rich – !'
I say to myself: 'Hello! I'm not well. My vitality is low.'

D.H. Lawrence

To have blessings and to prize them is to be in Heaven; to have them and not to prize them is to be in Hell, I would say, upon Earth: To prize them and not to have them, is to be in Hell. Which is evident by the effects. To prize blessings while we have them is to enjoy them, and the effect thereof is contentation, pleasure, thanksgiving, happiness. To prize them when they are gone produceth envy, covetousness, repining, ingratitude, vexation, misery. But it was no great mistake to say, that to have blessings and not to prize them is to be in Hell. For it maketh them ineffectual, as if they were absent. Yea, in some respect it is worse than to be in Hell. It is more vicious, and more irrational.

Thomas Traherne (1637–1674): Century I in 'Centuries of Meditation'

Conversion, experience of

I felt my heart strangely warmed. I felt I did trust in Christ, in Christ alone for my salvation; and an assurance was given me that he had taken away my sin, even MINE, and saved me from the law of sin and death.

John Wesley's account of his 'evangelical conversion' 24 May, 1738 at 8.45 pm during a prayer meeting of Moravians at Aldersgate Street, London whilst Luther's Preface to Romans (1:17) was being read

Augustine of Hippo had an illegitimate son at 18 years old, toyed with Manichaean and Neoplatonist ideas, became a sceptic and is reputed to have prayed: 'Give me chastity and continence, but not yet!' As he began to turn to the Faith (under the prayerful influence of his mother, Monica) he recalled the words; 'How long, O Lord? Will you be angry for ever?' and heard, in his tears, the voice of a child telling him to read the book of Paul's Letter to the Romans, which he had just put down. Doing so, he recalled, 'I seized, opened, and in silence read the passage upon which my eyes first fell: 'Not in revelry and drunkenness, not in immorality or indecency, not in fighting or jealousy, but put on the Lord Jesus Christ and stop paying attention to your sinful nature and satisfying its desires.' No further would I read, nor was there any need, for instantly, at the end of this sentence, as though my heart was flooded with a light of peace, all the shadows of doubt melted away.'

St Augustine of Hippo: 'Confessions', (c. 400), describing his conversion about A.D. 386. [Reference is Romans 13. 13b–14]

Then I suddenly felt that I was born again and entered through open doors into paradise.

Martin Luther's description of his conversion

It also pleased God, by the revelation of his holiness and grace, which the great theologians taught me to find in the Bible, to bring home to me my sin in a way that submerged all the school questions in weight, urgency, and poignancy. I was turned from a Christian into a believer, from a lover of love to an object of grace.

P.T. Forsyth (1848 – 1921): 'Positive Preaching and the Modern Mind', (1907)

In 1779, Charles Simeon, then a Cambridge undergraduate, was required to prepare himself to receive Holy Communion. Spiritually, the skies were dark, but he came upon the phrase that 'the Jews knew what they did when they transferred their sin to the head of their offering.'

He later wrote of his conversion: 'I can transfer all my guilt to Another! I will not bear them on my soul a moment longer . . . Accordingly I sought to lay my sins upon the sacred head of Jesus; and on the Wednesday began to have a hope of mercy; on the Thursday that hope increased; on the Friday and Saturday it became more strong; and on the Sunday morning, Easter Day, April 4th, I awoke early with those words upon my heart and lips, 'Jesus Christ is risen today! Hallelujah! Hallelujah!' From that hour peace flowed in rich abundance into my soul, and at the Lord's Table in our Chapel (King's College) I had the sweetest access to God through my blessed Saviour.'

H.E. Hopkins: 'Charles Simeon of Cambridge', (Hodders, 1977)

The Reverend William Haslam was ordained in 1842 and served conscientiously as a parson in North Cornwall. In 1851, while preaching on the gospel of the day, which included the question, 'What think ye of Christ', a complete transformation happened, which he afterwards recognised as the work of the Holy Spirit. A local preacher in the congregation at the time jumped up and shouted, 'The parson is converted! Hallelujah!' and the congregation was stirred in praise of God. The parson himself, as the record says, 'joined in the outburst of praise, and, to make it more orderly . . . gave out the Doxology . . . and the people sang it with heart and voice, over and over again.' News spread rapidly 'that the parson was converted, and that by his own sermon, in his own pulpit!'

W. Haslam: 'From Death into Life', (Marshall, Morgan & Scott, 1880)

Billy Graham, world-famous evangelist, was converted in 1935 (aged 17 years) at an evangelistic rally in his native Charlotte, North Carolina. He went forward to commit himself to Christ and recalled: 'I had no emotion. I saw a lady next to me weeping and I thought to myself, well, it's not real with me because I had no tears over it. It was just a simple declaration that I wanted Christ in my heart. And from then on I could tell a change inside – that was the beginning of a whole new pattern of life.'

Billy Graham: Interview in the Saturday Review of The Times, (26 January, 1993)

The theologian Jurgen Moltmann was a 19-year old prisoner of war in Nottinghamshire, in 1945, when he experienced a 'rebirth to a new life':
The experience of misery and forsakenness and daily humiliation gradually built up into an experience of God...

It was the experience of God's presence in the dark night of the soul: 'If I make my bed in hell, behold, thou art there.' A well-meaning army chaplain had given me a New Testament. I thought it was out of place. I would rather have had something to eat. But then I became fascinated by the Psalms (which were printed in an appendix) and especially Psalm 39: 'I was dumb with silence, I held my peace, even from good; and my sorrow was stirred' (but the German is much stronger – 'I have to eat up my grief within myself') . . . 'Hold thou not thy peace at my tears: for I am a stranger with thee, and a sojourner, as all my fathers were.'

These psalms gave me the words for my own suffering. They opened my eyes to the God who is with those 'that are of a broken heart'.

J. Moltmann: 'Experiences of God', (S.C.M., 1980)

A Jewish boy who attended Notre Dame University returned home for vacation and met the family's rabbi. After a while, the rabbi asked,
'They aren't trying to convert you at Notre Dame, are they?'

'No, Father!' came the unthinking reply.

Source unknown

Bernie ran with a loose crowd who drank at the Moonlite Bay roadhouse and boasted of having gotten girls in the family way, and Bernie came to church one Sunday night on a dare from his chums and sat in back and smirked at Rev. Osterhus until the evangelist would stand it no longer – he leaped from the pulpit! Dashed to the back pew! Seized the young man by the neck before he could slither away! Hauled him out and up to the altar! Threw him against the rail! The sinner fell weeping to the floor, and the man of God knelt over him, one knee in the small of his back, and prayed ferociously for light to dawn in his blackened soul. When Bernie stood up, he was reborn, and he yelled, 'Thank you, Jesus!' over and over, tears pouring down his cheeks – 'Now there was what I call preaching!' says . . . Bernie's brother, a deacon and Pastor Ingqvist's faithful critic.

Garrison Keillor: 'Lake Wobegon Days', (1985): 'Revival'

Conversion, doctrine of

. . . not by migrating from humanity in order to enter the church but by migrating more fully into humanity through incorporation into the new humanity of Christ.

Douglas Webster: 'Not Ashamed', (1970)

One real conversion in a great city is something more splendid than the spectacle of a whole remote village going to the sacraments. The one is an essentially religious event, a thing of grace; the other is to a large extent a sociological phenomenon, even though it may be a means of God's Grace.

Karl Rahner, S.J: 'Mission and Grace', (1963)

The work of conversion consisteth in two parts.
I. The well informing of the judgement in the necessary points.
II. The change of the will, by the efficacy of this truth.

Richard Baxter: 'The Reformed Pastor', (1655)

Conversion is not the smooth, easy-going process some seem to think it, otherwise man's heart would never have been compared to fallow ground, and God's Word to the plough.

John Bunyan (1628–88)

For many years I have been convinced (in my evangelistic work) that in our pragmatic age it is actually dangerous to invite people to 'give themselves to Jesus Christ' unless they have first been brought to see in very specific terms what that self-giving is immediately going to mean in a change of attitude and action . . . this is the point of John the Baptist preceding the Christ.

A person needs to be brought to the point of recognising a certain moral demand, recognising furthermore that he has not got what it takes to meet that demand, and then, in one and the same spiritual movement, committing himself to meet it and grasping at the spiritual resources which Christ offers to make it possible for him to do so. Better still, and truer to life, if at the same time the person recognises that the whole of this experience . . . is even more significant if it is a corporate one.

Bishop John Taylor (c. 1975), [former General Secretary of the Church Missionary Society, later Bishop of Winchester]

[Conversion to Judaism] . . . crucially determines for all time the convert's personal status, his marital rights and restrictions as well as his religious allegiance, and in the case of a female affecting her offspring for all generations to come.

. . . To effect a total religious commitment for a lifetime, and through the children beyond, more than a declaration of intent is required. It is brought about by radical changes inside the person's heart, determining all his future loyalties, his thinking, feelings and actions, the mould of his very personality, in many respects even more bindingly and incisively than the commitment involved in a bond of marriage or in the adoption of a child. A conversion, in the Jewish view, is the most delicate heart operation to which a person could ever submit, and the onus rests on the applicant to prove that he is adequately prepared to undergo such an operation.

. . . It must be enlightening to view a conversion as a religious naturalisation . . . For the grant of citizenship, countries usually require a residence period of at least two years, fluency in the vernacular, and ready submission to the laws of the land. No one questions these demands. Any alien declaring his readiness to observe all the country's laws except one would be refused his naturalisation, and it would not help him to argue that there are many native citizens who also sometimes transgress one regulation or another. In these matters it is all or nothing.

. . . True proselytes live up to the qualifications so concisely expressed by the most famous of them all, when Ruth the Moabite pledged: 'Where you go, I will go; and where you lodge for the night, I will lodge' – sharing the misfortunes as well as the fortunes of the Jewish people . . .; 'your people will be my people' – identifying with Jewish national aspirations . . .; 'and your God will be my God' – serving as a witness to Israel's religious commitment; 'where you die, I will die, and there I shall be buried' (Ruth 1:16–17) – defending Jewish beliefs and practices even to the grave.

Lord Immanuel Jacobovits, Chief Rabbi of Great Britain and the Commonwealth: in 'The Times', (15 May, 1989)

1) The communication [of the gospel cross-culturally] has to be in the language of the receptor culture. It has to be such that it accepts, at least provisionally, the way of understanding things that is embodied in that language; if it does not do so, it will simply be an unmeaning sound that cannot change anything.
2) However, if it is truly the communication of the gospel, it will call radically into question that way of understanding embodied in the language it uses. If it is truly revelation, it will involve contradiction, and call for conversion, for a radical *metanoia*, a U-turn of the mind.
3) Finally, this radical conversion can never be the achievement of any human persuasion, however, eloquent. It can only be the work of God.

True conversion, therefore, which is the proper end toward which the communication of the gospel looks, can only be a work of God, a kind of miracle – not natural but supernatural.

Lesslie Newbigin: 'Foolishness to the Greeks', (S.C.M., 1986)

Another description of conversion would be a 'paradigm shift'. In the natural sciences, a paradigm shift is a change which has not resulted from a step-by-step reasoning from the presuppositions of an earlier view, but from a new vision which calls for a complete re-orientation.

Source unknown

The world of today is one of which no Christian map can be made. Our task with this world is to convert it. Its need can be met . . . by the shattering impact upon its self-sufficiency and arrogance of the Son of God crucified, risen and ascended, pouring forth that explosive and disruptive energy which is the Holy Ghost.

Archbishop William Temple (of Canterbury): 'Towards the Conversion of England'

Conversion, the Scriptures

As he [Saul] was going along and approaching Damascus, suddenly a light from heaven flashed around him. He fell to the ground and heard a voice saying to him, 'Saul, Saul, why do you persecute me?' He asked, 'Who are you, Lord?' The reply came, 'I am Jesus, whom you are persecuting. But get up and enter the city, and you will be told what you are to do.' . . .

Ananias went and entered the house [in Damascus where Saul was staying]. He laid his hands on Saul and said, 'Brother Saul, the Lord Jesus, who appeared to you on your way here, has sent me so that you may regain your sight and be filled with the Holy Spirit.' And immediately something like scales fell from his eyes, and his sight was restored. Then he got up and was baptised, and after taking some food, he regained his strength. For several days he was with the disciples in Damascus, and immediately he began to proclaim Jesus in the synagogues, saying, 'He is the Son of God.'

Acts 9:3–6, 17–20

Paul relates this on a number of other occasions, describing his conversion thus:

Last of all, as to one untimely born, he appeared also to me.

1 Corinthians 15:8

The jailer [at Philippi, after the earthquake] called for lights, and rushing in, he fell down trembling before Paul and Silas. Then he brought them outside and said, 'Sirs, what must I do to be saved?' They answered, 'Believe on the Lord Jesus and you will be saved, you and your household.' They spoke the word of the Lord to him and to all who were in his house. At the same hour of the night he took them and washed their wounds; then he and his entire family were baptized without delay.

Acts 16:29–33

Conviction

The eighteenth century deistic philosopher, David Hume, who had rejected historical Christianity, was going to hear George Whitefield preach when he was met by a friend. 'But surely you don't believe what Whitefield preaches, do you?'

'No, I don't,' Hume replied, 'but *he* does.'

James Black: 'The Mystery of Preaching', (James Clarke, 1924)

. . . to handle issues of eternal life and death as if we were discussing nothing more serious than the weather, and to do it in a listless and lackadaisical manner, is to be inexcusably frivolous.

John R.W. Stott: 'I Believe in Preaching', (Hodders, 1982)

I'm a man of no convictions – at least, I *think* I am.

Christopher Hampton: 'The Philanthropist', (1970)

Our message of the gospel came to you not in word only, but also in power and in the Holy Spirit and with full conviction; just as you know what kind of persons we proved to be among you for your sake.

1 Thessalonians 1:5

Cooking

It is said that Matthew Arnold (1822–88) pointed to a plate of pancakes when eating at a friends' home, and said to his wife: 'Do try one, my dear, they are not nearly so nasty as they look.'

Archbishop Richard Chenevix Trench (1807–86) retired from the see of Dublin at the age of 77 years and spent his last two years in London. On returning to visit his successor Lord Plunkett in Dublin, his memory lapsed and he forgot that he was no longer the host, remarking to his wife, 'I'm afraid, my love, that we must put this cook down among our failures.'

Correction

Honest criticism is hard to take, particularly from a relative, a friend, an acquaintance or a stranger.

Franklin P. Jones

We need to correct one another at times, and must not forget that even if a friend's corrections make us smart, they are worth far more to us than all the false endearments of those who do not love us at all.

Aelred of Rievaulx (1110–1163): 'The Mirror of Charity'

My child, do not despise the LORD's discipline or be weary of his reproof, for the LORD reproves the one he loves, as a father the son in whom he delights.

Proverbs 3:11, 12 (quoted in Hebrews 12:5, 6)

Courage

The pastor of an institution for epileptics and the mentally ill, when told of Hitler's intention to exterminate the incurables and insane:

. . . as long as I am free, you do not touch one of my patients. I cannot change to fit the times or the wishes of the Fuehrer. I stand under orders from our Lord Jesus Christ.

Quoted by John Foster

If you can keep your head when all about you are losing theirs, it's just possible you haven't grasped the situation.

Jean Kerr: 'Please Don't Eat the Daisies', (1957)

Colonel Cathcart had courage and never hesitated to volunteer his men for any target available.

Joseph Heller: 'Catch 22', (1961)

Better to live one day as a lion than a hundred years as a sheep.

Italian proverb, variously quoted

Courage . . . is the indispensable requisite of any true ministry. . . If you are afraid of men and a slave to their opinion, go and do something else. Go and make shoes to fit them. Go even and paint pictures which you know are bad but which suit their bad taste. But do not keep on all your life preaching sermons which shall say not what God sent you to declare, but what they hire you to say. Be courageous. Be independent.

Phillips Brooks: 'Lectures on Preaching', (1877 Yale Lectures) (Brooks was Rector of Holy Trinity Boston and Bishop of Massachusetts)

Creation

Genesis is rather like the game of snakes and ladders!

Anonymous

To find out what really happened when the earth was created, engineers spent weeks gathering information, checking and rechecking it and feeding it into the computer. The great moment came: all was complete, everybody gathered around, a button was pressed, the great computer spun into action, relays opened and closed, lights flashed and bells rang; finally, a typed message emerged: 'SEE GENESIS 1. 1'.

Source unknown

The probability of life originating from accident is comparable to the probability of a dictionary resulting from an explosion in a printing works.

Edward Conklin

Genesis retired in favour of geology.

Horton Davies: on Charles Darwin's, 'The Origin of Species' (1833) and 'The Descent of Man', (1840)

I can trace my ancestry back to a protoplasmal primordial atomic globule. Consequently, my family pride is something 'inconceivable'.

W.S. Gilbert (1836–1911): 'The Mikado'

To see a World in a Grain of Sand,
And a Heaven in a Wild Flower,
Hold Infinity in the palm of your
Hand,
And Eternity in an hour.

William Blake (1757 – 1827): 'Auguries of Innocence', I

One of the most celebrated cases in American legal history was the Scopes case, which concerned the right of a schoolteacher to cast doubt on the assertion that the world was created at 9.00 a.m., Eastern Standard Time, on 23 October, 4004 B.C.

From the 'Oxford Book of Legal Anecdotes', Michael Gilbert, Ed., (Oxford, 1986)

Our Lord showed me a little thing, the size of a hazelnut, lying in the palm of my hand, as round as a ball. I looked at it and thought, 'What can this be?' And I was answered, 'It is all that is made.' I wondered how it could survive, for I thought that being so small it might suddenly disintegrate. And I was answered in my understanding: 'It lasts and always will because God loves it.' And so everything has its being through the love of God.

Julian of Norwich (c.1342 – 1416): 'The first revelation'

And God said, 'Let there be light!' and there was light. And *when* there was light, God *saw* the date, *that* it was a Monday, and He *got* down to work; for, verily he had a Big Job *to do*. And God made pottery shards and silurian molluscs and Pre-Cambrian limestone strata; and flints and Jurassic mastodon tusks and Pithecanthcopus erectus skulls and Cretaceous Placentalia made he; and those cave paintings at Lascaux. And that was *that* for the first day.

Tony Hendra & Sean Kelly: 'The Book of Creation', (in Playboy, 1982)

A world which has lost its vision of the sacredness of creation has also lost its commitment to the dignity of human life. Only now is our western society becoming aware of living on a planet of which we are a part, and that God the Creator and redeemer is at work with the whole of his creation.

Esther de Waal: 'A World Made Whole', (1991)

'Do you know who made you?'
'Nobody, as I knows on,' said the child, with a short laugh . . . 'I 'spect I grow'd.'

Harriet Beecher Stowe (1811 – 1896): 'Uncle Tom's Cabin', (1852), Chapter 20

Creeds

Paramount, for all Christians, is the Bible. Here is the inspired record and interpretation of God's love . . . We need this authoritative testimony to set us on the right path . . . The authority of the Creeds derives from the fact that they are regarded as stating and defining rightly certain central beliefs which are found, explicitly or implicitly, in Scripture.

'The Nature of Christian Belief', (Church House Publishing: London, 1986)

A man's liberty to travel is not cramped by signposts: on the contrary, they save his time by showing what roads he must avoid if he wishes to reach his destination. The creeds perform the same function.

C.B. Moss

Cricket

You have two sides: one out in the field and one in.
Each man that's in in the side that's in, goes out,
and when he's out he comes in
and the next man goes in until he's out.
When they are all out,
the side that's out comes in
and the side that's been in goes out
and tries to get those coming in out.
Sometimes you get men still in and not out.
When both sides have been in and out,
including the not-outs,
that's the end of the game.
Howzat!

Marylebone Cricket Club (The Editor was attempting, in vain, to explain the rules of the game of cricket to some young people in Uganda. For some years he had occasionally looked for this definition, but he came across a copy in Kampala. It amused the adults.)

Personally, I have always looked upon cricket as organised loafing.

Archbishop William Temple, (writing in 1925) (Bishop David Sheppard, a former England player, would not agree.)

Crime

After an incident in Croydon involving a prison van and a concrete mixer, police are looking for eighteen hardened criminals.

The Two Ronnies: (B.B.C. Television)

Cross, The, doctrine of

Christ was content to give up the glories of the Creator and be made even in the likeness of the fallen creatures; and not only to share the disgrace, but to suffer the punishment due to the meanest and vilest of them all.

John Wesley, on Philippians 2:5–9

Mori missus.
(Sent to die)

Tertullian (155–220)

He who came to bear our sins must also die our death. Death is the word which sums up the whole liability of man in relation to sin, and therefore, when Christ came to give himself for our sins, he did it by dying.

James Denny: 'The Death of Christ', (1902)

The blood of Abel cried for vengeance: the blood of Christ for remission.

Desiderius Erasmus, quoting Jewish tradition and Hebrews 12:24

Tom Paine [author of *The Rights of Man* and *The Age of Reason*] compared God with a passionate man who killed his son when he could not revenge himself in any other way.

Our radical sickness calls for a radical cure – and that can only come by way of the cross.

Archbishop Donald Coggan: (of Canterbury): in 'Convictions', (Hodders, 1975), 'Canterbury Enthronement'

We cannot think of God apart from Jesus Christ, and we cannot think of Jesus Christ apart from his passion and death.

John MacQuarrie: 'The Humility of God', (1978)

Cross, The, faith in

If you want to understand the Christian message, you must start with the wounds of Christ.

Martin Luther

There are some sciences that may be learned by the head, but the science of Christ crucified can only be learned by the heart.

Charles H. Spurgeon

Lamb of God, I fall before thee
Humbly trusting in Thy Cross;
That alone be all my glory,
All things else I count but loss.
Jesu, all my hope and joy
Flow from thee, thy sov'reign good.
Hope and love and faith and patience
All were purchased by his Blood.

Lutheran Chorale from 'St Matthew Passion': (J.S. Bach, 1729)

The message of the cross must not be severed from the whole of saving history (*Heilsgeschichte*). As it is false to speak of forgiveness without pointing to the cross, it is false also to isolate the cross from the rest of the life of Christ.

Emil Brunner: 'The Scandal of Christianity', (1948, S.C.M., 1951), Lecture IV, 'The Mediator'

A faith centred on the cross will certainly feel tongue-tied with its burden at times. We must learn the prayer of silence. There is no other way.

David Runcorn: 'Silence', (1986)

'Tis I, whose sin now binds thee,
With anguish deep surrounds thee,
And nails thee to the tree:
The torture thou art feeling,
Thy patient love revealing,
'Tis I should bear it, I alone.

Lutheran Chorale from 'St Matthew Passion': (J.S. Bach, 1729)

What from man's side is called the crucifixion of God's ambassador, that, from God's side, signifies the highest revelation of divine love.

Emil Brunner: 'The Letter to the Romans', 1938', (Lutterworth 1959)

. . . the cross means that God refuses to verify himself. 'Let the Christ, the King of Israel, come down now from the cross, that we may see and believe.' But he stays where he is.

Professor C. Kingsley Barrett: in Durham Cathedral, (1968)

. . . the essence of the gospel as witnessed in Scripture is that God in Jesus Christ has declared his reconciliation to us by means of the cross. We do not need to approach him by other means. If we try to do so, we are doubting his mercy.

A.T. & R.P.C. Hanson: 'The Identity of the Church', (S.C.M., 1987)

Now I saw in my dream, that the highway up which Christian was to go, was fenced on either side with a wall, and that wall was called Salvation. Up this way, therefore, did burdened Christian run, but not without difficulty because of the load on his back.

He ran thus till he came at a place somewhat ascending, and upon that place stood a cross, and a little below, in the bottom, a sepulchre. So I saw in my dream, that just as Christian came up with the cross, his burden loosed from off his shoulders, and fell from off his back, and began to tumble, and so continued to do till it came to the mouth of the sepulchre, where it fell in, and I saw it no more.

Then was Christian glad and lightsome, and said, with a merry heart. 'He hath given me rest by his sorrow, and life by his death.'

. . . He looked therefore and looked again, even till the springs that were in his head sent the waters down his cheeks. Now . . . behold, three Shining Ones came to him and saluted him with 'Peace be to thee.' So the first said to him, 'Thy sins be forgiven thee,' the second stripped him of his rags, and clothed him 'with a change of raiment'; the third also set a mark on his forehead, and gave him a roll with a seal upon it, which he bade him look on as he ran, and that he should give it in at the Celestial Gate. So they went their way . . . Then Christian gave three leaps for joy, and went on singing.

John Bunyan (1628 – 88): 'The Pilgrim's Progress'

We think that Paradise and Calvary,
Christ's Cross, and Adam's tree,
  stood in one place;
Look, Lord, and find both Adams
  met in me;
As the first Adam's sweat surrounds
  my face,
May the last Adam's blood my soul
  embrace.
So, in his purple wrapp'd receive me,
  Lord,
By these his thorns give me his other
  Crown;
And as to others' souls I preach'd thy
  word,
Be this my Text, my Sermon to mine
  own:
Therefore that he may raise, the
  Lord throws down.

John Donne: 'A Hymn to God in My Sicknesse'

Lie still, O sacred limbs, lie sleeping,
And I will lay aside my weeping;
Lie still: I too may rest in peace.
The grave that was appointed you
To close the sum of suffering due
Shall be my path to heaven, from hell
  my full release.

Lutheran Chorale from the 'St John Passion', (J. S. Bach, 1723)

Cross, The, today

We must give up the vain idea that we can ever make the cross of Christ acceptable by polishing and varnishing and painting and gilding it, and sawing off the corners.

Bishop J.C. Ryle (of Liverpool, 1882–1900): 'Knots Untied'

Calvary takes place in Cardiff, and Bethlehem in Bangor.

Gwennap: 'St. David'

Jesus was crucified not in a cathedral between two candles, but on a cross between two thieves.

George F. MacLeod (Founder of the Iona Community)

Jesus now has many lovers of his heavenly Kingdom, but few bearers of his cross.

Thomas à Kempis

The nearest some of us people ever get to bearing the cross is the one that will be planted on top of them in the cemetery.

Robert M.E. Paterson, (1987)

For fourteen hours yesterday I was at work – teaching Christ to lift his cross by numbers, and how to adjust his crown; and not to imagine his thirst until after the last halt. I attended his Supper to see that there were no complaints; and inspected his feet that they should be worthy of the nails. I see to it that he is dumb, and stands at attention before his accusers. With a piece of silver I buy him every day, and with maps I make him familiar with the topography of Golgotha.

Wilfred Owen, War Poet: Letter written in July 1918. (Owen died just a few months later, before the end of Great War)

. . . once the cross is made of none effect . . . then there ceases to be any place for a gospel.

Max Warren: 'Interpreters', (1936)

For the Indian Hindus, Christianity made no impact by describing the furniture of Heaven or the temperature of Hell; what made them listen was when the church preached the Lord Jesus Christ who gave himself up for us all.

Bishop Victor Premasager (of Medak, South India): Address to Church Missionary Society General Council, (1986)

. . . sadly, a cross to a clergyman is about as shocking as an invitation to a Mothers' Union coffee morning.

Richard MacKenna: 'God for Nothing', (Churchman, 1985)

There was a day when I took a party of students to visit the Church of the Holy Sepulchre [in Jerusalem]. The city was eerily quiet because there had been a riot that morning. Rumours had been flying around that some young Palestinians had been shot by some (again young) Israeli soldiers. Just before we turned the corner to enter the courtyard of the church, we saw some streaks and patches of blood on the stones in front of us. We stopped silent, our gaze held in horrified fascination. And then an old woman started shrieking in Arabic, 'They killed him, they killed him!' and there suddenly, so near to where Christ's crucifixion had taken place, Calvary seemed to have happened yet again through the passionate loves which turn to hate of those who dwell in the Holy City. The Christians of the Holy Land, whatever their race, desperately need our prayers for, and commitment to, peace.

Clare Amos: 'A Many-Coloured Mosaic', (C.M.S., 1987)

. . . for the Christian, the cross is the place where he looks for understanding of life and of himself. It is the most complete statement we have, or the most vivid clue, as to the nature of being. It is also the challenge that tells us where we need to go in order to be in touch with the deepest levels of our own reality.

Richard MacKenna: 'God for Nothing', (Churchman, 1984/85)

It is the cross-bearers, the failed, the broken, the empty, unlovely, unprestigious, unglamorous, who are the real body of Christ. No resurrection without crucifixion, no life without death first – the Christian paradoxes at the heart of the gospel – but we are terrified to put them into practice because in our heart of hearts we believe that the folly of the cross *is* folly; we pay lip service to it, but never dare light the blue touch-paper.

Richard MacKenna: 'God for Nothing', (Churchman 1984/85)

[The distinctiveness of the Christian gospel] is to be looked for in its *weakness*, in its *inability* to prove itself or force its way.

Another way of saying this is to submit that Christianity is unique because of the *cross of Jesus Christ*. But then the cross must be seen for what it is: not as a sign of strength, but as proof of weakness and vulnerability. The cross confronts us not with the power of God, but with God's weakness. A cross cannot feature in a divine beauty contest: who would ever think of suggesting a cross as a sign of beauty and strength?

And yet, this is precisely what Christians have often been tempted to do. We have done unimaginable things with the cross and in the name of the cross. Like Constantine and thousands of others since his time, we brandish it as a weapon, as a club, with which to clobber our own and God's enemies. Sometimes we try to hide it from the probing eyes of others, for a cross is such an embarrassment in public. At other times we wallow, masochistically, in the pain caused by the cross, since this makes us feel so much more virtuous; we even devise stratagems to make it heavier and more uncomfortable than it already is. Alternatively, we attempt to fit the cross with a handle, so as to make the carrying easier. We can then 'whistle and light-footedly follow Jesus "from victory to victory" . . . If necessary, we can even walk ahead of Jesus instead of "follow him".'

The gospel picture of the cross, and of a faith based on the cross, is, however, a very different one. Helpless, pain-racked in body and spirit, a victim of trumped-up charges, taunted by the bystanders, Jesus hung between two thieves.

David J Bosch: 'The Vulnerability of Mission', (Selly Oak Colleges, 1991), pages 5–6 (Quoting Kosuke Koyama: No Handle on the Cross, [Orbis Books, 1976])

Culture

Culture is one of God's tools: he doesn't skip culture in the Bible.

Darrell Whiteman: Seminar at the Lausanne II Congress in Manila, (July 1989)

The culture and history of Britain, its art, music, law, literature, architecture, even political ideology, are incomprehensible if the Christian dimension is left out. General ignorance of even the basic tenets and texts of Christianity is a modern educational scandal . . .

To teach this dimension respectfully and sympathetically is not indoctrination . . . to convey sympathy requires skill, and skill requires training. R.E. is too important to be left to amateur enthusiasts in the staff room.

The Times First Leader: (5 August, 1992)

. . . the gospel is a radical judgement upon every culture. The incarnate Word was rejected by human culture in one of its noblest forms. The commentary on the crucifixion of Jesus was the suicide of Judas: what future is there for a humanity which crucifies the Word by which it exists? But the gospel is at the same time an affirmation of new possibilities for human culture. In raising the crucified Jesus from the dead, God opened the way for new possibilities.

Lesslie Newbigin: in the Church Times (20 August, 1992), 'Truth for our Time'

Since Christianity is a historical religion that fulfils its task by engaging with rather than withdrawing from human culture, it is in constant danger of so adapting itself to the context in which it is set as to dilute and neutralise its own nature and message. It becomes an echo, not a prophetic word, a benediction of the spirit of the age rather than a challenge to it.

Richard Holloway: in the Church Times (28 August, 1992), 'Missionary energy laced with moralism'

Si fueris Romae, Romano vivito more;
Si fueri alibi, vivito sicut ibi.
(If you are in Rome, live in the Roman way;
if you are elsewhere, live as they do there.)

Ambrose of Milan, (340–397)

The Coca-colonisation of the world.

Theodore Rusack. (Coca Cola first went on sale in 1886)

D

Death, inevitability of

Do not go gentle into that good night,
Old age should burn and rave at
close of day;
Rage, rage against the dying of the
light.

Dylan Thomas: Do not go gentle (1951) from 'Collected Poems 1934–52' (Dent, 1952)

Cowards die many times before their
deaths;
The valiant taste of death but once.
Of all the wonders that I yet have
heard,
It seems to me most strange that men
should fear,
Seeing that death, a necessary end,
Will come when it will come.

William Shakespeare: 'Julius Caesar', II.ii.30, Caesar to Calphurnia

Life is an energy-process. Like every energy-process, it is in principle irreversible and is therefore directed towards a goal. That goal is a state of rest. In the long run everything that happens is, as it were, no more than the initial disturbance of a perpetual state of rest which forever attempts to re-establish itself . . . Thoughts of death pile up to an astonishing degree as the years increase.

C.G. Jung: 'The Soul and Death'

And come he slow, or come he fast,
It is but Death who comes at last.

Sir Walter Scott, (1771 – 1832)

The undiscover'd county from whose
bourne
No traveller returns.

William Shakespeare (1564–1616): 'Hamlet'

We're none of us ready for death, we thrust it out of our consciousness; one of the most tragic things about so many funerals is not just the sense of shock at the terrible intruder, reminding everyone of their own mortality, but also the sense of lost time, of missed opportunities. We live as if we were immortal, but time is not on our side; by the time the funeral comes, it's too late to say, 'If only . . .' But the real problem of death concerns not sadness or a sense of loss, not even our own mortality; it is to do with the question that mortality asks us – what, after all, is this whole rigmarole about? Are we born to die, and does that inevitable death make all our achievements, our dreams, hopes, loves and longings of as much worth as an empty cigarette packet? At the end of the game, says the Spanish proverb, king and pawn go back into the same box.

Richard MacKenna: 'God for Nothing', (Churchman, 1984/85)

Before the journey that awaits us all,
No man becomes so wise that he has
not
Need to think out, before his going
hence,
What judgement will be given to his
soul
After his death, of evil or of good.

The Venerable Bede's Death Song, (AD 735)

We're all cremated equal.

Goodman Ace: quoted in the New Yorker, (1977)

Death, hope beyond

'This is the day the Lord hath made, let us rejoice and be glad in it.' We will go to our death singing.

James Guthrie, on being wakened by his mournful servant on the day of Guthrie's execution

That longed-for moment
When we say 'good-night' to the world.

Gwennap: 'St. David'

As Martin Luther's daughter, Magdalene (aged 14), lay very ill in September 1542, he said: 'I love her very much but, dear God, if it is your will to take her, I submit to you.' Then he said to her as she lay in bed: 'Magdalene, my dear little daughter, would you like to stay here with your father, or would you willingly go to your Father yonder?' She answered: 'Darling father, as God wills.' Then he said: 'Dearest child, the spirit is willing but the flesh is weak.' Then he turned away and said: 'I love her very much; if my flesh is so strong, what can my spirit do? God has given no bishop so great a gift in a thousand years as he has given me in her. I am angry with myself that I cannot rejoice in my heart and be thankful as I ought.'

As Magdalene was dying, Luther knelt by her bed and wept bitterly, praying that God might free her. Then she died, falling asleep in her father's arms,

As they laid her in the coffin, he said: 'Darling, 'Lena, you will rise and shine like a star, yes, like the sun . . . I am happy in spirit, but the flesh is sorrowful and will not be content, the parting grieves me beyond measure. . . . I have sent a saint to heaven.'

Luther subsequently wrote the following poem for his wife:

I, Lena, Luther's beloved child,
Sleep gently here with all the saints
And lie at peace and rest;
Now I am our God's own guest.
I was a child of death, it is true,
My mother bore me out of mortal
seed;

Now I live and am rich in God.
For this I thank Christ's death and
  blood.

Rupp & Drewery, Ed.: 'Martin Luther'

Martin Luther's last sermon (before he died in Eiselben in February 1546) was on Matthew 12:25 ('a country divided against itself') and he urged his hearers to cling to the Lord and Master who calls the weak and the weary to himself, ending: 'I could say more, but I am weak, so I will leave it alone.'

Justas Jonas, a long-standing friend of Martin Luther, stood at the reformer's bed-side as he lay dying: 'Reverend father, will you die stead-fast in Christ and the doctrines you have preached?'
'Yes,' replied Luther in a clear voice for the last time.

(18 February, 1546)

Dietrich Bonhoeffer sent a last message to his friend, the English Bishop George Bell: 'Tell him that for me this is the end but also the beginning.'
The following morning he was executed by the Nazis.

To my question, whether we might not fortify our minds for the approach of death, he (Dr. Samuel Johnson) answered, in a passion, 'No, Sir, let it alone. It matters not how a man dies, but how he lives. The act of dying is not of importance, it lasts so short a time.'

James Boswell: 'Life of Johnson', (1791)

I shall hear in Heaven.

Last words of Ludwig van Beethoven, (1827)

My hopes are with the Dead: anon
My place with them will be
And I with them shall travel on
Through all Futurity;
Yet leaving here a name, I trust,
That will not perish in the dust.

Robert Southey: 'My days among the dead'

Death, scepticism, etc.

Nothing in his life
Became him like the leaving it.

William Shakespeare (1564 – 1616): 'Macbeth' I.iv.7

Such was the popularity of Charles Dickens' serialised novels that they sometimes caused a scandal. Thomas Carlyle told a story of a clergyman who had been administering 'ghostly consolation' to a sick person and, after leaving the room, heard the sick person exclaim: 'Well, thank God, *Pickwick* will be out in ten days any way!'

James Sutherland, Ed: 'The Oxford Book of Literary Anecdotes', (1975)

There are no problems in a cemetery.

Dr. Martin Lloyd-Jones

Death, questioning

One of the functions of death is that it questions life. One of the interesting features of the terminal phase of life is that most people find, when they realise the point they have reached, that is throws them back onto questioning what their entire life has been about. That is perhaps the major function of looking at [the problems and questions of life and death] while there is still time to do something about it.

Dr. Michael A. Simpson: in 'Simple Faith?' (1978)

There is nothing that focuses the issues of life so clearly as death.

David MacInnes: in 'David Watson', (1985)

Death is a fearful thing:
The wearied and most loathed
  worldly life
that age, ache, penury and
  imprisonment
can lay on nature, is a paradise
to what we fear of death.

William Shakespeare: 'Measure for Measure' III.iii

It is clear that the New Testament writers were not always precise in the use they made of language to do with life after death.

Michael Mitton: 'The Quick and the Dead', (Grove Pastoral Booklet 32, 1987)

Many of the people who plan to become Christians at the eleventh hour unfortunately die at 10.30.

Pam Weaver

If there were not dying people anxious to make sure of receiving full custom-house facilities at the frontier, the curé would be in a bad way. Happily there are always people feeling pretty small at such times. So long as humanity is afraid of the next world, the position of a man who hands out passports for the hereafter is really unassailable. The Curé Ponosse may therefore rest assured of continuing to exercise a dictatorship based on sheer fright. Humble and patient, he makes no attempt to restrain the blasphemies of men still in the full vigour of life. But he waits for them at the corner where the great Reaper will appear . . .

Gabriel Chevalier: 'Clochemerle', (1936), chapter 11

He who pretends to look on death without fear lies. All men are afraid of dying, this is the great law of sentient beings, without which the entire human species would soon be destroyed.

Jean-Jacques Rousseau (1712–78): 'Julie or The New Eloise'

Death, dead funny

Waldo is one of those people who would be enormously improved by death.

Saki (Hector Hugh Munro, 1870–1916)

The reports of my death are greatly exaggerated.

Mark Twain (1835–1910): Telegram from Europe to the Associated Press

When someone, who did not know of the death of Sir Arthur Sullivan, asked Sir William Gilbert if he was still composing, the dead musician's colleague replied: 'On the contrary; he is decomposing.'

Source unknown

Dean Inge (1860–1954) received an angry letter from a critic of one of his newspaper articles: 'I am praying nightly for your death. And it may interest you to know that in two other cases I have had great success.'

Asked how he would like to achieve immortality, Woody Allen replied: 'By not dying.'

The last thing you want to do is the last thing you will do.

Anonymous

George, 1st Marquess Curzon, went to great trouble to adorn the tomb of his first wife and to prepare his own in Kedleston Church. Not long after his death, his widow visited the vault to look at his coffin. On an adjacent ledge, she noticed a postcard which bore, in his handwriting, the words: 'Reserved for the second Lady Curzon.'

Source unknown

Robin Maugham reporting a conversation with his uncle, Somerset Maugham, shortly before the author's death in 1965:
'Dying,' he said to me, 'is a very dull, dreary affair.' Suddenly he smiled, 'And my advice to you is to have nothing whatever to do with it.'

I'm not afraid to die. I just don't want to be there when it happens.

Woody Allen: Getting Even

Death is nature's way of telling you to slow down.

Source unknown

I am ready to meet my Maker. Whether my Maker is prepared for the ordeal of meeting me is another matter.

Winston Churchill: on his 75th birthday, (1949)

Few men by their death can have given such deep satisfaction to so many.

William Connor: in the Casandra column of the Daily Mirror, on the death of Joseph Stalin, (1953)

Death, the Scriptures

When this perishable body puts on imperishability, and this mortal body puts on immortality, then the saying that is written will be fulfilled:
'Death has been swallowed up in victory.'
'Where, O death, is your sting?'
The sting of death is sin, and the power of sin is the law. But thanks be to God, who gives us the victory through our Lord Jesus Christ.

1 Corinthians 15:54–57

Death penalty

Depend upon it, Sir, when a man knows he is to be hanged in a fortnight, it concentrates his mind wonderfully.

Samuel Johnson, (1709–84): in 'Boswell's Life of Johnson'

Debate

We must avoid the common confusion of speaking as those that difference not between verbal and real errors, and that tear their brethren as heretics, before they understand them. And we must learn to see the true state of controversies, and reduce them to the very point where the difference lieth, and not make them seem greater than they are.

Richard Baxter: 'The Reformed Pastor', (1655)

Most debates are a head-on clash between the pigheaded and the cloth-eared to the tune of the Anvil Chorus.

Philip Howard: in The Times, (2 February, 1987)

Deception

A shopkeeper put up a sign 'For the Blind', put a bowl beside it, and left it on the counter. When there was enough money in the bowl, he removed it and erected a blind for the shop window with the money.

You can fool some of the people all of the time, and all of the people some of the time, but you cannot fool all of the people all the time.

Abraham Lincoln

Indeed, it is not in human nature to deceive others for any long time, without in a measure deceiving ourselves too.

John Henry Newman (1801–1890)

Democracy

Nor is the people's judgement always true:
The most may err as grossly as the few.

John Dryden (1631 – 1700): 'Absalom and Achitophel'

It has been said that democracy is the worst form of government, except all those other forms that have been tried from time to time.

Winston Churchill: in the House of Commons, (November, 1947)

Man's capacity for justice makes democracy possible. His inclination to injustice makes democracy necessary.

Reinhold Niebuhr (1892–1971)

Israel moves from a theocracy to a monarchy, via a kind of democracy.
All the elders of Israel gathered together and came to Samuel at Ramah, and said to him, 'You are old and your sons do not follow in your ways; appoint for us, then, a king to govern us, like other nations.' But the thing displeased Samuel when they said, 'Give us a king to govern us.' Samuel prayed to the LORD, and the LORD said to Samuel, 'Listen to the voice of the people in all that they say to you; for they have not rejected you, but they have rejected me from being king over them.'

I Samuel 8:4–7

Desert – *see also* SILENCE

. . . the desert is the place where God's people learn hard lessons of life and faith. It is a place to learn the real priorities and there are no margins for error. In the desert there is no room for luxuries and no respect for human status or strength. To contemplate the desert, then, is to understand the call to walk by faith in God alone. It is a place that simplifies us, down to our true selves, until we are ready to meet the God of life and death.

David Runcorn: 'Silence', (Grove Books, 1986)

Yahweh is first and foremost a God of the wilderness.

Kenneth Leech

. . . our God is the God of the desert. He is the 'three mile an hour God'. He walks with his people.

David Runcorn: 'Silence', (Grove Books, 1986)

Despair

Nature has let us down,
God seems to have left the receiver off the hook,
and time is running out.

Köestler

When you say: 'O stuff-it, Lord; I'm fed up!' and you stop trying, at that moment, God has a chance to get through to you.

Father Bruce Davies, (1986)

weeks are different days and weeks when they are held together by these regular, useless times.

Henri Nouwen: 'Gracias', (Harper & Row, 1983)

Secret discipline without worldliness becomes pure ghetto: worldliness without secret discipline pure boulevard.

Eberhard Bethge (Dietrich Bonhoeffer's closest friend and his first biographer)

Athletes exercise self-control in all things; they do it to receive a perishable wreath, but we an imperishable one.

1 Corinthians 9:25

A bishop, as God's steward, must be blameless; he must not be arrogant or quick-tempered or addicted to wine or violent or greedy for gain; but he must be hospitable, a lover of goodness, prudent, upright, devout, and self-controlled.

Titus 1:7, 8

Diversity

The only war that we must wage today is the war to make the world safe for diversity.

U Thant, (former Secretary General of the United Nations)

Doctors

Once there was a famous preacher whose brother was a doctor. The two were very much alike and they were often mistaken for each other.

One of the vicar's parishioners met the doctor in the street one day and congratulated him on his fine sermon the previous Sunday.

'Oh, I'm afraid you're mistaken,' said the doctor. 'My brother is the one who preaches; I'm the one who practises!'

Don Lewis, Ed: 'More Revd. Sirs, Ladies and Gentlemen'

Earnings: Doctors earn at least £100,000 a year. Even so, they never seem to be there when you need them.
Workload: Time hangs heavy for most doctors. Because of this they generally mooch about the surgery all day on the off-chance of a phone call from a patient in need of a prescription renewal.
Glands: Doctors never understand that you are fat because of your glands – unless you visit them privately.
Prescribing: Doctors generally like to put people on lots of medications which are of no benefit whatever, have potentially lethal side-effects and turn the patient into a gibbering drug addict.
Experience: Old doctors are immensely clever people. They can immediately tell what's wrong with a patient without examining him or talking to him.
Youth: Young doctors, particularly those in hospitals, are always students, even after they have qualified. They know nothing at all and are liable to try experiments on you.
The appointment: Doctors absolutely hate being given a straightforward account of an illness. They prefer to hear who you were speaking to, what time it was and what shopping you were doing when you first noticed the pain. If possible, show the doctor your purchases.
Writing: Always write legibly to a doctor – you cannot expect him to understand scrawl. It is the doctor's job to write illegibly, and he may feel threatened if you adopt that role.

From 'Sixteen Things You Did Not Know About Doctors'

'Is there hope?' the sick man said.
The silent doctor shook his head,
And took his leave with sighs of
sorrow,
Despairing of his fee tomorrow

John Gay: 'Fables', I

Doctrine

Christian apologetics is in crisis today. Cut loose from its missionary and evangelistic setting, it has been caught between the opposing tendencies of a broad conservative movement ('Don't persuade, proclaim!') and a broad liberal movement ('Don't debate, dialogue!'). In the process, apologetics has been either widely misunderstood (as an abject apology) or narrowly defined (in a purely defensive role) and critically constricted (to certain types of argument and certain levels of educational development). Its concern and capacity to persuade real people has almost been lost.

Os Guinness in 'The Mind on Fire': Blaise Pascal, Ed. J.M. Houston, (1989)

A Sunday School teacher asked her pupils if they understood the meaning of 'false doctrine'.

'Yes,' said a little boy. 'False doctrine is when you get the wrong kind of medicine.'

Anonymous

The request for decision [in preaching] without doctrine is an offence to human beings, for it is little less than mindless manipulation.

John R.W. Stott: 'I Believe in Preaching', (Hodders, 1982)

... if we wish to understand the nature of Christian doctrine, we must from the outset recognise that it is concerned with certain historical facts and their signification . . . The facts about the historical Jesus are therefore the data of theology . . . The supreme object of the Christian faith is thus the person of Jesus himself; no one theology or system of doctrine must be identified with the Christian religion. Historical Christianity (by which phrase is meant the mainstream of the development of Christian thought from the first century to the twentieth) is consequently not a system of ideas, but an attitude towards a certain historical person; and for this reason it is not possible or desirable for us to attempt to separate the religion of Jesus from the religion about Jesus. For the content of the gospel is Jesus himself, not a creed or a doctrine or a theory about him . . . Doctrine is not the gospel, but only an attempt to explain the significance of the gospel.

Alan Richardson: 'Creeds in the Making', (SCM, 1935), chapter 1

Neither the Old Testament nor the New Testament has any conception of a religion without this intolerance [of weak doctrine]. As there is only one God, so there can be only one gospel. If God has really done something in Christ on which the salvation of the world depends, and if he has made it known, then it is a Christian duty to be intolerant of everything which ignores, denies, or explains it away. The man who perverts it is the worst enemy of God and men . . . Intolerance like this is, indeed, an essential element in the true religion. Intolerance in this sense has its counterpart in comprehension; it is when we have the only gospel, and not till then, that we have the gospel for all.

James Denny: 'The Death of Christ', (1902), chapter 3, on Galatians 1

A clash of doctrines is not a disaster – it is an opportunity.

Alfred North Whitehead (1861–1947)

Any stigma is good enough to beat a dogma with.

Anonymous

I have been told by many people that they have turned away from the church because they have encountered the kind of absolutes which allow no space for questioning and make no attempt to begin where they are.

Bishop David Sheppard: in The Times, (6 May, 1991), 'Look, listen'

Nobody has any right to preach who has not mighty affirmations to make concerning God's Son Jesus Christ – affirmations in which there is no ambiguity.

James Denny: on 2 Corinthians

... what an expenditure of effort is put into the preaching of the Christian faith up and down the land! But – again with exceptions – is it not the institutionally assured platitudes which are preached?

Gerhard Ebeling: 'The Nature of Faith'

The preachers that have moved and held men have always preached doctrine. No exhortation to good life that does not put behind it some truth as deep as eternity can seize and hold the conscience. Preach doctrine, preach all the doctrine that you know, and learn forever more and more; but preach it always, not that men may believe it, but that men may be saved by believing it.

Phillips Brooks (1835–93, latterly Bishop of Massachusetts): 'Yale Lectures on Preaching', (1877)

If the tempter's voice is listened to ('Just a thought or two from the Gospel of the day') . . . The results are easy to see. We shall rear a generation of Christians accustomed to the Eucharist but foreigners to the many great truths of the Christian faith. They have never had the opportunity of listening, Sunday by Sunday, to a steady, intelligent, interesting exposition of the things most surely believed among us . . . They dare not speak, lest they make fools of themselves . . . They are spiritual Peter Pans. [Peter Pan's secret for flying was to think a happy thought, 'any happy little thought will do'.]

Archbishop Donald Coggan (of Canterbury): 'On Preaching', (1975/78)

Doubt

Suppression of doubt does nobody any good. Rather let it come out into the open where it can be faced. Truth is big enough and strong enough to stand the consequences.

Archbishop Donald Coggan: 'Christ and Our Crises', (B.B.C. Broadcasts, April, 1973)

. . . like many Christians, you manfully keep your doubts to yourself and lock your 'simple faith' and 'everyday life' into separate compartments, trustingly refusing to use on your faith the same questioning approach that you would apply to any other corner of your life, and wrestling with a growing sense of unease and discontent which you dimly feel may be sinful. Is it any wonder that, in church after church, you hear the confused appeal, 'Please can we have more teaching?' Teaching about what? Not sure, but something to ease the pain. Because of course the other thing we all know is that Christians *never feel doubt*, or, if they do, they've got to keep it to themselves.

Richard MacKenna: 'God for Nothing', (Churchman 1984/85)

Mourning after an absent God is an evidence of love as strong as rejoicing in a present one. Nay further, a man may be more decisively the servant of God and goodness while doubting his [God's] existence, and in the anguish of his soul crying for light, than while resting in a common creed, and coldly serving him. There has been one at least whose apparent forsakenness, and whose seeming doubt, bears the stamp of the majesty of Faith: 'My God, my God, why hast thou forsaken me?'

F.W. Robertson (1816–53): 'Sermons on Religion and Life'

To believe with certainty we must begin with doubting.

Polish saying

The wise are prone to doubt.

Greek saying

Thomas (who was called the Twin), one of the twelve, was not with them when Jesus came. So the other disciples told him, 'We have seen the Lord.' But he said to them, 'Unless I see the marks of the nails in his hands, and put my finger in the mark of the nails and my hand in his side, I will not believe.'

A week later his disciples were again in the house, and Thomas was with them. Although the doors were shut, Jesus came and stood among them and said, 'Peace be with you.' Then he said to Thomas, 'Put your finger here and see my hands. Reach out your hand and put it in my side. Do not doubt but believe.' Thomas answered him, 'My Lord and my God!' Jesus said to him, 'Have you believed because you have seen me? Blessed are those who have not seen and yet have come to believe.'

John 20:24–29

You, beloved, . . . have mercy on some who are wavering.

Jude 22

Dreams

The dreamers of the day are the dangerous men.

T.E. Lawrence (Lawrence of Arabia)

In the Bible God sometimes uses dreams to communicate (eg. through Daniel or Saint Paul). Joseph (Genesis 30–50) had a number of dreams and interpreted dreams. His brothers described him as 'this dreamer' in Genesis 37:19.

I will pour out my spirit on all flesh;

your sons and your daughters shall prophesy,
your old men shall dream dreams,
and your young men shall see visions.

Joel 2:28

Drink

A Vicar heard his doorbell ring at midnight and went down thinking it was an urgent caller. When he opened the door the man outside reeled a little and said:
'Did you know your spire's crooked?'
It was just as well, because he didn't!

(Bishop Michael Baughan: when Rector of Holy Trinity Church, Platt, Manchester)

The saintly Bishop King of Lincoln had gone for a walk one warm summer morning at Folkestone and had lain down on the shingly beach. When it came to getting up, his rheumatism made the effort impossible and he had to call for help from a little girl. 'This is very kind of you, my dear; but do you really think you're strong enough?' he asked. 'Oh yes,' answered the child. 'I've often helped my daddy when he was much drunker than you.'

From Derek Nimmo: 'Oh Come On All Ye Faithful', (Robson Books, 1986)

When Methodist preachers came
  down
A-preaching that drinking is sinful,
I'll wager the rascals a crown
They always preach best with a
  skinful.

But when you come down with your
  pence,
For a slice of their scurvy religion,
I'll leave it to all men of sense,
But you, my good friend, are the
  pigeon.

Oliver Goldsmith: Song from 'She Stoops to Conquer'

E

Earth

Earth, a planet named for its finely ground rock containing organic material that, given sunlight and moisture, can produce plant life that may support advanced life forms such as Catholics or Lutherans.

Garrison Keillor: 'Lake Wobegon Days', (1985), 'Spring'

Easter – *see* RESURRECTION

Easter eggs

Eggs were given as symbolic gifts by the Christians of Egypt to their believing friends as symbols of the new life of Easter after the penitence of Lent.

The Mothers' Union was asked to bring decorated eggs for an Easter Service – the eggs to be given to a local hospital. The Vicar explained to the members: 'As you enter church, ladies, will you please lay your eggs in the font.'

Anonymous

Economics

Neither for Luther nor Calvin would it have appeared as anything other than incomprehensible blasphemy to suggest that human behaviour in the sphere of economics was outside the jurisdiction of theology. On the contrary, buying and selling, hiring labour and working for a master, amassing wealth and enclosing land – these are precisely the human activities in greatest need of the reminder that every man stands under the law of God and will be accountable to God for his treatment of his neighbour.

Lesslie Newbigin: 'Foolishness to the Greeks', (S.C.M., 1986)

If all economists were laid end to end, they would not reach a conclusion.

Attributed to George Bernard Shaw

Education – *see also* KNOWLEDGE

Aristotle was asked how much educated men were superior to the uneducated. 'As much,' he replied, 'as the living are to the dead.'

Cited 'with great warmth' on occasions by Dr Samuel Johnson

James Boswell asked Dr Samuel Johnson what was best to teach children first:
Sir, it is no matter what you teach them first, any more than what leg you shall put into your breeches first. Sir, you may stand disputing which is best to put in first, but in the mean time your breech is bare. Sir, while you are considering which of two things you should teach your child first, another boy has learnt them both.

The Mock Turtle's opinion on the most important aspects of one's schooling:
Reeling and writhing of course, to begin with, and the different branches of Arithmetic, – Ambition, Distraction, Uglification and Derision.

Lewis Carroll: 'Alice's Adventures in Wonderland'

You cannot exclude values from the classroom because they are everywhere. The humanist, said T.E. Hulme, rejects heaven and hell only to replace them with heavens and hells more to his liking. . . . Ridiculing 'trendy' teachers is a standard crowd pleaser at party conferences as are rallying cries for a return to 'traditional values'.

Newspaper leader (source unknown)

The Church took a wrong turning when it substituted the technique of the classroom for the technique of the community in religious education.

Emil Brunner: quoted in the report 'Growing Churches', (1957)

Generally speaking, we are more firmly convinced by reasons that we have discovered for ourselves, than by those which are given to us by others.

Blaise Pascal (1623–1662)

It is not difficult to produce sophisticated men and women by collecting them to learn certain subjects. But it is not sophisticated men and women that a good university tries to produce. It is men and women whose knowledge goes with character, and with reverence for persons and for the things of the mind.

Archbishop Michael Ramsey, in the House of Lords, 11 December, 1963

. . . people, by what they understand, are best led to what they understand not.

George Herbert (1593–1633): in the 'Country Parson'

Education is too expensive? Try ignorance.

'Body Shop' slogan

The little girl came home very excited: 'I've been moved up from Class 2 to Class 3.'
'That's wonderful,' replied her mother. 'Why was that?'
'Because they're painting Class 2,' came the reply.

Public schools are the nurseries of all vice and immorality. All the wicked fellows whom I remember at the university were bred in them.

Henry Fielding: 'Joseph Andrews', (1742), Book III, Chapter 5, Parson Adams

Academics as a class are the most pusillanimous of mankind because they are best at inventing apparently good reasons for avoiding unpleasant duties.

A.T. & R.P.C. Hanson: 'The Identity of the Church', (S.C.M., 1987)

Efficiency

A company chairman had been given tickets to a performance of Schubert's 'Unfinished' Symphony. He couldn't go, and passed them on to his work study consultant. The next morning, the chairman asked him how he had enjoyed the performance, and was handed a memorandum which read:
For considerable periods, the four oboe players had nothing to do. The number should be reduced, and their work spread over the whole

orchestra, thus eliminating peaks of inactivity.

All of the 12 violins were playing identical notes. This seemed to be unnecessary duplication, and the staff of this section should be drastically cut.

Much effort was absorbed in the playing of demi-semi-quavers. Now this appears to be an excessive refinement, and it is recommended that all notes should be rounded up to the nearest semi-quaver.

No useful purpose is served by repeating with horns the passage that had already been played by the strings. If all such redundant passages were eliminated, the concert could be reduced from two hours to 20 minutes.

If Schubert had attended to these matters, he would probably have been able to finish his symphony after all.

Source unknown

Elections

The Vicar (anxious not to reveal political bias) announced that, whichever party won the forthcoming General Election, they would sing a hymn of praise to the Almighty. If the Tories were to win, *'Now thank we all our God'*. If the Labour party were to win, *'Our God, our help in ages past'*. If the Liberals were to win, *'God moves in his mysterious ways'*.

Anonymous

Emotions

. . . religious excitement will convert and strengthen a Soul as little as the dinner bell with replace a meal.

A.J. Mason

Don't tell me of your feelings. A traveller would be glad of fine weather, but, if he be a man of business, he will go on.

John Newton, (converted slave-trader, cleric and writer)

'What do you think of God?' the teacher asked. After a pause the young pupil replied, 'He's not a *think*, he's a *feel*.'

Related by Paul Frost

You taught me to be nice, so that now I am so full of niceness, I have no sense of right and wrong, no outrage, no passion. 'If you can't say something nice, don't say anything at all,' you said, so I am very quiet, which most people think is politeness. I call it repression.

Garrison Keillor: 'Lake Wobegon Days' (1985), News, '95 Theses 95'

In the temple he (Jesus) found people selling cattle, sheep and doves, and the money changers seated at their tables . . . He told those who were selling the doves, 'Take these things out of here! Stop making my Father's house a market-place!' His disciples remembered that it was written, 'Zeal for your house will consume me.'

John 2:14–17 (quoting Psalm 69:9)

(When they took him to the burial place of Lazarus, his friend,)
Jesus began to weep. So the Jews said, 'See how he loved him!'

John 11:35, 36

England and The English

The English, 'the most pernicious race of little odious vermin that nature ever suffered to crawl upon the surface of the earth.'

Jonathan Swift: Gulliver's Travels (part two)

The God to be worshipped in them [Wren's churches] was a God of order, of reason, of light; a God with whom well-behaved, reasonable, enlightened Englishmen felt at home.

David Edwards: 'Christian England', (volume 2, 1983)

This phlegmatic moderation is both the English strength and the English weakness. Although they balance on a knife-edge between excessive zeal and unbelief, it is the broad, blunt edge of the blade and really not such an uncomfortable place to sit on. The English find it remarkably easy to resist enthusiasm, whereas this lumpen inertia constantly threatens to overwhelm any spiritual sense they might have.

From the Introduction to 'The English Spirit', (D.L.T., 1987)

At every one of those concerts in England you will find rows of weary people who are there, not because they really like classical music, but because they think they ought to like it. Well, there is the same thing in heaven. A number of people sit there in glory, not because they are happy, but because they think they owe it to their position to be in heaven. They are almost all English.

George Bernard Shaw: 'Man and Superman'

. . .the English are never happy to stray too far from Scripture; they tend not to use their imaginations; their devotions are centred on Christ; they are uneasy about the Holy Spirit. These characteristics are not of course to be seen in every writer; nor are they exclusive to the English. Taken together and as a whole, however, they do form a distinct English tradition.

Introduction to 'The English Spirit', (D.L.T., 1987)

The English think incompetence is the same thing as sincerity.

Quentin Crisp: in The New York Times, (1977)

English (language)

When the American people get through with the English language, it will look as if it has been run over by a musical comedy.

Finley Peter Dunne: 'Mr. Dooley at His Best', (1938)

Be an American. Speak English.

Bumper-sticker in Hispanic Florida

Enthusiasm

How I long for a little ordinary human enthusiasm. Vast enthusiasm – that's all. I want to hear a warm, thrilling voice cry out, 'Hallelujah! Hallelujah! I'm alive!'

John Osborne: 'Look Back in Anger', (1956)

My temper is not very susceptible of enthusiasm, and the enthusiasm which I do not feel I have ever scorned to affect.

Source unknown

Dick Royds, for 19 years Vicar of Clunbury, Herefordshire, an old-fashioned evangelical:

I am a negligible scholar. I am an incoherent preacher. I am a futile administrator. I do not give wine-and-cheese parties in the nave of my church. I do not even serve Bovril and biscuits in the vestry. *But* I am a fanatical Evangelical and Erastian half crazy with ambition (to become the Rural Dean of Clun).

On failing to be appointed to another parish he wrote to Richard Hill:

I should ruthlessly have stamped out all enthusiasm, progress and initiative. No original thought or bright idea would have been allowed to pollute my tranquil incumbency and I doubt if the Parochial Church Council would have ever met. They would have received neither strong meat nor milk from me, but a kind of indeterminate theological custard, wholly uncontaminated by 'enthusiasm'.

Environment

The human being was made to breathe the good air of nature, but what he breathes is an obscure compound of acids and coal tars. He was created for a living environment, but he dwells in a lunar world of stone, cement, asphalt, glass, cast iron and steel. The trees wilt and blanch among sterile and stone façades. Cats and dogs disappear little by little in the city, going the way of the horse. Only rats and men remain to populate a dead world.

Jacques Ellul

. . . worrying is less work that doing something to fix the worry. This is especially true if we're careful to pick the biggest possible problems to worry about. Everybody wants to save the earth; nobody wants to help Mom do the dishes.

P.J. O'Rourke: 'All the Trouble in the World', (1994), 'Fashionable Worries'

God saw everything that he had made, and indeed, it was very good.

Genesis 1:31

The LORD God planted a garden in Eden, in the east; and there he put the man whom he had formed. Out of the ground the LORD God made to grow every tree that is pleasant to the sight and good for food, the tree of life also in the midst of the garden, and the tree of the knowledge of good and evil....

The LORD God took the man and put him in the garden of Eden to till it and keep it. And the LORD God commanded the man, 'You may freely eat of every tree of the garden; but of the tree of the knowledge of good and evil you shall not eat, for in the day that you eat of it you shall die.'

Genesis 2:8, 9, 15–17

In him (God's beloved Son) all things in heaven and on earth were created, things visible and invisible, whether thrones or dominions or rulers or powers – all things have been created through him and for him. He himself is before all things, and in him all things hold together.

Colossians 1:16, 17

Epitaphs

Life's like an inn
Where travellers stay;
Some only breakfast and away –
Others to dinner stay and are full fed –
The oldest only, sup and go to bed.
Long is his bill who lingers out the day;
Who goes the soonest has the least to pay.

Unverified tombstone inscription

In a vault underneath
Lie interred Several of the Saunderses
Late of this Parish.
Particulars the Last Day will disclose.

Tombstone in Tetbury, Gloucestershire

Here lies John Higley
Whose Father and Mother were drowned
in the Passage from America
Had they both lived
they would have been buried here.

Unverified Irish tombstone

John Baskerville, a celebrated type-founder and printer from Birmingham, (1706–75), was a determined atheist and had this inscription on his cone-shaped monument (which was overturned and his remains desecrated).

Stranger, Beneath this cone in
UNCONSECRATED Ground,
A friend to the liberties of mankind,
Directed his body to be inured.
May the example contribute to
emancipate thy mind
from the idle fears of
SUPERSTITION
and the wicked arts of priesthood.

To the memory of Thomas Hause.
Lord, thy grace is free -why not for me?
And the Lord answered and said,
Because thy debts ain't paid.

Tombstone at Coggleshall, Essex

Here lies in a horizontal position the
outside case of
Thomas Hinde, Clock and Watch maker,
Who departed this life wound up
in hope of being taken in hand by his Maker
and being thoroughly cleaned,
repaired, and set a-going
in the world to come,
On the 15th of August, 1836, in the
19th year of his life.

A tombstone in Bolsover, Derbyshire

O Cruel Death, How could you be so unkind,
To take him before, and leave me behind?
You should have taken both of us, if either,
Which would have been more
pleasing to the survivor.

Tombstone in St. Philip's Cathedral, Birmingham

M.S. Donald Robertson
Born 1st of January, 1785. Died 4th of
June, 1848. Aged 63 years.
He was a peaceable quiet man, and,
to all appearance, a sincere Christian.
His death was very much regretted -
which was caused by the stupidity of
Lawrence Tulloch of Clotherton
who sold him *nitre* instead of
Epsom Salts,
by which he was killed in the space of
three hours after taking a dose of it.

Tombstone in Cross Kirk

Sacred to the memory
of Major James Brush

who was killed
by the accidental discharge of a pistol
by his orderly, 14th April, 1831.
Well done, good and faithful servant.

Tombstone in Woolwich (unverified)

Erected to the Memory of John
McFarlane
– drowned in the Water of Leith –
By a few affectionate Friends

Tombstone in Edinburgh

The Honourable George Napier . . .
descendant of the inventor of
Logarithms . . .
Tho' but a private Gentleman embarrassed with a large family, (etc) . . .
In Him great Stature, Strength and
Comeliness were combined with
dauntless Courage,
and his Mind was as Strong and
Comely as his Person.
Nature and Study had fitted him for
any Station however high,
for any Enterprise however difficult,
But this opportunity was never given,
and this master Spirit passed away
unknown.
In 1804, at the Age of 51, He sank
under Sickness
produced by incessant toil in the
Public Service.

Memorial tablet in porch of Redland Parish Church, Bristol

Thorpe's Corpse

Unverified

Robert Ross (1869–1918) said that at the end of his stormy career as a literary editor, the appropriate inscription on his tombstone would be:

Here lies one whose name is writ in
hot water.

James Sutherland, Ed.: 'Oxford Book of Literary Anecdotes', (1975)

Beneath this smooth stone
By the bone of his bone
Sleeps Master John Gill;
By lies when alive
This attorney did thrive,
And now that he's dead he lies still.

Unverified

A tombstone in Hastings, Sussex:

16 January, 1751,
Joseph Bain.
Good peppell as you pafs by
I pray you on me caft an I,
For as you am fo wounce wous I;
And as i am fo muft you be,
Therefor prepare to follow me.

Reputedly chalked below was the rejoinder:

To follow you I'm not content,
Unless I know which way you went.

Unverified – because the chalk had washed off

A tombstone in Yorkshire ought to have included a brief tribute to the deceased woman, but the stonemason made an error: he wrote 'LORD, SHE WERE THIN'. It was pointed out to him that he had missed out an 'E' from the text, so the mason soon made a correction.
The family were later astonished to see the new inscription: 'E, LORD, SHE WERE THIN'.

Source unknown

Travellers I will relate a prodigy:
On the day whereupon the aforesaid
Thomas Carter
breathed out his soul, a Sudbury
camel passed
through the eye of a needle.
Go – and if thou art wealthy –
do likewise.
Farewell.

Tombstone in Sudbury

Brigham Young
Born on this spot 1801
A man of much courage and superb
equipment.

Memorial to the polygamous Brigham Young, Mormon leader

The body of Benjamin Franklin,
Printer,
(Like the cover of an old book,
its contents torn out and stript of its
lettering and gilding),
Lies here, food for worms. But the
work itself shall not be lost,
For it will, as he believed, appear once
more
In a new and more elegant edition,
Revised and corrected by The
Author.

Epitaph composed for Benjamin Franklin but never executed

Thos. Woodcock.
Here lie the remains of Thomas
Woodhen,
The most amiable of Husbands
And excellent of men.
His real name was Woodcock,
But it wouldn't come in Rhyme.

Tombstone in Dunoon

Robert Lives, Esq, a Barrister.
So great a lover of peace,
that when a contention arose between
Life and Death
he immediately yielded up his Ghost
to end the dispute, August 12th, 1819.

Tombstone in Richmond, Surrey

Equality

All animals are equal, but some animals are more equal than others.

George Orwell (Eric Blair, 1903–1950): 'Animal Farm'

Winston S Churchill (Prime Minister) liked pigs:
Dogs look up to men; cats look down on men: pigs just treat us as equals.

Eternity

. . . eternal life will not be a bore. I have often thought to myself that I know that I should want eternal life because I am told that God promises it to me and, of course, it is impolite not to want what God promises. But I have often wondered whether going on and on wouldn't be an awful bore. Of course, if we went on and on as we are now we should soon discover, as Sartre put it, that hell is other people. We only have to look in a mirror to see that, unless we are transformed, heaven will be hell, supposing we spend our lives there. That is why it must be transformation, growth and development. But I have begun to get glimpses, especially through other people, that eternity could be infinitely worth it precisely because there will always be more to discover.

Bishop David Jenkins (of Durham): 'God, Jesus and Life in the Spirit', (S.C.M., 1988)

High up in the North, in the land called Svithjod, there stands a rock. It is 100 miles high and 100 miles wide. Once every 1,000 years, a little bird comes to this rock to sharpen its beak. When the rock has thus been worn away, then a single day of eternity will have gone by.

Hendrik Willem Van Loon: 'The Story of Mankind'

Eternity is a terrible thought. I mean, where's it going to end?

Tom Stoppard: 'Rosencrantz and Guildenstern Are Dead'

Cricket is a game which the British, not being a spiritual people, had to invent in order to have some concept of eternity.

Lord Mancroft

The Christian is living between the Already and the Not Yet.

Anonymous

I am getting old now and death does not worry me. It's the eternal rest I think I shall find difficult.

Edna Nicholas: Letter, (1992)

Ethics – *see also* VALUES

'Surely an atheist, moved neither by hope of heaven nor fear of hell, would feel free to defy laws and run amok?' [asked Severo, cardinal prince of Grandinsula.]

'No doubt for a believer, desire to please God is a strong motive,' said Palinor. 'But a rational man may have sufficient reasons in this world to concede the necessity for laws and the benefits of obeying them. I think for most people in Aclar [Palinor's home], a desire to stand well in the eyes of the neighbours is reason enough.'

Jill Paton Walsh: 'Knowledge of Angels', (Green Bay / Black Swan: 1994/1995), Chapter 8

The greatest happiness of the greatest number is the foundation of morals and legislation.

Jeremy Bentham (1748–1832): 'The Commonplace Book'

There is no route from faithless immorality back to religious morality that does not pass through religion itself. A yearning for values can lead to religion, and is indeed a major highway. But religion calls for much more than morality; it seeks conversion. Classical Protestantism insists that morality follows conversion, and that the moral life is one of the fruits of justification by faith – after the event.

The doctrine rests on paradox: it is only after one realises the impossibility of being saved by one's best efforts at being good, after coming face to face with one's utter wretchedness, that one is ready to be saved at all. To stress morality without faith is to incur the ultimate Reformation anathema for the preaching of salvation by good works, the heresy known as Pelagianism. (And this is no longer a specifically Protestant doctrine: there is no salvation by good works in Catholicism.)

Clifford Longley: in The Times, (27 October, 1989), 'A consumer's guide to God'

In the Bible, people who innovated tended to get smote, and that at a time when God smote hard: when he smited you stayed smitten, smiting was no slap on the wrist. Mrs Tollerud illustrated this in Sunday School with a flannelgraph: a cloth-covered board on which she placed cloth figures and moved them around. The Liberals got kicked out of Paradise, they got flooded upon, and Pharaoh, though decent in some ways, when he didn't obey God, God made a mess of Egypt, dumping locusts, frogs, blood, lice, hail, and flies on them and then turning day to night. She took down the figure of Pharaoh the ruler and put up the figure of Pharaoh with his hands over his face. It made us think twice about striking out in new directions. But knowing right from wrong is the easy part. Knowing is not the problem.

Garrison Keillor: 'Lake Wobegon Days', (1985), 'Summer'

Eucharist, doctrine

In the mass the bread changed into Christ's flesh, even if it was not 'the sort of flesh from which red sausages are made.'

Martin Luther: Sermon on John 6:51, (1531)

The first service is a Bible-Class-cum-Prayer-Meeting and the second service is a Meal.

Michael Perry: 'Experiment in Worship', (1967), describing the typical Eucharist (actually referring to the new Series II service of the Church of England)

Thomas Aquinas laid it down (Summa Theologica Q.78) that the moment of consecration of each element was the last instant of the Dominical Words of Institution (the central acts of the Last Supper as recorded in Mark 14 and 1 Corinthians 11) over each element.

The conclusion cannot be escaped (from this and the elevation of the host from 1208 and the word 'transubstantiation' by the Lateran Council in 1215) that, whatever refinements may have been devised by sophisticated theologians, in popular faith and practice the recital of the Institution Narrative came perilously near to being regarded as a magical incantation which produced miraculous effects by its mere utterance.

Geoffrey Cuming: 'He Gave Thanks', (1981)

Teaching comes first: the Eucharist is the end-product of the preaching of the word, duly listened to and translated into action . . . The pattern is clear. Ministry is a service of the whole gospel, of the word of God, of the Saviour whose teachings must first be heard and believed if he is sincerely and fruitfully to be received in the Eucharist.

Michael Richards: in The Times, (1 August, 1987)

In the Russian Orthodox liturgy, the priest declares, as he breaks the bread into four parts:

The Lamb of God is broken and distributed,
and, though broken, is not divided,
though eaten, is never consumed,
but hallows those who share it.

Without the communion there is no identifiable body of Christ to be his presence in the world. Without the communion there is nothing from which we can be sent out into the world. Without the communion there is no testable Christian centre or point of focus to which enquirers in the world can be pointed, into which converts can be introduced through baptism. And without that eschatological feast which is communion, a feast of love and of the reign of God, we are modelling nothing about the transformation of society which is our larger task in mission. This is our deliverance from a privatised personal discipleship into marching in and with the people of God on the mission of God has given them. This is our glimpse of glory together, a glimpse which itself stirs us in our mission.

Colin Buchanan: 'The Heart of Sunday Worship', (Grove Worship, 1992)

. . . the doctrine that either the priest or the people offer Christ as a sacrifice or offer Christ's sacrifice in the eucharist is wholly uncongenial because it contradicts Scripture, reverses the proper relation of the believer to Christ, leads inevitably to doctrinal and ecclesiastical developments which history has shown to be disastrous for the welfare of the Christian church, and obscures the authentic, original, entirely sound, early Christian doctrine of sacrifice.

R.P.C. Hanson: 'Eucharistic Offering in the Early Church', (Grove Liturgical Study, 1979)

We do not offer Christ as a sacrifice for our sins, in the eucharist or on any other occasion. To do that would be inevitably to return to the old anxious nagging at God which is ultimately a confession of lack of faith. Instead we joyfully and thankfully accept the sacrifice which Christ has achieved and offered for us, and which is a gift, the gift of God to man, and try to live lives worthy of this gift. Sacrifice therefore becomes something which God graciously gives to man, not something which man anxiously offers to God. In this view the eucharist becomes what its very early name implied, above all an occasion of thanksgiving, with which are united, of course, communion in Christ and our offering of ourselves in Christ to God.

R.P.C. Hanson: 'Eucharistic Offering in the Early Church', (Grove Liturgical Study, 1979)

Some Christians worry a great deal about the means and meaning of consecrating a piece of bread and a cup of wine, yet so easily forget that these are simply means of consecrating the people of God.

Robert M.E. Paterson, (1995)

Eucharist, devotion

Your profiting [at the Lord's Supper] will for the most part be proportioned to your preparation.

Charles Simeon (1759–1836): 'Horae Homileticae', Sermon no. 1980

There we see Christ crucified, as it were, before our eyes: there we contemplate the most stupendous mysteries: there we commemorate the greatest of all mercies: there we are admitted to most familiar fellowship with God.

Charles Simeon (1759–1836)

Martin Bucer affirmed that Christ is present in the sacrament, but the Lord is not food for the stomach, rather he is food 'of faith for the new inner man, "so that we become one bone and one flesh with him".'

Martin Bucer, quoting John Jewel

[It should] be sufficient for me presenting myself at the Lord's table to know what there I receive from him, without searching or inquiring of the manner how Christ performeth his promise.

Richard Hooker: 'Of the Laws of Ecclesiastical Polity', Book V, lxvii, 12

Richard L Thulin told the story of an elderly parishioner, Agnes, whose gentle, intelligent nature had been transformed by dementia into something totally different. He often shared the sacramental meal with her and, as she received the bread, always beamed, 'Oh boy, does that taste good!'

I worried about her comprehension. And yet I knew that she did not have to be introduced to broken bread. She herself was broken. She herself existed as scraps torn from some wholeness: broken in body, crumbled in mind, split off from friendship, sliced away from all securities. Brokenness was the final question, not comprehension. I was broken as she, bringing only scraps of fidelity, bits and pieces of love, crumbs of hope. When Agnes took the bread and exclaimed, 'Oh boy, does that taste good!' I think she was saying, 'Brother Richard, both of us have tasted the kindness of the Lord.'

I also admitted that it was not easy for me to visit Agnes. I never knew what to expect. But more than that, at each succeeding visit a lifetime of deep bitterness and rancour gushed out in a vitriolic flood . . . Often I become defensive and sometimes outright angry. And yet we were two broken people eating broken bread in which we were given to one another. I think that I learned in that nursing home why I need to eat Christ's meal often. I need to eat at this table of a family made one in Christ until the language, manners, memories and tastes of that family become mine. I need to eat here until I am moved and softened to friendliness and service.

Agnes has been long dead. I think of her frequently. She and I, along with all who share this meal, are still brothers and sisters. Each time we gather at this table we advance the great and coming day when Agnes, you and I and the whole church, will feast with God in glory. Oh boy, Agnes, does that taste good!

Richard L Thulin: 'Journeys toward Narrative Preaching', (Pilgrim Press, 1990)

Eucharist, practice

Canon Arthur H. Couratin, a foremost Anglo-Catholic liturgical scholar, on the subject of the presiding priest facing the congregation at the Eucharist:
If you must go round behind the altar, old boy, don't kneel down, or you'll look like the head of John the Baptist on a platter.

Richard MacKenna describes a 'dirty, back-street church in Fulham where I celebrated the Eucharist for six or seven elderly, decrepit people and the church almost trembled with the presence of mystery.'

'God for Nothing', (Churchman, 1984/85)

. . . many will sit in church and say to themselves as the service starts, 'Oh, it's communion this morning.' That is to treat the communion not as central, but as an interesting variant on non-sacramental services. There is no evidence anywhere of worshippers being either taught or expected to alternate between morning and evening themselves in order to be in communion, and the only people who would become weekly communicants through this pattern would be the consistent 'twicers'. People become communicant by accident, rather than design.

Colin Buchanan: 'The Heart of Sunday Worship', (Grove Worship, 1992)

Sometimes Communion makes me feel strong all over though. I think it's the taste apart from anything else of course. The bread and wine in your mouth, and you can smell it off the others back in the pew, all part of the same thing. I don't know.

Adam Thorpe: 'Ulverton', (1992), chapter 11, Violet Nightingale's diary for 12 April, 1953

Evangelicals, history

. . . the leaders of the Anglican Evangelicals are not content to hand over the Catholic heritage of the Church of England to any mere section within it.

Alan Richardson, (c. 1950)

I am an Evangelical. I have never felt under any constraint to apologise for that designation, one of great and lofty lineage, not least within our own Anglican Communion. I like the word in its simple form, unhyphenated with others, whose usual associations, in Britain at any rate, is with the platforms of political parties.

Max Warren: 'The Sevenfold Secret'

When, in 1768, six Evangelical students were expelled from St Edmund Hall, Oxford, Dr. Samuel Johnson (who had himself failed to graduate) commented: 'A cow is a very good animal in a field but we turn her out of a garden.'

Gladstone's observation as the spiritual initiative passed from Evangelicals to others was:
The Evangelical movement filled men so full with the wine of spiritual life that larger and better vessels were required to hold it.

Evangelicals in the Church of England have never been a party. They have always been obstinate individualists – this is their strength, and in part also their weakness.

Bishop Stephen Neill: 'Anglicanism', (1958–77)

By this grand word Evangelical I mean the Evangelicalism of Paul and the apostles, that of Luther and the other Reformers, that of Wesley and of many other Christians in many different denominations in all parts of the world; and finally, I mean that Evangelicalism which is deep in the heart of the Church of England.

Canon Bryan Green: in the Church Times, (11 January, 1991), 'The manifesto of a liberated Evangelical'

Evangelicals, doctrine

Evangelicals are orthodox in doctrine, and enthusiastically orthodox.

Elliott-Binns, (1928)

We are moving into a situation in which, if Christianity is to continue as a significant force, it will have to recover something of the missionary energy that characterised the early church. It seems to be the case, so far, that only Evangelical versions of Christianity are in possession of this energy. This certainly seems to be the case within the Anglican Church. It is entirely possible, therefore, that it is the Evangelical version of Christianity that will survive and become dominant.

Bishop Richard Holloway: in the Church Times (28 August, 1992), 'Missionary energy laced with moralism'

Evangelicals seem to find it hard to think in dialectical terms [in systematic reasoning] and can hardly endure to live with unresolved questions and amidst tensions. This may partly explain why conservative Christians have problems with the teaching of Jesus on the Kingdom of God.

Peter Kuzmic: History and Eschatology, Evangelical Views, (in Bruce Nicholls, Ed. 'In Word and Deed', Paternoster, 1985)

Evangelicals, criticism of

It has always been the weakness of Evangelicals to quarrel over trifles, and to vilify one another for alleged adherence to tenets which have never been either precisely defined or adequately understood.

Bishop Stephen Neill: 'Anglicanism', (1958–77)

Some Evangelicals in their dismissal of other Christian styles are the obverse of the Anglo-papal absurdists in the Church of England who claim both loyalty to the Holy See and membership of a church that defined itself historically by separating from Rome.

Bishop Richard Holloway: in the Church Times (28 August, 1992), 'Missionary energy laced with moralism'

S.W.E.G. = Slimy Wet Evangelical Grin

Anonymous

Censoriousness has ever been the most unpleasant of all evangelical weaknesses.

Hugh Evan Hopkins: 'Charles Simeon of Cambridge', (1977)

F. J. Chavasse urged evangelicals to avoid an 'excessive individualism' and to 'entreat the Spirit of God to grant us the humility which hesitates to believe that, at all times and in all things, our own opinion must be right. We must crush under foot the temptation to imagine that if our fellow-Evangelicals do not hold exactly what we hold, or express themselves exactly as we do, it is our duty to decline to work with them because they are not sound.'

Islington Conference, (1927)

Part of the difficulty I find with enthusiastic Evangelicals is the way they have developed a particular cultural style; it is sometimes difficult to separate their message from their medium, and not everyone likes or can copy their medium of expression. I'm not an easy smiler, for instance, so I feel a bit uncomfortable in the presence of the Evangelical smile. Nor does the Evangelical method of extempore prayer, with its constant repetition of 'Lord, I just want to tell you, Lord', and other incantatory phrases sit well with my natural grimness. I deeply admire much about Conservative Evangelicals, and I believe that the future of the Christian cause lies to a great extent in their hands; but I do wish they'd calm down a bit and recognise that not all God's children can imitate their apparently unfailing enthusiasm and good nature. Some of us need to growl now and again, even at God.

Bishop Richard Holloway (of Edinburgh): Review in the Church Times, (4 April, 1985)

. . . some [Christians] have obviously observed humans smiling and laughing and noticed that this has a good effect on other humans, so they have evolved a whole repertoire of teeth-baring smiles and hearty laughs, just to prove what fun it all is, how nice and deeply loving they are, what joy in the Lord if you enrol here; but the smiles and laughs are not for where you are, loving and accepting you, comrades on the same journey: they are the smiles of the great white shark in *Jaws* who has spied another potential mouthful, another feather in the Lord's cap.

Richard MacKenna: 'God for Nothing', (Churchman, 1984/85)

I hope that they [Evangelicals] will be first Anglicans before they are Evangelicals. Indeed, any party which becomes more important than our Church risks destroying our ecclesiology and is potentially demonic.

Archbishop George Carey (when Bishop-designate of Bath & Wells): Letter to the Church Times, (20th November, 1987)

Extreme evangelical Protestantism has in itself a fissiparous, centrifugal tendency which would inhibit it from desiring reunion in any circumstances. Extreme fundamentalism runs out into lunatic deviations.

A.T. & R.P.C. Hanson: 'The Identity of the Church', (S.C.M., 1987)

The Evangelical Protestant mind has never relished complexity. Indeed its crusading genius, whether in religion or politics, has always been towards an over-simplification of issues and the substitution of inspiration and zeal for critical analysis and serious reflection.

N. K. Clifford: 'His Dominion: A Vision in Crisis', (Studies in Religion 2, 1973)

Evangelicals have been deeply sinful in being anti-intellectual ever since the 1820's and 1830's. . . . Evangelicals need to repent of their refusal to think Christianly and to develop the mind of Christ.

From 'Persuasion for the New World: An Interview with Os Guinness', (1992)

The scandal of the evangelical mind is that there is not much of an evangelical mind . . . Evangelical inattention to intellectual life is a curiosity for several reasons. One of the self-defining convictions of modern evangelicalism has been its adherence to the Bible as the revealed word of God. Most evangelicals also acknowledge that in the Scriptures God stands revealed plainly as the author of nature, as the sustainer of human institutions (family, work, and government), and as the source of harmony, creativity, and beauty. Yet it has been precisely these Bible-believers *par excellence* who have neglected sober analysis of nature, human society and the arts.

Mark A. Noll: 'The Scandal of the Evangelical Mind', (Eerdmans, 1994)

Evangelicals, characteristics

SIR, Could we not place a ten year moratorium on the word 'evangelical', particularly when it is used as a noun in a self-assumed defence or appellation?

Instead let us ask ourselves how Christian we are.

Douglas Dales: Church of England Newspaper, (1973)

I stand before you unashamedly proud of the word 'evangelical', a word all too frequently qualified by adjectives which seem to detract from its pristine beauty and strength.

Max Warren: first address to the Church Missionary Society General Committee as General Secretary, (1942)

When we seek to understand the strength of the Victorian Evangelicals, we ought to see Shaftesbury finding a ragged boy asleep in the roller used in Regent's Park. . . The Victorian Evangelicals did not merely condemn. Nor did they live only among the respectable. They followed their Master in seeking out the lost. And without intending to do this, they laid the foundations of the twentieth-century Welfare State by putting into practice their acknowledgement of a duty to interfere in the results of the working of the laws of capitalist economics.

David Edwards: 'Christian England', (volume 3, 1984)

. . . Evangelicalism has managed to maintain, in all its forms, one characteristic difference from other varieties of Anglican belief, namely its emphasis on conversion.

. . . 'turning from sin in repentance' *(Lausanne Conference 1973)*, a passage from spiritual death to spiritual life. Stated thus, it is impossible to dispute that this is an essential component of Christianity, whatever denominational or party label might be given to it: and that is a truth the Church of England at large tends to dismiss too sniffily.

Clifford Longley: in The Times, (10 September, 1988)

An evangelical is one who
emphasises:
the primacy of God's grace in salvation,
the uniqueness of Christ's work in reconciliation,
the gift of the Spirit in the life of the believer,
the necessity of faith in receiving God's life,
the supremacy of the Scriptures in understanding the truth,
the centrality of mission in the Church's life,
and who, with all the Church, worships one God: Father, Son and Holy Spirit.

Robert M.E. Paterson, (1989)

Beware of the Evangellyfish who stings his victim with a text and moves off swiftly.

Anonymous

The trouble with born-again Christians is that they are an even bigger pain the second time around.

Herb Caen: San Francisco Chronicle, (1981)

Evangelism, crusades

Urbanus, convert to Christ and citizen of Rome, unto the Saints in Britain, greetings:

I write to acquaint you of the doings of saints in Rome in these latter times and my fervent prayer and hope is that you may be made to think by what I say.

We have of late been much exercised about the needs of our fellow-citizens and there has arisen amongst us a committee formed by those who are prominent amongst us and supported by the many Christian sects in our city. Indeed so much was the concern we felt that we agreed to hold a great meeting in our largest auditorium, namely the Colosseum. It is, of course, common knowledge to all those who think about such things that the former ideas of evangelism are now so completely useless that we must learn to communicate to our generation in the manner they would understand. Because of this our Committee arranged not another evangelistic meeting but this time – a Christian Circus!

One of us, Helvidius, who was a leading Jester in Caesar's court, was the chief personality and he was very funny. Without contradiction, he made us laugh many, many times, especially when he poked fun at the old fashioned things in the church. We had some very good music, and a group calling themselves The Once Vestal Virgins sang with an abandon I have only seen matched in my former days when I was a regular attender at the theatre. I did not catch much of their words but their actions were very lively. Drusus, the deacon from our church, thought they were too scantily dressed, but I fear he does not keep step with the times.

Our Committee had many clever ideas and the programme was abundantly different. There was the Gospel Chariot Race and also something called The Gladiators. I thought it not becoming of some youths in the crowd to laugh when some of the wooden swords broke but, as you know, some of the unconverted are very cynical. One sometimes wonders whether they should be allowed to attend our meetings.

Time would fail me to tell of the various acts we had. Tumblers, wrestlers, singers and actors all took part. But I must speak of the Grand

share with all humanity the gospel of God made known in Jesus Christ.

Douglas Webster: 'Not Ashamed', (1970)

Evangelism is a sharing of gladness.

Source unknown

These early Christians (in the Acts of the Apostles) were led by the Spirit to the main task of bringing people to God through Christ, and were not permitted to enjoy fascinating side-tracks.

J. B. Phillips

Unless the Church reaches out, it passes out . . . Anyone who is not prepared to pass the gospel on to others, knows not the first thing of the Christian faith.

H. Lewis Clarke: Archidiaconal Charge, (1985)

The triune God is the author of evangelism.

Kuyper

Evangelism is one beggar telling another where to get bread.

D. T. Niles

To evangelise is so to present Christ Jesus in the power of the Holy Spirit that men shall come to put their trust in God through him, to accept him as their Saviour, and to serve him as their King in the fellowship of the church.

The Archbishops' Committee of enquiry on the Evangelistic Work of the Church, (1918)

[Evangelism goes wrong when we] feel that numerical growth is God's primary purpose for the church . . . Qualitative growth becomes a means towards attracting converts rather than existing as an end in itself.

Robert Zuercher: in Third Way, (March, 1980), 'Growing a Church'

It is quite clear from the New Testament that the very existence of the church was of evangelistic significance. It was from the outset a community with a difference. It was marked by intense fellowship, a new quality of love, an awareness of the holy, and a deep sense of the presence of the Spirit. Evangelism is always meant to be a joint activity of the whole church, a shared responsibility. The evangelist is never preaching in his or her own right, but as the mouthpiece of the church . . .

In every parish the community spirit should be fostered if the parish is to be in action evangelistically . . . St. Paul makes it clear that the role of the Christian ministry is to rouse and equip the congregation for the corporate task of evangelism.

Douglas Webster: 'What is Evangelism?', (1959)

I'm all for involvement with other people in our evangelism, but we must beware when we evangelise in potentially compromising situations that we don't get drawn into their ways. A fisherman who wants to catch fish stays in the boat, or, if he wades into the water, keeps his feet firmly on the river-bed – he doesn't jump in and thrash about with the fishes!

Canon George Lindsay, Sermon, (1972)

The Four P's:
1. Presence evangelism
2. Proclamation evangelism
3. Persuasion evangelism
4. Propagation evangelism

Source unknown

Is there any such thing as distance-evangelism? No! We have to touch people.

Leighton Ford: at the Lausanne II Congress in Manila, (July 1989)

The willingness to consider is an important part of the dynamics of evangelism. In true evangelism we are not coercing people to believe or taking advantage of an inability to escape from exposure to the gospel. In evangelism we are resourcing the search of those who are willing to be open to the gospel itself.

'All God's Children': (National Survey, Church House Publishing, 1991), section 2.19.

The man-in-the-street is not now a Christian who happened not to go to church last Sunday. And so church worship in turn is that of a small, gathered, and somewhat committed, community with distinctive group agenda, and not a kind of general activity of a vaguely Christian population, any or all of whom might be present on occasion.

Colin Buchanan: 'The Heart of Sunday Worship', (Grove Worship, 1992)

. . .the churches must – as a matter of urgency – invest new energies and resources into the evangelism of those millions of children at present beyond the reach of any congregation. We need to attempt to be a major contributor in the market place of experiences within which today's children live. This is not something that the churches can take in their stride – it calls for a fundamental change. It also calls for the facing of a number of difficult social, pastoral and theological questions. . .

'All God's Children': (National Society, Church House Publishing, 1991), section 3.42

The Parable of the Sower (Alternative Version):

A farmer once gave his labourer a bag of seed to sow on his field but as he went he began to reason with himself, 'It seems a shame to just throw this seed around! Some of it will certainly fall onto the path and those birds will get it, sure's eggs is eggs! I'll be careful and avoid the paths.' Then, as he walked, he saw the rocky soil and he thought, 'It won't be much use sowing the seed here: it'll grow all right, but then it'll soon dry up and that will be the end of it. I'll make sure I don't waste seed on the rocky bits!' As he plodded on with his basket, he came across a big patch of weeds, and murmured, 'It'll be no good sowing any seed near there, the suckers will soon come out and grow round the corn, and the good seed will have been wasted – I'll leave that bit.' At last he reached some good soil and he thought he'd begin to sow – carefully, mind you, in case he upset the neighbours by throwing a handful of seed across their land – when it was time to go home. 'Ah well,' he thought, 'there'll be another time.'

Robert M.E. Paterson, (c 1990)

The Parable of the Orange Trees:

I dreamed I drove on a Florida road, still and straight and empty. On either side were groves of orange trees, so that as I turned to look at them from time to time, line after line of trees stretched back endlessly from the road – their boughs heavy with round yellow fruit. This was harvest time. My wonder grew as the miles slipped by. How could the harvest be gathered? Suddenly I realised that for all the hours I had driven (and this was how I knew I must be dreaming), I had seen no other person. The groves were empty of people. No other car had passed me. No houses were to be seen beside the highway. I was alone in a forest of orange trees.

But at last I saw some orange pickers. Far from the highway, almost on the horizon, lost in the vast wilderness of unpicked fruit, I could discern a tiny group of them working steadily. And many miles later I saw another group. I could not be sure, but I suspected that the earth beneath me was shaking with silent laughter at the hopelessness of their task. Yet the pickers went on picking.

The sun had long passed its zenith, and the shadows were lengthening when, without any warning, I turned a corner of the road to see a notice,

'LEAVING NEGLECTED COUNTY – ENTERING HOME COUNTY'.

The contrast was so startling that I scarcely had time to take in the notice. I had to slow down, for all at once the traffic was heavy. People by the thousands swarmed the road and crowded the walks. Even more startling was the transformation in the orange groves. Orange groves were still there, and orange trees in abundance, but now, far from being silent and empty, they were filled with the laughter and singing of multitudes of people. Indeed it was the people I noticed rather than the trees. People – and houses.

I parked the car at the roadside and mingled with the crowd. Smart gowns, neat shoes, showy hats, expensive suits and starched shirts made me a little conscious of my work clothes. Everyone seemed so fresh, and poised and cheerful.

'Is it a holiday?' I asked a well-dressed women with whom I fell in step. She looked a little startled for a moment, and then her face relaxed with a gracious smile or gracious condescension.

'You're a stranger, aren't you?' she

said, and, before I could reply, 'This is Orange Day.' She must have seen a puzzled look on my face, for she went on, 'It is so good to turn aside from one's labours and pick oranges one day of the week.'

'But don't you pick oranges every day?' I asked.

'One *may* pick oranges at any time,' she said. 'We should always be *ready* to pick oranges, but Orange Day is the day that we devote especially to orange picking.'

I left here and made my way further into the trees. Most of the people were carrying a book. Bound beautifully in leather, and edged and lettered in gold, I was able to discern on the spine of one of them the words 'Orange Picker's Manual'.

By and by I noticed that around one of the orange trees seats had been arranged, rising upward in tiers from the ground. They were almost full – but as I approached the group, a smiling well-dressed gentleman shook my hand and conducted me to a seat.

There, around the foot of the orange tree, I could see a number of people. One of them was addressing all the people on the seats and, just as I got to my seat, everyone rose to his feet and began to sing. The man next to me shared with me his song book. It was called *Songs of the Orange Groves*. They sang for some time, and the song leader waved his arms with a strange and frenzied abandon, exhorting the people in the intervals between the songs to sing more loudly. I steadily grew more puzzled. 'When do we start to pick oranges?' I asked the man who had loaned me his book.

'It's not long now,' he told me. 'We like to get everyone warmed upon first. Besides, we want to make the oranges feel at home.' I thought he was joking – but his face was serious.

After a while a rather fat man took over from the song leader and, after reading two sentences from his well-thumbed copy of *The Orange Picker's Manual*, began to make a speech. I wasn't clear whether he was addressing the people or the oranges.

I glanced behind me and saw a number of groups of people similar to our own group gathering around an occasional tree and being addressed by other fat men. Some of the trees had no one around them.

'Which trees do we pick from?' I asked the man beside me. He did not seem to understand, so I pointed to the trees round about.

'This is our tree,' he said, pointing to the one we were gathered around.

'But there are too many of us to pick from just one tree,' I protested. 'Why, there are more people than oranges!'

'But *we* don't pick oranges,' the man explained. '*We* haven't been called. That's Pastor Orange Picker's job. We're here to support him. Besides we haven't been to college. You need to know how an orange thinks before you can pick it successfully – orange psychology, you know. Most of these folk here,' he went on, pointing to the congregation, 'have never been to Manual School.'

'Manual School,' I whispered. 'What's that?'

'It's where they go to study the *Orange Pickers' Manual*, my informant went on. 'It's very hard to understand. You need years of study before it makes sense.'

'I see,' I murmured; 'I had no idea that picking oranges was so difficult.'

The fat man at the front was still making his speech. His face was red, and he appeared to be indignant about something. So far as I could see there was rivalry with some of the other orange-picking groups. But a moment later a glow came on his face. 'But we are not forsaken,' he said. 'We have much to be thankful for. Last week we saw *three oranges* brought into our baskets, and we are now completely debt free from the money we owed on the new cushion covers that grace the seats you now sit on.'

'Isn't it wonderful?' the man next to me murmured. I made no reply. I felt that something must be wrong somewhere. All this seemed to be a very roundabout way of picking oranges. The fat man was reaching a climax in his speech. The atmosphere seemed tense. Then with a very dramatic gesture he reached for two of the oranges, plucked them from the branch, and placed them in the basket at his feet. The applause was deafening.

'Do we start on the picking now?' I asked my informant.

'What in the world do you think we are doing?' he hissed. 'What do you suppose this tremendous effort has been made for? There's more orange-picking talent in this group than in the rest of Home County. Thousands of dollars have been spent on the tree you're looking at.'

I apologised quickly. 'I wasn't being critical,' I said. 'And I'm sure the fat man must be a very good orange-picker – but surely the rest of us could try. After all, there are so many oranges that need picking. We've all got a pair of hands, and we could read the *Manual*.

'When you've been in the business as long as I have, you'll realise that it's not as simple as that,' he replied. 'There isn't time, for one thing. We have our work to do, our families to care for, and our homes to look after. We . . .'

But I wasn't listening. Light was beginning to dawn on me. Whatever these people were, they were not orange pickers. Orange picking was just a form of entertainment for their weekends. I tried one or two more of the groups around the trees. Not all of them had such high academic standards for orange pickers. Some held classes on orange picking. I tried to tell them of the trees I had seen in Neglected County but they seemed to have little interest. 'We haven't picked the oranges here yet,' was their usual reply.

The sun was setting in my dreams and, growing tired of the noise and activity all around me, I got in the car and began to drive back again along the road I had come. Soon all around me again were the vast and empty orange groves. But there were changes. Something had happened in my absence. Everywhere the ground was littered with fallen fruit. And as I watched it seemed that before my eyes the trees began to rain oranges. Many of them lay on the ground. I felt there was something so strange about it all, and my bewilderment increased as I thought of all the people in Home County.

Then, booming through the trees, there came a voice which said: 'The harvest truly is plenteous, but the labourers are few; pray ye therefore the Lord of the harvest, that he will sent forth labourers into the harvest.' (Matthew 9.:37 & 38)

And I awakened – for it was only a dream.

From John White: Inter-Varsity magazine

Evangelism, service

[For evangelicals,] conversion happens when one claims to believe in Jesus' atonement and then feels forgiveness and inner peace. Becoming a Christian is not seen to require any fundamental changes such as an acceptance of particular ways of behaving . . . One can become an evangelical Christian and still be a racialist, for example . . .

People can become Christians and then be told *later* that following Christ means rejecting racialism or loving one's enemy . . . This certainly violates the biblical understanding of salvation in which people are told to repent, to change their way of thinking and living and *thereby* be saved . . . The story of Zacchaeus is a case in point.

It is possible to so desire persons to respond positively to the gospel that we edit the content out of the salvation message.

. . . the gospel is unfortunately not being proclaimed when all we do as the church is to try to persuade people to pray a short prayer in which they invite Jesus to come into their hearts. Unless the gospel we speak includes the fact that false lords have to be dethroned, unless the gospel we live loudly proclaims that we are ordering our lives in a radically new way under Jesus' lordship, unless the gospel we invite others to accept is an invitation to join with other Christians in a celebration of freedom from wealth, status-seeking, power-seeking and the use of violence, we have not proclaimed the gospel at all. When persons are asked to invite Jesus into their hearts, they must know the directions Jesus is going to take them and they must be able to see these new directions being lived out in the church.

Of course we Christians want the church to grow. Only let us take care that what we are promoting is *church* growth rather than an enlargement of a manure heap. Let us also keep in mind that many will reject Christ and that if the church is truly being Christ's body, as many will probably try to destroy it, as will try to join it.

Robert Zuercher: in Third Way, (March 1980), 'Growing a Church'

We cannot institutionalise the world into God's Kingdom . . . It is only the fulfilment of its role as a servant that entitles the church to present Christ to the world it serves . . .

Evangelism must always be sensitive to distinguish between opportunity and exploitation. There is a danger in too closely linking service with Christian propaganda. To respond to human need and so demonstrate the divine love is not the same thing as the attempt to induce a response to Christ from those we help. Too much attention to the latter (the response) may remove all meaning from the former (the demonstration of God's love). But where love operates, the Holy Spirit can be trusted to direct human response. In service-evangelism the Christian must be more concerned with the integrity of the service than with the promptitude of the response.

Douglas Webster: 'What is Evangelism?', (1959)

The church and the Christian alike are committed to service as the expression of the love and compassion of God in the name of Jesus Christ. Unless the church is at home in the sphere of service, it is unlikely to be relevant when it turns to evangelism.

Douglas Webster: 'What is Evangelism?', (1959)

Evangelism is the process by which people and communities are confronted with the Good News.

Mark Oxbrow: at the Welsh Partnership for World Mission, (1991)

Lifestyle evangelism does not offer a programme or formula to win others for Christ but rather a way of life, i.e. an attitude and lifestyle by which a group of Christians committed to their Lord and to one another share the whole of their lives with others. And since Christ is the centre of their individual and corporate lives, NATURALLY this will include sharing him.

Ross Pilkington

Society no longer evangelises for the church.

Raymond Fung, (1987)

. . . funnily enough, it's when I'm making the least demands on them (people outside the Church), simply trying to love them and to be their servant, that they start taking what I believe in seriously, and want to know about the things that have started me on my journey.

Richard MacKenna: 'God for Nothing', (Churchman, 1984/85)

Evangelism must begin with the costly loving of those who cannot afford the price we set.

Robert M.E. Paterson, (1989)

[In the Third World] we cannot preach the gospel outside the context of poverty . . . fulfilling the great commission and the great commandment at the same time.

Eduardo Maling: at the Lausanne II Congress in Manila, (July 1989)

To use the classroom for evangelism on behalf of the teacher's personal creed is not likely to be acceptable to parents . . .

In a curriculum which claims to contain all the important things a child needs to know, however, neglecting religion makes an implied statement that it does not matter. Similarly, to treat all religions as equal, in the name of wayward notions of political correctness, can convey that they are all equally untrue. Neither of these two common approaches is as unbiased as it pretends . . .

In the past, schools have approached R.E. as a branch of ethics or civics or even sociology, to the detriment of religion.

Times First Leader, (5 August, 1992)

There are various aspects to being a preaching people, but none is more important than a commitment to your own locality. It was rural ministry that taught me this lesson – something one learns with more difficulty in the city, though it is equally important there. Whatever your locality, if your church is to preach in it, it must be 100% committed to it and to sharing the burden of its problems.

Robert M. E. Paterson: 'Short, Sharp and Off the Point', (MARC Europe, 1987)

University students are used to tackling concepts, ideas, and evaluating their validity. The working-class person is more likely to ask, 'Well, does it work?' than 'Is it true?' Inner city proclamation requires demonstration, which is a long-term process. So-called decisions for Christ may be made by inner-city folk after evangelistic preaching but they rarely last. So if I want to make a breakthrough to large numbers of people who do not think in a rarefied, intellectual way, then I may have to rethink the way that I proclaim the gospel . . .

Better to err on the side of identification than to err on the side of separation.

Tony Adamson: 'Inner City Evangelism', (Grove Evangelism, 1993)

When Christians make evangelism the sun around which all other church activities must circle like planets, our motives become seriously distorted; for example, we do not offer service to the needy in order that we may evangelise them, but because, as with evangelism, our Lord asks us to do it in response to his love. The first priority for the church is worship, which focuses our minds on the Lord who loves the world and calls us to join him in service in every area of life.

Bishop David Sheppard: in The Times, (6 May, 1991)

Evangelism, criticisms

There is something incongruous about *all* attempts to evangelise the unchurched by means of services. You are, in effect, inviting people to sing as though they had a certain relationship with God, and then preaching as if they hadn't.

Peter A. Cousins, (1976)

Unfortunately, some forms of evangelism today encourage people to remain thoroughly self-centred, instead of urging them to become God-centred. In this advertising age it is all too easy to present Christ as the one who will meet all your needs. Are you anxious? Christ will bring you peace! Are you lost? Christ will give you new direction! Are you depressed? Christ will fill your life with joy! All this is true, and it is part of the good news of Christ that he longs to meet the deepest needs of each one of us. But that by itself is only half of the story. On its own it mirrors the deceitful approach of the false cults. In practice many of our needs will be met as we give ourselves in service both to Jesus and to others. It is those who are willing to lose their lives who will find them.

David Watson: 'Discipleship', (1981)

Churches should not worship Deus Numericus.

Robert M. E. Paterson

Lack of modesty often reduces evangelism to propaganda, and campaigns are launched in a circus atmosphere which distorts the truth by careful (and not always honest) selectivity from the Bible and the world of experience, in order to pressurise people into conversion or conformity. Respect forbids us to use people as pawns in an evangelistic game, using the tricks of the trade to compel an acceptance which, otherwise, they would not countenance in a less high pressure atmosphere. The evangelist must respect the liberty of others because he knows that God respects his liberty. Even the most convinced Christian has to realise that other people are not insincere, or even necessarily wrong, because they do not happen to agree with him.

Edward Patey: 'Open the Doors', (Mowbrays, 1978)

It is inexcusable for an evangelist to make Christ sound boring, but some succeed in doing so.

Edward Patey: 'Open the Doors', (Mowbrays, 1978)

People are not digits to be added up.

Peter Kuzmic: at the Lausanne II Congress in Manila, (July 1989)

Much contemporary evangelism is manipulative, crass, cringe-making, guilt-inducing: can we discover an honourable evangelism that is filled with a longing for souls to meet Christ and to know God, and yet respects them and their integrity, respects their minds, their experience, and wishes to affirm and not denounce their humanity?

Bishop Richard Holloway (of Edinburgh): in the Church Times, (20 October, 1989), 'A Call to Catholics'

... it is easy to see a Christianity that is 'pasteurised', like milk; it is treated and bottled before being served out. You get an evangelism that is not definite, annoys nobody, challenges nobody, transforms nobody, an evangelism that is not about radical change but a gradual osmosis into the ecclesiastical system. That is a very far cry from Jesus, the most extreme radical the world has ever seen, who was always challenging men and women to leave the cherished areas of their selfish lives and come, follow him. The church has often domesticated Jesus and emasculated the good news.

Michael Green: 'Evangelism Through the Local Church', (Nelson)

Too much of our talk about evangelism is radically Pelagian – as though it was *our* business to convert people to Christianity. That is God's business, and many and mysterious are the ways he sets about it. Our business is to be faithful in telling the story ... we can and must invite people to recognise that all human knowledge has to depend upon the acceptance of something given, something taken for granted, and that all human being is an adventure of faith in which we are invited to take risks. The alternative is the false security that comes from accepting as given the assumptions of our society.

Bishop Lesslie Newbigin: in the Church Times, (20 August, 1992), 'Truth for our Time'

Bob and Verna drive a white van with hundreds of Scripture verses printed on it, such as 'The wages of sin is death' ... The white gospel van draws plenty of stares with all that writing, which Verna painted freehand, so it doesn't look slick or professional, but it's the word, and as Bob says, 'Once you've seen the van, you can't say you never heard the Gospel. You have no excuse. Anyone who's seen it will have to answer to God someday.'

Garrison Keillor: Lake Wobegon Days, (1985): 'Revival'

Examinations

There was once a young man who wished to be ordained in the Primitive Methodist Church, but failed on many occasions to pass the biblical examination. A last, the examiners took pity on him and asked the simple question: 'Now, Mr. Jones, can you tell us who was Saul?'

'He was a King of Israel,' Mr. Jones replied.

'Excellent. Thank you, that is all.'

At the door, Mr. Jones turned and said, 'His other name was Paul.'

Moral: never volunteer what you have not been asked.

Allegedly related by Sir Ernest Bruce Charles to Sir Charles Russell

Exegesis

No one comes to any text with a completely vacant mind. Everyone comes with a pre-understanding; without this no understanding is possible. But the reader must also, in a sense, place a temporary moratorium on his judgement, allow the text to speak in its own way, and accept the possibility that the pre-understanding will be changed into a new understanding.

Bishop Lesslie Newbigin: 'Foolishness to the Greeks', (S.C.M., 1986)

Martin Luther likened biblical exegesis to Moses striking the rock until water gushed out for the thirsty people (Exodus 17:1–7).
The rod is faith, under which Scripture opens, and faith is the confident hope of hearing the voice of God from the book and of being addressed directly. But the rod of faith must be wielded with the help of scholarship and research: the exegete must be clear in his thinking and in his reading of the text.

From Luther's Works

The canon (of Scripture) is the primary authority for the faith, and the words and concepts of Scripture are to be interpreted historically in the contemporary horizon and then related to today. This is the sense of historical exegesis that evangelical theology accepts, the examination of the context of the time of writing and the application of the normal grammatical sense in interpreting the texts. The era of the apostles, their writings and the writings coming from their immediate spheres of influence under their supervision, these are normative.

Tim Bradshaw: 'The Olive Branch', (Latimer House – Paternoster Press, 1992)

The evangelical predilection, when faced with a world crisis, to use the Bible as a crystal ball instead of as a guide for sorting out the complex tangles of international morality was nowhere more evident than in the responses to the Gulf War in early 1991. Neither through the publishing of books nor through focused consideration in the periodicals did evangelicals engage in serious discussions of the morality of the war, the use of the United Nations in the wake of the collapse of Communism, the significance of oil for job creation or wealth formation throughout the world, the history of Western efforts at intervention in the Middle East, or other topics fairly crying out for serious Christian analysis. Indeed, evangelicals gobbled up more than half a million copies of each of several self-assured, populist explanations of how the Gulf crisis was fulfilling the details of obscure biblical prophecies.

Mark A. Noll: 'The Scandal of the Evangelical Mind', (Eerdmans, 1994)

Evangelical theory of authority rests on a scriptural base which stresses the horizon of the author of the text as a vital control, as well as attempting to link this with the modern horizon of meaning. The text is authoritative.

Tim Bradshaw: 'The Olive Branch', (Paternoster, 1992)

The biblical preacher is fundamentally one who brings the past witness of the Bible into the present day – he is, to use a frightful word, a contemporiser . . . It is the privilege of the preacher to contemporise what he finds in the Bible, bringing the Bible to the present day and placing today's people into the Bible.

Robert M.E. Paterson: 'Short, Sharp and Off the Point', (MARC Europe, 1987)

Johannes Staupiz, Augustinian Prior of Wittenberg in the sixteenth century (and mentor of Martin Luther) embarked on a series of sermons on the Book of Job in the monastery church at Tubingen in 1498. When he reached 'the tenth or eleventh chapter' he realised that his preaching 'was tormenting Job more than his wretched boils . . . I am stopping. Job and I are both glad.'

O Schell: 'Martin Luther', (Tubingen, 1930)

A true sermon bridges the gulf between the biblical and the modern worlds, and must be equally earthed in both.

John Stott: 'I Believe in Preaching', (Hodders, 1982)

[Give a text] its just meaning, its natural bearing and its legitimate use . . . My endeavour is to bring out of Scripture what is there, and not to thrust in what I think might be there.

Charles Simeon (1759–1836): 'Horae Homileticae', Preface and comment to publisher, (1833)

The preacher, for example, must be an exegete, able by special study and constant application to wrestle with the ancient texts and to indicate their relevance to the people to whom he ministers. Not only is he an exegete; he is a *hermeneut*; and Hermes, be it noted, was the *messenger* of the gods.

Archbishop Donald Coggan (of Canterbury): Convictions, (Hodders, 1975), 'Spirituality'

When I ordain a priest in the church of God, the only thing I hand him (as I have said elsewhere) is a Bible. When I consecrate a bishop in the church of God, the only thing I hand him is a Bible... That is why we may not call it preaching when a man gives his own ideas and then, almost fortuitously, attaches a text to them!

It is the task of the preacher to be an exegete, but an exegete in a special sense. When he has wrestled with the ancient text, it is his responsibility to indicate its relevance to the people to whom he is sent. He is more than an exegete. He is a hermeneut...

Archbishop Donald Coggan (of Canterbury): 'The Minister as a Man of God;' (4 October, 1966)

... evangelical preachers too often take routine texts, which they may easily prate about, but comparatively seldom choose texts which require study and thinking over.

Charles Simeon (1759–1836)

A sermon should be like a telescope; each successive division of it should be as an additional lens to bring the subject of your text nearer, and make it more distinct.

Charles Simeon: 'Horae Homileticae', (1833)

Mark the *character* of the passage (for example, declaration, precept, promise, invitation, appeal, etc). Mark the *spirit* of the passage (it may be tender and compassionate, or indignant or menacing; but whatever it be, let that be the spirit of your discourse).

Charles Simeon: 'Horae Homileticae', (1833), xxi

Existentialism – *see also* IDEALISM

Cogito, ergo sum (I think, therefore I am)

Réné Descartes (1596–1650): 'Les discours de la méthode'

Experience

Experience by itself proves nothing. If a man doubts whether he is dreaming or waking, no experiment can solve his doubt, since every experiment may itself be part of the dream. Experience proves this, or that, or nothing, according to the preconceptions we bring to it.

C.S. Lewis: 'Miracles', (1942); in 'God in the Dock', (Collins 1979)

Experts

An expert is a man who knows that you don't.

Anonymous

F

Facts

Comment is free but facts are sacred.

C. P. Scott (1846–1932): Manchester Guardian, (6 May, 1926)

Bishop Lesslie Newbigin describes our current 'cosmopolitan culture' as one where we divide everything into 'facts' and 'beliefs'. 'Facts' – like one and one are two – are universally true. 'Beliefs' deal with such areas as religion and value systems and as such they are *not* seen as being universally true according to our 'reigning tradition, etc.' Thus the Battle of Hastings is seen as a 'fact' but the Resurrection is a 'belief' and belongs to the realm of private opinions.... For the Christian any 'reigning tradition' in a culture needs to be judged by the life, death and resurrection of Christ – not the other way around.

'All God's Children': (National Society/Church House Publishing, 1991), section 3.11

Faith, in Christ

Make thee clean, my heart, from sin:
Unto Jesus give thou welcome.
So within my cleansèd breast
Shall he rest,
Dwelling evermore within me.
World, depart; let Jesus in!

Lutheran Chorale: in 'St Matthew Passion' by J.S. Bach (1729)

Faith means belonging to God:
I, with my body and soul, both in life and death, am not my own but belong to my faithful Saviour Jesus Christ . . . who makes me heartily willing and ready henceforth to live unto him.

John Wesley

Archbishop William Temple (1881–1944) wrote: 'I do not believe in any creed', by which he meant that, although creeds are used to express, conserve and deepen faith, that faith is not in a formula, however historic; faith is distinctly personal and rests on one person, Christ the Lord.

Faith is Christ really becoming my Lord, and Christ cannot become my Lord in any other way save by my knowing and my acknowledging him in whom God claims me as his own.

Emil Brunner: 'The Letter to the Romans', (1938; Lutterworth, 1959), on Romans 1:1–7

Blaise Pascal (1623–1662) imagines the words of Christ:
I do not intend you to believe me and submit to me without a reason. I cannot claim the right to force you into this position. Nor do I claim to explain reasons for everything. It is only in order to reconcile these contradictions that I wish to show you clearly, by convincing proofs, marks of divinity within me, which will convince you who I am, and establish my authority by miracles and proofs you cannot reject. Then you will believe the things I teach, and you will find no other reason for rejecting them, except that you cannot know of yourself whether they are true or not.

Now this alone is the Christian way, that I turn away from my sin and want nothing more to do with it, and turn alone to Christ's righteousness, so that I know for certain that Christ's goodness, merit, innocence, and holiness are mine, as surely as I know that this body is mine. In his name I live, I die, and pass away, for he died for us and was resurrected for us. I am not good and just, but Christ is. He in whose name I am baptised, receive the Holy Sacrament, study the Catechism – he will embrace us if only we trust in him.

Martin Luther: Table Talk

Faith, its nature

You cannot know what the word 'God' means until you are at the end of your strength, and can hope only in God . . . The true God is the God a man finds when he can no longer help himself, and he puts his hope in him alone. To hope in God alone, not in the power of self, one's ability or knowledge, means faith, means being God's own.

Emil Brunner: 'Our Faith', (1936), chapter 21

By this act of believing, man surrenders himself and reckons only with God . . . in this act of believing, man gives God his place.

Emil Brunner: 'The Letter to the Romans', (1938; Lutterworth, 1959), on Romans 4:1–25

People, especially religious people in churches, are always trying 'to limit the risk, curtail the openness, contract the freedom and avoid that commitment of faith which is the falling into the risk and the abyss of love.'

Bishop David Jenkins (of Durham): at Church of England General Synod, (6 July, 1986)

Christianity is not a Theory, or a Speculation, but a Life; not a Philosophy of Life, but a Living Process . . . *Try it* . . . He who begins by loving Christianity better than Truth will proceed by loving his own Sect or Church better than Christianity, and end by loving himself better than all . . . Faith is a total act of the soul; it is the whole state of the mind, or it is not at all, and in this consists its power, as well as its exclusive worth.

Samuel Taylor Coleridge

Faith is trust in what we cannot see. And so, if we are to have room for faith, the things in which we put our trust must be unseen. Indeed, they cannot be more hidden than when they appear to be the opposite things, the opposite feelings and the opposite experiences.

Martin Luther (1483–1546): 'De Servo Arbitrio'

Faith is indeed nothing but living in the light of that which is to come. Therefore faith is living by day, not night-life.

Emil Brunner: 'The Letter to the Romans', (1938; Lutterworth, 1959)

Faith is not a work because its focus is not the believer but the one who is believed.

Richard Hooker (1554–1600)

Faith is precisely the ability to live with uncertainty.

Bishop Ian Ramsey (of Durham)

The older I grow and the more I abandon myself to God's will, the less I value intelligence that wants to know and will that wants to do; and as the only element of salvation I recognise faith, which can wait patiently, without asking too many questions.

Umberto Eco: 'The Name of the Rose' (tr. William Weaver, Picador, 1984), Adso

Come now, little child.
Turn awhile from your daily work;
hide yourself for a little time from your restless thoughts,
cast away your troublesome cares;
put aside your wearisome distractions.
Give yourself a little leisure to talk
with God,
and rest awhile in him.
Enter the secret chamber of your
heart,
shutting out everything but God,
and that which may keep you in
seeking him.
And when you've closed the door,
seek him.
Now, my whole heart, say to God:
'I seek your face;
your face, O Lord, do I seek.'
I will seek you by desiring you,
and desire you in seeking you.
I will find you by loving you,
and love you in finding you.
I praise and give thanks to you
that you have made me in your image,
so that I can remember you,
think of you,
love you.
But so darkened is your image in me
by the smoke of my sins,
that it is useless unless you restore it.
I do not seek, O Lord, to search out
your depths,
but only in some measure to understand your truth,
which my heart believes and loves.
I do not seek to understand so that I
may believe,
but I believe so that I may understand.
For this I know to be true
that unless I first believe, I shall not
understand.

Anselm of Canterbury: 'Proslogion'

Grant, Lord, that we may hold to you
without parting,
Worship you without wearying,
Serve you without failing;
Faithfully seek you,
Happily find you,
And for ever possess you,
The only God,
Blessed, now and for ever.

Prayer of Anselm of Canterbury

Let me seek you in my desire,
let me desire you in my seeking.
let me find you by loving you,
let me love you when I find you.

Prayer of Anselm of Canterbury

Christian faith is a Way – of perceiving life, receiving life, practising life and pursuing life. Finding oneself on that Way, or choosing or seeking to go on that Way are very much matters of receiving a gift, coming up against a demand which is also an offer, being engaged by a possibility and a presence which will not let you go, catching glimpses of an enticement or a provocation which must be followed up.

Bishop David Jenkins (of Durham): 'God, Jesus and Life in the Spirit', (S.C.M., 1988)

I said to the man who stood at the gate of the year: 'Give me a light that I may tread safely into the unknown.'

And he replied: 'Go out into the darkness and put your hand into the hand of God. That shall be to you better than a light, and safer than a known way.'

Minnie Louise Haskins: 'God Knows'
(Quoted by King George VI in his Christmas Broadcast, 1939, at the beginning of the Second World War)

It is better to suffer wrong than to do it, and happier to be sometimes cheated than not to trust.

Dr. Samuel Johnson

Scepticism is the beginning of faith.

Oscar Wilde: 'Picture of Dorian Gray', (1891)

God is not affected by our mutability: our changes do not alter him. When we are restless, he remains serene and calm: When we are low, selfish, mean, or dispirited, he is still the unalterable I AM. The same yesterday, today, and for ever, in whom is no variableness, neither shadow of turning. What God is in himself, not what we may chance to feel him in this or that moment to be, that is our hope. 'My soul, hope thou *in God*.'

F.W. Robertson (1816–53): 'Sermons on Religion and Life'

Faith is much better than belief. Belief is when someone *else* does the thinking.

E.M. Forster: 'Two Cheers for Democracy', (1951)

Faith, contrasted with

Describing 'the conservatism of the committed':

In Kierkegaard's analogy, its attitude to truth is like swimming with one foot on the bottom – rather than trusting yourself over 70,000 fathoms. For those who cannot swim it is certainly better than that of fundamentalism – which keeps both feet flatly on the bottom. But a *church* that cannot swim is in serious peril. For it is not free to obey its Lord's command to launch out into the deep. And if too many of its members, let alone its instructors, are in that condition, it will not be able to survive, let alone give a lead, in the modern world.

Bishop John A.T. Robinson: 'Can we trust the New Testament?', (Mowbrays, 1977)

How does man receive what belongs to God? Through faith; that is, by man receiving what God gives to him. Faith means here, where it is a question of God's justification of a sinner, man's trusting what God says to him although it goes against all his experience, turning upside-down all his customary ideas of right and wrong. The sinner is righteous.

Emil Brunner: 'The Letter to the Romans', (1938; Lutterworth, 1959), on Romans 3:21–31

The parson was preaching about the relationship between *fact* and *faith*. 'That you are sitting in front of me in church is fact,' he said. 'That I am speaking to you from the pulpit is fact. But it is only faith that makes me believe you are listening to me.'

Source unknown

A man or woman is meant to live the life of faith. Doctrine is important; biblical orthodoxy is crucial, but not in and of themselves. Faith is more than a concept, it is living daily. We are to integrate our doctrine and theological thinking with the way we live, act and worship. We are experiential beings . . .

Being a Christian is not a static affair; it is a life-long experience.

Gavin J. McGrath: 'Grace & Duty in Puritan Spirituality', (Grove Spirituality, 1991)

The classic Anglican confession of faith is: 'Vicar, I know what I believe, but I cannot say it.' A more rigorous analysis might be that the speaker does *not* know what he or she believes. The clergy often connive at this, by saying, 'Some things are too deep for words,' and such-like apologies. I find that extraordinary . . . God is revealed by word, it was the Word who became flesh, it is the word with which we are put in trust, and the word of God is good *news* for the world. If we cannot say it, it is almost certainly not because it is too profound for us, but because we are vague and foggy and ignorant about its contents and unpracticed at expressing it informally. And thus we have no message for the world around us.

Colin Buchanan: 'The Heart of Sunday Worship', (Grove Worship, 1992)

IN GOD WE TRUST.
All others pay cash.

T-shirt slogan

A teacher asked his class of young children whether they believed in Santa Claus.

'Yes, of course!' said the little ones.

The older ones shook their heads generously.

The little girls said nothing.

A future scientist declared: '*I* know who it is!'

One lad, with an eye to gain asserted: 'I believe in it all; I can believe anything.'

Source unknown (Stephen Laycock commented: 'That boy, I realised, would one day be a bishop.')

We have not lost faith, but we have transferred it from God to the medical profession.

George Bernard Shaw

Faith, by grace

For righteousness by faith is the righteousness of God, his act, his gift; it is free as God himself is free. God is also not fettered by his signs. Only one condition always stands . . . only faith can partake of it. '*To all* who believe'; that always means: 'Only to those who believe'.

Emil Brunner: 'The Letter to the Romans', (1938; Lutterworth, 1959), on Romans 4. 1–25

For the question here is whether man becomes 'righteous' of himself or through the gift of God. If that inheritance can be obtained also along the path of the Law, then faith is done for, then faith is not faith and promise not promise; then Jesus Christ is not the Saviour for all nor is he the one apart from whom there is no salvation.

Emil Brunner: 'The Letter to the Romans', (1938; Lutterworth, 1959), on Romans 4. 1–25

Freedom from the Law does not mean freedom from God but freedom for God. For faith is the exact opposite from being loosed from God; it is not an indirect but an immediate relationship with God. Faith knows: I belong to God from the very start . . . The only choice before man is whom he wants to obey; never whether he wishes to be obedient.

Emil Brunner: 'The Letter to the Romans', (1938; Lutterworth, 1959)

Luther struggled to faith with Romans 1:17, 'For in the gospel the righteousness of God is revealed through faith for faith'...

I hated the expression 'righteousness of God', for through the tradition and practice of all the doctors I had been taught to understand it philosophically, as the so-called 'formal' – or, to use another word, 'active' – righteousness through which God is just and punishes sinners and the unjust. But I could not love the righteous God, the God who punishes. I hated him . . . I was very displeased with God, if not in secret blasphemy, then certainly with mighty grumbling, and said: Should it not be enough for miserable sinners eternally damned by original sin to be oppressed by all sorts of calamity through the law of the Ten Commandments? Must God add suffering to suffering even through the gospel and also threaten us with his righteousness and his wrath through the gospel, too? . . . I pondered incessantly, day and night, until I gave heed to the context of the words, namely, 'For in the gospel the righteousness of God is revealed, as it is written: "The just shall live by faith"'. Then I began to understand the righteousness of God as a righteousness by which a just man lives as by a gift of God, that means by faith. I realised that it was to be understood this way: the righteousness of God is revealed through the gospel, namely the so-called 'passive' righteousness we receive, through which God justifies us by faith through grace and mercy . . . Now I felt as if I had been born again: the gates had been opened and I had entered Paradise itself.

Martin Luther: 'Works'

The father of an epileptic boy said: 'If you are able to do anything, have pity on us and help us!' Jesus said to him, 'If you are able! – All things can be done for the one who believes.'

Mark 9:22b, 23

These (the words of the gospel) are written so that you may come to believe that Jesus is the Messiah, the Son of God, and that through believing you may have life in his name.

John 20:31

Since we are surrounded by so great a cloud of witnesses, let us also lay aside every weight and the sin that clings so closely, and let us run with perseverance the race that is set before us, looking to Jesus the pioneer and perfecter of our faith.

Hebrews 12:1, 2a

Fall, The

The first *pair* ate the first *apple*.

Anonymous

R.T. Glover commented that the Greeks thought a man had only to follow his nose and he would arrive at blessedness. But the Greeks had forgotten that man has a broken nose.

Archbishop Donald Coggan (of Canterbury): 'The Relevance of the Bible for Today', (15 March, 1967)

We have to realise that in the New Testament the concept of sin is not, as in our modern use of the word, a merely moral one, but it embraces man's whole existence and his whole understanding of himself and the whole of life, let me say his philosophy, his ideologies and religion, as well as his personal life.

Emil Brunner: 'The Scandal of Christianity', (1948; S.C.M., 1951), Lecture I

Life is a maze in which we take the wrong turning before we have learned to walk.

Cyril Connolly: 'The Unquiet Grave', (1944)

(Adam and Eve) heard the sound of the LORD God walking in the garden at the time of the evening breeze, and the man and his wife hid themselves from the presence of the LORD God among the trees of the garden. But the LORD God called to the man, and said to him, 'Where are you?' He said, 'I heard the sound of you in the garden, and I was afraid, because I was naked; and I hid myself' . . .

The LORD God said, 'See, the man has become like one of us, knowing good and evil; and now, he might reach out his hand and take also from the tree of life, and eat, and live for ever' – therefore the LORD God sent him forth from the garden of Eden, to till the ground from which he was taken. He drove out the man; and at the east of the garden of Eden he placed the cherubim, and a sword flaming and turning to guard the way to the tree of life.

Genesis 3;8–10, 22–24

All have sinned and fall short of the glory of God.

Romans 3:23

Fame

When Dr. Samuel Johnson was present at a famous literary party hosted by Mrs. Montagu, he noticed that the ladies were gawping at him as though he were a monster or a strange creature from another continent. His retort was simple: 'Ladies, I am tame; you may stroke me.'

James Stevenson, Ed: 'The Oxford Book of Literary Anecdotes', (1975)

Every effect that one produces gives one an enemy. To be popular one must be a mediocrity.

Oscar Wilde: 'The Picture of Dorian Gray', (1891)

Family

You are like to see no general reformation, till you procure family reformation.

Richard Baxter: 'The Reformed Pastor', (1655)

The life of religion and the welfare and glory of church and State, dependeth much on family government and duty. If we suffer the neglect of this, we undo all.

Richard Baxter: 'The Reformed Pastor', (1655)

The test of a man's religion is not what he is abroad, but what he is at home.

Charles Simeon (1759–1836)

Are we disheartened by the breakup of the family? Nobody who ever met my family is.

P.J. O'Rourke: 'All the Trouble in the World', (1994), 'Fashionable Worries'

The family, grounded on marriage freely contracted, monogamous and indissoluble, is and must be considered the first and essential cell of human society.

Pope John XXIII

In the context of a preacher whose precept of family life is very different from his practice:

What worries me is that the Vicar is not telling us all that home life is difficult and has, like every form of life, its own proper temptations and corruptions . . . The trouble is not that he is insincere but that he is a fool. He is not talking from his own experience at all: he is automatically reproducing a sentimental tradition – and it happens to be a false tradition. That is why the congregation have stopped listening to him.

C S Lewis: 'The Sermon and the Lunch', (1945)

If a house is divided against itself, that house will not be able to stand.

Mark 3:25

Fanaticism

Fanaticism consists in redoubling your effort when you have forgotten your aim.

George Santayana (1863–1952)

Fatalism

The fault, dear Brutus, is not in our stars,
But in ourselves, that we are underlings.

William Shakespeare (1564 – 1616): 'Julius Caesar', I.ii.139

The bitterest tragic element in life is belief in a brute Fate or Destiny.

Ralph Waldo Emerson (1803–82, a radical and atheist)

Fear

Archbishop Richard Chenevix Trench (of Dublin, 1864–84), who retired to London two years before he died and who suffered greatly from creeping paralysis, was heard at the Lord Mayor's banquet to mutter: 'Total insensibility of the left limb come at last!' (a creeping paralysis he had been dreading). A little while later, the lady sitting next to him turned to the Archbishop and said: 'Your Grace, if it is any consolation to you, it is my leg you have been pinching for the last half an hour!'

Source unknown

Just because you're paranoid it doesn't mean they aren't out to get you.

Anonymous

Fellowship

Between the giant collective (the whole Church) and the lonely individual there must be a fellowship which is large enough to be corporate and small enough to be intimate, or at least personal. Fellowship of this kind can have converting power.

Douglas Webster: 'What is Evangelism?', (1959)

Just as surely God desires to lead us to a knowledge of genuine Christian fellowship, so surely must we be overwhelmed by a great disillusionment with others, with Christians in general, and, if we are fortunate, with ourselves . . . God is not a God of the emotions but the God of truth. Only that fellowship which faces such disillusionment with all its unhappy and ugly aspects, begins to be what it should be in God's sight . . . when the morning mists of dreams vanish, then dawns the bright day of Christian fellowship.

Dietrich Bonhoeffer

. . . too easily church fellowship can become a temple built on the Mount of Transfiguration.

John Poulton: in 'David Watson', (1985)

The more deeply we commit ourselves to loving fellowship with others, the more we shall be hurt . . . Jesus had to bear all this from his own disciples, and if we want to follow him we must do the same.

David Watson: 'Discipleship', (1981)

(The converts on the Day of Pentecost) devoted themselves to the apostles' teaching and fellowship, to the breaking of bread and the prayers . . .

All who believed were together and had all things in common; they would sell their possessions and goods and distribute the proceeds to all, as any had need. Day by day, as they spent much time together in the temple, they broke bread at home and ate their food with glad and generous hearts.

Acts 2:42, 44–46

Contribute to the needs of the saints; extend hospitality to strangers.

Romans 12:13

Let us consider how to provoke one another to love and good deeds, not neglecting to meet together, as is the habit of some, but encouraging one another, and all the more as you see the Day approaching.

Hebrews 10:24, 25

Fiction

Jonathan Swift was delighted with the stir caused by his satirical *Gulliver's Travels.* Among comments he reported from Dublin to Alexander Pope was of the Irish bishop who said, 'that book was full of improbable lies, and for his part he hardly believed a word of it.'

James Sutherland, Ed: 'The Oxford Book of Literary Anecdotes', (1975)

Miss Prism describes her novel:
The good ended happily, and the bad unhappily. That's what Fiction means.

Oscar Wilde (1854–1900): 'The Importance of Being Earnest', Act 2. (1895)

Finance

An actuary is someone who has given up accountancy because he couldn't stand the excitement.

Anonymous

Annual income twenty pounds, annual expenditure nineteen nineteen six, (£19/19/6 = £19.97½), result happiness. Annual income twenty pounds, annual expenditure twenty pounds ought and six (£20.02½), result misery.

Charles Dickens (1812–1870): 'David Copperfield'

I can get no remedy against this consumption of the purse; borrowing only lingers and lingers it out, but the disease is incurable

William Shakespeare (1564–1616): 'Henry IV' Part 2

What is killing the church's mission today is the failure of Christian people to see that goods and services cost the church as much as they cost individuals.

Source unknown

Fish, An Ancient Christian Cryptogram

ICHTHUS – The Fish – ΙΧΘΥΣ
An early Christian sign of identification during times of persecution.
One Christian drew an arc on the ground and the other drew another arc, completing the fish sign. The name is also a word puzzle for 'Jesus Christ, Son of God, Saviour'

Flattery

Imitation is the sincerest form of flattery.

Charles Caleb Colton, (1780–1832)

A nice old lady sitting next to P.G. Wodehouse (1881–1975) at dinner raved about his work and the number of his books her son had bought as soon as they were published. But Wodehouse was surprised when she concluded: 'And when I tell him that I have actually been sitting at dinner with Edgar Wallace (1875–1932) I don't know what he will say.'

Flattery is like a cigarette – it's all right so long as you don't inhale.

Adlai Stevenson: in a speech, (1961)

Flood, The

It is an interesting question as to whether Noah risked taking woodworm into the Ark.

Source unknown

Professionals built the *Titanic.* Amateurs built the Ark.

Anonymous

Noah and God strike a bargain:
And God said unto Noah, Make thee an ark of gopher wood; rooms shalt thou make in the ark, and the length of the ark shall be 300 cubits.
And of every living thing of all flesh, two of every sort shalt thou bring into the ark, to keep them alive with thee.
And Noah said, Sign here, and leavest Thou a deposit.
And the LORD signed here and left a deposit.
And Noah was 600 years old when the flood of the waters was upon the Earth.
And the LORD said unto Noah, Where is the ark which I commanded thee to build?
And Noah saith unto the LORD, Verily I have had three carpenters off ill. The gopher wood supplier hath let me down – yea, even though the gopher wood hath been on order for nigh upon twelve months. The damp course specialist also hath not turned up. What can I do, O LORD?

And God said unto Noah, I want that ark finished even after seven days and seven nights.
And Noah said, Verily, it will be so.
And it was not so.
And the LORD saith unto Noah, What seemeth to be the trouble this time?
And Noah saith unto the LORD, Mine sub-contractor hath gone bankrupt. The pitch which Thou commandest me to put on the outside and on the inside of the ark hath not arrived. The plumber hath gone on strike. Noah rent his garments and said, The glazier departeth for holiday in Majorca – yea, even though I offeredst him double-time. Shem, my son, who helped me on the ark side of the business, hath formed a pop band with his brothers Ham and Japeth. LORD, I am undone!
And God said in his wrath, Noah, do not thou mucketh me about! The end of all flesh is come before me; for the Earth is filled with violence through them; and behold, I will destroy them with the Earth. How canst I destroy them with the Earth if thou art incapable of completing the job that thou wast contracted to do?
And Noah said, Lo! the contract will be fulfillèd.
And Lo! it was not fulfillèd.
And Noah saith unto the LORD, The gopher wood is definitely in the warehouse. Verily and the gopher wood supplier waiteth only upon his servant to find the invoices before he delivereth up the gopher wood unto me.
Then the LORD grew angry and said, Scrubbeth thou round the gopher wood – useth something else. What about the animals? Of fowls after their kind, and of cattle after their kind, and of every sort after their kind have I ordered to come unto thee, to keep them alive. Where, for example, are the giraffes?
And Noah saith unto the LORD, They are expected today.
And where are the clean beasts, the male and the female, to keep their seed alive upon the face of all the Earth?
And Noah saith, The van cometh on Tuesday; truly, truly I say unto Thee, it shall be so.
And the LORD said unto Noah, What about the unicorns?
But Noah wrung his hands and wept, saying, LORD, LORD, they are a discontinued line. Thou canst not get unicorns for love nor money.
And God said, Come thou off it, Noah! I have left thee with a deposit, and thou has signed a contract. Where are the monkeys and the bears and the hippopotami, and the elephants and the zebras and the hartebeests, two of each kind; and of the fowls of the air by sevens, male and female? What didst thou do with the woodworm?
Noah made reply unto the LORD, These have been delivered unto the wrong address, but hath been promised for Friday; all save the fowls of the air by sevens, for it hath just been told me that fowls of the air are sold in half-dozens.
And God replied unto Noah, saying, Thou hast not made an ark of gopher wood, nor hast thou lined it with pitch within and without; and thou hast failed to bring of every sort into the ark. What dost thou say, Noah?
Noah kissed the earth and said, LORD, LORD, thou knowest in thy wisdom what it is like with delivery dates.
And the LORD in his wisdom said, Noah, my son, I knowest. Why else dost thou think I have caused a flood to descend upon the Earth?

Keith Waterhouse: 'Waterhouse at Large'

Forgiveness

Everyone says forgiveness is a lovely idea, until they have something to forgive.

C.S. Lewis

A wise man will make haste to forgive, because he knows the true value of time.

Dr Samuel Johnson

To err is human, to forgive, divine.

Alexander Pope (1688–1744): 'An Essay on Criticism', l. 525

Sunday 9 February:
Mrs. Flushpool asked the first question.

She said, 'I find it strange, Reverend – I cannot call you Father as I have scriptural reservations – that on your previous visit you barely mentioned the judgement of God on sin committed in the natural. Perhaps you do not feel sinful?'

Father John blinked. 'Oh, I'm a ratbag,' he declared, with enthusiasm, 'but I do feel so *very* forgiven. You see, God's crazy about me, just as he's crazy about you. Salvation was his idea you know – not ours.' He pointed at Mrs. Flushpool. 'If you were to commit a foul sin with every person in your street, and then you said to God, 'I really am honestly and sincerely most awfully sorry,' he would say, 'Great! Let's start all over again.' Marvellous, isn't it?'

Mrs. Flushpool, presumably wrestling inwardly with the image of herself committing foul sins with every person in her street, splashed back down into her seat, looking rather breathless. Leonard Thynn leaned across and whispered in my ear, 'He knows a different God to the one I do. His God's *nice!*'

Adrian Plass: 'The Sacred Diary of Adrian Plass', (1987)

Forgiveness is when someone smacks you on the bottom and you have to turn the other cheek.

Adrian Plass: 'The Sacred Diary of Adrian Plass', (1987)

God is generous in his forgiveness; for however much wrong a man does to God, he is a hundred times more ready to forgive than that wretched soul would be to ask forgiveness.

From 'The Mirrors of St. Edmund', (of Abingdon, 1175–1240)

What we encounter in Martin Luther is not the mediaeval battle cry 'God wishes it' – *deus vult,* but 'God does it' – *deus facit.*

Heiko O. Oberman: 'Luther', (Yale, (1982/89)

It is a grievous error to think that one could make amends for his sins, as God forgives sins without recompense, out of unlimited grace at all times, and demands nothing in return but living a proper life from then on.

Martin Luther: 'Works'

It's far easier to forgive an enemy after you've got even with him.

Olin Miller

My favourite verse in the Bible – now that I am reaching the Goal – is Hebrews 10.17: 'their sins and wicked deeds I will remember no more.' I imagine my sins being deposited in a deep lake where a large notice says 'No fishing'.

Lilian Swatkins, aged 84, in a letter to the editor, May 1994

And forgive us our debts, as we also have forgiven our debtors.

Matthew 6.:12

Jesus speaks to Simon the Pharisee about the sinful woman:
'I tell you, her sins, which were many, have been forgiven; hence she has shown great love. But the one to whom little is forgiven, loves little.' Then he said to her, 'Your sins are forgiven.' But those who were at the table with him began to say among themselves, 'Who is this who even forgives sins?'

Luke 7:47–49

If God is for us, who is against us? He who did not withhold his own Son, but gave him up for all of us, will he not with him also give us everything else? Who will bring any charge against God's elect? It is God who justifies. Who is to condemn? It is Christ Jesus who died, yes, who was raised, who is at the right hand of God, who indeed intercedes for us.

Romans 8:31b–34

God made you alive together with him, when he forgave us all our trespasses, erasing the record that stood against us with its legal demands. He set this aside, nailing it to the cross.

Colossians 2:13b, 14

France and the French

France in August, when you can travel through the entire country without encountering a single pesky Frenchman or being bothered with anything that's open for business.

P.J. O'Rourke: 'Holidays in Hell', (1988)

The French are masters of 'the dog ate my homework' school of diplomatic relations. French unofficial position, that is, the opinion of taxi drivers, bartenders, the concierge at the hotel and those old women they keep in the bathrooms, was no easier to figure out. I'd ask and get a nudge, a smirk, pursed lips, shrugged shoulders, knowing rolls of the eyes, waved hands, knitted brows – the whole panoply of Froggy visual tricks.

P.J. O'Rourke: 'Holidays in Hell', (1988)

. . . where gentler manners reign.
. . . honour forms the social temper here.
. . . all are taught an avarice of praise;
They please, are pleas'd, they give to get esteem,
Till, seeming bless'd, they grow to what they seem.
. . . For praise too dearly lov'd, or warmly sought,
Enfeebles all internal strength of thought . . .

Oliver Goldsmith: 'The Traveller', (1764)

In the mid nineteenth century, it was commonly said of French politics that the people wore their hearts on the left and their wallets on the right.

Freedom

[God] whose service is perfect freedom . . .

1662 Book of Common Prayer: Collect at Morning Prayer Whom to serve (as a slave) is to reign (as a king)

L'homme est ne libere, et partout il est dans les fers.
(Man is born free, and everywhere he is in chains.)

Jean-Jacques Rousseau (1712–1778)

A freedom that leads to fear and anxiety has lost its value; better authority with security than freedom with fear.

Paul Tillich

You cannot make men believe that a way of life is good when it spreads poverty, misery, disease and death. Men cannot be everlastingly loyal unless they are free.

President Franklin D. Roosevelt, (1945): from 'Public Papers and Addresses'

Liberty means responsibility. That is why most men dread it.

George Bernard Shaw: 'Maxims for Revolutionists', (1903)

I may disagree with what you say, but I will defend to death your right to say it.

Voltaire

Friendship

A man, Sir, should keep his friendship in constant repair.

Dr Samuel Johnson (1709–84): 'Boswell's Life of Johnson' (This has been taken as a reference to Ecclesiasticus 6:17 and James 4:4.)

Your friend is the man who knows all about you, and still likes you.

Elbert Hubbard: 'The Notebook', (1927)

. . . it is such a great joy to have the consolation of someone's affection – someone to whom one is deeply united by the bonds of love; someone in whom our weary spirit may find rest, and to whom we may pour out our souls . . . someone whose conversation is as sweet as a song in the tedium of our daily life. He must be someone whose soul will be to us a refuge to creep into when the world is altogether too much for us; someone to whom we can confide all our thoughts. His spirit will give us the comforting kiss that heals all the sickness of our preoccupied hearts. He will weep with us when we are troubled, and rejoice with us when we are happy, and he will always be there to consult when we are in doubt. And we will be so deeply bound to him in our hearts that even when he is far away we shall find him together with us in spirit, together and alone.

Aelred of Rievaulx (1110–1163)

Fun

People must not do things for fun. We are not here for fun. There is no reference to fun in any Act of Parliament.

Sir Alan Patrick Herbert: 'Uncommon Law'

A nation's fun will tell you more about that nation than anything except its jails.

P.J. O'Rourke: 'Holidays in Hell', (1988)

Fundamentalism

I believe that fundamentalists, wherever they are in the world and whatever religion they profess, have a great deal in common; that their shared attitudes towards change, diversity, deviance, dogma, and sex far outweigh the differences wrought by worshipping Jesus, Jahweh, or Allah.

Anonymous (1984)

Langdon Gilkey remarked that even the most devout fundamentalist in Texas, when prospecting for oil, consults the geologists and not the biblical scholars.

How the Church can Minister Scholars

Future

God will have other generations to succeed us... let us thank him that we have had our time... The gospel dieth not when I die: the church dieth not: the praises of God die not: the world dieth not: and perhaps it shall grow better, and those prayers shall be answered which seemed lost...

Richard Baxter

Think of tomorrow, what will it bring
you?
How can you face it all alone?
Though everything seems fine,
tomorrow is a long, long time.

The Crossbeats, pop group, (c. 1970)

In the twentieth century, war will be dead, the scaffold will be dead, hatred will be dead, frontier boundaries will be dead, dogmas will be dead; man will live. He will possess something higher than all these – a great country, the whole earth, and a great hope, the whole heaven.

Victor Marie Hugo (1882–1885): 'The Future of Man'

William Farish was an extraordinary character and early supporter of the Church Missionary Society; he is said to have once mounted his horse on one side and dismounted on the other, thinking he had completed his journey; on another occasion, boiled his watch while timing it with an egg! When in 1837, he suggested to a Parliamentary Committee that trains might one day travel at 60 miles an hour they dismissed him as of unsound mind. He is said to have told students that in time men would very probably voyage through the air by yet undiscovered agencies of impulsive powers.

From the 'Christian Observer', (September and October, 1937)

Jesus Christ is always future shock.

John Poulton, (later bishop)

We know something of the power of the Holy Spirit. We are open to learn more of him. We await the surprises of tomorrow.

Archbishop Donald Coggan: Canterbury Enthronement, (24 January, 1975)

You are orphans in an age of no tomorrow.

Joan Baez, (c. 1970)

Christians are better able to cope with change than anyone else because they know that God is in the future.

John Dixon, (1981)

Space may produce new Worlds.

John Milton (1608–74): 'Paradise Lost'

Christians engaged in ministry can always be expectant because they are living in God's 'Today', and there is no knowing what may happen and there are no limits to his grace.

Douglas Webster: 'Not Ashamed', (1970), referring to Psalm 95 and Hebrews 3 & 4

You show me the path of life. In your presence there is fulness of joy;
in your right hand are pleasures for evermore.

Psalm 16:11

All things are yours, whether Paul or Apollos or Cephas or the world or life or death or the present or the future – all belong to you, and you belong to Christ, and Christ belongs to God.

1 Corinthians 3:21b–23

G

Gambling

The whore and gambler, by the state
Licensed, build that nation's fate

William Blake (1757–1827): 'Auguries of Innocence'

Gambling provides a substitute for hope, very necessary in a world where there is not much hope around, but potentially confusing when offered by those whose message ought to be about something better.

Archbishop John Habgood, (as Bishop of Durham): Diocesan Newsletter, (1975)

Generosity

Benevolence is a natural instinct of the human mind. When **A** sees **B** in grievous distress, his conscience always urges him to entreat **C** to help him.

Sydney Smith (1771–1845)

The man who gives little with a smile gives more than the man who gives much with a frown.

Jewish saying

The most generous person is the one with the least to give.

French saying

The point is this: the one who sows sparingly will also reap sparingly, and the one who sows bountifully will also reap bountifully. Each of you must give as you have made up your mind, not reluctantly or under compulsion, for God loves a cheerful giver . . .

He who supplies seed to the sower and bread for food will supply and multiply your seed for sowing and increase the harvest of your righteousness. You will be enriched in every way for your great generosity, which will produce thanksgiving to God through us; for the rendering of this ministry not only supplies the needs of the saints but also overflows with many thanksgivings to God.

2 Corinthians 9:6, 7, 10–12

Genius

Genius is one per cent inspiration and ninety-nine per cent perspiration.

Thomas Alva Edison (1847–1931)

Oscar Wilde to the customs official who asked whether he had anything to declare:
'No. I have nothing to declare – except my genius.'

Gifts

Each one has a place in the community of Christ, and ought to fill it, but he ought not to be everywhere and want to take part in everything . . .

Take note of what God gives you, then you will also know the task he sets you.

Emil Brunner: 'The Letter to the Romans', (1938; Lutterworth, 1959), on Romans 12:3–8

Many look with one eye at what they give and seven at what they receive.

German proverb

It is easy to want things from the Lord and yet not want the Lord himself; as though the gift could ever be preferable to the Giver.

Augustine of Hippo (354–430)

When a group of people sets out to do a jigsaw, they need three pieces of information:

i. what is to be done;
ii. what has or has not been done;
iii. what is the shape of the piece one is holding.

And so, in the church, it is necessary to discover:

i. the purpose of God's mission in a particular context;
ii. the present situation;
iii. the gifts available.

Group exercise

Giving

We can no longer rely on dead men's money – nor toy with stewardship – nor fail to tithe our income in a businesslike fashion. The truth is that when confidence revives, and love of God waxes warm, and faith burns bright, financial problems have a strange way of solving themselves.

Archbishop Donald Coggan: 'Canterbury Enthronement', (25 January, 1975)

By a strange Christian logic, we find in every case that 'keepers' become poor and miserable while 'givers' have all they need in abundance.

Bishop Benjamin N.Y. Vaughan, (of Swansea and Brecon,1981)

None of us is too poor to give. Giving is part of believing in the God who gives.

Bishop Victor Premasagar (of Medak, India, 1986)

Bishop Azariah used to describe how the poorest people in his care were so anxious to share some of God's grace to them, that they would set aside a handful of rice from every two cupfuls used at a meal; this would then accumulate in the week and be offered in worship on Sunday. Only a few grains less at each meal enabled them to share with others God's grace to them.

Bishop Victor Premasagar (of Medak, India, 1986)

The complaint known as 'cirrhosis of the giver' was discovered early in the life of the church by Ananias and Sapphira (Acts 5). It is an acute condition which renders the patient's hand immovable when he is called upon to raise it in the direction of the wallet or purse and then to the offering plate. The remedy is to remove the patient from the house of God since it is clinically observable that this condition does not occur in other places such as the supermarket, restaurants or clubs. Of course, the best therapy, a sure and lasting cure, is to get right with God, as this is a condition symptomatic of a more serious problem: heart-trouble.

Tom Saunders, (Churchwarden of Gabalfa, October, 1986)

To sacrifice something is to make it holy by giving it away for love.

Buechner

At the Harvest Festival in church the area behind the pulpit was piled high with tins of fruit for the old-age pensioners. We had collected the tinned fruit from door to door. Most of it came from old-age pensioners.

Clive James: 'Unreliable Memoirs', (1980)

A little girl and her mother were in a bus: 'Please give Mummy a sweet,' said mother. She gave her a sweet paper. She changed her mind and took out all the sweets and gave her the box; then, thinking again, she replaced the sweets, closed the lid and said, 'I'll save it for you.'

Anonymous

There was a new minister at the Baptist Chapel and, on his first Sunday, he preached an impressive sermon on the text: 'It is easier for a camel to pass through the eye of a needle than for a rich man to enter the kingdom of Heaven.'

After the service, the deacons came up to him in serious mood. 'You shouldn't have preached that sermon with Mr. Evans in the congregation. He is our wealthiest benefactor and our best giver.'

So the minister went to Mr. Evans and apologised if he had caused any offence. 'No offence taken, young man,' Mr. Evans replied. 'It's a pretty poor sermon that doesn't hit me somewhere!'

Anonymous

Tithing: Conclusive proof that the average churchgoer earns around £10.00 per week.

Martin Wroe, Adrian Reith & Simon Parkes: 'The Church-English Dictionary', (1991)

One sends presents at all sorts of times – at Christmas, on Anniversaries, on Birthdays, and even (if you happen to be Winnie the Pooh) on UNBIRTHDAYS!

From A.A. Milne

Then [after a conversation with a rich man] Jesus looked around and said to his disciples, 'How hard it will be for those who have wealth to enter the kingdom of God!' And the disciples were perplexed at these words. But Jesus said to them again, 'Children, how hard it is to enter the kingdom of God! It is easier for a camel to go through the eye of a needle than for someone who is rich to enter the kingdom of God.' They were greatly astounded and said to one another, 'Then who can be saved?' Jesus looked at them and said, 'For mortals it is impossible, but not for God; for God all things are possible.'

Mark 10:23–27

[Jesus said] 'No slave can serve two masters; for a slave will either hate the one and love the other, or be devoted to the one and despise the other. You cannot serve God and wealth. The Pharisees, who were lovers of money, heard all this, and they ridiculed him. So he said to them, 'You are those who justify yourselves in the sight of others; but God knows your hearts; for what is prized by human beings is an abomination in the sight of God.'

Luke 16:13–15

Come now, you rich people, weep and wail for the miseries that are coming to you. Your riches have rotted, and your clothes are moth-eaten. Your gold and silver have rusted, and their rust will be evidence against you, and it will eat up your flesh like fire. You have laid up treasure for the last days. Listen! The wages of the labourers who mowed your fields, which you kept back by fraud, cry out, and the cries of the harvesters have reached the ears of the Lord of hosts. You have lived on the earth in luxury and pleasure; you have fattened your hearts in a day of slaughter.

James 5:1–6

God, doctrine of

In essence secular humanism is a monism of matter and energy [all is matter and energy] while cosmic humanism has a monism of spirit [all is God].

Douglas R. Groothuis: 'Unmaking the New Age', (I.V.F., U.S.A., 1986)

God has his centre everywhere, and his circumference nowhere.

St. Bonaventure (13th century scholastic, the 'Prince of Mystics')

God – World = God.
[God minus the World equals God.]

Archbishop William Temple (of York and Canterbury)

Richard Porson (1759–1808), a sceptic and Principal Librarian to the London Institution, was walking with a friend and discussing the doctrine of the Trinity. A buggy came along with three men in it. 'There,' said the friend, 'is an illustration of the Trinity.'

'No,' replied Porson, 'you must show me *one* man in *three* buggies, if you can.'

It has often been remarked that Protestant theology since Schleiermacher has had a continual tendency to become a kind of anthropology. It has become the study of an aspect of human experience. The Bible, on the other hand, is dominated by the figure of the living God who acts, speaks, calls and expects an answer. The biblical language is as much about God, about the created cosmos, and about the world of public events as about what can be called 'religious experience'.

Bishop Lesslie Newbigin: 'Foolishness to the Greeks', (S.C.M., 1986)

Most people are aware
not of the presence of God,
nor of the presence of his absence,
but of the absence of his presence.

Source unknown

Rat and Mole see Pan (the god of nature) on an island in the Thames:
'This is the place of my song-dream, the place the music played to me,' whispered the Rat, as if in a trance. 'Here, in this holy place, here if anywhere, surely we shall find him!'

Then suddenly, the Mole felt a great Awe fall upon him . . . It was no panic terror – indeed he felt wonderfully at peace and happy – but it was an awe that smote and held him and, without seeing, he knew it could only mean that some august Presence was very, very near.

. . . he looked in the very eyes of the Friend and Helper . . . All this he saw, for one moment breathless and intense, vivid on the morning sky; and still, as he looked, he lived; and still, as he lived, he wondered.

'Rat!' he found breath to whisper, shaking. 'Are you afraid?'

'Afraid?' murmured the Rat, his eyes shining with unutterable love. 'Afraid of *him?* O, never, never! And yet – and yet – O, Mole, I *am* afraid!'

Then the two animals, crouching to the earth, bowed their heads and did worship.

Kenneth Grahame: 'The Wind in the Willows', (1908), chapter VII

God is very disturbing – both for religious people who want religion to protect them from the world, and for worldly people who do not want to be reminded or confronted by anything more than their own ideas, aims, achievements and enjoyments.

Bishop David Jenkins (of Durham): in The Times, (5 July, 1987)

In God there is nothing of creativeness and in the world there is nothing of divinity. The being of God and the being of creatures are totally different.

Emil Brunner: 'The Scandal of Christianity', (1948; S.C.M., 1951), Lecture II, 'The Triune God'

Whoever cannot bear the thought that God is the absolutely free Lord forgets that he is a creature, who is placing himself on the same level with the Creator.

Emil Brunner: 'The Letter to the Romans', (1938; Lutterworth, 1959)

God is personal and relates personally to us. How dear this insight is to evangelical Christians; how important this is to all who hear the missionary call at home or overseas; and how easy, how destructive, it is to revert, under the pressure of complexity or the call to full obedience, to a narrow individual response to a God who is impersonal and remote.

Source unknown

The propensity of my countrymen to discuss their church instead of discussing the reason for it – to discuss their religion in isolation from any consideration of the existence of a deity – has always amazed me. I wonder whether, perhaps, I have missed something obvious; whether part of my brain is absent.

How is it possible – would somebody please explain – to hold and canvass vigorous opinions on whether women should be priests or the Church of England 'established', whether prayers should be said or sung, or the Bible read in the King James or more modern versions, what vestments should be worn, what music played, what bells rung, what hands clapped or incense used . . . How is it possible, I ask, so much as to begin such enquiries, or to feel remotely interested in the answers, without first determining the question to which they are mere postscripts? Does the God of the New Testament exist? . . .

For if God exists then our Godless existence falls apart. And if God does not exist then surely the church falls apart!

Forms of prayer? Hats or not hats? *Thou* or *you*? What would it matter? Would we discuss how to address the Loch Ness Monster if we did not believe in the Loch Ness Monster? Would we pay money into a pension policy if the insurance company were a fiction?

I simply cannot understand why all those millions of my countrymen who mumble that they are 'probably' believers can regard their uncertainty as less than a personal emergency.

The New Testament offers a picture: a God who does not sound at all vague to me. He has sent his son to Earth. He has distinct plans both for his son and for mankind. He knows each of us personally and can communicate directly with us. We are capable of forming a direct relationship, individually, with him, and are commended to try. We are told this can be done only through his son. And we are offered the prospect of eternal life – an afterlife in happy, blissful or glorious circumstances – if we live this life in a certain manner.

Friends, if I believe that, or even a tenth of that, how could I care which version of the prayer book was being used? I would drop my job, sell my house, throw away my possessions, leave my acquaintances and set out into the world burning with a desire to know more and, when I had found out more, to act upon it and tell others.

How is it possible to be indifferent to the possibility, if one believes it to be a possibility, that a being of this order makes demands of this order upon you or me . . .? I am unable to understand how *anyone* who believed what is written in the Bible could choose to spend his waking hours in any other endeavour . . .

The church and all its forms of worship, and the moral law to which it testifies, are all secondary facts: the primary fact (if fact it be) would be God . . .

No amount of breast-beating about the importance of a role for religion advances us an inch further towards a proof of the central fact upon which a religion must be predicated and without which it must fall: the existence of a deity. Nobody of any intellectual stature since Bishop Joseph Butler in the early 18th century has candidly tried to argue backwards from the want of a religion to its validity. Yet this is the argument now being advanced, under cover of some intemperate vacuities about 'moral panic'.

I fully accept that there is a need for God in this world. Whether, however, there is a God, is an altogether different question.

Matthew Parris: in The Times, (12 April, 1993), 'Why do people debate the future of the church when they have not made up their minds about the existence of God?'

The glory of God is the living man; and the life of man is the vision of God.

Irenaeus

Archbishop John Habgood (of York) received a letter from a student:
We are doing God this term. Please send full information and leaflets.

Deus comprehensus not est. (Any god which you can comprehend is not God.)

St. Augustine of Hippo (354–430)

God, activity of

Called or not called, God is always there.

Carl Jung

If my servants ask thee about Me, lo, I am near.

The Qur'an

God is not, as we so often make him appear to be, only interested in 'religion', nor is He a kind of super-ecclesiastic!

Archbishop Donald Coggan (of Canterbury): 'Convictions' (Hodders, 1975), 'Great Themes'

. . . the encounter at the burning bush was no seminar.

Aidan Kavanagh

God never leaves identical fingerprints.

Anonymous – see also Psalm 77:19

No matter how much I probe and
  prod
I cannot quite believe in God.
But oh! I hope to God that he
Unswervingly believes in me!

E.Y. Harburg: 'Rhymes for the Irrelevant', (1965)

A Librarian was asked by a child where to look up a book about God. The Librarian asked the child what he wanted to know about God. 'Well,' said the child, 'for a start, what does he do?'

Anonymous

A misprint in Her Majesty's Stationery Office monthly catalogue refers to a 'European agreement concerning the internal carriage of gods by road'

(N.U./H.M.S.O., 92 1 139025 7).

Deus absconditus:

(The God who escapes all attempts to 'capture' him in our minds or emotions.)

God cares for his mother

Sub-heading in a Scripture Union teaching book. (The reference is, in fact, to the raising of the widow 's son at Nain.)

God, trust in

They [Palinor and Beneditx] reached the end of the walk and turned before he [Palinor] said, 'Well, to start with, I do not find the world around me puzzling in the way you do. I am not amazed to find that things move, things change, things operate as causes or arise as effects. Whereas you assert that these things are so mysterious they must have some cause – you call it God – which is outside the material universe, I am content to think that material things have material causes, and things contrived, like fountains, shall we say, have causes in human ingenuity and human will. Your attempt to prove otherwise seems nearly scandalous to me.'

'Scandalous? What do you mean, Palinor?'

'First you say that nothing moves without a mover. Then you say that after all there must be something which moves without a mover, or else the process could not start. This is an argument whose conclusion contradicts one of its premises. But, Beneditx, much more important is another difference between us. Living as you do, here on Grandinsula, you are surrounded by belief; it seems to you that disbelievers must prove their point. But logically, you must see, this is not so. It is always a person who proposes something for belief who must prove it; the burden of proof must lie with those who suggest that in addition to what we can see and feel around us, there is a God. And even your philosopher saint [Thomas

Aquinas], I think – you will correct me if I am wrong – agreed that things which can be explained by fewer principles should not be explained by more.'

'But it seemed to him obvious that there would be no explanation of the world around us without postulating God. He needed even to discuss whether so self-evident a proposition could be demonstrated.'

'Your proofs all call God into the issue to be an *explanation,*' Palinor, said. 'But God is a useless explanation – he explains too much. Potentially he explains everything, and to explain everything is to explain nothing.'

'I do not understand you.'

'You can explain one thing in terms of another. I can explain the behaviour of fountains by saying it is a law of nature that water flows in such a way; I can explain the growth of vines by saying that all plants reach toward the light, and the orderly curve of these tendrils above our heads by saying that the gardener tied them thus. These explanations refer to something else, something else in the material world. But if you explain by reference to God, you explain too much. God's will could indeed explain why water flows downhill; but it would equally, and likewise, explain why it flowed uphill, if it did. It will explain every state of affairs, and would equally explain any conceivable alternative state of affairs. But for that precise reason it cannot therefore explain why water flows downhill and not uphill; it makes no distinction between what happens and what does not. I cannot see, therefore, how one could use what happens as evidence for God's existence.'

'Give me time to think,' said Beneditx. 'That is a new idea to me.'

'Beneditx, do you require me to come to believe in a weak God, or a strong one?'

'What do you mean, my friend?'

'A weak God – such as an explanation for a falling stone, or the excellence of a bird's wing in flight – or a strong God, such as the God of Abraham?'

'They are the same. The difference is only that one might reach, by pure unaided reason, your 'weak' God; knowledge of the God of Abraham is given us through revelation.'

Jill Paton Walsh: 'Knowledge of Angels', (Green Bay / Black Swan, 1994/1995), Chapter 23

It is a terrible thing to fall into the hands of the living God [Hebrews 10:31.]. It is more terrible to fall out of them.

D. H. Lawrence, (1885–1930)

. . . the very word 'God' used in so many of the prayers is, as someone has said, 'a beckoning word'.

John Carden: 'Another Day', (Triangle S.P.C.K., 1986)

I laugh when I hear that the fish in the water is thirsty.
I laugh when I hear that men go on pilgrimage to find God.

Kabir: Inscribed on the goldfish pond at Edwardes College, Peshawar, Pakistan

'O God, if there be a God, save my soul, if I have a soul!'

The prayer of a common soldier before the Battle of Blenheim (1704), as quoted by Sir William Wyndham in 1715 and later by J.H. Newman in 'Apologia pro Vita sua'

Those who think that they possess God are possessed by something more like the devil! We cannot possess God, but God again and again possesses us. As Augustine says, every time we find him, we find him because he has already found us. That is why discipleship, exploration, getting back to the basics and trying again and going deeper is absolutely of the essence of knowing God and serving God and having faith in him. He cannot be pinned down and he will not be pinned down, but he is always creating, sustaining, promising, coming and, therefore, always to be discovered as being and always to be worshipped.

Bishop David Jenkins (of Durham): 'God, Jesus and Life in the Spirit', (S.C.M., 1988)

Supposing a prisoner in the dungeon – not knowing whether sentence has been passed on him, and with only an hour left to find out – knows there is time enough to have his sentence revoked. It would not be natural for him to spend that hour wasting his time playing a game, indifferent as to whether the sentence has been passed. So it is surely beyond all nature that man is indifferent to how things are being weighed in the hands of God. It is not only the zeal of those who seek him that proves God's existence, but also the blindness of those who do not seek him.

Blaise Pascal (1623–1662)

. . . addicted to the pleasing of God. . .

Richard Baxter: 'The Reformed Pastor', (1655)

God, scepticism about

God is dead . . . Are we not straying through an infinite nothing?

Friedrich Wilhelm Nietzsche

I know there are many voices raised in disbelief that anyone can still think there is a God who loves, who hears our prayers and whose will is our good. They point to the bloodstains of human history, not least in the church, and ask, in anger, contempt or amusement, for evidence of this good and gracious God. They suspect that faith is simply a shelter for the weak in mind and spirit against the storms of life or nostalgia for a bygone age.

. . . God has not left himself without witnesses.

Archbishop George Carey: Canterbury Enthronement, (19 April, 1991)

The idea of God is a *brockenspecter*, that is, the projection of the human ego on the cosmos.

Feuerbach

When Laplace was criticised for having omitted God from his system of thought, he replied, 'I had no need of that hypothesis.'

God becomes a tyrant whom you're terrified of displacing and on whom rests your personal survival, so you have got to keep him sweet, and nothing is good or bad in itself but simply a means to an end: heaven or hell. Because it is to do with personal survival, and because it relates to a God 'out there' – something or someone outside the world – worship of this God can be profoundly selfish; the church becomes a Noah's Ark into which you crawl for safety and then watch everyone else drowning, and your main criterion when you meet someone will be, 'Does he belong – is he one of us?' And if he isn't, then no matter how good or right or true he is, he's still not a member. And because you are in the ark of safety, you are somehow removed from real life, set apart from other people and their concerns, busy with higher things. 'I always look forward to funerals,' the young curate said to me, 'they're such a marvellous opportunity for evangelisation.' In other words, get 'em while they're down. And as people find the traditional God increasingly irrelevant and boring, it is only when they are weak and vulnerable that the Noah's Ark Church is able to pounce.

Richard MacKenna: 'God for Nothing', (Churchman, 1984/85)

How can I believe in God when just last week I got my tongue caught in the roller of an electric typewriter?

Woody Allen

You have taught me to worship a god who is like you, who shares your thinking exactly, who is going to slap me one if I don't straighten out fast. I am very uneasy every Sunday, which is cloudy and deathly still and filled with silent accusing whispers.

Garrison Keillor: 'Lake Wobegon Days', (1985), News, '95 Theses 95'

Someone asked [Bertrand] Russell at some meeting: 'Lord Russell, what will you say when you die and are brought face to face with your Maker?' ' He replied without hesitation: 'God,' I shall say, 'God, why did you make the evidence for your existence so insufficient?'

Professor A.J. Ayer: quoted in the Evening Standard, (1984)

Not only is there no God, but try getting a plumber at weekends.

Woody Allen: 'Getting Even', (1972)

I read the book of Job last night – I don't think God comes well out of it.

Virginia Woolf: 'Letters Vol. II', 1912–22, (published 1975)

Is man one of God's blunders or is God one of man's blunders?

Friedrich Wilhelm Nietzsche

God lives in the bathroom, or so my father thinks. Every morning he goes up to the door and shouts, 'O God, are you still in there?'

Anonymous

Goodness

She went about doing good to others. And you could tell the others by their hunted look!

C.S. Lewis

There was a man in Jerusalem whose name was Simeon; this man was righteous and devout, looking forward to the consolation of Israel, and the Holy Spirit rested on him.

Luke 2:25

[Barnabas] was a good man, full of the Holy Spirit and of faith.

Acts 11:24

Gospel, content

The gospel itself can no more change than the Norman Conquest or Shakespeare's Hamlet. It is a part of the human heritage.

Douglas Webster: J.C. Jones 'Lecture', (1969), also in 'Not Ashamed', (1970)

The gospel is described in the New Testament as the 'Gospel of God'. It is neither the invention nor the possession of man; it is God's. It is therefore not pride or obstinacy which makes us declare categorically that the essence of the gospel can neither be reduced nor altered. It is a humble recognition of the fact that the gospel is God's, and is therefore true for all men and for all time.

Evangelical Alliance Commission on Evangelism: 'On the Other Side'

Karl Barth has said, 'Religion is unbelief'. That is, 'The Gospel is something utterly new, a complete break with anything previously known; all other religion is man's attempt to justify himself and is to that extent victim of demonic powers.'

Douglas Webster: 'Not Ashamed', (1970)

. . . the basic Christian gospel, the foundation on which all doctrine must rest, is not a statement about, or an offer of, religious experience. It is a statement about what God has done: God in Christ has manifested himself in saving power for the benefit of all who approach him in faith. There is nothing here, except the reference to faith . . . that necessarily implies religious experience. The gospel is therefore first and foremost a claim concerning God, not concerning man, though man is, of course, necessarily involved.

A.T. & R.P.C. Hanson: 'The Identity of the Church', (S.C.M., 1987)

... the deepest truth which Christianity enshrines is that the one sole true God has poured himself out in love in Jesus Christ for our final and decisive salvation, calling us to return to him in love.

A.T. & R.P.C. Hanson: 'The Identity of the Church', (S.C.M., 1987)

. . . the narcissism which is so prevalent in our culture, the mentality which is interested only in its own selfhood and not in the realities of a world beyond the self. Gnostics of all ages have used the word 'Christ' to designate something which is a product of their own reflection on experience; but Jesus is not that. The name 'Jesus' does not designate a plastic idea which can be moulded to suit my experience. And it is Jesus, no other, who is the Christ.

The gospel is an account of things which have happened. We do not discover it by interrogating our own experience. We have to be told. In that sense, the gospel necessarily comes from outside . . .

In the effort to be understood, the church has to take the risk that the story will simply be domesticated into the existing culture . . . The particular form of domestication which threatens the integrity of the church's witness today is its relegation to the private sector in a culture which makes a sharp distinction between a public world of facts and a private world of beliefs . . .

There can be no escape from the question of public truth. In our narcissistic culture the questions are always about 'What is meaningful for me'. The important question is not this, but

'What is the meaning which God has given to the whole creation?' And if it is true that God has done those things which we affirm week by week in our liturgies, then that has to be the starting-point for all our thinking, the clue for all our exploration, the criterion for all our action. If it is true, it is public truth.

Bishop Lesslie Newbigin: in the Church Times, (20 August, 1992), 'Truth for our Time'

Though the gospel is capable of doctrinal exposition, though it is eminently fertile in moral results, yet its substance is neither a dogmatic system nor an ethical code, but a person and a life.

Bishop J.B. Lightfoot (of Durham): 'The Epistle to the Philippians', (1903)

Gospel, proclamation of

The gospel, after all, is not an idea but an event, the response to which means a new creation in the midst of the old . . . If beliefs are to spread, they have to be embodied and expressed in the people who hold them.

Douglas Webster: 'Not Ashamed', (1970)

The church's primary task is to proclaim the gospel in each new generation and in every society. The gospel is more than a cultural inheritance.

Douglas Webster: 'Not Ashamed', (1970)

The big theme of the gospel is God and man. Therefore it is one of the essentials of the gospel that there should not be a single theme in this world which is not touched upon by the gospel.

Gerhard Bergmann: 'The Relevance of the Gospel Today'

. . . the announcement that in the series of events that have their centre in the life, ministry, death, and resurrection of Jesus Christ, something has happened that alters the total human situation and must therefore call into question every human culture.

Bishop Lesslie Newbigin: 'Foolishness to the Greeks', (S.P.C.K., 1986)

Gospel, 'whole' (holistic)

Half-gospels [to either physical *or* spiritual needs] have no future.

P.T. Forsyth

Half-gospels (which ignore socio-political responsibility) are like mules; they have neither pride of ancestry nor hope of posterity.

Peter Kuzmic: at the Lausanne II Congress in Manila, (July, 1979)

To separate word from action is to put asunder things that God has joined together. To separate the spiritual from the social is to be blind to the fact that they are the outside and the inside of the same thing. As ever for Christians, Jesus is the supreme example. His social concern and his spiritual concern went hand-in-hand. His presence embodying the kingdom of God was matched by his words explaining the kingdom. The two are not opposed to each other; they are complementary.

Michael Green: 'Evangelism Through the Local Church', (Nelson)

The New Testament does not drive a wedge between the personal and the social gospel.

Peter Kuzmic: at the Lausanne II Congress in Manila, (July, 1989)

Gospel, foolishness of

The scandal of Christianity exists as a scandal only so long as we are full of ourselves. To believe in the cross of Christ is no scandal for those who have seen how perverted is their own wisdom, the wisdom of natural man. It is the very corrective for this perversion of our sight, it makes us look straight again, who by sin have become cross-eyed. The foolishness of the gospel is divine wisdom to all those who have been healed of the perversion which consists in making man's reason and goodness the judge of all truth, that perversion which places man instead of God in the centre of the universe. The gospel is identical with the healing of this perversion, which in its depth and real significance is diabolical. It is the victory of God's light over the powers of darkness.

Emil Brunner: 'The Scandal of Christianity', (1948), last words of final lecture V, (S.C.M., 1951)

The frightening thing about the Christian message is that it has nothing to do with our wandering around looking pious and wonderful (the Action Man Pale Galilean Kit,) but focuses our attention on the cross, on suffering. Here, it says, is the key to meaning.

Richard MacKenna: 'God for Nothing', (Churchman, 1984/85)

In the gospel declared progressively to mankind down the centuries, and uniquely and fully in Jesus Christ, there is a grace, an unconditional love accepting us as we are, giving us the power to repent, giving us faith and therefore taking away all merit as we seek to be brought by God into true relationship with himself. We cannot earn it – he gives it. He accepts us as we are, to use us as we are.

What a glorious gospel, liberated, with plenty of doubts and questions left, but nevertheless based on the authority of believers down the centuries experienced by us today. If we have experienced this grace, then it is well worth sharing by word and life with all with whom we come in contact.

Such a gospel is not just an individual understanding of God's acceptance. It carries with it the fact that this world and all creatures in the world are God's creation. Therefore, they are all embraced with this unconditional love, as all societies are embraced.

. . . No doubt God's love embraces all creatures and all societies, but within that all-embracing love he wants us, us as individuals, to love him back.

Canon Bryan Green, in the Church Times, (11 January, 1991), 'The manifesto of a liberated Evangelical'

Gospel, the Scriptures

When [Jesus] came to Nazareth, where he had been brought up, he went to the synagogue on the sabbath day, as was his custom. He stood up to read, and the scroll of the prophet Isaiah was given to him. He unrolled the scroll and found the place where it was written:

'The Spirit of the Lord is upon me, because he has anointed me to bring good news to the poor.
He has sent me to proclaim release to the captives and recovery of sight to the blind,
to let the oppressed go free, to proclaim the year of the Lord's favour.'

And he rolled up the scroll, gave it back to the attendant, and sat down. The eyes of all in the synagogue were fixed on him. Then he began to say to them, 'Today this scripture has been fulfilled in your hearing.'

Luke 4:16–21 (quoting Isaiah 61:1, 2)

[Jesus] said to them [the crowds], 'I must proclaim the good news of the kingdom of God to the other cities also; for I was sent for this purpose.'

Luke 4:43

I am not ashamed of the gospel; it is the power of God for salvation to everyone who has faith, to the Jew first and also to the Greek. For in it the righteousness of God is revealed through faith for faith; as it is written, 'The one who is righteous will live by faith'.

Romans 1:16, 17 (citing a version of Habakkuk 2:4)

Gospels, The four

In 1846, John William Burgon (later Vicar of St. Mary's Oxford and Dean of Chichester) asked Martin Joseph Routh (1755–1854), the President of Magdalen College, Oxford, for advice on reading matter in religion.

I think, sir, were I you, sir, – that I would – first of all – read the – the Gospel according to St. Matthew. (pause) And after I had read the Gospel according to St. Matthew – I would – were I you, sir – go on to read – the Gospel according to St. Mark. (pause) I think, sir, when I had read the Gospel according to St. Mark, I would go on, sir, yes! go on to – to the – the Gospel – according to – St. Luke, sir. (pause) Well, sir, and when I had read those three gospels, sir, were I in your place, I would go on – yes, I would certainly go on to read the Gospel according to St. John.

Burgon later recollected:

For an instant I had felt an inclination to laugh. But by this time a very different set of feelings came over me. Here was a theologian of ninety-one, who, after surveying the entire field of sacred science, had come back to the point he had started from; and had nothing better to advise me to read than the Gospel!

Source unknown

Government

The Circumlocution Office went on mechanically, every day, keeping this wonderful, all sufficient wheel of statesmanship turning. How not to do it, in motion. Because the Circumlocution Office was down upon any ill-advised public servant who was going to do it, or who appeared to be by any surprising accident in remote danger of doing it, with a minute, and a memorandum, and a letter of instructions, extinguished him.

Charles H. Dickens: 'Little Dorrit'

He that goeth about to persuade a multitude that they are not so well governed as they ought to be, shall never want attentive and favourable hearers.

Richard Hooker (c.1554–1600)

For really I think that the poorest he that is in England hath a life to live, as the greatest he; and therefore truly, Sir [General Oliver Cromwell], I think it's clear, that every man that is to live under a government ought first by his own consent to put himself under that government; and I do think that the poorest man in England is not at all bound in a strict sense to that government that he hath not had a voice to put himself under....

From The Putney Debates of 1647, in A.S.P. Woodhouse, Ed: 'Puritanism and Liberty', (1974)

Democracy means government by the uneducated, while aristocracy means government by the badly educated.

G.K. Chesterton: in the New York Times, (1931)

Grace

The preoccupation with church planting, with congregational development often at the expense of depth, suggests the presence of an understanding of God that is still profoundly Pelagian, whereas the thing that is worth celebrating in the Christian gospel is that it is free.

There is more than a whiff of justification by works in the energies and apparent competitiveness of some evangelical groups; and in their moralism . . . there is a tendency to turn the gospel from grace to law, to give people the impression that their salvation is something they have to win for themselves, whereas the good thing about Christianity that makes it *good* news is that God saves us through Christ by grace. 'Amazing Grace' used to be the great love song of evangelicalism. What happened to it?

Bishop Richard Holloway: in Church Times 28 August, 1992, 'Missionary energy laced with moralism'

Great
Riches
At
Christ's
Expense

Source unknown

This grace, which indeed costs man nothing, cost God his Son. He let Jesus Christ die as a proof of his righteousness, so that forgiveness is not going to be misunderstood as a passing-over of guilt.

Emil Brunner: 'The Letter to the Romans', (1938; Lutterworth, 1959), on Romans 3;21–31

Each of us desperately needs this transformation to take place within us if we are to change anything in the world 'round us. If you are divided within yourself, how can you restore the ruins outside yourself? We need continually to receive Christ's forgiveness and healing deep within us . . . This is what the word 'grace' means, a love that makes a new wholeness.

Bishop Simon Barrington Ward: Enthronement at Coventry, (4 January, 1986)

The grace of God is always *personal,* but it is never *private.*

Anonymous

Grace is free and undeserved; it defines the new covenant. By grace, believers enter into the covenant in which they receive God's free and wonderful reconciliation through Jesus. Their Christian life is supported by grace and the Holy Spirit.

A definition of Puritan doctrine, as expounded typically in the 17th century, from an unknown source.

Grace is free and undeserved; our slavish efforts at a moral life do not win God's attention and favour. We are at peace with God, adopted children through his glorious pardon in Christ. On account of God's sovereign grace we are intimate with God.

Gavin J. McGrath: 'Grace & Duty in Puritan Spirituality', (Grove Spirituality, 1991)

If we are to give you love, says the church, then you must first deserve it . . . when treated like that, we realise in the end that we are not loved but *conned.*

Richard MacKenna: 'God for Nothing', (Churchman, 1984/85)

Batter my heart, three person'd God; for you
As yet but knocke, breathe, shine, and seeks to mend;
That I may rise, and stand, o'erthrow mee, and bend
Your force, to breake, blowe, burn and make me new.
I, like an usurpt towne, t'another due,
Labour t'admit you, but Oh, to no end.
Reason your viceroy in mee, mee should defend,
But is captiv'd, and proves weake or untrue.
Yet dearly I love you, and would be loved faine,
But am betroth'd unto your enemie;
Divorce mee, untie, or breake that knot againe,
Take mee to you, imprison me, for I
Except you enthrall me, never shall be free,
Nor ever chast, except you ravish mee.

John Donne (1572–1631): 'Holy Sonnet XIV'

. . . without total grace there will be total hell.

Bishop David Jenkins (of Durham): 'God, Jesus and Life in the Spirit', (S.C.M., 1988)

Cheap grace is the deadly enemy of the Church. We are fighting today for costly grace. (Cheap grace is) the preaching of forgiveness without requiring repentance, baptism without church discipline, communion without confession, absolution without personal confession. Cheap grace is grace without discipleship, grace without the cross.

Dietrich Bonhoeffer: 'The Cost of Discipleship'

He [the God and Father of our Lord Jesus Christ] destined us for adoption as his children through Jesus Christ, according to the good pleasure of his will, to the praise of his glorious grace that he freely bestowed on us in the Beloved. In him we have redemption through his blood, the forgiveness of our trespasses, according to the riches of his grace that he lavished on us.

Ephesians 1:5–8

God, who is rich in mercy, out of the great love with which he loved us even when we were dead through our trespasses, made us alive together with Christ – by grace you have been saved – and raised us up with him and seated us with him in the heavenly places in Christ Jesus, so that in the ages to come he might show the immeasurable riches of his grace in kindness toward us in Christ Jesus. For by grace you have been saved through faith, and this is not your own doing; it is the gift of God – not the result of works, so that no one may boast. For we are what he has made us, created in Christ Jesus for good works, which God prepared beforehand to be our way of life.

Ephesians 2:4–10

Grace (before food)

Heavenly Father, bless us,
And keep us all alive;
There's ten of us to dinner
And not enough for five

Hodge's Grace

The family had special guests to dinner – a couple new to the church they attended. Little James's party piece was to say grace, but tonight he would not perform.

'Go on!' his mother cajoled. 'Just say the prayer Daddy said at breakfast.'

'O.K. O God, it's not those awful

people coming for dinner tonight? Amen.'

During the air raids on London in the Second World War (1939–45) a little boy was trained by his parents to react to the air raid siren by running under the specially strengthened table which would provide some sort of protection in the event of a strike nearby. One day, mum and dad went next door for half an hour, reminding Peter what to do if the warning sounded and adding, uncharacteristically, 'And say your prayers.'

The siren went off while the parents were next door, so they rushed back home in time to hear Peter, from under the table, saying, 'For what we are about to receive, may the Lord make us truly thankful.'

Some hae meat, and canna eat,
And some wad eat that want it;
But we hae meat and we can eat,
And sae the Lord be thankit.

Robert Burns: 'The Selkirk Grace'

Graveyards

Distress has been expressed at a churchyard which has not been used for burial for thirty years and is in a very bad state. Voluntary bodies have been asked to help remedy the situation.

From a national newspaper, (19 June, 1974)

Greed

I'm a fan of big American corporations. At least, I used to be. I thought they embodied that true basis of the American character: utopian greed. Their vision of the future always combined mercantile rapacity with such courageous lack of common sense.

P.J. O'Rourke: 'Holidays in Hell', (1988)

The true test of meanness is the ability to peel an orange in your pocket.

Source unknown

She liked whate'er
She looked on, and her looks went everywhere.

Robert Browning (1812–1889): 'My Last Duchess'

Wealth is treacherous; the arrogant do not endure.
They open their throats wide as Sheol;
like Death they never have enough.

Habakkuk 2:5

Be sure of this, that no fornicator or impure person, or one who is greedy (that is, an idolater), has any inheritance in the kingdom of Christ and of God.

Ephesians 5:5

Growth

Growth is the only evidence of life.

Axiom often quoted by John Henry Newman when young. Derived from Thomas Scott's 'The Force of Truth'

You gotta be a baby if you're gonna grow.

Jesus People Song, (c. 1971)

Do not be afraid of growing slowly, simply be afraid of not growing at all.

Chinese saying

Some [seed] fell into good soil, and when it grew, it produced a hundredfold . . .

As for [the seed] in the good soil, these are the ones who, when they hear the word, hold it fast in an honest and good heart, and bear fruit with patient endurance.

Luke 8:8a, 15

I planted, Apollos watered, but God gave the growth. So neither the one who plants nor the one who waters is anything, but only God who gives the growth.

1 Corinthians 3:6, 7

Grow in the grace and knowledge of our Lord and Saviour Jesus Christ. To him be the glory both now and to the day of eternity. Amen.

2 Peter 3:18

Guidance

Who brought me hither will bring me hence;
No other guide I seek.

John Milton

He leads me in right paths for his name's sake.
Even though I walk through the darkest valley, I fear no evil;
for you are with me; your rod and your staff – they comfort me.

Psalm 23:3, 4

Let the peace of Christ rule in your hearts, to which indeed you were called in the one body. And be thankful. Let the word of Christ dwell in you richly; teach and admonish one another in all wisdom.

Colossians 3:15, 16a

H

Harvest thanksgiving

R. S. Hawker of Morwenstow, in Cornwall, an eccentric and scholarly parson, began the first Harvest Thanksgiving in 1843. It is said that his curate once tidied up his church of all books and papers, and put them in a wheelbarrow. The curate went to the parsonage and asked Hawker what to do with it. He was told to put himself on top and dispose of it all quickly. Hawker was neither High, Low nor Broad Church; he described conversion as 'a spasm of the ganglions'; his interest was in the Eastern churches which he believed (with some justification) were the mother of Celtic Christianity. His little parish, a few miles north of Bude, existed mainly on the illicit proceeds of smuggling, wrecking and poaching and, in a day of sombre church buildings, his was full of colour and activity. He wore an alb (a long white, sleeved robe), a cope (a long, liturgical cloak made from heavy fabric) and scarlet gloves (fulfilling what he thought was an ancient Eastern tradition) at services; he dressed extraordinarily – on his wedding-day in London he wore a blue fisherman's jersey, a claret coat, wading-boots up to the hips and a pink hat without a brim! He revived the rural deanery synod, studied Cornish customs and wrote poetry. From 1834–1875 he was a strange and whimsical figure in the church.

In introducing Harvest Thanksgivings, he appealed thus to his parishioners:

Brethren, God has been good to us. He has filled our garners. He has opened his hand and filled all things living with plenteousness. Let us offer a sacrifice of thanksgiving among such as keep Holy Day. Let us gather together in the Chancel of our Church, on the first Sunday in October, and there receive, in the Bread of the New Corn, that Blessed Sacrament which was ordained to strengthen and refresh our souls.

A preacher at a Harvest Family Service asked the children to name some of the things they saw on display in church. Carrots, potatoes, peas and cabbage were all mentioned.

'Good,' said the preacher. 'Now can anyone give me a word that covers all these things?'

'Gravy,' came the prompt reply.

Source unknown

A correspondent wrote to *The Times* in 1992 that a young reader in church at Harvest Thanksgiving had reported Jesus as saying: 'Take no thought for the marrow.' (compare Matthew 6:34, Authorised Version). The writer's wife had leaned over and whispered, 'No, it's the pumpkins you've got to watch!'

The Times: (10 October, 1992)

Healing

Among my patients in the second half of life – that is to say, over thirty-five – there has not been one whose problem in the last resort was not that of *finding* a religious outlook on life. It is safe to say that every one of them fell ill because he had *lost* that which the living religions of every age have given to their followers, and none of them has been really healed who did not regain his religious outlook . . .

It is indeed high time for the clergyman and the psychotherapists to join forces to meet this great spiritual task.

Carl Jung: 'Modern Man in Search of a Soul'

Humpty Dumpty sat on a wall,
Humpty Dumpty had a great fall:
This gave him the feeling
To seek Inner Healing,
And now he's no problems at all.

Anonymous

Peter said [to the beggar lame from birth], 'I have no silver or gold, but what I have I give you; in the name of Jesus Christ of Nazareth, stand up and walk.' And he took him by the right hand and raised him up; and immediately his feet and ankles were made strong. Jumping up, he stood and began to walk, and he entered the temple with them, walking and leaping and praising God. All the people saw him walking and praising God, and they recognised him as the one who used to sit and ask for alms at the Beautiful Gate of the temple; and they were filled with wonder and amazement at what had happened to him.

Acts 3:6–10

Are any among you sick? They should call for the elders of the church and have them pray over them, anointing them with oil in the name of the Lord. The prayer of faith will save the sick, and the Lord will raise them up; and anyone who has committed sins will be forgiven.

James 5:14, 15

Heaven

The inextinguishable laughter of heaven.

Sir Thomas Browne

[Judging by the stories in the Bible] there are going to be some surprises in heaven.

Colin Chapman: at the Lausanne Congress II in Manila, (July, 1989)

Small boy: Where do animals go when they die?
Small girl: All good animals go to heaven, but the bad ones go to the Natural History Museum.

Punch cartoon, illustrated by E.H. Shepard, (1929)

When I enter that beautiful city
and the saints all around me appear,
I hope that someone will tell me,
'It was *you* who invited me here.'

Source unknown

Sydney Smith (1771–1845) reckoned that in heaven, as he said, 'I will be more respectful to the upper clergy.'

The late F.W.H. Myers asked a man at a dinner table what he thought would happen to him when he died. Though the man tried to avoid the question, he found himself pressed by Myers. Eventually he replied, 'Oh well, I suppose I shall inherit eternal bliss, but I wish you wouldn't talk about such unpleasant subjects.'

From Bertrand Russell: Stoicism and Mental Health, (1928). A similar story is reported in Russell's 'Unpopular Essays', (1950)

Then I saw a new heaven and a new earth; for the first heaven and the first earth had passed away, and the sea was no more. And I saw the holy city, the new Jerusalem, coming down out of heaven from God, prepared as a bride adorned for her husband. And I heard a loud voice from the throne saying,
'See, the home of God is among mortals.
He will dwell with them as their God;
and they will be his peoples,
and God himself will be with them; he will wipe every tear from their eyes.
Death will be no more; mourning and crying and pain will be no more,
for the first things have passed away.'

And the one who was seated on the throne said, 'See, I am making all things new.' Also he said, 'Write this, for these words are trustworthy and true.' Then he said to me, 'It is done! I am the Alpha and the Omega, the beginning and the end. To the thirsty I will give water as a gift from the spring of the water of life.'

Revelation 21:1–6

I saw no temple in the [heavenly] city, for its temple is the Lord God the Almighty and the Lamb. And the city has no need of sun or moon to shine on it, for the glory of God is its light, and its lamp is the Lamb. The nations will walk by its light, and the kings of the earth will bring their glory into it. Its gates will never be shut by day – and there will be night there. People will bring into it the glory and honour of the nations. But nothing unclean will enter it, nor anyone who practises abomination or falsehood, but only those who are written in the Lamb's book of life.

Revelation 21;22–27

Hell

O God,
If thou wilt not have mercy on my soul,

Yet for Christ's sake, whose blood
hath ransomed me,
Impose some end on my incessant
pain:
Let Faustus live in hell a thousand
years,
A hundred thousand, and at last be
saved.
O, no end is limited to damnèd souls

Christopher Marlowe: 'Doctor Faustus', (c 1592)

The way to Hell is paved with good intentions.

Portuguese Proverb

There are undoubtedly some very direct and terrifying statements [in the Bible]. But there are also plenty of passages with a picture of the end as a gathering up of the whole created order in Christ. Furthermore there are insights into the nature of God derived from the whole story of Christ's death and resurrection and the promise of forgiveness – insights which seem to make the idea of everlasting punishment incompatible with the main thrust of the gospel. The biblical interpreter has to make sense of all this and more, not because he or she is liberal or conservative, modern or traditionalist, but because the questions are there in the Bible itself . . .

We need to recognise the dangers of self-centredness, faithlessness and despair. But the paralysing fear of punishment, which dogged some earlier Christians, has, I believe, no place in the Christian gospel.

Archbishop John Habgood (of York): in The Independent, (July, 1991): 'This is not Hell'

One way of reconciling these opposites [the doctrine of Hell which makes fear the motive for evangelism, or the doctrine of Hell as a statement of the seriousness of moral choices] is to say that we create Hell for ourselves. It is not an objective reality, not a place or state created by God as a means of executing his justice, but is the way we experience self-absorption, despair, and unwillingness to open ourselves to his love. Heaven, by contrast, is not self-centred but is the God-given fulfilment of all his intentions for us. There is therefore a real lostness from which we need to be rescued. But it is not a lostness imposed upon us by God as a punishment, and therefore raises no question about God's moral goodness or his love towards us.

Archbishop John Habgood (of York): in The Independent, (July, 1991): 'This is not Hell'

[Hell is] a place where the Germans are the police, the Swedish are the comedians, the Italians are the defence force, Frenchmen dig the roads, the Belgians are the pop singers, the Spanish run the railways, the Turks cook the food, the Irish are the waiters, the Greeks run the government and the common language is Dutch.

David Frost and Antony Jay: 'To England with Love', (1967)

. . . the safest road to Hell is the gradual one – the gentle slope, soft underfoot, without sudden turnings, without milestones, without signposts.

C.S. Lewis: 'The Screwtape Letters', (Geoffrey Bles, 1942), Letter XII

Faust: How comes it, then, that thou
art out of hell?
Mephistophilis: Why, this is hell, nor
am I out of it.
Think'st thou that I, who saw the
face of God,
And tasted the eternal joys of
heaven,
Am not tormented with ten thousand
hells
In being depriv'd of everlasting
bliss?

Christopher Marlowe: 'Doctor Faustus', (c 1592)

The first three Gospels and some of the other New Testament books give clear evidence for the doctrine of eternal punishment – Jesus himself clearly accepts the classic illustration of Jerusalem's rubbish dump, Gehenna (see Matthew 5:22, 29, 30; Mark 9:43; Luke 10:15; etc.)

The apostle John, on the other hand, writes of the same eternal issues in terms of life and death, not heaven and hell, (see John 3;15, 16; 5:21–26; 6:50; 8:21, 51; 10:28; 11:25, 26; 1 John 2:25; 3:14; 4:19; 5:11–20; and many more) – as also does Paul (Romans 6:23 and elsewhere).

In contrast to both, there are a few verses in Saint Paul's letters which do more than hint at universal salvation (see Romans 8:20–22; 11:25–36; 1 Corinthians 15:22; 2 Corinthians 5:14–19; Colossians 1:20), and this is also found in James 2:12, 13. But there are Pauline texts which assume the doctrine of hell (Galatians 1:8,9; Philippians 3:19; 1 Thessalonians 2:3).

It simply will not do to opt exclusively for the doctrine of hell (because it's more convenient for evangelism), and to explain that, in Saint John's many references, he must have meant 'hell' when he wrote about 'death', excusing Saint Paul's universalist references by intricate exegesis and by churning out some jargon which means, in effect, that the teaching of the Synoptic Gospels is normative, so other references must be made to conform!

Robert M.E. Paterson, (1987)

Heresay – *see also* PARADOX

As a Roman Catholic, I thank God for the heretics. Heresy is only another word for freedom of thought.

Graham Greene

Heresy is not so much the propagation of error as the promotion of one truth at the expense of others.

Traditional

Hinduism

Since Hinduism, with its many gods, has no problem with God in the Christian revelation, only with his uniqueness, J.N. Farquhar described the Christian faith as 'the Crown of Hinduism'.

Missionary Conference at Jerusalem, (1928)

First, the message of morality and the good life, . . . the normal way of salvation for the Hindu, is precisely what the Christian knows can *not* save him. The solidarity of human sin means that any attempt to 'turn over a new leaf' without help from above at every stage is doomed to failure. Secondly, the road of pseudo-mysticism, of an ahistorical 'faith' which amounts to a sort of modern gnosticism, is also ruled out. Man needs remaking, and not merely enlightening, since he is sinful and not merely muddled; and the work of remaking man is achieved only by 'Jesus Christ come in the flesh'. Those who put forward as Christianity a form of 'salvation' which is not earthed both to the historical Jesus and to real Christian faith and living in this life, and who speak instead of a vague 'experience of God' to which these things are secondary, are ignoring the deepest needs of man, not to mention the remedy which God has provided.

Michael Sadgrove and Tom Wright: Jesus Christ the Only Saviour, in 'Obeying Christ in a Changing World', (Fountain, 1977)

History

History is bunk.

Henry Ford (1863–1947): 'Remark in court, '(July, 1919)

History is all around us and is no preserve of scholars.

A. Cooke

Miss Ruth Etchells found quietness of spirit in gazing at 'the most wonderful view in the world' [across the River Wear to the Cathedral and Castle at Durham]. 'Sitting there and just watching the water flowing quietly, and pondering on the lives that have been lived on these river banks and in those historic buildings, makes me conscious of being part of a living history that we are still making. And the marvellous thing is that we are making it in God's time and under his will. It is not possible to live and work in Durham, and in my job (a college principal) in particular, and not be most sharply aware of the Christian continuum – and that is the greatest calling in the world.'

The Church Times, (30 May, 1986)

Upon that point [the life of Jesus Christ] all history converges.

Max Warren: 'The Uniqueness of Jesus Christ', (1969)

Max Warren, Alan Richardson and Lesslie Newbigin all argued against any division of sacred and secular, including the concept of 'saving or sacred history', if, by that, is meant abstracting the history of the people of God from the general continuum of history. There may have been what can be called 'directional events' in biblical history but there can be no divorce between these events and the rest of history.

. . . real history, secular history, the history of which we are a part. What other history is there? There are not different histories but there are different ways of understanding history . . . it can be understood theistically or atheistically . . . The long-running debate about the relationship between the Jesus of history and the Christ of faith is simply one manifestation of the illusion that has haunted our culture ever since the Enlightenment. There is only one Jesus, and there is only one history. The question is whether the faith that finds its focus in Jesus is the faith with which we seek to understand the whole of history, or whether we limit this faith to a private world of religion and hand over the public history of the world to other principles of explanation.

Lesslie Newbigin: 'Foolishness to the Greeks', (S.C.M., 1986)

. . . historians are not dispassionate observers, we study history in order to intervene in history – in order to understand and affect the present.

Bishop Ian Cundy (of Peterborough): 'Historical aspects of the Doctrine of the Church', (1989)

As typical modern people, most of us are prone to the curse of 'homo-up-to-datum', Daniel Boorstin's apt term for the illusion that the closer we are to instant total information, the nearer we are to wisdom. Of its many consequences, one of the most fatuous is that we seem to know everything about the last twenty-four hours but next to nothing about the last twenty-four years, let alone the last twenty-four centuries.

O.S. Guinness: in 'The Mind on Fire', Blaise Pascal, Ed. J. M. Houston, (1989)

A man's eyes should be plucked out if he can only see the past.

A Russian proverb

The Moving Finger writes; and having writ,
Moves on; nor all thy Piety nor Wit
Shall lure it back to cancel half a line,
Nor all thy tears wash out a Word of it.

Rubáiyát of Omar Khayam, Tr. Edward Fitzgerald (1809–83)

Holiness

My people's greatest need is my own personal holiness.

Robert Murray McCheyne (1813–1843)

The destined end of man is not happiness, nor health, but holiness. God . . . is not an eternal blessing-machine for men; he did not come to save men out of pity; he came to save men because he had created them to be holy.

Oswald Chambers

If only I may grow firmer, simpler, quieter, warmer.

Dag Hammarskjold: 'Markings'

If you want to be holy, don't try!

Bishop John V. Taylor, (1989)

If it is God's will, then do it with all your strength; and if it is not his will, then suffer death rather than attempt it. If you ask me, 'What is God's will?' I will answer that his will is that you become holy.

Edmund of Abingdon, (1175–1240)

God did not call us to impurity but in holiness.

1 Thessalonians 4:7

As he who called you is holy, be holy yourselves in all your conduct; for it is written, 'You shall be holy, for I am holy'.

1 Peter 1:15, 16 (referring to Leviticus 11:44, 45; 19:2)

Holy places

. . . the 'holiest place' of all for Christians is an empty tomb: surely a sign that our resurrection faith is called to transcend particular places and sanctuaries. And yet holy places rightly used can remind us of the earthly and material dimension of the Christian faith. The incarnation is concerned with the particular, God taking human flesh at a particular time and in a particular place.

Archbishop Joseph Raya, Greek Catholic Archbishop of Galilee: in 'A Many-Coloured Mosaic', (Clare Amos, C.M.S., 1987)

For the blood of Thy martyrs and
saints
Shall enrich the earth, shall create
the holy places.
For wherever a saint has dwelt,
wherever a martyr has
given his blood for the blood of
Christ,
There is holy ground, and the
sanctity shall not depart from it
Though armies trample over it,
though sightseers come
with guide-books looking over
it;
From where the western seas gnaw at
the coast of Iona,
To the death in the desert, the prayer
in forgotten places by
the broken imperial column,
From such ground springs that which
forever renews the earth
Though it is forever denied.

T.S. Eliot: 'Murder in the Cathedral', (1935), Part II, lines 628–636 (Faber and Faber, 1965)

Holy Communion – *see* EUCHARIST

Holy Spirit – *see* SPIRIT

Honesty

Robert Tyre Jones, said to be the best golfer of his time (in the 1920's), during a national championship, drove a ball into the woods. He went after it alone and accidentally touched it while practising his shot. Stepping out of the woods he signalled his fault, thus losing the championship. When he was praised for his sportsmanship, he said, 'You might as well praise a man for not robbing a bank.'

Source unknown

Better to be poor and walk in integrity than to be crooked in one's way even though rich.

Proverbs 28:6

Your iniquities have been barriers
between you and your God . . .
For our transgressions before you are
many, and our sins testify against
us.
Our transgressions indeed are with
us, and we know our iniquities:
transgressing, and denying the LORD,
and turning away from following
our God,
talking oppression and revolt,
conceiving lying words and
uttering them from the heart.
Justice is turned back, and
righteousness stands at a distance;
for truth stumbles in the public
square, and uprightness cannot
enter.
Truth is lacking, and whoever turns
from evil is despoiled.
The LORD saw it, and it displeased
him that there was no justice.

Isaiah 59:2a, 12–15

Hope

When the Christian speaks of confidence, he does *not* mean a kind of starry-eyed optimism based on a theory of human progress and perfectibility. Rather, he means hope, based on the resurrection-victory of Jesus.

Archbishop Dr F. Donald Coggan: 'Enthronement at Canterbury', (25 January, 1975)

All which happens in the world happens through hope. No husbandman would sow a seed of corn if he did not hope it would spring up and bring forth the ear. How much more are we helped on by hope in the way to eternal life.

Martin Luther (1483- 1546)

While there's tea there's hope.

Sir Arthur Wing Pinero, (1855–1934)

[Hope is] vivid anticipation.

Bishop B .F. Wescott, (on Hebrews 10. 23)

Safe shall be my going,
Secretly armed against all death's
endeavour;
Safe though all safety's lost; safe
where men fall;
And if these poor limbs die, safest of
all.

Rupert Brooke

The New Testament conception of hope has nothing at all to do with any this-worldly prospects; it is as far removed as possible from any notion of an earthly Utopia or any secular optimism.

Alan Richardson: 'A Theological Word Book of the Bible', (S.C.M., 1950)

Look away from yourself and look to God!

Augustine of Hippo (354–430): To a person who thought of little except his sins

At the end of all things. At the end of time. At the end of the world – there stands God. Our ultimate confidence lies not in some secular utopianism but in living with Christ.

Archbishop Robert Runcie: at the Anglican Consultative Council, (Nigeria, 1984)

The Godward look is the secret of Christian hope . . . [It] is not simply a trembling, hesitant hope that perhaps the promises of God may be true. It is the confident expectation that they cannot be anything else than true.

William Barclay: 'New Testament Words', (S.C.M., 1964)

What oxygen is to lungs, such is hope for the meaning of life.

Emil Brunner

He brought light out of darkness, not out of a lesser light; he can bring your summer out of winter, though you have no spring; though in the ways of fortune, or understanding, or conscience, you have been benighted until now, wintered and frozen, clouded and eclipsed, damped and benumbed, smothered and stupefied 'till now, now God comes to you, *not* as in the dawning of the day, not as in the bud of the spring, but as the sun at noon.

John Donne (1572–1631)

A mediaeval king gave his new court jester the fool's sceptre and told him to keep it until he met a bigger fool than himself. Years later the king lay dying and sent for the jester. 'I'm going on a long journey,' he said.

'Where are you going, and how will you travel?' asked the jester.

'I don't know,' replied the king.

'Have you made any provision for the journey, your majesty?'

'No.'

The jester handed the king his fool's sceptre: 'Then this belongs to you.'

Traditional

. . . how do I explain any of that [the purposes of God in an apparently meaningless life] to the little boy down the road with all the drainage tubes coming out of his skull, where the medics have tried to remove the cancer in his brain? Do I tell his mother that she will be a better woman because of it? The danger of all the arguments that try to justify the ways of God to man is that you are liable to feel rather like a laboratory rat put through a series of tests and mazes to see how well you perform; or as if you are being put through an assault course with a reward at the end if you get over all the obstacles without grumbling. I can think of no answer in the world to give to that mother or her son. I would like to believe that, in the greater context of what we may know and experience after death, all this suffering will seem less important, less total; and in a strange way, the beauty of their love and courage makes me think I see something like light breaking through – but no pat answers, no book of rules. They confront together all the pressures of the absurd, as mankind has always had to confront them. Nothing anyone can say can make them less real.

Richard MacKenna: 'God for Nothing', (Churchman, 1984/85)

Hope: The lived belief that with God no situation is the end of the story.

Martin Wroe, Adrian Reith & Simon Parkes: 'The Church-English Dictionary', (1991)

I can cope with despair: it's hope I can't take.

John Cleese: in the film 'Clockwise'

The needy shall not always bé
forgotten,
nor the hope of the poor perish
forever.

Psalm 9:18

May the God of hope fill you with all joy and peace in believing, so that you may abound in hope by the power of the Holy Spirit.

Romans 15:13

Humanity

God made man in his own image, but man has taken his revenge in kind.

Voltaire

If you do not believe in any ultimate mystery in the world, then there can be no ultimate mystery in the human self. Opposing this is the view that the self will always remain beyond science. This can be asserted for reasons of faith – human self-consciousness is a God-given creation and lies beyond human reason.

Bryan Appleyard: in The Times Saturday Review, (25 April, 1992), 'Science and spirit'

. . . the open-endedness, the valuelessness, the apparent objectivity and effectiveness of science have progressively stripped away any reason to value one way of life, one system, above another. Modern scientific attitudes – because of science's effectiveness rather than any conspiracy by scientists – destroy purpose in life, reduce us all to a condition of blank, adolescent nihilism.

Bryan Appleyard: in The Times Saturday Review, (25 April, 1992), 'Science and spirit'

The glory and the scum of the universe.

Blaise Pascal

I love the human race. All of my family belong to it; and some of my wife's family, too.

Anonymous

Question: What is man's chief end?
Answer: Man's chief end is to glorify God, and to enjoy him for ever.

The Shorter Westminster Catechism (1647–8): The first question

No man is an Iland, intire of it selfe; every man is a peece of the Continent, a part of the maine; if a Clod bee washed away by the Sea, Europe is the lesse, as well as if a Promontorie were, as well as if a Mannor of thy friends or of thine owne were: any mans death diminishes me, because I am involved in Mankinde; And therefore never send to know for whom the bell tolls; it tolls for thee.

John Donne: 'Devotions upon Emergent Occasions', XVII

Man becomes, as it were, the sex organs of the machine world.

Marshall Mcluhan, (c. 1970)

The little man.

President Franklin D Roosevelt, describing the ordinary American citizen without power or position

An old story tells of a rabbi asking his disciples how they could know when the night is ended and the dawn coming. One asked whether it could be when you could tell that an animal in the distance is a sheep or a dog. Another asked whether it could be when you could tell that a tree in the distance is a fig or an olive. 'No,' replied the rabbi. 'It is when you look at the face of any man or woman and see that he or she is your brother or sister. If you cannot do this, no matter what time of day it is, it is still the night.'

From John Carden: 'Another Day', (Triangle 1986)

Grant us, O Lord, that we may never forget that every man is the son of a King.

Hebrew Hasidim

Human rights

Either no member of the human race has any natural rights or they all have the same; and anyone who votes against the rights of another, of whatever religion, colour or sex, has from that moment denied his own.

Marquis de Condorcet (late 18th century, France)

I think I can see him [St Paul] growing increasingly impatient with talk about a charter of *rights*, and bringing us back, with inexorable logic, to the need, rather, for a charter of duties. You and I must both die one day. I want to know how to die. I want to be able to teach other people how to die. There *is* a judgement day, and we must prepare ourselves for it. We have duties. I feel this very strongly. Duty is a stern word. But then there is an element of iron in the Christian ethic which is very important.

Archbishop Donald Coggan (of Canterbury)

Humility

If only I had a little more humility. I'd be perfect.

Attributed to Ted Turner

What the world needs is more geniuses with humility. There are so few of us left.

Oscar Levant

Woman to cleric: I pride myself in my humility.

I am well aware that I am the 'umblest person going. . . .
We are so very 'umble.

Charles H. Dickens: 'David Copperfield', (Uriah Heep)

Humility is not a highly regarded virtue nowadays; it can have strong overtones of hypocrisy and false modesty, and can be just another way of manipulating people by presenting a seemingly unaggressive front, like Uriah Heap, the devious villain in *David Copperfield*. But true humility is something that starts from strength.

Richard MacKenna: 'God for Nothing', (Churchman, 1984/85)

Humility is not a mere ornament of a Christian, but an essential part of the new creature. It is a contradiction to be a true Christian and not humble.

Richard Baxter: 'The Reformed Pastor', (1655)

Humility is a chocolate biscuit lying with the plain side up.

Robert M.E. Paterson, (1970)

Humility is not simply the most important of all the virtues, it is the condition for all the virtues.

Malcolm Muggeridge, (1981)

The Christian pilgrimage begins with bowed head and bent knee; there is no way into the kingdom of God except by the exaltation of those who have humbled themselves.

John R.W. Stott: 'I Believe in Preaching', (Hodders, 1982)

Beware of too sublime a sense
Of your own worth and consequence.
The man who dreams himself so great,
And his importance of such weight,
That all around in all that's done
Must move and act for Him alone,
Will learn in school of tribulation
The folly of his expectation.

William Cowper: 'The Retired Cat', 1791, (published 1815)

Give me humility. If thou, Lord, had travelled in a sedan chair, how would the woman have touched thy garment's hem?

Henry Martyn (1781–1812): reflection on Matthew chapter 9

The greatest among you will be your servant. All who exalt themselves will be humbled, and all who humble themselves will be exalted.

Matthew 23:11, 12

A dispute also arose among them [the disciples at the Last Supper] as to which of them was to be regarded as the greatest. But he said to them, 'The kings of the Gentiles lord it over them; and those in authority over them are called benefactors. But not so with you; rather the greatest among you must become like the youngest, and the leader like one who serves. For who is greater, the one who is at the table or the one who serves? Is it not the one at the table? But I am among you as one who serves.

Luke 22:24–27

All of you must clothe yourselves with humility in your dealings with one another, for 'God opposes the proud, but gives grace to the humble.' Humble yourselves under the mighty hand of God, so that he may exalt you in due time.

1 Peter 5:5b, 6

Humour

I received the following letter after a broadcast:

> 'Dear Sir, I was very shocked to hear you say on the radio this morning that Christians ought to have a sense of humour and a sense of proportion. I think that, because ministers of religion have been saying this kind of thing, the Devil is out and about and not where he ought to be, in chains in the Abyss. Perhaps you too, Sir, are a limb of Satan.
> I remain,
> Your sincere friend . . .'

The listener obviously took life very seriously, and certainly there is every justification for doing so in the present state of the world. But do we take seriously enough the root causes of our problems? An editorial on the attempted assassination of the Pope suggested that the basic factor is 'the trivialisation of sin'. It is there in violence and brutality, in the contempt for the sanctity of human life, in the inhumanity which exploits and corrupts for profit or power. If we do not take sin seriously enough, perhaps we take ourselves too seriously. In the posturing of politicians and propagandists there is often an element of the ridiculous of which they seem utterly unaware. But, as Proverbs xxvi, 12, suggests, 'There is more hope for a fool than for a man wise in his own conceit'.

The same can be true of us as individuals when we fail to keep that sense of humour about ourselves which is far more important than our ability to laugh at other people. Being able to laugh at oneself is not only part of the humility which makes us easier to live with. It also depends on having that sense of proportion which is as aware of goodness as it is of evil, which can know compassion as well as joy, and which begins its prayers with thanksgiving even in times of crisis.

Fenton Morley: in the Church Times, (1981)

Laughter is holy.

Canon Edwyn Davies, (1985)

The poor human race 'has unquestionably one really effective weapon – laughter . . . Only laughter can blow it (humbug) to rags and atoms in a blast. Against the assault of laughter nothing can stand.'

Mark Twain

[Laughter is] 'the converse face of mysticism' [Malcolm Muggeridge] since the mystic reaches upwards towards God, while the humorist recognises our human inability to find him. This paradox he [Muggeridge] sees illustrated in the great cathedrals of mediaeval Europe which have both 'a steeple climbing into the sky' and 'a gargoyle grinning down at the earth'.

John R.W. Stott: 'I Believe in Preaching', (Hodders, 1982)

It is important to remind ourselves often that the cultivation of a right sense of humour can be one of the forms of piety. Cultivate a sense of humour in yourself about other people and in other people about yourself: learn to laugh rather than to be vexed by other people's foibles, but learn the ability also to let other people laugh at your own.

Gerald Vann (1906–1963): 'The Divine Pity'

Hymns – *see also* MUSIC AND SINGING

Hymns are praises of God with singing; hymns and songs containing praises of God.
If there be praise and not praise of God it is not a hymn.
If there is praise of God and it is not sung, it is not a hymn.
It is necessary, therefore, if it is to be a hymn, that it has these three things: both praise and praise of God and that it be sung.

St. Augustine of Hippo (354–430)

If I were a Cassowary
On the plains of Timbuctoo,
I would eat a missionary,
Cassock, band and hymn-book too.

Bishop Samuel Wilberforce ('Soapy Sam', 1805–1873)

Sir,
The hymn 'Onward Christian Soldiers', sung to the right tune and in a not-too-brisk tempo, makes a very good egg-timer. If you put the egg into boiling water and sing all five verses and chorus, the egg will be just right when you come to 'Amen'.

Letter in the Daily Telegraph, (1983)

Dear Lord and Father of mankind,
Forgive our foolish ways;
For most of us, when asked our mind,
Admit we still most pleasure find
In hymns of ancient days,
In hymns of ancient days.
The simple lyrics, for a start,
Of many a modern song
Are far too trite to touch the heart;
Enshrine no poetry, no art;
And go on much too long . . .
O, for a rest from jollity
And syncopated praise!
What happened to tranquillity?
The silence of eternity
Is hard to hear these days . . .
Send thy deep hush subduing all
Those happy claps that drown
The tender whisper of thy call;
Triumphalism is not all,
For sometimes we feel down . . .
Drop thy still dews of quietness

Till all our strummings cease;
Take from our souls the strain and stress
Of always having to be blessed;
Give us a bit of peace . . .
Breathe through the beats of praise guitar
Thy coolness and thy balm;
Let drum be dumb, bring back the lyre,
Enough of earthquake, wind and fire,
Let's hear it for some calm . . .

Peter Baker (discovered on the Internet, 1996)

Hypocrisy

Oh, for a forty-parson-power to chant
Thy praise, hypocrisy!

George Gordon, Lord Byron, (1788–1824): Don Juan

Of all villainy there is none more base than that of the hypocrite, who, at the moment he is most false, takes care to appear most virtuous.

Cicero

No man, for any considerable period, can wear one face to himself and another to the multitude, without finally getting bewildered as to which may be the true.

Nathaniel Hawthorne

No man is a hypocrite in his pleasures.

Dr. Samuel Johnson

And thus I clothe my naked villainy
With old odd ends stolen out of holy writ;
And seem a saint, when most I play the devil . . .

William Shakespeare: 'Richard III', I.3

The clergyman who affects worldliness in order to 'relate' to those outside the church is only the latest in the parade of ecclesiastical hypocrites.

Source unknown

Solemn prayers, rapturous devotions, are but repeated hypocrisies unless the heart and mind be conformable to them.

William Law

Of Belial:
A fairer person lost not heaven; he seemed
For dignity *compos'd* and high exploit:
But all was false and hollow; though his tongue
Dropt manna, and could make the *worse* appear
The *better* reason, to perplex and dash
Maturest counsels.

John Milton: 'Paradise Lost', Book 2, lines 110–115

We are not hypocrites in our sleep.

William Hazlitt: 'On Dreams'

He that speaks me fair and loves me not,
I'll speak him fair and trust him not.

John Ray: 'English Proverbs'

Freud called this moral gymnastics [saying that since God loves to forgive, why should our sin offend him so much] 'projection' . . . In a word, 'hypocrisy'.

John R.W. Stott: at the Lausanne II Congress in Manila, (July, 1989)

When Christian missionaries went first to the Hindus, the Hindus said 'It is not true!' – so the Christians taught the truth.

Then they said: 'It is not new!' – so the Christians explained about new life.

Eventually they said: 'It is not *you!'*

Source unknown

After a quantity of wine had been drunk over dinner at the Beef Steak Club in Covent Garden, Lord Sandwich unguardedly teased Samuel Foote (1720–77): 'Foote, I have often wondered what catastrophe would bring *you* to your end; but I think you must either die of the pox, or the halter.' Foote's reply was instantaneous: 'My Lord, *that* will depend upon one or two contingencies – whether I embrace your Lordship's mistress, or your Lordship's principles.'

James Stevenson, Ed: 'Oxford Book of Literary Anecdotes', (1975)

Adlai Stevenson (in 1956) described an acquaintance:
He is the kind of politician who would cut down a redwood tree and then mount the stump to make a speech for conservation.

Normally I take a live-and-let-live attitude towards refried Jesus-wheezing TV preachers. They've got their role in life, and I've got mine. Their role is to be sanctimonious panhandlers. My role is to have a good time. They don't pray for cocaine and orgies. I don't go on the tube and ask people to send me $100. But when a place like *Heritage U.S.A.* [a Christian resort and amusement park created by discredited television evangelists Jim and Tammy Bakker] starts advertising fun in the sun and *Heritage's* founders start having drug blasts and zany extramarital frolics, I feel they're stepping on my turf.

P.J. O'Rourke: 'Holidays in Hell', (1988)

. . . we must be distinguished not by our clothes but by our teaching; not by our dress but by our life-style; not by our costume but by our purity of heart.

Pope Celestine I, (c 425)

I

Idealism – *see also* EXISTENTIALISM, and PHILOSOPHY

After we came out of the church [at Harwich], we stood talking for some time of Bishop Berkeley's ingenious sophistry to prove the non-existence of matter,[1] and that every thing in the universe is merely ideal. I observed, that though we are satisfied his doctrine is not true, it is impossible to refute it. I shall never forget the alacrity with which Johnson answered, striking his foot with mighty force against a large stone, till he rebounded from it, 'I refute it *thus.*'

James Boswell: 'The Life of Samuel Johnson'

[1] Ideas are the things which really exist. Material things exist only insofar as they are perceived. But ideas are *not* the product of human minds because God is responsible for the existence of ideas. (George Berkeley, 1685–1753)

There once was a man who said,
'God
Must think it exceedingly odd
If he finds that this tree
Continues to be
When there's no one about in the
Quad.'

Attributed Ronald A Knox (1888–1957): 'Limerick on Idealism'

Dear Sir, Your astonishment's odd,
I'm always about in the Quad;
And that's why the tree
will continue to be
Since observed by, Yours faithfully,
God.

Anonymous reply

Ignorance

When Dr. Samuel Johnson (1709–1784) was asked by a lady why, in his Dictionary he defined 'pastern' as the 'knee' of a horse, he replied, 'Ignorance, madam, pure ignorance.'

(1755)

Imagination

Imagination is more important than knowledge.

Albert Einstein, (1879–1955): 'On Science'

The soul without imagination is what an observatory would be without a telescope.

Henry Ward Beecher (1813–1887)

Incarnation of the Word – *see also* CHRISTMAS and JESUS CHRIST

Run, shepherds, run, where Bethl'em blest appears,
We bring the best news, be not dismayed;
A Saviour there is born, more old than years,
Amidst the rolling Heaven this Earth who stayed . . .

William Drummond, (1584–1649)

. . . the Christian story is precisely the story of one grand miracle, the Christian assertion being that what is beyond all space and time, what is uncreated, eternal, came into nature, into human nature, descended into his own universe, and rose again, bringing nature up with him. It is precisely one great miracle. If you take that away there is nothing specifically Christian left. There may be many admirable human things which Christianity shares with all other systems in the world, but there would be nothing specifically Christian.

C.S. Lewis: 'The Grand Miracle', (1945), in 'God in the Dock', (Collins, 1979)

O hearken, for this is wonder!
Light looked down and beheld
Darkness;
'Thither will I go,' said Light.
Peace looked down and beheld war.
'Thither will I go,' said Peace.
Love looked down and beheld
Hatred.
'Thither will I go,' said Love.
So came Light, and shone.
So came Peace, and gave rest.
So came Love, and brought life.
And the Word was made flesh, and
dwelt among us.

Laurence Housman: from Brother Sun, in 'Little Plays of St. Francis'

There is a story of a young lady who asked Dr. Jowett, 'Oh Master, do tell me – what do you think about God?' To which the Master replied, 'That, my dear young lady, is a very unimportant question; the only thing that signifies is what he thinks about me.' . . . In the New Testament, if it is true at all, we are face to face with God; if that is not true, the New Testament is written under an illusion from end to end . . . The men who wrote the books of the New Testament believed that in Jesus Christ, God Himself lived and walked about among them. 'The Word was made flesh and dwelt among us.' They start from there.

Archbishop William Temple (of Canterbury, 1881–1944): 'The Universality of Christ'

The Word became flesh and lived among us, and we have seen his glory, the glory as of the father's only son, full of grace and truth.

John 1:14

Many deceivers have gone out into the world, those who do not confess that Jesus Christ has come in the flesh; any such person is the deceiver and the antichrist!

2 John 7

Intelligence

For God's sake give me the young man who has brains enough to make a fool of himself.

Robert Louis Stevenson: 'Crabbed Age and Youth'

A woman especially, if she have the misfortune of knowing any thing, should conceal it as well as she can.

Jane Austen (1775–1817): 'Northanger Abbey', chapter 14

I am a Bear of Very Little Brain, and long words Bother me.

A.A. Milne (1882–1956): 'Winnie the Pooh', (1926), chapter 4

Why, I ask myself, are you all here? It must be because you are not all there.

Lewis Clarke at an Annual Archdeacon's Visitation (about 1985)

Ireland and the Irish

Two Irish Republicans were looking at a traffic light.
One commented to the other, 'They don't leave much time for the Unionists to cross, do they?'

(Many Protestant Unionists are 'Orangemen', and the colour of Irish Nationalism is green.)

12th July commemorates the Battle of the Boyne in 1690, when the Protestant King William III (of Orange) defeated the forces of the Roman Catholic Jacobites, supported by Louis XIV of France.

An Englishman stumbles on a full-scale Orange march in Belfast and does not understand what is going on, so he asks the man standing next to him. 'It's the Twelfth,' the man answers.

'I'm afraid I still don't understand.'

'It's the Twelfth of July,' the Irishman replies.

'I know what the date is, but what's all this about?' asks the Englishman.

'Ach, away home to England and read your Bible, man!'

Tony Gray: from 'The Orange Order', (1972)

Islam

After Saturday comes Sunday.

The threat of extremist Muslim groups to deal with Christians after the Jews

A gigantic, oil-powered alternative to modernity.

Anonymous

The strength and weakness of Islam has always been its intense conservatism. It is essentially the Religion of the Book and that Book is the Qur'an, transcribed from a tablet preserved in heaven and revealed to the Prophet once and for all time as literally the word of God . . . In the past Islam has shown considerable powers of adaptation to different climates of thought. Reactionary forces, however, are firmly entrenched, and it cannot be denied that the stability of Islamic civilisation has been preserved throughout the ages by its unfailing adherence to its fundamental doctrine of unconditional submission to the will and precepts of Allah as revealed by his prophet Muhammad.

E O James: 'History of Religions', (Hodder and Stoughton, 1964; first published 1956)
[Recent history, a generation and more after this book was first published, has proved the accuracy of these assertions.]

Israel

Even in Old Testament times, to make a straight identification between Israel as the people of God and the then ethnic nation state in any of its stages was questionable and questioned.

Christopher Wright: Ecclesiology – 'A Biblical Perspective', (1989)

J

Jealousy

I'm not a jealous woman, but I can't see what he sees in her.

Sir Alan Patrick Herbert

In the course of a casual conversation, a husband asked his wife, 'If I died tomorrow, would you marry again?'

'Certainly not,' she replied.

'Why? Don't you like being married?'

'Of course I do, my dear,' she said, 'so perhaps I would think about it.'

'If you were to marry again, would you take my pictures down and put up some of him?' the husband persisted, becoming a little annoyed.

'I suppose so.'

'And would you sleep in our bed?'

'Possibly.'

At this the man's anger overcame him. 'And would you let him use my golf clubs?' 'Certainly not! He's left-handed,' came the reply

Anonymous

Jesus Christ – *see also* CHRISTMAS, CROSS, INCARNATION, etc.

Come, my Way, my Truth, my life:
Such a Way, as gives us breath:
Such a Truth, as ends all strife:
And such a Life, as killeth death.

Come, my Light, my Feast, my
  Strength;
Such a Light, as shows a feast:
Such a Feast, as mends in length:
Such a Strength, as makes his guest.

Come, my Joy, my Love, my Heart:
Such a Joy, as none can move:
Such a Love, as none can part:
Such a Heart, as joyes in love.

George Herbert (1593–1633): 'The Call'

The name of Jesus is powerfully evocative. Can you imagine any hymn which would begin: 'Mary Baker Eddy, let me to thy bosom fly!'?

Source unknown, probably Fenton Morley

If we cannot say with total conviction that Jesus of Nazareth is for all men and every man then we have little left worth saying.

Sir Kenneth Grubb: Church Missionary Society Annual General Meeting, (1969)

A young slave woman in the USA learned from white children how to recognise the name 'Jesus' in print; so she would spend long hours with a Bible, opened at random, tracing her finger along each line until she came across the name.

Raboteau: 'Slave Religion', (Oxford, 1978)

. . . all around us are the Greeks who, whether they know it or not, want to see Jesus; and the Jesus they want to see is not an ecclesiasticized Jesus, tamed, domesticated, conventionalised, carefully orthodox, but the Son of Man, whose lifting up on the cross was the very glory of God who so loved the world that he gave his only Son, that all men might believe and live.

Professor Charles Kingsley Barrett, (October 1968)

JESU is in my heart, his sacred name
Is deeply carved there: but th'other week
A great affliction broke the little frame,
Ev'n all to pieces: which I went to seek:
And first I found the corner, where was ***J***,
After, where ***ES***, and next where ***U*** was graved.
When I had got these parcels, instantly
I sat me down to spell them, and perceived
That to my broken heart he was ***I ease you***,
and to my whole is ***JESU***.

George Herbert (1593–1633): 'JESU'

. . . what else can be the meaning of the word Christian but just this indispensable connection with an historical event and person as the centre of this religion? Christian faith is faith in Jesus Christ as the supreme revelation of God. You cannot believe as a Christian without looking or pointing to this event of the past, without facing the divine revelation as having happened there and then.

Emil Brunner: 'The Scandal of Christianity', (1948; S.C.M., 1951), Lecture I, 'Historical Revelation'

The saying is sure and worthy of full acceptance, that Christ Jesus came into the world to save sinners – of whom I am the foremost.

1 Timothy 1:15

Let us run with perseverance the race that is set before us, looking to Jesus the pioneer and perfecter of our faith, who for the sake of the joy that was set before him endured the cross, disregarding its shame, and has taken his seat at the right hand of the throne of God.

Hebrews 12:1c, 2

Jesus Christ is the same yesterday and today and for ever.

Hebrews 13:8

Jews

How odd
of God
to choose
the Jews.

Attributed to William Norman Ewer and to Hilaire Belloc.

To which there have been many rejoinders, such as:
Not odd
of God.
Goyim
Annoy'im.

Journalism

P.J. O'Rourke describes capturing three illegal aliens on the Mexican border:
I just got over-excited, temporarily forgot I was a journalist and started acting like a law-abiding citizen.

From 'Holidays in Hell', (1988)

An admiring lady praised G.K. Chesterton: 'You seem to know everything!'

'I know nothing, madam,' the author replied. 'I am a journalist.'

Joy

Joy is not gush; joy is not jolliness. Joy is perfect acquiescence in the will of God.

Prebendary Webb-Peploe

Some Christians seem to have a ministry to make people feel miserable and guilty and they regularly check-up that their victims don't backslide into happiness.

Adrian Plass: 'The Sacred Diary of Adrian Plass aged 37½', (1987)

And in perfect acquiescence, is there not perfect rest?

Frances Ridley Havergal

Joy is the serious business of heaven.

C.S. Lewis: 'Surprised by Joy'

. . . there are but two lessons for the Christian to learn: the one is to enjoy

God in everything; the other is, to enjoy everything in God.

Charles Simeon (1759–1836): 'Sermon on Ecclesiastes'

If our faith is important to us, I used to muse, why shouldn't we too be moved to express our faith in ways that are true to us as individuals? Instead we sing glorious hymns like *Praise, my soul, the King of Heaven* as if we are paying the milk bill; or, if we are Anglicans, we sing the *Te Deum* 'We praise you, O Lord, we acknowledge you to be the Lord' (originally intended as a triumphant anthem against the opposition of all who reject Christ) as if we are taking a dose of cod liver oil!

George Carey (later archbishop): 'The Church in the Market Place', (Kingsway, 1984)

After visiting a puritan family, Sydney Smith (1774–1845) wrote:
I endeavoured in vain to give them more cheerful ideas of religion, to teach them that God is not a jealous, childish, merciless tyrant; that he is best served by a regular tenor of good actions – not by bad singing, ill-composed prayers and eternal apprehensiveness. But the luxury of false religion is to be unhappy.

This seems a cheerful world, Donatus, when I view it from this fair garden, under the shadow of these vines, But if I climbed some great mountain and looked out over the wide lands, you know very well what I would see. Brigands on the high road, pirates on the seas, in the amphitheatres men murdered to please the applauding crowds, under all roofs misery and selfishness. It is really a bad world, Donatus, an incredibly bad world. Yet in the midst of it I have found a quiet and holy people. They have discovered a joy which is a thousand times better than any pleasure of this sinful life. They are despised and persecuted, but they care not. They have overcome the world. These people, Donatus, are the Christians . . . and I am one of them.

Cyprian, (Bishop of Carthage 248–258) [He suffered under the ban on Christian assembly in the Empire.]

The fruit of the Spirit is love, joy, peace, patience, kindness, generosity, faithfulness, gentleness and self-control.

Galatians 5:22

Judgement

One night a friend questioned Peter Marshall about whether he really thought we shall ever have to stand before God on a Judgement Day and hear the roll-call of our sins.

'Yes, the Bible makes it quite clear,' Peter answered promptly. 'Some day, somewhere, somehow, there will be an accounting for each of us.' He paused and seemed lost in thought for a while, then said, 'I think I may have to go through the agony of hearing all my sins recited in the presence of God. But I believe it will be like this – Jesus will come over and lay his hand across my shoulders and say to the Father, 'Yes, all these things are true, but I'm here to cover up for Peter. He is sorry for all his sins, and by a transaction made between us, I am now solely responsible for them!'

Suddenly Peter smiled, 'And sister, if I'm wrong about that, ***I'm sunk.***'

Catherine Marshall: 'A Man Called Peter', biography of Peter Marshall, chaplain of U.S. Senate

Since the Bible stresses that judgement is the prerogative of God and not of man, and since the Gospels constantly highlight the surprising and paradoxical nature of Christ's salvation and judgement, a degree of reverent agnosticism may be no bad thing.

Walter Moberley: 'Perdition', (April, 1986)

We are as harsh in our judgement of others as we are lenient in our judgement of ourselves.

John Stott at Lausanne II Congress in Manila, (July, 1989)

The Politically Correct culture . . . chimes with the way the country [the U.S.A.] is fleeing from risk and moral judgement into the realm of 'victimology'. Every guest on a talk show is a 'survivor' of some kind, blaming everything from the alcoholism to bankruptcy on negligent parents or low self-esteem.

Charles Bremner: in The Times, (1992), 'Sense and Sensitivity'

When the Son of Man comes in his glory, and all the angels with him, then he will sit on the throne of his glory. All the nations will be gathered before him, and he will separate people one from another as a shepherd separates the sheep from the goats, and he will put the sheep at his right hand and the goats at the left.

Matthew 25. 31–33 (Then Jesus gave the basis for this judgement)

Why do you pass judgement on your brother or sister? Or you, why do you despise your brother or sister? For we will all stand before the judgement seat of God. For it is written, 'As I live, says the Lord, every knee shall bow to me, and every tongue shall give praise to God.' So then, each of us will be accountable to God.

Romans 14:10–12

Just as it is appointed for mortals to die once, and after that the judgement, so Christ, having been offered once to bear the sins of many, will appear a second time, not to deal with sin, but to save those who are eagerly waiting for him.

Hebrews 9:27, 28

Justice – *see also* JUDGEMENT *and* MERCY

Thwackum was for doing justice and leaving mercy to Heaven.

Henry Fielding, (1707–54): Tom Jones [Thwackum was Tom's clerical tutor]

The Long Silence

At the end of time, billions of people were scattered on a great plain before God's throne. Most shrank back from the brilliant light before them. But some groups near the front talked heatedly – not with cringing shame, but with belligerence.

'How can God judge us? How can He know about suffering?' snapped a pert young brunette. She ripped open a sleeve to reveal a tattooed number from a Nazi concentration camp. 'We endured terror, beatings, torture, death!'

In another group a Negro boy lowered his collar. 'What about this?' he demanded, showing an ugly rope burn. 'Lynched for no crime but being black! We have suffocated in slave ships, been wrenched from loved ones, toiled till only death gave release.'

In another group, a young girl stared with sullen eyes. On her forehead was the stamp 'illegitimate'. 'To endure my stigma,' she murmured, 'was beyond, beyond . . .' and her voice trailed off, to be taken up by others.

Far out across the plain were hundreds of such groups. Each had a complaint against God for the evil and suffering he permitted in his world. How lucky God was to live in heaven where all was sweetness and light, where there was no weeping, no fear, no hunger, no hatred. Indeed, what did God know of what humanity had been forced to endure in this world? After all, God leads a pretty sheltered life, they said.

So each of these groups sent forth a leader, chosen because he had suffered the most. There was a Jew, a Negro, an untouchable from India, an illegitimate, a horribly deformed arthritic, a person from Hiroshima, and one from a Siberian slave camp. In the centre of the plain they consulted with each other. At last they were ready to present their case. It was rather simple. Before God would be qualified to be their judge, he must endure what they had endured. Their decision was that God should be sentenced to live on earth – as a man! But, because he was God, they set certain safeguards to be sure he could not use his divine powers to help himself:

Let him be born a Jew.

Let the legitimacy of his birth be doubted so that none will know who is really his father.

Give him a work so difficult that even his family will think he is out of his mind when he tries to do it.

Let him try to describe what no other man has ever seen, tasted, heard or smelled. Let him try to describe God to man.

Let him be betrayed by his dearest friends.

Let him be indicted on false charges, tried before a prejudiced jury, convicted by a cowardly judge.

At last, let him see what it means to be terribly alone, completely abandoned by every living thing.

Let him be tortured, and then let him die. Let him die so that there can be no doubt he died. Let there be a great host of witnesses to verify it.

As each leader announced his portion of the sentence, loud murmurs of approval went up from the great throng of people assembled. When the last had finished pronouncing sentence, there was a long silence.

Those who had spoken their judgement of God quietly departed. No one uttered a word. No one moved. For suddenly all knew. God had already served his sentence.

Source unknown

'Justice' was done, and the President of the Immortals, in Aeschylean phrase, had ended his sport with Tess.

Thomas Hardy: 'Tess of the D'Urbervilles', (1891), comment on the execution of Tess

The love of justice in most men is only the fear of suffering injustice . . .
Everyone complains of his memory but no one complains of his judgement.

Duc François de La Rochefoucauld, (1613–1680)

The rain it raineth on the just
And also on the unjust fella:
But chiefly on the just, because
The unjust steals the just's umbrella.

Lord Bowen (Walter Sichel, 1835–1894): 'Sands of Time'

It is simply not true that regenerated people as a matter of course act justly towards their neighbours. In my own country (South Africa), some of the worst racists are born-again Christians.

David Bosch: 'Missionalia', (April 1988)

Commenting on the translation of *dikaiosune* in the New Testament as *righteousness,* rather than its equally good rendering as *justice,* Lesslie Newbigin notes that it is easy to see why this 'has seduced evangelical Christians into a mental separation between *righteousness* as an inward and spiritual state and *justice* as an outward and political program. But to accept this dichotomy is to abandon the gospel and surrender to the pressure of our pagan culture.'

Lesslie Newbigin: 'Foolishness to the Greeks', (S.C.M, 1986)

A prisoner, protesting his innocence after being found guilty and sentenced, is said to have been told by the judge: 'These are not courts of justice, they are courts of law.'

Source unknown

K

Kindness

Matthew Gregory 'Monk' Lewis admitted to becoming emotional when anyone said anything kind to him. At Oatlands his eyes were red because the Duchess of York had said something *so* kind to him. 'Never mind, Lewis,' said Colonel Armstrong, 'never mind, don't cry. *She could not mean it.'*

James Stevenson, Ed: 'The Oxford Book of Literary Anecdotes', (1975)

On *Human Kindness Day,* 10 May, 1975, in Washington D.C., there were 600 arrests, 150 smashed windows, 42 looted refreshment stands, 17 stonings of uniformed officers, 33 fires, 120 cases of public brawling and 14 destroyed cars.

Miss Carol Kirkendall, a spokeswoman for the organisers, said that 'although sporadic rock-throwing, public mayhem and purse-snatchings had been a sadness, a lot of beautiful things were going on out there.'

Stephen Pile, Ed: 'The Return of Heroic Failures', (1988)

Kingdom of God (or of Heaven)

. . . should not our chief concern, like Jesus', be with the gospel *of the Kingdom* in which evangelism and social involvement, though different, are so intrinsically intertwined that it is futile to try to unravel them, and prioritise them? The holistic gospel of the Kingdom does not get tied up in post-enlightenment dualist knots, trying to answer unnecessary questions.

Our prayer, following the Master's, 'Your Kingdom come, your will be done on earth as it is in heaven' and our whole life in response to that *are of eternal* importance. The biblical doctrine of the resurrection of the body shows that eternal significance is given not just to 'spiritual' matters.

Graham Kings: 'Evangelicals in Search of Catholicity', Church Missionary Society Report, (1989)

God's kingdom is creation healed.

Hans Kung

Jesus put before the crowds another parable:

'The kingdom of heaven may be compared to someone who sowed good seed in his field; but while everybody was asleep, an enemy came and sowed weeds among the wheat, and then went away . . .'.

'The kingdom of heaven is like a mustard seed that someone took and sowed in his field; it is the smallest of all the seeds, but when it has grown it is the greatest of shrubs and becomes a tree, so that the birds of the air come and make nests in its branches . . .'.

'The kingdom of heaven is like yeast that a woman took and mixed in with three measures of flour until all of it was leavened . . .'.

'The kingdom of heaven is like treasure hidden in a field, which someone found and hid; then in his joy he goes and sells all that he has and buys that field . . .'.

'The kingdom of heaven is like a net that was thrown into the sea and caught fish of every kind . . .'.

'. . . every scribe who has been trained for the kingdom of heaven is like the master of a household who brings out of his treasure what is new and what is old.'

Matthew 13:24, 25, 31–33, 44, 47, 52

Jesus said to the seventy missionaries: Whenever you enter a town and its people welcome you, eat what is set before you; cure the sick who are there, and say to them, 'The kingdom of God has come near to you.' But whenever you enter a town and they do not welcome you, go out into its streets and say, 'Even the dust of your town that clings to our feet we wipe off in protest against you. Yet know this: the kingdom of God has come near.'

Luke 10:8–11

Knowledge – *see also* EDUCATION

And still they gazed, and still the wonder grew,
That one small head could carry all he knew.

Oliver Goldsmith, (1728–1774): 'The Deserted Village' [Writing of the schoolmaster-cleric; see also 'Preachers']

A *little learning* is a dang'rous thing;
Drink deep, or taste not the Pierian spring:
There shallow draughts intoxicate the brain,
And drinking largely sobers us again.

Alexander Pope (1688–1744)

The discovery of the uncertainty of knowledge must be made ever anew.

Heiko O. Oberman: 'Luther', (Yale, 1982–89)

Pious scholars are rare.

Blaise Pascal (1623–1662)

L

Laity

The laity has a ministry as real as that of the ordained ministry . . .

The fundamental lay ministry is to be a Christian, visibly and sometimes audibly, in the secular world. This *is* ministry.

Douglas Webster: 'Not Ashamed', (1970)

All professions are conspiracies against the laity.

George Bernard Shaw (1856–1950): 'The Doctor's Dilemma', (1906), Act I

Four priests were discussing the raising of Lazarus from death [John chapter 11] and why Christ asked the people to roll away the stone. They concluded that Jesus wanted to involve the laity.

Source unknown

Language, English as she is spoke

. . . it is easily possible to become pedantic about mixed metaphors and to forget that the English language is almost a graveyard of faded figures of speech.

W.E. Sangster: 'The Craft of Sermon Illustration', (1946)

The 'San Francisco Examiner' rejected a piece by Rudyard Kipling thus:
I'm sorry, Mr. Kipling, but you just don't know how to use the English language.

A chairman of a meeting to be addressed by Sir James Sexton, 'the Dockers' MP', at Hyde, Lancashire:
Comrades, list to the clarion call! The plank of progress is now ripe for plucking. Soon shall we see the Socialist avalanche descending from the mountain tops and, with its mailed fist, crushing beneath its iron heel the capitalist snake in the grass which is barring the progress of the flood-gates of democracy from walking hand-in-hand with the British lion over the rich fields of prosperity from which we draw the sweet milk of iron, coal, and cotton.

From Sir James Sexton: 'Agitator', cited by W.E. Sangster, (1946)

The evangelist of the 1960's disliked women in trouser-suits: 'I was walking through Manchester today,' one declared, 'and saw women wearing trousers. I wish I could have seen these women without them.'

Reported by the preacher, whose name the editor has forgotten

Richard Porson (1759–1808) regarded Gibbon's *Decline and Fall* as the greatest English work of the eighteenth century, yet is said to have suggested that 'there could not be a better exercise for a schoolboy than to turn a page of it into English.'

James Stevenson, Ed: 'The Oxford Book of Literary Anecdotes', (1975)

A fourteenth century monk complained about English speech, which he described as 'strange wlaffyng, chytering, harryng, and garrying grisbittyng' [strange stammering, chattering, snarling and grating tooth-gnashing].

A regulation about ground nuts says:
In the Nuts (unground), (other than ground nuts) Order, the expression 'nuts' shall have reference to such nuts, other than ground nuts, as would but for this amending Order not qualify as nuts (unground) (other than ground nuts) by reason of their being nuts (unground).

Stephen Pile, Ed.: 'The Return of Heroic Failures', (1988)

The best test of whether an Englishman can speak the language is to ask him to say 'Fire'.

Anonymous

Mrs. Crupp had indignantly assured him that there wasn't room to swing a cat there: but, as Mr. Dick justly observed to me, sitting on the foot of the bed, nursing his leg, 'You know, Trotwood, I don't want to swing a cat. I never do swing a cat. Therefore, what does *that* signify to me!'

Charles Dickens (1812–1870): 'David Copperfield'

Language, howlers, jargon, metaphor and political correctness

Examination howlers:
The Equator: a menagerie lion running round the earth through Africa.

From the U.S.A.and Britain

Blood circulates to the lower limbs by going down one leg and up the other.

From the U.S.A. and Britain

Water is composed of two gins, Oxygin and Hydrogin. Oxygin is pure gin, Hydrogin is gin and water.

From the U.S.A.

Vacuum: a large empty space where the Pope lives.

From the U.S.A.

The Fallopian Tube is named after the monk who first discovered it.

From Africa

Trees break wind for up to 200 metres.

From Britain

To prevent milk from going sour, keep it in the cow.

From the U.S.A.

A fossil is an extinct animal. The older it is, the more extinct it is.

From the U.S.A.
Joanna Bale: in The Times, (1996)

In memory of her late husband, Mrs. Laycock made a loving gift of oak clergy and choir stalls to match the existing panelling in the chancel.

Centenary Brochure of Christ Church, Blackpool, (1970)

Basic P.C.:

Differently-abled person (Handicapped person)
Temporarily-abled person (Able-bodied person)
Acceptional pre-woman (Backward girl)
Person of colour *or* Members of the African/Indian diaspora (Non-white persons)
Knowledge-base non-possessors (Ignorant persons)
Animal companion (Pet)
Unpaid sex worker (Wife)
Partner (Husband, wife, lover, mistress)
Domestic partner (As above but does the housework)
Significant sharer (Partner)
Coself (Himself/Herself)
Kindergarten students (Toddlers)
Sexually dysfunctional persons (Perverts)
Socially misaligned person (Serial killer)
Person of difficult-to-meet needs (Cannibal)
WASPs (White Anglo-Saxon Protestants)
DWEMs (Dead White European Males)
Motivationally dispossessed (Lazy)
Lookism (Noticing how someone looks)
Differently-sized (Fat)
Follicularly-challenged (Bald)
Cosmetically-different (Ugly)
Chronologically-gifted (Old)
Charm-free (Boring)
Correctional facility (Prison)
Impaired vertical clearance (Low bridge.)

From Henry Beard & Christopher Cerf: 'The Official Politically Correct Dictionary and Handbook', (Harper Collins, 1992)

Diplomatspeak is an international but tribal code of language perfected over centuries.

Full and frank exchange of ideas. (A row)
Businesslike (Cold and unfriendly.)
Matters of mutual interest (Areas where we disagree)
The Foreign Secretary expressed his concern (We don't like this one little bit)
With the full cooperation of our allies (This is one where we have gone it alone)
Protracted (This one will run and run)
Recalled for consultations (We're going to *get* you for this!)
A difficult situation (They're bombing our embassy)
It is well-known that . . . (Here comes another economy with the truth!)

Ariel, the B.B.C.'s in-house magazine, in August, 1992, had an advertisement for 'human resources assessment technologist corporate management development'.

The biota experienced a 100% mortality response. (All the fish died.)

Source unknown

You ask me what it is I do. Well actually, you know,
I'm partly a liaison man and partly P.R.O.
Essentially I integrate the current export drive
And basically I'm viable from ten o'clock till five.

Sir John Betjeman (1906–1984): 'Executive' from A Nip in the Air (1974 in John Betjeman's Collected Poems, Murray 1958)

A description of a group of elderly ladies at a prayer meeting:

They all wore funny hats and punctuated the meetings with 'Amens' and 'Hallelujahs' and a strange religious jargon from a bygone age, quite foreign to me . . . such phrases as 'O Lord, we lift so-and-so's leg up before thee' or 'O Lord, thou art the Great Undertaker!'

Andrew Maries: in 'David Watson', (1985)

The British Association was told:

In the meroblastic ova the biliminar blastoderm is discoid, but in the holoblastic vesicular.

Abergavenny Chronicle

This elderly geriatric female has multiple joint problems which limit perambulation. Absence of verbal intercourse aggravates her detachment from reality and reinforces isolationism. She is unable to relate to events at this point in time. Psychogeriatric consideration in the context of conceptual distortion, and paranoia is also a parameter in the total dimensions of her problems.

That is: this lady of 83 has arthritis, cannot get about, and is lonely, confused and frightened.

From the Guardian Weekly, (29 January, 1978); what Christopher Reed called 'psychobabble'

A traveller, with a horse and carriage, arrived at a hotel and gave the following instructions:
Extricate the quadruped from the vehicle as he has toiled strenuously ever since the golden orb appeared on the eastern horizon at break of day. Therefore, extend to him a munificent supply of nutritious victuals.

That is: The horse has worked hard all day. Please feed him well.

Anonymous

Mr Justice Staughton, a judge in the Commercial Court, wrote in the journal *Counsel* (1987) of his irritation at linguistic duplicity in courtrooms.

'With respect' means 'You are wrong'; 'With great respect' means 'You are utterly wrong'; 'With the utmost respect' means 'Send for the men in white coats'.

As the courtroom clock moves towards 1 pm, counsel might say: 'It might be of value to your Lordship if I were to inform you at this juncture that I have several more questions to ask of this witness which would take some little while.' The judge will reply: 'This seems a useful time to adjourn.' What they really mean is : 'Lunch?' 'Yes.'

Community Affairs delivers decentralised services with specific targeting and outreach techniques to achieve manifesto objectives. The front line interface with the public and community groups provides a catalyst input to services across the council, supporting initiatives in priority areas.

From the department of community affairs of a London Borough, (1987)

'In our approach to ultimate reality we tend to proceed either inductively or deductively,' said the professor of theology at a Korean mission.

The translator's version was more direct: 'I am here to tell you what Jesus Christ means to me.'

Retold by David H.C. Read: in the 'Lyman Beecher Lecture', (1974)

Jesus said unto them, 'Who do you say that I am?' And they replied, 'You are the eschatological manifestation of the Ground of our being; the kerygma manifested in conflict and decision-making in the humanising process.'

And Jesus said unto them, 'What did you say?'

Matthew 16:15, 16, (c 1972)

Real, generative, symbolising utilities aspiring to the elusiveness and transcendence of mutuality lead us to the true possibilities of meanings inherent in religions, decoded in the fertile excesses of organisational aims and objectives of atomised pastoral care structures.
(I wrote this down but I still don't know what it means!)

From a Clergy Conference lecture, (1995)

Reading one of Frances Bissell's recipes, I wonder what is a 'free-range hard-boiled egg'? Is it the one that rolled across the kitchen floor?
Yours faithfully, Joyse Wickes.

Letter to The Times Magazine, (January 1996)

'Is there any history of cardiac arrest in your family?' the doctor asked.
'Certainly not!' came the indignant reply. 'We never 'ad no trouble with the police.'

Sign in a Moscow Hotel:
If this is your first visit to Moscow, you are welcome to it.

(1976)

Language, theory

This thing here [a cricket bat] which looks like a wooden club, is actually several pieces of particular wood cunningly put together in a certain way so that the whole thing is sprung, like a dance floor. It's for hitting cricket balls with. If you get it right, the cricket ball will travel two hundred yards in four seconds, and all you've done is give it a knock like knocking the top off a bottle of stout, and it makes a noise like a trout taking a fly . . . *(He clucks his tongue to make the noise).* What we're trying to do is to write cricket bats, so that when we throw up an idea and give it a little knock, it might . . . *travel. (He clucks his tongue again and picks up the script of a badly-written play.)* Now, what we've got here is a lump of wood roughly the same shape trying to be a cricket bat, and if you hit a ball with it, the ball will travel about ten feet and you will drop the bat and dance about shouting 'Ouch!' with your hands stuck into your armpits. *(Indicating the cricket bat).* This isn't better because someone says it's better, or because there's a conspiracy by the M.C.C. to keep cudgels out of Lords. It's better because it's better.

Tom Stoppard: 'The Real Thing', (1982), Henry to Annie

Weasel words (eg. 'situation', 'parameter', 'objective', 'subjective') suck the meaning out of the words to which they are attached, as a weasel sucks eggs.
Chameleon words (eg. 'appropriate' or 'apposite') change their colour to conform to the prejudices of the reader or listener.
Existence words (eg. 'God exists') do not operate as 'action' verbs (eg. 'speak'), nor as 'quality' words (eg. 'wise'); existence is not an action, nor a perfection.

Various sources

A verb has a hard enough time of it in this world when it is all together. It's downright inhuman to split it up. But that's just what those Germans do. They take part of a verb and put it down here, like a stake, and they take the other part of it and put it away over yonder like another stake, and between these two limits they just shovel in German.

Mark Twain (1835–1910): Address to the Nineteenth Century Club, New York, (20 November, 1900)

I can't help somebody who thinks, or thinks he thinks, that editing a newspaper is censorship, or that throwing bricks is a demonstration while building tower blocks is social violence, or that unpalatable statement is provocation while disrupting the speaker is the exercise of free speech . . . Words don't deserve that kind of malarkey. They're innocent, neutral, precise, standing for this, describing that, meaning the other, so if you look after them you can build bridges across incomprehension and chaos. But when they get their corners knocked off, they're no good any more . . . I don't think writers are sacred, but words are. They deserve respect. If you get the right ones in the right order, you can nudge the world a little or make a poem which children will speak for you when you're dead.

Tom Stoppard: 'The Real Thing', (1982), Henry to Annie

There are two words which describe being alone:
'Loneliness' is a painful word;
'Solitude' is a glorious word.

Source unknown

There was a young curate of Kew
Who kept a tom cat in a pew;
He taught it to speak Alphabetical
  Greek,
but it never got further than μ
  [mew].
Said the curate, 'Dear Pussy, you
  know,
Is that really as far as you go?
If you only would try
You might get up to π, [pi]
Or even υ [upsilon] or ρ. [rho].'

Last things, The

Just because you don't know the meaning of 'eschatology', it's not the end of the world.

Anonymous

Murphy's Armageddon Observation: Those who don't learn from the past are condemned to write end time books.
Corollary: God doesn't read prophecy books.

Steve Dennis: 'Murphy Goes to Church', (I.V.F., 1993)

Last words

Die, my dear Doctor, that's the last thing I shall do!

Viscount Henry John Temple Palmerston (1784 – 1865), Prime Minister; also attributed to Spencer Perceval, assassinated in 1812

'What *is* the answer?'
After a short silence she laughed and added, 'In that case, what is the question?'

Last words of Gertrude Stein (1874 – 1946)

Charles II on his deathbed:
I am sorry, gentlemen, for being such a time a-dying.
(MacAulay, the 19th century historian, altered this to 'I am sorry, gentlemen, for taking such an unconscionable time a-dying.')

Why should I see her. She will only want me to give a message to Albert.

Last words of Benjamin Disraeli, referring to Queen Victoria, who had suggested visiting him, (1881)

Law and Lawyers

'If the law supposes that', said Mr Bumble . . . 'the law is a ass, a idiot.'

Charles Dickens (1812–70): 'Oliver Twist'

Sir John Latham, Chief Justice of the Australian High Court (1877–1964) was driving in Melbourne when he was caught contravening a traffic law. The Irish policeman asked him his name. 'John Latham,' he replied.

The constable said, 'You wouldn't be after being that same John Latham who is a barrister, now would you?'
'Yes. I am he.'
'And you wouldn't be after being that same John Latham who is the Commonwealth Attorney General?'
Sir John's hopes began to rise. 'Yes,' he said, 'I am he.'
'Well, you won't be able to plead ignorance of the law, now will you?'

Michael Gilbert, Ed: 'Oxford Book of Legal Anecdotes', (Oxford, 1986)

[America,] a country where there are almost as many lawyers as criminals . . .

Ben MacIntyre: in The Times, (13 December, 1993), Smart women buy perfect escort

Sir Henry Honeywood Curtis-Bennett, K.C., (1879–1936) advised:
If you are ever stopped by the police don't, for goodness sake, touch the car in any way, or you will be said to be leaning on it for support. Don't sway at all when you are walking, or you will be said to be staggering under the influence of drink. Spring smartly to attention. Stand upright outside the car, and say, 'I am not guilty of whatever you are about to charge me with doing.'

Michael Gilbert, Ed: 'Oxford Book of Legal Anecdotes', (Oxford, 1986)

Law, of God

The little word 'law' you must not understand in its human or everyday sense as applying to things you do or do not do. By human standards it is enough just to observe the law even though your heart may not be in it. Paul says that the law is spiritual. Since it is spiritual, no man keeps it unless everything he does comes from the bottom of his heart. But nobody has a heart like that. Only the Holy Spirit can give a man such a heart. Thus it comes about that faith alone justifies a man and fulfils the law, for faith brings the Holy Spirit through the merits of Christ.

Martin Luther

Knowledge of grace presupposes the law. Without the law there is no experience of the grace of God. Without the Sermon on the Mount there would be no Epistle to the Romans.

Emil Brunner

I'd give the Devil the benefit of law, for my own safety's sake.

Robert Bolt: 'A Man for all Seasons', (Thomas More)

God's precepts are light to the loving, heavy to the fearful.

Thomas Aquinas

Laws, of life

Parkinson's Law: Work expands so as to fill the time available for its completion.

C. Northcote Parkinson: (1957)

Jenning's Corollary: The chance of bread falling with the buttered side down is directly proportional to the cost of the carpet.

Peter's Principle: In a hierarchy, every employee tends to rise to his level of incompetence.

Lawrence J. Peter: (1969)

Murphy's Law: If something can go wrong, it will.

During World War II it was suggested to the War Office that, if the temperature of the Atlantic Ocean could be raised to boiling point, all the Nazi U-boats would have to surface and surrender! When asked how this was to be achieved, the source of the hot-tip replied: 'Don't ask me. I'm just paid to make the policy.'

Anonymous

Laziness

We cannot ever in this life be idle, for we must necessarily work, speak, deal with and exchange views with men, as Christ also, being made in the likeness of men, was found in human form as a man.

Martin Luther, (1489–1546): on Philippians 2

A police officer reprimanded a man caught kicking a tortoise. The man replied, 'But the stupid beast has been following me around all day!'

Quoted by Archbishop Stuart Blanch (of York); also quoted by Max Boyce as a man who stamped on a snail

Leadership

Citing Professor Gillian Stamp, 'Management is more about foreseeing and providing than overseeing and controlling,' Peter Baelz added: 'Responsibility flourishes in a soil of reciprocal trust. (I sometimes wonder whether, as a church, we are rather more concerned with not putting a foot wrong than we are with putting our best foot forward.)'

Address to the Governing Body of the Church in Wales, (15 April, 1993)

The leaders of the church are great compromisers, who cannot countenance rocking the boat. Sawing it in half has even less appeal . . . In their enthusiasm to acclaim the insights of the contemporary – no bad thing in itself – church leaders have failed to recognise their transience . . . The leadership of the church is no more and no less effective than the leadership of the other important institutions. This is because it is of the same manufacture. It shares the horror of critical thought that the 'safe men' have always demonstrated. Yet truth is advanced by testing and questioning. Without controversy there is stagnation . . . the 'safe men' run the church as they nearly always have done. But this has never prevented the prophets and the critics from telling them where to get off.

Edward Norman: in The Times, (1991), 'Siren voices from the pulpit'

Lent

In the third century church those to be baptised at Easter were required to spend the forty weekdays leading up to Easter in fasting, prayer and instruction.

Anonymous

When in 1863 Archbishop Longley complained to the Queen [Victoria] about the fact that the Prince of Wales was being married in the penitential season of Lent, she replied, 'In my young days there was no Lent.'

Robert E. Dolman: 'How Anglicans Turned Methodists into Dissenters', Lecture at Queen's College, Birmingham, (17 May, 1994)

Liberalism, in theology

P. T. Forsyth had begun his pilgrimage as a theological liberal but felt it was not enough:
Now we want to know what makes and keeps us free, and what we are free for.

A Muslim *earns* his place in paradise by displaying the Muslim virtues in life. Hence the importance of a high militant stand against sin, blasphemy, heresy.

In Christian eyes, redemption by faith and God's love are accessible to all sinners, and one must never assume a transgressor is lost beyond recall. While there is life, there is hope . . . But it also undergirds, in a sloppier, unfocussed form, the entire liberal philosophy of non-judgementalism.

Margot Lawrence: in the Daily Telegraph, (February 1990), 'The Bible said it best'

There are no liberals behind steering wheels.

Russell Baker: 'Poor Russell's Almanac', (1972)

A liberal is a conservative who's been mugged by reality.

Anonymous

If God had been a liberal, we wouldn't have had the Ten Commandments. We'd have had the Ten Suggestions.

Anonymous

Compulsion and Christianity! Why, the very terms are at variance with each other – the ideas are incompatible. In the language of Inspiration itself, Christianity has been called the 'Law of Liberty'.

William Wilberforce: in the House of Commons, (1813)

I was brought up puritanical: . . . Gradually, I began to see as I matured a little, rather vaguely, rather faintly and very slowly, that as I grew in grace I must be willing to change. I was in bondage to the legalism which Paul speaks about in Galatians. This is still with us in many circles, binding us, if we believe in the 'infallible Church', or the 'infallible book', or our 'infallible subjective self'. To me this last is perhaps the worst of all and does indicate a human pride which is not true nor right . . . Nevertheless, if you step out, you must expect much to be thrown at you. People distrust you, pulpits are closed to you because you are unsound in doctrine or not true to the Bible.

Bryan Green: in the Church Times: 'The manifesto of a liberated Evangelical', (11 January, 1991)

Jesus said, 'You have heard that it was said, "You shall love your neighbour and hate your enemy." But I say to you, Love your enemies and pray for those who persecute you, so that you may be children of your Father in heaven; for he makes his sun rise on the evil and on the good, and sends rain on the righteous and the unrighteous.'

Matthew 6:43–45

Liberation theology

The essential mark of a liberationist ecclesiology will be the making available of the Gospel texts to those without power in a form that is not filtered by the powerful. Put in this way one can see why an evangelical ecclesiology so naturally fits with a liberationist one. Making the unadulterated word available to the people is fundamental to evangelicalism.

. . . we must not underestimate the importance of evangelical support for the anti-slavery campaign and for the independence of the American Colonies. Social and political liberation belongs to our [evangelical] history.

Michael J. Williams: 'Socio-Political Aspects of the Theology of the Church', (1989)

Liberty

Licence they mean when they cry liberty.

John Milton (1608–74)

The condition upon which God hath given liberty to man is eternal vigilance; which condition if he break, servitude is at once the consequence of his crime, and the punishment of his guilt.

John Philpot Curran (1750–1817)

O Liberté! que de crimes on commet en ton nom! (O Liberty! What crimes are committed in your name!)

Madame Roland (Marie Jeanne Philipon, 1754–1793): remark on mounting the scaffold

Liberty is the luxury of self-discipline.

French saying

He is Jesus, Saviour[1], because he brings men out into a new spaciousness in every sense and term. He breaks through the false securities and shams and compensatory oppressions of human life in order that he may lead his new race out into the place of light and growth and expansion and enlargement. 'Salvation' means life at its highest level of experience. It means freedom from the cramping and confining limitations both of the world's prejudices and of our own timidities. The Hero-Saviour has won the decisive victory and thereby has brought near to man 'the glorious liberty of the children of God'.

F.W. Dillistone: 'Jesus and His Cross'

[1] 'Saviour', in Hebrew, is derived from a root which means 'to be spacious'.

Give me your tired, your poor,
Your huddled masses yearning to breathe free,
The wretched refuse of your teeming shore.
Send these, the homeless, tempest-tossed to me,
I lift my lamp beside the golden door.

Emma Lazarus: from 'The New Colossus' [Inscribed on the pedestal of the statue of Liberty, New York harbour]

Life

Lord Bowen (1835–94) in a speech at Baliol Hall, described the course of a busy life like that of an express train journey. You begin by taking a keen interest in all you see – your fellow-passengers and the view from the window. As the train gathers speed, the view loses its freshness and clarity as years come and go. The journey seems to be going on for ever and you are very comfortable but then you notice the train is slowing down and that you are approaching the terminus. You look up, and here is the official coming along to collect your ticket!

Michael Gilbert, Ed: 'The Oxford Book of Literary Anecdotes', (1986)

Life is one long process of growing tired.

Samuel Butler the Younger

Fear not that your life shall come to an end, but rather that it shall never have a beginning.

John Henry Newman

Life can only be understood backwards, but it must be lived forwards.

Søren Kirkegaard

Othello to Desdemona, who is sleeping, before he suffocates her:
Put out the light, and then put out the light:
If I quench thee, thou flaming minister,
I can again thy former light restore,
Should I repent me; but once put out thine,
Thou cunning pattern of excelling nature,
I know not where is that Promethian heat
That can thy light resume : when I have pluck'd the rose,
I cannot give it vital growth again,
It must needs wither;...

William Shakespeare (1564–1616): 'Othello', V.ii

And all our yesterdays have lighted fools
The way to dusty death. Out, out, brief candle!
Life's but a walking shadow, a poor player,
That struts and frets his hour upon the stage,
And then is heard no more; it is a tale
Told by an idiot, full of sound and fury,
Signifying nothing.

William Shakespeare (1564–1616): 'Macbeth', V.v.16

A reflection on life by one of King Edwin's chief advisers, about A.D. 627:
Your Majesty, when we compare the present life of man with that time of which we have no knowledge, it seems to me like the swift flight of a lone sparrow through the banqueting hall where you sit in the winter months to dine with your thanes and counsellors. Inside there is a comforting fire to warm the room; outside, the wintry storms of snow and rain are ranging. This sparrow flies swiftly in through one door of the hall, and out through another. While he is inside, he is safe from the winter storms; but after a few moments of comfort, he vanishes from sight into the darkness whence he came. Similarly, man appears on earth for a little while, but we know nothing of what went before this life and what follows. Therefore if this new teaching [Christianity] can reveal any more certain knowledge, it seems only right that we should follow it.

Bede (673–735): 'History of the English Church and People'

You know, Life – Life, is rather like opening a tin of sardines. We are all of us looking for the key. Some of us – some of us think we've found the key, don't we? We roll back the lid of the sardine tin of life, we reveal the sardines, the riches of Life therein, and we get them out, we enjoy them. But, you know, there's always a little piece in the corner you can't get out. I wonder – I wonder, is there a little piece in the corner of your life? I know there is in mine.

Alan Bennett: 'Beyond the Fringe', (1959)

Daniel O'Connell (1775–1847) became an extremely skilled and untiring cross-examiner, with a great knowledge of the wiles of some Irish witnesses in court! A story is told of him in which a witness in a case where a will had been forged after death, kept protesting that the testator 'had life in him' when the will was signed. Following up that hint, O'Connell eventually extracted the admission that the life in the deceased was a fly in his mouth!

Psychologists and others tell us that from 0–20 we are Egocentric
20–40 we are Familiacentric
40–60 we are Sociocentric
and that various themes dominate our lives in this order:

Childhood:	Hope
	Will
	Purpose
	Competence
	Fidelity
Young Adulthood:	Love
Adulthood:	Care
Maturity:	Wisdom.

Oh, isn't life a terrible thing, thank God?

Dylan Thomas: 'Under Milk Wood', (Dent, 1954)

We know that we have passed from death to life because we love one another. Whoever does not love abides in death.

1 John 3:14

This is the testimony: God gave us eternal life, and this life is in his Son. Whoever has the Son has life; whoever does not have the Son of God does not have life.

1 John 5:11, 12

Light

And we thank Thee that darkness reminds us of light.
O Light Invisible, we give Thee thanks for Thy great glory.

T.S. Eliot: Chorus X from The Rock from Selected Poems (Faber and Faber 1954)

The Reverend Sydney Smith (1771–1845) was a frequent visitor to the home of Samuel Rogers, the poet (1763–1855), and both were sharp-witted and sharp-tongued. Rogers had candles all round the dining room, high up, to show off the pictures.

Smith was asked how he liked the arrangement. 'Not at all; above, there is a blaze of light, and below, nothing but darkness and gnashing of teeth.'

Either we must confess our blindness and seek the opening of our eyes; or else we must accept the light and walk by it. What we may not do, yet all strive to do, is to keep our eyes half-open and live by half the light. That kind of sight holds us to our sin and our sin to us. But the only way of avoiding it is to look with eyes wide open upon ourselves and the world as the full light reveals it; but this is the surrender of faith, and pride resists it.

William Temple: 'Readings in St John's Gospel'

Jesus spoke to them [the people], saying, 'I am the light of the world. Whoever follows me will never walk in darkness but will have the light of life.'

John 8:12

You, beloved, are not in darkness, for that day [the day of the Lord] to surprise you like a thief; for you are all children of light and children of the day; we are not of the night or of darkness.

1 Thessalonians 5:4, 5

This is the message we have heard from him [Jesus Christ] and proclaim to you, that God is light and in him there is no darkness at all. If we say that we have fellowship with him while we are walking in darkness, we lie and do not do what is true; but if we walk in the light as he himself is in the light, we have fellowship with one another, and the blood of Jesus his Son cleanses us from all sin.

1 John 1:5–7

Whoever says, 'I am in the light,' while hating a brother or sister, is still in darkness. Whoever loves a brother or sister lives in the light, and in such a person there is no cause for stumbling. But whoever hates another believer is in the darkness, walks in the darkness, and does not know the way to go, because the darkness has brought on blindness.

1 John 2:9–11

Lord's Supper, The – *see* EUCHARIST

Love, what it is

Love, all alike, no seasoun knowes, nor clyme,
Nor houres, dayes, moneths, which are the rags of time.

John Donne (1572–1631): 'The Sunne Rising'

Love makes the world go 'round, and those in it a bit dizzy.

Anonymous

The only place where you can be safe from love is hell.

C. S. Lewis (1898–1963)

Love is love's reward.

John Dryden (1631–1700): 'Palamon and Arcite', II

It is impossible to love and be wise.

Francis Bacon (1561–1626): 'Of Love'

'Tis better to have loved and lost
Than never to have loved at all.

Alfred, Lord Tennyson (1809–1892): 'In Memoriam' XXVII

Samuel Butler (1835–1902) parodied these lines:
'Tis better to have loved and lost
Than never to have lost at all.

Love's not love
When it is mingled with regards that stand
Aloof from the entire point.

William Shakespeare (1564–1616): 'King Lear', I.i

Grant, O God, your protection; and in your protection, strength; and in strength, understanding; and in understanding, knowledge; and in knowledge, to know justice; and in knowing justice, to love it; and in loving, the love of all existence; and in the love of all existence, the love of God, of God and all goodness.

Ancient Welsh prayer

To love your enemies is frightening; it means wanting the best for the people who can hurt you worst and it makes you totally vulnerable.

Richard MacKenna: 'God for Nothing', (Churchman, 1984/85)

Feelings are not entirely ours to command. We are attracted towards some against our will, while towards others we can never experience a spontaneous affection. If we are moved solely by our feelings, that is not love. Real love means that we are still master of our acts, and we use our inclinations and attractions simply as guides in the direction which we choose to take. And the same is true when reason tells us what direction love must take. It is not reason which impels us to love, it is we ourselves who choose to love, taking reason as our guide.

Aelred of Rievaulx (1110–1163)

. . . the denigration of those we love always detaches us from them in some degree. Never touch your idols: the gilding will stick to your fingers.

Gustave Flaubert: 'Madame Bovary', 3:6, trans. Geoffrey Wall, 1992, (Penguin 1993)

The heart has its reasons
Which reason cannot know.

Blaise Pascal (1623–1662): 'Pensées', IV

My bicycle is called 'Charity': it's 'not puffed up'!

Anonymous reference to 1 Corinthians 13:4 (King James Version)

Heart-break is a far worse ailment than heart-failure.

Norman Autton, (1980)

I think continually of those who were truly great –
The names of those who in their lives fought for life,
Who wove at their hearts the fire's centre.

Stephen Spender: 'I Think Continually of Those'

Love, between people

She who has never lov'd, has never liv'd.

John Gay, (1685–1732): 'The Captives'

Love is like the measles; we all have to go through it.

Jerome K Jerome (1859–1927): 'Idle Thoughts, On Being in Love'

Who ever loved, that loved not at first sight?

Christopher Marlowe (1564–93): 'Hero and Leander', I, [quoted by William Shakespeare: As You Like It, III.v]

'You're a narcissist,' said the character in *Monty Python's Flying Circus*, coming across someone gazing rapturously in a mirror. 'No I'm not,' was the angry reply; 'a narcissist is someone who has a foolish infatuation with himself, but this is the real thing.'

The power of a glance has been so much abused in love stories, that it has come to be disbelieved in. Few people dare now to say that two beings have fallen in love because they have looked at each other. Yet it is in this way that love begins, and in this way only. The rest is only the rest and comes afterwards. Nothing is more real than these great shocks which two souls give each other in exchanging this spark.

Victor Hugo (1802–85): 'Les Miserables', III.iv

If thou must love me, let it be for
naught
Except for love's sake only.

Elizabeth Barrett Browning (1806–1861): 'Sonnets from the Portuguese', XIV

'You gave me the key to your heart,
my love;
Then why did you make me knock?'
'Oh, that was yesterday; saints above,
Last night I changed the lock.'

John Boyle O'Reilly (1844–1890): 'Constancy'

Yet each man kills the thing he loves,
By each let this be heard,
Some do it with a bitter look,
Some with a flattering word.
The coward does it with a kiss,
The brave man with a sword!

Oscar Wilde (1854–1900): 'The Ballad of Reading Gaol', (1896), I.vii

My bounty is as boundless as the sea,
My love as deep; the more I give to
thee
The more I have, for both are infinite.

William Shakespeare (1564–1616): 'Romeo and Juliet', II.ii

'Come, come,' said Tom's father, 'at
your time of life,
There's no longer excuse for thus
playing the rake –
It is time you should think, boy, of
taking a wife – '
'Why so it is, father – whose wife
shall I take?'

Thomas Moore (1779–1852): 'A Joke Versified'

Love that is not madness is not love.

Pedro Calderon de la Barca (1600–1681): 'El Mayor Monstruo los Zelos'

Where we really love, we often dread more than we desire the solemn moment that exchanges hope for certainty.

Anne Louise Germaine de Staël (1766–1817): 'Corinne', VIII.iv

Whom we love best, to them can we say least.

John Ray [or Wray] (1627–1705), Ed.: 'English Proverbs', (1670)

Love, and a cough, cannot be hid.

George Herbert (1593–1633): 'Jacula Prudentum'

Brutus, about Cassius, a one-time fellow conspirator in the murder of Julius Caesar, now turned enemy:
Thou hast describ'd
A hot friend cooling. Ever more,
Lucilius,
When love begins to sicken and decay
It useth an enforced ceremony.
There are no tricks in plain and
simple faith;
But hollow men, like horses hot at
hand,
Make gallant show and promise of
their mettle.

William Shakespeare: 'Julius Caesar', (1599), IV.ii.18–24

'Love never needs to say it's sorry' was the line made famous by the film *Love Story.* At the end of the film *What's Up Doc?* Barbara Streisand reminds Ryan O'Neal of this saying, to which he replies in the final line of that film: 'That's the dumbest thing I ever heard.'

Love, of God

Holding the beggar's child
Against my heart

Through blinding tears, I see
That as I hold the tiny, piteous thing
So God loves me.

Dr Kagawa

To him who is everywhere, men come not by travelling but by loving.

Augustine of Hippo, (354–430)

Father, as downland pond,
Fed by the visiting dews
Which every night respond
To what the days diffuse.
So, through the dark's deface,
Pooled may my spirit be;
Alembic of thy grace,
Thy love's distillery.

Thomas Browne (1605–82): 'An Evening Colloquy with God'

Ask nothing of God but the gift of love, which is the Holy Spirit. For all God's gifts there is none so good, so profitable, so worthy, so excellent as this. It is in this gift of love alone that God is both the giver and the gift.

Walter Hilton (died 1396)

I find myself caught up in what I can best, but inadequately, describe as a love affair with a 'mysterious artist'. 'Love affair' is not an adequate phrase because it is not simply – or even mainly – a matter of my 'being in love'. There is a very strong undertow of attracting, desiring and longing; but it is much more a matter of having a sense of being loved and, even more, of being given a chance of becoming involved in a love affair which is really about affairs of love which are meant to embrace, involve and fulfil everything. That is to say, one has a share in the love so that one may share in the loving – in the sense of extending it and enabling it to be more and more real. And the reason for trying to talk about 'a love affair with a mysterious *artist*' is that the whole business is to do with not merely sharing but actually building up that which is shared – and that which is to be shared. The work of the artist is nothing like finished. There is something to be created and someone, somehow, to be creative with.

Bishop David Jenkins (of Durham): 'God, Jesus and Life in the Spirit', (S.C.M., 1988)

Thy nature and thy name is Love.

Line repeated several times in Charles Wesley's hymn, 'Wrestling Jacob'

I am convinced that neither death, nor life, nor angels, nor rulers, nor things present, nor things to come, nor powers, nor height, not depth, nor anything else in all creation, will be able to separate us from the love of God in Christ Jesus our Lord.

Romans 8:38, 39

Beloved, let us love one another, because love is from God; everyone who loves is born of God and knows God. Whoever does not love does not know God, for God is love. God's love was revealed among us in this way: God sent his only Son into the world so that we might live through him. In this is love, not that we loved God but that he loved us and sent his Son to be the atoning sacrifice for our sins. Beloved, since God loved us so much, we also ought to love one another. No one has ever seen God; if we love one another, God lives in us and his love is perfected in us.

1 John 4:7–12

Love, for God

General Booth (founder of the Salvation Army): We must grow 'till our arms get right 'round the world.
Commented upon by Archbishop Donald Coggan in his Enthronement at Canterbury, (25 January, 1975):
Such an embrace will be costly. It will involve the abandonment of much that we have hitherto taken for granted. Our divisions [in the Church], will have to go . . . Our possessions will have to go . . . Our selfishness will have to go . . . Round the deprived millions our arms must go, and for that *we* must grow. Our most powerful arms will be the arms of prayer.

A story was told by Roy Pointer of meeting a Baptist Christian who told him that she'd been a Roman Catholic until she met some Baptists who loved her into the kingdom. Some weeks later, he met a Roman Catholic who told him that he'd been a Baptist until he met some Roman Catholics who loved him into the kingdom.

He prayeth best who loveth best

All things both great and small.

Samuel Taylor Coleridge (1772–1834): 'The Ancient Mariner', VII

Love bade me welcome: yet my soul drew back,
Guiltie of dust and sinne.
But quick-ey'd Love, observing me grow slack
From my first entrance in,
Drew nearer to me, sweetly questioning,
If I lack'd any thing.

'A guest,' I answer'd, 'worthy to be here.'
Love said, 'You shall be he.'
'I the unkinde, ungratefull? Ah my deare,
I cannot look on thee.'
Love took my hand, and smiling did reply,
'Who made the eyes but I?'

'Truth Lord, but I have marr'd them: let my shame
Go where it doth deserve.'
'And know you not,' sayes Love, 'who bore the blame?'
'My deare, then I will serve.'
'You must sit down,' sayes Love, 'and taste my meat.'
So I did sit and eat.

George Herbert (1593–1633): 'Love III'

It is only the man who loves God with all his being who will be able to love his neighbour as himself.

Archbishop William Temple (of Canterbury): 'Christus Veritas'

If I speak in the tongues of mortals and of angels, but do not have love, I am a noisy gong or a clanging cymbal . . .

Love is patient; love is kind; love is not envious or boastful or arrogant or rude. It does not insist on its own way; it is not irritable or resentful; it does not rejoice in wrongdoing, but rejoices in the truth. It bears all things, believes all things, hopes all things, endures all things. Love never ends. . . .

And now faith, hope, and love abide, these three; and the greatest of these is love.

1 Corinthians 13:1, 4–8a, 13

Luxury

. . . anything which costs more either in money, or in time, or vital energy than it contributes to his power of service [is for a Christian] a . . . culpable luxury.

Bishop Brooke Foss Wescott (of Durham)

M

Magic

Advice to anyone attending a magician's show:
Always watch the hand that's *not* performing the trick.

Management

Memorandum from Jordan Management Consultants, Jerusalem, to Jesus, son of Joseph, woodcrafter, Nazareth.
Dear Sir,
Thank you for submitting the résumés of the twelve men you have picked for management positions in your new organisation. All of them have now taken our battery of tests; we have not only run the results through our computer, but also arranged personal interviews for each of them with our psychologist and vocational aptitude consultant.

It is the staff opinion that most of your nominees are lacking in background, education and vocational aptitude for the type of enterprise you are undertaking. They do not have the team concept. We would recommend that you continue your search for persons of experience in managerial ability and proven capability.

Simon Peter is emotionally unstable and given to fits of temper.

Andrew has absolutely no qualities of leadership.

The two brothers, ***James and John***, the sons of Zebedee, place personal interest above company loyalty.

Thomas demonstrates a questioning attitude that would tend to undermine morale. We feel it is our duty to tell you that ***Matthew*** has been blacklisted by the Greater Jerusalem Better Business Bureau.

James, son of Alphaeus, and

Thaddaeus definitely have radical leanings, and they both registered a high score on the manic-depressive scale.

One of the candidates, however, shows great potential. He is a man of ability and resourcefulness, meets people well, has a keen business mind and has contacts in high places. He is highly motivated, ambitious and responsible. We recommend ***Judas Iscariot*** as your controller and right-hand man.

All the other profiles are self-explanatory.

We wish you success in your new venture.

Marriage

Dining with the Duchess of Marlborough, Bishop Gilbert Burnet (1643–1715) compared her (disgraced) husband, once a great general, to Belisarius. 'But,' replied the Duchess, 'how came it that such a man was so miserable and universally deserted?'
'Oh, madam,' exclaimed the prelate, 'he had such a brimstone of a wife.'

G.M. Trevelyan, in choosing to thank God for King Henry VIII (the founder of Trinity College, Cambridge), rather than his daughter, Queen Mary Tudor, commented, 'It's better to marry than to burn *(I Corinthians 7:9)*.

When you're a married man, Samivel, you'll understand a good many things as you don't understand now; but vether it's worth while goin' through so much to learn so little, as the charity-boy said when he got to the end of the alphabet, is a matter o' taste.

Charles Dickens (1812–70): 'Pickwick Papers'

Kissing don't last: Cookery do!

George Meredith (1828–1909)

Advice to persons about to marry – don't.

Punch Magazine, (1845)

A young man *married* is a young man *marred.*

William Shakespeare: 'All's Well that Ends Well', II.iii.315 [Also quoted by Rudyard Kipling in 'The Story of the Gadsbys']

Marriage in the law of this country is the union of one man with one woman, voluntarily entered into for life, to the exclusion of all others.

H.M. Register Offices: 'Notice to all couples to be married'

Marriage helps a man appreciate the wonders of the human voice. Every husband notices it the moment his wife stops scolding him to pick up the telephone.

Youth group leader to discussion group: 'What's the purpose of marriage?'
14 year old choirboy: 'Well, the marriage service says, Have kids, be happy and don't get divorced too soon.'

Source unrevealed

During a prayer after banns of marriage were read at St John's, Hebburn-on-Tyne:
We pray that they may have wisdom in the conduct of all their affairs.

It is said that mistletoe was abandoned in the Christmas decking of churches, together with kissing at the services, because both were found to encourage a frivolous view of marriage. Holly was substituted to indicate the dark monotony of marriage and the many thorns with which it abounds.

Canon Chasuble: The precept as well as the practice of the Primitive Church was distinctly against matrimony.
Miss Prism: That is obviously the reason why the Primitive Church has not lasted up to
the present day.

Oscar Wilde: 'The Importance of Being Ernest', (1895), Act 2

Who marrieth for love without money hath good nights and sorry days.

John Ray [or Wray] (1627–1705), Ed.: 'English Proverbs', (1670)

Another name for marriage is 'Holy Acrimony'.

Child's comment

Christians have only one marriage-partner. This is called monotony.

Child's comment

Ah Mozart! He was happily married – but his wife wasn't.

Victor Borge

Marriage is not a word but a sentence.

Anonymous

It has been said that a bride's attitude towards her betrothed can be summed up in three words: Aisle, Altar, Hymn.

Quoted by Frank Muir

Lord Russell of Killowen (Charles Russell, 1832–1900), a former Lord Chief Justice, was asked what was the maximum punishment for bigamy. Without hesitation, he replied: 'Two mothers-in-law.'

Michael Gilbert, Ed: Oxford Book of Legal Anecdotes, (Oxford, 1986)

Marriage is a woman's way of calling a meeting to order.

Anonymous

John Dryden (1631–1700), author and playwright, did not get on well with his wife, Lady Elizabeth. Thinking herself neglected, she exclaimed: 'Lord, Mr Dryden, how can you always be poring over those musty books? I wish I were a book, and then I should have more of your company.' 'Pray, my dear,' replied Dryden, 'if you do become a book, let it be an almanac, for then I shall change you every year.'

James Sutherland, Ed.: 'Oxford Book of Literary Anecdotes', (1975)

A College Professor, delivering a graduation address gave this advice to his listeners: Gentlemen, most of you will marry. Let me entreat you to love your wives. Be patient with them. When you are going out together, do not fret if she is not ready on time. Have a good book nearby. Read it while you wait. And, gentlemen, I assure you that you will be astonished at the amount of information you will acquire!

Source unknown

Before, when you were just engaged you felt you could eat her. Now you are married you wish you had.

Old saying

The great thing I always desired to find was a woman who was a real Christian, who was a real lady, and who was not a fool. Whether I was successful or not, others must judge better than I can, but I call God to witness that these were the points I kept steadily in mind.

Bishop John Charles Ryle (of Liverpool, 1876–1900)

A man is in general better pleased when he has a good dinner upon his table, than when his wife talks Greek.

Samuel Johnson (1709–1784): 'Miscellanies'

One good turn gets most of the duvet.

Anonymous

Be subject to one another out of reverence for Christ.

Wives, be subject to your husbands as you are to the Lord. For the husband is head of the wife just a Christ is head of the church, the body of which he is the Saviour. Just as the church is subject to Christ, so also wives ought to be, in everything, to their husbands.

Husbands, love your wives, just as Christ loved the church and gave himself up for her ... In the same way, husbands should love their wives as they do their own bodies . . . 'For this reason a man will leave his father and mother and be joined to his wife, and the two will become one flesh.'

Ephesians 5:21–25, 28, 31

Wives, be subject to your husbands, as is fitting in the Lord. Husbands, love your wives and never treat them harshly.

Colossians 3:18, 19

Martyrdom – *see* WITNESS

Mary, the Virgin

When Mary heard she was to be the mother of Jesus, she sang the 'Magna Carta'.

Child's comment

In a village church of the Dordogne, one meets a warm welcome and a hideous wooden reredos on the east wall. Dominating this 'period piece', dating from a time when Roman Catholicism in France was asserting itself against what it considered to be the twin evils of Protestantism and atheism, are enormous figures of the Virgin and Child. Mary is clearly the important figure with a crown on her head, but the curly-haired, active toddler she carries (paying scant attention to him) seems desperate to get away and have fun. Each time I see it, I am reminded of the Church's tendency to crown herself (with a 'catholic' or a 'charismatic' tiara) and to hang on to the Lord in the hope that he won't wander off.

Robert M.E. Paterson, (1996)

In response to the angel Gabriel announcing to Mary that she would conceive Jesus, the Son of the Most High:
Mary said, 'Here am I, the servant of the Lord; let it be with me according to your word.'
And when greeted by Elizabeth, who was then in the late stages of pregnancy:
Mary said,
'My soul magnifies the Lord, and my spirit rejoices in God my Saviour, for he has looked with favour on the lowliness of his servant.
Surely, from now on all generations will call me blessed;
for the Mighty One has done great things for me, and holy is his name.
His mercy is for those who fear him from generation to generation.
He has shown strength with his arm;
he has scattered the proud in the thoughts of their hearts.
He has brought down the powerful from their thrones, and lifted up the lowly;
he has filled the hungry with good things, and sent the rich away empty.
He has helped his servant Israel, in remembrance of his mercy,
according to the promise he made to our ancestors,
to Abraham and to his descendants for ever.'

Luke 1:38, 46–55

Simeon blessed them [the Holy Family] and said to his mother Mary, 'This child is destined for the falling and the rising of many in Israel, and to be a sign that will be opposed so that the inner thoughts of many will be revealed – and a sword will pierce your own soul, too.'

Luke 2:34, 35

[Jesus'] mother and his brothers came to him, but they could not reach him because of the crowd. And he was told, 'Your mother and your brothers are standing outside, wanting to see you.' But he said to them, 'My mother and my brothers are those who hear the word of God and do it.'

Luke 8:19–21

When the fulness of time had come, God sent his Son, born of a woman, born under the law, in order to redeem those who were under the law, so that we might receive adoption as children. And because you are children, God has sent the Spirit of his Son into our hearts, crying, 'Abba! Father!' So you are no longer a slave but a child, and if a child then also an heir, through God.

Galatians 4:4–7

Materialism

Every other country scorns American materialism while striving in every big and little way to match it.

Alistair Cooke: 'America', (1973)

Christianity and most other distinctive Western traditions are mistrusted [by advocates of the New Age movements] because they are associated with the materialist waste land into which we are said to have strayed.

Bryan Appleyard: in The Times, (17 June, 1992), 'The Selling of the New Age'

[Jesus told the crowd a parable]: The land of a rich man produced abundantly. And he thought to himself, 'What should I do, for I have no place to store my crops?' Then he said, 'I will do this; I will pull down my barns and build larger ones, and there I will store all my grain and my goods. And I will say to my soul, "Soul, you have ample goods laid up for many years; relax, eat, drink, be merry."' But God said to him, 'You fool! This very night your life is being demanded of you. And the things you have prepared, whose will they be?' So it is with those who store up treasures for themselves but are not rich toward God.

Luke 12:16–21

Maturity

The full realisation of one's immaturity.

Robert M.E. Paterson

The ability to cope with uncertainty.

Anonymous

To discover self while remaining selfless.

Liz Pettit

Media

A bishop and a chief rabbi were in a boat on the Sea of Galilee when a wind blew up and the rabbi's skull cap was blown into the water. The bishop got out of the boat, walked over the water and collected the cap, returning it to its owner. A reporter with a powerful camera lens was on the shore. The following day, the headlines in the newspaper read: 'BISHOP CAN'T SWIM'.

Bishop David Jenkins (of Durham)

Freedom of the press in Britain is freedom to print such of the proprietor's prejudices as the advertisers don't object to.

Hannah Swaffer (1879–1962): in conversation with Tom Driberg, (c 1928)

Report in The Times on a House of Lords debate on 26 April 1989:
Lord Ardwick [a retired sub-editor] seemed to know a bit about the people. 'The wages of sin,' he told their Lordships, 'is increased circulation.'

Matthew Parris: in The Times, 'Commons Sketch'

Lord Riddell is said to have told Frederick Greenwood that he owned the newspaper *News of the World* and, later, to have sent him a copy. On the next occasion they met, Riddell asked Greenwood for his opinion: 'I looked at it,' replied Greenwood, 'and then I put it in the wastepaper basket. And then I thought, 'If I leave it there the Cook may read it' – so I burned it!'

James Sutherland, Ed: 'The Oxford Book of Literary Anecdotes'

Dean Inge (1860–1954), after his retirement, became a regular contributor to a London newspaper and used to comment that he had once been a pillar of the church but was now just two columns in the *Evening Standard.*

Source unknown

[A newspaper is] a device unable to discriminate between a bicycle accident and the collapse of civilisation.

George Bernard Shaw (1856–1950)

On arriving in New York, Archbishop Michael Ramsey was asked by a reporter, 'Will you be going to any night clubs, Archbishop?'

With typical impish humour, he replied, 'Are there any night clubs in New York?' The headline the following day was 'Archbishop asks: ARE THERE ANY NIGHT CLUBS IN NEW YORK?'

Source unknown

It used to be said that the B.B.C. was 'an organisation for retired philosophers'.

Anonymous

Mediator

. . . this doctrine that Christ died 'for our sins' must be regarded as one of the oldest and most original pieces of Christian doctrine. It cannot be pushed aside or reduced to a shadow. In it is contained the important truth that Jesus Christ cannot simply be regarded as a teacher and a paradigm; he must be something more, a mediator, somebody who reconciles us to God, not only by his words and example, but by his very person.

A.T. & R.P.C. Hanson: 'The Identity of the Church', (S.C.M., 1987)

There is one God;
there is also one mediator between
God and humankind,
Christ Jesus, himself human,
who gave himself a ransom for all.

1 Timothy 2:5, 6

Memory

'Tis distance lends enchantment to the view.

Thomas Campbell (1777–1844): 'Pleasures of Hopes'

A retentive memory may be a good thing, but the ability to forget is the true token of greatness.

Elbert Hubbard: 'The Notebook', (1927)

They shall grow not old, as we that are left grow old. Age shall not weary them, nor the years condemn. At the going down of the sun and in the morning we will remember them.

Laurence Binyon (1869–1943): 'Poems for the Fallen'

Men

On the far flung field of battle,
In the bivouac of life,
You will find the Christian soldier
Represented by his wife.

Anonymous

The male is a domestic animal which, if treated with firmness and kindness, can be trained to do most things.

Jilly Cooper: in Cosmopolitan Magazine, (1972)

Mercy – *see also* JUSTICE

He reminds me of the man who murdered both his parents, and then, when sentence was about to be pronounced, pleaded for mercy on the grounds that he was an orphan.

Abraham Lincoln

John Newton, the slave-trader, in the story of his life, told how he had cried, 'almost without meaning, . . . "If this will not do, the Lord have mercy on me." . . . This was the first desire I had breathed for mercy for the space of many years.' He found that his blasphemy ceased and that he could pray.

Portia to Shylock:
The quality of mercy is not strain'd;
It droppeth as the gentle rain from heaven
Upon the place beneath. It is twice blest;
It blesseth him that gives and him that takes.
'Tis mightiest in the mightiest; it becomes
The thronèd monarch better than his crown;
His sceptre shows the force of temporal power,
The attribute to awe and majesty,
Wherein doth sit the dread and fear of kings;
But mercy is above this sceptred sway,
It is enthronèd in the heart of kings,
It is an attribute of God himself;
And earthly power doth then show likest God's
When mercy seasons justice. Therefore, Jew,
Though justice be thy plea, consider this –
That in the course of justice none of us
Should see salvation; we do pray for mercy,
And that same prayer doth teach us all to render
The deeds of mercy.

William Shakespeare: 'The Merchant of Venice', IV.i.179–197

Wherefore have mercy upon me, O Lord, whose property is always to have mercy; for although my sins be great, yet thy mercy is greater.

Part of the final prayer of Archbishop Thomas Cranmer (of Canterbury) before his execution at the stake in Oxford, on 21 March 1556
[The expression, 'whose property is always to have mercy', appears in the 'Prayer of Humble Access' of Cranmer's Prayer Books of 1549 and 1552 and subsequent editions]

All occasions invite his mercies, and all times are his seasons.

John Donne (1571–1631)

Your theology wasn't happy about the idea of mercy and forgiveness, which only gave comfort to enemies, and so, although you recited the Lord's Prayer every Sunday, you remembered your debtors and managed not to speak to certain people – a major feat when you live in a town so small and attend the same church as they, an act of true dedication.

Garrison Keillor: 'Lake Wobegon Days', 1985, News, '95 Theses 95'

Speak and so act as those who are to be judged by the law of liberty. For judgement will be without mercy to anyone who has shown no mercy; mercy triumphs over judgement.

James 2:12, 13

Merit

Buddhists, like Christians, believe that actions in this life affect the future life: they differ in that good actions to the Buddhist are the way of storing up eternal merit, they talk of 'making merit' by good actions. A Buddhist monk reckons he's doing a lot of good by begging because he sees that as giving other people opportunities to earn merit. The Christian sees good deeds as his least duty because he recognises he has been redeemed by God. The first move for the Christian is God's.

Anonymous

A parking space . . . is the most prayed-for concept in Christian theology. Believed to be a kind of Nirvana-like state wherein are focused all kinds of accumulated hopes and fears. Confusion with Eastern thinking often creeps in here because even though Christian theology allows no sense of deserving special treatment – when it comes to the parking space it is sometimes felt that one is 'owed' one, considering that you were just pipped at the post for the last two spaces and you really are in a terrific hurry to get on with the Lord's work.

Martin Wroe, Adrian Reith, Simon Parkes: 'The Church-English Dictionary', (1991)

Methodism

We have the character of Methodism complete: It is Christian godliness without Christian order.

William Jones of Nayland: 'The Life of George Horne', (1830)

The grand breach [with Anglicanism] is now between the regular and irregular clergy.

John Wesley: Letter to James Rouquet, (20 March, 1761)

John Wesley was forced to take the gospel 'into the fields', a practice he strongly disliked, on Monday 2 April, 1739, in a brick field near what is now Temple Meads Station, Bristol. His Journal records:

At four in the afternoon, I submitted to be more vile and proclaimed in the highways the glad tidings of salvation . . . The scripture on which I spoke was this, The Spirit of the Lord is upon me, because he hath anointed me to preach the Gospel to the Poor.[1]

William Webb was present and wrote this account 50 years later:

I went to the place appointed out of curiosity, and heard that great and good man; but with much uneasiness all the time, not knowing what was the matter with me; nor could I relate to any part of the sermon, being much confused in my mind and filled with astonishment at the minister. For I had never seen such proceedings before, it being quite a new thing to preach in the open air and not in Church or Chapel. This was the first sermon Mr. Wesley preached in Bristol. When it was ended I was induced to follow him, but, at the same time, knew not why I did so, being shut up in ignorance and gross darkness, through the multitude of my sins and the hardness of my heart.[2]

Comparing Western religion with Mid-Eastern aspirations:

I wonder what a Methodist homeland would be like – mandatory stay-pressed shirts, federal regulations about keeping feet off furniture and automatic death penalty for anybody with crab grass in his lawn.

P.J. O'Rourke: 'Holidays in Hell', (1988)

Mind, The

It hath been thought a vast commendation of a painter to say his figures seem to breathe; but surely it is a much greater and nobler applause, that they appear to think.

Henry Fielding: Preface to 'Joseph Andrews', (1742)

For a journey into the undefined
The mind
Should not be overweight.

From a U.S.P.G. Missionary's prayer, 'For a missionary packing', quoted in full in John Carden: 'Another Day', (Triangle – S.P.C.K., 1986)

The Christian mind has succumbed to the secular drift with a degree of weakness and nervelessness unmatched in Christian history. It is difficult to do justice in word to the complete loss of intellectual morale in the twentieth-century Church. One cannot characterise it without having recourse to language which will sound hysterical and melodramatic. There is

[1] *Wesley's Journal*, (Epworth Press), i. 173.

[2] Etheridge: *The Life of Adam Clarke*, (London, 1858).

no longer a Christian mind. There is still, of course, a Christian ethic, a Christian practice, and a Christian spirituality . . . But as a *thinking* being, the modern Christian has succumbed to secularisation.

Harry Blamires: 'The Christian Mind', (1963)

It is a solemn thought that by our anti-intellectualism, in which we either refuse or cannot be bothered to listen to God's word, we may be storing up for ourselves the judgement of Almighty God . . . Perhaps the current mood (cultivated in some Christian groups) of anti-intellectualism begins now to be seen as the serious evil it is. It is not true piety at all but part of the fashion of the world and therefore a form of worldliness.

John R W Stott: 'Your Mind Matters', (1972)

In an age when attitudes to knowledge are strung out between technicians and fanatics, between knowledge-eunuchs and knowledge-hustlers, the distinctive Christian mind – sharp, objective and critical, but committed and worshipping – is all too rare.

Os Guinness: in 'The Mind on Fire', Blaise Pascal, Ed. J.M. Houston, (1989)

The problem is not only to win souls but to save minds. If you win the whole world and lose the mind of the world, you will discover that you have not won the world. Indeed it may turn out that you have actually lost the world.

Charles Malik: 'The Two Tasks', (Westchester, 1990)

We may preach with all the fervour of a reformer, and yet succeed only in winning a straggler here and there, if we permit the whole collective thought of the nation or of the world to be controlled by ideas which, by the resistless force of logic, prevent Christianity from being regarded as anything more than a harmless delusion . . . What is today a matter of academic speculation, begins to-morrow to move armies and pull down empires.

J. Gresham Machen: 'Christianity and Culture', (Princeton Theological Review 11, 1913)

Ministry, theory – *see also* SERVICE

Ministry is the vocation of the whole people of God to live out their baptism into Christ's death and resurrection. Quite simply, it is to be him in his world.

For this there is no mysterious technique to be mastered: rather it is to be what we were created to be. Jesus is honoured as perfect man not because he turned his back on humanity, but because he embraced it with a thoroughness none of us have dared to equal . . .

For at the centre of all ministry there must be passion. Jesus wept. While ministry involves that total commitment to life which led Jesus to be condemned as a glutton and a wine-bibber, its very vulnerableness leads to suffering . . .

Ministry then can never be comfortable. The words come cold and cheerless, and we prefer to ignore them: Take up your cross and follow me. Ministry has to be lived out in the tension of being stretched out on that bloodied wood. It is not a path for those who do not want to be troubled. It is based on painful failure.

But to look for any other way than the way of suffering is to mistake the very nature of God who bids us follow. Ministry then is not about exercising power but surrendering all that one has and is to the transforming love of him whose essential characteristic is his powerlessness. That is the risk to which the disciple is invited.

Anthony Phillips: The Times, (11 July, 1987)

. . . a bishop's principal responsibility was the proclamation of the gospel. The word of God spoken, heard, thought about, obeyed and continually re-expressed in actions as in words, gives meaning and reality to the life of the Church and of the individual Christian . . . It is only by their correct understanding and communication of the gospel that they (the church's ministers) can hope to build a Christian community. Attempts to make the church work simply by clever organisation or ritual performance may have some success

Ministry Mix for Effective Churches

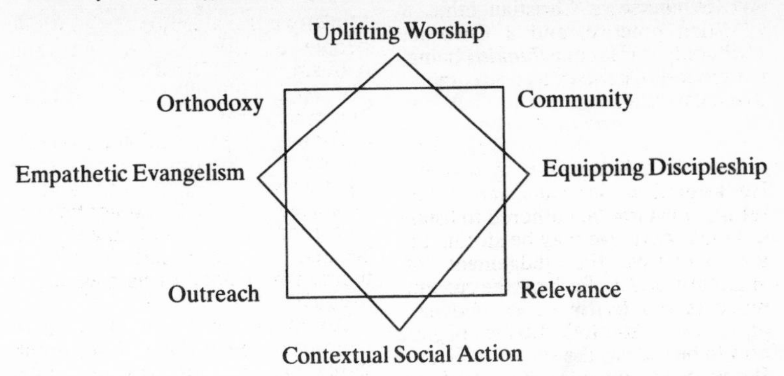

Donald C Posterski & Irwin Barker: 'Where's a Good Church?', (Wood Lake, 1993)

but they do not generate an authentic Church.

Canon Michael Richards: in The Times, (1 August, 1987)

Whatever each individual can do with his own power should not be done by the community: whatever the subordinate community and authority do not do, the supreme community has no need to do. The behaviour of the community in regard to the individual, and that of the superior community in regard to the subordinate community, is subsidiarity. This is the meaning of the principle of subsidiarity, which allows as much liberty as possible and as much association as necessary. But this implies, too, that the community has no right to shut itself off like a sect. Its autonomy is not absolute, but in many ways relative, inasmuch as subsidiarity carries with it an obligation to solidarity, to a solidarity with other communities, with the regional church and the universal church.

Hans Kung: 'Why Priests?'

To each is given the manifestation of the Spirit for the common good . . .

Just as the body is one and has many members, and all the members of the body, though many, are one body, so it is with Christ . . .

Now you are the body of Christ and individually members of it.

1 Corinthians 12:7, 12, 27

He who descended is the same one who ascended far above all the heavens, so that he might fill all things. The gifts he gave were that some would be apostles, some prophets, some evangelists, some pastors and teachers, to equip the saints for the work of ministry, for building up the body of Christ, until all of us come to the unity of the faith and of the knowledge of the Son of God, to maturity, to the measure of the full stature of Christ.

Ephesians 4:10–13

Ministry, every member

. . . in the apostolic church ministry is essentially a group activity. It is never seen as a solitary job and there is nothing monarchical about it.

Douglas Webster: 'Not Ashamed', (1970)

. . . the main work of Christ's church will be done by the witness of the faithful laity. But if that witness is to be intelligent and infectious, it will demand an adequate supply of full-time, well equipped, highly qualified clergy whose primary task will be to train the front line troops for their warfare.

Archbishop Dr F. Donald Coggan: 'Enthronement at Canterbury', (25 January, 1975)

A Very Incompetent Rector – By a Veteran of the Vestry:
This will have to be anonymous because I don't want to hurt our rector's feelings. I am very fond of him as a man and as a friend, but his incompetence as a priest is something else. It first surfaced soon after he had arrived. We were ready to have our Every-Member Canvass organised. The previous rector had devoted a lot of time to that – he made sure every detail was just the way he wanted it. But, for the last two or three years, things had been drying up, and we hoped the new rector was going to bring some new ideas and some new approaches. Did he? He didn't bring a thing! He did not seem to know what an Every-Member Canvass was all about. So two members of the vestry took the whole thing in hand that year. They worked so hard that the parish income was increased by fifteen per cent.

After showing the new rector how to do it, they naturally assumed he would get it all organised the next year; but, when the time came, he had hardly done anything. So our two vestrymen put their shoulders to the wheel once more. Again a fifteen per cent increase.

They swore they would never do it again, but somehow or other it worked out that way. So, when our parish was named at the diocesan convention as being in the top five for stewardship in the diocese, this is why it was. It had nothing to do with the rector.

Then there was Christian education. Our older rector had been a great one for Sunday school. He selected the teachers and told them exactly what to teach. Our Sunday school was very small in those days, but he said quality, not quantity, was what counted.

When our present rector came, he couldn't get it together. He asked the vestry to establish a Christian education committee, and, since he couldn't seem to train the teachers himself, he had them all go to a diocesan training conference. They reorganised our programme, and it did get off the ground.

For some reason they couldn't seem to keep it small any more. Finally they said they couldn't handle it between services on Sunday morning. That was a blow, although it finally did work out all right. We moved the whole Christian education operation to Tuesday night.

We usually have Evensong, then classes for both kids and adults. There are refreshments at the end for those who want to stay. Some of us older folks usually sit around for three-quarters of an hour or so afterwards. We call it the Tuesday Night Club.

Our rector didn't have much of what you would call social sense, but his wife always seemed to know how to make it a party. She still comes almost every week. The week before last was the senior warden's birthday. He brought some champagne and we put on some records and danced until past 11, but that is another story.

Our present Christian education programme is strictly the result of popular initiative. Our rector in fact said so himself. That is one thing about him: he was always an honest man. Then there was the pastoral calling. In spite of his being lame in one leg, he got around very well. I never heard people complain that he was not calling on the sick or shut-ins. He was the one who complained himself.

He said there were five different hospitals within a thirty-mile radius where different members of the parish went when they were sick, and he also showed the vestry a list of Episcopalians he had found in nursing-homes, in the State asylum, and even in the prison. I must say I had never heard of most of those people before. Anyhow, the vestry encouraged him to get together a group of people to do pastoral calling. They had some training sessions with some people from other parishes in our deanery. Now they do a lot of the calling. It seems like an odd system to me. Of course the rector or the deacon continued to bring Holy Communion and that sort of thing.

Now about the deacon: that was a real surprise to me. Judge Hardapple has been a deacon in the Baptist Church ever since I can remember, but that seems to be different. I never knew we had deacons in the Episcopal Church, but when I heard about it I was all for it. Anyhow, it would be better than having a curate, which we could hardly afford, even with increased income, now that we are supporting that missionary project.

Anyhow, with the rector's inability to do so many things, it was obvious he had to have help. Several of us agreed that Charlie Mendoza was the right guy. He had always given a lot of time to the church, and he worked with the Scouts – one more thing our rector didn't seem to know how to do. He also trained the acolytes – many of the same kids – since you-know-who never seemed to get that done either.

Charlie is not the sort of guy to spend much time with books, if you see what I mean; and our rector, as I have said, probably wouldn't know how to teach a cat to drink cream. You could have knocked me over with a feather when the bishop told everyone that, out of the whole group who took examinations to become deacons, Mendoza got the highest grade!

The previous rector was a great one at reading the Bible lessons in the service. We all loved to hear him. Our present rector seemed to have a good voice, but he said he had to save it for his sermon. So we had to have lay readers do the Old Testament lessons and epistles. Since Charlie was ordained, he always reads the gospel.

Our parish had never had lay-people do these readings before, and I guess we were pretty terrible. So a training course was started. A professor from the Lutheran college gave us some talks on the meaning of St Paul's Epistles, and a teacher from the high school, one of our own parishioners, trained us in speaking more clearly. I have to admit it was useful. Anyhow, the rector then preached. Now his sermons were really pretty good – although they certainly should have been, since he himself admitted that he had to start working on them four or five days ahead. Even so, he couldn't seem to handle it always, for he had Charlie preach about once a month. Sometimes he had lay-people do it too. I don't know whether that is really legal in the Episcopal Church, but folks didn't seem to mind. Once he even had four different people speak for three minutes each on what they thought the gospel meant that Sunday! I could go on to tell you quite a few other strange things that were done in the past several years here, but you probably get the picture.

Then there was that Wednesday. I was home from work that day and, since I was heading up a vestry committee, I stopped by the parish house to check out a few things. The secretary told me she thought the rector was in the church. That seemed to me like an odd place to be at 10.30 on Wednesday morning, but I went over and looked in.

It was all dark, and I didn't think anyone was there. Then I saw him kneeling on the step right in front of the altar, with his arms stretched out. He didn't move a muscle. I tiptoed up to the front of the church and said a prayer myself.

He still didn't know anyone was there and he started to pray out loud. His voice was so strange I can hear him still. Maybe, if I write down what I remember, I can think about it better and perhaps understand what it meant. It was about like this:

'Almighty and everlasting God (or something like that), I thank you that I have done the work you sent me here to do. It has not been easy to be silent when I had so much to say, or to be patient when things moved so slowly, or to watch people make mistakes which I knew how to avoid. I thank you for upholding me by your Holy Spirit. Now accept my offering through Jesus Christ, our great High Priest.'

I tiptoed out as I had come in. That afternoon they took him off in the ambulance. It turned out to be seven years, to the very day, that he had been here. Later on his wife told my wife that he had been in a lot of pain for a long time, but he just wouldn't go to the hospital.

Now we have given him a prolonged leave of absence. I think I have pretty well explained why our parish just happens to be in such a thriving condition, even though we now only have a supply priest coming in on Sundays. I guess what I can't explain is why, during the past seven years, belonging to the church has become the most important thing in my life.

From The Church Times, (14 December, 1979), reprinted from 'The Living Church'

Most people think of those who are involved in the local church as belonging to two categories – the clergy and the laity. The clergy are professionals. The laity are amateurs . . .

Such a hard and fast distinction between the professionals and the amateurs is not only damaging to the mission of the local church, it has little relationship with the picture of ministry found in the New Testament.

. . . he [the professional minister] will know that the ministry of the local church cannot be confined to the activities of one man. The front line of the church is the laity, and a primary task of the ordained and separated ministry is to train and equip the people of God for their role of mission in the world . . . So everyone, whatever his title or role in the local church, must recognise that his primary engagement is in the mission of the Church.

Edward Patey: 'Open the Doors', (Mowbrays, 1978)

In a truly healthy society, each man would see himself as partly responsible for the whole of it, rather than wholly responsible for a part of it.

James Mathers: in 'W.C.C. Contact 4', (1976)

Like the rest of the church, the pastor has to be struck to the roots of his/her soul by the unimaginable liberty of prayer, the grace of forgiveness, the awesomeness of faith. On a more mundane level and practically speaking, it is not the pastor who 'lets' the congregation in. It is the entire congregation, the church, the faith community which 'lets' one of their number, ordained for this purpose, preside.

Robert Horda: 'Strong, Loving and Wise', (the Liturgical Conference, 1987)

In the immense cathedral which is the universe of God, each man, whether scholar or manual labourer, is called to act as the priest of his whole life – to take all that is human and to turn it into an offering and a hymn of glory.

From an Orthodox saying

The priest does not cease to belong to the laity when he is ordained to the priesthood – he is given a special commission and function in it. The Ministry is the ministry of the whole Church and it is to be exercised by the whole Church.

Bishop Barry

Ministry, ordained

. . . every minister should be a man that hath much insight into the Tempter's wiles.

Richard Baxter: 'The Reformed Pastor', (1655)

We [ordained ministers] must spend all the time necessary with those who need our time. Otherwise we behave like a spiritual watering-can, sprinkling a little water all over the garden.

Norman Autton, (1980)

R.W. Dale (1829–1895), the great Congregational minister of Carr's Lane Chapel, Birmingham, towards the end of his life warned a young preacher, Charles Silvester Home: 'My lad, remember our temptation is not as a rule money.' And, pointing through the open vestry door to the crowded church, he added: 'That is our temptation.'

There is a sense in which every minister of the gospel is diminished by his ministry. If he has any self-knowledge at all, his ministry makes him less confident in himself, less assured, less doctrinaire and therefore sometimes less secure. He becomes more aware of the dark places in his own life and in the lives of others.

Archbishop Stuart Blanch: 'David Watson', (1985)

I do not envy the clergyman's life as an easy life, nor do I envy the clergyman who makes it an easy life.

Dr. Samuel Johnson

The three lessons which a minister has to learn, 1. Humility, 2. Humility, 3. Humility.

John Thornton: to Charles Simeon, (1788)

The ministers of Christ are generally either unduly exalted or undeservedly deprecated, by those around them: but they should discharge their duties with felicity, without any regard to the opinions of men, and approve themselves to him who will judge them righteously in the last day.

Charles Simeon(1759–1836): 'Horae Homileticae', Sermon no. 1952

The most tragic part of a bishop's life is that in which he has to deal with clergy who have *not* taken heed to themselves, when the bishop has perhaps to terminate a priest's ministry, or, almost equally tragically, to watch its formal continuance when the joy and power have gone from it, when prayer and sacrament and Bible study have died, and only the husk of the ministry remains. And all the time the bishop knows that this *could* happen to him.
'Keep watch over yourselves and over all the flock.' It is a word of warning.

Archbishop F. Donald Coggan: An Ordination Charge (on Acts 20 & John 16), in 'Convictions', (Hodders, 1975)

One of the functions of the ordained ministry is to multiply, not to monopolise, ministry.

John R.W. Stott, (1988)

It is very remarkable that none of the words which the church came eventually to use for the various grades in ordained ministry has a cultic or sacerdotal significance. In secular Greek a *diakonos* [deacon] meant any sort of servant. A *presbuteros* [presbyter, from which comes 'priest'] simply meant an older man. An *episkopos* [bishop] was any sort of overseer, from an inspector of markets to an auditor of temple finances.

A.T. & R.P.C. Hanson: 'The Identity of the Church', (S.C.M., 1987)

. . . the idea of the servant is not just empty rhetoric. Clergy, bishops, archdeacons, deans, vicars, curates, cardinals, popes, ministers really are very *unimportant;* if necessary, we should dump the lot, because the only absolute imperative for the church is that it must fulfil its mission.

Richard MacKenna: 'God for Nothing', (Churchman 1984/85)

The Affair:
It all started so innocently. Here I was doing God's work. I was happy. I wasn't looking for an affair. But it happens to pastors, and the results can be devastating.

I saw a real need. My pastor's heart responded to her needs. My efforts on her behalf were met with warmth, understanding, and acceptance. I felt needed. I saw in her eyes sparks of excitement for my godly attention, and it felt good. It was innocent and well meaning, not intended to foster an affair.

It was good to be appreciated. The bottom line was that she made me feel important. No, I did not want to be unfaithful to my wife. True, our marriage wasn't as exciting as it had been earlier. My wife and I got involved in different interests and activities. Our time schedules were so full that we hardly saw each other, and when we did we were both so tired that it was flat – no excitement.

But with her it was different – electric, powerful, energising.

Then there were the kids. My own kids were doing well in school, with two loving parents providing for all their needs. Her kids? Little support, massive needs, lots of hurting. They needed me more than my own kids. After all, my kids have my wife, even when I'm not there. Slowly the 'friend' became a mistress. There were the extra hours of counselling that couldn't wait. There were more and more 'evening appointments' that took me away from home. I could sense my wife's anxiety and puzzlement, but I kept spending more time with 'her'. My spouse kept quiet about what was going on, but I could detect a smouldering resentment that drove us even further apart, and made my contacts with 'her' even more desirable to me. It was easy to rationalise that if my wife were more attuned to my needs, I might spend more time at home.

Soon I noticed a subtle shift in my own attitude. At home I was husband and dad. That's fine, I guess. But with *her* I was a hero! She appreciated everything I did, and looked at me with loving, longing, unquestioning eyes. I enjoyed spending time with her. She fed my ego and I craved more of her delicacies.

One day she called me and gave an open invitation: 'I know it may be hard to get away, but I want you for a whole weekend. It's a little place up in the mountains, and honestly, I need you. No one else will do. Please say yes!' Her voice was plaintive and sincere. Heady stuff this. When did my spouse last make such a clear invitation and show that same eagerness to have me with her?

I know I should have said no, but there was a part of me that needed the recognition. Part of me wanted to be wanted. Besides, the Bible says we are to comfort the widow, the lonely, the needy, the hurting. My own family is well cared for. They don't need that much of my attention. And here's one who craves my presence, can't get along without me. I said yes. Not once, but again and again, and again. I was hooked into a full-blown affair. I loved my mistress, and she returned that love to me.

My family was not cut off. Just there. We had no animosity at home, just less and less involvement. My wife and I went from being lovers to being roommates.

My mistress and I had lots of exciting experiences together: picnics at the beach; long evenings of discussion; talk of the future for both of us. We even prayed together. In fact, we prayed together lots. That is one of the things that made the affair seem so right, so positive, so acceptable. Our intimacies increased to the point where I felt responsible for her every need, and she called on me for every major decision. Our lives seemed to blend together in a warm bond of loving trust and mutual joy.

Then a cold splash of reality hit me like a bucket of ice water. She's not my bride, and never will be. She informed me that she belongs to someone else. I had to make some tough decisions. Caught between needing and wanting her attention and affection, and drawing on my own somewhat neglected marriage for those needs to be met, I felt like a fool.

I felt so vulnerable, so ashamed. So scared of admitting what had gone on. What would I tell my wife and my own children? How about, 'Oh, hi there, family – I'm back. Sorry to have had an affair. Hope it didn't hurt you too much?' Or 'Well, to tell the truth, I just got caught up with my own ego needs and began to invest in the affair until there was nothing left for the family.' Or could my wife understand how the involvement had moved her out of my affection focus, yet I still loved her as my wife? Could I manage to overcome the affair and still have a marriage and family?

I didn't want it to be this way. It began with sincere devotion and paying attention to her needs (strange – it started with her needing me, and changed to my needing her). Then my love and affection began to produce results in her. It fed my ego. It seemed so right, it felt so good! We were both so happy. But she began to pull me away from my own family responsibilities. I began to realise that sometimes I'd rather be with her than with my own wife and children. That's when I began to see the danger.

The affair, I sensed, could destroy everything. It is the affair pastors don't want to face or talk about – the affair with their church.

Richard O. Stenbakken: in 'Ministry', (March, 1993)

I suspect that the emphasis placed of late – and rightly placed – on the ministry of the whole people of God has had the side-effect of obscuring the role of the ordained ministry. We who exercise this ministry have been brought up with our own various models of how it should be exercised. Do we now need a new model, which will express and nourish the relationships which deeper insight into the meaning of the body of Christ has revealed? As a cockshy, how about that of a good and godly Rep.?

Peter Baelz: Address to the Governing Body of the Church in Wales, (15 April, 1993)

Right across denominational lines, the church has tended to define its ministry mainly in terms of what pastors may do that others may not, and these definitions usually owe more to the past than to the present. In short, the church selects its ministers carefully, accepting their call from God, trains them rigorously in certain specialist ministries and then ordains them. At that point, their pastoral specialism is transformed into that of an ordained watering-can, sprinkling God's pastoral favour on the largest number of people who can be sprinkled upon in their homes; their leadership specialism is called to account . . . and their preaching specialism (the most particular specialism of all) is squeezed out by the pressures of time and so underrated by the people that the clergy themselves come to accept its low value.

Robert M.E. Paterson: 'Short, Sharp and Off the Point', (MARC Europe, 1987)

The necessity for a consistent lifestyle does not only mean that he [the Minister] seeks God's grace, like any other Christian, to lead a holy life, but that the whole of his life bears the stamp of reality and integrity on it. Too many pastors, priests and lay preachers hide behind their office and status because they are frightened that people outside the close circle of their friends will discover some of the emptiness inside. The preacher must seek to be what he preaches and to preach what he is in the grace of God.

Robert M.E. Paterson: 'Short, Sharp and Off the Point', (MARC Europe, 1987)

There is a custom in the Roman Catholic Church and in parts of the Anglican Communion known as 'concelebration', by which a number of presbyters (sometimes with a bishop) jointly lead the Eucharistic Prayer at a Communion. The custom has its origins and its only justification in the requirement that Roman Catholic priests should receive the sacrament daily. On other occasions it can have a powerful negative impact: 'We're the boys (and/or girls) who do the business. This is *our* club. We may delegate a few bits and pieces to you laity, but the church is really a priestly cabal.'

Robert M.E. Paterson, (1994)

The liturgical functions of the ordained arise out of pastoral responsibility. Separating liturgical function and pastoral oversight tends to reduce liturgical presidency to an isolated ritual function.

The International Anglican Liturgical Consultation, (Dublin, 1995), Principle 6

. . . a bishop's primary responsibility was to the proclamation of the gospel. The word of God spoken, heard, thought about, obeyed and continually re-expressed in actions as in words, gives meaning and reality to the life of the church and of the individual Christian . . . It is only by their correct understanding and communication of the gospel that they (the church's ministers) can hope to build a Christian community. Attempts to make the church work simply by clever organisation or ritual performance may have some success, but they do not generate an authentic church.

Canon Michael Richards: in The Times, (1 August, 1987)

There is a sense in which [Pope] Leo XIII was quite right*, the reformed Church of England had no intention of ordaining sacrificing priests. But then neither had the early church. The earliest Roman ordinals contain no suggestion of ordaining sacrificing priests.

A.T. & R.P.C. Hanson: 'The Identity of the Church', (S.C.M., 1987)

[The reference is to the papal bull, 'Apostolicae Curae', 1896, declaring Anglican orders 'absolutely null and utterly void'.]*

It has been reasoned, indeed, that he (a minister) may in a guarded and secondary sense be called, officially, a *sacerdos (priest)*, as he is in some respects the representative of the congregation to God and of God to the congregation. But such reasoning and usage is absent from the New Testament, in which the pastoral aspect of the ministry is (to say the least) very far more conspicuous than the representative.

Bishop C.F.D. Moule (of Durham)

If any man will live as faithfully as he preaches . . . he will lose his popularity with the upper classes, and will get no Bishopric.

Charles Simeon (1759–1836)

New Presbyter is but Old Priest writ Large.

John Milton (1608–74): Sonnet 'On the New Forces of Conscience under the Long Parliament'

And that is what an evangelist is – not necessarily a person with a striking style; not always a person with great charismatic gifts, but one who makes it easier for others to believe in God . . . Every minister of the gospel is diminished by his ministry.

Archbishop Stuart Blanch: in 'David Watson', (1985)

Jesus told his disciples they were to be 'fishers of men' (AV Matthew 4:19; Mark 1:17) but we have taught most of our ministers to be keepers of aquaria.

Attributed to Bishop Oliver Tompkins (of Bristol)

Ministry, dedication to

It is not the possession of extraordinary gifts that makes extraordinary usefulness, but the dedication of what we have to the service of God.

F.W. Robertson

Watch continually over your own spirit, and do all in love; we must grow downwards in humility to soar heavenward. I should recommend your having a watchful eye over yourself, for generally speaking as is the minister so are the people.

John Thornton: to Charles Simeon on the latter's becoming Vicar of Holy Trinity, Cambridge, (November, 1782)

Minutes

A Parochial Church Council minute read:
Since the former secretary has left the area and the former minutes could not be found, it was proposed, seconded and carried, that the minutes of the last meeting be adopted as they would have been read had they been found.

Source unknown

Miracles

Miracles are gifts rather than guarantees, given to faith, and perceived by faith, and they always involve a mysterious collaboration and convergence between the intervening power of God and human responses of faith, obedience and activity.

Bishop David Jenkins (of Durham): at the Church of England General Synod, (6 July, 1986)

A *Harris* poll for *The Spectator* (December 1986) noted that 86% of the 'believers' in the Top People Religious Survey said they thought the miracles of Christ really happened, while only 64% accepted the Virgin Birth. Clifford Longley commented [*The Times* 15.12.86]: 'It is called straining at a gnat while swallowing a camel.'

C.S. Lewis argues the procedure is flawed which evaluates a miracle thus:
Assuming that the story is fake, we could thus explain how it arose.

C.S. Lewis: 'Miracles', (1942), in 'God in the Dock', (Collins, 1979)

The experience of a miracle in fact requires two conditions. First we must believe in a normal stability of nature, which means we must recognise that the data offered by our senses recur in regular patterns. Secondly, we must believe in some reality beyond nature. When both beliefs are held, and not till then, can we approach with an open mind the various reports which claim that this super- or extra-natural reality has sometimes invaded and disturbed the sensuous content of space and time which makes our 'natural' world.

. . . modern people have an almost aesthetic dislike of miracles. Admitting that God can, they doubt if he would. To violate the laws he himself has imposed on his creation seems to them arbitrary, clumsy, a theatrical device only fit to impress savages – a solecism against the grammar of the universe.

C.S. Lewis: 'Miracles', (1942), in 'God in the Dock', (Collins, 1979

Misprints

In an obituary in St Mary's Parish Magazine, Swansea, the editor wished to say 'she was a chatty soul', but the printer missed the 'h'. The mistake was spotted at proof-reading!

Robert Barker and Martin Lucas, the King's printers at London, printed an edition of the Bible of 1,000 copies in which the word 'not' was omitted from the seventh commandment [forbidding adultery]. The Archbishop of Canterbury (Dr. William Laud) and King Charles I took the case to the Court of Star Chamber where a fine of £3,000 was imposed.

A piece of land between a volcano and the sea should have been described as 'strewn with erratic blocks' but what was printed was that the scene was 'strewn with erotic blacks'.

Psalm 119:161 was rendered 'Printers have persecuted me without a cause' in an early version of the 1611 Bible.

We are delighted to announce the birth of David John, the latest sin of the Vicarage.

Anonymous

Mission, theory

As fire exists by burning, so the church exists by mission.

Emil Brunner

Mission is not a population drive for heaven.

D. T. Niles

. . . the place of missions in the life of the church must be the central place and none other.

Archbishop Randall Davidson (of Canterbury), at the World Missionary Conference, (Edinburgh, 1910)

Fundamentally, mission is the work of God.

Bishop John V. Taylor (of Winchester)

Mission is the joyous and loving response of the Christian community to the universal and exclusive claims of the triune God who has revealed himself definitively in Jesus Christ. It involves crossing all human boundaries by Christians who are called individually and corporately to proclaim God's purposes. By their witness and service, they summon fellow-sinners to turn to God and share in his promised kingdom, for right response to God is inseparable from the calling of the nations and offer of a new life to all who will hear.

Dr. Ian Breward

. . . the key to world evangelisation is not in technological and communication networks but in churches sending away the best that God has given them.

Archbishop David Penman (of Melbourne): at Lausanne II Congress in Manila, July 1989

The history of the church tells us that when the Christian church parts company with Christian mission which is eschatological in nature, she loses her inner dynamic to become open and creative for the future; she loses her incentive for action. She lives on her past. She becomes more and more a liturgical church. The priestly function of the clergy overshadows the prophetic function. The clergy become preoccupied with the church as an institution and the activities of church members are directed to the conservation of the church as an institution. This kind of church has no passion for the world. And with the loss of passion for the world, she loses passion for God.

Choan-Seng Song: Christian Mission in Reconstruction – An Asian Attempt, (Madras, 1975)

It is of the very essence of the church's mission that it should continue the work which Jesus did. The members of the church are the limbs of his body, thus ensuring that the kind of things he did, the kind of person he proved to be among men, are continued and that his influence is extended throughout the world. That is the mission of the church at home and abroad. That is your mission if you are a disciple of Jesus.

Archbishop F. Donald Coggan (of Canterbury): The Ministry of Counselling, from 'Convictions', (Hodders 1975)

God in the name of Christ on behalf of the world. God intends that all that his people are and say and do in the ordinariness of life as much as in its high moments should, at one and the same time, be mission and worship.

Jim Punton: 'Christian Mission Today', (F.Y.T.)

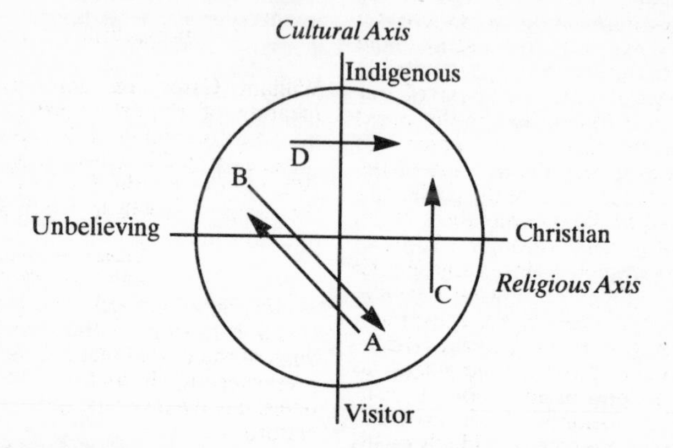

A is a missionary who has exported his/her home culture with the gospel, so **B** has become a Christian on the terms of the missionary's home culture.
C is a good cross-cultural missionary who helps **D** to become a Christian within his/her own culture.

The source of mission is God himself. He is a sending God; one might almost say a centrifugal God. So we find him sending prophets, sending his Son, sending his Spirit, and also his people.

We must see mission as an activity, almost an attribute of God. It begins with God and it continues with God. He hasn't given the task to others and withdrawn, but draws men in Christ into participation in his mission. So we see the Christian community as a function of God's mission. His mission is not a function of the Christian community. The community does not send missionaries; the community is by its nature a community of missionaries sent by God. The people of God are true to the name only as they are in mission with God.

Jim Punton: 'Christian Mission Today', (F.Y.T.)

In mission, the church faces the world in the name of Christ on behalf of God . . . In worship the church faces

The motive for mission must be found in the source of mission which is the heart of God. It is the love of God, that persistent, irrepressible care he has for man in his need, rebellion, arrogance and estrangement. 'God so loved'. The early Christian community could say: 'The love of Christ leaves us no choice'.

Jim Punton: 'Christian Mission Today', (F.Y.T.)

Mission is not only Christianity looking outward into the world, but also looking forward into the future. It sees a future filled with Christ and dominated by Christ. He is already Lord. He is the Omega point to which all converge. His destiny is to complete, to unify, to fill all things.

Douglas Webster: 'Not Ashamed', (1970)

The roots of the church are in mission, God's mission in which he calls the church to engage. Separate the church from God's mission and it loses its passion, its passion for God. That is a hard judgement.

Bishop Harry Moore: J.C. Jones Memorial Lecture, (1989)

We are called to share his (the Mediator's) apostolic ministry;... His mission is from the Father without intermediary, and ours is from the Father through him. But as there is a need at times to check our sense of the dignity of our status, so it is impossible to exaggerate the greatness of our calling. It is to continue in the world that divine mission of which the inauguration was the sending of the Son by the Father to be the Redeemer of the world. We are members of the body of Christ, through whom he would accomplish his purpose. All accounts of the charge given to his disciples by the risen Lord agree in its content; they were to go forth to be his witnesses, to proclaim the gospel, to make disciples of all nations, to continue the mission of the Incarnation. For this purpose they could rely on his presence and the power of the Holy Spirit. This is the primary purpose for which the Spirit is given: that we may bear witness to Christ. We must not expect the gift (the Spirit) while we ignore the purpose (mission). A church which ceases to be missionary will not be, and cannot rightly expect to be, 'spiritual'.

Archbishop William Temple: 'Readings in St. John's Gospel', on John 20. 21–22

Mission, world mission

An artist was engaged to paint the picture of a 'dying church'. It was assumed he would portray a ramshackle building, with broken windows and neglected grounds. But when it was unveiled the painting was of a fine Gothic church, stately, elegant and expensive – glorious stained glass, carved wooden stalls, a rood screen, a great organ and comfortable pews. Everyone was bewildered, but one day an old man who had spent much time looking at the painting solved the problem. There in an inconspicuous corner the artist had painted-in a box on the wall labelled **'FOR MISSIONS.'** Covering the box were cobwebs!

Source unknown

No responsible church leader today would deny that Europe and North America are as much areas of mission as are Asia and Africa, and in this respect, our understanding of mission has changed considerably from that of a century ago.

Douglas Webster: 'Not Ashamed', (1970)

William Carey, on approaching a meeting of Baptist ministers about overseas mission in 1786, was told by the chairman: 'Sit down, young man! When it pleases the Lord to convert the heathen, he will do it without your help or mine.'

Carey founded the Baptist Missionary Society in 1792

. . . to spread abroad among barbarians and heathen natives the knowledge of the gospel seems to be highly preposterous, in so far as it anticipates, nay even reverses, the order of Nature.

Resolution of the General Assembly of the Church of Scotland, (1796)

The church is confronted today, as in no previous generation, with a literally world-wide opportunity to make Christ known.

Edinburgh Missionary Conference, (1910)

Mission, home mission

Too many clergy are heard to say, 'Until my parishioners get out of their houses and into the church, God help the church.' They should realise that until the church has got out of the pews into the homes and work-places, God help the world, and the church!

Robert M.E. Paterson, (1980)

I am convinced that God is teaching our church in these days how to recover the attitudes of a missionary situation, and our survival as an effective church of the nation depends upon our readiness to learn that lesson . . . We often seem to have nothing to say to our fellow-countrymen except 'come back to church!' That betrays a favourite illusion of some clergymen that every person they pass in the high-street is a recently-lapsed Anglican . . . That is the attitude of Christendom, and Christendom has gone.

Bishop John V. Taylor (of Winchester): in the Winchester Churchman, (March 1985)

The task of mission is not so much to get the heathen into the church as to get the Christians out of the church into the world which is the proper sphere of witness.

Edward Patey: 'Open the Doors', (Mowbrays, 1978)

It [our society] is a pagan society, and its paganism, having been born out of the rejection of Christianity, is far more resistant to the gospel than the pre-Christian paganism with which cross-cultural missions have been familiar. Here, surely, is the most challenging missionary frontier of our time.

Lesslie Newbigin: 'Foolishness to the Greeks', (S.C.M. 1986)

Mission, word and action

It will be woe to us if we preach religion instead of the gospel; woe to us if we seek to hive off the importance of the past and fail to build on those foundations for the future; woe to us if we preach a message that looks only towards inner piety and does not relate our faith to the world around.

And that earthed gospel takes us directly into the market-place of the world. No church can or should avoid political comment when freedom, dignity and worth are threatened. The cross of Jesus Christ firmly roots us in human concerns and needs – and places us alongside the oppressed, the dispossessed, the homeless, the poor and the starving millions of our planet.

Archbishop George Carey; Enthronement at Canterbury, (19 April, 1991)

Is it not the case that we often go into battle as Christians with thermos flasks, sun-glasses and deck chairs in hands instead of the sword of the Spirit, the helmet of salvation, the shield of faith, the breastplate of righteousness?

Source unknown

Missionary earnestness is incompatible with prudery.

Emil Brunner: 'The Letter to the Romans', (1938; Lutterworth, 1959), on Romans 1. 18–32

Mission, being missionary

If the local church is to be faithful to its mission, it must know both the gospel and the people to whom the gospel is to be proclaimed.

Edward Patey: 'Open the Doors', (Mowbrays, 1978)

Mission in Christ's way means accepting that there will be no earthly security. It is not a question of getting so used to a new culture that you feel comfortable with it, but a question of being willing to be uncomfortable in whatever culture you are sent to, in order to share its suffering, its growth and whatever disturbing the Lord wants to do in that community.

Helen Old: 'Time for a Change', (Church Missionary Society, 1990)

Before the church can actively engage in mission, it must itself be renewed for mission. Nothing hinders the mission of the church, both its evangelistic and its social mission, more than its failure to be what it claims to be, and to practice what it preaches.

If we preach the cross, then we must ourselves take up the cross and follow Christ, dying to our own self-centredness in order to live for others, loving, forgiving and serving our enemies, and overcoming evil with good.

If we preach the Resurrection, then we must ourselves live in its power, experiencing deliverance from the bondage of sin and fear of death, and eagerly expecting the completion of the new creation when Christ returns.

If we preach the Ascension, then we must ourselves submit to the universal authority of the reigning Christ, longing that every tongue should confess him as Lord and that more and more of human society should come under his rule.

If we preach Pentecost, we must ourselves demonstrate the power of the Holy Spirit in our lives, as he makes Christ in us and binds us together in love.

If we preach the church as God's new and reconciled community, then we must set ourselves resolutely against the re-erection of the racial, social and sexual barriers which Christ abolished (Ephesians 2:11; Galatians 3:28), and must seek his grace to become the united, accepting, caring and supportive fellowship which he means us to be.

1978 Lambeth Conference: A statement given to the delegates

Coming into fellowship with Christ we find in ourselves an overmastering impulse to share him with others. We are constrained by the love of Christ and by obedience to his last command.

Jerusalem Missionary Council, (1928)

What would have been the state of the whole world if the same mind had been in Christ that is in us? . . . It may be said perhaps, 'Why are we to waste our strength upon the heathen? Is there not scope for the labours of us all at home?' I answer, 'It is well for us that the apostles did not argue thus.'

Charles Simeon (1759–1836)

We affirm that God is both the Creator and the Judge of all men. We, therefore, should share his concern for justice and reconciliation throughout human society and for the liberation of men from every kind of oppression . . . Although reconciliation with man is not reconciliation with God, nor is social action evangelism, nor is political liberation salvation, nevertheless we affirm that evangelism and socio-political involvement are both part of our Christian duty. [Both are necessary expressions of] our doctrines of God and Man, our love for our neighbour and our obedience to Jesus Christ.

The Lausanne Covenant, (1974)

Although this had never been their original aim the *peregrini* (pilgrims) soon began to find themselves missionaries preaching the gospel. The inter-connection of exile and mission lay of course deep in Celtic tradition, for the word had come to Ireland through a man who himself knew the unassuageable pain of exile [Patrick] . . . In a remarkably short time after they themselves had received the faith, the Celtic world was bringing that faith back to Europe. All over the continent Christianity, which had been battered and beaten by successive waves of barbarian hordes, was given new life by men bringing the light of Christ from the West, from the furthest outpost of the Western world.

Esther de Waal: 'A World Made Whole', (Fount, 1991)

We need all the saints, and the foreign missionary is not a temporary but an abiding necessity for the life of the church, provided always that the movement of missionaries is multi-directional, all churches both sending and receiving. The work of God is to be spoken in every tongue, but it can never be domesticated in any.

Lesslie Newbigin: 'Foolishness to the Greeks', (S.C.M., 1986)

When ferocious cannibals captured a hapless missionary he had the privilege of giving them their first real taste of Christianity.

Source unknown

Mission, Scripture

You [apostles] will receive power when the Holy Spirit has come upon you; and you will be my witnesses in Jerusalem, in all Judea and Samaria, and to the ends of the earth.

Acts 1:8

How are they to call on one in whom they have not believed? And how are they to believe in one of whom they have never heard? And how are they to hear without someone to proclaim him? And how are they to proclaim him unless they are sent? As it is written, 'How beautiful are the feet of those who bring good news!' But not all have obeyed the good news; for Isaiah says, 'Lord, who has believed our message?' So faith comes from what is heard, and what is heard comes through the word of Christ.

Romans 10:14–17

Modernity

Modernity [not Modernism] can lead to 'the loss of the mandate of heaven . . . We know all about the immediate and nothing about the ultimate.'

Os Guinness: at Lausanne II Congress in Manila, (July, 1989)

Modern advertising techniques (since c.1920) say: 'Simplify thought. Magnify images. Intensify emotion.'

To test the truth, ask: 'What is being said? Is it true? What of it?'

Source unknown

Modernity preaches a gospel of 'by bread alone and by sex alone'.

Os Guinness: at Lausanne II Congress in Manila, (July 1989)

Modesty

The English instinctively admire any man who has no talent and is modest about it.

James Agee

Monarchy

The Sovereign has, under a constitutional monarchy such as ours, three rights – the right to be consulted, the right to encourage, the right to warn.

Walter Bagehot (1827–1877): 'The English Constitution', (1867)

A republican is a sinner mentioned in the gospels.

Child's comment

Money

Mammon enthroned showed himself a consummate ass.

Sidney Dark: 'The People's Archbishop', (James Clarke, 1942)

No one would have remembered the Good Samaritan if he had only had good intentions. He had money as well.

Margaret Thatcher, Conservative Prime Minister and monetarist

The meek shall inherit the earth, but not the mineral rights.

Paul Getty, multi-millionaire

Jesus said, 'Do not store up for yourselves treasures on earth, where moth and rust consume and where thieves break in and steal; but store up for yourselves treasures in heaven, where neither moth nor rust consumes and where thieves do not break in and steal. For where your treasure is, there your heart will be also.'

Matthew 6:19–21

[Jesus] sat down opposite the [temple] treasury, and watched the crowd putting money into the treasury. Many rich people put in large sums. A poor widow came and put in two small copper coins, which are worth a penny. Then he called his disciples and said to them, 'Truly I tell you, this poor widow has put in more than all those who are contributing to the treasury. For all of them have contributed out of their abundance; but she out of her poverty has put in everything she had, all she had to live on.'

Mark 12:41–44

Moralism

The curse of moralism is not the fact that the action is being undertaken seriously, but the self-deception of the unredeemed man who regards the action as done in his strength . . . It is the delusion of moralism, even of the religiously 'deepened' moralism, that man can extricate himself from sin by treating God's command seriously in practice, climbing up, as it were.

Emil Brunner: 'The Letter to the Romans', (1938; Lutterworth, 1959), on Romans 2:1–29

Morality – *see also* ETHICS

Luther's new morality was not ascetic or unworldly. It was directed toward the world – not to transform it into a monastery but to let it remain the world and become what is was, God's good creation.

Heiko A. Oberman: 'Luther', (Yale, 1982/89)

The most fundamental aspect of moral development consists not in unthinking adherence to a set of rules and regulations, but in building and strengthening of *positive* sentiments for people and ideals.

Epple: 'Adolescence and Morality'

New knowledge alters the human situation. The function of morals is to control the human situation as apprehended in any culture. Hence an inevitable relationship exists between new knowledge and moral change.

Hemming

. . . capitalism cannot now reinvent Protestant Christianity, nor any other system of religious faith, just because it needs values to assert its human face.

Clifford Longley: in The Times, (27 October, 1989), 'A consumer's guide to God'

Authenticity is more crucial than methodology: the question is not only 'How shall they hear?' but also 'What shall they see?' As we have seen with the tele-evangelists [1988/89 scandals in the U.S.A.], charisma without character is catastrophic.

Peter Kuzmic: at Lausanne II Congress in Manila, (July, 1989)

Motivation

The last temptation is the greatest treason:
To do the right deed for the wrong reason.

T.S. Eliot: 'Murder in the Cathedral', (1935), Part 1 (Faber and Faber 1965)

The child that speaks the truth for the sake of the praise of truth, is not truthful. The man who is honest because honesty is the best policy, has not integrity in his heart. He who endeavours to be humble, and holy, and perfect, in order to win heaven, has only a counterfeit religion. God for his own sake – goodness because it is good – truth because it is lovely – this is the Christian's aim. The prize is only an incentive: inseparable from success, but not the aim itself.

F.W. Robertson (1816–1853): 'Sermons on Religion and Life'

Music – *see also* HYMNS AND SINGING

Music, the greatest good that mortals know,
And all of heaven we have below.

Joseph Addison (1762–1719): 'A Song for St Cecilia's Day'

It's better than it sounds!

Mark Twain: on Wagner's music

The art of music is 'a most wonderful and glorious gift of God, which has the power to drive out Satan and to resist temptations and evil thoughts.'

Martin Luther (1483–1546)

I suffer when the clergyman decides – for reasons best known to himself – to intone the prayers, but does not realise that he drops about half a tone each time. I suffer when the organist over-sentimentalises a canticle by liberal use of *tremolo,* and converts the *Magnificat* (which is the nearest thing in the New Testament to the 'Red Flag') into slop! I suffer – and here the totally unmusical join the musical – when people will sing nonsense, for example, lusty confirmation candidates being forced to describe themselves as 'frail and trembling sheep', and thoughtful congregations being made to sing Coverdale's version of Psalm 22:29: 'all such as be fat upon earth have eaten and worshipped'. What on earth does that mean? . . .

If the clergy would not insist, in small parish churches, on aping cathedrals, but would make worship the beautifully simple thing which it is meant to be, we should be saved much agony (and I suspect would . . . have many more level-headed laity within our doors).

Archbishop Donald Coggan: 'Music in Church', at Westminster Choir College, Princeton, New Jersey, (25 May, 1966)

After the first performance of *The Marriage of Figaro,* the Emperor Ferdinand told Mozart, 'Far too noisy, my dear Mozart. Far too many notes.'

I would say that this does not belong to the art which I am in the habit of considering music.

A. Oulibicheff, reviewing Beethoven's Fifth Symphony

Praise [God] with trumpet sound;
praise him with lute and harp!
Praise him with tambourine and dance; praise him with strings and pipe!
Praise him with clanging cymbals;
praise him with loud clashing cymbals!
Let everything that breathes praise the LORD!

Psalm 150:3–6

I heard a voice from heaven like the sound of many waters and like the sound of loud thunder; the voice I heard was like the sound of harpists playing on their harps, and they sing a new song before the throne and before the four living creatures and before the elders.

Revelation 14:2, 3

Mystery (Secret)

Mystery means not the inexplicable but the inexhaustible.

Dewi Morgan: in The Times, (21 December, 1985)

With all wisdom and insight he [the God and Father of our Lord Jesus Christ] has made known to us the mystery of his will, according to his good pleasure that he set forth in Christ, as a plan for the fulness of time, to gather up all things in him, things in heaven and things on earth.

Ephesians 1:8b–10

Pray also for me, so that when I speak, a message may be given to me to make known with boldness the mystery of the gospel, for which I am an ambassador in chains. Pray that I may declare it boldly, as I must speak.

Ephesians 6:19, 20

I became its [the gospel's] servant according to God's commission that was given to me for you, to make the word of God fully known, the mystery that has been hidden throughout the ages and generations but has now been revealed to his saints. To them God chose to make known how great among the Gentiles are the riches of the glory of this mystery, which is Christ in you, the hope of glory.

Colossians 1:25–27

Pray for us as well that God will open to us a door for the word, that we may declare the mystery of Christ, for which I am in prison, so that I may reveal it clearly, as I should.

Colossians 4:3, 4

Without any doubt, the mystery of
  our religion is great:
He was revealed in flesh, vindicated
  in spirit, seen by angels,
proclaimed among Gentiles, believed
  in throughout the world, taken up
  in glory.

1 Timothy 3:16

Myth

'Myth' is a word less than 150 years old.

A myth is a story which is told but which is not literally true, or an idea or image which is applied to someone or something but which does not literally apply, but which invites a particular attitude in its hearers.

Dr. Maurice Wiles

You cannot *study* pleasure in the moment of the nuptial embrace, nor repentance while repenting, nor analyse the nature of humour while roaring with laughter. But when else can you really know these things? 'If only my toothache would stop, I could write another chapter about pain.' But once it stops, what do I know about pain? . . .

It is only while receiving the myth as a story that you experience the principle correctly.

C.S. Lewis: 'Myth became Fact', (1944), in God in the Dock, (Collins 1979)

N

Naivete

It's a joy to be naive. The less naive I become, the harder I find it is to serve.

Roderick R Hewitt: Address to Church in Wales Board of Mission Council, (1996)

Nationality

The Duke of Wellington was born in Ireland but denied that he was Irish.

Because a man is born in a stable, that does not make him a horse.

Navigation

On 31 August 1986, a Mr. Sebury set out from Newport, Gwent, to cross the Atlantic in a 15-foot sloop equipped with a bucketful of cheese, five litres of orange juice and an Ordnance Survey map of the Welsh coast. Three days later, very seasick and with a broken engine and mast down, he was found drifting in a Royal Navy torpedo range. When a vessel came out to warn him, Mr. Rebury shouted, 'Take me ashore and sink the boat!'

Late that year he tried again and reached Milford Haven.

Stephen Pile, Ed: 'The Return of Heroic Failures', (1988)

A grandfather aged 84 has established an unenviable record by spending the best – or worst – part of two days driving round the M25 London orbital route in search of his daughter's home. The ordeal of William Allen, of Leyland, Lancashire, was disclosed yesterday when his son-in-law rang Capital Radio to thank the police for rescuing him. A motorist had found Mr. Allen in a confused state parked in a layby. Sid Cordier called the police and Mr. Allen was taken to the local station, where it transpired that he had left home without his address book.

He knew that his daughter, Joan Belcher, lived near an airport in a town beginning with the letter R. But he ended up in Reigate, near Gatwick, when he should have been in Ruislip, near Heathrow.

Quite how many circuits Mr. Allen completed will probably never be known. But his daughter said he told her that he had driven through a tunnel several times. She said: 'He must have been driving round and round the M25 for hours. I know he left home before 7 am and I didn't see him until 2 am two days later. He was very embarrassed by the whole thing, but he has gone back home now and is still driving his car.'

Last November Bob Flemming, from Kent, made at least one circuit of the M25 believing that he was heading north. It was not until he asked police where the turn-off was for Durham that he realised he was still only 15 miles from where he started.

John Young: in The Times, (1991)

Am at Market Harborough. Where ought I to be?

Telegram from G.K. Chesterton to his wife (1874–1936)

New age, The

Confronted with all this ['psycho-babble, dim-witted meandering and a morbid fascination with one's own private feelings'], Christians may well be alarmed. Far from being a benign and companionable form of spirituality, much New Age thinking is an explicit assault on the self-denying heart of western religion.

. . . its strength lies in its flabby plurality, the way it unquestioningly embraces every idea, however crazy, and then flaunts it as the symptom of the dawning of a new era.

. . . By saying nothing clearly, it becomes all things to all men. By making no demands, it wins easy converts – hippie values, says one sceptic, for a yuppie lifestyle.

Bryan Appleyard: in The Times, (17 June, 1992), 'The Selling of the New Age'

Nominalism

Some people may be known as 'four wheeler Christians', in that they only ever come to church on four wheels: in a pram (for the baptism), in a limousine (for the wedding) and in a hearse (for the funeral).

Source unknown

Diary Dates in Church

So when were you last in church? Was it your own wedding, or Uncle David's funeral, or your baby's christening? Well, weekends do tend to rush by, what with the car to clean and the lawn to cut. After all, you do try to lead the sort of life that might be called Christian without actually going to church: that is, not hurting other people and, indeed, helping them if you can. You do not feel that the church has got much to do with the rush of modern life and keeping up with the work and the bills and the family or the decorating. Church-going does not seem important enough to fit in the time.

Understandable. Everyone is entitled to his own opinion. If you do not regard the church as part of your life there is no reason why you should attend a service. But, if the church is not important enough to be given some of your time, would you not agree that it is hypocritical to use it for the major rituals of baptism, marriage and burial? For that is exactly what we do. We use the church in the laziest, unthinking, insensitive way, primitives touching wood to avert the Evil Eye.

A mother: 'We went along to see the Vicar to arrange the christening but he wanted to see us at church occasionally first, and we weren't going to do that so Mandy was never christened.'

You can regularly hear about vicars who refuse to christen a child whose parents just want 'to have him done'. It is a pretty custom, with the baby all rosy, and relatives gathering to admire, but it is a symbol far greater than that. Once you have registered the birth, the baby legally exists. the christening is the occasion when the baby becomes a member of the church. Put yourself in the clergyman's place when parents he has never laid eyes on, and knows he never will again, turn up and say 'We want him done'. Would you demand some understanding of the deep reasons behind the ceremony, or would you just hope that if the child is sent to Sunday School, even if only so that Dad can get a bit of quiet, it must assimilate knowledge of the Christian ethos.

Some clergymen get awkward about the sponsors at the christening – and why not? The majority of godparents, if they were honest, would refuse point-blank to be a party to the fraud. Being a godparent is not just producing some silver napkin rings for the christening. You are sponsoring an incapable infant: promising on its behalf that one day it will fulfil the promise you gave and become a full member of the church. Do you keep your tongue in your cheek, or ignore the words?

Or would you have the gall to pop up when the child is an adolescent, and say 'Now what about confirmation?', especially if you never attend Holy Communion yourself? In 1970, 466 out of every 1,000 live births were baptised by the Church of England (47%), and 19.7 in every 1,000 in the 12–20 age group were confirmed (2%). Touching wood in infancy is apparently sufficient for the majority.

Bride-to-be, quoted in a newspaper diary item: 'Neither of us has been to a church for 10 years, so we felt it would be hypocritical to have a religious ceremony.' I retain this 16 months old cutting as a rarity.

You can be legally married in a registry office. But, of course, the administrative offices of our towns do not provide the same setting as a church. You cannot get the full queen-for-a-day sweep-down-the-aisle effect. Nor, for that matter, the background to the pictures for the album that a church porch and approach offer. Recently one vicar found a wedding couple who had just married in the local registry office posing for pictures outside his church!

A funeral director: 'Only once in the last two years have I specifically been requested not to arrange a service because the man who had died was an atheist. Normally it goes like this: I ask the widow the denomination of her husband. After a bit of thought she says C. of E. So I go along to the vicar and he says, yes, that the man was in his parish, though he had never ever met him. And the vicar still comes along to conduct the service.'

Unlike other rituals, the clergy do not participate at funerals in the hope that the involved party may be drawn towards the church, of course, but in the hope that the family may find their comfort there.

In our hypocritical attitude to the church we seem to treat it like a free National Health Service: expected to be there, sound and functioning, to provide the trappings for major rituals, but otherwise ignored, and unsupported either by financial contribution or the expenditure of our time. When you last went to church for a wedding, christening or funeral, did you at least put something into the church maintenance box?

Diary Dates in Church, Betty Jerman: in The Telegraph Magazine, (1973) © Telegraph Group Ltd, London 1973 (The statistics quoted are no longer accurate)

Notices, church

Don't let worry kill you. The Church can help.

Please pray for all who are sick of this church.

For those who have children but don't know it, there is a Nursery in the hall.

On Easter Eve we will hold an important Baptism service in the North and South transepts. Candidates will be baptised at both ends.

On Tuesday at 2.00 pm, there will be a meeting of the Little Mothers' Club. All women who would like to become little mothers please see the Rector soon.

The Toddlers' Service will end with 'Little drops of Water' by one of the children, and the others will join in.

The members of the Ladies' Prayer Circle have cast off clothing of every kind. Come and see what they have to offer on Wednesday evening at 7.30.

The theme of this evening's sermon will be, 'What is Hell?' Come and hear the choir's latest anthem.

Obedience

Enthusiasm is no substitute for obedience.

Michael Griffith

It is a vain thought to flee from the work that God appoints us, for the sake of finding a greater blessing, instead of seeking it where alone it is to be found – in loving obedience.

George Eliot (Mary Anne Evans)

Every revelation of God is a demand, and the way to knowledge of God is by obedience.

Archbishop William Temple (of Canterbury)

. . . if saints have usually a double share in the miseries of this life, I that am none ought not to repine at what my wise Creator hath appointed for me, but labour (as indeed I do daily) to submit mine to his will, and possess my soul in patience and peace.

Richard Hooker (1554–1600): when George Cranmer sympathised with him that his fortunes were no better than they were

Chaucer's picture of the Parson in the Prologue of the Canterbury Tales is idealistic and ironical:

He waited after no pompe and
reverence,
Ne maked him a spiced conscience,
But Christes loore and his apostles
twelve
He taught, but first he folwed it
hymselve.

A prayer for obedience:

You alone know what is expedient for me. You are the Sovereign Master. Do whatever pleases you. Give me or take away from me. Confirm my will to yours, and grant that with a humble and perfect submission, and in holy confidence, I may dispose myself utterly to you. May I receive the orders of your everlasting, provident care. May I equally adore whatever proceeds from you.

Blaise Pascal: 'Asking God to Use Sickness in His Life', (1659 or 1660)

The Methodist Act of Covenant:

I am no longer my own but yours.
Put me to what you will,
rank me with who you will;
put me to doing, put me to suffering;
let me be employed for you or laid
aside for you,
exalted for you or brought low for
you;
let me be full, let me be empty;

let me have all things, let me have nothing.
I freely and willingly yield all things to your pleasure and disposal.
And now, O glorious and blessed God, Father, Son and Holy Spirit,
you are mine and I am yours.
So be it.
And the covenant which I have now made on earth,
let it be ratified in heaven. Amen.

The promise that he would inherit the world did not come to Abraham or to his descendants through the law but through the righteousness of faith. If it is the adherents of the law who are to be the heirs, faith is null and the promise is void. For the law brings wrath; but where there is no law, neither is there violation. For this reason it depends on faith, in order that the promise may rest on grace . . .

Romans 4:13–16a

In the presence of God, who gives life to all things, and of Christ Jesus, who in his testimony before Pontius Pilate made the good confession, I charge you to keep the commandment without spot or blame until the manifestation of our Lord Jesus Christ . . .

1 Timothy 6:13, 14

Occult, The

Dear Friend,
On Christmas Day 1968 my wife and I went to a party in a neighbour's home. During the evening we were introduced to a new 'party game'. The letters of the alphabet were placed in a circle around the table, and the words 'yes' and 'no' placed opposite each other. An upturned wineglass was then put in the centre on which we all put our index finger. We asked the glass 'Is anybody there?' and sometimes the glass would move around the letters spelling words and forming sentences. Each accused the others of pushing the glass, and the whole thing was treated as a joke.

The following day my wife, her sister and myself decided to play the 'game' together. This time we contacted a spirit which said it was my wife's grandmother who had died two years before. Indeed many of the idiosyncrasies of her Cornish manner and speech were faithfully reproduced. By now we were beginning to take this more seriously as so many questions were being answered accurately.

At this time I was working on night shift, and that night I told a friend what we had been doing. He asked if this had in any way affected my oft-pronounced atheistic convictions, and I had to confess that they were under pressure.

We continued talking to this spirit for several weeks, sometimes spending whole afternoons and evenings in contact with what we believed to be the spirit of Carol's grandmother. After a while the glass began to say 'god is listening' and by now we were convinced that this was so. Then quite dramatically one night, the glass took on an entirely new personality saying 'god is here'. The glass moved with such dominating force that we had difficulty in following it. I was told shortly afterwards that I was in the 'Black Book' and would have to pay the consequences. This was the start of a dreadful phase of fear for me. I went and fetched my Bible, long neglected and blew the dust off it. I turned its pages and opened and read Job chapter 23.

My wife Carol was undergoing a completely different experience. The spirit flirted with her until she was captivated by its flatteries. We discovered at this time that we were able to discern the voice of the spirit without using the glass; we had been slowly tutored in this as we had tried to anticipate the movements of the glass, and guess what it was trying to say to us. We were told of a task that we would have to undertake for this 'god spirit'. However, we had a disagreement with the spirit at this time, and our relationship with the spirit began to deteriorate. This was the start of a very real fear campaign. The glass refused to work for us, and yet we could still hear the voice in our minds, which became so inextricably mixed up with our thoughts that we were completely at its mercy. Conflicting thoughts were injected into our already confused minds, driving us steadily towards insanity. I was told that I would be inflicted with blindness, or that my wife or one of the children would die. Always one of us was under terrible pressure, sleep became a fearful thing filled with obscene and terrifying dreams. We got at most two or three hours sleep spending the rest of the night praying to this 'god' for mercy for each other and the children. It would be impossible to describe the full horror of the situation, the conviction of our own sinful condition, and the fact that having offended the 'god' we were eternally damned. (If hell is nothing more than conviction of sin without a hope of forgiveness, then that is torment indeed.) On reflection our minds were completely deranged, and our home and children totally neglected.

On the morning of February 14th, 1969, after a particularly dreadful night, we decided to go and seek help from the local Methodist minister, Rev Allen Fisher. We knew him only because he had christened our younger daughter. We saw him at 11.15 am. and told him all we could think of. He listened with concern, prayed with us, and we left two hours later, promising that he would call later in the day. I had had a dream previously of going to work in a very demented condition, and of being told to pull myself together. That afternoon it came true and I was sent home from work. Again I went to see Mr Fisher, leaving Carol a little calmer at home. Later she phoned in terror, as she feared that the spirit would appear if she was alone in the house. Mr Fisher came into our home and sat and talked about the true nature of God, and how he had given his only Son Jesus Christ, that we should have a way back to him. He pointed us to Revelation chapter 3 verse 20: 'Behold I stand at the door and knock, if any man hear my voice and open the door I will come in . . .' He explained that the door was our hearts, that the handle was on the inside, that Jesus was waiting to come in and save us. All we had to do was open the door. Late that night we knelt down and prayed very simply, confessing our sinful condition, claiming forgiveness in Jesus Christ's name and asking him to come into our lives. That night for the first time for weeks we slept soundly . . .

However, although we had an inner calm and peace, there still raged a spiritual battle. The enemy still tried, as he does with all newly-born Christians, to destroy our new-found faith in Jesus Christ. The following day as Carol and I were walking in Wolverhampton we both suddenly stopped. We had both heard a voice saying 'So you think you have escaped'. Strange thoughts and doubts concerning the Scriptures came into our minds, but through it all we clung to Jesus Christ and the living reality of the miracle He had performed in us. Satan is extremely active when anyone turns to the Lord, and Carol and I were in a very vulnerable position, due to the turbulence of mind we had gone through. Yet with the Lord's guidance three things contributed to our spiritual victory: constant prayer, regular guided Bible reading, and fellowship with born again Christian friends.

Now, it is the Lord's voice we listen for as we pray and read the Bible. The devil knows that One mightier than he now dominates our thoughts.

Yours sincerely
John and Carol Cockerill.

Christian Publicity Organisation, Worthing

Saul died for his unfaithfulness; he was unfaithful to the LORD in that he did not keep the command of the LORD; moreover, he had consulted a medium, seeking guidance, and did not seek guidance from the LORD. Therefore the LORD put him to death and turned the kingdom over to David son of Jesse.

1 Chronicles 10:13, 14

See to it that no one takes you captive through philosophy and empty deceit, according to human tradition, according to the elemental spirits of the universe, and not according to Christ. For in him the whole fulness of deity dwells bodily, and you have come to fulness in him, who is the head of every ruler and authority . . . He disarmed the rulers and authorities and made a public example of them, triumphing over them in it.

Colossians 2:8–10, 15

Opera

It *moves* me [ie. pop music], the way people are supposed to be moved by *real* music. I was taken once to Covent Garden to hear a woman called Callas in a sort of foreign musical with no dancing which people were donating kidneys to get tickets for. The idea was that I would be cured of my strange disability. As though the place were a kind of Lourdes, except that instead of the front steps being littered with wooden legs, it would be tin ears. My illness at the time took the form of believing the Righteous Brothers' recording of *You've Lost that Lovin' Feelin'* on the *London* label was possibly the most haunting, the most deeply moving noise ever produced by the human spirit, and this female vocalist person was going to set me right.

Tom Stoppard: 'The Real Thing', (1982), Henry to Max

Orthodox churches, The

The Orthodox ('right believing') Churches are a loose federation of self-governing churches, sometimes known as 'the Church of the Seven Councils', as they lay stress on the councils of the church held at Nicea (325 & 787), Constantinople (381, 553 & 680–1), Ephesus (431) and Chalcedon (451). The five patriarchates, in order, are Rome (now the primatial see of the Roman Catholic Church), Constantinople, Alexandria, Antioch and Jerusalem, and there are a range of national churches in Eastern Europe and the Mediterranean.

In the Orthodox tradition, priests are married but bishops (chosen from the religious life) are not. In many the method of selecting a bishop is that several candidates are considered and a shortlist is drawn up, based on an assessment of personal gifts and diocesan needs. A form of lottery then takes place (often a child is asked to pick one of a number of unmarked envelopes) in the context of prayer for the guidance of the Holy Spirit. The Orthodox Christian sees this as a way of ensuring that careful thought goes into the preparation, and the Spirit's will (rather than human choice) leads to the right person being elected. This accords with the practice found in Acts 1:21–26 which is often misunderstood in the Western (Roman Catholic and Reformed) Church.

Worship in an Orthodox Church is a lengthy and complex act with little congregational participation (people come and go, sit or stand) but with a deep sense of being caught up into the continual worship of heaven. One of the vital precepts of Orthodoxy is that human beings are most truly themselves when they adore.

P

Pain

When Thomas Babington MacAulay (1800–59) was a child, he was taken by his father to visit Lady Waldegrave at Strawberry Hill. A servant spilt some hot coffee on the boy's legs and the hostess was naturally very concerned and compassionate. After a while, she enquired how he was feeling, only to be told, 'Thank you, madam, the agony is abated.'

James Sutherland, Ed: 'The Oxford Book of Literary Anecdotes', (1975)

Paradox

The truth is not in the middle, and not in one extreme; but in both extremes . . . As wheels in a complicated machine may move in opposite directions and yet subserve one common end, so may truths *apparently opposite* be perfectly reconcilable with each other, and equally subserve the purposes of God in the accomplishment of man's salvation . . .

Many think that the opposite to right must be wrong; but the opposite to right may be right . . .

The human mind is very fond of fetters, and is apt to forget them for itself.

Charles Simeon (1759–1836)

Both aspects [judgement and universal reconciliation] remain juxtaposed in their harsh incompatibility . . . And the one, by its very absoluteness, logically excludes the other . . .

We must listen to the voice which speaks of world judgement as to the voice of God himself, in order that we may fear him; we must listen to the voice which speaks of universal redemption as to the voice of God himself, in order that we may love him. Only through this indissoluble duality do we grasp the duality of God's being which yet is one: his holiness and his love. Hence the criterion of all genuine theology is this – does it lead to the cry, 'God be merciful to me, a sinner!' and, beyond it, to the exclamation, 'Thanks be to God, who gives us the victory through Jesus Christ our Lord!'

Emil Brunner: 'Eternal Hope', (1953; Lutterworth, 1959), Chapter 17

The classical theory is that heresy is not so much plain error, as the result of overemphasis on one side of a two-sided truth – that Jesus Christ was true God and true man, for instance. Heresy often starts when 'and' tends to become 'or' in such apparent paradoxes, for instance the classic heresies that Christ was more God than man (Docetism), or more man than God (Arianism) . . . Heretics do not like paradoxes, and insist on resolving them.

Clifford Longley: in The Times, 2 March, (1991), 'Both sides of the truth'

Parents

To lose one parent, Mr Worthing, may be regarded as a misfortune; to lose both looks like carelessness.

Oscar Wilde: 'The Importance of Being Earnest', (1895), Act 1, Lady Bracknell

The fifth commandment is, 'Humour your father and mother.'

Anonymous

Children begin by loving their parents; after a time they judge them; rarely, if ever, do they forgive them.

Oscar Wilde: 'A Woman of No Importance', (1893), Act 1

Honour your father and your mother, so that your days may be long in the land that the LORD your God is giving you.

Exodus 20:12

Hear, O Israel: The LORD is our God, the LORD alone. You shall love the LORD your God with all your heart, and with all your soul, and with all your might. Keep these words that I am commanding you today in your heart. Recite them to your children and talk about them when you are at home and when you are away, when you lie down and when you rise.

Deuteronomy 6:4–7

Children, obey your parents in everything, for this is your acceptable duty in the Lord. Fathers, do not provoke your children, or they may lose heart.

Colossians 3:20, 21

Parliament

Britain alone of the great nation States . . . elaborated [during the seventeenth and eighteenth centuries] a system by which a debating club of elected persons could successfully govern an Empire in peace and war.

J.M. Trevelyan: 'A History of England', (1926), The Prologue (This sweeping epigram, typical of Trevelyan, was questioned by the reviewer in the 'American Historical Review' with the question: 'Surely Britain lost America in the seventeenth century?')

When James Harris (1709–80) – author of two books, one on grammar and the other on virtue – took his seat in the House of Commons, Charles Townsend queried: 'What the devil brings him here? I am sure he will find neither the one nor the other in the Commons.'

James Sutherland, Ed: 'The Oxford Book of Literary Anecdotes', (1975)

Partisanship

Labels should be used as a means of identifying theological tradition, not as offensive weapons.

Frances Gumley & Brian Redhead: 'Protestors for Paradise', (B.B.C. Books, 1993)

It is a great and common sin throughout the Christian world to take up religion in a way of faction; and instead of a love and tender care of the universal church, to confine that love and respect to a party.

Richard Baxter: 'The Reformed Pastor', (1655)

Past, the

Do you remember the past – when flying was dangerous and sex was safe?

Source unknown

Pastoral care

Our Lord's Commandment was, 'Feed my Sheep', not 'Teach my performing dogs new tricks' nor 'Try experiments on my rats!'

C.S. Lewis: 'Letters to Malcolm on Prayer'

Mrs. Huff is up the miff tree
On a seat fixed good and firm;
And she'd like to tell the pastor
A few things to make him squirm.

Mrs. Huff was sick abed, sir,
Yes sir, sick abed a week!
And the pastor didn't call, sir,
Never even took a peek

When I asked her if the doctor
Called to see her, she said, 'Sure!'
And she looked as if she thought I
Needed some good mental cure.

Then I asked her how the doctor
Knew that sickness laid her low,
And she said that she had called him
On the 'phone and told him so.

Now the doctor gets his bill paid
With a nicely written cheque;
But the pastor, for not knowing,
Simply gets it in the neck!

Anonymous

What patients in hospital need is love. Their world is a large and empty room and they need human figures to enter it.

Norman Autton, (1980)

A woman complained to her vicar that she wouldn't come to church until he had visited her. A few days later he saw her queuing outside a cinema. 'I see the cinema manager's been to see you,' he commented.

Anonymous

Their lean and flashy songs
Grate on their scrannel pipes of wretched straw,
The hungry sheep look up, and are not fed.

John Milton, (1608–1674): 'Lycidas', 1.163. Ronald Knox parodied the last line to: 'The sheep look fed up and are not hungry!'

Patience

Not without design does God write the music of our lives. Be it ours to learn the time, and not be discouraged at the rests. If we say sadly to ourselves, 'There is no music in a rest', let us not forget 'There is the making of music in it'. The making of music is often a slow and painful process in this life. How patiently God works to teach us! How long he waits for us to learn the lesson.

John Ruskin

'How do you eat an elephant?'
'One mouthful at a time.'

Anonymous old saying, repeated by Archbishop Desmond Tutu (of Cape Town)

Slow me down, Lord!
Ease the pounding of my heart by the quieting of my mind.
Steady my hurried pace with a vision of the Eternal reach of time.
Give me, amidst the confusion of my day,
the calmness of the Everlasting hills.
Break the tensions of my nerves and muscles
with the soothing music of the singing streams that live in my memory.
Help me to know the restoring power of sleep.
Teach me the art of taking minute vacations,
of slowing down to look at a flower, to chat with a friend,
to pat a dog, to read a few lines from a good book.
Remind me each day of the fable of the hare and the tortoise
that I may know that the race is not always to the swift;

that there is more to life than
measuring its speed.
Let me look upward into the
branches of the towering oak,
and know that it grew great and
strong because it grew slowly and
well.
Slow me down, Lord,
and inspire me to send my roots deep
into the soil of life's enduring
values.
That I may grow towards the sky of
my greater destiny.

Source unknown

Patriotism

Dulce et decorum est pro patria mori.
(It is a fine and seemly thing to die for one's native land)

Quintus Horatius Flaccus Horace (65–08 BC)

'My country, right or wrong' is a thing no patriot would think of saying except in a desperate case. It is like saying, 'My mother, drunk or sober'.

G K Chesterton: The Defendant

Describing the death of a soldier gassed in the trenches during the Great War (1914–18):
If in some smothering dreams, you
too could pace
Behind the wagon that we flung him
in,
And watch the white eyes writhing in
his face,
His hanging face, like a devil's sick of
sin;
If you could hear, at every jolt, the
blood
Come gargling from the froth-
corrupted lungs,
Bitter as the cud
Of vile, incurable sores on innocent
tongues, –
My friend, you would not tell with
such high zest
To children ardent for some desper-
ate glory,
The old lie: Dulce et decorum est
Pro patria mori.

Wilfred Owen: Dulce et Decorum Est

Peace

If I must choose between peace and righteousness I choose righteousness.

Theodore Roosevelt (1858–1919): 'Unwise Peace Treaties'

I asked a Rabbi what 'Shalom' meant and his answer was 'completeness, wholeness, right relations between God and man and between man and man'. I believe than when people want to know what this peace of God is about, they look at us as individuals and as a corporate company of Christians and we communicate what we are. And our communicating of God's peace is a long term business with no short cuts.

Bishop David Sheppard (of Liverpool): at the Church Pastoral-Aid Society Annual Meeting, (1974)

A rural dean from York turned to greet his neighbour in the pew with, 'The peace of the Lord,' and received the immediate response, 'I don't believe in it!'

Source unknown (c. 1980)

Peace without justice is an empty kind of peace.

Archbishop George Carey (of Canterbury): in Sudan, (1995)

Pentecostal churches – *see* CHARISMATICS, SPIRIT

Persecution – *see also* WITNESS

The soul, when it is starved of food, thrives the better;
So Christians, when they are punished, increase daily all the more.

Anonymous Letter to Diognetus, (2nd half of the 2nd Century AD)

Let the Church face the fact – and face it unblinkered – that it is in for a time of tribulation. If we are fools enough, for Christ's sake, to follow him, then we must face tribulation and even crucifixion – and no whining when that comes, no complaining when the winds are contrary. No crying to the world, for the sake of popularity, 'peace, peace, when there is no peace'! No 'healing of the wounds of my people lightly'! Our radical sickness calls for a radical cure – and that can only come by way of the cross.

Archbishop Donald Coggan: Enthronement at Canterbury, (25 January, 1975)

No. For the Church is stronger for this
action [Thomas à Becket's murder],
Triumphant in adversity. It is fortified
By persecution: supreme, so long as
men will die for it.

T.S. Eliot: 'Murder in the Cathedral', (1935), Part II, lines 590ff (Faber and Faber 1965)

Opposition may become sweet to a man when he has christened it 'persecution'.

George Eliot (Mary Anne Evans)

Christians have burnt each other,
quite persuaded
That all the Apostles would have
done as they did.

Lord George Byron (1788–1824): 'Don Juan'

Whoever is right, the persecutor must be wrong.

William Penn

Oscar Wilde [at a party held by the Bishop of London] is reported to have referred to a possible dinner engagement thus: 'I should be like a poor lion in a den of Daniels.'

On the first night of George Bernard Shaw's play *Arms and the Man* on 21 April, 1894, Shaw took a curtain call and there was a solitary hiss from the gallery, after the cheers subsided. It was from a literary critic who had misunderstood the play. Shaw bowed to him [R. Goulding Bright] and said, 'I quite agree with you, sir, but what can two do against so many?'

James Sutherland, Ed: 'The Oxford Book of Literary Anecdotes', (1975)

Today the devil is endangering the church with the greatest conceivable persecutions, namely without persecution, with tolerance and security. Woe to us, who are so dazzled by our comforts and well-being that we fall into the devil's trap.

Martin Luther: 'Works'

. . . the two fundamental principles of Passover. A people who were once slaves must never enslave others. And to have faith is not simply to believe that God is on your side. When God brings about a victory, he remains the God who suffers with the victims of that victory.

. . . those who have eaten the bread of affliction must give others bread, not affliction.

Rabbi Dr. Jonathan Sacks, then Chief Rabbi-elect: in The Times, (Good Friday, 29 March 1991), 'The world might weep'

Perseverance

There are but two roads that lead to an important goal and to the doing of great things: strength and perseverance. Strength is the lot of but a few privileged men; but austere perseverance, harsh and continuous, may be employed by the smallest of us and rarely fails of its purpose, for its silent power grows irresistibly greater with time.

Goethe

By perseverance the snail reached the Ark

Charles Haddon Spurgeon

The man who moved the mountain began by carrying away small stones.

Chinese Proverb

Great oaks from little acorns grow.

Anonymous

Little strokes fell great oaks.

Benjamin Franklin (1706–90)

[Jesus said] 'You will be hated by all because of my name. But the one who endures to the end will be saved.'

Matthew 10:22

[Jesus said] 'As for [the seed] in the good soil, these are the ones who, when they hear the word, hold it fast in an honest and good heart, and bear fruit with patient endurance.'

Luke 8:15

We have become partners of Christ, if only we hold our first confidence firm to the end.

Hebrews 3:14

God is not unjust; he will not overlook your work and the love that you showed for his sake in serving the saints, as you still do. And we want each of you to show the same diligence so as to realise the full assurance of hope to the very end, so that you may not become sluggish, but imitators of those who through faith and patience inherit the promises.

Hebrews 6:10–12

Pessimism

'Twixt the optimist and the pessimist
The difference is droll:
The optimist sees the doughnut
But the pessimist sees the hole.

McLandburgh Wilson: 'Optimist and Pessimist'

Philosophy

. . . no man that hath not the vitals of theology is capable of going beyond a fool in philosophy.

Richard Baxter: 'The Reformed Pastor', (1655)

Two rival philosophers were travelling in the same railway carriage. They hardly spoke for fear that what one said would be corrected by the logic of the other. Eventually one spoke up:

'I see the sheep in the fields have been sheared early this year!'

Silence followed until eventually the other philosopher replied: 'Yes, they have – at least on this side!'

BBC Radio 4, (7 April, 1985)

On a Metaphysician: A blind man in a dark room looking for a black hat which isn't there.

Attributed to Lord Bowen (1835–94)

Dieu d'Abraham, d'Isaac et de Jacob non des philosophes.
(The God of Abraham, Isaac and Jacob – of revelation – is not the philosophers' god.)

From a document (sometimes called his 'spiritual testament') found after his death sewn into the jacket of Blaise Pascal (1623–62)

The point of philosophy is to start with something so simple as to seem not worth stating, and to end with something so paradoxical that no one will believe it.

Bertrand Russell: 'Logic and Knowledge', (1956)

Pilgrimage

Let us concern ourselves with heavenly things, not human ones, and like pilgrims always sigh for our homeland, long for our homeland. It is the end of the road that travellers look for and desire, and because we are travellers and pilgrims through this world, it is the road's end, that is of our lives, that we should always be thinking about. For that road's end is our true homeland . . . Don't let us love the road rather than the land to which it leads, lest we lose our homeland altogether . . . So then, while we are on the road, as travellers, as pilgrims, as guests of the world, let us not get entangled with any earthly desires and lusts . . . Christians must travel in perpetual pilgrimage as guests of the world.

St. Columbanus, Abbot of Bangor, Ireland, (sixth century), who travelled to France and Italy

To go to Rome
Is much of trouble, little of profit;
The King whom thou seekest here,
Unless thou bring Him with thee, thou wilt not find.

Old Irish Poem in a collection edited by Kumo Meyer

Planning

Waiting upon the Spirit is the prerequisite of all we shall think and say and do. But our need to wait upon the Spirit must not be made an excuse for dodging rigorous analysis, planning and difficult decisions. In New Testament language, the time of the coming of the kingdom is known to God alone. But we are to prepare for its coming as well as pray for it, and so be ready to enter it when it comes. Gerd Theissen, German Theologian and sociologist, has put it in a nutshell: 'The church is a plannable institution which aims at offering opportunities for an unplannable event that escapes all institutionalising; the event of the Holy Spirit who blows where he wills.'

Peter Baelz: Address to the Governing Body of the Church in Wales, (15 April, 1993)

Reconnaissance is worth a thousand men.

Military saying

[Jesus said] 'Which of you, intending to build a tower, does not first sit down and estimate the cost, to see whether he has enough to complete it? Otherwise, when he has laid a foundation and is not able to finish, all who see it will begin to ridicule him, saying, 'This fellow began to build and was not able to finish.' Or what king, going out to wage war against another king, will not sit down first and consider whether he is able with ten thousand to oppose the one who comes against him with twenty thousand? If he cannot, then, while the other is still far away, he sends a delegation and asks for the terms of peace. So therefore, none of you can become my disciple if you do not give up all your possessions.'

Luke 14:28–33

Pluralism

For some Christians . . . the words of the church's sermon . . . no longer bite as they did from the lips of Jesus and the apostles . . . for they have relaxed into the club mentality of a civilisation which has become increasingly pluralist, undogmatic and flabbily tolerant.

Ian D. Bunting: 'Preaching at Communion', Part One, (Grove, 1981)

Poetry

Poets, of course, attempt to give shape to human existence in words. But they do not content themselves with platitudes. As far as the poet is concerned, words are not graves in which deep and disturbing flashes of understanding are finally laid to rest; they are the attempt to pin down moments of perception, they are little incarnations of thought which, for the moment at least, are partially valid as describing something important about the human condition. Occasionally the poet seizes words that will outlive their maker and tease new understanding out of succeeding generations.

John C. King: 'The Gospel Shrinkers', (Hodders, 1970)

Sir, I admit your gen'ral rule
That every poet is a fool;
But you yourself may serve to show it,
That every fool is not a poet.

Alexander Pope (1688–1744): 'Epigram from the French'

It was said that the policemen of Dublin became used to W.B. Yeats' strange antics as a young man: 'Shure,' they said, ''tisn't mad he is, nor yet drink taken. 'Tis the poethry that's disturbin' his head,' and they left him alone.

Recollection of Katharine Tynan (1861–1931)

The crown of literature is poetry. It is its end and aim. It is the sublimest activity of the human mind. It is the achievement of beauty and delicacy. The writer of prose can only stand aside when the poet passes.

W. Somerset Maughan: in the Saturday Review, (1957)

'Ah! so you are a poet, my dear sir,' he [Alexandre Bourdillat] went on. 'An excellent thing to be, a poet. A man who succeeds in that line may go far. Victor Hugo *[a novelist]* ended up as a millionaire *[far from it]*. I had a friend once who wrote little things. He died in the workhouse, poor man. Oh! I don't want to discourage you. And how many feet have your verses?'

'I write in all meters, Monsieur le Ministre.'

'How clever of you! And what type of poetry, eh? Sad, gay, humorous? Little ditties, perhaps? People like those things.'

'I write every kind, Monsieur le Ministre.'

'Better and better! So you are a real poet, like the members of the Academy. Splendid, splendid! Well, I may tell you that so far as I am concerned, poetry –'

For the second time since his arrival in Clochemerle, the ex-Minister displayed the ability to say the right thing at the right moment which contributes so greatly to the popularity of politicians. He smiled in the modest way he had when making the statement 'I am a self-made man.'

'I know less about feet in verses than feet in centipedes. You understand, Monsieur Samotherace, I was at the Ministry of Agriculture.'

Gabriel Chevalier: 'Clochemerle', (1936), chapter 5

Politics and Politicians

William Pitt the Elder (1708–1778), Earl of Chatham and Prime Minister, was a man of tireless energy. One day he asked his self-seeking adviser, the Duke of Newcastle to come to his house to discuss plans. The duke found him in bed in a cold room. Pitt had much to say and the duke found the cold unbearable; at last, spying another bed in the room, he crept into it, and the two statesmen were found talking and gesticulating at one another from under the bed clothes.

From Williams: William Pitt

He never said a foolish thing,
Nor ever did a wise one.
Verse on King Charles II, to which the king replied:
This is very true: for my words are my own and my actions are those of my ministers.

I am not one of those who has ever held the view that the church, to put it into colloquial language, should not interfere with politics. I believe that the church has a very heavy responsibility to point to the ills in our society, to do so frankly and fearlessly and for us to accept the criticism based on the principles for which the church stands. That is a very solemn responsibility of the church. But we also have to recognise that modern knowledge has become so specialised and the problems of our communal life so complex, that by the very nature of affairs there are fewer and fewer church leaders who can have detailed knowledge of the problems which arise in our society. It is therefore when they address their minds to the solutions to the problems to which they have so rightly pointed for our attention that difficulties arise.

Edward Heath, Prime Minister

He that goeth about to persuade a multitude, that they are not so well governed as they ought to be, shall never want of attentive and favourable hearers.

Richard Hooker (1554–1600): 'Laws of Ecclesiastical Polity'

We stand immovably on this eternal rock; what is morally wrong can never be politically right.

Hugh Price Hughes, (1890), while President of the Wesleyan Methodist Conference

An honest politician is one who, when he is bought, will stay bought.

Simon Cameron (1789–1889)

A politician is a person who faces every question with an open mouth.

Adlai Stevenson

Politics – the gentle art of getting votes from the poor and campaign funds from the rich by promising to protect each from the other.

Oscar Ameringer

Die Politik ist die Lehre von Möglichen.
(Politics is the art of the possible.)

Prince Bismarck (1815–98): conversation with Meyer von Waldeck, (11 August, 1867)

Every Communist must grasp the truth: Political power grows out of the barrel of a gun.

Mao Tse-Tung (1893–1976): 'Selected Works', (Peking, 1961), Vol 2, (6 November 1938)

. . . a sophisticated rhetorician inebriated with the exuberance of his own verbosity, and gifted with an egotistical imagination that can at all times command an interminable and inconsistent series of arguments to malign an opponent and to glorify himself.

Benjamin Disraeli: on Ewart Gladstone

A group of politicians deciding to dump a President because his morals are bad is like the Mafia getting together to bump off the Godfather for not going to church on Sunday.

Russell Baker: in The New York Times during the 'Watergate' scandal which brought down President Richard Nixon, (1974)

Nothing is politically right which is morally wrong.

Daniel O'Connell (1775–1847), Irish politician and lawyer

We the Ladies of the Sunflower League of Little Knitting, appeal to Mr. Khrushchev (of the Soviet Union) to take away the Iron Curtain, providing he doesn't sell it to Herr Krupps to melt down for bullets.

Based on a Giles Cartoon, (c. 1965)

. . . the earliest church never availed itself of the protection it would have had under Roman law as a *cultus privatus* dedicated to the pursuit of a purely personal and spiritual salvation for its members. Such private religion flourished as vigorously in the world of the Eastern Mediterranean as it does in North America today. It was permitted by the imperial authorities for the same reason that its counterparts are permitted today: it did not challenge the political order. Why, then, did the church refuse this protection? When did it have to engage in a battle to the death with the imperial powers? Because, true to its roots in the Old Testament, it could not accept relegation to a private sphere of purely inward and personal religion. It knew itself to be the bearer of the promise of the reign of Yahweh over all nations. It refused the names by which the many religious societies called themselves, and which critics such as Celsus applied to the church (*thiasos, hieranos*); it called itself the *ecclesia tou theou*, the public assembly to which God is calling all men everywhere without distinction. This made a collision with the imperial power inevitable – as inevitable as the Cross . . .

For the modern church to accept this position is to do exactly what the early church refused to do and what the Bible forbids us to do. It is, in effect, to deny that Christ is, simply and finally, the truth by which all other claims to truth are to be tested. It is to abandon its calling.

Lesslie Newbigin: 'Foolishness to the Greeks', (S.C.M., 1986)

Christians can never seek refuge in a ghetto where their faith is not proclaimed as public truth for all. They can never agree that there is one law for themselves and another for the world. They can never admit that there are areas of human life where the writ of Christ does not run. They can never accept that there are orders of creation or powers or dominions that exist otherwise than to serve Christ. Whatever the institutional relationship between the church and the state – and there are many possible relationships, no one of which is necessarily the right one for all times and places – the church can never cease to remind governments that they are under the rule of Christ and that he alone is the judge of all they do.

Lesslie Newbigin: 'Foolishness to the Greeks', (S.C.M., 1986)

Lloyd George described Éamon de Valera, the Irish politician:
Negotiating with him is like trying to pick up mercury with a fork.

Ye friends of truth, ye statesmen, who survey
The Rich man's joys increase, the poor's decay,
'Tis yours to judge, how wide the limits stand
Between a splendid and a happy land.

Oliver Goldsmith (1728–1774): 'The Deserted Village'

[Jesus said] 'Give therefore to the emperor the things that are the emperor's, and to God the things that are God's.'

Matthew 22:21b

Pilate therefore said to him, 'Do you refuse to speak to me? Do you not know that I have power to release you, and power to crucify you?' Jesus answered him, 'You would have no power over me unless it had been given you from above . . .'

John 19:10, 11a

Let every person be subject to the governing authorities; for there is no authority except from God, and those authorities that exist have been instituted by God. Therefore whoever resists authority resists what God has appointed, and those who resist will incur judgement. For rulers are not a terror to good conduct but to bad. Do you wish to have no fear of the authority? Then do what is good . . . But if you do what is wrong, you should be afraid, for the authority does not bear the sword in vain! It is the servant of God to execute wrath on the wrongdoer. Therefore one must be subject, not only because of wrath but also because of conscience. For the same reason you also pay taxes, for the authorities are God's servants, busy with this very thing.

Pay to all what is due them – taxes to whom taxes are due, revenue to whom revenue is due, respect to whom respect is due, honour to whom honour is due.

Romans 13:1–7

Pope, Bishop of Rome

. . . from the tyranny of the Bishop of Rome and all his detestable enormities, Good Lord deliver us.

Litany in the 1549 and 1552 Books of Common Prayer [This petition was removed by Queen Elizabeth I]

Some Protestants are for ever looking for a Pope under the bed.

Comment on some aspects of ecumenical relations

Possessions

The raw challenge of Jesus to the wealthy, and his warnings about the eternal peril of letting possessions take control of us, are equally noticeable by their absence from many people's preaching.

David Prior: 'The Suffering and the Glory', (1985)

[Jesus said] 'No one can serve two masters: for a slave will either hate the one and love the other, or be devoted to the one and despise the other. You cannot serve God and wealth.'

Matthew 6:24

Jesus said to them [the crowd], 'Take care! Be on your guard against all kinds of greed; for one's life does not consist in the abundance of possessions.'

Luke 12:15

Poverty

Poverty is an anomaly to rich people. It is very difficult [for them] to make out why people who want dinner do not ring the bell.

Walter Bagehot (1826–1877)

We cannot preserve slums in order to make them breeding-grounds for saints.

Julius Nyrere

There are three categories of poor people in the Bible:
i. The people who are always poor because their needs grow with their wealth *(penes)*.
ii. The oppressed, defeated, helpless, powerless poor *(ptochoi)*.
iii. The poor in spirit, for the sake of the kingdom of God.

I believe that there is a divine bias to the disadvantaged, and that the church needs to be much more faithful in reflecting it . . .

If we can put ourselves in the shoes of the poor and disadvantaged, we may see how matters appear to their consciousness . . . They are to do with the righteousness of God which has a persistent tendency to favour those at a disadvantage. They are to do with God taking flesh in the person of Jesus, living out his life in a special relation to the poor.

Bishop David Sheppard (of Liverpool): 'Bias to the Poor', (Hodders 1983)

The struggle for justice needs to be placed in the context of the gratuitous love of God. Not in order to be left demanding for justice, but to understand its meaning . . .

To be a Christian, for us, is to enter into the world of the poor. We are not committed to the poor if we are committed to a culture, a race, a discriminated sex, a social class. We are committed to the poor if we have friends among poor persons. I am not taking a romantic way of talking about the poor. To have friends is to share our lives with them, and to consider them our equals. Love is only possible between equals.

Father Custavo Gutierrez, Professor of Theology and Roman Catholic priest in an inner-city Peruvian parish: Lambeth Conference, (20 July, 1988)

This speaker [at the C.O.P.E.C. Conference in 1941 at Malvern, who assumed that only *extremes* of ill-spent wealth should be censured] evidently agreed with Wesley that the Christian should 'gain all he can, save all he can, give all he can,' and his speech illustrated the complete and comfortable ignorance of the causes of poverty cherished by Christians who are lucky enough to have plenty of cash in the bank.

Sidney Dark: 'The People's Archbishop', (James Clarke, 1942)

The prosperous are still living in luxury and paying little attention to the poor outside their door or half a world away. The rich fools are still going for bigger and better and losing their souls in the process. The unjust businessmen are still obsessed by their margins of profit and will end up without friends in eternity. Wealthy, upright, leaders still want to believe they can have eternal life without any significant parting with their goods for the benefit of the poor. Religious leaders still pass by those on the other side who have been robbed on the highways of life and economics.

Tom Houston: a paraphrase of Luke's Gospel at the Lausanne Congress II in Manila, (July 1989); from 'Proclaim Christ Until He Comes', (W.W. Publications, 1990)

It is not enough for Dives to throw a half-crown to Lazarus when he sees him crouching on his doorstep. He must see to it that Lazarus is medically treated for his sores and that he is properly fed every day, and he must see to it, too, that social conditions are so changed that there will never again be a Lazarus compelled to pick up the crumbs that fall down from the rich man's table.

Sidney Dark: 'The People's Archbishop', (James Clarke, 1942)

Shadows in the mist
We pretend they don't exist
They're the victims of the rich
They're the shadows in the mist.
In the eyes of the world they are
nothing
But they are treasures in the eyes of
God.

Garth Hewitt, (1989)

We saw beauty in the ashes
We saw treasure in the dust
We saw joy come out of mourning
We saw diamonds in the rough
And though the image may look
broken
We saw Jesus shining through
And on each forgotten feature
He was writing 'I love you'.

Come and stand with the broken
Come and learn from the poor
Take the side of those forgotten
Let the image be restored.

Garth Hewitt, (1989)

In the parable, it was the one lost sheep that the shepherd went in search of (Matthew 18:12; Luke 15:4): it was not the only sheep in the flock, and we are not told that it was the most valuable – save in so far as the most desperately in need has, while the need lasts, a peculiar value in the eyes of Love.

C.S. Lewis: 'Dogma and the Universe', (1943), in 'God in the Dock', (Collins, 1979)

Poverty is a knee-level view from your bit of pavement; a battered, upturned cooking pot and countable ribs; coughing from your steel-banded lungs, alone, with your face to the wall; shrunken breasts and a three-year old who cannot stand; the ringed fingers, the eyes averted and a five-pence piece in your hand; smoking the babus' cigarette butts to quieten the fiend in your belly; a husband without a job, without a square meal a day, without energy, without hope; being at the mercy of everyone further up the ladder because you are a threat to their self-respect; a hut of tins and rags and plastic bags in a warren of huts you cannot stand up in, where your neighbours live at one arm's length across the lane; a man who cries out in silence; nobody listening, for everyone's talking; the prayer withheld; the hand withheld – yours and mine.

LORD, TEACH US TO HATE OUR POVERTY OF SPIRIT.

A Litany from Calcutta

Lawrence was a Deacon of the Church of Rome in the third century and was martyred during a persecution of the church.

When it was realised that Lawrence was the keeper of the church treasures, he was arrested and ordered to give them up. He asked for a day's grace, after which he promised to produce the church's most treasured possessions. All night long he hurried around Rome's poorest streets and alleys, and in the morning appeared before the court with a crowd of poor, maimed, lame, blind and sick people. 'These,' he said, 'are what the church holds most dear and counts her greatest treasures. The gold you seek is simply metal and serves to incite people to all kinds of crimes. The light of heaven, which these people enjoy, is the true gold!'

Traditional

Smoky Mountain, a rubbish tip in Metro Manila, is home to 17,000 people.
There are some kinds of desolation that leave you impotent . . .

There is suffering on earth, I know. And plenty of that suffering is in the Philippines. But if I can't subtract from the world's sum of misery, do I have to add to it personally? It's one of these questions I mean to take up if ever I get religion.

P.J. O'Rourke: 'Holidays in Hell', (1988)

Fortune, that arrant whore,
Ne'er turns the key to th'poor.

William Shakespeare: 'King Lear', (1605/06), Song by the Fool, II.iv.50–51

Jesus said, 'Blessed are the poor in spirit, for theirs is the kingdom of heaven.'

Matthew 5:3

Jesus answered them (the disciples of John the Baptist), 'Go and tell John what you have seen and heard: the blind receive their sight, the lame walk, the lepers are cleansed, the deaf hear, the dead are raised, the poor have good news brought to them. And blessed is anyone who takes no offence at me.'

Luke 7:22, 23

You know the generous act of our Lord Jesus Christ, that though he was rich, yet for your sakes he became poor, so that by his poverty you might become rich.

2 Corinthians 8:9

How does God's love abide in anyone who has the world's goods and sees a brother or sister in need and yet refuses help? Little children, let us love, not in word or speech, but in truth and action.

1 John 3:17, 18

Power

Power tends to corrupt, and absolute power corrupts absolutely.

First Baron Acton (1834–1902)

. . . power is subordinate to love and love exerts its power by self-sacrifice.

Archbishop William Temple (of Canterbury)

Right without might is helpless, whereas might without right is tyrannical. Right without might is challenged because there are always unjust people around. Power without justice is to be condemned. Justice and power must therefore be combined so that we can ensure that what is right is strong, and what is strong is just.

Blaise Pascal (1623–1662)

Prayer, what is it?

'Prayer and helplessness are inseparable.' Only the person who is helpless can truly pray. If I feel sinful or abandoned, cold or depressed, doubting or dishonest, the feeling of helplessness this awareness induces is not my barrier but my way into prayer. 'Prayer therefore simply consists in telling God day by day in what ways we feel that we are helpless.' The Psalms encourage this view.

John Goldingay: 'Praying the Psalms', (Grove Spirituality, 1993); quoting Otto Hallesby: 'Prayer', (I.V.F., 1948)

The victory of the church over the Roman Empire was not won by seizing the levers of power; it was won when the victims knelt down in the Colosseum and prayed in the name of Jesus for the Emperor.

Bishop Lesslie Newbigin: 'The Gospel in a Pluralist Society', (S.P.C.K., 1989)

Prayer is praise, worship and thanksgiving to God.
Prayer is the unending conversation with God about everything that concerns us and ours.
Sometimes prayer is arguing with God about life's mysteries.
Prayer is interceding on behalf of others near and far, high and low, rich and poor, weak and strong.
Prayer is meditating on the working of God in history, the greatness of God in nature, the goodness of God in his providences and the promises of God in Scripture.
Prayer is being totally honest with yourself in the presence of God.

Prayer is recovering from the brink of despair, the depth of failure, the isolation of loneliness.
Prayer is intensive care in acute suffering and sickness.
Prayer is refining our dreams about the future in the light of the will of God.
Prayer is waiting on God when he is long in coming.
Prayer is the cry for justice when it does not come.
Prayer is walking with God all day and every day.

Tom Houston: in World Evangelisation, No. 68, (1994), 'Prayer and Spiritual Warfare'

There are so many prayer success stories that one hears about, all to do with this benevolent God on tap who seems to be on the end of the private line, but somehow they don't fit in with my experience of life, and I'm tired of feeling guilty and saying that if I believed more strongly I'd see that sort of thing happen too. In fact, I've seen the other side of the coin – the bewilderment when tragedy hits a deeply good and believing family and people start saying, 'Why did God allow it? How did he let this happen?', as if there were someone sitting in a heavenly control room, stopping this, allowing that, presumably according to some deeply laid plan – although it feels more like whimsy – but capable of being cajoled if everyone would only pray hard enough. And as long as the image of the control room is there, worship will be tinged with self-interest; we shall be siding with where we think the power is: now, if we could only find the secret of tapping it effectively . . .

Richard MacKenna: 'God for Nothing', (Churchman, 1984/85)

A.C.T.S. (the order of prayer): **A**doration, **C**onfession, **T**hanksgiving, **S**upplication.

From the Community of the Resurrection, Mirfield

What a man is on his knees before God, that he is – and nothing more.

Robert Murray McCheyne (1813–1843)

Real prayer is offering what you can see and grasping what is happening, however painful and beastly it is, and waiting on God with it, almost as though you have it in your hands.

Alan Amos: in an interview, (1983)

. . . prayer is not instructing God in his duties or ordering from him what we want. It is co-operating with him in fulfilling his purposes to which we must humbly submit. He reigns – we serve.

Belfry Trust Newsletter, (7 March 1984), announcing death of David Watson (18 February, 1984)

The gift of prayer is one of the noblest and most useful in the Christian life, and therefore to be sought with earnest desire and diligence; and in order to attain it, we must avoid these two extremes:

I. A confining ourselves entirely to precomposed forms of prayer.

II. An entire dependence on sudden motions and suggestions of thought . . .

Do not affect to pray long, for the sake of length, or to stretch out your matter by labour and toil of thought, beyond the furniture of your own spirit. God is not the more pleased with prayers, merely because they are long, nor are Christians ever the more edified. It is much better to make up by the frequency of our devotions what we want in the length of them, when we feel our spirits dry, and our hearts straitened. We may also cry to God for the aid of his own Holy Spirit, even in the middle of our prayer, to carry us forward in that work: but every man is not fit to pray long. God has bestowed a variety of natural, as well as spiritual talents and gifts upon men; nor is the best Christian, or a saint of the greatest gifts, always fit for long prayers.

Isaac Watts (1674–1748)

Real prayer leads to action, leads to us doing what we can for people. But it also saves us from fantasies of omnipotence, of imagining that we can do for people what we manifestly can't do, and from the anxiety and guilt-feelings such fantasies evoke. And praying for people also makes us sensitive to their deepest needs which are generally not their most obvious ones. By means of our prayer God succours people in the very centre and core of their being, and that is what they need most.

Harry A. Williams: 'Becoming What I Am'

Prayer is often regarded, even by genuinely religious people, as chiefly a means to various ends; it is a way of getting things done. That is true, so far as it goes; but, like so many half-truths, it is in practice as misleading as a complete falsehood. Prayer which is mainly occupied with a result to be obtained is comparatively powerless to obtain results. The real significance of prayer lies in the fact that it is the effort and attitude of the souls which makes possible the unity of the human spirit with God; it is therefore itself the supreme aim of human existence.

Archbishop William Temple (of Canterbury): 'Christus Veritas'

Screwtape writes to his diabolical pupil, Wormwood:
Don't forget to use the 'heads I win, tails you lose' argument. If the thing he prays for doesn't happen, then that is one more proof that petitionary prayers don't work; if it does happen, he will, of course, be able to see some of the physical causes which led up to it and 'therefore it would have happened anyway', and thus a granted prayer becomes just as good a proof as a denied one that prayers are ineffective.

C.S. Lewis (1898–1963): 'The Screwtape Letters'

John Chapman, Anglican, Roman Catholic, Jesuit and eventually Benedictine abbot (1865–1933) wrote letters which form a spiritual diary:
19 December 1919:
The one real proof that you have the *right kind of prayer for you,* is not that it always goes easily and always succeeds, but that it really does you good and changes your life.
13 October 1925:
. . . it seems to be a fact that God *always gives breathing-spaces.*

Prayer gives a man the opportunity of getting to know a gentleman he hardly ever meets. I do not mean his Maker, but himself.

Dean William Inge (of St. Paul's, London, 1911–1934)

Intercession, which has been described as the search for our part in the work of God, is an essential element in the missionary dimension of worship.

Edward Patey: 'Open the Doors', (Mowbrays, 1978)

God help us, without doubting, to obtain all these petitions, and suffer us not to doubt that thou *hast* heard us and *wilt* hear us in them all; that it is 'Yea' and not 'Nay' and not 'Perhaps'. Therefore we say with joy, 'Amen', and it is true and certain. Amen.

Martin Luther: on the Lord's Prayer

Prayer, praying

The things, good Lord, that your servants pray for, give us also grace to labour for.

Sir Thomas More

Where there is no prayer in the pew, there is no power in the pulpit.

Cecil G.C. Lillingstone, (January 1905)

We are helpless to put prayer into words and generally feel as if the failure to 'say it right' is a failure in the prayer itself. That is not so.

David Runcorn: 'Silence', (1986)

Charles Spurgeon was asked by an American why he was so successful; Spurgeon's reply was: 'My people pray for me.'

'I look at him, and he looks at me, and we are one together.' It matters little whether or not words are spoken . . . When the man of faith presses his littleness close to God's greatness in prayer, his ignorance close to God's wisdom, his weakness close to God's strength, yes, and (greatly daring) his sinfulness close to God's holy forgiving, it is personal indeed. . . .

God's fatherly care reaches to the least significant, for 'significance' is a human term which has no significance for the Heavenly Father . . .

Meanwhile, when I pray – even when I am at my coldest and most formal – I 'chip in'; I take my part in the great orchestra; I am one with angels and archangels and all the company of heaven . . .

The saints would appear to tell us

that about the *only* prayer that matters is: 'Thy will be done.'

Archbishop Donald Coggan (of Canterbury): 'Faith and Prayer', Methodist Preacher's Handbook, (1972)

O Lord! thou knowest how busy I must be this day: if I forget thee, do not thou forget me.

The prayer of Sir Jacob Astley before the Battle of Edghill (1642), in which he was wounded. It appears in the 'Memoires' of Sir Philip Warwick, (1701), and is found in other versions, (apparently quoting from this source)

Describing 'a different and important sort of prayer above and beyond words; a stillness and silence and a waiting on God':
Isn't one of the greatest gifts of the church the chance to offer such a space? And isn't it in danger of snatching it back if it shows itself frightened of mystery, solitude, failure, darkness – of everything, in fact, that confronts us most with the pressure of Being? 'Not by might, nor by power, but by my Spirit, says the Lord of Hosts' (Zechariah 4:6).

Richard MacKenna: 'God for Nothing', (Churchman, 1984/85)

Dr. Samuel Johnson, speaking to James Boswell of what was taken for madness:
My poor friend Smart showed the disturbance of his mind by falling upon his knees and saying his prayers in the street, or in any other unusual place. Now although, rationally speaking, it is a greater madness not to pray at all than to pray as Smart did, I am afraid there are so many people who do not pray, that their understanding is not called in question.

Prayer, abuse and problems of

A brother of the bride's father, both noted Christians, was asked to say grace at the wedding breakfast and began with classic jargon:
Let us just bow our heads together.

(1987)

The idea of reading a prayer was sacrilege to us [as Sanctified Brethren]: 'If a man can't remember what he wants to say to God, let him sit down and think a little harder,' Grandpa said.

Garrison Keillor: 'Lake Wobegon Days', (1985), Sumus Quod Sumus

Garrison Keillor tells the story of a Lutheran pastor who
. . . is no longer in the ministry. He is vice-president for sales at Devotional Systems, Inc., maker of quadraphonic sanctuary speakers for high fidelity sermons, home devotional programmes on floppy disks, and individual biofeed back systems in the pews. Two wires with electrodes hang from each hymnal rack, which the faithful press to their temples as they pray, attempting to bring the needle on the biometer into the reverence zone. For some reason, prayer doesn't accomplish that so well as, say, thinking about food, but DSI is working on it and thinks this may be a breakthrough in the worship of the future.

Garrison Keillor: 'Lake Wobegon Days', (1985), Sumus Quod Sumus

Worship on Christmas Day: Wednesday December 25th:
Enjoyed it all very much except for a point halfway through the prayer-time, when George Farmer, who was sitting behind me, stood up and began to swing his fist from side to side as he prayed fervently for good will among God's people.

Suddenly felt a heavy blow on the side of my head and slumped forward, momentarily stunned. Shook my head to clear it, and realised to my amazement that Farmer was still ranting on as if nothing had happened!

Didn't feel much good will.

I said to him afterwards, 'I forgive you for punching me in the head, George.'

He said, 'Did I really do that?'

Gerald said, 'Yes you did. It was on your twenty-fifth 'just' – I was counting.'
Went home.

Adrian Plass: 'The Sacred Diary of Adrian Plass'

Bobbie's birthday was next week. That night, after saying his prayers, he added the following prayer in a very loud voice:

'Dear God, I pray that I will get a new bicycle, and an electric train for my birthday. Amen.'
'Why are you praying so loudly?' asked his brother. 'God isn't deaf.'
'I know', replied Bobbie, 'But Grandma is!'

Anonymous

Father expected a good deal of God. He didn't actually accuse God of inefficiency, but when he prayed his tone was loud and angry, like that of a dissatisfied guest in a carelessly managed hotel.

Clarence Day: 'God and My Father'

While our brother is finishing his prayer, we will sing our last hymn . . .

Charles H. Spurgeon

I sat in the church
(I'd gone to break bread);
the pastor began to assure us
that we could spend time
with our minds fixed on God
– but somebody thought of a chorus:

Gordon Bailey: 'Patchwork Quilt', (1975)

. . . if my prayer is centred on myself, if it seeks the enrichment of my own self, it will be my greatest potential distraction.

Thomas Merton: 'Thoughts in Solitude'

It is said that some nonconformist ministers in 'The Long Prayer' commonly used a tone of easy formality with the Almighty, such as might be used by a leader of a deputation interviewing a trusted but not too well informed superior.

Anonymous

Kill him, O Lord, kill him! We cannot kill him without being hanged ourselves, but thou canst kill him.

Welsh minister's prayer recalled by Lloyd George (from his childhood)

A type of answer [to prayer] which may have an impeccable scriptural pedigree, and which may have been adopted in entire good faith, may nevertheless act as a pointer to a subtle spiritual sickness, if it is taken as the final word on the subject . . . using God as a conversation-stopper . . . effectively puts an end to any further discussion.

. . . to believe that one has reached an ultimate point of knowing the mind of God under the conditions of earthly existence, especially when there are all-too-human motives and explanations ready to hand, is to risk using God as a convenient excuse for not facing facts . . . God . . . is not an excuse for any failure to use our best powers in the unravelling of that truth.

Archbishop John Habgood (of York): in The Independent, (9 May, 1987)

A five-year old insisted on changing the Lord's Prayer by saying: 'Give us today our daily chips.' His teacher gently corrected him and told him that the word was 'bread'.
'Oh, no!' was the reply. 'I've got plenty of bread; what I want is chips.'

Anonymous

'I'll pray for you', that glib turn-off, but never, 'I'll watch with you'.

Richard MacKenna: 'God for Nothing', (Churchman, 1984/85)

The first goal scored by Roberto Rivelino of the Corinthians in a game against Rio Preto at Bahia Stadium came as a surprise to the goalie, Senor Irandir, who was on his knees saying his pre-match prayers in the goal mouth.

Stephen Pile, Ed: 'The Book of Heroic Failures', (1979)

. . . perhaps the reason why some of us seem unable to grow as people or as Christians is that our prayer life is used as a shield against the pressures of reality and an evasion of the questions that life (or God?) is asking us.

Richard MacKenna: 'God for Nothing,' (Churchman, 1984/85)

. . . when we consider with a religious seriousness the manifold weaknesses of the strongest devotions in time of Prayer, it is a sad consideration. I throw myself downe in my Chamber, and I call in, and invite God, and his Angels thither.

And when they are there, I neglect God and his Angels, for the noise of a Flie, for the ratling of a Coach, for the whining of a doore; I talke on, in the same posture of praying; eyes lifted up; knees bowed downe; as though I prayed to God; and, if God, or his

Angels should aske me, when I last thought of God in that prayer, I cannot tell. Sometimes I finde that I had forgot what I was about, but when I began to forget it, I cannot tell. A memory of yester days pleasures, a feare of tomorrows dangers, a straw under my knee, a noise in mine eare, a light in mine eye, an any thing, a nothing, a fancy, a chimera in my brain, troubles me in my prayer. So certainly there is nothing, nothing in spiritual things, perfect in this world. I turn to hearty and earnest prayer to God, and I fix my thoughts strongly (as I thinke) upon him, and before I have perfected one petition . . . the spirit of slumber closes mine eyes and I pray drowsily; or the spirit of deviation, and vaine repetition, and I pray giddily, and circularly, and return againe and againe to that I have said before, and perceive not that I do so . . . I consider not mine own purpose in prayer; and by this advantage, this door of inconsideration, enters the seducing spirit, the spirit of error, and I pray not only negligently, but erroneously, dangerously for such things as disconduce to the glory of God, and my true happiness, if they were granted.

John Donne (1572–1631): Sermon at the funeral of Sir William Cokayne

It is amusing to see souls who, while they are at prayer, fancy they are willing to be despised and publicly insulted for the love of God, yet afterwards do all they can to hide their small defects; if anyone unjustly accuses them of a fault, God deliver us from their outcries! Let those who cannot bear such things take no notice of the splendid plan they make when alone . . . Prayer does not consist of such fancies.

St. Theresa of Avila (1515–1582): 'The Interior Castle'

A schoolboy emerged desperate from a Geography examination with this prayer: 'Dear God, *please* make Paris the capital of Turkey!'

Anonymous

Prayer, discipline of

'Twould ring the bells of heaven the
loudest peal for years.
If parson lost his sense and people
came to theirs.
And he and they together knelt
down with angry prayers.
For tamed and shabby tigers
And dancing dogs and bears,
And wretched, blind pit ponies
And little hunted hares.

Ralph Hodgson

Pray as you can and do not pray as you can't. Take yourself as you find yourself and start from there.

Dom. John Chapman

I must say my prayers today whether I feel devout or not; but that is only as I must learn my grammar if I am ever to read the poets.

C.S. Lewis (1898–1963): 'Letters to Malcolm'

. . . prayer and love are really learned in the hour when faith becomes impossible. Struggle is the fruit of faithfulness in the desert – not the failure of it.

David Runcorn: 'Silence', (1986)

I am so busy that I find I cannot do with less than four hours a day in the presence of God.

Martin Luther (1483 – 1546)

. . . perhaps one of the reasons why the Third Collect is placed in [the Anglican service of] Evensong*, is to prevent us getting too polite, to remind us that the closing of day and the falling of darkness is a time not for relaxing the grip, but a time of increased Christian responsibility; is a time to be kept through and in Jesus Christ our Lord, caring and praying for those who cry out in any kind of fear in the dark, sore, lonesome, inarticulate places of the world, our own hearts included.

John Carden: 'Another Day', (Triangle, 1986)

** Lighten our darkness, we beseech thee, O Lord; and by thy great mercy defend us from all perils and dangers of this night; for the love of thy only Son, our Saviour Jesus Christ. Amen.*

If a concert pianist stops practising four hours a day,
after a day or two he notices it's bad,
after a week his manager notices,

after two or three weeks his audience notices.
Seven days without prayer make one weak.

Prayer, joy of

Give us this day our daily discovery.

Prayer of Dr. Randell Harris (a Quaker)

Lord, I am like a bicycle and my tyres are flat.
Blow me up, and then ride me!

An African boy's prayer

Prayer the Churches banquet,
Angels age,
Gods breath in man returning to his birth,
The soul in paraphrase, heart in pilgrimage,
The Christian plummet sounding heaven and earth.

Engine against th'Almightie, sinners towre,
Reversed thunder, Christ-side-piercing spear,
The six-daies world-transposing in an houre,
A kinde of tune, which all things heare and fear;

Softnesse, and peace, and joy, and love, and blisse,
Exalted Manna, gladness of the best,
Heaven in ordinarie, man well drest,
The milkie way, the bird of Paradise,

Church-bells beyond the starres heard, the souls bloud,
The land of spices; something understood.

George Herbert (1593–1633): 'Prayer'

The time of business does not with me differ from the time of prayer, and in the noise and clatter of my kitchen, while several persons are at the same time calling for different things, I possess God in as great tranquillity as if I were upon my knees at the Blessed Sacrament.

Brother Lawrence: from 'The Practice of the Presence of God', (English translation, 1892)

And Satan trembles, when he sees
The weakest saint upon his knees.

William Cowper (1731–1800)

Prayer, the Scriptures

[Jesus said] 'Ask, and it will be given you; search, and you will find; knock, and the door will be opened for you. For everyone who asks receives, and everyone who searches finds, and for everyone who knocks, the door will be opened. Is there anyone among you who, if your child asks for bread, will give a stone? Or if a child asks for a fish, will give a snake? If you then, who are evil, know how to give good gifts to your children, how much more will your Father in heaven give good things to those who ask him!'

Matthew 7:7–11

Devote yourselves to prayer, keeping alert in it with thanksgiving.

Colossians 4:2

Since, then, we have a great high priest who has passed through the heavens, Jesus, the Son of God, let us hold fast to our confession. For we do not have a high priest who is unable to sympathise with our weaknesses, but we have one who in every respect has been tested as we are, yet without sin. Let us therefore approach the throne of grace with boldness, so that we may receive mercy and find grace to help in time of need.

Hebrews 4:14–16

This is the boldness we have in him, that if we ask anything according to his will, he hears us. And if we know that he hears us in whatever we ask, we know that we have obtained the requests made of him.

1 John 5:14, 15

Prayer Book (The Books of Common Prayer, 1549–1662)

The Book of Common Prayer, next to the Bible itself, is the authoritative standard of doctrine of the Anglican Communion.

Lambeth Conference Encyclical Letter, (1897)

The Conference holds that the Book of Common Prayer has been, and is, so strong a bond of unity throughout the whole Angl ican Communion that great care must be taken to ensure that revisions of the Book shall be in accordance with the doctrine and accepted liturgical worship of the Anglican Communion.

Resolution 78 of Lambeth Conference, (1948)

In a large village to the west of Truro, Cornwall, in about 1740, there was no church, nor Bible; but there was a one-volume Prayer Book and New Testament, the property of the old woman who kept the inn. This she kept, along with a copy of Daniel Defoe's *Robinson Crusoe* on a shelf in the kitchen. One Summer's evening, in a violent storm, many villagers gathered at the inn for the comfort and safety of the sacred book. To be doubly-sure, Jack, the innkeeper's apprentice, who had learned to read and was therefore a prodigy, was sent for and everyone fell to their knees in the drinking room.

Jack went to fetch the Prayer Book, but, in all the confusion, took down *Robinson Crusoe* by mistake: he fell on his knees and read as fast as he could – often misreading the words. At length, when he stumbled over the name 'Friday', his mistress called out: 'Why Jack! thee hast got the wrong book! Sure thee'st reading prayers out of *Robinson Crusoe*!'

Jack was deeply wounded at this insult and continued to read, declaring that '*Robinson Crusoe* would as soon stop thunder as the Prayer Book.'

Related in more detail in a letter by Richard Polwhele in 1822 and referring to this incident as having happened 'about 80 years ago'

A principal of Trevelyan College, Durham (then a women's college) came across a male student of theology in the corridor of her college at an improper hour of the night. 'Young man,' she said, 'you have erred and strayed from your ways like a lost sheep.'

'With respect, not at all, Principal,' came the prompt reply. 'I am simply following the devices and desires of my own heart.'

Anonymous source

Those who make light of the Prayers, and regard them only as a kind of decent prelude to the Sermon show that 'they know not what spirit they are of': since all the preaching in the universe will be of no use without prayer . . . A congregation uniting fervently in the prayers of our liturgy would afford as complete a picture of heaven as ever yet was beheld on earth. The finest sight short of heaven would be a whole congregation using the prayers of the Liturgy in the true spirit of them.

Charles Simeon: 'Horae Homileticae', (1833), Sermon 333 and elsewhere

I believe there is no Liturgy in the world, either in ancient or modern language, which breathes more solid, scriptural, rational piety, than the Common Prayer of the Church of England.

John Wesley, cited in R. Davies & G. Rupp (Eds.): 'A History of The Methodist Church in Great Britain', Vol. I, (Epworth, 1965)

Take the prayers that are offered on any Sabbath in the places out of the establishment; have them all written down . . . then compare them with the prayers that have been offered in all the churches of the kingdom; and see what comparison the extemporaneous effusions will bear with our precomposed forms; . . . proceed to do it for a year; and . . . methinks there is scarcely a man in the kingdom that would not fall down on his knees and bless God for the liturgy of the established church.

Charles Simeon, preaching in November 1811 during a controversy which followed the founding of the British and Foreign Bible Society

Prayer should be short, without giving God Almighty reasons why he should grant this or that; he knows best what is good for us . . .

If a servant that has been fed with good beef, goes into that part of England where salmon is plenty, at first he is pleased with his salmon, and despises his beef, but, after he has been there a while, he grows weary of his salmon, and wishes for his good beef again. We have a while been much taken with this praying by the Spirit [during the Commonwealth]; but in time we may grow weary of it, and wish for our Common Prayer.

John Seldon (1584–1654): from his 'Table Talk'

Preachers

The kind of preacher the church needs most:
...an authoritative gospel in a humble personality.

P.T. Forsyth: 'Positive Preaching and the Modern Mind', (Independent, 1907)

Believe it, brethren, God never saved any man for being a preacher, nor because he was an able preacher; but because he was a justified, sanctified man, and consequently faithful in his Master's work.

Richard Baxter: 'The Reformed Pastor', (1655)

I am convinced that a major influence on our preaching is the image of the preacher we carry with us as we prepare and as we stand to preach. The primary persona can be the scholar, the counsellor, the moralist or the motivational speaker, among others. Whilst most of us invoke one or more of these roles in any given series of Sundays, there is usually one persona that is primary. For me, that preaching persona is the story-teller. Indeed storytelling has provided my primary self-image throughout my life.

Michael E Williams: 'Journey toward Narrative Preaching', (Pilgrim Press, 1990)

First, I reads myself full, next I thinks myself clear, next I prays myself hot, then I lets go.

An American preacher's technique of preparation and delivery

A Methodist Church selection panel was interviewing a candidate for the ministry. The candidate, who was a shy young man, explained that he would never set the River Thames on fire. 'My dear young brother,' replied Dr. W.E. Sangster, 'I'm not interested to know if you could set the Thames on fire. What I want to know is this: if I picked you up by the scruff of your neck and dropped you into the Thames, would it sizzle?'

Original source unknown

Our sermons will never catch fire unless the fire of the Holy Spirit burns in our hearts and we are ourselves 'aglow with the Spirit'. [Romans 12:11].

John R.W. Stott: 'I Believe in Preaching', (Hodders, 1982)

[Preaching is] theology coming from a man who is on fire.

Martyn Lloyd-Jones

I constantly find myself wishing that we twentieth-century preachers could learn to weep again.

John R.W. Stott: 'I Believe in Preaching', (Hodders, 1982)

All of us who are Christian preachers are finite, fallen, frail and fallible creatures ... The power belongs to Christ and is exerted through his Spirit. The words we speak in human weakness the Holy Spirit carries home by his power to the mind, heart, conscience and will of the hearers.

John R.W. Stott: 'I Believe in Preaching', (Hodders, 1982)

It became clearer to me the more I preach that I dare not urge others to do what I am not willing to put into practice myself. In some ways the most beautiful words from the Roman ordination rite are spoken at the *traditio* (the 'handing on') of the Gospel Book to new deacons: 'Receive the gospel of Christ, whose herald you now are. Believe what you read, teach what you believe, and practise what you teach'. These words can have a haunting quality if they are taken seriously, for precisely this commitment to the truth of the biblical text is communicated by the very manner in which the preacher speaks. Successful preaching is ultimately the establishment of trust between the preacher and the congregation – or I should say – the rest of the assembly. In fact it is only preachers who recognise the need for the correction that I just made, namely that the preacher is a member of the assembly *before* he or she holds office in the church, it is only such preachers who ultimately serve the purposes of the gathered church. I do not mean to argue that a preacher must always be a member of the congregation to which he or she preaches, but rather that the preacher must be able to relate on some level to the assembly and basically to consider him or herself more of a member of the assembly than set over it.

John F. Baldovin, S.J.: 'Biblical Preaching in the Liturgy', at Societas Liturgica Congress XIII, (Toronto, 1991)

Who, having been called to be a preacher, would stoop to be a king?

Thomas Carlyle

The teacher is like a candle which is consumed in illuminating others.

Italian Proverb

Some clergy prepare their sermons; others prepare themselves.

Bishop Samuel Wilberforce (of Winchester, 'Soapy Sam', 1805–73)

. . . consider Almighty God himself as speaking to you by your minister. Ministers come not in their own name. They are sent by Christ. It is his message they bring. Their word is not their own but his.

Charles Simeon (1759–1835): to the people of Holy Trinity Church, Cambridge

He who preaches Christ cannot accept worship of himself and must become so careful about publicity that he avoids any danger of self-exaltation.

Teddy Saunders: in 'David Watson', (1985)

. . . be also very careful . . . that you preach to yourselves the sermons that you study, before you preach them to others . . .

He preacheth not heartily to his people, that will not pray for them.

Richard Baxter: 'The Reformed Pastor', (1655)

God forbid, that every man that can take unto himself boldness to speak an hour together in a church, upon a text, should be admitted for a preacher, though he mean never so well.

Francis Bacon, Lord Keeper (Chancellor) of England (1560–1626): 'On the Importance of an Educated Ministry'

What you *are* speaks so loudly that I cannot hear what you *say!*

Anonymous

He that *means* as he speaks, will surely *do* as he speaks.

Richard Baxter: 'The Reformed Pastor', (1655)

. . . there is One there 'in whose sight' we preach. The King of kings is in the congregation. We cannot prate or strut before *him.*

Archbishop Donald Coggan (of Canterbury): 'On Preaching', (1975/78)

The preacher is not a lone figure, preaching what appeals to him most and leaving the rest unsaid. He is, rather, the last in the apostolic line of those through whose preaching God's salvation in Christ continues. Through him the gospel reverberates.

Archbishop Donald Coggan (of Canterbury): 'On Preaching', (1975/78)

Talking overmuch about oneself is a fearful fault in a preacher and it is hardly less heinous when he constantly talks about his own wife and children.

W E Sangster: 'The Craft of Sermon Illustration', (1946)

Truth from his lips prevail'd with
 double sway,
And fools, who came to scoff,
 remain'd to pray . . .
His ready smile a parent's warmth
 express'd,
Their welfare pleas'd him, and their
 cares distress'd;
To them his heart, his love, his griefs
 were given,
But all his serious thoughts had rest
 in Heaven . . .
In arguing too, the parson own'd his
 skill,
For e'en though vanquish'd, he could
 argue still;
While words of learned length and
 thund'ring sound
Amazed the gazing rustics rang'd
 around,
And still they gazed, and still the
 wonder grew,
That one small head could carry all
 he knew.

Oliver Goldsmith (whose father was a country parson in Ireland): 'The Deserted Village', (1770), from lines 179–216

Preaching, what it is

'What right have I,' the curate or vicar may ask, 'to preach to these people Sunday by Sunday? Many of them are better educated than I am; very many of them far more experienced in life and affairs. Who am I to harangue them?' He does well to ask such questions and to ask them sincerely. Who indeed is he? Who am I? But if he can find no answer to these questions, it will go ill with him and with his ministry. Authority matters . . . The Spirit of the Lord is upon him, and his aim is so to set his sail so as to catch the Wind. Unless this is a reality – the great reality of his life – he may read his people an essay Sunday by Sunday, he may give them a few good thoughts drawn from the papers with a dash of Scripture added, but he cannot *preach*. For to preach a man must know the authority of being under authority . . .

He alone can exercise an authoritative ministry who often has recourse to the secret place of the Most High, who has learned to listen to the God who speaks, who knows the meaning of obedience, who can say not merely, 'I hold this view', but 'I am held by this God'.

Archbishop Donald Coggan (of Canterbury): Convictions, 'Spirituality', (Hodders, 1975)

. . . of all the actions of the Christian ministry preaching is the highest, and the test of our reverence for our profession is our performance of the preacher's duty . . . Never allow yourself to take a mean view of your duty as a preacher . . . In a sense we may say truly that all activities of the pastorate are gathered up in the ministry of preaching.

Bishop Hensley Henson: 'Church & Parson in England', (Hodders, 1964)

Preaching is the proclamation and sharing of a gift received, a tradition of revelation come alive, a way opened up. It is therefore at the heart of worship which gathers together the life and faith of the people of the Way, which confronts us with our shortcomings along the way, and enables us to celebrate, not our failures and our faithlessness, but God's faithfulness and restoring purpose. So preaching is to do also with deepening faith, renewing faith and extending faith. God's gift and presence is to be shared and allowed to grow because God gives, in and through the worship and the preaching, constant reminders and challenges of his repeated and redeeming givingness. Preaching is also an attempt to reach out beyond the faithful (who always require to be challenged, judged, renewed and expanded in their faith) to listeners and seekers, and the heedless and the lost in the world at large. For God is the giver who wills and wishes to give to all, so that all may share in the rich environment of his giving, not only by receiving, but also by giving themselves. So preaching is at the heart of worship, is directed to celebrating and deepening discipleship, and is an invitation and instrument of mission.

Bishop David Jenkins (of Durham): 'God, Jesus and the Life of the Spirit', (S.C.M., 1988)

If of these two things you can do only one – either hear the mass or hear the sermon – you should let the mass go, rather than the sermon . . . There is less peril for your soul in not hearing mass than in not hearing the sermon.

St. Bernardino of Siena, O.S.F., (1380–1444): in Charles Smyth, 'The Art of Preaching', (S.P.C.K., 1940)

Preaching is the bringing of truth through personality.

Phillips Brooks (1835–93): in the first of the 1877 Lyman Beecher Lectures at Yale

Preachers cannot . . . escape the duty of disturbing the complacent.

John R.W. Stott: 'I Believe in Preaching', (Hodders, 1982)

My grand point in preaching is to break the hard heart and to heal the broken one.

John Newton (1725–1807)

. . . the true function of a preacher is to disturb the comfortable and to comfort the disturbed.

Chad Walsh: 'Campus Goods on Trial', (Macmillan, 1962)

Since no one can be saved who has not first believed, priests, as co-workers with their bishops, have as their primary duty the proclamation of the gospel of God to all . . . The task of priests is not to teach their own wisdom but God's word, and to summon all men urgently to conversion and to holiness. Such preaching must not present God's word in a general and abstract fashion only, but it must apply the perennial truth of the gospel to the concrete circumstances of life.

Decree of the Ministry and Life of Priests, from W.M. Abbott, Ed: 'The Documents of Vatican II', (Chapman, 1967)

Too many sermons are written 'in the imperative mode' whereas biblical religion 'is written largely in the revealing language of the indicative mode . . . A sermon is by its very nature a revelation, not an exhortation.'

Theodorc Parker Ferris: 'Go Tell the People', 1950, (Scribner, 1951)

Lord, how can man preach thy eternall word?
He is a brittle crazie glasse:
Yet in thy temple thou dost him afford
This glorious and transcendent place,
To be a window, through thy grace.

But when thou dost anneal in glass thy storie,
Making thy life to shine within
The holy Preachers: then the light and glorie
More rev'rend grows, & more doth win:
Which else shows watrish, bleak, & thin.

Doctrine and life, colours and light, in one
When they combine and mingle, bring
A strong regard and awe: but speech alone
Doth vanish like a flaring thing,
And in the eare, not conscience ring.

George Herbert (1593–1633): 'The Windows'

Preaching is indispensable to Christianity. Without preaching a necessary part of its authenticity has been lost.

John Stott: 'I Believe in Preaching', (Hodders, 1982)

To love to preach is one thing – to love those to whom we preach, quite another.

Richard Cecil

The test of a preacher is that his congregation goes away saying, *not* 'What a lovely sermon!' but 'I will do something.'

Bishop Francis de Sales (1567–1622): 'On the Preacher and Preaching'

Charles Simeon's test for every sermon:
Does it uniformly tend
TO HUMBLE THE SINNER?
TO EXALT THE SAVIOUR?
TO PROMOTE HOLINESS?
If in one single instance it lose sight of any of these points, let it be condemned without mercy.

Charles Simeon: 'Preface to Horae Homileticae', (1834)

. . . it is a mistake to suppose that men of science [knowledge] will not be pleased unless the sermon be abstruse or profound.

Charles Simeon (1759–1836)

When we know our people we will know how to bring a word from the Lord.

Ian D Bunting, 'Preaching at Communion', part II, (1982)

A sermon . . . should have something of the quality of a knock on the door.

H. H. Farmer: 'The Servant of the Word', (1941)

Preaching *is* a tyranny. I refer not only to the fact that Sunday comes round with an inexorable regularity and makes demands which needs must be met. I refer also to the fact that we know that we must not offer to the Lord a second-rate offering: only the best we can produce will do. I think of the demands which this makes on a man's freshness and devotion and thinking and praying. A tyranny indeed! But a *joyful* tyranny – who would be without it who has been called and commissioned? I suppose a mother finds the care of her family in the early years demanding and tyrannical. But deprive her of her brood, and you have the epitome of bereavement and misery.

Archbishop Donald Coggan (of Canterbury): 'On Preaching', (1975/78)

. . . if I preach only what I have experienced, then my hearers will have to live on an impoverished diet.

Archbishop Donald Coggan (of Canterbury): 'On Preaching', (1975/78)

I do not ask that men should sing my praises,
Or flaming headlines spread my name abroad,
I only pray that, as I voice the Message,
Men may find God.

Anonymous

I am convinced that preaching has primacy over theology, and that theology merely works back to investigate the basis of that which it has already heard proclaimed. It seems to me to be a perversion when contemporary theology is regarded – especially by many of the more avid young disciples of the masters – as an undertaking which first must investigate the possibility of preaching and lay down the conditions for it. This false primacy of theology seems to me to be one of the decisive reasons for the current spiritual and homiletical paralysis of which we are all aware. The fact is that the primary decisions are reached in the preaching, where the active Word becomes Event. Here is where the great theological themes begin to take shape. They are not first posited by theology in the form of *a priori* constructions.

Helmut Theilicke: 'How Modern Should Theology Be?', (1967)

Preaching is the medium through which God contemporises his historic self disclosure in Christ, and offers man the opportunity to respond in faith.

R.H. Mounce

. . . to preach Christianity and to preach Christ are not identical – the one is a system of thought and practice, the other is the revelation of a person.

J. G. Davies: 'Worship and Mission', (1966)

Preaching, what it is not

Our preaching must not be articulate snoring.

Charles H. Spurgeon: 'Lectures', (Second Series, 1882)

Charles H. Spurgeon used to remind his preaching-classes that they were called to feed sheep, not pasture giraffes!

Aubrey de Vere said that listening to F.D. Maurice (1805–72) preach was 'like eating pea-soup with a fork'; and Benjamin Jowett was no less acerbic about a Maurice sermon: 'Well! all that I could make out was that today was yesterday, and this would the same as the next.'

King Charles II asked Dr. Edward Stillingfleet (1635–99), how it was that the archbishop always read his sermons before the King when in other circumstances, he preached without a book. Stillingfleet replied that the awe of so noble an audience, where he saw nothing that was not greatly superior to him, but chiefly the seeing before him, so great and wise a prince, made him afraid to trust himself.

Stillingfleet was emboldened to ask the King why he read *his* speeches to Parliament when he could have none of the same reason. 'Why truly, doctor,' said the King, 'your question is a very pertinent one, and so will be my answer. I have asked them so often, and for so much money, that I am ashamed to look them in the face.'

Joseph Parker warned Charles Spurgeon in 1890:

The universe is not divided into plain black and white as you suppose . . . Believe me you really are not infallible.

Anthony Trollope – a cynic about preaching and youthful preachers – wrote of his hope that 'Clergymen who could not preach would be such blessings that they would be bribed to adhere to their incompetence.'

'Barchester Towers', (1857), Dent Everyman edition, (1906)

Brevity may be the soul of wit, but the preacher is not a wit . . . A Christianity of short sermons is a Christianity of short fibre.

P.T. Forsyth: 'Positive Preaching and the Modern Mind', (Independent, 1907)

How few ministers do preach with all their might? . . . Alas, we speak so drowsily or gently, that sleeping sinners cannot hear. The blow falls so light that hard-hearted persons cannot feel it. . . . Such a work as preaching for men's salvation should be done with all our might – that the people can *feel* us preach when they hear us.

Richard Baxter: 'The Reformed Pastor', (1655)

. . . the tendency (in the Parish Communion movement of which

Bishop Buchanan generally approves) was for the sermon to go down to a seven-minute 'liturgical homily' – tidy, churchy, related to the theme of the Sunday, very often related to receiving communion, quite probably poker-faced, passionless and powerless – or so it seemed to the sermon-centred evangelicals.

Colin Buchanan: 'The Heart of Sunday Worship', (Grove Worship, 1992)

The form must not betray the content.

Anonymous

Actors speak of things imaginary as if they were real, while you preachers too often speak of things real as if they were imaginary

Thomas Betterton (1635–1710): 'Reply to the Archbishop of Canterbury', (1690)

If you, as a preacher, sometimes feel bored, that's no bad thing. God may want you to be bored in order to help you to understand what it's like to listen to one of your own sermons.

Bruce Davies, (1986)

When you preach the gospel, beware of preaching it as the religion which explains everything.

Dr. Albert Schweitzer (1875–1965)

Little girl to her mum, in church: 'Why does daddy always say a prayer before his sermons?'

'To ask God to help him when he's preaching.'

Quick as a flash, the little girl asked, 'So why doesn't he?'

If we banish from the pulpit those topics which are most relevant in the world, it is not surprising that our people wonder if our preaching is relevant to their lives.

John R W Stott, (1985)

Moralistic sermons, telling people what to do without helping them to *understand* how to do it are 'a few helpful hints for harmful habits'.

Ian D Bunting: 'Preaching at Communion', part I, (1981)

We have preached a faith which has barely touched upon the everyday lives of our people and has not fully reflected the scandalous intrusion of the incarnate Christ into our murky world.

Ian D Bunting: 'Preaching at Communion', part I, (1981)

Nice sermon, Vicar. Short, sharp and off the point!

A Northampton churchgoer, (c 1980)
(Used as the title of a book, 1987)

Preaching, biblical

The strength of the church lies in the gospel it proclaims – thus in its preaching – today, as it always has. And since the church stands under the authority of the word, it follows that the best preaching – nay, the only proper preaching – is biblical preaching. Only biblical preaching carries with it the authority of the word. If, therefore, the Christian pulpit is ever to regain the power and respect which rightfully belongs to it, it will be through a return to biblical preaching.

John Bright: 'The Authority of the Old Testament', (S.C.M., 1976)

Though the preacher speaks words which, because they belong to the Bible, are not entirely his own, he is not at liberty to utter words which he would not be willing to defend. He has no right to stand in the pulpit and to prattle on about things he does not believe and has no intention of practising . . . The preacher who relies entirely on his role, without any conviction that what he says is true, ought to stop preaching, for his own sake and for the sake of his people.

Robert M.E. Paterson: 'Short, Sharp and Off the Point', (MARC Europe, 1987)

The task of the preacher is thus very similar to the task of the theologian – to illuminate this community's faith in the light of the classic and normative story of the faith [the Bible] and the present situation in light of the tradition of the text and the experience of the community.

John F. Baldovin, S.J.: 'Biblical Preaching in the Liturgy', at Societas Liturgica Congress XIII, (Toronto, 1991)

The task [of the preacher with regard to the biblical text] is two-fold. It requires the preacher to enter into the world of the text, . . . to wrestle with the meaning of the text in its original setting, to muse on the text, to study it and re-translate it into his or her own language. This process means allowing the text its power over oneself. In itself it is an act of submission. It is also an act of critical submission, for I take it that no treatment of the Bible or other classic expressions of Christian faith can be done today with a hermeneutic of suspicion...

The second aspect of the preacher's task is to connect the text and its world to her or his own contemporary experience and that of the assembly which she or he serves. The successful combination of these two tasks is what can only be called a charism or a grace. It includes wit, imagination, style, honesty, courage and might even include sleeplessness, physical discomfort and anxiety – what Walter Burghardt has called 'The Cost of Preaching'. It is not without good reason that Karl Barth's comment that the preacher must have the Bible in one hand and the daily newspaper in the other has been quoted so often.

John F. Baldovin, S.J.: 'Biblical Preaching in the Liturgy', at Societas Liturgica Congress XIII, (Toronto, 1991)

Preaching, abuse of

Sermonettes breed Christianettes.

Variously attributed to George Campbell Morgan (of Westminster Chapel) and Stuart Holden (of St. Paul's, Portman Square)

Robin Pittman (*Times* letters, 1991) recalled playing 'sermon cricket: a run for the mention of 'I' and a wicket for the mention of 'God'.' He continued, 'I remember well the headmaster colleague who scored an effortless 93 for 2.'

... no one thinks that it [preaching] makes any difference except for the time it takes. No one expects to learn anything there. A man listens to preaching three or four years and does not learn enough to give answer concerning one article of the Creed: I know this from daily experience.

Martin Luther: Works Volume 6, (1932), 'The German Mass and Order of Service'

Half an hour seems like five minutes when one is preaching extempore.

Robert Francis Kilvert (1840–79)

Describing a fellow cleric: 'He drew water out of rock like Moses and hit the people harder than Moses hit the rock.'

Robert Francis Kilvert (1840–79)

Joseph Parker (1830–1902) once asked an aspiring preacher to deliver his best sermon, and afterwards commented: 'For the last half hour you have not been trying to get something into my mind but something off yours. You are like a man anxious to get rid of a sack of coals.'

Albert Dawson: Joseph Parker

The preacher had laboured for 28 minutes on a children's talk about the parable of the wheat and weeds, and at the end he asked the congregation to tell him his text. After silence, someone suggested: 'O Timothy, avoid profane and vain babblings'.

Anonymous: see I Timothy 6:20 and 2 Timothy 2:16 (AV)

Archbishop Whately said of a preacher that 'he aimed at nothing, and hit it.'

R.W. Dale: 'Nine lectures on Preaching', Yale Lectures, (1876)

God have mercy on any congregation that is subjected Sunday by Sunday to a report of the preacher's reading for the previous week.

Jerry Vines: 'A Practical Guide to Sermon Preparation', (Moody, 1985)

Someone has said that flattery is soft-soaping a person until he can't see for suds. There is too much flattery in modern preaching.

Jerry Vines: 'A Practical Guide to Sermon Preparation', (Moody, 1985)

Possible compliments of a preacher after the service:

a. Splendid! I particularly liked the ending.
b. When will you be preaching next?
c. You have such a gift for preaching off-the-cuff.
d. Your sermon reminded me of something that happened to me recently on a visit to *Disney World.*
e. Do you practise your delivery a great deal?
f. Your detailed treatment of Aramaic Targums was particularly moving.

g. That sermon was even better than the last time you preached it.
h. It is a shame that more people don't hear your sermons.
i. I couldn't quite make out whether you were saying 'resurrection' or 'insurrection'.
j. You have such an unique preaching style!
k. The power! The beauty! The control! Wasn't the music magnificent?
l. I hope you keep your sermons, Vicar; for your *next* parish, I mean.
m. I remember a sermon in which *[insert the name of a well-known preacher]* said exactly the same thing.
n. Where in the world did you learn to preach like that?
o. Isn't that baby who cried all through your sermon adorable?

Anonymous

When the speaker had talked ten minutes I was so impressed I decided I would give every cent I had with me. After another ten minutes I concluded that I would throw into the treasure all the silver I had with me. Ten minutes later I decided I wouldn't give anything. At the end of the talk, still ten minutes later, as the contribution plate came around, I was so utterly exhausted by the arguments, that I extracted two dollars for my own use.

Mark Twain

[Uncle Val, a Lutheran deacon] . . . says of the pastor's sermons, 'He mumbles. He murmurs. It's a lot of on-the-one-hand-this, on-the-other-hand-that. He never comes straight out. He never puts the hay down where the goats can get it. It's a lot of talk, and many a Sunday I've walked away with no idea *what* he said. Can't remember even where he started from. You never had that problem with the old preachers. There was never a moment's doubt. It was Repent or Be Dammed. We need that. This guy, he tries to please everybody. Just once I wish he'd raise his voice and pound on the pulpit. That way I'd know he wasn't talking in his sleep.'

Garrison Keillor: 'Lake Wobegon Days', (1985), 'Revival'

The homily which followed the reading sounded less like a learned discourse than a spontaneous outburst of sour grapes on the part of the priest, nettled by the poor turn-out. Once upon a time, he complained, the church had been the centre of the community, a privileged place where the people gathered to experience the presence of God. Now what did we see? The shops, discotheques, night clubs, beer bars and fast food outlets were all turning people away, while the churches had never been so empty. The touristic passing trade had by this time largely dispersed, but this line of argument appeared to risk alienating even the core of the congregation, reminding them painfully of their status as a marginalised and anachronistic minority, representatives of an outmoded way of thinking. Coughing, shuffling and inattention became endemic.

Michael Dibden: 'Cabal', (1992)

Preaching, humour in

O Lord we thank thee for the words of Duncan's awe-ful sermon tonight.

Tim Cross: An extempore prayer, (1989)

Many preachers indulge in the ritual removal of the watch and the placing of it on the pulpit desk. The family of one such preacher described this ceremony as 'Dad's most meaningless gesture'.

Anonymous source

The vicar could no longer contain his annoyance at the woman in his congregation who always closed her eyes throughout his sermons. When he asked her why she did it, her reply was simple: 'I'm not sleeping, Vicar; I just find that it's easier to work out tomorrow's shopping list with my eyes closed.'

Source unknown

At the end of a three-hour sermon by the Reverend Edward Tatham (Rector of Lincoln College, Oxford, 1792–1834), only one member of the congregation was left in the church, and he was found to be dead.

Dr. Robert South (1634–1716), preaching before King Charles II, noticed that the royal entourage was falling asleep and some began to snore: 'Lord Lauderdale, let me entreat you to rouse yourself; you snore so loud that you will wake the King!'

Samuel Taylor Coleridge (1772–1834) to Charles Lamb (1775–1834):
'I believe . . . that you have heard me preach?'
To which Lamb replied: 'I? I never heard you do anything less.'

James Sutherland, Ed: 'Oxford Book of Literary Anecdotes', (1975)

A Chaplain who had preached the Assize sermon was fishing for compliments. On asking a judge what he thought of the discourse, he was a little taken aback by the reply.

It was a divine sermon. For it was like the peace of God which passeth all understanding. And like his mercy, it seemed to endure for ever.

Related by Henry Hawkins (Lord Brampton, 1817–1907)

W.H. Auden described a preacher as 'a person who talks in someone else's sleep.'

Sydney Smith devised the worst punishment imaginable. 'Sir,' he said to an adversary, 'you deserve to be preached to death by wild curates.'

The vicar was ill and a local curate had come to preach. From the pulpit, he noticed a piece of cardboard filling a gap in a beautiful stained glass window.

'You know,' he said, 'as I stand here in place of your excellent preacher today, I feel like the cardboard in that window – a poor substitute.'

After the service, one of the wardens thanked him kindly and added: 'I want you to know that you weren't a piece of cardboard today, you were a real pane.'

Source unknown

It is said that the lips of some preachers ought to be hermeneutically sealed.

Anonymous

The minister had been taken ill and would be absent for several weeks, so a visiting preacher had been called on at very short notice. At the end of his sermon he apologised: 'I'm afraid I didn't have time to prepare my sermon; I just relied on the Holy Spirit. But next week I'll have time to do better.'

Source unknown

The preacher was introduced to the congregation with a very long eulogy about his abilities, personality, etc. When he began his sermon, he thanked his host: 'After such an introduction, I can hardly wait to hear what I've got to say.'

Anonymous (variously attributed)

Preaching, importance of

A good, honest and painful sermon.

Samuel Pepys: 'Diary of 1661'

For the sake of the proclaimed word the world exists with all of its words. In the sermon the foundation of a new world is laid. Here the original word becomes audible. There is no evading or getting away from the spoken word of the sermon, nothing releases us from the necessity of this witness, not even cult or liturgy . . . The preacher should be assured that Christ enters the congregation through those words which he proclaims from the Scripture.

Dietrich Bonhoeffer, in C.E. Fant: 'Bonhoeffer: Worldly Preaching', (Nelson, 1975)

Archbishop Michael Ramsey, late in life, reflected: 'I loved to preach – if I felt that they wanted to know. If I got no reaction, I felt depressed. Preaching and talking about God is a dialogue. It is a giving and receiving.' He preferred notes to a full text: 'The object of notes is to get it into the head beforehand. If I construct sentences, I read them, and that has led to several disasters. My head and my eyes are not in harmony.'

From Owen Chadwick: 'Michael Ramsey, A Life', (Oxford, 1991)

If the church ever dispenses with preaching it signs its own death warrant.

John Stott, (c. 1974)

Servant of God, I am bitter and
 desolate,

What do I care for perfection of phrase?
Cursed be your humour, your poise, your diction,
See how my soul turns to ashes within me.
You who have vowed to declare your Redeemer,
Give me the words that would save.

Margaret Chaplin Anderson: 'A Wail from a Distressed Soul'

A bee is a small animal which makes sweet honey, but which nevertheless can sting. So the preacher has the sweetest consolations, yet when roused to anger he can say biting and stinging things.

Martin Luther in P. Smith and H.P. Gallinger, Ed: 'Conversations with Luther'

Better, far, to preach a little above their [the congregation's] capacity than below it.

Archbishop Donald Coggan (of Canterbury): 'On Preaching', (1975/78)

When I preach I regard neither doctors nor magistrates, of whom I have above forty in my congregation; I have all my eyes on the servant-maids and on the children. And if the learned men are not well pleased with what they hear, well, the door is open.

Martin Luther (1483–1546)

Unlike liturgical structures and liturgical prayers, homilies are unique to the moment when they are preached; they are unrepeatable. Yet homilies are also like the liturgy in that they tend to be delivered by the same person or few persons week after week, month after month. In this sense, preaching is a cumulative enterprise. In the context of the ongoing worship of a community, the homily is not a discrete entity but an aspect of the creative engagement between minister and community, the engagement of faith that characterises, challenges, encourages the community as a whole. Each homily may be new but it tends to carry with it the credibility of the person who does the preaching – his or her own faith commitment to the people and to Christian faith. This is the irreducible element in preaching for which no amount of preparation or even rhetorical skill can substitute. It demands men and women who can serve as living and breathing (if imperfect) ikons of what both the Bible and the liturgy are about.

John F. Baldovin, S.J.: 'Biblical Preaching in the Liturgy', at Societas Liturgica Congress XIII, (Toronto, 1991)

Christ only once heard Mass . . . but he laid great stress on prayer and preaching, especially on preaching.

Humbert de Romans (died 1277), Dominican Minister General, in Charles Smyth: 'The Art of Preaching, (S.P.C.K., 1940)

As the nineteenth century drew to a close the influence of the pulpit was reaching its zenith. The cult of the popular preacher was as Victorian as the railway lines which made his peripatetic career possible.

Adrian Burdon: 'The Preaching Service', (Alcuin/GROW Liturgical Study 17, 1991)

Preaching, technique

Who has not heard a wearisome preacher ambling forward with phrases like these? 'I heard the other day of a story which I think might illustrate this point, and which I would now like to pass on to you. You may judge yourself whether or not it does, indeed, illustrate what I want to say . . .'

Bah! He is nearly as boring as Thackeray who, in some of his books, can hardly get a character on the way without explaining why he chose this character . . . and not that! (citing *Vanity Fair* Chapter VI).

W.E. Sangster: 'The Craft of Sermon Illustration', (1946)

I must be able to look my people in the eye . . . for preaching is an essay in co-operation.

Archbishop Donald Coggan (of Canterbury)

Preach to their eyes!

Robert M.E. Paterson, (1986)

As long as I can discover no connection between the gospel and the problems of my life, then it has nothing to say to me and I am not interested. And that is precisely why the gospel must be preached afresh and told in new ways to every generation, since every generation has its own unique questions. This is why the gospel must constantly be forwarded to a new address, because the recipient is repeatedly changing his place of residence.

. . . In short, if the basic questions of life have shifted, then I must redirect the message of the gospel. Otherwise I am answering questions that have never even been asked. And upon hearing such answers, my opposite number will just shake his head and say, 'That's no concern of mine. It has nothing to do with me.'

Helmut Theilicke: 'How Modern Should Theology Be?', (1967)

Little girl to the Rector:
'Why are you dressed like that?'
'Because I am the Rector.'
'What do you do?'
'I suppose I tell people about God.'
'And *do* you know all about God?'

Bruce Davies

The expertise of the pulpit can only be learned slowly and, it may well be, with a strange mixture of pain and joy.

Archbishop Donald Coggan (of Canterbury)

I believe the method observed by the famous Lord Falkland, in some of his writings, would not be an ill one for young divines: I was assured by an old person of quality who knew him well that when he doubted whether a word were perfectly intelligible or no, he used to consult one of his lady's chambermaids (not the waiting-woman, because it was possible she might be conversant in romances), and by her judgement was guided whether to receive or reject it. And if that great person thought such a caution necessary in treatises offered to the learned world, it will be sure at least as proper in sermons, when the meanest hearer is supposed to be concerned, and where very often a lady's chambermaid may be allowed to equal half the congregation, both as to quality and understanding.

Jonathan Swift, referring to Lucius Cary, Viscount Falkland (1610–1643)

The simplicity of John Wesley's preaching was his glory. This simplicity had not been easily attained, but was the result of many years of effort . . . [He] read his sermons to an intelligent maid-servant who agreed to stop him every time he came to a word she did not understand. She shouted 'Stop sir!' so often that Wesley became impatient. He schooled himself thereafter to express himself clearly and simply and was rewarded by the knowledge that the congregation could understand his message.

Adrian Burdon: 'The Preaching Service', (Alcuin/GROW Liturgical Study 17, 1991)

I am convinced that the best a preacher can do week-in and week-out with sensitivity to the liturgical assembly, to the assembly's act of thanksgiving, and to the Scriptures that are determined for the day, is to discern one thing that needs to be said in this situation and say it imaginatively enough to have an impact. In my experience many a promising homily flounders on the shoals of overambition.

John F. Baldovin, S.J.: 'Biblical Preaching in the Liturgy', at Societas Liturgica Congress XIII, (Toronto, 1991)

. . . there are a number of styles that might adequately convey the biblical message for people today. Often in reading literature on homiletics one gets the impression that the hunt is on for *the one* perfect style of preaching or sermon preparation. I am convinced that no such single style or method exists, for the simple reason that assemblies which gather for worship differ and they differ greatly – even given their common humanity. While it may be permissible, even expected, to preach for an hour in one culture, for example, it may be just as unthinkable to do so in another.

John F. Baldovin, S.J.: 'Biblical Preaching in the Liturgy', at Societas Liturgica Congress XIII, (Toronto, 1991)

Charles Simeon (1759–1836) used to ask young, would-be preachers who came to him to imagine they had to fill some narrow-mouthed glass vessels with water: would they do so with a large pail filled to overflowing or 'with a tea-kettle with a nice spout'?

Endeavour to rivet their attention to your message for a reasonable time; but remember that the mind, and especially among the generality of persons or the uneducated, will only bear a certain amount of tension ... It is the want of a good and impressive delivery that destroys the usefulness of a great proportion of pious ministers.

Charles Simeon (1759–1836)

I preach usually to the small door in the west gallery of Trinity Church. It is a good central spot for me to direct my countenance to, it is a fair average of the more distant parts of the congregation. When I perceive that the door distinctly hears me, then I know all the congregation may.

Charles Simeon (1759–1836), [referring to Holy Trinity Church, Cambridge]

... only speak from *love* to man and not from the *fear* of man, and God will both accept and prosper you.

Charles Simeon (1759–1836)

... after preaching in his own chapel at Peasholm Green [John Wesley] went in his canonicals to Mr. Cordeaux's Church. Mr. Cordeaux saw that he was a clergyman, and, without knowing who he was, offered him his pulpit. After the service, he asked the clerk if he knew who the stranger was. The clerk replied, 'Sir, he is the vagabond Wesley, against whom you warned us.' 'Aye, indeed!' said the astonished rector, 'we are trapped; but never mind, we have had a good sermon.'

Source unknown

Advice given to Henry Cecil Leon (1902–76) by Robert Fortune, who took Cecil as his pupil:
'Just tell the tale, my dear fellow, just tell the judge the tale.'

Michael Gilbert, Ed: 'Oxford Book of Legal Anecdotes', (1986) [In 1968, the same advice was given to the editor and his fellow students by J.P. (Jim) Hickenbotham, a great teacher of preachers]

... I confess that in the pulpit I am often seized with 'communication frustration', for a message burns within me, but I am unable to convey to others what I am thinking, let alone feeling. And seldom if ever do I leave the pulpit without a sense of partial failure, a mood of penitence, a cry to God for forgiveness, and a resolve to look to him for grace to do better in future.

John Stott: 'I Believe in Preaching', (Hodders, 1982)

Bishop J.C. Ryle advised preachers to use short sentences:
Preach as if you were asthmatical.

The first element on which your preaching will largely depend for power and success, you will perhaps be surprised to learn, is *Imagination*, which I regard as the most important of all the elements that go to make the preacher.

H.W. Beecher: 'Yale Lectures on Preaching', (1872)

Preaching should be talking 'to a person' rather than merely 'spraying the solar system with words'.

Dick Sheppard, from H.E. Luccock: 'The Best of Dick Sheppard', (1951)

The three essentials of a sermon: truth, clarity and passion.

George Campbell Morgan: 'Preaching', (1937)

If elephants can be trained to dance, lions to play, and leopards to hunt, surely preachers can be taught to preach.

Desiderius Erasmus (1466–1536)

The phrase 'return home' will not come as any surprise to preachers within the black tradition. Every black preacher understands that for the sermon to happen, it must move to a final celebrative event – a *dénouement.* Again, there is no coincidence in all this, because, in fact, jazz improvisation grew directly out of the black preaching experience.

Eugene L. Lowry: in 'Journeys toward Narrative Preaching', (Pilgrim Press, 1990)

I have made this letter longer than usual, only because I have not had time to make it shorter.

Blaise Pascal (1623 – 1662)

Preaching, the Scriptures

We have renounced the shameful things that one hides; we refuse to practise cunning or to falsify God's word; but by the open statement of the truth we commend ourselves to the conscience of everyone in the sight of God.

2 Corinthians 4:2

Until I (the Apostle Paul) arrive, give attention to the public reading of scripture, to exhorting, to teaching.

1 Timothy 4:13

In the presence of God and of Christ Jesus, who is to judge the living and the dead, and in view of his appearing and his kingdom, I solemnly urge you: proclaim the message; be persistent whether the time is favourable or unfavourable; convince, rebuke, and encourage, with the utmost patience in teaching. For the time is coming when people will not put up with sound doctrine, but having itching ears, they will accumulate for themselves teachers to suit their own desires, and will turn away from listening to the truth and wander away to myths. As for you, always be sober, endure suffering, do the work of an evangelist, carry out your ministry fully.

2 Timothy 4:1–5

Predestination

George Morley, later Bishop of Winchester in the seventeenth century was asked: 'What did the English Puritans hold?' and was told, 'The doctrine of Predestination.'

'And what did the other English Clergy hold?' Morley asked. 'The best offices in the Church of England,' came the reply.

Source unknown

Although whatever comes about, I
mean,
Must therefore be foreknown – as
who can doubt? –
And though it does not come *because*
foreseen,
Yet it still follows, and one can't get
out
Of this, that things which *are* to come
about
Must be foreseen; or, if foreseen,
take shape
Inevitably; there is no escape.
And this is quite sufficient anyway
To prove free choice in us a mere
pretence;
What an absurdity it is to say
That temporal happenings – the
things of sense -
Are causes of eternal prescience!
Now truly, it's as false as it is odd
To say things cause the Providence of
God!

Geoffrey Chaucer: Troilus and Criseyde, (written 1382–6/7). [An aside on the nature of foreknowledge and predestination.] Book 4, stanzas 151–152, translated by Neville Coghill

There once was a man who said,
'Sham!
I've just realised what I am;
For I find that I move
In predestinate grooves -
Not even a 'bus but a tram!'

Professor H.E.W.Turner

It is written in the letter to the Romans that God has the right to do with his creature what he will, that if he will he can also make vessels of wrath (Romans 9:20–22); but it does not say that he has predestined men from eternity to be vessels of wrath (9:22) of whom he says in the eleventh chapter that they are finally to be saved (11:23ff.). In this matter Paul and the entire Bible are consistently illogical. The Scriptures refuse, as it were, to draw the conclusion which logic would like to draw from the concept of eternal election into the opposite direction.

Emil Brunner: 'The Letter to the Romans', (1938; Lutterworth, 1959), Appendix

John Wesley and George Whitefield disagreed on their understanding of the relationship between predestination and free will.

Wesley: I'm so sinful and yet have been saved. Therefore it must be possible for anyone to be saved.

Whitefield: I am so sinful and yet have been saved. Only the predestined will of God could have saved me.

Anonymous

God has never confused the elect with the élite.

Anonymous

Election . . . is the summons to service.

H.H. Rowley

Saint Peter was taking a party of newcomers around heaven to enable them to get their bearings. When they reached one house, he asked them to take off their shoes and tiptoe past. 'Why do we have to do that?' asked one. 'Oh, they think they're the only ones here and it would be a pity to disappoint them,' replied Peter.

. . . none will be lost whom God can save without destroying in them his own gift of free will.

E B Pusey: 'What is of Faith as to Everlasting Punishment?', (his last book)

Prejudice

. . . perhaps I'd realise where I'm standing. Or at least that I'm standing *somewhere.* There is, I suppose, a world of objects which have a certain form, like this coffee mug. I turn it, and it has no handle. I tilt it, and it has no cavity. But there is something real here which is always a mug with a handle. I suppose. But politics, justice, patriotism – they aren't even like coffee mugs. There's nothing real there separate from our perception of them. So if you try to change them as though there was something there to change, you'll get frustrated, and frustration will finally make you violent. If you know this and proceed with humility, you may perhaps alter people's perceptions so that they behave a little differently at that axis of behaviour where we locate politics or justice; but if you don't know this, then you're acting on a mistake. Prejudice is the expression of this mistake.

Tom Stoppard: 'The Real Thing', (1982), Henry to Annie

Pressure-groups

Tuesday February 11th:
On the way home today, met Mr. Lamberton-Pincey, who runs a little group called 'Spot it and Stop it' in the church. They look for things to ban.

Adrian Plass: 'The Sacred Diary of Adrian Plass', (1987)

Professionalism

Don't hire a master to paint you a masterpiece and then assign a roomful of schoolboy-artists to look over his shoulder and suggest improvements.

Robert Townsend: 'Up the Organisation'

Progress

What we call 'Progress' is the exchange of one nuisance for another nuisance.

Henry Havelock Ellis (1859–1939): 'Impressions and Comments'

Man invents a machine : he is its master and it is his pride. It is all part of Man's ambition and vanity, part of his pride in the creative skill that distinguishes him from the beasts, an elaboration of that primitive tool-making without which he would still be living in a cave. Then suddenly, one morning – as with motor cars or nuclear bombs – he wakes up to find that he hates the . . . things. It is too late. He has made them, he would be without them, but by their mere existence they enslave him. He has eaten of the fruit of the tree of knowledge; he can never go back.'

R. Furneaux Jordan: The Penguin W. Heath Robinson', (1966)

Prophecy

Christianity is prophetic through and through. When the prophets are silent and the word of God is in short supply, the church withers and dies. If there are prophets today, their hands are tied and their mouths gagged by the clumsy democratic processes of church institutions. It is, alas, as true today as it was in Jesus' day that prophecy is seldom heard within the establishment. For prophecy comes by the Spirit of God, not by consensus or debate.

Michael Harper, (c. 1978)

Most of us are not poor enough in spirit to be prophets.

Anonymous

What constitutes the prophet is exact and rigorous proclamation of . . . God's decision, today . . . But it is not just this unveiling of the intention of

God that makes a man a prophet. It is also the proclamation of an order: 'Listen to the word of God'.

Jacques Ellul: 'The Politics of God and the Politics of Man', (1972)

. . . the true prophet will probably have to endure loneliness and censure even in the house of those who might be expected to be his friends . . . It is hard enough to stand out against 'the world' – how much more difficult to stand out *contra ecclesiam!*

Archbishop Donald Coggan (of Canterbury): 'On Preaching', (1975/78)

Hosea looked into his own heart and found it broken . . . He looked into the heart of God and found it a broken heart, too. It was *this* that made him the preacher he was – and, for that matter, is.

Archbishop Donald Coggan (of Canterbury): 'On Preaching', (1975/78)

The prophets whom we should look for are not the plants forced in the hot-house of sectarian religious experience, but those great men and women who, usually swimming against the current of the age, have spoken unwelcome but forceful truths to the church.

A.T. & R.P.C. Hanson: 'The Identity of the Church', (S.C.M., 1987)

The prophet lives with God rather than with his fellow-men; and he is confident that the word which he speaks is the word of God.

Benjamin Jowett (1817–93)

Prosperity and Success – *see also* MATERIALISM

William Tyndale translated Genesis 39:2 (The Lord was with Joseph and he became a successful man):
And the Lorde was with Joseph, and he was a luckie felowe.

You have spoken harsh words against me, says the LORD. Yet you say, 'How have we spoken against you?' You have said, 'It is vain to serve God. What do we profit by keeping his command or by going about as mourners before the LORD of hosts? Now we count the arrogant happy; evildoers not only prosper, but, when they put God to the test, they escape.

Then those who revered the LORD spoke with one another. The LORD took note and listened, and a book of remembrance was written before him of those who revered the LORD and thought on his name. They shall be mine, says the LORD of hosts, my special possession on the day when I act, and I will spare them as parents spare their children who serve them. Then once more you shall see the difference between the righteous and the wicked, between one who serves God and the one who does not serve him.

Malachi 3:13–18

If I must boast, I will boast of the things that show my weakness . . .
He [the Lord] said to me, 'My grace is sufficient for you, for power is made perfect in weakness.' So I will boast all the more gladly of my weaknesses, so that the power of Christ may dwell in me.

2 Corinthians 11:30; 12:9

As for those who in the present age are rich, command them not to be haughty, or to set their hopes on the uncertainty of riches, but rather on God who richly provides us with everything for our enjoyment. They are to do good, to be rich in good works, generous, and ready to share, thus storing up for themselves the treasure of a good foundation for the future, so that they may take hold of the life that really is life.

1 Timothy 6:17–19

Prostitution

George Bernard Shaw once asked a woman at dinner whether she would go to bed with him for £10,000. The 'lady' hesitatingly agreed, so George Bernard Shaw asked if she would do the same for £2.

'Certainly not!' the lady cried. 'What do you take me for?'

'We have already established that,' said Shaw. 'What we are trying to establish now is the price.'

Protest

The story of Christian protest from the late 1800's to 1950 is dominated by an absence of protest, by the shameful silence of those who knew the truth about the concentration camps but shut their eyes against what they did not want to see and, to protect themselves and their families, pretended that sanity ruled in the mad house.

Frances Gumley & Brian Redhead: 'Protestors for Paradise', (B.B.C. Books, 1993)

Protestantism

The evangelical estates [of Germany] lodged 'protests' against the decision [of the Diet of Speyer] to affirm the Diet of Worms' condemnation of Luther on April 19–20, 1529, thus gaining themselves the name 'Protestants'. The Protestants objected to the Diet's assumption of authority 'as in matters of God's honour and the salvation of our souls, each estate must stand for itself before God.'

A positive testimony to the supremacy of God's word lies at the heart of Protestantism.

A Skevington-Wood: T.S.F. Magazine, (1971)

. . . the life of Protestantism depends on the survival of that against which it protests .

T.S. Eliot: 'Notes towards the definition of Culture', (1948)

The three great elements of modern civilisation, Gunpowder, Printing and the Protestant Religion.

Thomas Carlyle (1795–1881)

Providence

In the late 18th century, a Scottish coach company advertised that its coach would run six times a week, 'God willing', and at least twice a week 'whether or no'.

Related by C. Wordsworth

A lady sitting next to a bishop at a dinner observed in the course of conversation, 'My Aunt was prevented at the last moment from sailing in the ship which sank last week. Would you not call that the intervention of providence?'

'I can't tell', replied the bishop, 'because I do not know your aunt!'

Source unknown

I never saw a wild thing
sorry for itself.
A small bird will drop frozen dead
from a bough
without ever having felt sorry for
itself.

D.H. Lawrence

If you see a blind man, kick him; why should you be kinder than God?

Anonymous

All Nature is but Art, unknown to
thee;
All Chance, Direction, which thou
canst not see;
All Discord, Harmony, not understood;
All partial Evil, universal Good.

Alexander Pope

[Jesus said] 'Do not worry, saying, "What will we eat?" or "What will we wear?" For it is the Gentiles who strive for all these things; and indeed your heavenly Father knows that you need all these things. But strive first for the kingdom of God and his righteousness, and all these things will be given to you as well. So do not worry about tomorrow, for tomorrow will bring worries of its own. Today's trouble is enough for today.'

Matthew 6:31–34

No testing has overtaken you that is not common to everyone. God is faithful, and he will not let you be tested beyond your strength, but with the testing he will also provide the way out so that you may be able to endure it.

1 Corinthians 10:13

Psalms

You cannot imagine the great benefit of learning psalms by heart; for when you are under any temptation, or are in any affliction, or when you lie waking in the night, or when sick, these psalms will come into your mind; and the devout repeating them will yield you most seasonable consolations.

Bishop Thomas Ken (1637–1711): 'Directions for Prayer for the Diocese of Bath and Wells'

Psalm 23:
The Rule Book is my shepherd:
I shall not work.
It maketh me to lie down on the job:
it leadeth me beside the still factories,
it restoreth my insurance benefit.

Yea, though I walk through the valley of the shadow of unemployment
I will fear no recrimination, for the union is with me:
its restrictive practices and shop stewards, they comfort me.
It prepareth a works committee before me
in the presence of my employers:
it anointeth my hand with pay rises and my credit limit runneth over.
Surely work bonuses and restrictive practices shall follow me
all the days of my life:
and I shall dwell in a fine house for ever.

Source unknown

Never was a piece of experimental divinity (the Psalter) so nobly written, or so justly reverenced and admired. But it must be acknowledged still that there are a thousand lines in it which were not made for a church in our day to assume as its own.

Isaac Watts: quoted in 'The Broadcast Psalter', (1948)

Psychology

Psychoanalysis is confession without absolution.

G.K. Chesterton (1874–1936)

Did you hear what the white rat said to the other white rat? 'I've got that psychologist so well trained that every time I ring the bell he brings me something to eat.'

David Mercer: 'A Suitable Case for Treatment', (B.B.C., 1962)

Public Speaking

There is a lot of mimicry involved (in preaching and public speaking): if some world-famous preacher has a particularly pronounced fancy accent, it won't be long before people training for ministry pick it up and begin the slide that will develop in their early years of ministry into something much admired by sermon-cassetteers but quite foreign to people outside the sacred portals of the church. The funny voices of their preachers seem to be perfectly acceptable, even a distinct advantage, to some Christians today; those who are more discerning will be tempted to question whether the preacher's message is as phony as his accent!

Robert M.E. Paterson: 'Short, Sharp and Off the Point', (MARC Europe, 1987)

John Duke Coleridge (Lord Coleridge, 1820–94, Lord Chief Justice) once rose to reply to a toast at a Baliol College dinner with the words: 'I, my lords and gentlemen, have been asked to respond for Oxford as a whole. And, my lords and gentlemen, what a whole Oxford is.'

Michael Gilbert, Ed: 'Oxford Book of Legal Anecdotes', (Oxford, 1986)

An ORATOR is a man who says what he thinks and feels what he says.

William Jennings Bryan (1860–1925): 'The Peerless Leader'

A description of William G. McAdoo's public speaking (he was an unsuccessful Democratic contender for nomination in the U.S. presidential campaigns of 1920 and 1924):
His speeches left the impression of an army of pompous phrases moving over the landscape in search of an idea; sometimes these meandering words would actually capture a struggling thought and bear it triumphantly a prisoner in their midst, until it died of servitude and over-work.

An after-dinner speech should be like a lady's dress: long enough to cover the subject and short enough to make it interesting.

Anonymous

A speech is like a love-affair. Any fool can start it, but to end it requires considerable skill.

Lord Mancroft

Speeches are like babies – easy to conceive but hard to deliver.

Pat O'Malley

The human brain starts working the moment you are born and never stops until you stand up to speak in public.

Sir George Jessel

When you have nothing to say, say nothing.

Charles Caleb Colton (1780–1832)

. . . you must, he [Rudolphe] thought, beware of turgid speeches masking commonplace passions; as though the soil's abundance does not sometimes spill over in the most decrepit metaphors, since no one can give the exact measure of their needs, their ideas, their afflictions, and since human speech is like a cracked cauldron on which we knock out tunes for dancing bears, when we wish to conjure pity from the stars.

Gustave Flaubert: 'Madame Bovary', Part 2, in translation by Geoffrey Wall, (1992; Penguin, 1993)

A Christian was sent to the lions before the Emperor Nero in the arena. He called the first lion over to him, whispered in his ear and the lion retreated as meek as a Persian pussy cat. Fiercer lions were sent in, but each time the same thing happened. Nero finally offered to release the Christian if he would tell him what were the mysterious words that he said to the lions. The Christian explained: 'It's quite simple; I just said, "After dinner you've got to make a speech!"'

Source unknown; quoted by David Watson (c. 1970)

Sir Horace [later Lord] Davey (1833–1907) had great difficulty in getting elected to a seat in the House of Commons because he was a very uninspiring orator. 'You should try a bit of repartee sometimes, Sir 'Orace,' said one of his many election agents after a stormy public meeting. The forlorn candidate agreed. 'Tell me,' he added sadly, 'what ought I to say if somebody calls out, "Speak up, you old toad!"?'.

Michael Gilbert, Ed: 'Oxford Book of Legal Anecdotes', (Oxford, 1986)

Publicity

The sort of church news which gets into local newspapers is usually very trivial. Pictures of the crowning of a Rose Queen and accounts of who won a prize for guessing the weight of the vicar hardly commend the cause of Christ to the casual reader.

Edward Patey: 'Open the Doors', (Mowbrays, 1978)

[Some parish magazines are] platitudinous and trivial effusions which verge on the edge of parody. There is a tendency to use unctuous clericalisms of the 'May God's blessings be upon us this Lenten season' variety, but this is the style hardened readers have come to expect.

Edward Patey: 'Open the Doors', (Mowbrays, 1978)

A cartoon showed three bill-boards. One national title proclaimed a famine and refugees; the second declared news of serious unemployment; the third, headed 'Parish Magazine' heralded 'Next month's Sidesmen's Rota' as its gripping lead.

Administry

Pulpits

. . . people are governed by pulpits more than the sword.

King Charles I

What a coronation is our taking of orders, and what an inthronisation is the coming up into a pulpit, where God invests his servants with his ordinance . . . 'Woe be unto thee if thou do not preach', and then enables him to preach peace, mercy, consolation, to the whole congregation.

John Donne (1572–1631), Dean of St Paul's

St Paul's Cross was described by Thomas Carlyle as 'a kind of *Times* newspaper, but edited by heaven itself . . . a most important entity.'

M. Cornford: 'Paul's Cross', (London, 1910)

For all its shortcomings, the pulpit is the place *par excellence* where Sunday by Sunday in thousands of places the gospel message is proclaimed. There are many other methods of evangelism besides preaching, but if the sermon is either neglected or treated casually, a major opportunity for proclaiming the gospel will be thrown away.

Edward Patey: 'Open the Doors', (Mowbray, 1978)

The abandonment of the pulpit can mean little more than a loss of confidence in preaching under the guise of a desire for informality.

David Kennedy: 'Understanding Anglican Worship', (Grove Worship, 1994)

The Country Parson preacheth constantly, the pulpit is his joy and his throne.

'George Herbert A Priest to the Temple', chapter 7, (1632, posthumously published, 1652), from edition by H.C. Beeching, (Blackwell, 1898)

The preachers who fail imagine themselves to be six foot above contradiction.

Anonymous

Little girl to her mother, on observing the signs of 'Hwyl' (spirit) in a Welsh non-conformist preacher:
Mummy, what will happen if he gets out of there?

Coward's Castle.

Anonymous

In the remodelling of St John's Church, Washington, D.C., 'The Church on Lafayette Square', in 1842, a number of improvements were introduced.
One distinct loss, however, was the substitution of a conventional pulpit for the graceful wine glass pulpit with its charming light spiral of steps by which the preacher mounted to an elevation commanding his audience. Wheels attached to the tripodal base had fitted into iron tracks laid in the floor and thus permitted shifting the pulpit from the front of the chancel toward the center of the church. As Bishop Ravenscroft later told the story, on one occasion when he was preaching under the dome, 'the pulpit ran away with me. It had been wheeled out of its place and fastened with a snap catch. I was conscious of the distinguished and notable audience before me (there is a Presidential pew), and was preaching to them with vigorous earnestness, when of a sudden I felt the pulpit beneath me to be gliding away. Faster and faster towards the side wall of the church it was moving, and gaining rapidly as it went. The congregation was agitated; I was helpless; and I assure you I was considerably out of countenance when we stopped suddenly, and with a bump at the end of our notable journey.' With the new stationary pulpit a similar hejira never recurred.

Constance McLaughlin Green: from the 'History of the Church, 1815–1970'

'When will you ecclesiastical architects,' I said, 'give us *Anglican* ecclesiastical architecture? Is it not time that a visitor from some other tradition than ours should be able to see, by the very architecture of the building, that Anglicanism is 'bifocal' in its means of grace, that the living God comes to us *both* in the sacrament of the body and blood of Christ *and* in the sacrament of the word?'

Archbishop Donald Coggan, at the dedication of a re-ordered church in the Diocese of York, where there was 'a poor, paltry little stand' instead of a pulpit: 'On Preaching', (SPCK, 1975/8)

Punctuality

Some people are never on time for fear that they will lose time by the other fellow's not being on time!

Anonymous

Purpose

Everything is born without reason, prolongs itself out of weakness, dies by chance.

Jean-Paul Sartre

Man is a useless passion. It is meaningless that we live and it is meaningless that we die.

Colin Wilson

[Twentieth century] Man now realises that he is an accident, that he is a completely futile being and that he has to play out the game without reason.

Francis Bacon

In the physics classroom the student learns what the 'facts' are and is expected at the end to believe the truth of what he has learned. In the religious education classroom he is invited to choose what he likes best. It is not surprising that the goods that are most often picked off the shelves are those with an Eastern provenance . . . not only exciting because of their newness to a Western student, they are also compatible with the modern scientific world-view in a way that Christianity is not . . .

The Eastern religions do not understand the world in terms of purpose. The symbol of the dance is an interpretation of music and change without invoking the idea of purpose.

The Bible, on the other hand, is dominated by the idea of divine purpose. This means that one has to say that value judgements are either right or wrong in that they are or are not directed to the end for which all things in fact exist.

Lesslie Newbigin: 'Foolishness to the Greeks', (S.C.M., 1986)

Usually we trust that nature has a master plan. But what was it she expected us to do with tobacco?

Bill Vaughan

At eye level on one of the main panels of a revolving door in a departmental store was a sticker which read:
By the time you have finished reading this, you will have made an idiot of yourself going round and round and round and round, and you'll probably go out the way you came in.

Source unknown

Pilate asked Jesus, 'So you are a king?' Jesus answered, 'You say that I am a king. For this I was born, and for this I came into the world, to testify to the truth. Everyone who belongs to the truth listens to my voice.'

John 18:37

No longer present your [bodily] members to sin as instruments of wickedness, but present yourselves to God as those who have been brought from death to life, and present your members to God as instruments of righteousness.

Romans 6:13

Q

Quotation

Books of quotations and anecdotes can be a great help but need to be used sparingly.

Robert M.E. Paterson: 'Short, Sharp and Off the Point', (MARC Europe, 1987)

With just enough of learning to misquote.

Lord George Byron (1788–1824): 'English Bards and Scottish Reviewers'

Turning over too many pages in the Bible can be troublesome:
'Moses fell sick . . . and the lot fell upon Aaron.'
'And Judas went and hanged himself . . . Go, and do thou likewise!'
'The catch was 153 fish . . . And the lot fell upon Matthias.'

R

Race

President Taft of the U.S.A. met an old Indian chief and asked the chief if he had any words of wisdom for the president. The chief's reply was incisive: 'Watch your immigration laws.'

Source unknown

Now in Christ Jesus you who once were far off have been brought near by the blood of Christ. For he is our peace; in his flesh he has made both groups [Jews and Gentiles] into one and has broken down the dividing wall, that is, the hostility between us. He has abolished the law with its commandments and ordinances, that he might create in himself one new humanity in place of the two, thus making peace, and might reconcile both groups to God in one body through the cross, thus putting to death that hostility through it. So he came and proclaimed peace to you who were far off and peace to those who were near; for through him both of us have access in one Spirit to the Father.

Ephesians 2:13–18

Radicalism

Today there is a tendency in the new radicalism to insist that evangelism must give way completely to service, proclamation to dialogue, mission aimed at persons to mission aimed at structures. A penitence for ineffectiveness becomes a rationalisation of failure, a belief in the power of the gospel is replaced by a belief in the power of reformed organisations, progress is decried and protest applauded, and the renewal of humanity is considered independently from the revival of the church. It is now possible to attend Christian conferences where prayer is regarded as a waste of time, action alone counts, and even then it is frequently just talk about action. At the end of this route we may have to confess with the poet Byron, 'I am ashes where once I was fire'.

Douglas Webster: 'Not Ashamed', (1970)

Realism

Don Quixote saw twenty or thirty windmills and, turning to his squire Sancho, he said: 'See how fortune favours us! Do you see those terrible giants in the distance? There are over thirty of them. But no matter; I'll fight these fierce enemies of God and man.'

'What giants?' replied Sancho.

'Those you see there with their huge arms – some as much as two leagues long.'

'O, take care, sir! They're only windmills. Those aren't arms, sir, it's just their sails . . .'

'Ah, my poor innocent friend – it's easy to see you don't know much about adventures. They are giants. I know what I'm talking about. If you're afraid, you had better keep out of the way and say your prayers, while I undertake this dangerous and unequal combat.'

Don Quixote spurred on his horse, paying no attention to his squire's protestations that the windmills were not giants with long arms! 'Hold!' he shouted. 'Hold, you cowardly brigands! A knight attacks you, single-handed!'

At that moment a light wind arose and the sails of the windmills began to turn. 'That won't help you,' cried the knight. Then, grasping his shield, he rushed with his lance at the sails of the windmill. With tremendous force, Don Quixote and his horse were swept from the ground then hurled violently to the earth again with such force that Sancho had difficulty setting his master on his feet again. Sancho's attempts to explain fell on deaf ears. 'Peace, peace!' cried our hero. 'In a life devoted to fighting, one has to face strong enemies. I know what my enemy the dreadful sorcerer has done: he changed the giants into windmills in order to rob me of the victory!'

Cervantes

'If you get excited, you are unrealistic,' they say. 'If you are depressed, you are realistic.'

Bishop Festo Kivengere, (1981)

Somehow God has become for most people and even for many practising Christians, unreal. The God we want must be real. He must be a convincing personal experience. The God who is not real to me, revealing and operating all that is deepest and most personal in my being, is no God to me.

Bernadine Bishop: 'The God I want'

Jesus said to Thomas, 'Put your finger here and see my hands. Reach out your hand and put it in my side. Do not doubt but believe.'

John 20:27

We look not at what can be seen, but at what cannot be seen; for what can be seen is temporary, but what cannot be seen is eternal.

2 Corinthians 4:18

Reason

'Would not conversation be much more rational than dancing?' asked Miss Bingley.

'Much more rational,' replied Mr Bingley, 'but much less like a ball.'

Jane Austen (1775–1817): 'Pride and Prejudice', Chapter 11

When the ultimate explanation of things is found in the creating, sustaining, judging, and redeeming work of a personal God, then science can be the servant of humanity, not its master. It is only this testimony that can save our culture from dissolving into the irrational fanaticism that is the child of total scepticism. It will perhaps be the greatest task of the church in the twenty-first century to be the bastion of rationality in a world of unreason. But for that, Christians will have to learn that conversion is a matter not only of the heart and the will, but also of the mind.

Lesslie Newbigin: 'Foolishness to the Greeks', (S.C.M., 1986)

Reason [in the Enlightenment way of thinking – 'those analytical and mathematical powers by which human beings could attain to a complete understanding of, and thus a full mastery of, nature – of reality in all its forms'] . . . is sovereign in this enterprise. It cannot bow before any authority other than what it calls the facts. No alleged divine revelation, no tradition however ancient, and no dogma however hallowed has the right to veto its exercise.

Lesslie Newbigin: 'Foolishness to the Greeks', (S.C.M., 1986)

Mankind suffers from two excesses: To exclude reason, and to live by nothing but reason.

Blaise Pascal (1623–1662)

The heart has its reasons which reason knows not of; we know this in innumerable ways.

Blaise Pascal (1623–1662)

Man is merely a reed, the weakest thing in nature; but he is a thinking reed. There is no need for the whole universe to take up arms to crush him; a vapour, a drop of water, is enough to kill him. But, though the universe were to crush him, man would still be nobler than his destroyer, because he knows he is dying, knows the universe has the advantage over him. But the universe knows nothing of this.

Thus all our dignity consists in thought. It is on thought that we must depend for our recovery, not on space and time, which we could never fill. Let us then strive to think aright; that is the basic principle of moral life.

Blaise Pascal (1623–1662)

The church has failed not only by dodging the offence which the gospel offers, but also by wrapping the gospel in language and concepts which are mere human primitiveness and superstition. Do not let us forget that all the treasures of wisdom are hid in Christ. The Christian message is not opposed to hard and deep thinking, granted that this thinking is done to honour God's wisdom and not man's. At the present time, when man is filled with his own wisdom, the gospel truth will hardly seize a man's heart without forcing upon him some hard thinking.

Emil Brunner: 'The Scandal of Christianity', (1948; S.C.M., 1951), Lecture V, 'Resurrection'

Reconciliation

If anyone is in Christ, there is a new creation: everything old has passed away; see, everything has become new! All this is from God, who reconciled us to himself through Christ, and has given us the ministry of reconciliation; that is, in Christ God was reconciling the world to himself, not counting their trespasses against them, and entrusting the message of reconciliation to us. So we are ambassadors for Christ, since God is making his appeal through us; we entreat you on behalf of Christ, be reconciled to God. For our sake he made him to be sin who knew no sin, so that in him we might become the righteousness of God.

2 Corinthians 5:17–21

In him [Christ] all the fulness of God was pleased to dwell, and through him God was pleased to reconcile to himself all things, whether on earth or in heaven, by making peace through the blood of his cross. And you who were once estranged and hostile in mind, doing evil deeds, he has now reconciled in his fleshly body through death, so as to present you holy and blameless and irreproachable before him.

Colossians 1:19–22

Redemption

[In Christ] Redemption entered the arena of sheltered humanity.

Bishop Festo Kivengere, (1981)

Having been tenant long to a rich
  Lord,
  Not thriving, I resolved to be bold,
  And make a suit unto him, to afford
A new small-rented lease, and cancel
  th' old.

In heaven at his manour I him sought:
They told me there, that he was lately gone
About some land, which he had dearly bought
Long since on earth, to take possession.

I straight return'd, and knowing his great birth,
Sought him accordingly in great resorts;
In cities, theatres, gardens, parks, and courts:
At length I heard a ragged noise and mirth

Of theeves and murderers: there I him espied,
Who straight, *Your suit is granted,* said, and died.

George Herbert (1593–1633): 'Redemption'

Put away from you all bitterness and wrath and anger and wrangling and slander, together with all malice, and be kind to one another, tender-hearted, forgiving one another, as God in Christ has forgiven you. Therefore be imitators of God, as beloved children, and live in love, as Christ loved us and gave himself up for us, a fragrant offering and sacrifice to God.

Ephesians 4:31 – 5:2

Reform

On Roman Catholic Emancipation:
My firm belief is that England will be compelled to grant ignominiously what she now refuses haughtily . . . If you think the thing must be done at some time or another, do it when you are calm and powerful and when you need not do it.

Sydney Smith, (1826)

'Sinners' were with me, 'Saints' against me. Strange the contradiction in human nature.

Entry from Lord Shaftesbury's Diary during the passing of the Mines and Collieries Bill, 1842

By what authority . . . do Anglicans regard themselves as priests? By the authority of their own governing body alone, which has permitted a married priesthood, consecrated bishops debarred from communion with the Roman Church, and officially declared that the Bishop of Rome has no jurisdiction in England. The Church of England took it upon itself to decide that these were matters of reform of Catholic faith important enough to cause the magisterium of the Roman Catholic Church to be set aside.

Professor Keith Ward: in The Church Times, (1992), 'Priesthood and the humanity of Jesus'

Reformation, The

The Reformation was at heart a return to early Christianity. Its aim was to restore the church to its pristine purity.

A Skevington Wood: T.S.F. Magazine, (volume 60, 1971)

Ecclesia reformata sed semper reformanda.
(The church reformed yet always in the process of being reformed.)

Traditional

Be of good cheer, Master Ridley, and play the man. We shall this day light such a candle, by God's grace, in England, as I trust shall never be put out.

Bishop Hugh Latimer (of Worcester) to Bishop Nicholas Ridley (of London), on 16 October, 1555, at the stake at Oxford: related by Foxe

The English Reformation was master-minded by a moderate scholar with a love of the past rather than a radical reformer.

From the Introduction to 'The English Spirit', an anthology of English Spirituality, (D.L.T., 1987)

Regeneration *see also* NEW BIRTH

Jesus said, 'You must be born again.' (John 3:3,5,7). Frederick Buechner's reply was not very different from that of Nicodemus:
At my age I have trouble getting into a cab – let alone a womb!

Source unknown

The one thing no one can ever do is to birth oneself. Birth is always the gift of another.

Eugene L. Lowry: 'Journeys toward Narrative Preaching', (Pilgrim Press, 1990)

Jesus said, 'Very truly, I tell you, no one can see the kingdom of God without being born from above[1].' Nicodemus said to him, 'How can anyone be born after having grown old? Can one enter a second time into the mother's womb and be born?' Jesus answered, 'Very truly, I tell you, no one can enter the kingdom of God without being born of water and the Spirit. What is born of the flesh is flesh, and what is born of the Spirit is spirit. Do not be astonished that I said to you, "You must be born from above."'

John 3:3–7

When the goodness and loving kindness of God our Saviour appeared, he saved us, not because of any works of righteousness that we had done, but according to his mercy, through the water of rebirth and renewal by the Holy Spirit.

Titus 3:4, 5

Relationships

Sustained and creative relationships have to be worked at; rarely do they occur spontaneously.

Peter Baelz: Address to the Governing Body of the Church in Wales, (1993)

Nothing is a greater impediment to being on good terms with others than being ill at ease with yourself.

Honoré de Balzac (1799–1850)

As God's chosen ones, holy and beloved, clothe yourselves with compassion, kindness, humility, meekness, and patience. Bear with one another and, if anyone has a complaint against another, forgive each other; just as the Lord has forgiven you, so you also must forgive. Above all, clothe yourselves with love, which binds everything together in perfect harmony.

Colossians 3:12–14

Conduct yourselves wisely towards outsiders, making the most of the time. Let your speech always be gracious. seasoned with salt, so that you may know how you ought to answer everyone.

Colossians 4:5, 6

[1] *Or* 'born anew'.

Religion – *see also* GOSPEL

Die Religion . . . ist das Opium des Volkes.
(Religion . . . is the opium of the people)

Karl Heinrich Marx (1818–1833)

Things have come to a pretty pass when religion is allowed to invade the sphere of private life.

Viscount William Lamb Melbourne (1779–1848)

Religion is unbelief.

Karl Barth

You don't actually discuss what you think about religion with anyone – it's like underwear – close to you and rather personal, and you don't talk about it.

Jackie Pullinger reflecting on religion at school

There are those who try to trap him [Christ] in their churches, preferably with enough stained glass to produce a dim religious light, in some vague belief he will be safe there. They forget the reaction of Jesus when Peter tried to guard him against crucifixion.

Dewi Morgan: in The Times, (21 December, 1985)

The churches will bring the people in to the extent they shut this world out.

Paul Johnson: in the Daily Mail, (28 December, 1985)!

The peace of God [is] the Christian phrase for civilisation; the kingdom of God [is] the ideal society of the future; [and] Christian principles need a basis outside dogma [since religion is] morality touched by emotion.

Matthew Arnold (1822–1888)

Religion is a refuge for fugitives from God.

Malcolm Muggeridge

Unfortunately, religion can turn out to be the biggest cover-up job of them all – the ultimate comfort blanket . . . If this is true, then religion must be a deeply retrogressive force in our lives, something that keeps us perpetually in a childish state. And there are certainly various pictures of God which fit this view, whether he is made the rubber stamp of approval for a plush lifestyle, a lucky charm, or the distant monarch on his throne, keeping careful tally of all the good little boys and girls.

Richard MacKenna: 'God for Nothing', (Churchman 1984/85)

Religion always hovers on the edge of blasphemy. It slips easily into travesties of itself. It is vulnerable to an internal reversal of aim which turns it from awed contemplation of and response to ultimate mystery, into an inflated and pretentious claim to superhuman wisdom and powers . . .

There must be some deep flaw in a concept of God which contracts rather than expands the dimensions of the world which believers inhabit.

Archbishop John Habgood (of York): in The Independent, (9 May, 1987)

Britain is not a religious place. It is likely that a majority of Tory conference fodder, as they bay for traditional values, as well as most of the Cabinet, are atheists. The nostalgia they feel for the English Hymnal, the Book of Common Prayer and the Authorised Version is terribly nice and respectable and entirely vacuous in religious terms . . .

They [the Education ministers] are aspiring to resurrect religion as a socially unifying force amid the widespread conviction that it is untrue.

Bryan Appleyard: in The Times, (5 August, 1992), 'Finding God in the classroom'

. . . the bane of parish work: somebody who has got religion. It's as embarrassing to a cleric of sensibility as 'poetry lovers' are to a poet.

Peter de Vires: 'The Mackerel Plaza', (1958)

Religions die when they are proved to be true. Science is the record of dead religions.

Oscar Wilde: 'Phrases and Philosophies for the Use of the Young', (1894)

There is no religion in England. If anyone mentions religion people begin to laugh.

Montesquieu, (1730)

Oliver Cromwell to Sir Thomas Chichele in the matters concerning religion:

I can tell you, sirs, what I would not have, though I cannot what I would.

From the Memoirs of Sir Philip Warwick, (1813)

Religion has become interested in religion and is, therefore, anaemic.

Pete Hammond: at the Lausanne II Congress, Manila, (July, 1989)

The time has come for Christianity and the other great world religions to think in terms of sharing a mission to the loveless and unloved masses of humanity.

Professor John Macquarrie

A man fell into a deep pit from which there was no escape.

Mohammed came along and told the man it was God's will that he was there and he should stay.

Buddha passed by and said the man must accept his suffering and contemplate his lot.

A Hindu monk came that way and said that it was man's place to suffer; the man should look to himself and mentally escape by seeking inner peace.

A Jew came along and offered the man advice on how to climb out.

Finally Jesus came along and jumped down into the pit so that the man could climb out on his shoulders.

Source unknown

. . . the whole world once very nearly died of broad-mindedness and the brotherhood of all religions.

G.K. Chesterton (1874–1936)

It is now commonplace to hear middle-class atheists say that it is better to have something to reject than to have nothing . . .

While well-meaning Christians were soberly assessing the virtues of neighbouring faiths, fundamentalist Muslims were blithely rejecting their overtures.

Bryan Appleyard: in The Times, (5 August, 1992), 'Finding God in the classroom'

When young they indulge their lusts, or at least pursue the world's vanities; as time goes on they get in a fair way of business, or other mode of making money; then they marry and settle; and their interest coinciding with their duty, they seem to be, and think themselves, respectable and religious men;

they grow attached to things as they are; they begin to have a zeal against vice and error; and they follow after peace with all men. Such conduct indeed, as far as it goes, is right and praiseworthy. Only, I say, it has not necessarily anything to do with religion at all.

John Henry Newman, (then Vicar of the University Church, Oxford): in a sermon, 'The Venture of Faith', (21 February, 1836)

. . . religion can be dangerous. It can arouse some quite ugly passions. And sometimes the more deeply people feel themselves to be committed, the more ready they are to exclude and condemn those who fail to measure up to their own way of seeing things.

Archbishop John Habgood (of York): in The Independent, (July, 1991), 'This is not Hell'

Religious Education

Britain is a plural society in which the secular predominates, though there is an odd tendency, shown in the popularity of church schools, for parents to want their children brought up in – or if not quite in, then adjacent to – a faith they do not themselves profess.

The Times: First Leader, (5 August, 1992)

By and large modern pupils (and their teachers, too) could not state a single coherent thing about Jesus. Moses and the bulrushes might have been on another planet . . .

Paradoxically, while dogma runs rife in the classroom in history or science, it was banished from the one sphere in which it properly belongs. So however else religion was to be taught, it was not to be taught as true nor as potentially attractive. This was paraded past bored classrooms, in the name of encouraging good race relations, a potted caricature of each of the many faithful, with most attention naturally to their rude and weird bits. And putting lots of them together helped them cancel each other out . . . And how telling a skinhead a few facts about Islam was supposed to make him less likely to bash a Pakistani was never explained.

Clifford Longley: in The Times, (8 August, 1992)

Repentance – *see also* CONFESSION

Repentance is a positive thing, a life-attitude of turning one's back on what is sinful and worthless, and turning one's face towards the living God.

Archbishop F Donald Coggan, Enthronement at Canterbury, (25 January, 1975)

[Repentance means] rejecting self-autonomy and joining the movement where Jesus is Lord.

Robert Zuercher: in 'Third Way', (1980)

You can start all over again . . . This is where we begin, then. Right in the middle of life where everything seems to have gone wrong. This is where each of us, king and shepherd, high and low, rich and poor, one with another can come to kneel and to be changed.

Bishop Simon Barrington-Ward, Enthronement at Coventry',(4 January, 1986)

God in Heaven, you have helped my life to grow like a tree. Now something has happened. Satan, like a bird, has carried in one twig of his own choosing after another. Before I knew it, he had built a dwelling place and was living in it. Tonight, my Father, I am throwing out both the bird and the nest. Amen.

Prayer of a Nigerian Christian

When Jesus urged men to repent, he was urging them to become as little children. He wasn't asking them to eat the dust. He was confronting them with the necessity of a radical change of outlook, a fundamental re-orientation of their lives, so that they would no longer trust for security in the persons they had built up – the drama of being me which I continuously stage for my own benefit – so that they would no longer trust that, but have the courage to become as receptive as little children, with all the openness to life, the taking down of the shutters and the throwing away of the armour which that entails.

Harry A. Williams: 'The True Wilderness'

How well composed the ninety-five theses [of Martin Luther] are is evident from the fact that the conclusion can already be deduced from the first thesis: 'When our Lord and Master Jesus Christ said 'Repent!' (Matthew 4:17), he willed the entire life of believers to be one of true repentance.' But as Staupitz [Augustinian prior and Luther's mentor] had impressed on his student, true repentance is love, a response to the love of God, and not fear of Hell. And true repentance leads through temptation, death, and Hell, for it is the path in imitation of Christ, which no one may spend money to evade. *Penance* is a misleading word, for genuine repentance is not imposed; it is granted as a gift.

Heiko O. Oberman: 'Luther', (Yale, 1982/89)

But let them [the dead] sleepe, Lord,
 and let mee mourn a space,
For, if above all these, my sinnes
 abound,
'Tis late to aske abundance of thy
 grace,
When wee are there; here on this
 holy ground,
Teach mee how to repent; for that's
 as good
As if thou hadst seal'd my pardon,
 with thy blood.

John Donne: 'Holy Sonnet VII'

In place of true contrition, you taught me to be apologetic. I apologise continually. I apologise for my own existence, a fact that I cannot change. For years, you told me I'd be sorry someday. I am.

Garrison Keillor: 'Lake Wobegon Days', (1985), News, '95 Theses 95'

Peter, in forgetfulness,
Thrice denied his Master:
One Look moved him to confess,
Weeping his disaster.
Jesus, turn to look on me
Who persist in sinning;
Set my fettered conscience free,
Free for new beginning.

Lutheran chorale from the St John Passion, by J.S. Bach, (1723)

Jesus said, 'I tell you, there will be more joy in heaven over one sinner who repents than over ninety-nine righteous persons who need no repentance.'

Luke 15:7

Peter said to the crowd [on the Day of Pentecost], 'Repent, and be baptized every one of you in the name of Jesus Christ so that your sins may be forgiven; and you will receive the gift of the Holy Spirit.'

Acts 2:38

My brothers and sisters, if anyone among you wanders from the truth and is brought back by another, you should know that whoever brings back a sinner from wandering will save the sinner's soul from death and will cover a multitude of sins.

James 5:19, 20

Reputation

Good name in men and woman's
 dear, my lord;
Is the immediate jewel of our souls:
Who steals my purse, steals trash; 'tis
 something, nothing;
'Twas mine, 'tis his, and has been
 slave to thousands:
But he that filches from me my good
 name
Robs me of that which not enriches
 him,
And makes me poor indeed.

William Shakespeare: 'Othello', III.3, 159–165, Iago

Rest

In the days of the Apostle John at Ephesus [died c. 100] a young hunter came to John's house with an unstrung bow. He found John playing with a tame dove and expressed surprise that the apostle should be so idle! John merely asked the young man why he carried his bow unstrung. He replied that this was the way for the bow to retain its strength and elasticity. 'Just so,' said John. 'Mind and body will not retain their usefulness unless they are at times unstrung.'

Traditional

Be still, and know that I am God!
I am exalted among the nations, I am exalted in the earth.

Psalm 46:10

Therefore, while the promise of entering his rest is still open, let us take care that none of you should seem to have failed to reach it. For indeed the good news came to us just as to them; but the message they heard did not benefit them, because they were not united by faith with those who listened. For we who have believed enter that rest, just as God has said, 'As in my anger I swore, 'They shall not enter my rest' . . .

Let us therefore make every effort to enter that rest, so that no one may fall through such disobedience as theirs.

Hebrews 4:1–3, 11

Resurrection

The death of Christ in the New Testament is the death of One who is alive for evermore.

James Denny: 'The Death of Christ'

The Resurrection is true not just in an historic sense, but also in an absolute sense. Lazarus was raised to die again. Jesus was raised absolutely.

Professor G.B. Caird, (1972)

The Gospels do not explain the Resurrection; the Resurrection explains the Gospels. Belief in the Resurrection is not an appendage to the Christian faith: It is the Christian faith.

John S. Whale

The door of the holy sepulchre is the portal through which we enter the kingdom of God.

Herbert F. Gallagher

'Who are you?' said the Prime Minister, opening the door.

'I am God' replied the stranger.

'I don't believe you,' sneered the Prime Minister. 'Show me a miracle.'

And God showed the Prime Minister the miracle of birth.

'Pah,' said the Prime Minister. 'My scientists are creating life in test-tubes and have more-or-less solved the secret of heredity. Artificial insemination is more certain than your lackadaisical method, and by cross-breeding we are producing fish and mammals to our design. Show me a miracle.'

And God caused the sky to darken and hailstones came pouring down.

'That's nothing,' said the Prime Minister, picking up the telephone to the Air Ministry. 'Send up a met. plane would you, old chap, and sprinkle the clouds with chloride crystals.' And the met. plane went up and sprinkled the clouds which had darkened the world and hailstones stopped pouring down and the sun shone brightly.

'Show me another,' said the Prime Minister. And God caused a plague of frogs to descend upon the land.

The Prime Minister picked up his telephone. 'Get the Min. of Agriculture,' he said to the operator, 'and instruct them to develop a frog-killer, just like myxomatosis killed rabbits.' And soon the land was free of frogs, and the people gave thanks to the Prime Minister and erected laboratories in his name.

'Show me another,' sneered the Prime Minister. And God caused the sea to divide. The Prime Minister picked up his direct-link-telephone to a nuclear submarine.

'Lob a few missiles into Antarctica and melt the ice-cap, please, old man.' And the ice-cap melted into water and the sea came rushing back.

'I will kill all the first-born,' said God.

'Paltry tricks,' said the Prime Minister. 'Watch this.' He pressed a button on his desk. And missiles flew to their preordained destinations and immense explosions split the world asunder, and radio-active dust clouds killed every mortal thing.

'I can raise the dead,' said God.

'Please,' said the Prime Minister in his cardboard coffin. 'Let me live again.'

'Why, who are *you*?', said God, closing the lid.

From Brian Morris: 'Genesis'

[The Resurrection is] either the supreme fact in history, or else a gigantic hoax.

Professor J.N.D. Anderson

If event without interpretation is blind, interpretation without event is empty.

Immanuel Kant

Our reasoning powers intact, our grasp of science and philosophy unshaken, we can possess the truth of the Resurrection – or rather, be possessed by it – by means of the gift of faith which is freely given to all who seek it. None needs make apology for accepting that gift, which enhances and does not diminish all that is human, the intellect included.

The Times: First leader, (6 April, 1985, Easter Eve)

Question: On what do you base your belief that there is life after death?
Answer: I go back primarily to the Resurrection of Jesus. I also go back to the question of justice. In the death and Resurrection of Christ, the power of death has been broken. He has, as it were, invaded that world [of death] and conquered it. The man who is 'in Christ' now, a member of his church and in living relationship with him, has forged such a relationship with Christ as cannot be broken by the physical dissolution of his body.

Archbishop F Donald Coggan (of Canterbury): 'Simple Faith?', (1978)

I cannot see that we have any liberty to declare the death and burial [of Christ] to have been physical, while the resurrection and appearances were not . . . When Paul wrote that 'Christ died, was buried, was raised and appeared', we may be sure he did not mean that he was raised *while still remaining buried*.

John R.W. Stott: in The Times, (6 April, 1985, Easter Eve)

The resurrection of Christ is the work of the God who was, who is and who is to be: it is a foretaste of the future in the present.

Bishop John V. Taylor (formerly of Winchester, 1989)

Awake sad heart, whom sorrow ever drowns;
Take up thine eyes, which feed on earth;
Unfold thy forehead gather'd into frowns:
Thy Saviour comes, and with him mirth:
Awake, awake;
And with a thankful heart his comforts take.
But thou dost still lament, and pine, and crie;
And feel his death, but not his victorie.

Arise sad heart; if thou dost not withstand,
Christ's resurrection thine may be:
Do not by hanging down break from the hand,
Which as it riseth, raiseth thee:
Arise, arise;
And with his buriall-linen drie thine eyes:
Christ left his grave-clothes, that we might, when grief
Draws tears, or bloud, not want an handkerchief.

George Herbert (1593–1633): 'The Dawning'

God's love goes beyond history, of which death is so characteristic a feature. Resurrection is eternal life breaking up the framework of historical existence.

Emil Brunner: 'The Scandal of Christianity', (1948; S.C.M., 1951), Lecture V, 'Resurrection'

[Schleiermacher] consistently speaks of this (the resurrection of Jesus from the dead) as a fact but absolutely denies that it has any bearing on faith in Jesus as Redeemer, which is the heart of the self-consciousness of the Christian believer.

Lesslie Newbigin: 'Foolishness To the Greeks', (S.C.M., 1986), referring to Schleiermacher's 'The Christian Faith'

The . . . statement [ie. that the tomb was empty] can be accepted (by the modern sceptic) as a fact only if the whole plausibility structure of contemporary Western culture is called into question. To accept it as a fact means that history has a meaning that cannot be found from any study of the regularities and recurrences of the past. It means that the whole existing order of nature and history is confronted by a new reality that gives it a new meaning. It means a radical contradiction of this world as it is. But the affirmation that this is so can be made only by a community that is itself engaged in that contradiction, is actually pitting its life against 'the ruler of this world' and – in fellowship with Jesus – is bearing the cost in its own life.

Lesslie Newbigin: 'Foolishness to the Greeks', (S.C.M., 1986)

Most glorious Lord of Lyfe! that, on this day,

Didst make Thy triumph over death and sin;
And, having harrowed hell, didst bring away
Captivity, thence captive, us to win:

This joyous day, deare Lord, with joy begin;
And grant that we, for whom thou didest dye,
Being with Thy deare blood clene washt from sin,
May live for ever in felicity!

And that Thy love we weighing worthily,
May likewise love Thee for the same againe;
And for Thy sake, that all lyke deare didst buy,
With love may one another entertayne!

So let us love, deare love, lyke as we ought,
– Love is the lesson which the Lord us taught.

Edmund Spenser (c. 1552–1599)

At first [in the church's life] the doctrine of the resurrection of Jesus was the cardinal teaching of Christianity.

Whether we like it or not, we cannot escape from the fact that historically Christianity was founded upon the belief in the resurrection...

We cannot understand the development of Christian doctrine unless we have a clear grasp of the facts which that doctrine was invented to explain. The chief fact which called for explanation was the disciples' experience of the resurrection of Jesus. Without the presupposition of this experience the historical formulations of Christian doctrine are meaningless.

Alan Richardson: 'Creeds in the Making', (S.C.M. 1935), Chapter 1

God raised Jesus up. It is absolutely clear that we should never have heard of the gospel of God, of the good news of God in Jesus, had it not been for the resurrection. In other words, had not the disillusioned disciples of Jesus of Nazareth met him after his death in a totally new way.

I think that it is essential to be clear about this, no matter what questions can be raised, and in other context indeed *need* to be raised, about the New Testament narratives.

Bishop David Jenkins (of Durham): 'God, Jesus and Life in the Spirit, '(S.C.M., 1988). (The Bishop is often quoted as not believing in the Resurrection)

The resurrection is the revelation to chosen witnesses of the fact that Jesus who died on the cross is indeed King – conqueror of death and sin, Lord and Saviour of all. The resurrection is not the reversal of a defeat but the proclamation of a victory. The King reigns from the tree. The reign of God has indeed come upon us, and its sign is not a golden throne but a wooden cross.

Lesslie Newbigin: 'Foolishness to the Greeks', (S.C.M., 1986)

Jesus said, 'As for the resurrection of the dead, have you not read what was said to you by God, "I am the God of Abraham, the God of Isaac, and the God of Jacob"? He is God not of the dead but of the living.'

Matthew 22:31, 32

Now if Christ is proclaimed as raised from the dead, how can some of you say there is no resurrection of the dead? If there is no resurrection of the dead, then Christ has not been raised; and if Christ has not been raised, then our proclamation has been in vain and your faith has been in vain. We are even found to be misrepresenting God, because we testified of God that he raised Christ – whom he did not raise if it is true that the dead are not raised. For if the dead are not raised, then Christ has not been raised. If Christ has not been raised, your faith is futile and you are still in your sins. Then those also who have died in Christ have perished. If for this life only we have hoped in Christ, we are of all people most to be pitied. But in fact Christ has been raised from the dead.

1 Corinthians 15:12–20

I want to know Christ and the power of his resurrection and the sharing of his sufferings by becoming like him in his death, if somehow I may attain the resurrection from the dead.

Philippians 3:10, 11

If you have been raised with Christ, seek the things that are above, where Christ is, seated at the right hand of God. Set your mind on things that are above, not on things that are on earth, for you have died, and your life is hidden with Christ in God. When Christ who is your life is revealed, then you also will be revealed with him in glory.

Colossians 3:1–4

Blessed be the God and Father of our Lord Jesus Christ! By his great mercy he has given us a new birth into a living hope through the resurrection of Jesus Christ from the dead.

1 Peter 1:3

Retirement

Vicar: I'm very sorry to be leaving this parish, but I expect that you will get a better man than me next time.
Parishioner : Not necessarily; that's what the last vicar said!

Revelation

. . . historical revelation is the great scandal or stumbling-block for natural man. Man, filled with his self-love and self-pride, does not want to be uncovered, because he does not want his pride to be infringed upon. To acknowledge historical revelation means to acknowledge that the truth is not in us, that the right revelation to God cannot be established from our side; that the breach between God and us is of such a nature that we can do nothing about it.

Emil Brunner: 'The Scandal of Christianity', (1948; S.C.M., 1951), Lecture I, 'Historical Revelation'

. . . there are truths of revelation, . . . propositions which express the results of correct thinking concerning revelation; but they are not themselves directly revealed. On the other hand, this does not involve the result that there need be anything vague or indefinite about revelation itself . . .

What is offered to man's apprehension in any specific revelation is not truth concerning God but the living God himself.

Archbishop William Temple (of Canterbury): 'Christus Veritas'

God's revelation is not given in order that one should know it, but that through it he may become the Lord.

Emil Brunner: 'The Letter to the Romans', (1938; Lutterworth, 1959)

Simeon, the aged, held the baby Jesus, one would assume, for less than a quarter of an hour. [Luke 2]. Yet he could say that he had seen a light for revelation. Life is so full of brief encounters.

Roland H. Bainton: 'Christmas letter', (1978)

Yet more there be who doubt God's
ways not just,
And to his own edicts, found contra-
dicting,
They give the reins to wandering
thought,
Regardless of his glory's diminution;
'Till by their own perplexities
involved
They ravel more, still less resolved,
But never find self-satisfying solution.

John Milton (1608–1674): 'Samson Agonistes'

Rhyme

There once was a man from Japan
Whose limericks never would scan:
When told this was so,
he replied, 'Yes, I know,
But I always try to get as many words
into the last line as I possibly can.'

Anonymous

Rime being no necessary Adjunct or true ornament of Poem or good Verse, in longer Works especially, but the Invention of a barbarous Age, to set off wretched matter and lame Meeter.

John Milton (1608–1674): The Verse of 'Paradise Lost', (1669)

Riddles

A rabbi was asked, 'Why do Jews answer a question with a question?'

'Why shouldn't Jews answer a question with a question?'

Anonymous

Jesus said, 'What will it profit them [would-be followers] to gain the whole world and forfeit their life? Indeed, what can they give in return for their life?'

Marks 8:36, 37

Ridicule

If Jesus Christ were to come today, people would not even crucify him. They would ask him to dinner, and hear what he had to say, and make fun of it.

Thomas Carlyle (1795–1889)

It has come, I know not how, to be taken for granted by many persons, that Christianity is not so much a subject for enquiry but that it is, now at length, discovered to be fictitious. And accordingly they treat as if, in the present age, this were an agreed point among all people of discernment and nothing remained, but to set it up as a principal subject of mirth and ridicule as it were by way of reprisals for having so long interrupted the pleasures of the world.

Bishop Joseph Butler, (1736)

Ritual

They destroy service by services.

E.W. Benson (then Dean of Lincoln): to the Archbishop of Canterbury

Confession is nine points of the law.

Source unknown, (1877)

... this childish mimicry of antiquated garments.

Archbishop A.C. Tait (of Canterbury, 1868–82)

What was the difference between Eve before and after the Fall? Before the fall she was Eve-angelical, after the Fall she wore vestments.

Anonymous

Clerical robes are 'a comforting reminder of less complicated days'.

Church Pastoral-Aid Society (c 1965)

Chasuble: From the Latin *chasius ublo*, meaning 'clothing of the people'. The chasuble is a gorgeous, colourful and highly distinctive overgarment, draped eye-catchingly and stunningly over clergy to indicate just how much they are 'one of us'.

Martin Wroe, Adrian Reith & Simon Parkes: 'The Church-English Dictionary', (1991)

Alas! can we think that the reformation is wrought when we cast out a few ceremonies and change some vestures and gestures and forms. Oh no, Sirs! It is the converting and saving of souls that is our business. That is the chiefest part of reformation that doth most good and tendeth most to the salvation of the people.

Richard Baxter: 'The Reformed Pastor', (1655)

S

Sacraments

. . . there is no true interpretation of the Sacraments except by reference to the death of Christ.

James Denny: 'The Death of Christ', (1902)

The Word must make the element a sacrament; otherwise it remains a mere element.

Martin Luther's 'Greater Catechism', (1529), section 245

A sacrament is something more than a divine poem, because it conveys (as is believed by those who make use of it) not only God's meaning to the mind, but God himself to the whole person of the worshipper. No doubt it is 'Grace' which is commonly spoken of as thus conveyed; but Grace is not something other than God, imparted by him; it is the very love of God (which is himself) approaching and seeking entry to the soul of man.

Archbishop William Temple (of Canterbury)

The two sacraments constitute the visible, tangible prop that makes it possible to resist the devil in God's name. Thus baptism and holy communion are the solid ground on which the certainty of a Christian's faith rests. It is therefore clear that there can be no greater danger than the undermining of these two sacraments. Making baptism and communion into the work of man destroys the foundation of Christian life because it makes God's truth and reality dependent on the powers of persuasion of the individual, subjective conscience.

Heiko O. Oberman: 'Luther', (Yale, 1982/89)

The sacraments of Baptism and the Lord's Supper are God's commitment to us, enabling our commitment to one another.

Bishop Rowan Williams, (of Monmouth, 1993)

. . . what matters is the intention of the church in the administration of any sacrament, and the question to determine is whether the minister is carrying out the intention of the church, whatever his private thought may be.

A.T. & R.P.C. Hanson: 'The Identity of the Church', (S.C.M., 1987)

The church's ordained ministers need to take care that the symbols they attach to the ministry of the sacraments in no way overshadow the ministry of the word, from which all sacraments proceed.

Robert M.E. Paterson, (1994)

Do you not know that all of us who have been baptized into Christ Jesus were baptized into his death? Therefore we have been buried with him by baptism into death, so that, just as Christ was raised from the dead by the glory of the Father, so we too might walk in newness of life.

Romans 6:3, 4

The cup of blessing that we bless, is it not a sharing in the blood of Christ? The bread that we break, is it not a sharing in the body of Christ? Because there is one bread, we who are many are one body, for we all partake of the one bread.

1 Corinthians 10:16, 17

I received from the Lord what I also handed on to you, that the Lord Jesus on the night when he was betrayed took a loaf of bread, and when he had given thanks, he broke it and said, 'This is my body that is for you. Do this in remembrance of me.' In the same way he took the cup also, after supper, saying, 'This cup is the new covenant in my blood. Do this, as often as you drink it, in remembrance of me.' For as often as you eat this bread and drink the cup, you proclaim the Lord's death until he comes.

1 Corinthians 11:23–26

When you were buried with him [Christ] in baptism, you were also raised with him through faith in the power of God, who raised him from the dead.

Colossians 2:12

Sacrifice

Under the [Old Testament] Law, sacrifices were offered continually, which in itself pointed to their ineffectiveness. Had they succeeded in doing what they were intended to do, that is, to remove sins, they would have ceased. Instead, they served only to remind worshippers of the sins which still excluded them from the presence of God. As Luther said of indulgences, the more you buy of them, the less sure you are of salvation. The writer [to the Hebrews] states categorically. 'It is impossible for the blood of bulls and goats to remove sins.' He was equally firm in his conviction . . . that 'without the shedding of blood, forgiveness is impossible.' So sacrifice there had to be.

Bishop J.J.A. Thomas (of Swansea and Brecon): 'The Letter to the Hebrews'

A chicken and a pig were passing a church one day. The noticeboard advertised 'Stewardship Weekend. Come and pledge your gift at a ham and egg supper.'

'Oh yes,' said the chicken, 'let's go along and do our bit for the church.'

'That's all very well for you,' replied the pig. 'Your part's a contribution, mine's a sacrifice.'

Anonymous

The Bible tells us that we share in the benefits secured by Christ's sacrifice, but where does it suggest that we share in the offering of it? The Bible exhorts us to offer ourselves to God through Christ, but where does it tell us that our sacrifice is incorporated into his?

James I. Packer: 'Eucharistic Sacrifice', (1962)

The essence of the Christian gospel is that man is saved not by the example of self-giving of our Lord, but through his sacrifice. A lamb is quite useless for any kind of *service*. Its only use is as a sacrifice in the Old Testament understanding of it.

Bishop B.N.Y. Vaughan (of Swansea and Brecon): 'The Book of Signs', [on John 1:29]

Saints

God creates out of nothing. 'Wonderful!' you say. Yes, to be sure, but he does what is still more wonderful: he makes saints out of sinners.

Søren Kierkegaard

Every saint has a bee in his halo.

E.V. Lucas

The saint is a saint, not because he is 'good' but because he is transparent for something that is more than he himself is.

Paul Tillich

The Apostle Paul consistently refers to the Christians to whom he was writing as 'saints' (people who have been set apart):
To all God's beloved in Rome, who are called to be saints . . . *(Romans 1:7)*
To the church of God that is in Corinth, to those who are sanctified in Christ Jesus, called to be saints . . . *(1 Corinthians 1:2)*
To the saints who are in Ephesus and are faithful in Christ Jesus. *(Ephesians 1:1)*
To all the saints in Christ Jesus who are in Philippi, with the bishops and deacons . . . *(Philippians 1:1)*
To the saints and faithful brothers and sisters in Christ at Colossae . . . *(Colossians 1:2)*

Since we are surrounded by so great a cloud of witnesses, let us also lay aside every weight and the sin that clings so closely, and let us run with perseverance the race that is set before us, looking to Jesus the pioneer and perfecter of our faith, who for the sake of the joy that was set before him endured the cross, disregarding its shame, and has taken his seat at the right hand of the throne of God.

Hebrews 12:1, 2

Salvation

Bishop Leonard Wilson, Bishop of Singapore (later of Birmingham) spoke of his internment as a Japanese Prisoner of War.
After my first beating, I was almost afraid to pray for courage lest I should have another opportunity of exercising it; but my unspoken prayer was there, and without God's help I doubt whether I would have come through. Long hours of ignoble pain were a severe test. In the middle of torture they asked me if I still believed in God. When by God's help, I said, 'I do,' they asked me why God did not save me. By the help of His Holy Spirit I said, 'God does save me. He does not save me by freeing me from pain or punishment, but he saves me by giving me the Spirit to bear it;' and when they asked me why I did not curse them I told them it was because I was a follower of Jesus Christ who taught us that we were all brethren.

B.B.C. broadcast, (13 October, 1946)

The Line to Heaven by Christ was made,
With heavenly truth the Rails were laid,
From Earth to Heaven the Line extends,
To Life Eternal where it ends.

Repentance is the Station then
Where passengers are taken in,
No fee for them is there to pay,
For Jesus is Himself the Way.

God's Word is the First Engineer –
It points the way to Heaven so clear.
Through tunnels dark and dreary here,
It does the way to Glory steer.

God's Love the Fire, His Truth the Steam,
Which drives the Engine and the Train.
All you who would to Glory ride,
Must come to Christ, in Him abide. . . .

Come then, poor Sinners, now's the time,
At any station on the Line,
If you'll repent and turn from sin,
The Train will stop and take you in.

Anonymous: 'Found in Voices', Vol 2

God save the people.
When wilt thou save the people?
O God of mercy, when?
The people, Lord, the people -
Not thrones and crowns, but men.
God save the people!

Stephen Schwartz: 'Godspell', (1971)

Bishop B.F. Wescott (of Durham) when approached by a young Salvation Army lady in a train, who asked him if he was saved, replied to this effect:

Do you mean, 'Have I been saved?', 'Am I saved?' or 'Will I be saved?' And the answer is that I have been saved [conversion], I know I am saved [assurance] and I know that at the end of time I will be saved [hope].

(Some versions of this story claim that he used New Testament Greek quotations)

Nothing can save us that is possible.
We who must die demand a miracle.

W.H. Auden (1939, after his conversion)

It is no use nagging at God asking him to save you because you have in yourself no inducements that can possibly persuade God to save you. And anyway it is perfectly unnecessary to nag, because God has, independently of your anxiety, gratuitously, unexpectedly and inexplicably, given you everything in the way of salvation that you could possibly want in Christ.

R.P.C. Hanson: 'Eucharistic Offering in the Early Church', (Grove Liturgical Study, 1979)

Satire

This places the boundary between, and distinguishes the satirist from the libeller: for the former privately corrects the fault for the benefit of the person, like a parent; the latter publicly exposes the person himself, as an example to others, like an executioner.

Henry Fielding: 'Joseph Andrews', (1742), Book III, Chapter 1

The end of satyr is reformation.

Daniel Defoe: 'The True-Born Englishman'

Scepticism

If you believe the doctors, nothing is wholesome; if you believe the theologians, nothing is innocent; if you believe the soldiers, nothing is safe.

Lord Salisbury (1830–1903): 'Letter to Lord Lytton', (15 June,1877)

Scholarship

The mouth of any scholar who pays compliments to another is a jar of honeyed venom.

Victor Hugo: 'Notre Dame de Paris', V. I; translated by Alban Krailsheimer

Science

Why does this magnificent applied science which saves work and makes life easier bring us so little happiness? The simple answer runs: Because we have not yet learned to make sensible use of it.

Albert Einstein (1879–1955)

In everything that relates to science, I am a whole Encyclopaedia behind the rest of the world.

Charles Lamb (1775–1834)

Science is for those who learn; poetry for those who know.

Joseph Roux (1834–1886): 'Meditations of a Parish Priest', 1

[Secular scientism teaches that . . .] To have discovered the cause of something is to have explained it. There is no need to invoke purpose or design as an explanation. There is no place for miracles or divine intervention in providence as categories of explanation. God may be conceived, as in eighteenth-century Deism, as the ultimate author of it all, but one does not need to know the author personally in order to read the book. Nature – the sum total of what exists – is the really real. And the scientist is the priest who can unlock for us the secrets of nature and give us the practical mastery of its workings.

Lesslie Newbigin: 'Foolishness to the Greeks', (S.C.M., 1986)

Narcissism [ie. 'self-cultivation to virtuousness'], as well as many other aspects of our society (including, I believe, their liberal-democratic basis), is the result of having only one agreed truth system, science, which depends for its effectiveness on its refusal to tell us anything positive about ourselves or our place in the world and yet still becoming, in our imaginations, The Truth.

Bryan Appleyard: in The Times Saturday Review, (25 April, 1992), 'Science and Spirit'

The message of all three theories [quantum mechanics, relativity and chaos theory – 'the three big weirdos'] is: classical science is wrong insofar as it claims to be a final interpretation of reality . . .

The oddest thing about . . . science . . . is not simply that it creates a cosmic machine that does not need us, but that science only actually works on the assumption that we do not exist.

This is a complex point that has been spotted and argued about by many 20th century scientists and philosophers. But it can be summarised simply: we observe nature with the assumption that out presence does not affect our observations. We are utterly neutral observers, the fact of our consciousness does not affect what we observe. To some this may seem like common sense; to me it seems like one of the wildest and most extreme demands ever placed upon the human imagination – yet it is a demand which, to a large extent, we still obey.

Bryan Appleyard: in The Times Saturday Review, (25 April, 1992), 'Science and Spirit'

Scientists . . . are at last coming clean: they, and only they, hold the key to the meaning, purpose and justification of human life. The truth or otherwise of this claim, as well as the question of whether it is the real underlying belief by which we conduct our lives, is the most urgent issue of our age. Indeed, I believe it is the only issue of our age, the decisive debate that shapes all others. If we do not begin to understand science, we cannot claim to understand the present.

Apart from the best-seller lists, there is other evidence that people are prepared to accept this outrageous claim.

Bryan Appleyard: in The Times Saturday Review, (25 April, 1992), 'Science and Spirit'

When a man sits with a pretty girl for an hour, it seems like a minute. But let him sit on a hot stove for a minute – and it's longer than any hour. That's relativity.

Albert Einstein (1879–1955)

Scotland and the Scots

The book 'Scotland and Her Tartans' was promoted by Angus and Robertson, booksellers, in this way:
'Look up your clan's kilt and see where you came from.'

The English went to war against the Scots and mustered their troops on the side of a great hill. First, they sent a scout to assess the enemy's numbers, but he did not return. So next they sent a hundred men, but only one returned, badly wounded. 'The others are all dead,' he gasped. 'Don't attack, there are two of them.'

The same story is told by Yorkshiremen, Lancastrians, Welshmen, etc.

Searching

Many people today have a muddled, half-awareness of God, side by side with genuine searchings and values. We need to enter with them on to serious middle ground on which they may discover that there is a good and purposeful creator God concerned with neighbourhood, nation and world, its quality of life, its developing – or crumbling – culture. Christians need to help one another to find the confidence to think through the issues which are of common importance to them and their neighbours and to speak of God on these middle ground matters.

Bishop David Sheppard (of Liverpool): in The Times, (6 May, 1991)

Second Coming of Christ

If Christ came back tomorrow, he'd have to change planes in Frankfurt.

P.J. O'Rourke: 'Holidays in Hell', (1988)

The penultimate verse of the New Testament has Jesus saying, 'Surely I come quickly.' And he wasn't coming over for a swim. (Note to kids: Finish that math assignment. Somehow the world never manages to end before your homework is due.)

P.J. O'Rourke: 'All the Trouble in the World', (1994), 'Fashionable Worries'

[Jesus said,] about that day or hour no one knows, neither the angels in heaven, nor the Son, but only the Father. Beware, keep alert; for you do not know when the time will come . . . And what I say to you I say to all: keep awake.

Mark 13:32, 33, 37

Secularism and Secularisation

The contrast now is between Christianity in all its forms, and a kind of secular agnostic materialism, the fundamental doctrine of which dismisses all religion as pie in the sky when you die; and worse than that, not even interestingly true or false, but irrelevant and inconceivable.

Clifford Longley: in The Times, (27 October 1989), 'A Consumer's Guide to God'

Secularisation: The separation of religious institutions (formal, informal and symbolic) from the wider society and its economy.

Anonymous

Self

To love oneself is the beginning of a lifelong romance.

Oscar Wilde

. . .the religious scene is littered with people who are in danger of replacing God with self-culture, anxiously watching themselves for signs of growth and grace. And so we shop around for a better church, better denomination, better religion, or even anxiously seek out religious books that will give us all the answers in exchange for the purchase price.

Richard MacKenna: 'God for Nothing', (Churchman, 1984/85)

'It is a case of each for himself,' said the elephant, as he danced among the chickens!

Bishop Charles Gore (of Oxford)

The message to be gleaned from this catalogue ['of psychobabble and dimwitted meandering'] and from other New Age literature has nothing to do with spirituality and harmony, and everything to do with the most egregious narcissism. Every technique, every therapy, every group counselling session encourages the belief that the only way forward is to pamper, analyse and neurotically fixate upon ourselves. Spirituality seems to these people to be no more than a morbid fascination with one's private feelings at the expense of all else.

Bryan Appleyard: in The Times, (17 June, 1992), 'The selling of the New Age'

O Lord, though knowest that I have nine houses in the City of London, and that I have lately purchased an estate in Essex. I beseech thee to preserve the two counties of Middlesex and Essex from fires and earthquakes. And, as I also have a mortgage in Hertfordshire, I beg thee also to have an eye for that county; and for the rest of the counties, thou mayest deal with them as thou art pleased.

Prayer of the Right Honourable John Ward, (1727)

When a man is wrapped up in himself, he makes a pretty small package.

John Ruskin (1819–1900)

A survey [in the 1980's] showed that 80% of popular Christian books are basically self-orientated, 'betraying a religion which is closer to psychology than faith.'

David Wells: at the Lausanne II Congress in Manila, (July, 1989)

Any clubs that would accept me as a member I wouldn't want to join.

Attributed to Groucho Marx

I am afraid to tell you who I am, because, if I tell you who I am, you may not like who I am, and it's all that I have.

John Powell: 'Why am I afraid to tell you who I am?'

You were taught to put away your former way of life, your old self, corrupt and deluded by its lusts, and to be renewed in the spirit of your minds, and to clothe yourselves with the new self, created according to the likeness of God in true righteousness and holiness.

Ephesians 4:22–24

The end of all things is near; therefore be serious and discipline yourselves for the sake of your prayers.

1 Peter 4:7

Service – *see also* MINISTRY

I cannot praise a fugitive and cloistered virtue, unexercised and unbreathed, that never sallies out and sees her adversary, but slinks out of the race where that immortal garland is to be run for, not without dust and heat.

John Milton (1608–74): 'Areopagitica'

It [the church] is here to serve, to incarnate the powerlessness and suffering of God in the world, to convey the continuing challenge and promise of Christ. That means that *all* Christians have a ministry, *all* are priests, to use the old terminology, and the only time you find the idea of priesthood in the New Testament, apart from the final and perfect priesthood of Christ, is in the sense that *all* Christians are priests. It also means that there is only one absolute imperative for the church: *it is here to fulfil its mission.* And all the hierarchies, ministries and structures are purely functional and must be judged and used in that light. Not 'how not to do it' but *'how to do it'*.

Richard MacKenna: 'God for Nothing', (Churchman, 1984/85)

There are other messages [than the quiet, unconscious ones], other stimuli to catch the eye and perhaps to persuade them that this is what Christianity is *really* about. For instance, they may turn on the TV and, before switching over to something more interesting, get a glimpse of a figure dressed up like a Barbie doll with jewels and golden crosses and purple dress and cloth-of-gold cloak – Diana Dors? Danny La Rue? No, a Christian servant. (Obviously, servanthood is an attitude of the heart, not a matter of externals, but you need to have it written on your heart very deeply for it to make any headway through all the tat.)

Richard MacKenna: 'God for Nothing', (Churchman 1984/85)

The only ones among you who will be really happy are those who sought and found how to serve.

Albert Schweitzer

Nobody can be a good pastor or teacher of others who is not first a good servant of Jesus Christ.

John R.W. Stott: 'I Believe in Preaching', (Hodders, 1982)

As you do him more service, so also more disservice than others. The nearer men stand to God, the greater dishonour hath he by their miscarriages; and the more will they be imputed by foolish men to God himself.

Richard Baxter: 'The Reformed Pastor', (1655)

I had rather wear out than rust out.

George Whitefield (1714–1770), towards the end of his life

The church exists to serve. It is only within this context that the church's evangelism can be earthed and relevant and effective. Service to the world must be the unchanging background to the church's witness. It is only the fulfilment of its role as a servant that entitles the church to present Christ to the world it serves. The mere fact of availability to people, with no motive except to love and care for them, may have immense evangelistic significance in the long run . . .

The Church and the Christian alike are committed to service as the expression of the love and compassion of God in the name of Jesus Christ. Unless the church is at home in the sphere of service, it is unlikely to be relevant when it turns to evangelism.

Douglas Webster: 'What is Evangelism?', (1959)

Instead of being an ornament to literature he was a blessing to his fellows; instead of the genius of his age, he was the servant of God.

The Gentleman's Magazine obituary of John Wesley, (1791)

Ministers of good things are like torches, a light to others, waste and destruction to themselves.

Richard Hooker (c. 1554–1600)

A church which is not organised for service as well as for services forfeits the right to call itself the church of Jesus Christ, however impeccable its orthodoxy and however impressive its worship. Service is not necessarily the characteristic of all those who go to services. But it ought to be! For service is the sign that the gospel is being taken seriously.

Edward Patey: 'Open the Doors', (Mowbrays, 1978)

. . . But Patience, to prevent
That murmur, soon replies: 'God doth not need
Either man's work or his own gifts; who best
Bear his mild yoke, they serve him best. His state
Is kingley; thousands at his bidding speed
And post o'er Land and Ocean without rest;
They also serve who only stand and wait.

John Milton (1608–1674): 'Sonnet on his Blindness'

Sister Brunnhilde was coaching a Krebsback on his catechism one morning in Our Lady lunchroom and suddenly asked a question out of order. 'Why did God make you?' she said sharply, as if it were an accusation. The boy opened his mouth, wavered, then looked at a spot on the linoleum and put his breakfast there. He ran to the lavatory, and Sister, after a moment's thought, strolled down the hall to the fifth-grade classroom 'Who wants to be a nurse when she grows up?' she asked. Six girls raised their hands, and she picked Betty Diener. 'Nurses help sick people in many different ways,' she told Betty as they walked to the lunchroom. 'They have many different jobs to do. Now here is one of them. The mop is in the kitchen. Be sure to use plenty of Pine-Sol.'

Garrison Keillor: 'Lake Wobegon Days', (1985), 'Home'

If I were ever in danger of getting above scrubology, I hope the sight of the old original would make me ashamed. Just now I often wish there were more opportunities for that kind of service, but the wish is rather a lazy one. It has always been an easier thing to me to serve others in *doing* something for them than by merely talking to them, especially when they seldom really want to hear what you have to say . . . However, whether I have many chances or few the old brush tells me to take them, to see to it that I live up to the old ideal, of anything and everything as a love service to souls and bodies for Jesus' sake. It tells me also that it is the spirit that sanctifies the work, as it truly did when I scrubbed the dining room in those dear old Training College days. So now we can – I can – you can do all in the spirit of the Lord Jesus. Isn't it wonderful to realise it?

Catherine Bramwell-Booth: in published letters to ex-cadets, (May, 1916)

Sex

A group of clergy touring Australia were accommodated in one town in a girl's school, empty because of the holidays. They found in their dormitory this notice: 'If you require a mistress during the night ring the bell.'

Source unknown

The weaker sex is the stronger sex because of the weakness of the stronger sex for the weaker sex.

Anonymous

Luther wanted to liberate the Christian faith from this distortion [that the sexual drive is incompatible with 'higher perfection']: he could not accept the oppression of people down to their most intimate moments and warned of its devastating effects on society. God-given celibacy does not elevate to a high, holier state, it is the result of a specific divine calling to undivided service to the word.

'This is the word of God by virtue of which . . . the passionate, natural inclination toward woman is created and maintained. It may not be prevented by vow and law. For it is God's word and work . . .

Whoever is ashamed of marriage is also ashamed of being human.'

Heiko O. Oberman [quoting Martin Luther]: 'Luther', (Yale, 1982/89)

After a fortnight's mission, the leader proposed a vote of thanks for the hospitality offered by the host church, during which he made a special mention of all the women he had been sleeping with for the last two weeks.

Source unknown

In the late 1970's during a rape trial at the Northern Crown Court, a juror fell asleep. The victim had been asked to repeat what her attacker had said to her prior to the alleged crime. Overcome with embarrassment, the girl was allowed to write down the remark and the paper was folded and passed along the jurors. It was, by all accounts, a significant claim of sexual intention.

An attractive blonde was sitting next to the sleeping juror and, after reading the note, she nudged him and passed on the paper. He read the note, blushed, read it again, winked at the blonde and slipped the paper into his pocket. When the judge asked him to pass on the paper to the next juror he refused to do so, saying it was 'a personal matter'.

Stephen Pile, Ed: 'The Book of Heroic Failures', (1979)

The body is meant not for fornication but for the Lord, and the Lord for the body . . . Shun fornication! Every sin that a person commits is outside the body; but the fornicator sins against the body itself. Or do you not know that your body is a temple of the Holy Spirit within you, which you have from God, and that you are not your own? For you were bought with a price; therefore glorify God in your body.

1 Corinthians 6:13b, 18–20

Shopping

Wishing to know the difference in price between two tins of pilchards on the supermarket shelves, the housewife asked the assistant, 'What's the difference between the tall tin of pilchards and the flat tin?'

The assistant's reply was simple: 'Those pilchards are standing up, and the others are lying down.'

Shop 'til you drop!

Source unknown

It is possible for a man to know the love of God even when his wife takes him shopping.

Source unknown

Sickness

Walter de la Mare (1873–1956), during a severe (though not fatal) illness was visited by his younger daughter. As she left, she asked: 'Is there nothing I could get for you, fruit or flowers?'

Her father answered, weakly, 'No, no, my dear; too late for fruit, too soon for flowers.'

Silence

Someone once described language as a 'cord of silence', and words are knots in it. If there is a cord of silence linking the words of Scripture it is found in the wilderness. We must learn to meditate on the silences of Scripture if we are to enter into the life and faith behind the words.

David Runcorn: 'Silence', (Grove, 1986)

Silence more musical than any song.

Christina Georgina Rossetti (1830–1894): 'Rest'

The true God is inexpressible in the mystery of his holiness. He is, and dwells in, silence. As Henri Nouwen says: 'silence alone shares something of God's infinity.' So the place of meeting must be the desert of loving silence.

David Runcorn: 'Silence', (Grove, 1986); quoting Nouwen, 'The Way of the Heart', (1981)

One Word the Father spoke, which Word was his Son, and this Word he ever speaks in eternal silence and in silence it must be heard by the soul.

St. John of the Cross (1542–91)

One way to nurture simplicity is through the discipline of silence. Society is dominated by the inane notion that action is the only reality. Please, for God's sake and your own, don't just do something, stand there!

David Runcorn: 'Silence', (Grove, 1986)

. . . sometimes, if he [Mahatma Gandhi] was too tired or the crowd too noisy, he would sit on the platform in silence until the audience, which often numbered two hundred thousand, became quiet. He then continued to sit in silence, and the men and women sat in silence, and he touched his palms together to bless them, and smiled and departed. This was communication without words, and the mass silence was an exercise in self-control and self-searching, a step therefore towards self-rule.

Louis Fischer: 'The Life of Mahatma Gandhi', (1982)

It may be with silence rather than words that we will ever draw near the Eternal Presence. What marked out this Wilderness God of the Hebrews from other gods was that he could *not* be expressed.

David Runcorn: 'Silence', (Grove, 1986)

Silence is the perfectest herald of joy.

William Shakespeare: 'Much Ado About Nothing'

. . . silence also assaults our notion of *usefulness*. What is the point of silence? What is the use of it? None at all on the face of it. But our assumptions about worth and usefulness need challenging themselves. Our culture still measures worth by activity and achievement. It is an approach to society that profoundly devalues the most vulnerable in our midst – not least the unemployed and the elderly at this time. Silence must profoundly disturb us in these false estimates of ourselves. It calls us to confess them, to die to them, and so to enter new life in Christ.

David Runcorn: 'Silence', (Grove, 1986)

Dietrich Bonhoeffer condemned a 'chattering', rather than a 'proclaiming' church. He longed for respectful silence before the word: 'The church's silence is silence before the word . . . The proclamation of Christ is the church speaking from a proper silence.'

From 'Christology'

Silence is not an abandoning of words. Silence expresses our reverence for words and reminds us to respect their truth and power.

David Runcorn: 'Silence', (Grove, 1986)

If only the Christian world could learn to speak through silence, through the quality of its mystery and being. The louder we talk, the less we believe, the less real our journey becomes.

Richard MacKenna: 'God for Nothing', (Churchman, 1984/85)

. . . it is *pauses* in which almost the chief excellence of reading consists.

Charles Simeon (1759–1836): advice to John Venn (the younger) on reading aloud

Simplicity

[Many of] today's frustrations [are caused by] a surplus of simple answers, coupled with a tremendous shortage of simple problems.

Paul Sweeney

Any fool can make simple things complicated, but the wise preacher makes difficult things plain.

Charles Simeon (1759–1836)

Complex problems have simple, easy-to-understand, wrong answers.

Anonymous

Jesus said, 'I tell you, do not worry about your life, what you will eat or what you will drink, or about your body, what you will wear. Is not life more than food, and the body more than clothing? Look at the birds of the air; they neither sow nor reap nor gather into barns, and yet your heavenly Father feeds them. Are you not of more value than they? And can any of you by worrying add a single hour to your span of life? And why do you worry about clothing? Consider the lilies of the field, how they grow; they neither toil nor spin, yet I tell you, even Solomon in all his glory was not clothed like one of these. But if God so clothes the grass of the field, which is alive today and tomorrow is thrown into the oven, will he not much more clothe you – you of little faith? Therefore do not worry, saying, 'What will we eat?' or 'What will we drink?' or 'What will we wear?' For it is the Gentiles who strive for all these things; and indeed your heavenly Father knows that you need all these things. But strive first for the kingdom of God and his righteousness, and all these things will be given to you as well. So do not worry about tomorrow, for tomorrow will bring worries of its own. Today's trouble is enough for today.'

Matthew 6:25–34

Sin – *see also* THE FALL

To call themselves 'miserable sinners' is with many people a kind of religious good manners, just as a man inscribes himself 'your humble servant'.

J.A. Spender

The ultimate proof of the sinner is that he does not know his own sin.

Martin Luther

He does not cleanse himself of his sins who denies them.

Latin Proverb

Sin is not hurtful because it is forbidden, but sin is forbidden because it is hurtful.

Benjamin Franklin

Unless we believe in him we are bound to be wrong in our whole idea about sin; for apart from that faith we have neither the stimulus nor the capacity to frame the true standard . . . We try to cure our symptoms – our habits of lying, or cheating, or resentment, or envy, or contempt, or impurity – but we leave the disease itself alone. But the disease is that we are self-centred, not God-centred: the cure for that is faith; if we do not at least seek after faith, it proves that we have not understood the nature of our trouble: if we knew our sickness, we should know our need of the physician.

William Temple: 'Readings in St John', (on John 16:9)

Thorough tatter'd clothes small vices do appear;
Robes and furr'd gowns hide all.
Plate sin with gold,
And the strong lance of justice hurtless breaks;
Arm it in rags, a pigmy's straw does pierce it.

William Shakespeare: 'King Lear', IV. vi

'Oh, holy father,' Alice said, ''twould *grieve* you, would it not?
To discover that I *was* a most disreputable lot!
Of all unhappy sinners, I'm the most unhappy one!'
The padre said, '*Whatever* have you *been* and *gone* and *done*?'

W.S. Gilbert: Bab Ballads, 'Gentle Alice Brown'

Other men's sins are before our eyes; our own are behind our back.

Seneca: 'De Ira'

The seven deadly sins . . . food, clothing, firing [heating], rent, taxes, respectability and children.

George Bernard Shaw: 'Major Barbara'

Sir,
What's wrong with the world?
I am.
Yours faithfully,
G.K. Chesterton.

Letter to The Times (Chesterton (1874–1936) later wrote works entitled 'What's Wrong with the World' and 'What's Right with the World')

Total depravity is not that in all respects man is as bad as he could be, but that in no respects is man as good as he should be.

James I. Packer

All mankind is divided into two groups: sinners who think that they are righteous, and saints who know that they are sinners.

Blaise Pascal

Around every sin camps an army of quacks making a living from telling the sinner it isn't his fault, it is an 'illness', etc. Humbug. Fatness is voluntary, like smoking.

Matthew Parris: in The Times, (1992)

I think if the church put in half the time on covetousness that it does on lust, this would be a better world for all of us.

Garrison Keillor: 'Lake Wobegon Days', (1985), 'Protestant'

By that ['the buggeration factor'] I mean the way in which, just when things are going splendidly and someone has a really good idea, some idiot comes along, produces something idiotic and everything actually gets . . . . up.

Bishop David Jenkins (of Durham): from 'God, Jesus and Life in the Spirit', (S.C.M., 1988)

Many preachers have taken to giving advice on how to cure the symptoms of the human predicament, how to deal with a sin here and a sin there. This would be a nice way of coping with spiritual hypochondriacs, but most people in our churches do not have imaginary spiritual problems, nor can their problems be cured by a dose of some comforting but ineffective placebo . . . the preacher must tackle principles of far greater importance: the eternal matter of our relationship with God in Christ, and our consequent relationships with one another.

Robert M.E. Paterson: 'Short, Sharp and Off the Point', (MARC Europe, 1987)

Every saint has a past and every sinner has a future.

Oscar Wilde

As for Jesus, there must be a lot of sin in Arkansas to support this much forgiveness. All sorts of Christian enterprises advertise on the radio shows. There are Christian bookstores, Christian day care centers, Christian drug and alcohol counseling centers. For all I know there are Christian strip joints. The girls don't disrobe. They don't dance or wear makeup either. I mean, this is Baptist territory. They sit in pews and take their clothes off in their hearts.

P.J. O'Rourke: 'Age and Guile', (Atlantic and Picador, 1995), 'Current and Recurrent Events', 1994

A soap manufacturer said to a priest, 'The gospel you preach hasn't done much good, for there's still a lot of wickedness and wicked people.' Later the priest remarked as they passed an exceedingly dirty child making mud pies, 'I see that soap has not done much good in the world, for there is still much dirt and dirty people.'

'Oh, well,' said the soapmaker, 'soap is useful only when it's applied.'

'Exactly,' the priest replied.

Source unknown

We know that those who are born of God do not sin, but the one who was born of God protects them, and the evil one does not touch them. We know that we are God's children, and that the whole world lies under the power of the evil one.

1 John 5:18, 19

Singing – *see also* HYMNS AND MUSIC

Swans sing before they die – 'twere
no bad thing
Did certain persons die before they
sing.

Samuel Taylor Coleridge (1772–1834): 'Epigram on a Volunteer Singer'

Let the word of Christ dwell in you richly; teach and admonish one another in all wisdom; and with gratitude in your hearts sing psalms, hymns and spiritual songs to God.

Colossians 3:16

They [the twenty-four elders and the four living creatures] sing a new song:
'You are worthy to take the scroll and to open its seals,
for you were slaughtered and by your blood you ransomed for God
saints from every tribe and language and people and nation;
you have made them to be a kingdom and priests serving our God,
and they will reign on earth.'

Then I looked, and I heard the voice of many angels surrounding the throne and the living creatures and the elders; they numbered myriads of myriads and thousands of thousands, singing with a full voice,

'Worthy is the Lamb that was slaughtered to receive power and wealth and wisdom and might and honour and glory and blessing!'

Then I heard every creature in heaven and on earth and under the earth and in the sea, and all that is in them, singing,

'To the one seated on the throne and to the Lamb be blessing and honour and glory and might for ever and ever!'

And the four living creatures said, 'Amen!' And the elders fell down and worshipped.

Revelation :9–14

Slavery

The peculiar characteristic of a slave is always to be in fear.

Saint Ambrose of Milan

There they are, cutting each other's throats, because one half of them prefer hiring their servants for life, and the other by the hour.

Thomas Carlyle (1795–1881) describing the American Civil War.

In the protracted [and ultimately successful] attempts to abolish the slave trade and slavery in British dominions, Granville Sharp, William Wilberforce and others came into conflict with many other Christians who were willing to recognise that the slaves were made in God's image and were of equal value in his sight, but believed that God had decreed their station in life. They supported their view with New Testament evidence, such as Ephesians 6:5–8; Colossians 3:22; 1 Timothy 6:1, 2; Titus 2:9:10; Philemon 15, 16.

Smoking

A custom loathsome to the eye, hateful to the nose, harmful to the brain, dangerous to the lungs, and in the black, stinking fume thereof, nearest resembling the horrible Stygian smoke of the pit that is bottomless.

James VI of Scotland and I of England (1566–1625): 'A Counterblast to Tobacco'

Stinking'st of the stinking kind,
Filth to the mouth and fog of the
mind.

Charles Lamb (1775–1834): 'A Farewell to Tobacco'

Social Action

Sunday December 22nd:
Speaker [who was a monk] kept quoting Mother Teresa of Calcutta, who is, of course, a *Roman Catholic!!*

Afterwards, Richard Cook whispered to us, 'Ah yes, but is she saved?'

Gerald whispered back, 'Ah yes, but how many filthy beggars have you washed this week, Richard?'

Adrian Plass: 'The Sacred Diary of Adrian Plass', (1987)

George Herbert (1593–1633) a celebrated Anglican priest and poet, used to travel twice a week to Salisbury Cathedral and then go on to a music meeting with friends. One day, Mr. Herbert was very late and arrived very dirty and dishevelled, an unknown sight! On his way to Salisbury, the parson had come across a poor man with a poorer horse that had fallen under its load; Mr. Herbert had unloaded the beast and loaded his own horse; he gave the man money and told him to be merciful to the horse.

One of the parson's friends told him he had not acted wisely in so dirty an employment but Herbert replied that he thought his actions would be music to him at midnight and that to have failed to have done so would have made discord in his conscience every time he passed the spot. 'For,' he said, 'if I be bound to pray for all that be in distress, I am sure that I am bound, so far as it is in my power, to practise what I pray for . . . And now let us tune our instruments.'

Izaak Walton: 'The Life of George Herbert'

The younger priests [of the 1920's] were vastly excited by the proper place of the *Gloria* in the Office of Holy Communion, but they were not interested by the proper place of the workers in a Christian society. The consequence was that the hold that the church had on the people in working-class parishes was largely lost, and the people's priests were content to minister to pious old ladies and rather unpleasant young men, who connected religion with the wearing of lace cottas.

Sidney Dark: 'The People's Archbishop', (James Clarke, 1942)

The service we can offer to alleviate the most desperate needs of human kind is no substitute for this good news.

Sir Kenneth Grubb: A.G.M. of the Church Missionary Society, (6 May, 1969)

Did Jesus come only to supply man's material needs and give him a happier human existence? This is not the gospel declared in the New Testament. The end of poverty will not mean the end of sin. And when all the problems which haunt us today – hunger, racism, war – are solved, man will still stand in need of forgiveness, of hope beyond the grave, and of entering the new humanity this side of it.

Douglas Webster: 'Not Ashamed', (1970)

It has been a strength of evangelicalism tenaciously to preserve the idea that the church's main mission is to win persons for Christ. This preservation has been particularly important at times when parts of the church would have done away with personal evangelism altogether in favour of programmes for social reform. But it has been a weakness of evangelicalism to separate the church's mission to individuals from the church's mission in society.

Evangelicals act as if the two are distinct and neatly distinguishable aspects of the gospel, as though people can be saved without necessarily making an impact on the broader society. But what did it mean to accept Christ in the New Testament? When the early Christians confessed Jesus as Lord, it was clear that they were at the same time rejecting the lordship of other powerful lords. They dethroned money by sharing their possessions. They dethroned power and status by become each other's servants. They dethroned Jewish religious tradition by accepting Gentiles as brothers and sisters. They dethroned the state by claiming that Jesus is Lord, not Caesar, and by refusing to fight in Caesar's army. Becoming a Christian had very specific historical relevance. The mission of the church was to proclaim Jesus' lordship by the way they lived together in stark contrast to the way in which a society dominated by other and oppressive lords lived. Accepting Christ was to participate in a new quality of life in community with other Christians.

Robert Zuercher: in Third Way,(1980), 'On Growing a Church'

Jesus said, 'When the Son of Man comes in his glory, and all the angels with him, then he will sit on the throne of his glory. All the nations will be gathered before him, and he will separate people one from another as a shepherd separates the sheep from the goats, and he will put the sheep at his right hand and the goats at the left. Then the king will say to those at his right hand, 'Come, you that are blessed by my Father, inherit the kingdom prepared for you from the foundation of the world; for I was hungry and you gave me food, I was thirsty and you gave me something to drink, I was a stranger and you welcomed me, I was naked and you gave me clothing, I was sick and you took care of me, I was in prison and you visited me . . . '"Truly I tell you, just as you did it to one of the least of these who are members of my family, you did it to me." Then he will say to those at his left hand, "You that are accursed, depart from me into the eternal fire prepared for the devil and his angels; for I was hungry and you gave me no food, I was thirsty and you gave me nothing to drink, I was a stranger and you did not welcome me, naked and you did not give me clothing, sick and in prison and you did not visit me . . . Truly I tell you, just as you did not do it to one of the least of these, you did not do it to me."'

Matthew 25:31–36, 40–45

Society

What is bad for the hive is bad for the bees themselves.

Marcus Aurelius (121–180)

A preaching of the gospel that calls men and women to accept Jesus as Saviour but does not make it clear that discipleship means commitment to a vision of society radically different from that which controls our public life today must be condemned as false.

Lesslie Newbigin: 'Foolishness to the Greeks', (S.C.M., 1986)

There is no such thing as 'Society', merely individuals.

Margaret Thatcher, Prime Minister

Solitude

The curfew tolls the knell of parting
 day,
The lowing herd wind slowly o'er the
 lea,
The ploughman homeward plods his
 weary way
And leaves the world to darkness
 and to me.

Thomas Gray (1716–1771): 'Elegy written in a Country Churchyard'

Spelling

Peter Sellers once received a letter from a fan of the *Goon Show* asking for a '*singed* photograph of yourself'. Egged on by his friends, Sellers took the writer at his spelling. With his cigarette lighter he burnt the edges of one of his publicity photographs, and sent it off to his fan.

A week later the fan wrote back: 'Thank you very much for the photograph, but I wonder if I could trouble you for another as this one is *signed* all round the edge.'

Source unknown

After hydrotherapy, rape the patient in a blanket.

Instructions to Health Service therapists issued in the 1960's, also found in First Aid examination answers about how to cure snake bites!

Spirit, The Holy

We knew something of the power of the Holy Spirit. We are open to learn more of him. We await the surprises of tomorrow.

Archbishop F. Donald Coggan: 'Enthronement at Canterbury', (25 January 1975)

Every time we say, 'I believe in the Holy Spirit,' we mean that we believe that there is a living God able and willing to enter human personality and change it.

J.B. Phillips

Before Christ sent the church into the world, he sent the Spirit into the church. The same order must be observed today.

John R.W. Stott

You can feel its breath [the Spirit's] on your face if, hearing it pass, you go out and stand in its course. 'So is everyone that is born of the Spirit.' Don't ask for credentials. Don't wait till you know the source of the wind before you let it refresh you, or its destination before you spread sail to it. It offers what you need; trust yourself to it.

Archbishop William Temple (of Canterbury): 'Readings in St John's Gospel', [on John 3]

Sir, the pretending to extraordinary revelation and gifts of the Holy Ghost is a horrid thing, a very horrid thing.

Bishop Joseph Butler (of Durham) to George Whitefield

I believe that the Holy Spirit is still the creating Spirit, and that he will give us every morning fresh freedom, joy and a new provision of hope, if we open our soul to him . . .

I believe in the surprises of the Holy Spirit. Why should we think that God's imagination and love might be exhausted?

Archbishop Donald Coggan (of Canterbury): in the Methodist Preacher's Handbook, (1972), 'Faith and Prayer'

[David Watson told his hearers that] the aim of being filled with the Holy Spirit was not primarily that we may feel better but that God would make us more useful in his service.

David Armstrong: in 'David Watson', (1985)

Wind and fire are never *safe* elements. They are full of risk and danger. . . What it will mean for me when the wind and the fire of the Holy Spirit come upon my sinfulness and selfishness, only *I* can find out in personal encounter with the living God.

Archbishop Donald Coggan (of Canterbury): 'Spirit of Flame', C.J. Cadoux Memorial Lecture, (24 February, 1965)

The Holy Spirit is God the evangelist.

James I. Packer: at the Lausanne II Congress, Manila, (July, 1989)

If you blunder into some church where 'the Spirit' has taken them over and they are all swaying around, arms raised, with beatific smiles on their faces, the similarity to auto-eroticism is unmistakable. They are getting off on God.

Richard MacKenna: 'God for Nothing', (Churchman, 1984/85)

The difficulty is that even among our own congregations of regular churchgoers – and might I not add even among the clergy? – so many are still unconverted, and have never experienced the life-giving movements of the Holy Spirit in their souls. Or if not wholly unconverted, many nominal Christians have not made a complete and whole-hearted surrender to the Spirit's guidance. Let me again assert my conviction that nothing but a rebaptism of the church with the Holy Ghost, a second Day of Pentecost, can save the world from disaster.

Peter Green: 'The Holy Ghost, the Comforter', (1933)

. . . it appears self-evident to me that there is not such a being as a Spiritless Christian. There are plenty of disobedient Christians around who refuse to allow the Holy Spirit to have his sovereign way in their lives, but there cannot be Christians unbaptised in the Holy Spirit. Impoverished and stunted they may be, but not without the Spirit of God.

George Carey (later Archbishop of Canterbury): 'The Church in the Market Place', (Kingsway, 1984)

. . .the keynote of spiritual fellowship is the centrality of Jesus. Although the Spirit gives us his gifts, his main role is to point us to Christ. He 'glorifies' Christ – this is the biblical teaching.

George Carey (later Archbishop of Canterbury): 'The Church in the Market Place', (Kingsway, 1984)

He [the Holy Spirit] is not a tame force carefully bottled in ecclesiastical institutions, available to be served out in rational doses according to the decision of the hierarchy or the ministry of specially illuminated saints. He is the Lord of the church, not subject to human control, and like the wind he blows wherever he chooses. He is capable of causing explosions within the structures of the church and bringing about discontinuities and surprises as his wisdom determines, His judgments are unsearchable and his ways past finding out.

A.T. & R.P.C. Hanson: 'The Identity of the Church', (S.C.M., 1987)

Garrison Keillor describes the polite but heated argument between Brother Louie (a charismatic) and Brother Mell (strictly reformed) on the subject of the Holy Spirit.

The thought of Uncle Louie speaking in tongues was fascinating to me. Uncle Louie worked at the bank, he spoke to me mostly about thrift and hard work. What tongue would he speak? Spanish? French? Or would it sound like gibberish? Louie said that speaking in tongues was the true sign, that those who believed *heard* and to those who didn't it was only gabble – what if he stood up and said, 'Freemalator, jasperator, hoo ha ha, wamalamagamanana, zis boom bah!' and everyone else said, 'Amen! That's right, brother! Praise God!' and *I* was the only one who said, 'Huh?'

'Lake Wobegon Days', (1985)

In the *Peterborough* column of the Daily Telegraph in 1993 was a report of a recent charismatic conference at Westminster Roman Catholic Cathedral. The congregation 'started burbling away, to the delight of an old and very traditionalist woman who had strayed in. 'How lovely,' she murmured, 'to hear the old Latin again.' '

Revival comes not when the roof is raised but when the floor drops away.

Quoted by Bishop Simon Barrington-Ward: Enthronement at Coventry, (4 January, 1986)

. . . the heart of renewal is commitment to Jesus Christ. He is never secondary to any movement of the Spirit. Neither for that matter is the Father. To enter more and more into his love and into the realisation of his care is the secret of all spiritually alive people.

George Carey (later Archbishop): The Church in the Market Place, (Kingsway, 1984)

Inspiration may better be described as 'in-Spiriting'.

James Robertson, (1982)

If you begin worrying as to whether you have the Spirit or not, you have not yet understood who he is . . .

The Holy Spirit is much nearer to us, much more intimately concerned in our life in the church and in our individual spiritual lives than we usually realise. The Holy Spirit is in fact God in whom we experience God, God in whom we return to God. We cannot invoke God through Christ except in the Holy Spirit; we cannot pray except in him. He is directly and immediately God whom we experience.

A.T. & R.P.C. Hanson: 'The Identity of the Church', (S.C.M., 1987)

I have one concern about some of the popular forms of evangelism which have evolved in the 1990's: they pay more attention to the Holy Spirit than to the Lord Jesus Christ. That cannot be justified by the evidence of the New Testament and it cannot be right.

Robert M.E. Paterson, (1995)

It is hard for an empty bag to stand upright.

Bishop John Charles Ryle (1816–1900)

Jesus said to them [the disciples], 'Peace be with you. As the Father has sent me, so I send you.' When he had said this, he breathed on them and said to them, 'Receive the Holy Spirit. If you forgive the sins of any, they are forgiven them; if you retain the sins of any, they are retained.'

John 20:21–23

You are not in the flesh; you are in the Spirit, since the Spirit of God dwells in you. Anyone who does not have the Spirit of Christ does not belong to him . . .

You did not receive a spirit of slavery to fall back into fear, but you have received a spirit of adoption. When we cry, 'Abba! Father!' it is that very Spirit bearing witness with our spirit that we are children of God, and if children, then heirs, heirs of God and joint heirs with Christ – if, in fact, we suffer with him so that we may also be glorified with him.

Romans 8:9, 15–17

I want you to understand that no one speaking by the Spirit of God ever says 'Let Jesus be cursed!' and no one can say 'Jesus is Lord' except by the Holy Spirit.

1 Corinthians 12:3

The fruit of the Spirit is love, joy, peace, patience, kindness, generosity, faithfulness, gentleness and self-control. There is no law against such things. And those who belong to Christ Jesus have crucified the flesh with its passions and desires. If we live by the Spirit, let us also be guided by the Spirit.

Galatians 5:22–25

Do not grieve the Holy Spirit of God, with which you were marked with a seal for the day of redemption.

Ephesians 4:30

Do not quench the Spirit.

1 Thessalonians 5:19

God did not give us a spirit of cowardice, but rather a spirit of power and of love and of self-discipline.

2 Timothy 1:7

By this we know that we abide in him (God) and he in us, because he has given us of his Spirit. And we have seen and do testify that the Father has sent his Son as the Saviour of the world.

1 John 4:13, 14

Spirituality

Spirituality is the basis and foundation of human life . . . It must underlie everything. To put it briefly, man is a spiritual being, and the proper work of his mind is to interpret the world according to his higher nature, and to conquer the material aspects of the world so as to bring them into subjection to the spirit.

Robert Bridges: 'The Spirit of Man', Introduction

. . . just as there is much going on in the black economy about which little is known officially, so there is much going on spiritually in this country which is also hidden – naturally for very different reasons – from the public gaze: charismatic meetings in private homes, small-scale religious charities providing all sorts of practical help on a neighbourly basis, and above all, countless individuals wrestling with their own souls as they try to find their personal way back to God.

Peregrine Worsthorne: in the Daily Telegraph, (January 1982), 'Is Faith Returning?'

Spoonerisms – *after Dr. William Archibald Spooner, 1844–1930, Warden of New College, Oxford*

I think there are only two Christian Socialists in Oxford, Dr. Rashdall and myself . . . and I'm not very much of a Socialist, and Dr. Rashdall isn't very much of a Christian.

Genuine Spoonerisms are rare, but one is authentic, his rendering of 1 Corinthians 13:12 (from the Authorised Version of the Bible) as 'see through a dark glassly'.

Drinking the health of the elderly Queen Victoria, 'A toast to the queer old dean', the order, 'You have tasted two whole worms and must leave on the next town drain', and 'Kinkering congs their titles take', are all apocryphal.

Curate to Archbishop:
More Grace your Cake?

Statistics

There are lies, . . . lies, and statistics.
Mark Twain

Figures can't lie, but liars can figure.
Anonymous

Stewardship

Stewardship is not a classroom exercise in fractions. It is a homework assignment in total living.
Kenneth L. Wilson

*Vicar:*What would you do for God if you owned two luxury homes?
Christian: I'd give one to the church.
Vicar: What would you do for God if you inherited £1 million?
Christian: I'd give half of it to the church.
Vicar: What would you do for God if you owned two pairs of trousers? *(Silence.)*
Christian: The problem is, I *do* own two pairs of trousers.
Source unknown

If I believed that the Christian faith was the source of eternal life, I reckon that to give back at least 60% of my income would not be asking too much.
David Furbank, (1994)

Success

. . . in religion, nothing fails like success.
Bishop Barnes (of Birmingham)

A suffering God is most strongly at work in defeat . . . I worry if we see success in worldly terms. The Old Testament, as Martin Buber pointed out, sees no intrinsic value in success. If it has to report a successful deed it makes certain that it also reports in detail all the failure involved in the success. For the prophets, failure 'is the breath in their nostrils' – they fight, but can never win.
Richard MacKenna: 'God for Nothing', (Churchman, 1984/85)

Anybody can sympathise with the sufferings of a friend, but it requires a very fine nature to sympathise with a friend's success.
Oscar Wilde: 'The Souls of Man under Socialism', (1891)

Suffering – *see also* WITNESS

The 'moment of decision' is the moment of 'suffering with Christ'. This is where the mission of the church should begin . . . If God's will for his followers is that they should share in his suffering, consequently we have to look at the suffering that there is in the world as the greatest opportunity we have for mission. Where there is suffering, there should be the beginning of missionary work . . . To be willing to suffer with your neighbour through Christ is the alphabet of missionary life and work. Without it no one will ever be able to know or understand what missionary work is about . . . Are you ready to be a missionary to share in the suffering and sorrow of the world? Then come and follow the Master, Jesus Christ. Amen.
Bishop Misaeri Kauma (of Namirembe, Uganda): 1980 Church Missionary Society Annual Sermon, (8 December, 1980)

Christians must imitate Christ, and suffer with him. [History has often told of God's] befooling them that have dreamed of glorious times.
Richard Baxter (1615–1691)

O child, the human heart can suffer. It holds more tears than the ocean holds waters. We never know how wide, how deep it is, until misery begins to unbind her clouds, and fills it with rushing blackness.
Charlotte Brontë: Shirley (Charlotte's brother and two sisters had, the year before, died of tuberculosis, a disease which would later kill her)

The frightening thing about the Christian message is that it has nothing to do with our wandering around looking pious and wonderful (the Action Man Pale Galilean Kit), but focuses our attention on the cross, on suffering. Here, it says, is the key to meaning.
Richard MacKenna: 'God for Nothing', (Churchman, Worthing, 1985)

. . . I have come to think that the only, the supreme prayer we can offer up during these hours when the road before us is shrouded in darkness, is that of our Master on the cross: Into thy hands I commend my spirit. To the hands that broke and gave life to the bread, that blessed and caressed, they were pierced; – to the hands that are as our hands, of which we can never say what they will do with the objects they hold, whether shatter them or care for them, but those whims, we may be sure, are full of kindness and will never do more than hold us close in a jealous grasp, – to the kindly and mighty hands that reach down to the very marrow of the soul, – that mould and create – to the hands through which so great a love is transmitted, – it is to these that it is good to surrender our souls, above all when we suffer or are afraid. And in so doing there is a great happiness and great merit.

Teilhard de Chardin: in one of his 'Letters from a soldier priest during the Great War', 1914–18

Teach me, O Lord, to accept these manacles as my wedding ring to Christ.

Prayer of a French Protestant of the 17th century condemned to the horror of the galleys because of his faith.
[Also attributed to John Knox, captured at St Andrews and forced to work on galleys for 19 months.]

Forgive them all the tortures done,
My thirst and my starvation;
For who would suffer more than One
Who died for our salvation.

One of three verses written during World War II by an English prisoner of war on the walls of his cell, before his execution by the Japanese

Jesus did not undergo every type of suffering; no individual person can. But the very fact that here was God not just sympathising or even empathising with us in our agonies from outside, but sharing what it can be like for us, revolutionises our whole attitude to him. It does not solve the problem of pain and evil, but it does help us to trust where we cannot understand. And of all the gods on offer in the world the crucified Christ is the only one of whom this it true.

Bishop John Austin Baker (of Salisbury): in the Church Times, (24 December, 1993), '. . . Who is God and Lord of all'

Unbar the door! unbar the door!
We are not here to triumph by
  fighting, by stratagem, or by
  resistance,
Not to fight with beasts as men. We
  have fought the beast
And have conquered. We have only
  to conquer
Now, by suffering. This is the easier
  victory.
Now is the triumph of the Cross, now
Open the door! I command it. OPEN
THE DOOR!

T.S. Eliot: 'Murder in the Cathedral', (1935), Part II, lines 345 ff. (Faber and Faber 1965)

Sunday

. . . there can be no certainty about primitive practice in the early church. We simply do not know. In such circumstances a certain measure of modest stillness and humility might be considered to be in order.

John C. King: 'The Gospel Shrinkers', (Hodders, 1970)

The Jewish Sabbath, like the rite of circumcision, has always been a symbol of national identity, and theologically, a sign of the covenant of the people of God. The early church had to face the question whether gentile Christians should be made to conform to these and other hallmarks of Jewish identity. The apostle Paul argued strongly against such judaising of converts.

As the church grew and Gentiles began to worship, the day of the Resurrection gained in importance at the expense of the old Sabbath. This means that Christian approaches to this issue are not based on legal or religious obligation; after all, few of us accept the need to be circumcised. However, the principle of a day of rest is given more than a religious undergirding in the Old Testament. It is seen as part of the rhythm of the created order, as illustrated in the story of the seven days of creation, and also as important to the maintenance of harmonious social order, in that the forth commandment is in part a demand for masters to give their servants a proper day of rest. For the Sabbath to work it had to be part of the law which regulated the affairs of Jewish society. It needed legal force: first, to protect the powerless (including slaves who would otherwise have no right to their rest day); and second, to prevent the unscrupulous from using their workers on the Sabbath to steal a march on their competitors . . .

When the church says no to widespread Sunday trading, it is out of concern for a society that in its materialist penchant for production and consumption is losing sight of those other values that make us truly human.

Bishop John Taylor: in The Times, (16 December, 1991), 'Society will pay the price'

Sunday clears away the rest of the whole week, not only as it refreshes the mind of notions of religion, but as it puts both the sexes upon appearing in their most agreeable forms.

Joseph Addison: in The Spectator, no. 112

. . . a 'Special' Sunday is finished. Christians – that is, lay Christians – themselves can hardly complain, for they have largely joined the world's ways, simply slipping in an hour or so for worship when other calls on their time did not squeeze worship into being an occasional or irregular activity . . .

Let there be no mistake. Christians are still interested in corporate worship. They still think the world needs converting to Christ either through worshipping or as a spur to worshipping. But we already find ourselves with thousands upon thousands of people to whom churchgoing on Sundays is not only alien but actually impossible. We might find that our congregations, far from being a cross-section of society, are a privileged and untypical remnant.

Bishop Colin Buchanan: Editorial in News of Liturgy, (December, 1993), commenting on a House of Commons vote on deregulation

At a Parochial Church Council meeting a member was trying to have the after-church *Traidcraft* stall closed on Sundays. When pressed as to whether she had ever made a purchase, she replied: 'Oh yes, I've taken things from the stall on a Sunday, but I've never paid until Monday.'

Source unrevealed, (1993)

Superstition

Religious belief, when not associated with active membership of a church, tends to be associated with superstitious belief . . . for those people who do not go to church yet say they are religious people and pray often, religious belief has moved quite far from the orthodox church position and is really much closer to what would normally be called superstition . . . there is a gulf between orthodox religion on the one hand and superstition and private religion on the other which really makes it impossible to describe the latter as a variant of the former.

Nicholas Abercrombie: in 'A Sociological Yearbook for Religion in Britain', (S.C.M.), volume iii

Swimming

I am not going to let my child anywhere near water until he can swim.

Source unknown

Symbolism

The Africa Inland Mission was very cautious about eucharistic discipline. The service always contained a reading from 1 Corinthians 11 including the warning verses 27–32. The Akambo tend to think in concrete ways and tend to have a 'magical' view of the world, therefore the reading of this passage was heard by them to give a magical nature to the Eucharist similar to their own religious traditions. Those who eat unworthily will receive a curse and not a blessing. The result was that the missionaries were heard to be mediaeval in their sacramental theology whereas in fact this was the exact opposite of what they were trying to convey.

Philip Tovey: 'Inculturation, The Eucharist in Africa', (Alcuin/Grove, 1988)

. . . in this matter-of-fact world, symbols have their uses.

Canon Paul Oestreicher: in Exeter Cathedral, (6 August 1986)

St John the Evangelist's symbol is the Eagle, reported to fly higher and further than all other birds; the only bird which can look straight into the Sun undazzled.

Traditional

Sympathy

Laugh, and the world laughs with you;
Weep, and you weep alone.

Ella Wheeler Wilcox: Solitude

Laugh, and the world laughs with you.
Weep, and you ruin your make-up.

Anonymous jibe at the above

T

Tact

A dontopedologist is one who puts his foot in it, every time he opens his mouth.

Reputed observation of Prince Philip, Duke of Edinburgh

Taxes

Tax Returns could be simplified:
1 How much did you earn?
2 How much is left?
3 How come?

Source unknown

Teaching – *see also* EDUCATION

'What does your mum do when you come home miserable from school after the teacher has told you off?'

Ten-year old boy: 'She calls the teacher names.'

Anthony Ellis, (1974)

If your plan is for one year, plant rice.
For 10 years, plant trees.
For 100 years, educate.

Kuan-tze

He who can, does. He who cannot, teaches.

George Bernard Shaw (1856–1950): 'Education in Maxims for Revolutionists', (1903)

Perhaps some churches keep their congregations up to date, but on the whole there seems to be a deceitful gap between what the clergy have picked up of modern studies and what they are prepared to let their congregations know.

Richard MacKenna: 'God for Nothing', (Churchman, 1984/85)

The Church of England must use the best modern teaching methods to explain Bible stories and tell the young what they need to know in order to understand a church service.

British industry has traditionally been remiss at training and its competitive position as a result has lagged. Likewise the Anglican Church can no longer expect others (eg. schools) to teach on its behalf. It must train a new generation of churchgoers, or it will go out of business.

Times Leading Article, (18 November, 1991)

Teeth

In defending a client who alleged that she had injured her jaw when a bus moved off too quickly, a Queen's Counsel appearing before Lord Goddard (Lord Chief Justice) alleged:
Through this most unfortunate accident, caused by the gross negligence of the servant of the Defendant Company, my unfortunate client suffered this most grievous injury to her jaw with the dire result that she could not, for quite a long time afterwards, bite her bottom with her top teeth.

James Sutherland, Ed: 'Oxford Book of Legal Anecdotes', (1986)

The preacher was in full spate describing the torments of hell. 'There will be wailing and gnashing of teeth,' he boomed.

'That lets me off,' called out an old man. 'I've got no teeth.'

'Teeth,' said the preacher, 'will be provided.'

Welsh source unknown

Bishop Hensley-Henson (first of Hereford then of Durham) had a habit of raising his hand in a large flowing gesture and touching his lips just prior to an outburst of rhetoric. During a School of Pastoral Theology at Durham University which he was giving on the subject of Preaching, an ordinand dared to ask him the origin of this enthralling gesture. 'When you have false teeth, young man,' said the bishop, 'you'll know!'

Source unknown

An elderly cleric was preaching in the cathedral when, with a burst of eloquence, his false teeth fell out and crashed to the pavement below. The aged canon looked down at the nearly deaf virger below and, in a bellowed whisper, asked: 'Toombes, are they broken?'

The reply was heard throughout the cathedral: 'Smashed to HATOMS Sir!'

The Virger Magazine, (1986)

Telephone

Remember that as a teenager you are at the last stage in your life when you will be happy to hear that the phone is for you.

Fran Lebowitz: 'Tips for Teens', (1981)

Television

Advice on being interviewed on television:

1. Be prepared – find out in advance as much as you can about the interview.
2. Make sure you are clear in your own mind what your case is.
3. Go into every interview with three key points in mind, and ensure that you make them whatever questions are asked.
4. Television is a visual medium. What you look like and the general impression you create have much more impact on most people than anything you say. Make sure that your appearance and manner reflect your desired image.
5. Use examples where possible – a good example is worth a thousand words of abstract argument.
6. Adopt a conversational and lively style, and avoid jargon.

Source unknown

'Television?' The word is half Latin and half Greek. No good can come of it.

Attributed to C.P. Scott (1846–1932)

The child who frequently watches television tunes into a hyperactive world – and further, a world that is slickly presented. Small wonder that he frequently uses the word 'boring' to describe the world that takes place away from the small screen. 'Real' life, however, includes those times which are boring – and there is no remote control button to punch in search of something more exciting.

'All God's Children', (National Society/Church House Publishing, 1991), section 3.18

All the world's a set and all the men and women merely spectators.

Anonymous, with apologies to William Shakespeare

With its appetite for visual sensation, its tabloid dependence on pictures, television has an inherent tendency to distort and to trivialise. Disaster, violence, disruption, were the staple of TV's diet. Television's appetite for them was insatiable. This appetite, this lust for visible action and violent happenings, is itself an invitation to create more of the same for TV to project.

Robin Day: 'Grand Inquisitor', (Pan 1989)

A fashionable lady was asked if she had ever read a certain classic novel. 'No,' she replied, 'I have not read it, but I saw it sterilised on television.'

Anonymous

Temptation

I couldn't help it. I can resist everything except temptation.

Oscar Wilde: 'Lady Windermere's Fan', (1892), Act 1

I can't help birds flying over my head, but I can stop them building a nest under my hat.

Martin Luther

No testing has overtaken you that is not common to everyone. God is faithful, and he will not let you be tested beyond your strength, but with the testing he will also provide the way out so that you may be able to endure it.

1 Corinthians 10:13

Thankfulness

A thankful heart is not only the greatest virtue but the parent of all other virtues.

Cicero

The atheist's most embarrassing moment is when he feels profoundly thankful for something but can't think of anybody to thank for it.

Mary Ann Vincent

There are three kinds of giving: grudge giving, duty giving and thanksgiving.

Robert N. Rodenmayer

. . . nor did he [Bede, 673–735] forget to give thanks to God with uplifted hands. I tell it, and it is true, that never have I seen with my eyes or heard with my ears anyone so painstaking in giving thanks to the living God.

Cuthbert, writing to Cuthwin (both former students of the Venerable Bede), about the last days of the old scholar

One of the ancient rabbinical teachers commented that Daniel in the den of lions had one consolation which had sometimes been overlooked: when the dreadful banquet was over he would not be called on for a vote of thanks.

O give thanks to the LORD for he is good,
for his steadfast love endures forever.

Psalm 136:1

Ten lepers were cleansed of their disease by Jesus and told to show themselves to the priests:
One of them, when he saw that he was healed, turned back, praising God with a loud voice. He prostrated himself at Jesus' feet and thanked him. And he was a Samaritan. Then Jesus asked, 'Were not ten made clean? But the other nine, where are they? Was none of them found to return and give praise to God except this foreigner?' Then he said to him, 'Get up and go on your way; your faith has made you well.'

Luke 17:15–19

Whatever you do, in word or deed, do everything in the name of the Lord Jesus, giving thanks to God the Father through him.

Colossians 3:17

Theft

A Syrian soldier stops a Volkswagen Beetle and demands that the driver open the trunk. The driver begins to open the luggage compartment at the front of the car. 'No!' says the Syrian, 'I said the *trunk*.'

'This *is* the trunk,' says the driver.

'I am not a donkey,' says the Syrian, pointing to the back of the car. 'Open the trunk!' So the driver does as he's told, exposing the VW's engine. 'Aha!' says the Syrian. 'You have stolen a motor. Furthermore, you have just done it because it's still running.'

P.J. O'Rourke: 'Holidays in Hell', (1988)

Theology

I haven't the faintest interest in theology which does not help us to evangelise . . . [the] theology which helps us to evangelise [is the theology which recognises] the centrality, the gravity, the inevitableness and the glory of the death of Christ.

James Denny, (1902)

All theology is a story told on earth about heaven.

Philip Toynbee

The clergyman is a popular hermit and a jobbing theologian.

Robin Bennett, (c. 1980)

Anglican theological colleges have now trained a whole generation of priests with a minimal knowledge of classical Anglican divinity or its methods. Clergy without a sense of there being some authority in the historic experience of the church may well came to think that theology is the latest fashionable theory of theologians.

Gareth Bennett: Preface to Crockford's Clerical Directory, (December, 1987) (The Controversy surrounding this Preface led to Dr. Bennett's suicide)

[Theology] . . . must never again be left in the hands of a scholarly or priestly elite, but must be reclaimed as an essential component of every Christian's kit-bag.

Bishop Harry Moore: Church Missionary Society Newsletter 483, (1988)

I bring you theology and your hearts sink.

James I Packer: at the Lausanne II Congress in Manila, (July, 1989)

Theology is taught by God, teaches God, and leads us to God.

Thomas Aquinas

We must never allow our strategy to overcome our theology.

Caesar Molegatsi: at Lausanne II Congress in Manila, (July, 1989)

To judge by the strenuous regularity with which clergy deny that they know anything about or have any use for theology, one could well conclude that theology has no effect at all on the church. But in fact even the loose intellectual permissiveness of the Church of England can be seen to be affected by theology in the long run.

A.T. & R.P.C. Hanson: 'The Identity of the Church', (S.C.M., 1987)

. . . Jesus is not a theologian but the despair of theologians. No systematic treatment can do justice to the richness and variety of his thought.

R.M. Grant & D. Tracy: 'A Short History of the Interpretation of the Bible', (S.C.M., 1963 & 1984)

No formula which expresses clearly the thought of one generation can convey the same meaning to the generation that follows.

Bishop B.F. Wescott (of Durham)

A rabbi asked two of his students what came into their minds when they saw a bird flying high in the sky. One said it reminded him of the flight of the human spirit to God. The other wondered if the bird were to die in flight and its body to fall in a hedgerow between two fields, whose property would it be? The rabbi concluded that the second student was the true theologian.

Source unknown

. . . many modern churchgoers are receiving almost no help to put together the jigsaw of biblical theology, and, when they start barely knowing what they are trying to do, they feel quite content if they can put together a few pieces round the edges of belief. It is not really their fault: they need proper training in the faith in the first place, and consistent teaching after that, to help them in their own piecing together of what God has revealed of himself and his world.

Robert M.E. Paterson: 'Short, Sharp and Off the Point', (MARC Europe, 1987)

To be a theologian is to be exposed to the vision of heaven and to the tragedies of mankind.

Archbishop Michael Ramsey (of Canterbury): 'Looking into the Future'

There is probably no document of human spiritual history where passion of feeling, power of thought and inexorableness of will are so permeated by one another as here (The Letter of Paul to the Romans). In the face of this volcanic original production in which everything surges red hot out of the depths of the divine mystery of love, the cheap contrast between life and doctrine, theology and piety, passes away.

Emil Brunner: 'The Letter to the Romans', (1938; Lutterworth, 1959)

Thought

Robert Southey (1774–1843) told a Quaker lady about his exceedingly ordered life: so many hours for one language or another, so long for poetry, prose and translation, and so on. 'And, pray, when dost thou think, friend?' she asked a very discomfited poet!

The church has ceased to count because the church has ceased to think.

R.H. Tawney

The LORD gives wisdom;
from his mouth come knowledge and understanding;
he stores up sound wisdom for the upright;
he is a shield to those who walk blamelessly,
guarding the paths of justice and preserving the way of his faithful ones.

Proverbs 2:6–8

Do not deceive yourselves. If you think that you are wise in this age, you should become fools so that you may become wise. For the wisdom of this world is foolishness with God. For it is written,
'He catches the wise in their craftiness,' and again,
'The Lord knows the thoughts of the wise, that they are futile.'

1 Corinthians 3:18–20

Time

The man who marries the spirit of the age soon finds himself a widower.

Anonymous

Sic transit gloria mundi.
(Thus passes away the glory of the world.)

Thomas à Kempis: 'Imitation of Christ'

I'm glad to see you've been early of late.
You were always behind before;
But now you are first at last, I see,
Lately first to come in at the door.

Adapted from an autograph book of 1896

Remember that time is money.

Benjamin Franklin (1706 – 1790): advice to a young tradesman

Dost thou love life? Then do not squander time, for that's the stuff life is made of.

Benjamin Franklin (1706–1790)

He who neglects the present moment throws away all he has.

Johann C.F. von Schiller (1759–1805)

Adam to Eve: We live in times of transition, my dear.

Anonymous

Time never takes time off.

Augustine of Hippo (354–430)

We all find time to do what we really want to do.

Anonymous

If a man has no time or only a short time for seeing people, you can be fairly sure that he is neither very important nor very busy.

John Spencer Churchill (1650–1722)

Do not walk through time without leaving worthy evidence of your passing.

Pope John XXIII (1881–1963)

Come what, come may, time and the hour run through the roughest day.

William Shakespeare (1564–1616): 'Macbeth', I. iii.137

Anno Domini – that's the most fatal complaint of all in the end.

James Hilton: 'Goodbye, Mr. Chips'

When a Mr. Bill Hancock complained to his local council that the buses on the Hanley to Bagnall route in Staffordshire regularly sailed past queues of up to 30 people, Councillor Arthur Cholerton replied that if the buses stopped to pick up passengers they would disrupt the timetable.

Stephen Pile, Ed: 'The Book of Heroic Failures', (1979)

One of Voltare's characters (Zadig) is asked a question:
What of all things in the world, is the longest and the shortest, the swiftest and the slowest, the most divisible and the most extended, the most neglected and the most regretted, without which nothing can be done, which devours all that is petty and enlivens all that is great?
The answer, said Zadig, is 'Time'.

Zadig – a 'Mystery of Fate'

Mummies are Egyptians that were pressed for time.

Anonymous

When I was a kid, I had no watch. I used to tell the time by my violin. I used to practise in the middle of the night and the neighbours would yell, 'Fine time to practise the violin, three o'clock in the morning!'

Henry Youngman

Punctuality is something that, if you have it, there's often no one around to share it with you.

Anonymous

Westerners* have watches. Africans have time.

African saying

*(*The Swahili word for a 'westerner' means 'one who spins around'.)*

For everything there is a season, and a time for every matter under heaven:
a time to be born, and a time to die;
a time to plant, and a time to pluck up what is planted;
a time to kill, and a time to heal;

a time to break down and a time to build up;
a time to weep and a time to laugh;
a time to mourn, and a time to dance;
a time to throw away stones, and a time to gather stones together;
a time to embrace, and a time to refrain from embracing;
a time to seek, and a time to lose;
a time to keep and a time to throw away;
a time to tear, and a time to sew;
a time to keep silence, and a time to speak;
a time to love, and a time to hate;
a time for war, and a time for peace.

Ecclesiastes 3:1–9

Toleration

He [Jesus] was compassionate towards the repentant; he was certainly not tolerant of the rest. The sharp edges of real Christian morality have become blunted as the memory of it recedes.

Clifford Longley: in The Times, (27 October, 1989), 'A consumer's guide to God'

To dwell above with saints we love,
That will be bliss and glory;
To dwell below with saints we know,
That's quite another story.

Anonymous:

Tradition

In 1 Corinthians 15:3 ('I handed on to you as of first importance what I in turn had received'), Paul is saying: 'This gospel is not my invention: I didn't begin it all! The gospel's too important to be a private doctrine. I am just a link in a chain. I got it from source, from the apostles, and I've passed it on to you.'

From time to time we've had 'reformist' Christians who've attempted to scratch out church history and begin all over again, as if the past 2,000 years have never happened. And evangelicals have done this time and again. The result is they make the same mistakes as were made in the early days of the church, and the movements they give rise to lack depth and breadth and stability, and they never last, because they lack a crucial ingredient. I wouldn't be an Anglican evangelical if I didn't believe in the importance of continuity from the very earliest days of apostolic Christianity. A continuity that has sometimes diverged and needed reformation, a continuity that has sometimes learnt truth by walking on the brink of heresy and stepping back just in time, a continuity in which worldliness has run side-by-side with quite remarkable heroism and holiness.

Bishop John Taylor (of St. Albans): National Evangelical Anglican Congress, (1988)

On 8 April 1546, a small group of about thirty bishops, almost all Italians, changed the whole course of the history of the church. They affirmed that the church receives with equal veneration (*pari veneratione*) the Holy Scriptures of the Old and New Testament, and the traditions, *written and unwritten*, which have been preserved since the time of the apostles. [This statement was later affirmed in a Plenary Session of the Council of Trent.]

The Church of England stands simply and uncompromisingly for the Catholic position held by the church through the centuries (see Article VI of the XXXIX Articles) . . . From this standard the Church of Rome has departed, with disastrous consequences to itself. The Tridentine Church is not the great historic church of West.

Bishop Stephen Neill: 'Anglicanism'

The problem with revivalism for the life of the mind . . . lay precisely in its antitraditionalism. Revivals called people to Christ as a way of escaping tradition, including traditional learning. They called upon individuals to take the step of faith for themselves. In so doing, they often left the impression that individual believers could accept nothing from others. Everything of value in the Christian life had to come from the individual's own choice – not just personal faith but every scrap of wisdom, understanding and conviction about the faith.

Mark A. Noll: 'The Scandal of the Evangelical Mind', (Eerdmans, 1994)

Jesus said, 'You abandon the commandment of God and hold to human tradition.'

Mark 7:8

Translation

Language is used to convey emotion as well as precision. Traditional phrases such as the Lord's Prayer are part of our national poetic heritage. We know them in our sleep. There is a case for retaining such ancestral spells as 'for now we see through a glass, darkly' for nostalgia and national team spirit. But scholars and ecclesiastics have a duty also continually to translate into our shifting language, to try to catch the rainbow of the original meaning . . . We must continually translate. But, as with all poetry, we should never claim that any version is definitive. Especially not for bigotry, or political or show-off reasons. The Lord knows what we mean. We are the ones who lose the meaning in the mumbo-jumbo.

Philip Howard: in The Times, (1996), 'Translation needs both the old familiarity and the new accuracy'

The story is told that the late Professor C.H. Dodd and his New English Bible Committee were stumped in their search for a more modern version of the words 'the fatted calf' in the parable of the Prodigal Son [Luke 15].

Finally, armed with their list of alternatives, Professor Dodd went to London's Smithfield meat market. Giving the list to one of the men there, Professor Dodd asked, 'Which if any, of these terms would you use to describe a calf about to be slaughtered?'

The man read the list through with care, shook his head and returned the piece of paper. 'We shouldn't say any o'them, guv'nor,' he said. 'You see, we've got technical terms for these things. We always calls 'em "fatted calves".'

Source unknown

Helmut Theilicke asks why there should be preaching, 'instead of letting the word of God ring forth in the way it was written':

'The way it was written?' What would that mean? If I were to read the Bible to you in its original Hebrew and Greek, hardly anyone would understand it. At the very least it must be translated. But what does it mean to translate? It obviously means that I must take the old story and put it into the language of today. And this must be done repeatedly; even the best known translations of the Bible have parts that are no longer understandable. But translating means more than a mere recasting in words. It means making 'relevant' too, so that the hearer remarks, 'Why, that has to do with me!'

Helmut Theilicke: 'How Modern Should Theology Be?', (1967)

In translation work in Australia, translators had asked aborigines what this-and-that object was called. The Kangaroo got its name that way, but it turns out that 'Kangaroo' means 'I don't know what you mean'.

Bible Society, (1980)

[A word] means what people think it means, and if the meaning is confused and uncertain, the confusion and uncertainty will transmit itself to doctrine. It could not be otherwise. Theology and doctrine has no 'pure' language in which to express itself, only the language commonly available.

Clifford Longley: in The Times, (2 December, 1985)

In the Sahara desert, far from any ocean there is no word for 'Anchor'. But the Moré people have a perfect parallel in picketing peg 'We have a sure and steadfast picketing peg for the soul', as the hymn might be rendered.

Bible Society

Hypocrites specialise in rapid transformation on the outside – camouflaging their dirtiness. In the language of the Malagasy Republic their word is taken from the practice of an untidy housewife as 'one who spreads a clean raffia carpet' on an unswept floor.

See Luke 12:1–2 (Bible Society)

On the Equator, the Karré people had difficulty in translating 'the Comforter'. They found the right phrase from a line of porters carrying heavy loads on their heads. If one porter is completely exhausted and someone sees him lying prostrate and stoops down to pick him up and supports him, he is known as 'the one who falls down beside us'. This is their expression for the Holy Spirit in St John's Gospel.

Bible Society

Fellowship implies common interest, a willingness to listen to one another. The Mazatecs of Mexico say 'the two are dovetailed' – the dovetail joint that is close and fits perfectly together.

See 1 John 1:3 (Bible Society)

In the Maasai language in Kenya there isn't an equivalent word for 'pioneer', so the phrase they have chosen is 'one who treads on the thorns ahead'.

Hebrews 12:2 (Bible Society)

In West Africa the act of faith is described simply as 'committing oneself to be held'. This is exactly the same phrase used to describe a mother's careful commitment of her child into the arms of someone else, whilst she has to work.

Mark 11:22 (Bible Society)

The chief god of the Caroline Islands in the Ponapean language is the 'Thunder God'. So when translators wanted to describe the name Jesus gave to James and John, the sons of Zebedee, 'The Sons of Thunder', they realised a change was necessary.

The name was probably given because James and John were hot-tempered and unpredictable and the local Christians explained 'We have our own name for that – "pwurien ikem"' – a phrase which described the unpredictable darting of a small fish among the corals on the reef. So this was the name given to James and John in the Ponapean version.

Bible Society

We must sometimes get away from the Authorised Version, if for no other reason, simply *because* it is so beautiful and so solemn. Beauty exalts, but beauty also lulls. Early associations endear but they also confuse. Through that beautiful solemnity the transporting or horrifying realities of which the book tells may come to us as blunted and disarmed and we may only sigh with tranquil veneration when we ought to be burning with shame or struck dumb with terror or carried out of ourselves by ravishing hopes and adorations.

C.S. Lewis: 'Modern Translations of the Bible', (1947)

All the words in any language derive their meaning, their resonance in the minds of those who use them, from a whole world of experience and a whole way of grasping that experience. So there are no exact translations.

Lesslie Newbigin: 'Foolishness to the Greeks', (S.C.M. 1986)

Poetry is what gets lost in translation.

Attributed to Robert Frost (1874–1963)

To ordinary Japanese, the staple food is rice. To say Jesus said, 'I am the bread of life,' is to say that Jesus implied he was the food of foreigners, Westerners. It makes better sense to translate the words 'I am the rice of life'.

Masao Takenaka: the origin of the title 'God is Rice', (World Council of Churches, 1986)

By trying to translate our doctrines into vulgar speech we discover how much we understand them ourselves. Our failure to translate may sometimes be due to our ignorance of the vernacular; much more often it exposes the fact that we do not exactly know what we mean.

C.S. Lewis: 'God in the Dock', (1948; Collins, 1979)

Martin Luther knew that a good translator had to be bilingual. 'Spelling' did not imply a slavishly literal, word-for-word rendering; it was the thorough comprehension of the linguistic usage of the Scriptures. That is the secret of the originality and power of the Luther Bible. Command of one's own language and the ability to use it to its best presupposes listening to the way the common people speak: 'One must ask the mother at home, the children in the street, the man at the market, and listen to how they speak, and translate accordingly. That way they will understand and notice that one is speaking German to them.'

Heiko O. Oberman: 'Luther', (Yale, 1982/89), quoting Luther's Works.

Heiko Oberman comments on the completion of the Wittenberg Bible in September 1534:
The translation played a major role in shaping the modern German language, yet it became a genuine folk Bible, carrying the cause of the Reformation into every house, because Luther made use of living, colloquial German in his translation. He had truly listened to the common people – the language of the common man was not too lowly to be the language of God.

It is not possible to reproduce a foreign idiom in one's native tongue. The proper method of translation is to seek a vocabulary neither too free nor too literal, but to select the most fitting terms according to the usage of the language adopted . . .

I try to speak as folk do in the market-place. Didactic, philosophical, and sententious books are, therefore, hard to translate, but narrative is easy. In reading Moses I make him so German that no one would know that he was a Jew.

Martin Luther, (1489–1546)

A computer translation of 'Out of sight, out of mind' for Russian students came up with 'Invisible idiot'.

Source unknown

Travel

Being in a ship is being in a jail, with the chance of being drowned.

Dr. Samuel Johnson, (16 March, 1759)

What would be a road hazard anywhere else, in the Third World is probably the road.

How do you translate kilometres into miles? Most people don't know this, but one kilometre = ten miles, exactly. True a kilometre is only 62 per cent of a mile, but if something is one hundred kilometres away, read that as one thousand miles because the roads are 620 per cent worse than anything you've ever seen . . .

It's important to understand that in the Third World most driving is done with the horn, or 'Egyptian Brake Pedal', as it is known. There is a precise and complicated etiquette of horn use. Honk your horn only under the following circumstances:

1. When anything blocks the road.
2. When anything doesn't.
3. When anything might.
4. At red lights.
5. At green lights.
6. At all other times.

P.J. O'Rourke: 'Holidays in Hell', (1988)

George, 1st Marquess Curzon, Viceroy of India at the end of the 19th century, described his first trip on a bus:
This omnibus business is not what it is reported to be. I hailed one at the bottom of Whitehall and told the man to take me to Carlton House Terrace. But the fellow flatly refused.

A person who does not travel is like a man who reads only one page of a book.

St. Augustine of Hippo (354–430)

There are two kinds of military road-block, the kind where you slow down so they can look you over, and the kind where you come to a full stop so they can steal your luggage. The important thing is that you must *never* stop at the slow-down kind of road-block. If you stop, they'll think you're a terrorist about to attack them, and they'll shoot you. And you must *always* stop at the full-stop kind of road-block. If you just slow down, they'll think you're a terrorist about to attack them, and they'll shoot you. How do you tell the difference between the two kinds of road block? Here's the fun part: you can't!

P.J. O'Rourke: 'Holidays in Hell', (1988)

Truth

The truth is rarely pure, and never simple.

Oscar Wilde: 'The Importance of Being Earnest', (1895), Act I

Habit for him was all the test of truth,
'It must be right: I've done it from my youth.'

George Crabbe (1754–1832)

History teems with instances of truth put down by persecution . . . It is a piece of idle sentimentality that truth, merely as truth, has any inherent power denied to error, of prevailing against the dungeon and the stake.

John Stuart Mill (1806–73): 'On Liberty'

Truth, in matters of religion, is simply the opinion that has survived.

Oscar Wilde: 'The Critic as an Artist'

Hard are the ways of truth, and rough to walk.

John Milton: 'Paradise Regained', 1. 478

God offers every mind its choice between truth and repose. Take which you please – you can never have both.

R.W. Emerson: 'Intellect'

In denying the lawfulness of telling a lie to a sick man, for fear of alarming him:

You have no business with consequences; you are to tell the truth.

Samuel Johnson in James Boswell: 'Life of Samuel Johnson', (13 June, 1784)

Christianity is not a drug which suits some complaints and not others. It is either sheer illusion or else it is the truth. But if it is the truth, if the universe happens to be constituted in this way, the question is not whether the God of Christianity suits us, but whether we suit him.

Archbishop William Temple (of York and Canterbury)

We should consider ourselves as liable to err no less than others. To imagine that we are in possession of all truth, and to take for granted that all who differ from us must of necessity be wrong, is not consistent with Christian modesty.

Charles Simeon (1759–1836): 'Appeal to Men of Wisdom', Sermon 1993 from Horae Homileticae

You daren't handle high explosives; but you're all ready to handle honesty and truth and justice and the whole duty of man, and kill one another at that game. What a country! What a world!

George Bernard Shaw (1856–1950): 'Major Barbara', (1907), Act 3

Lord, help me never to use my reason against the truth.

Jewish prayer

For it is not much knowledge that fills and satisfies the soul, but an intimate understanding and relish of the truth.

Ignatius of Loyola (1491–1556): 'Spiritual Exercises', (c. 1522–25), paragraph 2

. . . in these days if we do not burn our theological opponents at the stake it is not necessarily because we are better men than our fathers, but at least in part because we care less passionately for the truth.

Professor Charles Kingsley Barrett: Sermon in Durham Cathedral, (October, 1968)

One of the gifts Christians are good at is polarisation; in fact, we are probably better at it than any other group.

Tom Houston: at the Lausanne II Congress in Manila, (July, 1989)

There is no substitute, in short, for the only claim that Christianity has ever been able to make: not that it is good for you, but that it is true. And that is a claim that can be approached only in the appropriate terms. Does God exist? If so, did he, does he still, reveal himself through his Son? Is the revelation accessible today? And so to the desperately awkward question which everyone on this road must face: what must I do to be saved? To which the startling answer is waiting: there is nothing you can do, but it has been done for you already. One is then at the heart of the matter, but there are those who go sadly away. The problem is not what Christianity offers, but what it demands; and the rest is grace.

Clifford Longley: in The Times, (27 October, 1989), 'A consumer's guide to God'

Christian truth is not such as can be preserved either by pious ignorance or timid conservatism.

A.T. & R.P.C. Hanson: 'The Identity of the Church', (S.C.M. 1987)

The Antichrist can be born from piety itself, from excessive love of God or of the truth, as the heretic is born from the saint and the possessed from the seer. Fear prophets, Adso, and those prepared to die for the truth, for as a rule they make many others die with them, often before them, at times instead of them . . . Perhaps the mission of those who love mankind is to make people laugh at the truth, *to make truth laugh*, because the only truth lies in learning to free ourselves from insane passion for the truth.

Umberto Eco: 'The Name of the Rose', (1980), translated by William Weaver, (Picador, 1985), William to his assistant

The ultimate question is not whether something is useful but whether it is true.

Graham Kings: 'Evangelicals in Search of Catholicity', (Church Missionary Society report, 1989)

The church witnesses to that true end for which all creation and all human beings exist, the truth by which all alleged values are to be judged. And truth must be public truth, truth for all. A private truth for a limited circle of believers is not truth at all.

Lesslie Newbigin: 'Foolishness to the Greeks', (S.C.M)

There is never a duel with the truth. The truth always wins and we are not afraid of it. The truth is no coward. The truth does not need the law. The truth does not need forces of government . . . The truth is imperishable, eternal and immortal and needs no human agency to support it.

Dudley Malone, during the celebrated 'Scopes case' in which a teacher sought the right to teach that creation may not have happened at 9.00 a.m. on 23 October, 4004 B.C.

People are driven from the church not so much by stern truth that makes them uneasy as by weak nothings that make them contemptuous.

George Buttrick: 'Jesus Came Preaching', 1931 Yale Lectures (Scribner, 1931)

I do not care one straw about popularity, for I know that it is generally purchased by a sacrifice of the truth.

Hensley Henson,(later Bishop) soon after being elected Head of Oxford House, Bethnal Green, (1887): from 'Retrospect of an Unimportant Life', (O.U.P., volume I, 1942)

A truth that's told with bad intent
Beats all the lies you can invent.

William Blake, (1757–1827)

Winston Churchill once described Stanley Baldwin (three times Conservative Prime Minister between 1923 and 1937) thus:

He occasionally stumbled over the truth, but hastily picked himself up and hurried off as if nothing had happened.

I don't want any yes-men around me. I want everybody to tell me the truth even if it costs them their jobs.

Samuel Goldwyn

Lake Wobegon Lutheran Church's new Christmas Pageant (of which it had 20 copies):

And the spirit of truth came upon them, and it gave them a great brightness, and naturally they were worried. And the spirit of truth said, 'Don't worry. I've come with good news that should make you really happy, for there is born today a child who shall be a symbol of new beginnings and possibilities.' And suddenly there was with the spirit of truth a multitude of truths, praising goodness and saying, 'It's wonderful! Peace on earth and real understanding among people.'

The purchase price was nonrefundable.

Garrison Keillor: 'Lake Wobegon Days', (1985), 'Winter'

It is false piety to preserve peace at the expense of truth. It is also false zeal to preserve truth at the expense of clarity.

Blaise Pascal, (1623–1662)

Man's sensitivity to trivia, and his insensitivity to matters of major importance, reveal he has a strange disorder.

Blaise Pascal, (1623–1662)

It is the spirit of the age to believe that any fact, no matter how suspect, is superior to any imaginative exercise, no matter how true.

Gore Vidal: 'Encounter', (1967)

And, after what is a lie. 'Tis but
The truth in Masquerade

Lord George Byron (1788–1824): 'Don Juan'

U

Unity

Little boy blue, come blow on your
horn,
The sheep are not fed and the lambs
are new-born.
But where are the boys who look
after the flocks?
They're building a house with
liturgical blocks.

A comment on the abortive Anglo-Methodist reunion scheme of the mid–1960's

The Methodists bring down the sheep
from the mountains,
the Roman Catholics let them gambol
in the fields,
the Presbyterians put them in order,
the Baptists dip them,
and the Church of England fleeces
them.

Source unknown (19th century)

We of the church today stubbornly refuse to kick down these crazy barriers . . . refuse to upset our inherited prejudices . . . while the world slips into the embrace of evil.

Bishop Benjamin N.Y. Vaughan (of Swansea and Brecon): Sermon, (2 October, 1982)

Of Anglicanism: A bridge is there to be trampled over.

Irish proverb, quoted by David Bleakley, (1985)

'Father Abraham, whom have you in heaven? Any Episcopalians? . . . Presbyterians? . . . Independents or Seceders? . . . Have you any Methodists?'
And Abraham's answer: 'We don't know those names here.'

George Whitefield, preaching in Philadelphia, (c. 1745)

If persons be Christians in their lives and . . . if they acknowledge the eternal Son of God for their Master and their Lord, . . . why then should I hate such persons whom God loves and who love God? . . . cling to the creed of the apostles; and in all other things an honest endeavour to find out what truth we can.

Bishop Jeremy Taylor, (1647)

In necessary things, unity;
in doubtful things, liberty;
in everything, charity.

Richard Baxter's motto (1615–91)

Evangelism is the test of true ecumenism.

Philip Potter, General Secretary of the World Council of Churches

If necessity is laid upon us to preach that God reconciles, then we cannot rest content with our scandalous divisions. 'The love of Christ compels a burning desire for unity' Archbishop Benson declared years ago. Indeed it does, for that love requires of its messengers the love of Christ for each other.

Archbishop George Carey: Canterbury Enthronement, (19 April, 1991)

[The questions we ask about ministry, sacraments, orthodoxy, soundness, etc.] are important. They show whether we – my brother and I – have rightly or wrongly, adequately or inadequately, understood the fact that Christ died for us. But this basic fact is so incomparably more important that the rest fades, or ought to fade, into obscurity, like the stars when the sun comes up.

Professor Charles Kingsley Barrett, Sermon in Durham Cathedral, (October, 1968)

If two people agree entirely on everything, one of them is retarded.

Luis Palau, (1989)

The suggestion that there is nothing we can learn from those of other traditions, or in other churches, about our understanding of Christian truth, our spiritual life, both individual and corporate, or our Christian witness in both word and action is at worst sheer arrogance and at best myopia.

Ian Cundy (later Bishop of Peterborough): 'Historical Aspects of the Doctrine of the Church', (1989)

There is one *'Christian Viewpoint'*, one place where Christians stand together and look out on life, and the one Christian viewpoint is the cross: 'I, if I am lifted up from the earth, will draw all men to myself.'

Professor Charles Kingsley Barrett: Sermon in Durham Cathedral, (October, 1968)

God does not recognise our divisions, even the most hallowed and ancient of them. If there is schism in the church, it is internal schism and we are all guilty of it. Despite our strenuous efforts through the centuries, we have not succeeded in dividing the church ontologically (in its being). It is still one in God's eyes. Nor can any one denomination, however large, claim to be that church to the exclusion of everyone else.

A.T. & R.P.C. Hanson: 'The Identity of the Church', (S.C.M., 1987)

If the apostle Peter had done a course under Donald McGavran or Peter Wagner he could have easily stood up to Paul at Antioch (Galatians 2. 11ff.) and said, 'Your theological talk of the crucial unity between Jews and Gentiles is OK, but let's have that spiritual unity in 2 separate churches in Antioch, then we will reach more Jews and more Gentiles, won't we?' The apostle Paul, in reply, perhaps would have used even stronger language than he does in Galatians.

Graham Kings: 'Evangelicals in Search of Catholicity', (1989)

Of a truth unity and concord doth best become religion; yet is not unity the sure and certain mark whereby we know the church of God.

Bishop John Jewel (1522 – 1571): 'Works', Vol III

In the 16th century, Archbishop Thomas Cranmer tried to persuade the leaders of the continental Reformation to come to England to share their points of agreement. He failed.

The frustration of magnificent hopes does not necessarily brand them as fatuous . . . Cranmer is not to be judged merely on his record as the chief of the English Reformers. His espousal of a cause far wider than national reform – the integration of the severed Reformation churches of Europe – is evidence of a sincere ecumenicity and of a certain noble grandeur of design challenging to later generations.

John T. McNeill: 'A History of the Ecumenical Movement', 1517–1948, (1954)

It is the common observation of sociologists of religion that denominationalism is the religious aspect of secularisation . . . As Thomas Luckman says, 'Once religion is defined as a private affair the individual may choose from the assortment of ultimate meanings as he sees fit.' The denomination provides a shelter for those who have made the same choice. It is thus in principle unable to confront the state and society as a whole with the claim with which the Jews confronted Pilate – the claim of the truth. It is not, in any biblical sense, the church.

Lesslie Newbigin: 'Foolishness to the Greeks', (S.C.M., 1986); Quoting T. Luckman, 'The Invisible Religion'

We were 'exclusive' Brethren, a branch that believed in keeping itself pure of false doctrine by avoiding association with the impure. Some Brethren assemblies, mostly in larger cities, were not so strict and broke bread with strangers – we referred to them as 'the so-called Open Brethren', the 'so-called' implying the shakiness of their position – whereas we made sure that any who fellowshipped with us were straight on all the details of the Faith, as set forth by the first Brethren who left the Anglican Church in 1865 to worship on the basis of correct principles . . . united in their opposition to the pomp and corruption of the Christian aristocracy. Unfortunately, once freed of the worldly Anglicans, these firebrands were not content to worship in peace but turned their guns on each other . . . if Believer **A** is associated with Believer **B** who has somehow associated himself with **C** who holds a False Doctrine, must **D** break off association with **A**, even though **A** does not hold the Doctrine, to avoid the taint? The correct answer is: Yes. Some Brethren, however, felt that **D** should only speak with **A** and urge him to break off with **B**. The Brethren who felt otherwise promptly broke off with them. This was the Bedford Question, one of several controversies that, inside of two years, split the Brethren into three branches.

Once having tasted the pleasure of being correct and defending True Doctrine, they kept right on and broke up at every opportunity, until, by the time I came along, there were dozens of tiny Brethren groups, none of which were speaking to any of the others.

His Grandpa commented on this situation:

'Anyone that wants to come to us and admit their mistake, we're perfectly happy to sit and listen to them and then come to a decision about accepting them back.'

Garrison Keillor: 'Lake Wobegon Days', (1985), 'Protestant'

A man ran to stop another man from flinging himself off a bridge into the River Thames.

'Why are you killing yourself?' he asked.

'I've nothing to live for!'

'Don't you believe in God?'

'Yes, I do.'

'What a coincidence! So do I. Are you a Jew, Hindu, Moslem, Buddhist or Christian?'

'Christian.'

'What a coincidence! So am I. Protestant or Catholic?'

'Protestant.'

'What a coincidence! So am I. Anglican, Baptist, Methodist or Presbyterian?'

'Baptist.'

'What a coincidence! So am I. "Strict and Particular" or "General"?'

'Strict and Particular.'

'What a coincidence! So am I. Premillennial or Amillennial?'

'Premillennial.'

'What a coincidence! So am I. "Partial rapture" or "Full rapture"?'

'Partial rapture.'

On hearing this the rescuer sprang on his victim and pushed him into the river, shouting, 'Die, infidel!'

Source unknown

Modern schemes for unity tend so often to neglect doctrinal differences that we get Alice-in-Wonderland plans of 'all have won and all shall have prizes'.

Anonymous

. . . it is a most perverse imagination that separation is the only cure for church disorders.

John Owen, one-time Vice Chancellor of Oxford University

Blackmail is levied in ecclesiastical circles when a minority within a church threatens to break off from the majority and either form a separate body or join some other already existing body if something takes place within that church to which the minority is opposed. *[On the contrary, 'refusing to give in to it']* . . . is not a refusal to make concessions to the weaker brethren. People who threaten to leave the church are not weaker brethren, but men and women who are prepared to divide the church for the sake of gaining their ends.

A T and R P C Hanson: 'The Identity of the Church', (S.C.M., 1987)

Universalism

'The popular mind of which I am thinking is now largely dominated by Universalism (that is, the conviction that the world is getting better every day and that all will in any case be saved); and, wherever this conception prevails, it follows that the 'clergyman' is regarded, not as a warrior or a 'captain of the host of the Lord'. . . – for the whole military metaphor then becomes inappropriate – but rather as a kind of restaurant-car attendant, who may help, supplying adventitious comforts, to make the journey to the next world less tedious and uncomfortable than it might otherwise have been, but does not directly assist the passenger to arrive at his destination.

But where the infinite horror of sin, the existence of evil spirits, and the possibility of eternal loss are wholeheartedly accepted, there life becomes almost synonymous with war; the church is an army, in which the Son of God himself is the commander-in-chief; its dioceses and parishes, its religious orders, congregations, and guilds are so many divisions, battalions, companies, and platoons, moving forward in the great unending attack upon the trenches of the evil power; its weapons are the Sacraments, the Scriptures, and the prayers of the saints; and its ministers are conceived as a *corps* of officers, a knightly brotherhood of keen-eyed, disciplined, finely trained men, who are prepared to spend and be spent in the cause to which they have devoted their lives.'

Dated as some of this language may be the passage nevertheless presents a view of the ministry which cannot but command respect and will always attract men of high quality if taught by the church with sufficient conviction.

Crockford's Clerical Directory: Editorial, (1975)

V

Values – *see also* ETHICS *and* MORALITY

The truth is mightier than eloquence,
the Spirit greater than genius,
faith more than education.

Martin Luther: 'Table Talk'

A farmer was showing a friend around when they came across a pig with a wooden leg. The visitor expressed some surprise.

The farmer praised this special pig. 'One night when we were all a-bed, the farm caught fire. But the pig saw it, broke out of the sty, called the fire brigade, threw buckets of water on the fire, then rushed into the farmhouse and rescued me, my wife and the children.'

'So he must have lost a leg in the fire?' enquired the visitor.

'Oh no! But a very special pig like that – you don't eat it all at once!'

Anonymous

Even when we have accepted high standards for ourselves, we have hesitated to call others to live by them. But this is sheer arrogance masquerading as kindness. You cannot insult a man more atrociously than by offering him a lower standard than your own.

Archbishop William Temple (of Canterbury): in a World War II broadcast

It is my belief that it is the value-free, pseudo-objective mechanistic and terrifyingly effective, scientific mode of thought that has led to our inability to sustain or defend the very heart of our culture. Dimly, our moral patriarchs in the Church of England or in right-wing American think-tanks witter on about the evils of poverty or the iniquity of pornography . . . But, when pressed, they have nothing positive to say. Paralysed by the scientific-liberal idea that all attitudes and ways of life must be viewed objectively and without prejudice, they fell asleep over lunch while science beavers away at making consciousness. . . .

There is an answer to all this, but it is not easily understood. It is not an anti-scientific answer, although it does involve the humbling of science and the ridiculing of some of its more absurd and incoherent rhetoric. As Bloom [Alan Bloom: *The Closing of the American Mind*] and others have pointed out, only when science has been returned to it proper place as a part, but only a small part, of the totality of human culture, can it really become science again.

Bryan Appleyard: in The Times Saturday Review, (25 April, 1992), 'Science and Spirit'

The great enlightenment figures struggled to find a new way of defining the specifically human. This was to prove a truly heroic enterprise because of the odds they were fighting against. For, as time passed and technology improved, science became ever more devastatingly effective. First it explained the cosmos to those who were qualified to look. But later it produced machines, cured diseases and generated wealth so effectively that everybody was affected. Science was so flamboyantly good at these things that it must be right, it must be The Truth.

But if it *was* right in *that* way, then humankind was a purposeless nothing. Trying to discover meaning or morality in such circumstances was pointless. It was no good pretending: we were alone with whatever values we could construct in the privacy of our own heads.

'A dog,' said Charles Darwin bleakly, 'might as well speculate on the mind of Newton. Let each man hope and believe what he can.'

And Freud wrote, with his characteristic tragic sense: 'Thus I have not the courage to rise up before my fellow men as a prophet, and I bow to their reproach that I can offer them no consolation...'

This is the bitter message of classical science. This is The Truth, but it has no place for us; we can find no basis for our values in the world.

Bryan Appleyard: in The Times Saturday Review, (25 April, 1992), 'Science and Spirit'

Violence

The interesting thing about staring down a gun barrel is how small the hole is where the bullet comes out, yet what a big difference it would make to your social schedule.

P.J. O'Rourke: 'Holidays in Hell',(1988)

A little girl of three knocked her five your old brother out with a punch. Her mother gasped in horror. 'Katie! How *could* you do such a thing?'

'The Lord gave me strength,' Katie replied proudly.

Anonymous

Now the earth was corrupt in God's sight, and the earth was filled with violence.

Genesis 6:11

Violence shall no more be heard in
 your land,
devastation or destruction within
 your borders;
you shall call your walls Salvation,
 and your gates Praise.

Isaiah 60:18

Vision

I discovered a common malaise in churches that were in advance stages of ecclesiastical terminal illness – lack of vision. Unless the minister and at least some of the people have a spiritual vision which sees beyond the difficulties of the human situation, everything will seem hopeless. Vision thus becomes the driving force of prayer and the wheels of change are set in motion. It is important also for this vision to be shared with others so that it may gently permeate the life of the church, creating expectancy and awareness of what is possible.

George Carey (later Archbishop): 'The Church in the Market Place', (Kingsway, 1984)

If you want a definition of water, don't ask a fish.

Chinese Proverb

There is nothing as powerful as an idea whose time has now come.

Victor Hugo

The dwarf who stands on the giant's shoulders can indeed see farther than the giant himself, especially if the dwarf puts on his spectacles. But notwithstanding our broader perspective, we miss that lofty institution and giant heart, which we cannot acquire.

Heinrich Heine, (1971)

During the night [at Troas on his second missionary journey] Paul had a vision: there stood a man of Macedonia pleading with him and saying, 'Come over to Macedonia and help us.' When he had seen the vision, we immediately tried to cross over to Macedonia, being convinced that God had called us to proclaim the good news to them.

Acts 16:9, 10: Luke records the mission of the gospel to Europe

Vocation

When Christ calls a man, he bids him come and die. It may be a death like that of the first disciples who had to leave home and work to follow him, or it may be a death like Luther's, who had to leave the monastery and go out into the world. But it is the same death every time – death in Jesus Christ, the death of the old man at his call. That is why the rich young man was so loath to follow Jesus, for the cost of following was the death of his will. In fact every command of Jesus is a call to die, with all our affections and lusts. But we do not want to die, and therefore Jesus Christ and his call are necessarily our death and our life.

Dietrich Bonhoeffer: 'The Cost of Discipleship.' (The first sentence is quoted at the beginning of Bishop George Bell's life of Bonhoeffer)

The LORD came and stood there [in the temple], calling as before, 'Samuel! Samuel!' And Samuel said, 'Speak, for your servant is listening.'

1 Samuel 3:10

In his vision of the majesty of the Lord, Isaiah recounts:
I heard the voice of the Lord saying, 'Whom shall I send, and who will go for us?' And I said, 'Here am I; send me!' And he said, 'Go and say to this people: "Keep listening, but do not comprehend; keep looking, but do not understand," Make the mind of this people dull, and stop their ears, and shut their eyes, so that they may not look with their eyes, and listen with their ears, and comprehend with their minds, and turn and be healed.'

Isaiah 6:8–10

I pray that the God of our Lord Jesus Christ, the Father of glory, may give you a spirit of wisdom and revelation as you come to know him, so that, with the eyes of your heart enlightened, you may know what is the hope to which he has called you, what are the riches of his glorious inheritance among the saints . . .

Ephesians 1:17, 18

Wales and the Welsh

Sir James Cassels (1877–1972) recalled the case of an English circuit judge in Wales. The defendant's counsel asked for permission to speak in Welsh in his closing speech and the judge agreed.

Despite the judge's summing up – which made it clear that the jury should find the defendant guilty – the jury found the man not guilty, unanimously, without leaving the court.

The judge was curious and later asked a Welsh-speaking court attendant for a translation. It was: 'The prosecutor is English; the prosecution counsel is English; the judge is English. But the prisoner is Welsh; I'm Welsh; and you're Welsh. Do your duty.'

Michael Gilbert, Ed: 'The Oxford Book of Literary Anecdotes', (1986)

There are still parts of Wales where the only concession to gaiety is a striped shroud.

Gwyn Thomas: in Punch, (1958)

There are three varieties of Celt in British politics, one coming from Ulster, one from Scotland and the third from Wales. They all have this in common: they are aggrieved. Politics, for them, is the pursuit of grievance. Grievance is their meat and drink, grievance their waking cry and daily song; and before they go to sleep at night they kneel in silent prayer: 'Lord, why are the English so horrible to us?'

. . . Your Ulster grievance is a wild, paranoid fantasy . . . Your Scots grievance, on the other hand, is a demand with menaces . . .

But your Welsh grievance is different from both. It is a sort of continuous, censorious whine, a tugging at the sleeve. Never threatening, it carries always a hint of moral reproof. In pious sing-song the Englishman is informed that his injustice is an affront not so much to Wales, as to Heaven. Unlike your Scot, your Welshman is not trying to pick a fight, just letting you know what God thinks of your behaviour.

Matthew Paris: in The Times, (20 July, 1993), 'Political Sketch'

A formal oath never binds them [the Welsh]. They have no respect for their plighted word, and the truth means nothing to them . . . To a people so cunning and crafty this seems no great burden, for they take it all very lightly.

Giraldus Cambrensis, Archdeacon of Brecon: 'Descriptio Cambriae', (12th century)

War

The purpose of all war is peace.

Augustine of Hippo (354–430)

Lyndon B. Johnson, a former President of the U.S.A., said, in December 1969, that the thought of picking up his telephone receiver at 4.00 am. and finding that America was involved in World War III, terrified him.

[Johnson had been J.F. Kennedy's Vice President when Kennedy was assassinated in 1963]

In war, whichever side may call itself the victor, there are no winners, but all are losers.

Neville Chamberlain (1869–1940): Speech, (1938)

Dulce bellum inexpertis.
(War is sweet to those who do not experience it)

Latin proverb cited by Erasmus (1465–1536)

There never was a good war, or a bad peace.

Benjamin Franklin: 'Letter to Quincey', (1773)

For what can War, but endless wars still breed?

John Milton (1608–74): 'Sonnet On the Lord General Fairfax'

War, that mad game the world so loves to play.

Jonathan Swift: 'Ode to Sir William Temple'

In war, actions of great importance are (often) the result of trivial causes.

Julius Caesar: 'De Bello Gallico', I. xxi

The war is just which is necessary:

Machiavelli: 'The Prince'

War must be for the sake of peace.

Aristotle: 'Politics VII'

We are mad, not only individually, but nationally. We check manslaughter and isolated murders; but what of war and the much vaunted crime of slaughtering whole people?

Seneca: 'Ad Lucilium', XCV

God heard the embattled nations
sing and shout,
'Gott strafe England*' and 'God save
the King';
God this, God that and God the
other thing.
'Good God!' said God, 'I've got my
work cut out.'

J.C. Squire: Poem written during the Great War, 1914–18
(Gott strafe England = God punish England)*

The lights are going out all over Europe. We shall not see them lit again in our lifetime.

Sir Edward Grey, as Europe slid into the Great War, (3 August 1914)

Weakness

I asked God for strength, that I
might achieve,
I was made weak, that I might learn
humbly to obey.
I asked for health, that I might do
greater things,
I was given infirmity, that I might do
better things.
I asked for power, that I might have
the praise of men,
I was given weakness, that I might
face the need of God.

An anonymous soldier in the American Civil War

Pray that the weak shall be strong and the strong shall be just.

Senator Jovito Salonga, President of the Philippine Senate, (1989)

The Apostle Paul describes a 'thorn in the flesh':
He (The Lord) said to me, 'My grace is sufficient for you, for power is made perfect in weakness.' So, I will boast all the more gladly of my weaknesses, so that the power of Christ may dwell in me. Therefore I am content with weaknesses, insults, hardships, persecutions and calamities for the sake of Christ; for whenever I am weak, then I am strong.

2 Corinthians 12:9, 10

Wealth

A cat appeared at Trinity Cathedral, Sacramento, North California. It was fat and had been well treated, and had long white fur. Around its neck was a chain with a medallion on which was inscribed – 'I am an Episcopalian.'

Anonymous, (1975)

Weather

The English winter – ending in July,
To recommence in August.

Lord G. Byron (1788–1824): 'Don Juan'

Weddings – *see also* MARRIAGE

One man brought 16 brides to church for a wedding – 'Because,' he said, 'the Prayer Book lists four better, four worse, four richer, and four poorer.'

Anonymous

In 1980, Grigory Romanov, the mayor of Leningrad [St. Petersburg] persuaded the director of the Heritage Museum to lend him Catherine the Great's tea service for the occasion of his daughter's wedding. Late in the proceedings a guest rose to his feet and dropped a cup. Thinking this was some kind of toast, all the guests rose to their feet, took a drink and hurled the entire service into the fireplace!

Stephen Pile, Ed: 'The Return of Heroic Failures', (1988)

Wilderness – *see* DESERT

Wisdom

Education . . . has produced a vast population able to read but unable to distinguish what is worth reading.

G.M. Trevelyan: 'English Social History', (1st Edition, 1944)

F.E. Smith, Earl of Birkenhead (1872–193) was a barrister. On one occasion a judge commented to him: 'I have read your case, Mr. Smith, and am no wiser now than I was when I started.'
'Possibly not, my Lord,' was Smith's reply, 'but far better informed.'

The fear of the LORD is the
beginning of knowledge;
fools despise wisdom and instruction.

Proverbs 1:7

Trust in the LORD with all your heart,
and do not rely on your own insight.
In all your ways acknowledge him,
and he will make straight your paths.

Proverbs 3:5, 6

The fear of the LORD is the
beginning of wisdom,
and the knowledge of the Holy One
is insight.

Proverbs 9:10

Since, in the wisdom of God, the world did not know God through wisdom, God decided, through the foolishness of our proclamation, to save those who believe . . .

For God's foolishness is wiser than human wisdom, and God's weakness is stronger than human strength . . .

He [God] is the source of your life in Christ Jesus, who became for us wisdom from God, and righteousness and sanctification and redemption, in order that, as it is written, 'Let the one who boasts, boast in the Lord.'

1 Corinthians 1:21, 25, 30, 31

Wit

Brevity is the soul of wit.

William Shakespeare (1564–1616): 'Hamlet', II. ii. 90

It takes wit to think up a sharp remark, and wisdom not to say it.

Bill Hinton, (1995)

Witness – *see also* MARTYRDOM

. . . *marturia* has to do with bearing costly witness as to how God's work in Christ has affected our lives. The most costly way to do this is, of course, to die for the faith. Numerous Christians, right down the ages, have done just this; they have accepted death rather than renounce or hide their faith. Such a courageous testimony to hope based on faith has often had the result of vindicating the faith itself. One of Athanasius' central arguments for the truth of Christ's Resurrection was based on the observed reality that Christians of all kinds – men, women, children, the old and the young – were willing to die for their belief that God had raised Jesus Christ from the dead and would raise them to a transformed life in a similar manner.

Bishop Michael Nazir-Ali: 'Evangelisation in Contemporary Cultures', (1993)

One sphere of a Christian's witness is, of course, the way he fulfils his secular vocation and does his daily job. This is not directly evangelistic at all, though it is a prerequisite for any subsequent evangelistic witness . . . The power of example can reach where words can never go. This must always be the central content of the Christian's witness: without it, words do not count. But in all his witness, unself-conscious as it must be, his prayer and his goal will be to lead other people to know Jesus Christ as their Saviour, not just intellectually but personally.

Douglas Webster: 'What is Evangelism?', (1959)

To be a witness means to live in such a way that one's life would not make sense if God did not exist.

Source unknown

The messenger's personal life is at least half of his message.

James I. Packer: at the Lausanne II Congress, Manila, (July, 1989)

Our problem is not with the gospel but with its messengers . . . . Evangelism is a question of *being* before it is an agenda for *doing* . . . Charisma without character is catastrophic.

Peter Kuzmic: at the Lausanne II Congress, Manila, (July, 1989)

As a Christian, I must witness for Christ, if necessary using words.

Unattributable comment of Francis of Assisi (1182–1226)

It is no use walking anywhere to preach unless we preach as we walk.

Francis of Assisi (1182–1226)

A church should not absorb the attention and time of Christians to such a degree that they end up by having no time to get involved in trade union activities, local politics, community welfare work and so on.

George Carey (later Archbishop): 'The Church in the Market Place', (Kingsway, 1984)

If Christians wish us to believe in their redeemer, why don't they look a little more redeemed?

Friedrich Nietzche (1844–1900)

Four Christians were rushing through a station to catch a train. As they ran, they knocked over a boy's apple cart. Three of them caught the train but the fourth stopped to pick up the apples and missed the train. The boy with the cart was blind and asked the fourth Christian: 'Sir, are you Jesus?'

Source unknown

Our claim that God took flesh in Jesus Christ touches hurt people effectively when they meet Christians, motivated by that belief, involving themselves in service where the hurts are greatest.

Bishop David Sheppard (of Liverpool): in The Times, (6 May, 1991)

I cannot hear a word you are saying because what you *are* shouts so loudly in my ears.

African proverb

'How do you like that bird I sent you home for your birthday? . . . You cooked it? . . . Mamma, that was a South American parrot – he spoke five languages! . . . He should have SAID something!'

George Jessel: 'Phone Call to Mama'

Is it an accident, do you think, that the day of the first martyr follows immediately the day of the birth of Christ? By no means. Just as we rejoice and mourn at once, in the birth and in the Passion of Our Lord; so also, in a smaller figure, we both rejoice and mourn the death of martyrs . . .

Beloved, we do not think of a martyr simply as a good Christian who has been killed because he is a Christian: for that would be solely to mourn. We do not think of him simply as a good Christian who has been elevated to the company of the Saints: for that would be simply to rejoice: and neither our mourning nor our rejoicing is as the world's is. A Christian martyrdom is never an accident, for Saints are not made by accident. Still less is a Christian martyrdom the effect of a man's will to become a Saint, as a man by willing and contriving may become a ruler of men. A martyrdom is always the design of God, for his love of men, to warn them and to lead them, to bring them both back to his ways. It is never the design of man; for the true martyr is he who has become the instrument of God, who has lost his will in the will of God, and who no longer desires anything for himself, not even the glory of being a martyr.

T.S. Eliot: 'Murder in the Cathedral', (1935), the Interlude (Faber and Faber, 1965)

Semen est sanguis Christianorum. (Normally translated 'The blood of the martyrs is the seed of the Church')

Tertullian (c. 200)

Love makes the difference between an execution and a martyrdom.

Evelyn Underhill

It is not suffering, but the cause, which makes a martyr.

English Proverb

Thursday January 30th:
Flushpools arrived at about seven-thirty. We all sat down straight away in the dining room. Mrs Flushpool, who looks like a collection of black plastic bags half-filled with water, glanced around and said, 'Dear Anne, such a problem keeping a room of this size really clean. How we need the

presence of the mighty one, even in our most intimate wifely duties.'

Mr Flushpool, who bears a remarkable resemblance to those old photographs of Crippen, said, in a deep tomb-like voice, 'Amen to that!'

From that point onwards, Anne said hardly anything. Mrs Flushpool described at great length how she had been converted from fleshly works and appetites since being washed in the blood, and how, in consequence, she was now able to turn her back on those things that she used to do in what she called 'the natural'. Everything she said seemed to have a sort of dampness about it. She and her husband refused wine, saying that Christians should be ashamed to have it in the house, as it leads to carnal excess. At this point Mr Flushpool let out another sonorous 'Amen to that!' Coffee was also frowned on as something that was wont to stimulate inappropriately in the natural.

Gerald, with a perfectly straight face, asked Mrs Flushpool if she used to go swimming in the natural. She replied fervently that her bodily flesh would never again rouse any man to a fever of sensual lust.

Mr Flushpool opened his mouth very wide to say, 'Amen to that!' but thought twice and shut it.

Mrs Flushpool went on to talk, with gleaming eyes, about the dangers of the occult, becoming so vehement, that she started to froth slightly at the mouth, and had to use a red paper napkin.

Quite glad when they got up to go at about 10 o'clock. As she left, Mrs Flushpool said, 'Thank you so much for supper, dear Anne. You must come round to us soon, and have a proper meal.'

Through the closed door we heard a final 'Amen to that' as Mr Flushpool marched to his nightly fate.

Adrian Plass: 'The Sacred Diary of Adrian Plass', (1987)

Do not be ashamed, then, of the testimony about our Lord or of me his prisoner, but join with me in suffering for the gospel, relying on the power of God, who saved us and called us with a holy calling, not according to our works but according to his own purpose and grace.

2 Timothy 1:8, 9a

Beloved, do not be surprised at the fiery ordeal that is taking place among you to test you, as though something strange were happening to you. But rejoice insofar as you are sharing Christ's sufferings, so that you may also be glad and shout for joy when his glory is revealed. If you are reviled for the name of Christ, you are blessed, because the spirit of glory, which is the Spirit of God, is resting on you. But let none of you suffer as a murderer, a thief, a criminal, or even as a mischief maker. Yet if any of you suffers as a Christian, do not consider it a disgrace, but glorify God because you bear this name.

1 Peter 4:12–16

One of the elders addressed me,
saying, 'Who are these, robed in white, and where have they come from?' I said to him, 'Sir, you are the one that knows.' Then he said to me, 'These are they who have come out of the great ordeal; they have washed their robes and made them white in the blood of the Lamb.
For this reason they are before the throne of God,
and worship him day and night within his temple,
and the one who is seated on the throne will shelter them.
They will hunger no more, and thirst no more;
the sun will not strike them, nor any scorching heat;
for the Lamb at the centre of the throne will be their shepherd,
and he will guide them to springs of the water of life,
and God will wipe away every tear from their eyes.'

Revelation 7:13–17

Women

A woman has a strange instinct that tells her she is right, whether she is or not.

Anonymous male

She's the sort of woman now . . . one would almost feel disposed to bury for nothing: and do it neatly, too!

Charles Dickens (1872–1870): 'Martin Chuzzlewit'

And a woman is only a woman, but a good cigar is a Smoke.

Rudyard Kipling (1865–1936): 'The Betrothed'

Elle flotte, elle hesite; en un mot, elle est female. (She wavers, she hesitates: in a word, she is a woman.)

Jean Racine (1639–1699)

Thomas Aquinas considered whether a woman could receive holy orders because it would include the commission to preach. Woman, he said, is 'a malformed male', incapable of reflecting in her body the male Jesus who imaged God. She is, at best, an incomplete sign. The Genesis account of original sin subjected her to man, for she represents a danger in terms of sexual excitement. The mediaeval woman, moreover, was uneducated.

All things considered, according to his own best lights, Aquinas voted thumbs down to woman's rights.

Sister Camille D'Arienzo: in 'America', (c 1980)

David and Solomon lived right merry lives.
One had a thousand concubines,
the other a thousand wives.
But when, as they were growing old,
they began to have their qualms,
the one wrote the Proverbs
and the other wrote the Psalms.

Anonymous

Advice of the Duke of Newcastle to the future King Charles II (who was his pupil):
Above all, be civil to women.

Arguments out of a pretty mouth are unanswerable.

Joseph Addison (1672–1719): 'Women and Liberty'

The argument about awaiting the consent of the whole church is a way of postponing the ordination of women until the Greek Kalends. There will never be a time within the foreseeable future when what the proponents of this argument understand as the church will be sufficiently united to agree on anything.

A.T. & R.P.C. Hanson: 'The Identity of the Church', (S.C.M., 1987)

It is announced that the Liberation Society has engaged the services of two lady lecturers, and some of our contemporaries have been making merry over the fact. We hardly see why. If the ladies are to address their own sex only, there is surely no reason against.

Church Times Editorial: (16 September, 1892)

. . . if 'being male' is not an essential-kind property of humanity, then the Word did not have to possess it any more than the Word had to possess the property of speaking Aramaic.

It is not in question that the Word did possess the property of being male in fact . . . We are saved, no doubt, because Christ spoke Aramaic and because he was male, but we are not saved *by* the fact he spoke Aramaic or *by* his maleness. We are saved by the assumption of all essential-kind human properties into God, and by the free self-offering of those properties on the cross.

. . . a major theological issue at stake is whether priesthood represents the essential and full humanity of Christ as united indissolubly with divinity, rather than a set of contingent human properties which Jesus possessed. If the former, then to admit women to priesthood is no more than to confess their full humanity, as that humanity is revealed and transformed in Christ. That seems to me an important theological issue, the very reflection upon which can deepen our understanding of the incarnation and thus of the ground of our faith.

Professor Keith Ward: in the Church Times, (1992), 'Priesthood and the humanity of Jesus'

The first leader in 'The Times' following the vote in favour of the ordination of women as priests at the General Synod of the Church of England (11 November, 1992):
In this case, the Church of England has shown decisively that it values some principles more than absolute unity within its own ranks, or nervous solidarity with other Christian traditions. The woolliness of recent Anglican history may yet be forgiven.

By elevating women to the priesthood, the Church has proved itself responsive to the prevailing mood of the nation whose spiritual life it is supposed to serve, and acknowledged an argument that had become all but irresistible. . . . The ordination of women is unlikely to provoke a social catastrophe or encourage moral decline.

(12 November, 1992)

Sir, a woman's preaching is like a dog's walking on his hinder legs. It is not done well; but you are surprised to find it done at all.

Dr. Samuel Johnson

Sir,
Women have proved themselves eminently successful in such highly responsible posts, *inter alia,* as college principals, doctors, surgeons, judges, diplomats, Cabinet Ministers, Prime Ministers, and be it noted, as ministers of many national episcopal churches and non-conformist churches the world over. Yet they are still denied admission to the priesthood of the Church of England, and this despite the shortage of clergy.

It has now, however, been officially declared that there is no theological reason against their ordination to the priesthood.

I recall that the Archbishop of Canterbury [Dr. Donald Coggan] when Archbishop of York, in his sermon on the 13th centenary of the historic conference of the Celtic and Roman missions at the Synod of Whitby, preached at Whitby Abbey of which St Hilda was both the founder and first abbess, spoke of her as a seventh-century example of the emancipation of women and went on to say:

'I fancy that St Hilda looks steadily down through the centuries, centuries that have seen the emancipation of women in a way of which she can never have dreamed, and says to us: 'When will you awaken to the opportunities before you? How long will you cripple the church by letting your women do little more than provide the food after parish functions, mend the linen, clean the brasses (all good deeds) and otherwise serve as parish workers but *not* entrust them on a big scale with parts of responsibility equal to those carried by their brethren?'

This significant utterance by our scholarly and forward-looking Archbishop cannot but give powerful impetus to the campaign for the ordination of women to the priesthood.

Charles P. Hines: Letter to the Daily Telegraph, (6 February, 1976)
[On 1 January, 1976, the beginning of the U.N. International Women's Year, British women achieved full legal equality with men, except in the church's ministry.]

I'm afraid that women who want to be ordained are the same ones who want to 'wear the pants' in the family. They must be totally unable to understand that to be different is not to be inferior.

From an American magazine, (c. 1974/5)

Wonder

. . . wonder is a faculty much to be prized.

Archbishop Donald Coggan (of York, later of Canterbury): 'The Bible in the Modern World', Guildford Cathedral, (1965)

When the wonder has gone out of a man he is dead. When all comes to all, the most precious element in life is wonder. Love is a great emotion and power is power. But both love and power are based on wonder.

D.H. Lawrence (1885–1930): 'The Phoenix'

Since we are receiving a kingdom that cannot be shaken, let us give thanks, by which we offer to God an acceptable worship with reverence and awe; for indeed our God is a consuming fire.

Hebrews 12:28, 29

Great and amazing are your deeds,
  Lord God the Almighty!
Just and true are your ways, King of
  the nations!
Lord, who will not fear and glorify
  your name?
For you alone are holy.
All nations will come and worship
  before you,
for your judgements have been
  revealed.

Revelation 15:3b, 4

Word of God – *see also* BIBLE, CHRIST, *etc.*

Others can provide the social services, but no government can lead men to God. This is not to disparage for one moment works of compassion done in the name of Christ, or to deny that we find him when we minister to his needy ones, for that is a basic tenet of the gospel. What I assert is the truth of Christ's dictum that man cannot *live* on bread alone. He *must* have the word of God . . . I believe that it is a weak and enfeebled church which has a low doctrine of the word.

Archbishop Donald Coggan (of Canterbury): 'Retrospect and Prospect', (1974)

This living body of teaching, this proclamation of the perennial word of God, calls the church together and creates its distinctive character. Communion is above all a communion of faith. Sacramental communion of the correct outward observance of the rules prescribed by the bishops have no real content or significance apart from that teaching, which constantly needs reaffirmation if religious practice is to remain true to its aim . . .

The word of God, spoken, heard, thought about, obeyed and continually re-expressed in actions as in words, gives meaning and reality to the life of the church and of the individual Christian.

Canon Michael Richards: in The Times, (1 August, 1987)

It is only by their (the clergy's) correct understanding and communication of the gospel that they can hope to build a Christian community. Attempts to make the church work simply by clever organisation or ritual performance may have some success but they do not generate an authentic Church.

Eucharistic validity is not the prime consideration. Teaching comes first: the Eucharist is the end-product of the preaching of the word, duly listened to and translated into action.

Canon Michael Richards: in The Times, (1 August, 1987)

God's word is not anybody's word. The church has a right to be protected from heretics, cranks, and fanatics . . .

A state of affairs in which preaching has degenerated into a purely subjective expression of the preacher's own ideas is closely comparable to a state of affairs in which the Eucharist has degenerated into an individualistic rite in which I meet my Saviour and enjoy my religious emotion without any necessary reference to any of my fellow Christians.

A.T. & R.P.C. Hanson: 'The Identity of the Church', (S.C.M., 1987)

'The Word was made flesh' (John 1:14) is how St. John the Evangelist announced the miracle of Christ's birth. But, depending on the denomination, theology has transformed 'flesh' into either 'Church' or 'preaching' . . .

For Luther, this spiritualisation, this striving for the transcendental, was a perversion of Christianity. A just man does not become spiritual through faith, he *lives* out faith; and for this our life is created and intended by God.

Heiko O. Oberman: 'Luther', (Yale, 1982/89)

In the beginning was the Word, and the Word was with God, and the Word was God. He was in the beginning with God. All things came into being through him, and without him not one thing came into being. What has come into being in him was life, and the life was the light of all people.

John 1:1–4

Whatever was written in former days was written for our instruction, so that by steadfastness and by the encouragement of the scriptures we might have hope.

Romans 15:4

All scripture is inspired by God and is useful for teaching, for reproof, for correction and for training in righteousness, so that everyone who belongs to God may be proficient, equipped for every good work.

2 Timothy 3:16, 17

Be doers of the word, and not merely hearers who deceive themselves. For if any are hearers of the word and not doers, they are like those who look at themselves in a mirror; for they look at themselves and, on going away, immediately forget what they were like. But those who look into the perfect law, the law of liberty, and persevere, being not hearers who forget but doers who act – they will be blessed in their doing.

James 1:22–25

We declare to you what was from the beginning, what we have heard, what we have seen with our eyes, what we have looked at and touched with our hands, concerning the word of life – this life was revealed, and we have seen it and testify to it, and declare to you the eternal life that was with the Father and was revealed to us – we declare to you what we have seen and heard so that you also may have fellowship with us; and truly our fellowship is with the Father and with his Son Jesus Christ.

1 John 1:1–3

Work

Laborare est Orare. ('Prayer is work' or 'Work and prayer are one')

The Rule of St. Augustine of Hippo, commending monks to work for their living and to spend 8 hours a day in prayer; 8 hours at labour; 8 hours asleep

I like work; it fascinates me. I can sit and look at it for hours. I love to keep it by me: the idea of getting rid of it nearly breaks my heart.

Jerome K. Jerome (1859–1927): 'Three Men in a Boat'

The curse of Adam and the consolation of Eve.

Source unknown

Work hard, make money, go to church and wash behind the ears and all will be taken care of. The poor, condemned for laziness and thus ungodliness, voted with their feet.

Andrew Hibbert: in The Guardian, (March, 1986), on the 'Protestant Work Ethic'

I have spent my life laboriously doing nothing.

Hugo de Groot (Grotius), 17th century international lawyer

Nine out of ten practising Christians feel that men's work is always at the level of a spiritual encumbrance.

Teilhard de Chardin: 'Le Milieu Divin', (1957)

Their [most Christians] faith has seemed to them as applicable to the circumstances in which they work but not to the actual work itself.

Kenneth Adams: in The Times, (3 May, 1986)

The founder of the MacDonalds fast-food chain is said to have noted: 'I believe in God, my family and MacDonalds: when I go to the office, I reverse the order.'

Anonymous

It is not only prayer that gives God glory, but work.

Gerald Manley Hopkins: 'The Principle or Foundation', an address

Do not lag in zeal, be ardent in spirit, serve the Lord.

Romans 12:11

Whatever your task, put yourselves into it, as done for the Lord and not for your masters, since you know that from the Lord you will receive the inheritance as your reward; you serve the Lord Christ.

Colossians 3:23, 24

Now we command you, beloved, in the name of our Lord Jesus Christ, to keep away from believers who are living in idleness and not according to the tradition that they received from us. For you yourselves know how you ought to imitate us; we were not idle when we were with you, and we did not eat anyone's bread without paying for it; but with toil and labour we worked night and day, so that we might not burden any of you. This was not because we do not have that right, but in order to give you an example to imitate. For even when we were with you, we gave you this command: Anyone unwilling to work should not eat. For we hear that some of you are living in idleness, mere busybodies, not doing any work. Now such persons we command and exhort in the Lord Jesus Christ to do their work quietly and to earn their own living.

2 Thessalonians 3:6–12

Works

[Beware the] Dangers of inoperative orthodoxy.

Donald Guthrie

No man can earn the love of God, but once a man knows through faith that

God loves him, he knows (or he knows nothing of the meaning of Christianity), that he must spend all his life trying to live a life that is worthy of that love.

Professor William Barclay

The Church of Ireland's Archbishop D'Arcy and a Roman Catholic priest used to debate 'faith versus works'. One day they were going for a train and the priest recommended haste, but the Archbishop (looking at his watch) said there was plenty of time. They missed the train! 'I had great faith in that watch,' said the Archbishop.

'But it would have been better if it had had good works,' rejoined the priest!

Source unknown

Martin Luther (1483–1546) always advocated the necessity of good works in the life of the believer: 'I should be called *Doctor bonorum operam,* the Doctor of good works.'

Martin Luther: 'Table Talk'

In times past, one of the most controversial issues within the church was 'Faith or works?' – essentially a debate about divine grace.

Those days are past. Today a key issue is 'Faith-with-works or Faith-with-words?'; our churches half-filled with rows of entertained religious people who will turn up to anything as long as the cost and the risk are minimal. Their religion of words does not touch the world God sent his Son to save because the world has had enough of words alone and the world finds their unchallenging faith deeply unattractive.

Robert M.E. Paterson, (1993)

The opposite of sin in the Christian view is not virtue but faith. And faith means that you do not and cannot any longer feel compelled to nag anxiously at God. Late mediaeval religion had seemed to the Reformers to be in some of its aspects nothing more than a vast machine for clocking up merit with God, an elaborate means of pulling wires with God, whether through masses or pilgrimages, or invocation of highly-placed saints. Indeed the whole chantry system looked like a well organised and sophisticated mechanism for nagging God, motivated by an all-pervading anxiety about whether God should or would or could grant salvation to the individual.

R.P.C. Hanson: 'Eucharistic Offering in the Early Church', (Grove Liturgical Study, 1979)

In the days of great rivalry between Saint John's and St. Chad's Colleges, Durham, *John's* went rowing at 7.00 a.m., whilst *Chad's* went to Mass ['1662' Holy Communion]. One day in *Chad's* Chapel, as the priest reached the 'comfortable words', 'Hear also what St. John saith. . .', a shout was heard from the riverbank: 'Row harder, you devils! Row harder!'

The editor is assured of the truth of this (though he was in the boat at the time)

When the goodness and loving kindness of God our Saviour appeared, he saved us, not because of any works of righteousness that we had done, but according to his mercy, through the water of rebirth and renewal by the Holy Spirit. This Spirit he poured out on us richly through Jesus Christ our Saviour, so that, having been justified by grace, we might become heirs according to the hope of eternal life.

Titus 3:4–6

What good is it, my brothers and sisters, if you say you have faith but do not have works? Can faith save you? If a brother or sister is naked and lacks daily food, and one of you says to them, 'Go in peace; keep warm and eat your fill,' and yet you do not supply their bodily needs, what is the good of that? So faith by itself, if it has no works, is dead. But someone will say, 'You have faith and I have works.' Show me your faith apart from your works, and I by my works will show you my faith . . .

For just as the body without the spirit is dead, so faith without works is also dead.

James 2:14–18, 26

The voice of a great multitude in heaven:

'Let us rejoice and exult and give
him the glory,

for the marriage of the Lamb has
come, and his bride has made
herself ready;
to her it has been granted to be
clothed with fine linen, bright and
pure' –
for the fine linen is the righteous
deeds of the saints.

Revelation 19:7, 8

Worship

Adoration begins when we are captivated by the living God – not for what he does or promises – but just for who he is . . .

There is much worship that stops short of adoration. In doing so it remains on the level of appreciation or another way of offering thanks to God. But adoration is not appreciation but *abandonment* – abandonment before the wonder and beauty of God in all his glory.

David Runcorn: 'Silence', (Grove, 1987)

When Christian worship is dull and joyless, Jesus Christ has been left outside – that is the only possible explanation.

James S. Stewart

If the order of your worship service is so rigid that it can't be changed, it had better be changed.

Theodore A. Raedeke

Worship does not need an apology nor should it seem to depend on the goodwill and tolerance of unchurched visitors. If we don't believe in what we are doing, let us shut up shop. I still look forward with eager expectation to the day when the flabby question: 'Shall we sing hymn number 1023?' is answered by a joyous and resounding, 'No!'

Peter Cousins, (1976)

An elderly gent in the early years of the 20th century took his new – and large – ear trumpet with him to the service in his local Scottish Kirk. When one of the elders saw it, he warned: 'Wullie! One toot and ye're oot!'

Source unknown

Worship is the submission of all our nature to God. It is the quickening of conscience by his holiness; the nourishment of mind with his truth; the purifying of imagination with his beauty; the opening of the heart to his love; the surrender of the will to his purpose – and all this gathered up in adoration.

Archbishop William Temple (of Canterbury): 'Readings in St. John's Gospel', (1938/39)

If all men could pray at all times as some men can sometimes, then indeed we might prefer extempore to precomposed prayers.

Charles Simeon, (1759–1836)

Sung Matins did not die in most Anglican parishes. It committed suicide.

Robert M.E. Paterson, (1987)

At the end of a typical Sunday, Charles Simeon declared: 'I am an eight-day clock. Now I am wound up for another week.'

M.M. Preston: 'Memoranda of the Rev. Charles Simeon', (1759–1836)

What does Stan, in his Sunday clothes, think of in Church? The man himself could not have told. He was confused, because his wife was watching, and the words of worship expected too much. His body too, of which he was partly ashamed, made him kneel with an awkwardness that he did not connect with humility. But he was humbler. When he failed to rise to the heights of objective prayer he would examine himself, or the grain of the pews, finding such flaws in each that there was little hope of correction. At times, though, peace did descend, in a champing of horses' bits at a fence outside, in some word that suddenly lit, in birds bringing straws to build nests under the eaves, in words bearing promises, which could perhaps have been the grace of God.

Patrick White: 'The Tree Man'

'Nay, nay,' he [Silas] said, 'I know nothing o'church; I've never been to church.'

'No!' said Dolly, in a low tone of wonderment. Then bethinking herself of Silas' advent from an unknown country, she said, 'Could it ha' been as they'd no church where you was born?'

'Oh yes,' said Silas meditatively,

sitting in his usual posture of leaning on his knees and supporting his head. 'There was churches – a many – it was a big town. But I knew nothing of 'em; I went to chapel.'

Dolly was much puzzled at this new word, but she was rather afraid of inquiring further, lest 'chapel' might mean some haunt of wickedness. After a little thought, she said, 'Well, Master Marner, it's niver too late to turn over a new leaf; and if you've niver had no church, there's no telling the good it'll do you.

'For I feel so set up and comfortable as niver was when I've been and heard the prayers, and the singing to the praise and glory o' God, as Mr. Macey gives out; and Mr. Crackenthorp saying good words, and more partic'lar on Sacramen' Day. And if a bit o' trouble comes, I feel as I can put up wi' it, for I've looked for help i' the right quarter, and gev myself up to Them as we must all give ourselves up to at the last; and if we'n done our part, it isn't to be believed as Them as are above us 'ull be worse nor we are, and come short o' Their'n.'

Poor Dolly's exposition of her simple Raveloe theology fell rather unmeaningly on Silas's ears, for there was no word in it that would rouse a memory of what he had known as religion, and his comprehension was quite baffled by the plural pronoun, which was no heresy of Dolly's, but only her way of avoiding a presumptuous familiarity.

George Eliot: 'Silas Marner', (1861), chapter X

Twelve Reasons Why I Never Wash (or go to church):
1. I was forced to wash as a child.
2. I'm not dirty.
3. I'll wait until I'm older and then I'll be dirtier.
4. There are too many brands of soap to choose from.
5. People who wash are hypocrites.
6. None of my friends bother to wash.
7. Washing is boring.
8. I'm too busy to wash.
9. The water is always too cold.
10. Washing is a soap manufacturers' conspiracy to make money.
11. There are other ways of dealing with dirt, and I sometimes wash on special occasions.
12. You have to get up too early.

Source unknown

Symptoms of *Morbus Sabbaticus*:
1. Professing Christians are its most susceptible victims.
2. It is always worst on Sundays.
3. It lasts just one day per week.
4. The symptoms do not affect sleep, appetite, leisure activities or personal convenience.
5. The patient is averse to calling a doctor, though the doctor is supposed to know all about the patient's illness.
6. It is very infectious and spreads by personal contact with infected persons.
7. It is ultimately fatal, though death is usually slow.
8. It is worst when the weather is wet, but also occurs when it is dry, cold, hot, sunny, windy, or when someone's coming for lunch.
9. The patient normally blames the disease on another person.
10. Conversion is the only known cure.

Source unknown

After his retirement, Sir Charles Frederick Gill, K.C. (1851–1923), built a country house. The vicar once asked him why he never attended church. Gill was annoyed and replied: 'For two very good reasons, Sir. The first is that, as Recorder of Chichester, I am prayed for in the Cathedral every Sunday morning; and the second, that I have defended more clergymen at the Old Bailey than any living barrister.'

Michael Gilbert, Ed: 'Oxford Book of Legal Anecdotes', (Oxford, 1986)

The cumulative effect of most people trying to sit near the back is pretty grim. There is a variant on this, where everybody who arrives early sits at the end of the row, guarding it against all-comers. This provides a totally unwelcoming vista – the late-comer has to push past someone to get into a seat, and the sense of at least marginal mutual resentment is built into that embarrassment.

Colin Buchanan: 'The Heart of Sunday Worship', (Grove, 1992)

When our worship is at its best our feelings are deeply stirred.

Archbishop William Temple (of Canterbury): 'Worship and Life', (S.C.M., 1942)

A worship event composed of young and old alike, meeting together to worship with a sacred book nearly two thousand years old, and an order of worship not much younger, in a church building six hundred years old, singing hymns which are two hundred years old, led by a clergyman who is sixty years old, and using a liturgical text which is about twenty years old, whilst sitting on furniture that was replaced only last year, is inevitably the creation of the historic forces acting upon it.

Colin Buchanan: 'The Heart of Sunday Worship', (Grove, 1992)

We must not only worship God always, but the whole of us must worship God. Our very distractions must be worship, and we must have some kind of worship which will enable them so to be.

F.W. Faber (1814–1863)

On the first real warm Sunday [of the year], attendance is down at church, people deciding that, God being everywhere, they can worship anywhere – what Father Emil calls 'The Protestant fallacy'; he strolls around after Mass, surprising some absentees who were busy working with rakes and didn't see him coming. 'Oh! Father! My gosh! Didn't see you! Good morning.'

'Yes. Almost afternoon. Funny how the morning just slips away, don't it?'

'Yea, that's right, Father. That's for sure.'

'Such a beautiful day, it'd be a shame to have to be indoors on a day like this, now wouldn't it?'

'Well, that's true, Father. You got a point there.'

Garrison Keillor: 'Lake Wobegon Days', (1985), 'Spring'

When we worship we thus take the world into the presence of God with us, so that we can name God's name over it. We look the world in the face and look in the face the questions that trouble us – and the developments that excite us – and declare over them 'Yahweh is God', 'Jesus is Lord'. In the power of that confession we then take the world and its questions more seriously, because it carries with it the promise that they can be faced. In worship we affirm how we believe the world to be, despite what we see. We do not create this new world – it already exists as the real world, the world of God. In the light of affirming that it is the real world, we then live in the world in that conviction.

John Goldingay: 'Praying the Psalms', (Grove,1993)

Leitourgia or worship is, first of all, offering praise, thanksgiving and adoration to God, but it is also a powerful witness to the world. The New Testament clearly recognises the significance of worship for witness.

Bishop Michael Nazir-Ali: 'Evangelisation in Contemporary Cultures', (1993)

Worship is the people of God travelling home.

Robert M.E. Paterson, (1995)

Creativity of the Spontaneous Me Me variety condemns rite and symbol to lingering deaths by trivialisation.

Aidan Kavanagh: 'On Liturgical Theology'

In Coventry, a new cathedral has been built, according to the best recipe for achieving a noble result. Honest, sincere artists, 'the best'. have been grouped together to make a civilised stab at celebrating God and Man and Culture and Life through a collective act. So there is a new building, fine ideas, beautiful glass-work – only the ritual is threadbare. Those Ancient and Modern hymns, charming perhaps in a little country church, those numbers on the wall, those dog-collars and the lessons – they are sadly inadequate here. The new place cries out for a new ceremony, but of course it is the new ceremony that should have come first – it is the ceremony in all its meanings that should have dictated the shape of the place, as it did when all the great mosques and cathedrals and temples were built.

Peter Brook, (Director of the Royal Shakespeare Company), in 1968, quoted in Harmondsworth, 'The Empty Space', (Penguin, 1972)

By participating in a liturgy a Christian exposes himself to a number of doctrinal influences, of which he may not be directly aware. When he hears the Scriptures read in a service, he will, of course, hear what the passage teaches. But he may not be consciously aware that the very fact *that* the Scripture has been read expresses a doctrine.

Stephen W. Sykes: 'The Integrity of Anglicanism', (Mowbrays, 1978), chapter 3

... liturgical judgement is not a matter of liturgical archaeology.

Stephen W. Sykes: 'The Integrity of Anglicanism', (Mowbrays, 1978), chapter 7

Lex orandi, lex credendi (The law of prayer is the law of belief.)

Maxim expounded by Prosper of Aquitaine, (c. 390 – c. 463) but probably older

Liturgy is an activity through which a community celebrates its values, passes on its norms and recreates a sense of its own identity through memory and forgiveness. Liturgy can be described, therefore, as an activity tied up with the complexities of human needs and motivations.

Robin Green: 'Only Connect', (D.L.T., 1987)

Jesus freed people to take their humanity to God. Could there be a better definition of Christian Liturgy? The freedom to take our humanity to God.

Robin Green: 'Only Connect', (D.L.T., 1987)

The Benedicite
is a nicety
to relieve
the Te Deum.

Anonymous

Question: What is the difference between a liturgist and a terrorist?
Answer: You can negotiate with a terrorist.

The evangelical tendency . . . is towards a sort of aesthetic contraction and banality in which liturgy is fast food rather then *haute cuisine*. We know there are solid missionary reasons for this liturgical reductionism. It makes worship accessible to people in a way that the more developed liturgies do not. More people go to discos than high opera, and one of the courageous things about evangelicals is their ability to embrace bad taste for the sake of the gospel.

Nevertheless, there is a genuine problem here. The Christian life is a process of formation and sanctification; development is built into it. How much openness is there among Anglican evangelicals to appropriate liturgical development?

Bishop Richard Holloway (of Edinburgh): in the Church Times, (28 August, 1992), 'Missionary energy laced with moralism'

The truth . . . is that when we are taking part in the liturgy of the church we are in the real world, whereas a great deal of what goes on in the names of secular business is riddled with illusions.

Bishop Lesslie Newbigin: in the Church Times, (20 August, 1992), 'Truth for our time'

We must avoid on the one hand the dangers taught us by history of an inflexible and fixed liturgy which leaves no room for the freedom of the Holy Spirit. On the other hand we must avoid that 'squalid sluttery' and uninspired disorder which comes from disregarding the traditional patterns and forms of Christian worship.

Orders and Prayers for (Baptist) Church Worship, (1960)

In the liturgy God speaks to his people, and Christ is still proclaiming his gospel.

Vatican II: 'Constitution on the Sacred Liturgy', (December 1963)

. . . the new liturgy [of the Roman Catholic Church following the Second Vatican Council] was greeted with a long low moan from the faithful and even from the unfaithful – Arvonne's sister Rosalie who had not uttered a Pater Noster since the early days of the Eisenhower administration nevertheless mourned the Latin mass as if it were her dear departed mother – but Arvonne didn't pause for a moment. 'English,' she told Rosalie, 'is an excellent language. Look at Shakespeare. Look at Milton – if a Congregationalist could write like that, think what you could do if you actually knew something.'

Garrison Keillor: 'Lake Wobegon Days', (1985), 'Winter'

As surely as prayer belongs first in life and not in liturgy, so does the praise which recognises that God has overheard the people's cry even though that cry may not have been uttered with God in mind . . .

Praise and prayer belong first in life and derivatively in worship.

John Goldingay: 'Praying the Psalms', (Grove Spirituality, 1993)

For the language in which it [the Anglican liturgy of the sixteenth and seventeenth centuries] is wrote being constantly in flux, as all other living languages are, in every age some words that were in use in the former grow obsolete, and some phrases and expressions formerly in grace and fashion through disuse become uncouth and ridiculous, and always to continue these in our liturgy without correction would be to bring a disparagement upon the whole, and expose to contempt the worship of God among us.

Humphrey Prideaux, later Dean of Norwich: in 'Letter to a Friend', (c. 1689)

One other point at which a service could come to life was during 'the Peace'. Encouraged by the vicar, people left their pews and walked around the church to greet their friends and have a few words with them. The church seemed to come alive as it was filled with the murmur of dozens of conversations. Again there was a spark of life, but again it was not part of the written liturgy.

This was also its weakness. I turned to greet the lady sitting in the pew behind. I clasped her by the hand and said, 'The peace of the Lord be with you.' She replied, 'Pleased to meet you.' I felt flat, let down. I had greeted her with a Christian greeting and she had responded as if she had just been introduced to me at a tea-party.

The whole service left me with the impression that here was a congregation who had a liturgy, written in their service books, but they did not know how to use it. As a result they just plodded through it, and only felt free to express themselves when the set form of words was put aside for a moment and people did things in a more informal way.

It was not the content of what they were being asked to say that was the problem. They had chosen to have this order of service. They were aware of the way it uses the ideas and verbal images and in places the actual words of Scripture. Their problem was how to use this Christian liturgy as a means of worshipping God in spirit and in truth.

David Durston: in the Church of England Newspaper, (14 March, 1975)

A little boy was becoming restless during a church service. His mother leaned over: 'Ssh! This is God's house,' she said.

'Well,' said the child, 'if I were God, I'd move.'

Anonymous

I looked, and there was a great multitude that no one could count, from every nation, from all tribes and people and languages, standing before the throne and before the Lamb, robed in white, with palm branches in their hands. They cried out in a loud voice saying,

'Salvation belongs to our God who is seated on the throne, and to the Lamb!'

And all the angels stood around the throne and around the elders and the four living creatures, and they fell on their faces before the throne and worshipped God, singing,

'Amen! Blessing and glory and wisdom and thanksgiving and honour and power and might be to our God for ever and ever! Amen.'

Revelation 7:9–12

The throne of God and of the Lamb will be in it [the heavenly city], and his servants will worship him; they will see his face, and his name will be on their foreheads. And there will be no more night; they need no light of lamp or sun, for the Lord God will be their light, and they will reign for ever and ever.

Revelation 22:3b–5

Wrath

If we refuse to surrender to the love of God, we must feel the absoluteness of his will as wrath.

Emil Brunner: 'Our Faith', (1936; S.C.M., 1949)

Facing into the wind of God's grace.

Robert M.E. Paterson, (1988)

Johnnie, a little Scottish boy, was staying with his granny, and she gave him prunes for his tea. After six prunes he could eat no more and left two. Granny tried persuasion, then got angry, then threatened him with God's wrath: 'God will be very angry with you if you don't eat your prunes!' But Johnnie couldn't, so he was sent to bed, reassured that God was angry! A few minutes later, a fierce thunderstorm began and Granny began to repent of her incautious threatenings so up she went to Johnnie's room, where, to her amazement, she saw him gazing out of the window at the storm, saying: 'A' that fuss ower twa prunes!'

Gavin Reid, (1986)

Writers

Anyone can be a writer . . . it's infinitely easier to be a writer than to be a Christian.

Garrison Keillor

One of Richard Brinsley Sheridan's friends reproached him for flattering Gibbon. 'Why, what did I say of him?' 'You called him the luminous author, etc.' he was told.
'Luminous! Oh I meant *voluminous*.'

James Stevenson, Ed: 'The Oxford Book of Literary Anecdotes', (1975)

XYZ

Youth

Almost everything that is great has been done by youth.

Benjamin Disraeli

Young people will respond if the challenge is tough enough and hard enough. Youth wants a master and a controller. Young people were built for God, and without God as the centre of their lives they become frustrated and confused, desperately grasping for and searching for security.

Billy Graham

The world is passing through troublesome times. The young people of today think of nothing but themselves. They have no reverence for parents or old age. They are impatient of all restraint. They talk as if they knew everything, and what passes for wisdom with us is foolishness to them. As for girls, they are immodest and unwomanly in speech, behaviour and dress.

Peter the Hermit (c. 1050–1115)

When I was a boy of fourteen, my father was so ignorant I could hardly stand to have the man around. But when I got to be twenty-one, I was astonished at how much he had learned in seven years.

Mark Twain

When a nation's young men are conservative, its funeral bell is already rung.

Henry Ward Beecher: 'Proverbs from Plymouth Pulpit', (1887)

[What is clear is that] a theology which operates almost entirely in categories appropriate to adulthood will be severely restricted in its ability to further understanding with regard to that large proportion of humanity which, in various ways, is not adult and needs to be understood on its own terms.

Walter Moberley: 'Pedition', (Anvil, 1986)

When we are out of sympathy with the young, then I think our work in this world is over.

George MacDonald

INDEX OF SOURCES

A KEMPIS, Thomas
Books 34
Cross 66
Time 260
ABBOTT, W M
Preaching 207
ABERCROMBIE, Nicholas
Superstition 255
ABERGAVENNY CHRONICLE, The
Language 146
ACE, Goodman
Death 69
ACTON, J E E D
Power 197
ADAM-SMITH, George
Bible 29
ADAMS, Kenneth
Work 280
ADAMSON, Tony
Bible 25
Evangelism 98
ADDISON, Joseph
Music 179
Sunday 255
Women 277
ADMINISTRY
Publicity 222
ADOLFS, Robert
Church 48
AELRED OF RIEVAULX
Correction 63
Friendship 111
Love 154
AFRICAN BOY
Prayer 203
AFRICAN PROVERB
Witness 275
AGEE, James
Modesty 178
ALLEN, Woody
Death 71
God 119
AMBROSE OF MILAN
Culture 68
Slavery 247
AMERINGER, Oscar
Politics 193
AMOS, Alan
Prayer 198
AMOS, Clare
Cross 67
ANDERSON, J Norman D
Resurrection 232
ANDERSON, Margaret Chaplin
Preaching 213
ANDREWES, Lancelot
Christmas 44
Church 48
ANGUS and ROBERTSON
Scotland 240
ANSELM OF CANTERBURY
Atonement 19
Faith 103
APOSTOLIUS
Blindness 33
APPLEYARD, Bryan
Humanity 133
Materialism 160
New Age 181
Religion 229
Science 239
Self 240
Values 270
AQUINAS, Thomas
Angels 12
Eucharist 85
Law of God 149
Theology 259
ARAB CHRISTIAN SAYING
Christ, The 42
ARBUTHNOT, John
Anglicanism 15
ARIEL Magazine
Language 146
ARISTOTLE
War 273
ARMSTRONG, David
Spirit 250
ARNOLD, Matthew
Anglicanism 14
Christianity 42
Church 48
Cooking 63
Religion 228

ARNOLD, Thomas
Anglicanism 14
ARTICLES OF RELIGION, The XXXIX
Apocrypha 18
ASTLEY, Jacob
Prayer 200
ATHANASIUS
Witness 274
AUDEN, W H
Preaching 213
Salvation 239
AUGUSTINE OF HIPPO
Belief 22
Bishops 31
Church 46
Conversion 59
Gifts 113
God 117
Hope 132
Hymns 135
Love 156
Time 260
Travel 264
War 272
Work 280
AUSTEN, Jane
Intelligence 138
Reason 225
AUSTIN, George
Anglo-Catholicism 16
AUTTON, Norman
Communication 54
Love 154
Ministry 168
Pastoral Care 188
AYER, A J
God 119
BACON, Francis
Blessing 33
Books 34
Love 154
Preachers 206
Purpose 223
BAELZ, Peter
Leadership 150
Ministry 170
Planning 191
Relationships 228
BAEZ, Joan
Future 112
BAGEHOT, Walter
Monarchy 178
Poverty 195
BAILEY, Gordon
Prayer 201
BAIN, Joseph
Epitaphs 83
BAINTON, Roland H
Revelation 235
BAKER, John Austin
Suffering 254
BAKER, Peter
Hymns 135
BAKER, Russell
Liberalism 150
Politics 193
BALDOVIN, John F
Preachers 205
Preaching 210, 214, 215
BALDWIN, Stanley
Truth 266
BALE, Joanna
Language 145
BAPTIST CHURCH, The
Worship 285
BARCLAY, William
Hope 132
Works 281
BARKER, Ronnie and CORBETT, Ronnie
Crime 65
BARNES, Ernest William
Success 235
BARRETT, Charles Kingsley
Baptism 20
Cross 66
Jesus Christ 139
Truth 265
Unity 267
BARRINGTON WARD, Simon
Grace 123
Repentance 230
Spirit 251
BARRY, Alfred
Ministry 168
BARTH, Karl
Church 45
Preaching 210
Religion 228
BASKERVILLE, John
Epitaphs 82
BAUGHAN, Michael
Drink 78
BAXTER, Richard
Bible 29
Catechism 35
Church 47
Conscience 58
Conversion 60
Debate 72
Family 106
Future 112

God 119
Humility 134
Ministry 168
Partisanship 188
Philosophy 191
Preachers 205, 206
Preaching 209
Ritual 236
Service 242
Suffering 253
Unity 267
BEARD, H and CERF, C
Language 146
BEDE, Venerable
Death 69
Life 152
Thankfulness 258
BEECHER STOWE, Harriet
Creation 64
BEECHER, H W
Preaching 216
BEECHER, Harriet Ward
Youth 287
Imagination 137
BEECHING, H C
Pulpits 223
BEETHOVEN, Ludwig van
Death 70
BELFRY TRUST Newsletter
Prayer 198
BELL, David
Children 40
BELL, George
Vocation 271
BELLOC, Hillaire
Jews 140
BENNETT, Alan
Life 152
BENNETT, Gareth
Bishops 32
Theology 258
BENNETT, Robin
Theology 258
BENSON, E W
Bible 27
Ritual 236
BENTHAM, Jeremy
Ethics 84
BERGMANN, Gerhard
Gospel 121
BERKELEY, George
Idealism 137 (note)
BERKSON, M D
Christmas 44
BERNARDINO OF SIENA
Preaching 207
BETHGE, Eberhard
Discipline 75
BETJEMAN, John
Christmas 44
Church Buildings 50
Language 146
BETTERTON, Thomas
Preaching 210
BIBLE SOCIETY, The
Translation 262
BINYON, Laurence
Memory 162
BIRMINGHAM, St Philip's Cathedral
Epitaphs 82
BISHOP, Bernadine
Realism 225
BISMARCK, Otto von
Politics 193
BLACK, James
Conviction 62
BLAKE, William
Creation 64
Gambling 112
Truth 266
BLAMIRES, Harry
Mind 163
BLANCH, Stuart
Laziness 150
Ministry 168, 172
BLANDON, Nelba
Censorship 37
BLEAKLEY, David
Authority 20
BOARD, Dafydd Miles
Communication 55
BODY SHOP, The
Education 79
BOLSOVER
Epitaphs 82
BOLT, Robert
Law of God 149
BONAVENTURE
God 115
BONHOEFFER, Dietrich
Church 48
Death 70
Fellowship 107
Grace 124
Preaching 213
Silence 245
Vocation 271
BONYER, Louis
Bible 27
BOOK OF COMMON PRAYER
Freedom 111
Pope 195

BOORDE, Andrew
Blindness 33
BOORSTIN, Daniel
History 130
BOOTH, William
Love 156
BORGE, Victor
Marriage 159
BORLAND, Hal
Change 39
BOSCH, David J
Cross 67
Justice 143
BOSWELL, James
Death 70
Death Penalty 72
Education 79
Friendship 111
Idealism 137
Scotland 200
Truth 265
BOWEN, C S C
Philosophy 191
BOWEN, Euros
Church 46
BOYCE, Max
Laziness 150
BRADSHAW, Tim
Exegesis 100
BRAMWELL-BOOTH, Catherine
Service 243
BREMNER, Charles
Judgement 141
BREWARD, Ian
Mission 173
BRIDGES, Robert
Spirituality 252
BRIGHT, John
Bible 25
Preaching 210
BRITISH BROADCASTING CORPORATION
Media 161
Philosophy 191
BRONTE, Charlotte
Clerics 52
Suffering 253
BROOK, Peter
Worship 284
BROOKE, Rupert
Hope 131
BROOKS, Phillips
Courage 63
Doctrine 76
Preaching 207
BROWNE, Thomas
Heaven 127
Love 156
BROWNING, Elizabeth Barrett
Devil 73
Love 155
BROWNING, Robert
Beauty 22
Greed 125
BRUCE, Lenny
Church 48
BRUNNER, Emil
Cross 65
Discipleship 74
Education 79
Faith 102–105
Fall 106
Gifts 113
God 115
Gospel 121
Grace 123
Hope 132
Jesus Christ 140
Law of God 149
Mission 173, 176
Moralism 178
Paradox 187
Predestination 217
Reason 226
Resurrection 233
Revelation 235
Theology 259
Wrath 287
BRUSH, James
Epitaphs 82
BRYAN, William Jennings
Public Speaking 221
BUCER, Martin
Eucharist 86
BUCHAN, John
Atheism 19
BUCHANAN, Colin O
Baptism 20
Christianity 42
Eucharist 85
Evangelism 93
Faith 104
Preaching 209
Sunday 255
Worship 283, 284
BUECHNER, Frederick
Giving 114
Regeneration 227
BUNTING, Ian D
Pluralism 192
Preaching 208, 210
BUNYAN, John
Apocrypha 17
Conversion 60

Cross 66
BURDON, Adrian
Preaching 214, 215
BURGON, John William
Gospels 122
BURKE, Edmund
Apathy 17
Bereavement 23
BURNET, Gilbert
Marriage 158
BURNS, Robert
Clerics 52
Grace (food) 125
BUTLER, Joseph
Ridicule 236
Spirit 250
BUTLER, Samuel
Life 152
Love 154
BUTTRICK, George
Truth 266
BYATT, A S
Atonement 19
BYERS, Carl
Committees 54
BYRON, Lord (George Gordon)
Angels 12
Hypocrisy 136
Persecution 190
Quotation 224
Truth 266
Weather 273
CAEN, Herb
Evangelicals 90
CAIRD, G B
Resurrection 232
CALVIN, John
Bible 27
Bishops 32
Church 46
Discipleship 74
CAMBRIDGE INTELLIGENCER, The
Clerics 52
CAMERON, Simon
Politics 193
CAMPBELL, Thomas
Books 34
Memory 161
CAMPOLO, Tony
Christianity 42
CARDEN, John
God 118
Humanity 133
Mind 163
Prayer 202
CAREY, George
Apathy 17
Church 45
Church, its Mission 47
Evangelicals 89
God 119
Joy 141
Mission 176
Peace 189
Spirit 251
Unity 267
Vision 271
Witness 275
CAREY, William
Mission 175
CARLYLE, Thomas
Preachers 206
Protestantism 220
Pulpits 222
Ridicule 236
Slavery 247
CARROL, Lewis (Charles William Dodgson)
Education 79
CARTER, Thomas
Epitaphs 83
CARY, Lucius
Preaching 215
CATO, Marcius Porcius
Communication 54
CECIL, Richard
Preaching 208
CELESTINE I, Pope
Hypocrisy 137
CERVANTES
Realism 225
CHADWICK, Owen
Absent-mindedness 9
Preaching 213
CHAMBERLAIN, Neville
War 273
CHAMBERS, Oswald
Holiness 130
CHAPMAN, Colin
Heaven 127
CHAPMAN, John
Prayer 199, 202
CHARLES I, King
Pulpits 222
CHARLES II, King
Bishops 31
Last Words 149
Politics 193
Preaching 209
Women 277
CHARLES, Ernest Bruce
Examinations 99

CHAUCER, Geoffrey
Obedience 183
Predestination 217
CHESTERTON, G K
Bigotry 30
Celts 37
Government 123
Journalism 140
Navigation 181
Patriotism 189
Psychology 221
Religion 229
Sin 246
CHEVALIER, Gabriel
Bishops 31
Death 70
Poetry 192
CHEVASSE, F J
Evangelicals 88
CHINESE PROVERB
Perseverance 190
Vision 271
CHINESE SAYING
Growth 125
CHRISTIAN OBSERVER, The
Future 112
CHURCH OF ENGLAND
Creeds 64
Evangelism 93
Facts 101
Television 257
CHURCH OF SCOTLAND
Mission 175
CHURCH PASTORAL-AID SOCIETY
Ritual 236
CHURCH TIMES, The
History 129
Women 277
CHURCHILL, John Spencer
Time 260
CHURCHILL, Winston Spencer
Beauty 22
Death 71
Democracy 72
Equality 84
Truth 266
CICERO, Marcus Tullius
Hypocrisy 136
Thankfulness 258
CIVIL WAR (American)
Weakness 273
CLARKE, H Lewis
Evangelism 93
Intelligence 138
CLAUDIUS CAESAR
Britain 34
CLEESE, John
Hope 132
CLIFFORD, N K
Evangelicals 89
COCKERILL, John and Carol
Occult 184
COGGAN, F Donald
Anglicanism 13
Bible 24, 27
Bishops 30
Church 46
Clerics 51
Committees 54
Cross 65
Discipleship 74
Doctrine 77
Doubt 77
Exegesis 100, 101
Fall 106
Future 112
Giving 113
God 117
Hope 131
Human Rights 133
Love 156
Ministry 165, 169
Mission 173
Music 179
Persecution 189
Prayer 199
Preachers 206
Preaching 206, 208, 214, 215
Prophecy 219
Pulpits 223
Repentance 230
Resurrection 233
Spirit 250
Women 278
Wonder 278
Word 279
COGGLESHALL
Epitaphs 82
COLERIDGE, Samuel Taylor
Faith 102
Love 156
Preaching 213
Singing 247
COLTON, Charles Caleb
Flattery 108
Public Speaking 221
COLUMBANUS
Pilgrimage 191
CONKLIN, Edward
Creation 63
CONNOLLY, Cyril
Fall 106

CONNOR, Ralph
Abba 9
CONNOR, William
Death 71
COOKE, A
History 129
COOKE, Alistair
Materialism 160
COOPER, Anthony Ashley (Lord Shaftesbury)
Reform 227
COOPER, Jilly
Men 162
CORNFORD, M
Pulpits 222
CORONATION, The
Bible 24
COUNSEL Journal
Language 147
COURATIN, Arthur
Eucharist 87
COUSINS, Peter
Evangelism 98
Worship 282
COWPER, William
Humility 134
Prayer 203
CRABBE, George
Truth 264
CRANMER, Thomas
Mercy 162
CREIGHTON, Oswin
Church 47
CRISP, Quentin
England 81
CROCKFORDS Clerical Directory
Universalism 269
CROMWELL, Oliver
Religion 229
CROSS KIRK
Epitaphs 82
CROSS, Tim
Preaching 212
CROSSBEATS, The
Future 112
CUMING, Geoffrey
Eucharist 85
CUNDY, Ian
Catholicity 35
Choice 42
Church 45
History 130
Unity 267
CUNLIFFE, Christopher
Anglicanism 16
CURRAN, John Philpot
Charm 40
Liberty 151
CURTIS-BENNETT, Henry Honeywood
Law 149
CURZON, George
Class 51
Death 71
Travel 264
CUTHBERT OF LINDISFARNE
Thankfulness 258
CYPRIAN OF CARTHAGE
Joy 141
D'ARCY (Archbishop)
Works 281
D'ARIENZO, Camille
Women 277
DAILY TELEGRAPH, The
Christmas 44
Hymns 135
Spirit 251
DALE, R W
Ministry 168
Preaching 211
DALES, Douglas
Evangelicals 89
DARK, Sidney
Money 178
Poverty 195, 196
Social Action 248
DARWIN, Charles
Creation 63
DAVEY, Horace
Public Speaking 222
DAVIDSON, Randall
Compromise 57
Mission 173
DAVIES, Bruce
Despair 72
Preaching 210, 215
DAVIES, Edwyn
Humour 135
DAVIES, Horton
Creation 63
DAVIES, J G
Preaching 209
DAVIES, R and RUPP, G
Prayer Book 204
DAWSON, Albert
Preaching 211
DAWSON, E C
Anglo-Catholicism 17
DAY, Clarence
Prayer 201
DAY, Robin
Television 257

DE BALZAC, Honore
Relationships 228
DE CHARDIN, Teilhard
Suffering 254
Work 280
DE CONDORCET
Human Rights 133
DE GROOT, Hugo (Grotius)
Work 280
DE LA BARCA, Pedro Calderon
Love 155
DE LA MARE, Walter
Sickness 244
DE LA ROCHEFOUCAULD, Francois
Justice 143
DE ROMANS, Humbert
Preaching 214
DE SALES, Francis
Preaching 208
DE STAEL, Anne Louise Germaine
Love 155
DE VALERA, Eamon
Politics 194
DE VERE, Aubrey
Preaching 209
DE VIRES, Peter
Religion 229
DE WAAL, Esther
Celtic Christianity 37
Creation 64
Mission 177
DEFOE, Daniel
Devil 73
Satire 203
DENNY, James
Cross 65
Doctrine 76
Resurrection 232
Sacraments 236
Theology 258
DESCARTES, Rene
Existentialism 101
DIBDEN, Michael
Apathy 17
Christmas 44
Preaching 212
DICKENS, Charles Huffam
Finance 108
Government 123
Humility 134
Language 145
Law 149
Marriage 158
Women 276
DILLISTONE, F W
Liberty 151
DIOGNETUS, Letter to
Christians 43
Persecution 189
DISRAELI, Benjamin
Books 34
Death 71
Last Words 149
Politics 193
Youth 287
DIX, Gregory
Baptism 20
Bishops 31
DIXON, John
Future 112
DODD, C H
Translation 262
DOLMAN, Robert E
Lent 150
DONNA
Children 40
DONNE, John
Catholicity 36
Cross 66
Grace 124
Hope 132
Humanity 133
Love 154
Mercy 162
Prayer 201
Pulpits 222
Repentance 231
DOUGLAS, Norman
Advertising 10
DOUGLAS-HOME, William
Absent-mindedness 9
DRAKE, Francis
Commitment 53
DRUMMOND, William
Incarnation 137
DRYDEN, John
Democracy 72
Love 154
Marriage 159
DUNNE, Finley Peter
English 81
DUNOON
Epitaphs 83
DUNSTAN, Alan
Anglicanism 14
DURSTON, David
Worship 286
EBELING, Gerhard
Doctrine 76

ECO, Umberto
Devil 73
Faith 103
Truth 265
EDINBURGH
Epitaphs 83
EDINBURGH MISSIONARY CONFERENCE
Mission 175
EDISON, Thomas Alva
Genius 113
EDMUND OF ABINGDON
Forgiveness 110
Holiness 130
EDWARDS, Aled
Celtic Christianity 37
EDWARDS, David L
England 80
Evangelicals 89
EINSTEIN, Albert
Imagination 137
Science 239, 240
ELIOT, George (Mary Anne Evans)
Bereavement 23
Obedience 183
Persecution 190
Worship 282
ELIOT, Thomas Stearns
Ambition 12
Church 47, 49
Holy Places 131
Light 153
Motivation 179
Persecution 190
Protestantism 220
Suffering 254
Witness 275
ELLIOTT-BINNS
Evangelicals 87
ELLIS, Anthony
Teaching 256
ELLIS, Henry Havelock
Progress 218
ELLUL, Jacques
Environment 81
Prophecy 218
EMERSON, Ralph Waldo
Books 34
Fatalism 107
Truth 265
ENGLISH PRISONER OF WAR
Suffering 254
ENGLISH PROVERB
Witness 275
ENGLISH SAYING
Blindness 33
ENGLISH, Wilda
Christmas 44
EPISCOPAL CHURCH of the U.S.A.
Anglicanism 15
Wealth 273
EPPLE
Morality 178
ERASMUS, Desiderius
Christians 43
Cross 65
Preaching 216
War 273
EVANGELICAL ALLIANCE
Gospel 120
EWER, William Norman
Jews 140
FABER, F W
Worship 284
FANE, John
Bishops 31
FANT, C E
Preaching 213
FARMER, H H
Preaching 208
FENTON MORLEY
Humour 134
Jesus Christ 139
FENTON, James
Anglo-Catholicism 17
FENTON, John
Bible 27
FERRIS, Theodorc Parker
Preaching 208
FEUERBACH
God 119
FIELDING, Henry
Education 79
Justice 142
Mind 163
Satire 239
FINLEY, John
Change 39
FISCHER, Louis
Silence 244
FITZGERALD, Edward
History 130
FLAUBERT, Gustav
Love 154
Public Speaking 221
FOOT, Michael
Anglicanism 14
FORD, Henry
History 129
FORD, Leighton
Evangelism 93
FORSTER, E M
Faith 104

FORSYTH, P T
Bishops 32
Church 45
Conversion 59
Gospel 121
Liberalism 150
Preachers 205
Preaching 209
FOSTER, John
Courage 63
FRANCE, Anatole
Chance 37
FRANCH SAYING
Generosity 113
FRANCIS OF ASSISI
Witness 275
FRANKLIN, Benjamin
Epitaphs 83
Perseverance 190
Sin 246
Time 260
War 273
FRENCH PROTESTANT
Suffering 254
FRENCH SAYING
Beauty 22
France 111
Liberty 151
FROST, David and JAY, Anthony
Hell 128
FROST, Paul
Emotions 80
FROST, Robert
Translation 263
FULLER, John
Anglo-Catholicism 17
FUNG, Raymond
Care 35
Evangelism 97
FURBANK, David
Stewardship 253
GAITSKELL, Hugh
Cleanliness 51
GALLAGHER, Herbert F
Resurrection 232
GAY, John
Doctors 75
Love 154
GENTLEMAN'S MAGAZINE, The
Service 242
GEORGE VI, King
Faith 103
GEORGE, Lloyd
Politics 194
Prayer 201
GERMAN PROVERB
Gifts 113
GERMAN SAYING
Bereavement 23
GETTY, Paul
Money 178
GILBERT, Michael
Creation 64
Law 149
Life 152
Marriage 159
Preaching 216
Public Speaking 221, 222
Wales 272
Worship 283
GILBERT, W S
Creation 63
Sin 246
GILES Cartoon
Politics 193
GILKEY, Langdon
Fundamentalism 112
GILL, John
Epitaphs 83
GIRALDUS CAMBRENSIS
Wales 272
GLADSTONE, William Ewart
Evangelicals 87
GOBEY, Edward
Baptism 21
GOETHE
Perseverence 190
GOLDINGAY, John
Prayer 197
Worship 284, 286
GOLDSMITH, Oliver
Drink 78
France 111
Knowledge 144
Politics 194
Preachers 206
GOLDWYN, Samuel
Truth 266
GOLLANCZ, V
Change 38
GORE, Charles
Anglicanism 16
Christ, The 42
Self 241
GRAHAM, Billy
Christianity 42
Conversion 60
Youth 287
GRAHAME, Kenneth
God 115
GRANT, R M
Bible 29
GRANT, R M and TRACY, D
Theology 259

GRAVES, Robert
Britain 34
GRAY, Thomas
Boasting 33
Solitude 249
GRAY, Tony
Ireland 138
GREAT BIBLE, The
Charity 40
GREEK SAYING
Doubt 77
GREEN, Bryan
Agnosticism 11
Catholicity 36
Evangelicals 87
Gospel 122
Liberalism 151
GREEN, Constance McLaughlin
Pulpits 223
GREEN, Michael
Evangelism 99
Gospel 121
GREEN, Peter
Commitment 53
Spirit 250
GREEN, Robin
Worship 285
GREENE, Graham
Heresy 129
GREENFIELD, Douglas
Evangelism 92
GREENWOOD, Frederick
Media 161
GREGORY THE GREAT, Pope
Angels 12
GREY, Edward
War 273
GRIFFITH, Michael
Obedience 183
GROOTHIUS, Douglas R
God 115
GRUBB, Kenneth
Jesus Christ 139
Social Action 248
GUARDIAN WEEKLY, The
Language 147
GUINNESS, Os
Doctrine 75
Evangelicals 89
History 130
Mind 164
Modernity 177, 178
GUMLEY, F and REDHEAD, B
Partisanship 187
Protest 219
GUTHRIE, Donald
Works 280
GUTHRIE, James
Death 69
GUTIERREZ, Gustavo
Poverty 195
GWENNAP
Cross 66
Death 69
HABGOOD, John
Gambling 112
God 117
Hell 128
Prayer 201
Religion 229, 230
HALIFAX, Lord
Chance 37
HALLE, Edward
Bible 28
HALLESBY, Otto
Prayer 197
HAMMARSKJOLD, Dag
Holiness 130
HAMMOND, Peter
Religion 229
HAMPTON, Christopher
Conviction 62
HANDLEY, MacMATH, SAUNDERS, Van de WEYER
Anglicanism 13
England 80, 81
Reformation 227
HANSON, A T and R P C
Baptism 21
Bible 24
Bishops 30, 32
Church 45, 47
Cross 66
Education 79
Evangelicals 89
Gospel 120
Mediator 161
Ministry 169, 171
Prophecy 219
Sacraments 237
Spirit 251
Theology 259
Truth 265
Unity 267, 269
Women 277
Word 279
HANSON, Richard P C
Catholicity 35
Eucharist 86
Salvation 239
Works 281
HARBURG, E Y
God 117

HARDY, Thomas
Anglicanism 15
Christianity 42
Clerics 52
Justice 143
HARINGTON, John
Books 34
HARPER, Michael
Prophecy 218
HARRIES, Christopher
Anglicanism 16
HARRIET ANN
Children 40
HARRIS POLL
Miracles 172
HARRIS, Randell
Prayer 203
HASIDIM, The
Humanity 133
HASKINS, Minnie Louise
Faith 103
HASLAM, William
Conversion 59
HATCH, Nathan O
Bible 26
HAVERGAL, Frances Ridley
Joy 140
HAWKER, R S
Harvest 126
HAWKINS, Henry
Preaching 213
HAWTHORNE, Nathanael
Hypocrisy 136
HAZLITT, William
Hypocrisy 136
HEATH, Edward
Politics 193
HEINE, Heinrich
Vision 271
HELLER, Joseph
Courage 63
HELPS, Arthur
Books 34
HEMMING
Morality 178
HENDRA, Tony and KELLY, Sean
Creation 64
HENSON, H Hensley
Baptism 20
Preaching 207
Teeth 256
Truth 266
HERBERT, Alan Patrick
Fun 111
Jealousy 139
HERBERT, George
Education 79
Jesus Christ 139, 140
Love 155, 157
Prayer 202, 203
Preaching 208
Pulpits 223
Redemption 226
Resurrection 233
Social Action 248
HEWITT, Garth
Poverty 196
HEWITT, Roderick R
Naivete 180
HIBBERT, Andrew
Work 280
HIGLEY, John
Epitaphs 82
HILTON, James
Time 260
HILTON, Walter
Love 156
HINDE, Thomas
Epitaphs 82
HINES, Charles P
Women 278
HINTON, Reginald Charles (Bill)
Wit 274
HODGE, John
Grace (food) 124
HODGSON, Ralph
Prayer 202
HOLDEN, Stuart
Preaching 211
HOLLOWAY, Richard
Anglicanism 13, 16
Church 47
Culture 68
Evangelicals 87, 88
Evangelism 99
Grace 123
Worship 285
HOLMES, Oliver Wendell
Compromise 56
HOME, Charles Silvester
Ministry 168
HOOKER, Richard
Eucharist 86
Faith 103
Government 123
Obedience 183
Politics 193
Service 242
HOPKINS, Gerald Manley
Work 280

HOPKINS, Hugh Evan
Conversion 59
Evangelicals 88
HORACE, Quintus Horatius Flaccus
Patriotism 189
HORDA, Robert
Ministry 168
HOUSMAN, Laurence
Incarnation 138
HOUSTON, J M
Doctrine 75
Evangelism 92
HOUSTON, Tom
Bible 27
Poverty 196
Prayer 197
Truth 265
HOWARD, Philip
Debate 72
Translation 262
HUBBARD, Elbert
Friendship 111
Memory 161
HUGHES, Hugh Price
Politics 193
HUGHES, Ivor
Children 41
HUGO, Victor Marie
Future 112
Love 155
Scholarship 239
Vision 271
HUXLEY, Thomas Henry
Agnosticism 11
I.A.L.C.
Ministry 171
IGNATIUS OF ANTIOCH
Catholicity 35
IGNATIUS OF LOYOLA
Bishops 30
Truth 265
INGE, William
Church 46
Death 71
Media 161
Prayer 199
INGHAM, Michael
Bishops 32
IRENAEUS OF LYONS
God 117
IRISH POEM
Pilgrimage 191
IRISH PROVERB
Unity 267
ISLINGTON CONFERENCE
Evangelicals 88
ITALIAN PROVERB
Courage 63
Preachers 206
JACOBOVITS, Immanuel
Conversion 61
JAMES I / VI, King
Smoking 248
JAMES, Clive
Giving 114
JAMES, E O
Islam 139
JAMES, William
Choice 41
JEFFERSON, Thomas
Advertising 10
JENKINS, David
Bible 27, 28
Catholicity 36
Church 49
Eternity 84
Faith 102, 103
God 115, 118
Grace 124
Love 156
Media 161
Miracles 172
Preaching 207
Resurrection 234
Sin 246
JENNINGS
Laws 149
JEREMIAS, Joachim
Abba 9
JERMAN, Betty
Nominalism 181
JEROME, Jerome Klapka
Love 155
Work 280
JERUSALEM MISSIONARY COUNCIL
Hinduism 129
Mission 177
JESSEL, George
Public Speaking 221
Witness 275
JESUS PEOPLE
Growth 125
JEWEL, John
Bishops 33
Eucharist 86
Unity 268
JEWISH PRAYER
Truth 265
JEWISH SAYING
Bigotry 30
Generosity 113

JOHN OF THE CROSS
Silence 244
JOHN PAUL I, Pope
Evangelism 92
JOHN THE APOSTLE
Rest 231
JOHN THE EVANGELIST
Symbolism 256
JOHN XXIII, Pope
Family 106
Time 260
JOHNSON, Samuel
Ministry 169
JOHNSON, Lyndon B
War 272
JOHNSON, Paul
Religion 228
JOHNSON, Samuel
Age 11
Charity 40
Death 70
Death Penalty 72
Education 79
Evangelicals 87
Faith 103
Fame 106
Forgiveness 109
Friendship 111
Hypocrisy 136
Idealism 137
Ignorance 137
Marriage 159
Prayer 200
Travel 264
Truth 265
Women 278
JONES, Alwyn Rice
Change 39
JONES, Franklin P
Correction 63
JONES, William
Methodism 163
JORDAN MANAGEMENT CONSULTANTS
Management 157
JORDAN, R Fumeaux
Progress 218
JOWETT, Benjamin
Prophecy 219
JULIAN OF NORWICH
Creation 64
JULIUS CAESAR
Belief 22
War 273
JUNG, Carl G
Death 69
God 117
Healing 126
KABIR
God 118
KAFKA, Franz
Beauty 22
KAGAWA, Dr.
Love 155
KANT, Immanuel
Resurrection 232
KAUMA, Misaeri
Suffering 253
KAVANAGH, Aidan
God 117
Worship 284
KEILLOR, Garrison
Bible 26
Caution 36
Conversion 60
Earth 78
Emotions 80
Ethics 85
Evangelism 99
God 119
Mercy 162
Prayer 200
Preaching 212
Repentance 231
Service 243
Sin 246
Spirit 251
Truth 266
Unity 268
Worship 284, 285
Writers 287
KEN, Thomas
Psalms 220
KENNEDY, David
Pulpits 222
KERR, Jean
Courage 63
KEVIN
Children 40
KILVERT, Robert Francis
Preaching 211
KING JAMES VERSION, The
Charity 40
KING, Edward
Drink 78
KING, John C
Anglicanism 16
Catholicity 36
Poetry 192
Sunday 254
KINGS, Graham
Kingdom of God 143
Truth 266
Unity 268

KIPLING, Rudyard
Boasting 33
Language 145
Women 277
KIPLINGER MAGAZINE
Computers 57
KIRKEGAARD, Soren
Life 152
Saints 238
KIVENGERE, Festo
Realism 225
Redemption 226
KNEBEL, Fletcher
Committees 54
KNOX, John
Suffering 254
KNOX, Ronald A
Idealism 137
Pastoral Care 188
KOESTLER, Arthur
Despair 72
KOYAMA, Kosuke
Cross 67
KUAN-TZE
Teaching 256
KUNG, Hans
Kingdom of God 144
Ministry 165
KUYPER, Abraham
Evangelism 93
KUZMIC, Peter
Church 46
Evangelicals 87
Evangelism 99
Gospel 121
Morality 179
Witness 275
LAMB, Charles
Preaching 213
Science 239
Smoking 248
LAMBETH CONFERENCE (1897)
Prayer Book 203
LAMBETH CONFERENCE (1948)
Prayer Book 203
LAMBETH CONFERENCE (1978)
Mission 177
LANCASTER, John
Evangelism 90
LAPLACE
God 119
LATHAM, John
Law 149
LATIMER, Hugh
Bishops 31
Reformation 227
LATIN PROVERB
Sin 246
War 273
LAUSANNE COVENANT, The
Evangelism 92
Mission 177
LAW, William
Hypocrisy 136
LAWRENCE (Deacon)
Poverty 196
LAWRENCE, Brother
Charismatics 39
Prayer 203
LAWRENCE, D H
Contentment 58
God 118
Providence 220
Wonder 278
LAWRENCE, Margot
Liberalism 150
LAWRENCE, T E (Lawrence of Arabia)
Dreams 77
LAYCOCK, Stephen
Faith 104
LAZARUS, Emma
Liberty 152
LEACOCK, Stephen
Advertising 10
LEAN, V S
Choice 41
LEBOWITZ, Fran
Telephone 257
LEECH, Kenneth
Desert 72
LEO XIII, Pope
Bible 24
LEVANT, Oscar
Humility 134
LEVIN, Bernard
Change 39
LEWIS, C S
Agnosticism 11
Atonement 19
Chance 37
Change 39
Christianity 43
Communication 55
Devil 73
Experience 101
Family 106
Forgiveness 109
Goodness 120
Hell 128
Incarnation 137
Joy 140
Love 154

Miracles 172
Myth 180
Pastoral Care 188
Poverty 196
Prayer 199, 202
Translation 263
LEWIS, Don
Doctors 75
LEWIS, Matthew Gregory (Monk)
Kindness 143
LIGHTFOOT, Joseph Barber
Bishops 33
Gospel 121
LILLINGSTONE, Cecil G C
Prayer 199
LINCOLN, Abraham
Deception 72
Mercy 162
LINDSAY, George
Evangelism 93
LINKLETTER, Art
Age 10
LIVES, Robert
Epitaphs 84
LIVING CHURCH, The
Ministry 166
LLOYD-JONES, Martin
Death 70
Preachers 205
LONGLEY, Charles Thomas
Lent 150
LONGLEY, Clifford
Anglicanism 15
Anglo-Catholicism 17
Authority 20
Choice 41
Church Buildings 50
Commandments 53
Ethics 84
Evangelicals 90
Morality 178
Paradox 187
Religious Education 230
Secularism 241
Toleration 261
Translation 262
Truth 265
LOVE STORY
Love 155
LOWRY, Eugene L
Preaching 216
Regeneration 227
LUCAS, E V
Saints 238
LUCCOCK, H E
Preaching 216
LUTHER, Martin
Abba 9
Bible 24, 25, 27
Conversion 59
Cross 65
Death 69, 70
Devil 73
Eucharist 85
Exegesis 100
Faith 102, 106
Forgiveness 110
Hope 131
Law of God 149
Laziness 150
Music 179
Persecution 190
Prayer 199, 202
Preaching 211, 214
Sacraments 236
Sex 243
Sin 246
Temptation 257
Translation 263, 264
Values 270
Works 281
LYTTON, E R B
Scepticism 239
MACAULAY, R B
Last Words 149
MACDONALD, George
Youth 287
MACDONALDS
Work 280
MACHEN, J Gresham
Mind 164
MACHIAVELLI
Blindness 33
War 273
MACINNES, David
Clerics 51
Death 70
MACINTYRE, Ben
Law 149
MACKENNA, Richard
Christians 43
Church 47–49
Clerics 52
Cross 67
Death 69
Doubt 77
Eucharist 87
Evangelicals 89
Evangelism 97
God 119
Gospel 122
Grace 124
Hope 132

Humility 134
Love 154
Ministry 169
Prayer 198, 200, 201
Religion 228
Self 241
Service 242
Silence 245
Spirit 250
Success 253
Suffering 253
Teaching 256
MACKINNON
Bible 27
MACLOED, George F
Cross 66
MACQUARRIE, John
Cross 65
Religion 229
MALIK, Charles
Mind 164
MALING, Eduardo
Evangelism 97
MALONE, Dudley
Truth 266
MANCROFT (Lord)
Eternity 84
Public Speaking 221
MANN, Horace
Committees 54
MANN, Thomas
Communication 54
MAO TSE-TUNG
Politics 193
MARC cartoon
Class 51
MARCUS AURELIUS
Society 249
MARIES, Andrew
Language 146
MARLOWE, Christopher
Hell 127, 128
Love 155
MARSHALL, Catherine
Judgement 141
MARTYN, Henry
Humility 134
MARX, Groucho
Beauty 22
Self 241
MARX, Karl Heinrich
Communism 55
Religion 228
MARYLEBONE CRICKET CLUB
Cricket 64
MASCALL, Eric L
Devil 73
MASON, A J
Emotions 80
MATHERS, James
Ministry 168
MAUGHAM, Robin
Death 71
MAUGHAM, W Somerset
Death 71
Poetry 192
MAURICE, Frederick Denison
Preaching 209
MAY, Matthew
Computers 57
MCADOO, William G
Public Speaking 221
MCCHEYNE, Robert Murray
Holiness 130
Prayer 198
MCFARLANE, John
Epitaphs 83
McGEE, Archbishop
Anger 13
MCGRATH, Gavin
Faith 104
Grace 124
MCLUHAN, Marshall
Humanity 133
MCNEILL, John T
Unity 268
MELBOURNE, William Lamb
Religion 228
MENCKEN, H L
Birth Control 30
Bishops 31
Conscience 58
MERCER, David
Psychology 221
MEREDITH, George
Marriage 158
MERTON, Thomas
Prayer 201
METHODIST CHURCH
Obedience 183
MILITARY SAYING
Planning 191
MILL, John Stuart
Belief 22
Truth 265
MILLER, Olin
Forgiveness 110
MILNE, A A
Activism 10
Giving 114
Intelligence 138
MILTON, John
Books 34
Chance 37

Discipleship 74
Future 112
Guidance 125
Hypocrisy 136
Liberty 151
Ministry 172
Pastoral Care 188
Revelation 235
Rhyme 235
Service 242, 243
Truth 265
War 273

MIRFIELD (Community of the Resurrection)
Prayer 198

MISSAL, of the Roman Catholic Church
Bible 26

MITTON, Michael
Death 70

MOBERLEY, Walter
Judgement 141
Youth 287

MOLEGATSI, Caesar
Theology 259

MOLTMANN, Jurgen
Church 47
Conversion 60

MONTEFIORE, Hugh
Commandments 52

MONTESQUIEU
Religion 229

MOODY, D L
Bible 29

MOORE, Hannah
Bible 28

MOORE, Harry
Evangelism 92
Mission 174
Theology 258

MOORE, Thomas
Love 155

MOORMAN, J R H
Bishops 31

MORE, Richard D A
Devil 73

MORE, Thomas
Prayer 199

MORGAN, Dewi
Christ, The 42
Mystery 180
Religion 228

MORGAN, George Campbell
Preaching 211, 216

MORLEY, George
Predestination 217

MORRIS, Brian
Resurrection 232

MORROW, Dwight
Achievement 9

MOSS, C B
Creeds 64

MOTTISTONE, Lord
Christmas 43

MOULE, Charles F D
Ministry 171

MOULE, Handley
Church Buildings 50

MOUNCE, R H
Preaching 209

MOZART, Wolfgang Amadeus
Music 179

MUGGERIDGE, Malcolm
Humility 134
Humour 135
Religion 228

MUIR, Frank
Marriage 159

MUMFORD, Bob
Authority 20

MURPHY
Laws 150

MYERS, F H
Heaven 127

NAPIER, George
Epitaphs 83

NATIONAL LAMPOON
Britain 34

NAZIR-ALI, Michael
Church 46, 48
Witness 274
Worship 284

NEALE, John
Church 48

NEIL
Children 40

NEILL, Stephen
Anglicanism 14, 15
Evangelicals 87
Tradition 261

NELSON, Horatio
Blindness 33

NEVIN, John W
Bible 26

NEW STATESMAN, The
Anger 13

NEWBIGIN, Lesslie
Bible 24, 27
Conversion 61
Culture 68
Economics 78
Evangelism 99
Exegesis 99

God 115
Gospel 120, 121
History 130
Justice 143
Mission 176, 177
Politics 194
Prayer 197
Purpose 223
Reason 225, 226
Resurrection 233, 234
Science 239
Society 249
Translation 263
Truth 266
Unity 268
Worship 285
NEWCASTLE (Duke of)
Women 277
NEWMAN, John Henry
Agnosticism 11
Anglo-Catholicism 17
Deception 72
God 118
Growth 125
Life 152
Religion 229
NEWTON, John
Emotions 80
Mercy 162
Preaching 207
NICHOLAS, Edna
Eternity 84
NIEBUHR, Reinhold
Democracy 72
NIETZSCHE, Friedrich Wilhelm
God 119
Witness 275
NIGERIAN CHRISTIAN
Repentance 230
NILES, D T
Evangelism 93
Mission 173
NIMMO, Derek
Drink 78
NIXON, Richard
Politics 193
NIXON, Robin
Ascension 19
NOLL, Mark A
Communication 54
Evangelicals 89
Exegesis 100
Tradition 261
NORMAN, Edward
Anglicanism 14, 16
Arts 18
Leadership 150
NOUWEN, Henri
Discipline 74
Silence 244
NYRERE, Julius
Poverty 195
O'CONNELL, Daniel
Life 153
Politics 193
O'CONNOR, Frank
Clerics 52
O'DONOVAN, Oliver
Bible 28
O'MALLEY, Pat
Public Speaking 221
O'REILLY, John Boyle
Love 34
O'ROURKE, P J
Books 34
Church 47
Communism 55, 56
Environment 81
Family 106
France 110
Fun 111
Greed 125
Hypocrisy 136
Journalism 140
Methodism 163
Poverty 197
Second Coming 240
Sin 247
Theft 258
Travel 264
Violence 271
OBERMAN, Heiko O
Baptism 21
Devil 73
Forgiveness 110
Knowledge 144
Morality 178
Repentance 230
Sacraments 236
Sex 243
Translation 264
Word 279
ODDIE, William
Anglicanism 15
OESTREICHER, Paul
Symbolism 256
OFF THE WALL STREET JOURNAL, The
Computers 57
OLD, Helen
Mission 176
OLINGHOUSE, Lane
Children 40

OMAR KHAYAM
History 130
ORIGEN
Commitment 53
ORTHODOX SAYING
Ministry 168
ORWELL, George (Eric Blair)
Equality 84
OSBORNE, Derek
Age 11
OSBORNE, John
Enthusiasm 81
OULIBICHEFF, A
Music 179
OWEN, John
Unity 269
OWEN, Wilfred
Cross 67
Patriotism 189
OXBROW, Mark
Evangelism 97
PACKER, James I
Anglicanism 14
Sacrifice 237
Sin 246
Spirit 250
Theology 259
Witness 274
PAINE, Tom
Cross 65
PALAU, Luis
Unity 267
PARKER, Joseph
Preaching 209, 211
PARKER, Thomas H L
Bible 26
PARKINSON, C Northcote
Laws 149
PARRIS, Matthew
Age 11
Blessing 33
Christmas 43
God 116
Media 161
Sin 246
Wales 272
PASCAL, Blaise
Education 79
Evangelism 92
Faith 102
God 118
Humanity 133
Knowledge 144
Love 154
Obedience 183
Philosophy 191
Power 197
Preaching 216
Reason 226
Sin 246
Truth 266
PATERSON, Robert M E
Anglicanism 13
Bible 26
Birth Control 30
Change 39
Children 40
Church 47
Cross 66
Eucharist 86
Evangelicals 90
Evangelism 94, 97, 98
Exegesis 100
Hell 128
Humility 134
Mary 159
Maturity 161
Ministry 171
Mission 175
Preaching 210, 214
Public Speaking 221
Quotation 224
Sacraments 237
Sin 246
Spirit 251
Theology 259
Works 281
Worship 282, 284
Wrath 287
PATEY, Edward
Evangelism 92, 98, 99
Ministry 168
Mission 176
Prayer 199
Publicity 222
Pulpits 222
Service 242
PATRICK
Celtic Christianity 37
PAUL VI, Pope
Church 48
PEEL, Robert
Charm 40
PENMAN, David
Church 49
Mission 173
PENN, William
Persecution 190
PEPYS, Samuel
Preaching 213
PERCEVAL, Spencer
Last Words 148
PERRY, Michael
Eucharist 85

PETER THE HERMIT
Youth 287
PETER, Lawrence, J
Laws 149
PETTIT, Liz
Maturity 161
PHILIP, Prince
Tact 256
PHILLIPS, Anthony
Ministry 164
PHILLIPS, J B
Bible 29
Evangelism 93
Spirit 250
PILE, Stephen
Age 10
Kindness 143
Language 145
Navigation 180
Prayer 201
Sex 244
Time 260
Weddings 273
PILKINGTON, Ross
Evangelism 97
PINERO, Arthur Wing
Hope 131
PITT, William
Politics 193
PITTMAN, Robert
Preaching 211
PLASS, Adrian
Forgiveness 109, 110
Joy 140
Prayer 200
Pressure-groups 218
Social Action 248
Witness 275
PLUTARCH
Contentment 58
POINTER, Roy
Love 156
POLISH SAYING
Doubt 77
POLWHELE, Richard
Prayer Book 204
POLYCARP OF SMYRNA
Christ, The 42
POPE, Alexander
Forgiveness 109
Knowledge 144
Poetry 192
Providence 220
POPE, John Dickson
Care 35
PORSON, Richard
God 115
PORTUGUESE PROVERB
Hell 128
POSTERSKI, D C and BARKER, I
Ministry 165
POTTER, Philip
Unity 267
POULTON, John
Church 47
Fellowship 107
Future 112
POWELL, John
Self 241
PREMASAGAR, Victor
Cross 67
Giving 113
PRESTON, M M
Worship 282
PRICE, Eugenia
Christmas 44
PRIDEAUX, Humphrey
Worship 286
PRIOR, David
Church 46
Possessions 195
PROSPER OF AQUITAINE
Worship 285
PULLINGER, Jackie
Religion 228
PUNCH Magazine
Heaven 127
Marriage 158
PUNTON, Jim
Mission 174
PURITANS
Grace 123
PUSEY, E B
Predestination 218
PUTNEY DEBATES
Government 123
PYM, Francis
Clerics 51
PYTHON, Monty
Love 155
QUICK, Oliver
Confirmation 58
QUR'AN, The
God 117
RABOTEAU
Jesus Christ 139
RACINE, Jean
Women 277
RAEDEKE, Theodore A
Worship 282
RAHNER, Karl
Conversion 60
RAMSEY, Ian
Faith 103

RAMSEY, Michael
Absent-mindedness 9
Anglicanism 16
Church 48
Education 79
Media 161
Preaching 213
Theology 259
RASHDALL, Hastings
Spoonerisms 252
RAWLINSON, A E J
Catholicity 36
RAY, John (or WRAY)
Hypocrisy 136
Love 155
Marriage 158
RAYA, Joseph
Holy Places 130
READ, David H C
Language 147
RECONCILIATION, Rite of
Confession 57
REDLAND
Epitaphs 83
REGISTER OFFICES, Her Majesty's
Marriage 158
REID, Gavin
Wrath 287
RICE, John R
Christmas 44
RICHARDS, Michael
Eucharist 85
Ministry 164, 171
Word 279
RICHARDSON, Alan
Christianity 42
Doctrine 76
Evangelicals 87
History 130
Hope 131
Resurrection 234
RICHMOND
Epitaphs 84
RIDLEY, Nicholas
Reformation 227
RINKART, Martin
Apocrypha 18
ROBERTSON, Donald
Epitaphs 82
ROBERTSON, F W
Doubt 77
Faith 104
Ministry 172
Motivation 179
ROBERTSON, James
Church 45
Spirit 251
ROBINSON, John
Bible 26
ROBINSON, John A T
Bible 24
Faith 104
RODENMAYER, Robert N
Thankfulness 258
ROGERS, John
Bible 28
ROLAND, Madame (Marie Jeanne Philipon)
Liberty 151
ROOSEVELDT, Franklin D
Freedom 111
Humanity 133
ROOSEVELDT, Theodore
Peace 189
ROSS, Robert
Epitaphs 83
ROSSETTI, Christina
Silence 244
ROUSSEAU, Jean-Jacques
Death 71
Freedom 111
ROUTH, Martin Joseph
Gospels 122
ROUX, Joseph
Science 239
ROWLEY, H H
Predestination 218
ROYDS, Dick
Enthusiasm 81
RUNCIE, Robert
Bishops 31
Hope 132
RUNCORN, David
Communication 54
Cross 65
Desert 72
Prayer 199, 202
Silence 244, 245
Worship 282
RUPP and DREWERY
Death 69
RUSACK, Theodore
Culture 68
RUSKIN, John
Bereavement 23
Patience 188
Self 241
RUSSELL, Bertrand
Heaven 127
Philosophy 191
RUSSIAN ORTHODOX LITURGY
Eucharist 85
RUSSIAN PROVERB
History 130

RYLE, John Charles
Cross 66
Marriage 159
Preaching 216
Spirit 252
SACKS, Jonathan
Persecution 190
SADGROVE, M and WRIGHT, T
Hinduism 129
SAHL, Mort
Conservatism 558
SAKI (Hector Hugh Munro)
Death 71
SALISBURY (Lord)
Scepticism 239
SALONGA, Jovito
Weakness 273
SAN FRANCISCO EXAMINER, The
Language 145
SANGSTER, W E
Language 145
Preachers 205, 206
Preaching 214
SANTAYANA, George
Fanaticism 107
SARTRE, Jean-Paul
Communication 54
Purpose 223
SAUNDERS, Kate
Anglo-Catholicism 16
SAUNDERS, Teddy
Preachers 206
SAUNDERS, Thomas G
Giving 114
SCHELL, O
Exegesis 100
SCHLEIERMACHER, Friedrich Daniel Ernst
Resurrection 233
SCHWARTZ, Stephen
Salvation 238
SCHWEITZER, Albert
Preaching 210
Service 242
SCOPES CASE
Creation 64
SCOTLAND, Nigel
Church Buildings 50
SCOTT, C P
Facts 101
Television 257
SCOTT, Thomas
Growth 125
SCOTT, Walter
Death 69
SCRIPTURE UNION
God 117
SELDON, John
Prayer Book 204
SELLAR, W C and YEATMAN, R J
Angels 12
SELLERS, Peter
Spelling 249
SENECA, Lucius Annaeus
Sin 246
War 273
SEXTON, James
Language 145
SHAKESPEARE, William
Caution 36
Children 41
Death 68–70
Fatalism 107
Finance 108
Hypocrisy 136
Life 152
Love 154, 155
Marriage 158
Mercy 162
Poverty 197
Reputation 231
Silence 245
Sin 246
Television 257
Time 260
Wit 270
SHAW, George Bernard
Belief 22
Bible 28
Censorship 37
Economics 78
England 81
Faith 105
Freedom 111
Laity 144
Media 161
Persecution 190
Prostitution 219
Sin 246
Teaching 256
Truth 265
SHEPPARD, David
Doctrine 76
Evangelism 98
Peace 189
Poverty 195
Searching 240
Witness 275
SHEPPARD, Dick
Preaching 216
SHERIDAN, Richard Brinsley
Writers 287

SICHEL, Walter (Lord Bowen)
Justice 143
Life 152
SIDER, Ronald J
Church 47
SIMEON, Charles
Apocrypha 18
Baptism 20
Bereavement 23
Bible 24, 25, 27
Clerics 52
Conversion 59
Eucharist 86
Exegesis 100, 101
Family 106
Joy 140
Ministry 169, 172
Mission 177
Paradox 186
Prayer Book 204
Preachers 206
Preaching 208, 216
Silence 245
Simplicity 245
Truth 265
Worship 282
SIMPSON, Michael A
Death 70
SKEVINGTON-WOOD, A
Protestantism 220
Reformation 227
SMITH, F E
Wisdom 274
SMITH, P and GALLINGER, H P
Preaching 124
SMITH, Sydney
Bishops 32
Compassion 55
Generosity 113
Heaven 127
Joy 141
Light 153
Preaching 213
Reform 227
SMYTH, Charles
Preaching 207, 214
SONG, Choan-Seng
Mission 173
SOUTH, Robert
Preaching 212
SOUTHCOTT, Ernie
Church 48
SOUTHEY, Robert
Death 70
Thought 259
SPECTATOR, The
Miracles 172
SPENDER, J A
Sin 246
SPENDER, Stephen
Love 154
SPENSER, Edmund
Resurrection 233
SPOONER, William Archibald
Spoonerisms 252
SPURGEON, Charles Haddon
Cross 65
Evangelism 92
Perseverance 190
Prayer 199, 201
Preaching 209
SQUIRE, J C
War 273
ST JOHN PASSION
Cross 66
Repentance 231
ST MATTHEW PASSION
Commitment 53
Cross 65
Faith 101
STAFFORD, William
Anglicanism 14
STALIN, Joseph
Death 71
STAMP, Gillian
Leadership 150
STANTON, A H
Bible 26
STATIONERY OFFICE, Her Majesty's
God 117
STAUPITZ, Johannes
Exegesis 100
STEIN, Gertrude
Last Words 149
STENBAKKEN, Richard O
Ministry 169
STEVENSON, Adlai
Flattery 108
Hypocrisy 136
Politics 193
STEVENSON, James
Fame 106
Hypocrisy 136
Kindness 143
Language 145
Writers 287
STEVENSON, Robert Louis
Intelligence 138
STEWART, Dugald
Books 34
STEWART, James S
Worship 282

STILLINGFLEET, Edward
Preaching 209
STOCKMAN, Ralph
Bible 27
STOPPARD, Tom
Arts 18
Atheism 19
Eternity 84
Language 147, 148
Opera 186
Prejudice 218
STOTT, John R W
Authority 20
Bible 24
Church 46
Conviction 62
Doctrine 76
Evangelism 92
Exegesis 100
Humility 134
Humour 135
Hypocrisy 136
Judgement 141
Mind 164
Ministry 169
Preachers 205
Preaching 207, 208, 210, 213, 216
Resurrection 233
Service 242
Spirit 250
STRAUSS, D F
Bible 28
SUDBURY
Epitaphs 83
SUMNER, J B
Church Buildings 50
SUTHERLAND, James
Books 34
Death 70
Epitaphs 83
Fiction 108
Marriage 159
Media 161
Pain 186
Parliament 187
Persecution 190
Preaching 213
Teeth 256
SWAFFER, Hannah
Media 161
SWAHILI
Time 260
SWANSEA, St Mary's Church
Misprints 173
SWATKINS, Lilian
Forgiveness 110
SWEENEY, Paul
Simplicity 245
SWIFT, Jonathan
Clerics 52
England 80
Fiction 108
Preaching 215
War 273
SYKES, Stephen W
Anglicanism 14
Authority 20
Bishops 32
Catholicity 36
Worship 285
TAFT, William Howard
Race 224
TAIT, A C
Anglicanism 14
Ritual 236
TAKENAKA, Maseo
Translation 263
TALMUD, The
Care 35
TATHAM, Edward
Preaching 212
TAWNEY, R H
Thought 259
TAYLOR, Edward
Christ, The 42
TAYLOR, Jeremy
Unity 267
TAYLOR, John
Conversion 61
Sunday 254
Tradition 261
TAYLOR, John V
Evangelism 92
Holiness 130
Mission 173, 175
Resurrection 233
TAYLOR, Rowland
Bible 28
TEMPLE, Frederick
Bishops 30
TEMPLE, John Henry
Last Words 148
TEMPLE, William
Ascension 18
Bishops 30
Church 47
Conversion 62
Cricket 65
Faith 102
God 115
Incarnation 138
Light 153
Love 157

Mission 175
Obedience 183
Power 197
Prayer 199
Revelation 235
Sacraments 236
Sin 246
Spirit 250
Truth 265
Values 270
Worship 282, 284
TENNYSON, Alfred Lord
Ambition 12
Love 154
TERTULLIAN OF CARTHAGE
Cross 65
Witness 275
TETBURY
Epitaphs 82
THANT, U
Diversity 75
THATCHER, Margaret
Money 178
Society 249
THEILICKE, Helmut
Preaching 209, 214
Translation 262
THERESA OF AVILA
Prayer 202
THERESA, Mother
Evangelism 92
THOMAS, Dylan
Death 68
Life 153
THOMAS, Gwyn
Wales 272
THOMAS, John James Absalom
Sacrifice 237
THOMSON, James
Beauty 22
THORNTON, John
Ministry 169, 172
THORPE
Epitaphs 83
THORPE, Adam
Eucharist 87
THULIN, Richard L
Eucharist 86
TILLICH, Paul
Freedom 111
Saints 238
TIMES, The
Compromise 57
Culture 68
Evangelism 97
Harvest 126
Religious Education 230
Resurrection 232
Teaching 256
Women 277
TOLSTOY, Leo
Beauty 22
TOMPKINS, Oliver
Ministry 172
TOPLADY, Augustus Montague
Atonement 19
TOVEY, Philip
Symbolism 255
TOWNSEND, Robert
Professionalism 218
TOYNBEE, Philip
Theology 258
TRACY, D
Bible 29
TRAHERNE, Thomas
Contentment 58
TRENCH, Richard Chenevix
Cooking 63
Fear 107
TREVELYAN, G M
Marriage 158
Wisdom 274
TREVELYAN, J M
Parliament 187
TROLLOPE, Anthony
Preaching 209
TURNER, H E W
Predestination 217
TURNER, Ted
Humility 133
TUTU, Desmond
Patience 188
TWAIN, Mark (Samuel Langhorne Clemens)
Death 71
Humour 135
Language 148
Music 179
Preaching 212
Statistics 253
Youth 287
TYNAN, Katharine
Poetry 192
TYNDALE, William
Bible 28
Prosperity 219
ULLATHORNE, Bernard
Devil 73
UNDERHILL, Evelyn
Christianity 42
Witness 275
VAN LOON, Hendrik Willem
Eternity 84

VANN, Gerald
Humour 135
VATICAN II (Roman Catholic Council)
Preaching 207
Worship 285
VAUGHAN, Benjamin N Y
Giving 113
Sacrifice 237
Unity 267
VAUGHAN, Bill
Purpose 224
VENN, Henry
Church Buildings 50
VICTORIA, Queen
Lent 150
VIDAL, Gore
Truth 266
VIDLER, Alec R
Baptism 21
Devil 73
VINCENT, Mary Ann
Thankfulness 258
VINES, Jerry
Preaching 211
VIRGER Magazine, The
Teeth 257
VOLTAIRE, Francois Marie
Bigotry 30
Freedom 111
Humanity 132
Time 260
VON SCHILLER, Johann C F
Time 260
WAITE, Terry
Bereavement 23
WALSH, Chad
Preaching 207
WALSH, Jill Paton
Ethics 84
God 117
WALTON, Izaac
Social Action 248
WARD, John
Self 241
WARD, Keith
Reform 227
Women 277
WARREN, Max
Communication 54
Cross 67
Evangelicals 87, 89
History 129, 130
WARWICK, Philip
Prayer 200
Religion 229
WATERHOUSE, Keith
Flood 108
WATSON, David
Blindness 33
Choice 41
Christ, The 42
Church 46
Discipleship 74
Evangelism 92, 98
Fellowship 107
Public Speaking 222
Spirit 250
WATTS, Isaac
Prayer 198
Psalms 221
WATTS, Murray
Clerics 51
WEAVER, Pam
Death 70
WEBB, William
Methodism 163
WEBB-PEPLOE
Joy 140
WEBSTER, Douglas
Bible 29
Church 46, 47, 49
Conversion 60
Evangelism 92, 93, 97
Fellowship 107
Future 112
Gospel 120, 121
Laity 144
Ministry 165
Mission 174, 175
Radicalism 224
Service 242
Social Action 248
Witness 274
WELLS, David
Self 241
WELSH CHURCH LEADER
Compromise 56
WELSH PRAYER
Love 154
WELSH PREACHER
Teeth 256
WELSH SAYING
Atheism 19
WESCOTT, Brooke Foss
Hope 131
Luxury 157
Salvation 239
Theology 259
WESLEY, Charles
Beauty 22
Love 156

WESLEY, John
Activism 10
Church 45
Conversion 58
Cross 65
Evangelism 92
Faith 102
Methodism 163
Prayer Book 204
Preaching 215, 216
Predestination 217
Service 242
WEST, Frank H
Change 37
WEST, Mae
Beauty 22
Choice 41
WESTMINSTER CATECHISM (Shorter), The
Bible 24
Humanity 133
WHALE, John S
Resurrection 232
WHATLEY, Richard
Preaching 211
WHITE, John
Evangelism 94
WHITE, Patrick
Worship 282
WHITEFIELD, George
Charismatics 40
Predestination 217
Service 242
Unity 267
WHITEHEAD, Alfred North
Doctrine 76
WHITEMAN, Darrell
Culture 68
WICKES, Joyse
Language 147
WILBERFORCE, Samuel
Communication 54
Hymns 135
Preachers 206
WILBERFORCE, William
Compassion 55
Liberalism 151
WILCOX, Ella Wheeler
Sympathy 256
WILDE, Oscar
Anger 13
Baptism 21
Diaries 74
Faith 104
Fame 106
Fiction 108
Genius 113
Love 155
Marriage 158
Parents 187
Persecution 190
Religion 229
Self 241
Sin 247
Success 253
Temptation 257
Truth 264, 265
WILES, Maurice
Myth 180
WILLIAMS, Harry A
Activism 9
Anger 13
Prayer 198
Repentance 230
WILLIAMS, Michael E
Preachers 205
WILLIAMS, Michael J
Liberation Theology 151
WILLIAMS, Rowan D
Achievement 9
Church 48
Sacraments 237
WILSON, Colin
Purpose 223
WILSON, Craig
Christmas 44
WILSON, Harold
Committees 54
WILSON, Kenneth L
Stewardship 253
WILSON, Leonard
Salvation 238
WILSON, McLandburg
Pessimism 191
WINDHAM, William
God 118
WINTER, David
Bible 29
WOODCOCK, Thomas
Epitaphs 108
WOODHOUSE, A S P
Government 123
WOODRUFF, Douglas
Confession 57
WOOLF, Virginia
God 119
WOOLWICH
Epitaphs 82
WOOTTON, Henry
Ambassador 12
WORDSWORTH, C
Providence 220
WORSTHORNE, Peregrine
Clerics 52

Spirituality 252
WRAY, John – see **Ray**
WRIGHT, Chris
Church 45, 47
Israel 139
WROE, M, REITH, A and PARKES, S
Advent 10
Anglicanism 13
Anglo-Catholicism 17
Charismatics 39
Children 41
Clerics 52
Giving 114
Hope 132
Merit 163
Ritual 236
YOUNG, Brigham
Epitaphs 83
YOUNG, John
Navigation 181
YOUNGMAN, Henry
Time 260
ZIZIONLAS, John
Catholicity 35
ZUERCHER, Robert
Evangelism 93, 96
Repentance 230
Social Action 248

BIBLICAL INDEX BY THEME

Age
Ecclesiastes 12. 1–7
Angels
2 Corinthians 11. 14; Hebrews 1. 3b–5a; Revelation 5, 11, 12; 12. 7–9
Apocrypha
Sirach (Ecclesiasticus) 2. 10; 50. 22–24
Ascension
Luke 24. 50–53; Acts 1. 9–11
Atonement
John 1. 29; Hebrews 10. 11–14
Beauty
Psalm 27. 4; 29. 2; Isaiah 53. 2; 2 Corinthians 3. 18; 1 Peter 3. 4
Belief
Mark 9. 24; John 6. 35–37; 9. 35–39; 1 John 3. 23, 24
Bereavement
John 11. 21–27; Philippians 4. 6, 7
Boasting
Jeremiah 9. 24; 2 Corinthians 10. 17, 18; Ephesians 2. 8–10; Philippians 2. 3, 4; 3. 7–9
Care
Genesis 4. 9; Numbers 6. 24–26; John 21. 15–17
Chance
Ephesians 4. 27
Charismatics
1 Corinthians 7. 7; 1 Peter 4. 10
Church
Ephesians 3. 20, 21; 1 Peter 2. 4, 5, 9, 10
Commitment
Luke 8. 42b–48; 9. 62
Communication
1 Corinthians 13. 1
Confession
James 5. 16; 1 John 1. 8, 9
Conscience
1 John 3. 18–21
Conversion
Psalm 39; Ruth 1. 16, 17; Romans 13. 13, 14; Acts 9. 3–6, 17–20; 16. 29–33; 1 Corinthians 15.8;
Conviction
1 Thessalonians 1. 5
Correction
Proverbs 3. 11, 12; Hebrews 12. 5, 6
Cross
Philippians 2. 5–9; Hebrews 12. 24
Death
1 Corinthians 15. 54–57
Democracy
1 Samuel 8. 4–7
Despair
Psalm 22. 1, 2; 130. 1; 2 Corinthians 4. 8–10
Devil
Colossians 2. 15
Discipleship
Mark 8. 34, 35
Discipline
1 Corinthians 9. 25; Titus 1. 7, 8
Doubt
John 20. 24–29; Jude 22
Dreams
Genesis 37. 19; Joel 2. 28
Emotions
Psalm 69. 9; John 2. 14–17; 11. 35, 36
Environment
Genesis 1. 31; 2. 8, 9, 15–17; Colossians 1. 16, 17
Eucharist
John 6. 51
Faith
Mark 9. 22b, 23; John 20. 31; Romans 1.17; Hebrews 12. 1, 2a;
Fall
Genesis 3. 8–10, 22–24; Romans 3. 23
Family
Mark 3. 25
Fellowship
Acts 2. 42, 44–46; Romans 12. 13; Hebrews 10. 24, 25
Forgiveness
Matthew 6. 12; Luke 7. 47–49; Romans 8. 31b–34; Colossians 2. 13b, 14
Future
Psalm 16. 11; Psalm 95; 1 Corinthians 3. 21b–23; Hebrews 3 & 4
Generosity
2 Corinthians 9. 6, 7, 10–12
Giving
Mark 10. 23–27; Luke 16. 13–15; James 5. 1–6

God
Psalm 77. 19
Goodness
Luke 2. 25; Acts 11. 24
Gospel
Isaiah 61. 1, 2; Habakkuk 2. 4; Luke 4. 16–21; 4. 43; Romans 1. 16, 17
Grace
Ephesians 1. 5–8; 2. 4–10
Greed
Habakkuk 2. 5; Ephesians 5. 5
Growth
Luke 8. 8a, 15; 1 Corinthians 3. 6, 7; 2 Peter 3. 18
Guidance
Psalm 23. 4; Colossians 3. 15, 16a
Healing
Acts 3. 6–10; James 5. 14, 15
Heaven
Revelation 21. 1–6, 22–27
Holiness
Leviticus 11. 44, 45; 19. 2;
1 Thessalonians 4. 7; 1;
Peter 1. 15, 16;
Honesty
Proverbs 28. 6; Isaiah 59. 2a, 12–15
Hope
Psalm 9. 18; Romans 15. 13
Humility
Matthew 23. 11, 12; Luke 22. 24–27; 1 Peter 5. 5b, 6
Humour
Proverbs 26. 12
Incarnation
John 1. 14; 2 John 7
Jesus Christ
1 Timothy 1. 15;
Hebrews 12. 1c, 2; 13. 8
Joy
Galatians 5. 22
Judgement
Matthew 25. 31–33; Romans 14. 10–12; Hebrews 9. 27, 28
Kingdom of God
Matthew 13 (various); Luke 10. 8–11
Language
Matthew 16. 15, 16
Liberalism
Matthew 6. 43–45
Life
1 John 3. 14; 5. 11, 12
Light
John 8. 12; 1 Thessalonians 5. 4, 5;
1 John 1. 5–7; 2. 9–11
Love
1 Corinthians 13. 4;
Romans 8. 38, 39; 1 John 4. 7–12;
1 Corinthians 13. 1, 4–8a, 13
Marriage
Ephesians 5. 21–25, 28, 31;
Colossians 3. 18, 19
Mary
Luke 1. 38, 46–55; 2. 34, 35; 8. 19–21;
Galatians 4. 4–7
Materialism
Luke 12. 16–21
Mediator
1 Timothy 2. 5, 6
Mercy
James 2. 12, 13
Ministry
Matthew 4. 19; Mark 1. 7; Acts 20.28;
1 Corinthians 12. 7, 12, 27;
Ephesians 4. 10–13;
Mission
John 20.21; Acts 1. 8; Romans 10. 14–17; Galatians 3. 28;
Ephesians 2. 11;
Money
Matthew 6. 19–21; Mark 12. 41–44
Music
Psalm 150. 3–6; Revelation 14. 2, 3
Mystery
Ephesians 1. 8b–10; 6. 19, 20;
Colossians 1. 25–27; 4. 3, 4;
1 Timothy 3. 16
Obedience
Romans 4. 13–16a;
1 Timothy 6. 13, 14
Occult
1 Chronicles 10. 13, 14;
Colossians 2. 8–10, 15
Orthodox Churches
Acts 1. 21–26
Parents
Exodus 20. 12; Deuteronomy 6. 4–7;
Colossians 3. 20, 21
Perseverance
Matthew 10. 22; Luke 8. 15;
Hebrews 3. 14; 6. 10–12
Planning
Luke 14. 28–33
Politics
Matthew 22. 21b; John 19. 10, 11a;
Romans 13. 1–7
Possessions
Matthew 6. 24; Luke 12.15
Poverty
Matthew 5. 3; 18. 12; Luke 7. 22, 23;
15. 4; 2 Corinthians 8. 9;
1 John 3. 17, 18
Prayer
Zachariah 4. 6; Matthew 7. 7–11;
Colossians 4. 2; Hebrews 4. 14–16;
1 John 5. 14, 15
Preaching
2 Corinthians 4. 2; 1 Timothy 4. 13;

2 Timothy 4. 1–5
Predestination
Romans 9. 20–22; 11. 23 ff;
Prosperity
Genesis 39. 2; Malachi 3. 16–18; 2 Corinthians 11. 30; 12. 9; 1 Timothy 6. 17–19
Providence
Matthew 6. 31–34; 1 Corinthians 10. 13
Purpose
John 18. 37; Romans 6. 13
Race
Ephesians 2. 13–18
Realism
John 20. 27; 2 Corinthians 4. 18
Reconciliation
2 Corinthians 5. 17–21; Colossians 1. 19–22
Redemption
Ephesians 4.31–5.2
Regeneration
John 3. 3–7; Titus 3. 4, 5
Relationships
Colossians 3. 12–14; 4. 5, 6
Repentance
Matthew 4. 17; Luke 15. 7; Acts 2. 38; James 5. 19, 20
Rest
Psalm 46. 10; Hebrews 4. 1–3, 11
Resurrection
Matthew 22. 31, 32; 1 Corinthians 15. 12–20; Philippians 3. 10, 11; Colossians 3. 1–4; 1 Peter 1. 3
Riddles
Mark 8. 36, 37
Sacraments
Romans 6. 3, 4; 1 Corinthians 10. 16, 17; 11. 23–26; Colossians 2. 12
Saints
Romans 1. 7; 1 Corinthians 1. 2; Ephesians 1. 1; Hebrews 12. 1, 2; Philippians 1. 1
Second Coming
Mark 13. 32, 33, 37
Self
Ephesians 4. 22–24; 1 Peter 4. 7
Sex
1 Corinthians 6. 13b, 18–20
Simplicity
Matthew 6. 25–34
Sin
1 John 5. 18, 19
Singing
Colossians 3. 16; Revelation 5. 9–14
Slavery
1 Timothy 6. 1, 2; Colossians 3. 22; Ephesians 6. 5–8; Titus 2. 9, 10; Philemon 15, 16
Social Action
Matthew 25. 31–36, 40–45
Spirit
John 20. 21–23; Romans 8. 9, 15–17; 1 Corinthians 12. 3; Galatians 5. 22–25; Ephesians 4. 30; 1 Thessalonians 5. 19; 2 Timothy 1. 7; 1 John 4. 13, 14
Spoonerisms
1 Corinthians 13. 12
Symbolism
1 Corinthians 11. 27–32
Temptation
1 Corinthians 10. 13
Thankfulness
Psalm 136. 1; Luke 17. 12–19; Colossians 3. 17
Thought
Proverbs 2. 6–8; 1 Corinthians 3. 18–20
Time
Ecclesiastes 3. 1–9
Tradition
1 Corinthians 15. 3; Mark 7. 8
Unity
Galatians 2. 1 ff
Violence
Genesis 6. 11; Isaiah 60. 18
Vision
Acts 16. 9, 10
Vocation
1 Samuel 3. 10; Isaiah 6. 8–10; Ephesians 1. 17, 18
Weakness
2 Corinthians 12. 9, 10
Wisdom
Proverbs 1. 7; 3. 5, 6; 9. 10; 1 Corinthians 1. 21, 25, 30, 31
Witness
2 Timothy 1. 8, 9a; 1 Peter 4. 12–16; Revelation 7. 13–17
Wonder
Hebrews 12. 28, 29; Revelation 15. 3b, 4
Word
John 1. 1–4, 14; Romans 15. 4; 2 Timothy 3. 16; James 1. 22–25; 1 John 1. 1–3
Work
Romans 12. 11; Colossians 3. 23, 24; 2 Thessalonians 3. 6–12
Works
Titus 3. 4–6; James 2. 14–18, 26; Revelation 19. 7, 8
Worship
Revelation 7. 9–12; 22. 3b–5